Office of the Inspector General
U.S. Department of Justice

OVERSIGHT ★ INTEGRITY ★ GUIDANCE

A Review of Various Actions by the Federal Bureau of Investigation and Department of Justice in Advance of the 2016 Election

Oversight and Review Division 18-04

June 2018

Executive Summary

A Review of Various Actions by the Federal Bureau of Investigation and Department of Justice in Advance of the 2016 Election

Background

In response to requests from Congress, various organizations, and members of the public, the Department of Justice (Department) Office of the Inspector General (OIG) undertook this review of various actions by the Federal Bureau of Investigation (FBI) and the Department in connection with the investigation into former Secretary of State Hillary Clinton's use of a private email server. Our review included examining:

- Allegations that Department or FBI policies or procedures were not followed in connection with, or in actions leading up to or related to, then FBI Director James Comey's public announcement on July 5, 2016, and Comey's letters to Congress on October 28 and November 6, 2016;

- Allegations that certain investigative decisions were based on improper considerations;

- Allegations that then FBI Deputy Director Andrew McCabe should have been recused from participating in certain investigative matters;

- Allegations that the Department's then Assistant Attorney General for Legislative Affairs, Peter Kadzik, improperly disclosed non-public information and/or should have been recused from participating in certain matters;

- Allegations that Department and FBI employees improperly disclosed non-public information during the course of the investigation; and

- Allegations that decisions regarding the timing of the FBI's release of certain Freedom of Information Act (FOIA) documents on October 30 and November 1, 2016, and the use of a Twitter account to publicize this release, were influenced by improper considerations.

During the course of the review, the OIG discovered text messages and instant messages between some FBI employees on the investigative team, conducted using FBI mobile devices and computers, that expressed statements of hostility toward then candidate Donald Trump and statements of support for then candidate Clinton. We also identified messages that expressed opinions that were critical of the conduct and quality of the investigation. We included in our review an assessment of these messages and actions by the FBI employees.

OIG Methodology

The OIG reviewed significantly more than 1.2 million documents during the review and interviewed more than 100 witnesses, several on more than one occasion. These included former Director Comey, former Attorney General (AG) Loretta Lynch, former Deputy Attorney General (DAG) Sally Yates, FBI agents and supervisors and Department attorneys and supervisors who conducted the investigation, former and current members of the FBI's senior executive leadership, and former President Bill Clinton.

Conduct of the Midyear Investigation

The FBI and Department referred to the investigation as "Midyear Exam" or "Midyear." The Midyear investigation was opened by the FBI in July 2015 based on a referral from the Office of the Intelligence Community Inspector General (IC IG). The investigation was staffed by prosecutors from the Department's National Security Division (NSD) and the U.S. Attorney's Office for the Eastern District of Virginia (EDVA), and agents and analysts selected primarily from the FBI's Washington Field Office to work at FBI Headquarters.

The Midyear investigation focused on whether Clinton intended to transmit classified information on unclassified systems, knew that information included in unmarked emails was classified, or later became aware that information was classified and failed to report it. The Midyear team employed an investigative strategy that included three primary lines of inquiry: collection and examination of emails that traversed Clinton's servers and other relevant evidence, interviews of relevant witnesses, and analysis of whether classified information was compromised by hostile cyber intrusions.

As described in Chapter Five of our report, we selected for examination particular investigative decisions that were the subject of public or internal controversy. These included the following:

- The preference for consent over compulsory process to obtain evidence;

- Decisions not to obtain or seek to review certain evidence, such as the personal devices used by former Secretary Clinton's senior aides;

- The use of voluntary witness interviews;

i

Executive Summary

A Review of Various Actions by the Federal Bureau of Investigation and Department of Justice in Advance of the 2016 Election

- Decisions to enter into "letter use" or "Queen for a Day" immunity agreements with three witnesses;

- The use of consent agreements and "act of production" immunity to obtain the laptops used by Clinton's attorneys (Cheryl Mills and Heather Samuelson) to "cull" her personal and work-related emails; and

- The handling of Clinton's interview on July 2, 2016.

With regard to these investigative decisions, we found, as detailed in Chapter Five, that the Midyear team:

- Sought to obtain evidence whenever possible through consent but also used compulsory process, including grand jury subpoenas, search warrants, and 2703(d) orders (court orders for non-content email information) to obtain various evidence. We found that the prosecutors provided justifications for the preference for consent that were supported by Department and FBI policy and practice;

- Conducted voluntary witness interviews to obtain testimony, including from Clinton and her senior aides, and did not require any witnesses to testify before the grand jury. We found that one of the reasons for not using the grand jury for testimony involved concerns about exposing grand jurors to classified information;

- Did not seek to obtain every device, including those of Clinton's senior aides, or the contents of every email account through which a classified email may have traversed. We found that the reasons for not doing so were based on limitations the Midyear team imposed on the investigation's scope, the desire to complete the investigation well before the election, and the belief that the foregone evidence was likely of limited value. We further found that those reasons were, in part, in tension with Comey's response in October 2016 to the discovery of Clinton emails on the laptop of Anthony Weiner, the husband of Clinton's former Deputy Chief of Staff and personal assistant, Huma Abedin;

- Considered but did not seek permission from the Department to review certain highly classified materials that may have included information potentially relevant to the Midyear investigation. The classified appendix to this report describes in more detail the highly classified information, its potential relevance to

the Midyear investigation, the FBI's reasons for not seeking access to it, and our analysis;

- Granted letter use immunity and/or "Queen for a Day" immunity to three witnesses in exchange for their testimony after considering, as provided for in Department policy, the value of the witness's testimony, the witness's relative culpability, and the possibility of a successful prosecution;

- Used consent agreements and "act of production" immunity to obtain the culling laptops used by Mills and Samuelson, in part to avoid the uncertainty and delays of a potential motion to quash any subpoenas or search warrants. We found that these decisions were occurring at a time when Comey and the Midyear team had already concluded that there was likely no prosecutable case and believed it was unlikely the culling laptops would change the outcome of the investigation;

- Asked Clinton what appeared to be appropriate questions and made use of documents to challenge Clinton's testimony and assess her credibility during her interview. We found that, by the date of her interview, the Midyear team and Comey had concluded that the evidence did not support criminal charges (absent a confession or false statement by Clinton during the interview), and that the interview had little effect on the outcome of the investigation; and

- Allowed Mills and Samuelson to attend the Clinton interview as Clinton's counsel, even though they also were fact witnesses, because the Midyear team determined that the only way to exclude them was to subpoena Clinton to testify before the grand jury, an option that we found was not seriously considered. We found no persuasive evidence that Mills's or Samuelson's presence influenced Clinton's interview. Nevertheless, we found the decision to allow them to attend the interview was inconsistent with typical investigative strategy.

For each of these decisions, we analyzed whether there was evidence of improper considerations, including bias, and also whether the justifications offered for the decision were a pretext for improper, but unstated, considerations.

The question we considered was not whether a particular investigative decision was the ideal choice or one that could have been handled more effectively, but

Executive Summary

A Review of Various Actions by the Federal Bureau of Investigation and Department of Justice in Advance of the 2016 Election

whether the circumstances surrounding the decision indicated that it was based on considerations other than the merits of the investigation. If a choice made by the investigative team was among two or more reasonable alternatives, we did not find that it was improper even if we believed that an alternative decision would have been more effective.

Thus, a determination by the OIG that a decision was not unreasonable does not mean that the OIG has endorsed the decision or concluded that the decision was the most effective among the options considered. We took this approach because our role as an OIG is not to second-guess valid discretionary judgments made during the course of an investigation, and this approach is consistent with the OIG's handling of such questions in past reviews.

In undertaking our analysis, our task was made significantly more difficult because of text and instant messages exchanged on FBI devices and systems by five FBI employees involved in the Midyear investigation. These messages reflected political opinions in support of former Secretary Clinton and against her then political opponent, Donald Trump. Some of these text messages and instant messages mixed political commentary with discussions about the Midyear investigation, and raised concerns that political bias may have impacted investigative decisions.

In particular, we were concerned about text messages exchanged by FBI Deputy Assistant Director Peter Strzok and Lisa Page, Special Counsel to the Deputy Director, that potentially indicated or created the appearance that investigative decisions were impacted by bias or improper considerations. As we describe in Chapter Twelve of our report, most of the text messages raising such questions pertained to the Russia investigation, which was not a part of this review. Nonetheless, the suggestion in certain Russia-related text messages in August 2016 that Strzok might be willing to take official action to impact presidential candidate Trump's electoral prospects caused us to question the earlier Midyear investigative decisions in which Strzok was involved, and whether he took specific actions in the Midyear investigation based on his political views. As we describe Chapter Five of our report, we found that Strzok was not the sole decisionmaker for any of the specific Midyear investigative decisions we examined in that chapter. We further found evidence that in some instances Strzok and Page advocated for more aggressive investigative measures in the Midyear investigation,

such as the use of grand jury subpoenas and search warrants to obtain evidence.

There were clearly tensions and disagreements in a number of important areas between Midyear agents and prosecutors. However, we did not find documentary or testimonial evidence that improper considerations, including political bias, directly affected the specific investigative decisions we reviewed in Chapter Five, or that the justifications offered for these decisions were pretextual.

Nonetheless, these messages cast a cloud over the FBI's handling of the Midyear investigation and the investigation's credibility. But our review did not find evidence to connect the political views expressed in these messages to the specific investigative decisions that we reviewed; rather, consistent with the analytic approach described above, we found that these specific decisions were the result of discretionary judgments made during the course of an investigation by the Midyear agents and prosecutors and that these judgment calls were not unreasonable. The broader impact of these text and instant messages, including on such matters as the public perception of the FBI and the Midyear investigation, are discussed in Chapter Twelve of our report.

Comey's Public Statement on July 5

"Endgame" Discussions

As we describe in Chapter Six of the report, by the Spring of 2016, Comey and the Midyear team had determined that, absent an unexpected development, evidence to support a criminal prosecution of Clinton was lacking. Midyear team members told us that they based this assessment on a lack of evidence showing intent to place classified information on the server, or knowledge that the information was classified. We describe the factors that the Department took into account in its decision to decline prosecution in Chapter Seven of our report and below.

Comey told the OIG that as he began to realize the investigation was likely to result in a declination, he began to think of ways to credibly announce its closing. Comey engaged then DAG Yates in discussions in April 2016 about the "endgame" for the Midyear investigation. Comey said that he encouraged Yates to consider the most transparent options for announcing a declination. Yates told the OIG that, as a result of her

Executive Summary

A Review of Various Actions by the Federal Bureau of Investigation and Department of Justice in Advance of the 2016 Election

discussions with Comey, she thought the Department and FBI would jointly announce any declination.

Comey said he also told Yates that the closer they got to the political conventions, the more likely he would be to insist that a special counsel be appointed, because he did not believe the Department could credibly announce the closing of the investigation once Clinton was the Democratic Party nominee. However, we did not find evidence that Comey ever seriously considered requesting a special counsel; instead, he used the reference to a special counsel as an effort to induce the Department to move more quickly to obtain the Mills and Samuelson culling laptops and to complete the investigation.

Although Comey engaged with the Department in these "endgame" discussions, he told us that he was concerned that involvement by then AG Loretta Lynch in a declination announcement would result in "corrosive doubt" about whether the decision was objective and impartial because Lynch was appointed by a President from the same political party as Clinton. Comey cited other factors to us that he said caused him to be concerned by early May 2016 that Lynch could not credibly participate in announcing a declination:

- An alleged instruction from Lynch at a meeting in September 2015 to call the Midyear investigation a "matter" in statements to the media and Congress, which we describe in Chapter Four of our report;
- Statements made by then President Barack Obama about the Midyear investigation, which also are discussed in Chapter Four; and
- Concerns that certain classified information mentioning Lynch would leak, which we describe in Chapter Six and in the classified appendix.

As we discuss below and in Chapter Six of our report, the meeting between Lynch and former President Clinton on June 27, 2016 also played a role in Comey's decision to deliver a unilateral statement.

Comey did not raise any of these concerns with Lynch or Yates. Rather, unbeknownst to them, Comey began considering the possibility of an FBI-only public statement in late April and early May 2016. Comey told the OIG that a separate public statement was warranted by the "500-year flood" in which the FBI found itself, and that he weighed the need to preserve the credibility and integrity of the Department and the

FBI, and the need to protect "a sense of justice more broadly in the country—that things are fair not fixed, and they're done independently."

Comey's Draft Statement

Comey's initial draft statement, which he shared with FBI senior leadership on May 2, criticized Clinton's handling of classified information as "grossly negligent," but concluded that "no reasonable prosecutor" would bring a case based on the facts developed in the Midyear investigation. Over the course of the next 2 months, Comey's draft statement underwent various language changes, including the following:

- The description of Clinton's handling of classified information was changed from "grossly negligent" to "extremely careless;"
- A statement that the sheer volume of information classified as Secret supported an inference of gross negligence was removed and replaced with a statement that the classified information they discovered was "especially concerning because all of these emails were housed on servers not supported by full-time staff";
- A statement that the FBI assessed that it was "reasonably likely" that hostile actors gained access to Clinton's private email server was changed to "possible." The statement also acknowledged that the FBI investigation and its forensic analysis did not find evidence that Clinton's email server systems were compromised; and
- A paragraph summarizing the factors that led the FBI to assess that it was possible that hostile actors accessed Clinton's server was added, and at one point referenced Clinton's use of her private email for an exchange with then President Obama while in the territory of a foreign adversary. This reference later was changed to "another senior government official," and ultimately was omitted.

Each version of the statement criticized Clinton's handling of classified information. Comey told us that he included criticism of former Secretary Clinton's uncharged conduct because "unusual transparency...was necessary for an unprecedented situation," and that such transparency "was the best chance we had of having the American people have confidence that the justice system works[.]"

Executive Summary

A Review of Various Actions by the Federal Bureau of Investigation and Department of Justice in Advance of the 2016 Election

Other witnesses told the OIG that Comey included this criticism to avoid creating the appearance that the FBI was "letting [Clinton] off the hook," as well as to "messag[e]" the decision to the FBI workforce to emphasize that employees would be disciplined for similar conduct and to distinguish the Clinton investigation from the cases of other public figures who had been prosecuted for mishandling violations.

The Tarmac Meeting and Impact on Comey's Statement

On June 27, 2016, Lynch met with former President Clinton on Lynch's plane, which was parked on the tarmac at a Phoenix airport. This meeting was unplanned, and Lynch's staff told the OIG they received no notice that former President Clinton planned to board Lynch's plane. Both Lynch and former President Clinton told the OIG that they did not discuss the Midyear investigation or any other Department investigation during their conversation. Chapter Six of our report describes their testimony about the substance of their discussion.

Lynch told the OIG that she became increasingly concerned as the meeting "went on and on," and stated "that it was just too long a conversation to have had." Following this meeting, Lynch obtained an ethics opinion from the Departmental Ethics Office that she was not required to recuse herself from the Midyear investigation, and she decided not to voluntarily recuse herself either. In making this decision, Lynch told the OIG that stepping aside would create a misimpression that she and former President Clinton had discussed inappropriate topics, or that her role in the Midyear investigation somehow was greater than it was.

On July 1, during an interview with a reporter, Lynch stated that she was not recusing from the Midyear investigation, but that she "fully expect[ed]" to accept the recommendation of the career agents and prosecutors who conducted the investigation, "as is the common process." Then, in a follow up question, Lynch said "I'll be briefed on [the findings] and I will be accepting their recommendations." Lynch's statements created considerable public confusion about the status of her continuing involvement in the Midyear investigation.

Although we found no evidence that Lynch and former President Clinton discussed the Midyear investigation or engaged in other inappropriate discussion during their tarmac meeting, we also found that Lynch's failure to recognize the appearance problem created by former President Clinton's visit and to take action to cut the

visit short was an error in judgment. We further concluded that her efforts to respond to the meeting by explaining what her role would be in the investigation going forward created public confusion and did not adequately address the situation.

Comey told the OIG that he was "90 percent there, like highly likely" to make a separate public statement prior to the tarmac meeting, but that the tarmac meeting "tipped the scales" toward making his mind up to go forward with his own public statement.

Comey's Decision Not to Tell Department Leadership

Comey acknowledged that he made a conscious decision not to tell Department leadership about his plans to make a separate statement because he was concerned that they would instruct him not to do it. He also acknowledged that he made this decision when he first conceived of the idea to do the statement, even as he continued to engage the Department in discussions about the "endgame" for the investigation.

Comey admitted that he concealed his intentions from the Department until the morning of his press conference on July 5, and instructed his staff to do the same, to make it impracticable for Department leadership to prevent him from delivering his statement. We found that it was extraordinary and insubordinate for Comey to do so, and we found none of his reasons to be a persuasive basis for deviating from well-established Department policies in a way intentionally designed to avoid supervision by Department leadership over his actions.

On the morning of July 5, 2016, Comey contacted Lynch and Yates about his plans to make a public statement, but did so only after the FBI had notified the press—in fact, the Department first learned about Comey's press conference from a media inquiry, rather than from the FBI. When Comey did call Lynch that morning, he told her that he was not going to inform her about the substance of his planned press statement.

While Lynch asked Comey what the subject matter of the statement was going to be (Comey told her in response it would be about the Midyear investigation), she did not ask him to tell her what he intended to say about the Midyear investigation. We found that Lynch, having decided not to recuse herself, retained authority over both the final prosecution decision and the Department's management of the Midyear investigation. As such, we believe she should have instructed Comey

Executive Summary

A Review of Various Actions by the Federal Bureau of Investigation and Department of Justice in Advance of the 2016 Election

to tell her what he intended to say beforehand, and should have discussed it with Comey.

Comey's public statement announced that the FBI had completed its Midyear investigation, criticized Clinton and her senior aides as "extremely careless" in their handling of classified information, stated that the FBI was recommending that the Department decline prosecution of Clinton, and asserted that "no reasonable prosecutor" would prosecute Clinton based on the facts developed by the FBI during its investigation. We determined that Comey's decision to make this statement was the result of his belief that only he had the ability to credibly and authoritatively convey the rationale for the decision to not seek charges against Clinton, and that he needed to hold the press conference to protect the FBI and the Department from the extraordinary harm that he believed would have resulted had he failed to do so. While we found no evidence that Comey's statement was the result of bias or an effort to influence the election, we did not find his justifications for issuing the statement to be reasonable or persuasive.

We concluded that Comey's unilateral announcement was inconsistent with Department policy and violated long-standing Department practice and protocol by, among other things, criticizing Clinton's uncharged conduct. We also found that Comey usurped the authority of the Attorney General, and inadequately and incompletely described the legal position of Department prosecutors.

The Department's Declination Decision on July 6

Following Comey's public statement on July 5, the Midyear prosecutors finalized their recommendation that the Department decline prosecution of Clinton, her senior aides, and the senders of emails determined to contain classified information. On July 6, the Midyear prosecutors briefed Lynch, Yates, Comey, other members of Department and FBI leadership, and FBI Midyear team members about the basis for the declination recommendation. Lynch subsequently issued a short public statement that she met with the career prosecutors and agents who conducted the investigation and "received and accepted their unanimous recommendation" that the investigation be closed without charges.

We found that the prosecutors considered five federal statutes:

- 18 U.S.C. §§ 793(d) and (e) (willful mishandling of documents or information relating to the national defense);
- 18 U.S.C. § 793(f) (removal, loss, theft, abstraction, or destruction of documents or information relating to the national defense through gross negligence, or failure to report such removal, loss, theft, abstraction, or destruction);
- 18 U.S.C. § 1924 (unauthorized removal and retention of classified documents or material by government employees); and
- 18 U.S.C. § 2071 (concealment, removal, or mutilation of government records).

As described in Chapter Seven of our report, the prosecutors concluded that the evidence did not support prosecution under any of these statutes for various reasons, including that former Secretary Clinton and her senior aides lacked the intent to communicate classified information on unclassified systems. Critical to their conclusion was that the emails in question lacked proper classification markings, that the senders often refrained from using specific classified facts or terms in emails and worded emails carefully in an attempt to "talk around" classified information, that the emails were sent to other government officials in furtherance of their official duties, and that former Secretary Clinton relied on the judgment of State Department employees to properly handle classified information, among other facts.

We further found that the statute that required the most complex analysis by the prosecutors was Section 793(f)(1), the "gross negligence" provision that has been the focus of much of the criticism of the declination decision. As we describe in Chapters Two and Seven of our report, the prosecutors analyzed the legislative history of Section 793(f)(1), relevant case law, and the Department's prior interpretation of the statute. They concluded that Section 793(f)(1) likely required a state of mind that was "so gross as to almost suggest deliberate intention," criminally reckless, or "something that falls just short of being willful," as well as evidence that the individuals who sent emails containing classified information "knowingly" included or transferred such information onto unclassified systems.

The Midyear team concluded that such proof was lacking. We found that this interpretation of Section 793(f)(1) was consistent with the Department's historical approach in prior cases under different leadership, including in the 2008 decision not to

vi

Executive Summary
A Review of Various Actions by the Federal Bureau of Investigation and Department of Justice in Advance of the 2016 Election

prosecute former Attorney General Alberto Gonzales for mishandling classified documents.

We analyzed the Department's declination decision according to the same analytical standard that we applied to other decisions made during the investigation. We did not substitute the OIG's judgment for the judgments made by the Department, but rather sought to determine whether the decision was based on improper considerations, including political bias. We found no evidence that the conclusions by the prosecutors were affected by bias or other improper considerations; rather, we determined that they were based on the prosecutors' assessment of the facts, the law, and past Department practice.

We therefore concluded that these were legal and policy judgments involving core prosecutorial discretion that were for the Department to make.

Discovery in September 2016 of Emails on the Weiner Laptop

Discovery of Emails by the FBI's New York Field Office

In September 2016, the FBI's New York Field Office (NYO) and the U.S. Attorney's Office for the Southern District of New York (SDNY) began investigating former Congressman Anthony Weiner for his online relationship with a minor. A federal search warrant was obtained on September 26, 2016, for Weiner's iPhone, iPad, and laptop computer. The FBI obtained these devices the same day. The search warrant authorized the government to search for evidence relating to the following crimes: transmitting obscene material to a minor, sexual exploitation of children, and activities related to child pornography.

The Weiner case agent told the OIG that he began processing Weiner's devices on September 26, and that he noticed "within hours" that there were "over 300,000 emails on the laptop." He said that either that evening or the next morning, he saw at least one BlackBerry PIN message between Clinton and Abedin, as well as emails between them. He said that he recalled seeing emails associated with "about seven domains," such as yahoo.com, state.gov, clintonfoundation.org, clintonemail.com, and hillaryclinton.com. The case agent immediately notified his NYO chain of command, and the information was ultimately briefed to NYO Assistant Director in Charge (ADIC) William Sweeney on September 28.

Reporting of Emails to FBI Headquarters

As we describe in Chapter Nine of our report, Sweeney took the following steps to notify FBI Headquarters about the discovery of Midyear-related emails on the Weiner laptop:

- On September 28, during a secure video teleconference (SVTC), Sweeney reported that Weiner investigation agents had discovered 141,000 emails on Weiner's laptop that were potentially relevant to the Midyear investigation. The OIG determined that this SVTC was led by then Deputy Director Andrew McCabe, and that approximately 39 senior FBI executives likely would have participated. Comey was not present for the SVTC.

- Sweeney said he spoke again with McCabe on the evening of September 28. Sweeney said that during this call he informed McCabe that NYO personnel had continued processing the laptop and that they had now identified 347,000 emails on the laptop.

- Sweeney said he also called two FBI Executive Assistant Directors (EAD) on September 28 and informed them that the Weiner case team had discovered emails relevant to the Midyear investigation. One of the EADs told the OIG that he then called McCabe, and that McCabe told the EAD that he was aware of the emails. The EAD told us that "[T]here was no doubt in my mind when we finished that conversation that [McCabe] understood the, the gravity of what the find was."

- Sweeney said he also spoke to FBI Assistant Director E.W. "Bill" Priestap on September 28 and 29, 2016. Emails indicate that during their conversation on September 29, they discussed the limited scope of the Weiner search warrant (*i.e.*, the need to obtain additional legal process to review any Midyear-related email on the Weiner laptop).

Initial Response of FBI Headquarters

McCabe told the OIG that he considered the information provided by Sweeney to be "a big deal" and said he instructed Priestap to send a team to New York to review the emails on the Weiner laptop. McCabe told the OIG that he recalled talking to Comey about the issue "right around the time [McCabe] found out about it." McCabe described it as a "fly-by," where the Weiner

Executive Summary

A Review of Various Actions by the Federal Bureau of Investigation and Department of Justice in Advance of the 2016 Election

laptop was "like one in a list of things that we discussed."

Comey said that he recalled first learning about the additional emails on the Weiner laptop at some point in early October 2016, although he said it was possible this could have occurred in late September 2016. Comey told the OIG that this information "didn't index" with him, which he attributed to the way the information was presented to him and the fact that, "I don't know that I knew that [Weiner] was married to Huma Abedin at the time."

Text messages of FBI Deputy Assistant Director Peter Strzok indicated that he, McCabe, and Priestap discussed the Weiner laptop on September 28. Strzok said that he had initially planned to send a team to New York to review the emails, but a conference call with NYO was scheduled instead. The conference call took place on September 29, and five members of the FBI Midyear team participated. Notes from the conference call indicate the participants discussed the presence of a large volume of emails (350,000) on the Weiner laptop and specific domain names, including clintonemail.com and state.gov. The Midyear SSA said that NYO also mentioned seeing BlackBerry domain emails on the Weiner laptop.

Additional discussions took place on October 3 and 4, 2016. However, after October 4, we found no evidence that anyone associated with the Midyear investigation, including the entire leadership team at FBI Headquarters, took any action on the Weiner laptop issue until the week of October 24, and then did so only after the Weiner case agent expressed concerns to SDNY, prompting SDNY to contact the Office of the Deputy Attorney General (ODAG) on October 21 to raise concerns about the lack of action.

Reengagement of FBI Headquarters

On Friday, October 21, SDNY Deputy U.S. Attorney Joon Kim contacted ODAG and was put in touch with DAAG George Toscas, the most senior career Department official involved in the Midyear investigation. Thereafter, at Toscas's request, one of the Midyear prosecutors called Strzok. This was the first conversation that the FBI had with Midyear prosecutors about the Weiner laptop.

Toscas said he asked McCabe about the Weiner laptop on Monday, October 24, after a routine meeting between FBI and Department leadership. McCabe told us that this interaction with Toscas caused him to follow up with the FBI Midyear team about the Weiner laptop and to call McCord about the issue.

On October 26, NYO, SDNY, and Midyear team members participated in a conference call. The FBI Midyear team told the OIG that they learned important new information on this call, specifically: (1) that there was a large volume of emails on the Weiner laptop, particularly the potential for a large number of @clintonemail.com emails; and (2) that the presence of Blackberry data indicated that emails from Clinton's first three months as Secretary of State could be present on the laptop. However, as we describe above and in Chapter Nine of our report, these basic facts were known to the FBI by September 29, 2016.

The FBI Midyear team briefed McCabe about the information from the conference call on the evening of October 26, 2016. McCabe told us that he felt the situation was "absolutely urgent" and proposed that the FBI Midyear team meet with Comey the following day.

On October 27 at 5:20 a.m., McCabe emailed Comey stating that the Midyear team "has come across some additional actions they believe they need to take," and recommending that they meet that day to discuss the implications "if you have any space on your calendar." Comey stated that he did not know what this email was about when he received it and did not initially recall that he had been previously notified about the Weiner laptop.

We found that, by no later than September 29, FBI executives and the FBI Midyear team had learned virtually every fact that was cited by the FBI in late October as justification for obtaining the search warrant for the Weiner laptop, including that the laptop contained:

- Over 340,000 emails, some of which were from domains associated with Clinton, including state.gov, clintonfoundation.org, clintonemail.com, and hillaryclinton.com;
- Numerous emails between Clinton and Abedin;
- An unknown number of Blackberry communications on the laptop, including one or more messages between Clinton and Abedin, indicating the possibility that the laptop contained communications from the early months of Clinton's tenure; and
- Emails dated beginning in 2007 and covering the entire period of Clinton's tenure as Secretary of State.

Executive Summary

A Review of Various Actions by the Federal Bureau of Investigation and Department of Justice in Advance of the 2016 Election

As we describe in Chapter Nine of our report, the explanations we were given for the FBI's failure to take immediate action on the Weiner laptop fell into four general categories:

- The FBI Midyear team was waiting for additional information about the contents of the laptop from NYO, which was not provided until late October;

- The FBI Midyear team could not review the emails without additional legal authority, such as consent or a new search warrant;

- The FBI Midyear team and senior FBI officials did not believe that the information on the laptop was likely to be significant; and

- Key members of the FBI Midyear team had been reassigned to the investigation of Russian interference in the U.S. election, which was a higher priority.

We found these explanations to be unpersuasive justifications for not acting sooner, given the FBI leadership's conclusion about the importance of the information and that the FBI Midyear team had sufficient information to take action in early October and knew at that time that it would need a new search warrant to review any Clinton-Abedin emails. Moreover, given the FBI's extensive resources, the fact that Strzok and several other FBI members of the Midyear team had been assigned to the Russia investigation, which was extremely active during this September and October time period, was not an excuse for failing to take any action during this time period on the Weiner laptop.

The FBI's failure to act in late September or early October is even less justifiable when contrasted with the attention and resources that FBI management and some members of the Midyear team dedicated to other activities in connection with the Midyear investigation during the same period. As detailed in Chapter Eight, these activities included:

- The preparation of Comey's speech at the FBI's SAC Conference on October 12, a speech designed to help equip SACs to "bat down" misinformation about the July 5 declination decision;

- The preparation and distribution of detailed talking points to FBI SACs in mid-October in order, again, "to equip people who are going to be talking about it anyway with the actual facts

and [the FBI's] actual perspective on [the declination]"; and

- A briefing for retired FBI agents conducted on October 21 to describe the investigative decisions made during Midyear so as to arm former employees with facts so that they, too, might counter "falsehoods and exaggerations."

In assessing the decision to prioritize the Russia investigation over following up on the Midyear-related investigative lead discovered on the Weiner laptop, we were particularly concerned about text messages sent by Strzok and Page that potentially indicated or created the appearance that investigative decisions they made were impacted by bias or improper considerations. Most of the text messages raising such questions pertained to the Russia investigation, and the implication in some of these text messages, particularly Strzok's August 8 text message ("we'll stop" candidate Trump from being elected), was that Strzok might be willing to take official action to impact a presidential candidate's electoral prospects. Under these circumstances, we did not have confidence that Strzok's decision to prioritize the Russia investigation over following up on the Midyear-related investigative lead discovered on the Weiner laptop was free from bias.

We searched for evidence that the Weiner laptop was deliberately placed on the back-burner by others in the FBI to protect Clinton, but found no evidence in emails, text messages, instant messages, or documents that suggested an improper purpose. We also took note of the fact that numerous other FBI executives—including the approximately 39 who participated in the September 28 SVTC—were briefed on the potential existence of Midyear-related emails on the Weiner laptop. We also noted that the Russia investigation was under the supervision of Priestap—for whom we found no evidence of bias and who himself was aware of the Weiner laptop issue by September 29. However, we also did not identify a consistent or persuasive explanation for the FBI's failure to act for almost a month after learning of potential Midyear-related emails on the Weiner laptop.

The FBI's inaction had potentially far-reaching consequences. Comey told the OIG that, had he known about the laptop in the beginning of October and thought the email review could have been completed before the election, it may have affected his decision to notify Congress. Comey told the OIG, "I don't know [if] it would have put us in a different place, but I would have wanted to have the opportunity."

ix

Executive Summary

A Review of Various Actions by the Federal Bureau of Investigation and Department of Justice in Advance of the 2016 Election

Comey's Decision to Notify Congress on October 28

Following the briefing from the FBI Midyear team on October 27, 2016, Comey authorized the Midyear team to seek a search warrant, telling the OIG that "the volume of emails" and the presence of BlackBerry emails on the Weiner laptop were "two highly significant facts." As we describe in Chapter Thirteen of our report, McCabe joined this meeting by phone but was asked not to participate, and subsequently recused himself from the Midyear investigation on November 1, 2016.

The issue of notifying Congress of the Weiner laptop development was first raised at the October 27 briefing and, over the course of the next 24 hours, numerous additional discussions occurred within the FBI. As we describe in Chapter Ten of our report, the factors considered during those discussions included:

- Comey's belief that failure to disclose the existence of the emails would be an act of concealment;

- The belief that Comey had an obligation to update Congress because the discovery was potentially significant and made his prior testimony that the investigation was closed no longer true;

- An implicit assumption that Clinton would be elected President;

- Fear that the information would leak if the FBI failed to disclose it;

- Concern that failing to disclose would result in accusations that the FBI had "engineered a cover up" to help Clinton get elected;

- Concerns about protecting the reputation of the FBI;

- Concerns about the perceived illegitimacy of a Clinton presidency that would follow from a failure to disclose the discovery of the emails if they proved to be significant;

- Concerns about the electoral impact of any announcement; and

- The belief that the email review could not be completed before the election.

As a result of these discussions on October 27, Comey decided to notify Congress about the discovery of Midyear-related emails on the Weiner laptop. Comey

told us that, although he "believe[d] very strongly that our rule should be, we don't comment on pending investigations" and that it was a "very important norm" for the Department to avoid taking actions that could impact an imminent election, he felt he had an obligation to update Congress because the email discovery was potentially very significant and it made his prior testimony no longer true.

We found no evidence that Comey's decision to send the October 28 letter was influenced by political preferences. Instead, we found that his decision was the result of several interrelated factors that were connected to his concern that failing to send the letter would harm the FBI and his ability to lead it, and his view that candidate Clinton was going to win the presidency and that she would be perceived to be an illegitimate president if the public first learned of the information after the election. Although Comey told us that he "didn't make this decision because [he] thought it would leak otherwise," several FBI officials told us that the concern about leaks played a role in the decision.

Much like with his July 5 announcement, we found that in making this decision, Comey engaged in ad hoc decisionmaking based on his personal views even if it meant rejecting longstanding Department policy or practice. We found unpersuasive Comey's explanation as to why transparency was more important than Department policy and practice with regard to the reactivated Midyear investigation while, by contrast, Department policy and practice were more important to follow with regard to the Clinton Foundation and Russia investigations.

Comey's description of his choice as being between "two doors," one labeled "speak" and one labeled "conceal," was a false dichotomy. The two doors were actually labeled "follow policy/practice" and "depart from policy/practice." Although we acknowledge that Comey faced a difficult situation with unattractive choices, in proceeding as he did, we concluded that Comey made a serious error of judgment.

Department and FBI Leadership Discussions

On October 27, Comey instructed his Chief of Staff, James Rybicki, to reach out to the Department about his plan to notify Congress. As we describe in Chapter Ten of our report, Comey told the OIG that he decided to ask Rybicki to inform the Department rather than to contact Lynch or Yates directly because he did not "want to jam them and I wanted to offer them the

Executive Summary

A Review of Various Actions by the Federal Bureau of Investigation and Department of Justice in Advance of the 2016 Election

opportunity to think about and decide whether they wanted to be engaged on it." Rybicki and Axelrod spoke on the afternoon of October 27 and had "a series of phone calls" the rest of the day. Rybicki told Axelrod that Comey believed he had an obligation to notify Congress about the laptop in order to correct a misimpression that the Midyear investigation was closed.

Lynch, Yates, Axelrod, and their staffs had several discussions that same day as to whether Lynch or Yates should call Comey directly, but said they ultimately decided to have Axelrod communicate "the strong view that neither the DAG nor [AG] felt this letter should go out." Yates told us they were concerned that direct contact with Comey would be perceived as "strong-arming" him, and that based on her experience with Comey, he was likely to "push back hard" against input from Lynch or her, especially if accepting their input meant that he had to go back to his staff and explain that he was reversing his decision. She said that she viewed Rybicki as the person they needed to convince if they wanted to change Comey's mind. Accordingly, Axelrod informed Rybicki on October 27 of the Department's strong opposition to Comey's plan to send a letter.

Rybicki reported to Comey that the Department "recommend[ed] against" the Congressional notification and thought it was "a bad idea." Although Comey told us that he would not have sent the letter if Lynch or Yates had told him not to do so, he said he viewed their response as only a recommendation and interpreted their lack of direct engagement as saying "basically...it's up to you.... I honestly thought they were taking kind of a cowardly way out." The following day, October 28, Comey sent a letter to Congress stating, in part, that "the FBI has learned of the existence of emails that appear to be pertinent to the [Midyear] investigation."

Comey, Lynch, and Yates faced difficult choices in late October 2016. However, we found it extraordinary that Comey assessed that it was best that the FBI Director not speak directly with the Attorney General and Deputy Attorney General about how best to navigate this most important decision and mitigate the resulting harms, and that Comey's decision resulted in the Attorney General and Deputy Attorney General concluding that it would be counterproductive to speak directly with the FBI Director. We believe that open and candid communication among leaders in the Department and its components is essential for the effective functioning of the Department.

Text and Instant Messages, Use of Personal Email, and Alleged Improper Disclosures of Non-Public Information

Text Messages and Instant Messages

As we describe in Chapter Twelve, during our review we identified text messages and instant messages sent on FBI mobile devices or computer systems by five FBI employees who were assigned to the Midyear investigation. These included:

- Text messages exchanged between Strzok and Page;

- Instant messages exchanged between Agent 1, who was one of the four Midyear case agents, and Agent 5, who was a member of the filter team; and

- Instant messages sent by FBI Attorney 2, who was assigned to the Midyear investigation.

The text messages and instant messages sent by these employees included statements of hostility toward then candidate Trump and statements of support for candidate Clinton, and several appeared to mix political opinions with discussions about the Midyear investigation.

We found that the conduct of these five FBI employees brought discredit to themselves, sowed doubt about the FBI's handling of the Midyear investigation, and impacted the reputation of the FBI. Although our review did not find documentary or testimonial evidence directly connecting the political views these employees expressed in their text messages and instant messages to the specific investigative decisions we reviewed in Chapter Five, the conduct by these employees cast a cloud over the FBI Midyear investigation and sowed doubt the FBI's work on, and its handling of, the Midyear investigation. Moreover, the damage caused by their actions extends far beyond the scope of the Midyear investigation and goes to the heart of the FBI's reputation for neutral factfinding and political independence.

We were deeply troubled by text messages exchanged between Strzok and Page that potentially indicated or created the appearance that investigative decisions were impacted by bias or improper considerations. Most of the text messages raising such questions pertained to the Russia investigation, which was not a part of this review. Nonetheless, when one senior FBI official, Strzok, who was helping to lead the Russia

Executive Summary

A Review of Various Actions by the Federal Bureau of Investigation and Department of Justice in Advance of the 2016 Election

investigation at the time, conveys in a text message to another senior FBI official, Page, "No. No he won't. We'll stop it" in response to her question "[Trump's] not ever going to become president, right? Right?!", it is not only indicative of a biased state of mind but, even more seriously, implies a willingness to take official action to impact the presidential candidate's electoral prospects. This is antithetical to the core values of the FBI and the Department of Justice.

We do not question that the FBI employees who sent these messages are entitled to their own political views. However, we believe using FBI devices to send the messages discussed in Chapter Twelve—particularly the messages that intermix work-related discussions with political commentary—potentially implicate provisions in the FBI's Offense Code and Penalty Guidelines. At a minimum, we found that the employees' use of FBI systems and devices to send the identified messages demonstrated extremely poor judgment and a gross lack of professionalism. We therefore refer this information to the FBI for its handling and consideration of whether the messages sent by the five employees listed above violated the FBI's Offense Code of Conduct.

Use of Personal Email

As we also describe in Chapter Twelve, we learned during the course of our review that Comey, Strzok, and Page used their personal email accounts to conduct FBI business.

We identified numerous instances in which Comey used a personal email account to conduct unclassified FBI business. We found that, given the absence of exigent circumstances and the frequency with which the use of personal email occurred, Comey's use of a personal email account for unclassified FBI business to be inconsistent with Department policy.

We found that Strzok used his personal email accounts for official government business on several occasions, including forwarding an email from his FBI account to his personal email account about the proposed search warrant the Midyear team was seeking on the Weiner laptop. This email included a draft of the search warrant affidavit, which contained information from the Weiner investigation that appears to have been under seal at the time in the Southern District of New York and information obtained pursuant to a grand jury subpoena issued in the Eastern District of Virginia in the Midyear investigation. We refer to the FBI the issue of whether Strzok's use of personal email accounts violated FBI and Department policies.

Finally, when questioned, Page also told us she used personal email for work-related matters at times. She stated that she and Strzok sometimes used these forums for work-related discussions due to the technical limitations of FBI-issued phones. Page left the FBI on May 4, 2018.

Improper Disclosure of Non-Public Information

As we also describe in Chapter Twelve, among the issues we reviewed were allegations that Department and FBI employees improperly disclosed non-public information regarding the Midyear investigation. Although FBI policy strictly limits the employees who are authorized to speak to the media, we found that this policy appeared to be widely ignored during the period we reviewed.

We identified numerous FBI employees, at all levels of the organization and with no official reason to be in contact with the media, who were nevertheless in frequent contact with reporters. Attached to this report as Attachments E and F are two link charts that reflect the volume of communications that we identified between FBI employees and media representatives in April/May and October 2016. We have profound concerns about the volume and extent of unauthorized media contacts by FBI personnel that we have uncovered during our review.

In addition, we identified instances where FBI employees improperly received benefits from reporters, including tickets to sporting events, golfing outings, drinks and meals, and admittance to nonpublic social events. We will separately report on those investigations as they are concluded, consistent with the Inspector General Act, other applicable federal statutes, and OIG policy.

The harm caused by leaks, fear of potential leaks, and a culture of unauthorized media contacts is illustrated in Chapters Ten and Eleven of our report, where we detail the fact that these issues influenced FBI officials who were advising Comey on consequential investigative decisions in October 2016. The FBI updated its media policy in November 2017, restating its strict guidelines concerning media contacts, and identifying who is required to obtain authority before engaging members of the media, and when and where to report media contact. We do not believe the problem is with the FBI's policy, which we found to be clear and unambiguous. Rather, we concluded that these leaks highlight the need to change what appears to be a cultural attitude among many in the organization.

Executive Summary

A Review of Various Actions by the Federal Bureau of Investigation and Department of Justice in Advance of the 2016 Election

Recusal Issues

Former Deputy Director Andrew McCabe: As we describe in Chapter Thirteen, in 2015, McCabe's spouse, Dr. Jill McCabe, ran for a Virginia State Senate seat. During the campaign, Dr. McCabe's campaign committee received substantial monetary and in-kind contributions, totaling $675,288 or approximately 40 percent of the total contributions raised by Dr. McCabe for her state senate campaign, from then Governor McAuliffe's Political Action Committee (PAC) and from the Virginia Democratic Party. In addition, on June 26, 2015, Hillary Clinton was the featured speaker at a fundraiser in Virginia hosted by the Virginia Democratic Party and attended by Governor McAuliffe.

At the time his wife sought to run for state senate, McCabe was the Assistant Director in Charge of the FBI's Washington Field Office (WFO) and sought ethics advice from FBI ethics officials and attorneys. We found that FBI ethics officials and attorneys did not fully appreciate the potential significant implications to McCabe and the FBI from campaign donations to Dr. McCabe's campaign. The FBI did not implement any review of campaign donations to assess potential conflicts or appearance issues that could arise from the donations. On this issue, we believe McCabe did what he was supposed to do by notifying those responsible in the FBI for ethics issues and seeking their guidance.

After McCabe became FBI Deputy Director in February 2016, McCabe had an active role in the supervision of the Midyear investigation, and oversight of the Clinton Foundation investigation, until he recused himself from these investigations on November 1, 2016. McCabe voluntarily recused himself on November 1, at Comey's urging, as the result of an October 23 article in the Wall Street Journal identifying the substantial donations from McAuliffe's PAC and the Virginia Democratic Party to Dr. McCabe.

With respect to these investigations, we agreed with the FBI's chief ethics official that McCabe was not at any time required to recuse under the relevant authorities. However, voluntary recusal is always permissible with the approval of a supervisor or ethics official, which is what McCabe did on November 1. Had the FBI put in place a system for reviewing campaign donations to Dr. McCabe, which were public under Virginia law, the sizable donations from McAuliffe's PAC and the Virginia Democratic Party may have triggered prior consideration of the very appearance concerns raised in the October 23 WSJ article. Finally, we also found that McCabe did not fully comply with this recusal in a few

instances related to the Clinton Foundation investigation.

Former Assistant Attorney General Peter Kadzik: In Chapter Fourteen, we found that Kadzik demonstrated poor judgment by failing to recuse himself from Clinton-related matters under federal ethics regulations prior to November 2, 2016. Kadzik did not recognize the appearance of a conflict that he created when he initiated an effort to obtain employment for his son with the Clinton campaign while participating in Department discussions and communications about Clinton-related matters.

Kadzik also created an appearance of a conflict when he sent the Chairman of the Clinton Campaign and a longtime friend, John Podesta, the "Heads up" email that included the schedule for the release of former Secretary Clinton's emails proposed to the court in a FOIA litigation without knowing whether the information had yet been filed and made public. His willingness to do so raised a reasonable question about his ability to act impartially on Clinton-related matters in connection with his official duties.

Additionally, although Department leadership determined that Kadzik should be recused from Clinton-related matters upon learning of his "Heads up" email to Podesta, we found that Kadzik failed to strictly adhere to this recusal. Lastly, because the government information in the "Heads up" email had in fact been released publically, we did not find that Kadzik released non-public information or misused his official position.

FBI Records Vault Twitter Announcements

As we describe in Chapter Fifteen, on November 1, 2016, in response to multiple FOIA requests, the FBI Records Management Division (RMD) posted records to the FBI Records Vault, a page on the FBI's public website, concerning the "William J. Clinton Foundation." The @FBIRecordsVault Twitter account announced this posting later the same day. We concluded that these requests were processed according to RMD's internal procedures like other similarly-sized requests, and found no evidence that the FOIA response was expedited or delayed in order to impact the 2016 presidential election. We also found no evidence that improper political considerations influenced the FBI's use of the Twitter account to publicize the release.

Executive Summary

A Review of Various Actions by the Federal Bureau of Investigation and Department of Justice in Advance of the 2016 Election

Recommendations

Our report makes nine recommendations to the Department and the FBI to assist them in addressing the issues that we identified in this review:

- We recommend that the Department and the FBI consider developing guidance that identifies the risks associated with and alternatives to permitting a witness to attend a voluntary interview of another witness (including in the witness's capacity as counsel).

- We recommend that the Department consider making explicit that, except in situations where the law requires or permits disclosure, an investigating agency cannot publicly announce its recommended charging decision prior to consulting with the Attorney General, Deputy Attorney General, U.S. Attorney, or his or her designee, and cannot proceed without the approval of one of these officials.

- We recommend that the Department and the FBI consider adopting a policy addressing the appropriateness of Department employees discussing the conduct of uncharged individuals in public statements.

- We recommend that the Department consider providing guidance to agents and prosecutors concerning the taking of overt investigative steps, indictments, public announcements, or other actions that could impact an election.

- We recommend that the Office of the Deputy Attorney General take steps to improve the retention and monitoring of text messages Department-wide.

- We recommend that the FBI add a warning banner to all of the FBI's mobile phones and devices in order to further notify users that they have no reasonable expectation of privacy.

- We recommend that the FBI consider (a) assessing whether it has provided adequate training to employees about the proper use of text messages and instant messages, including any related discovery obligations, and (b) providing additional guidance about the allowable uses of FBI devices for any non-governmental purpose, including guidance about the use of FBI devices for political conversations.

- We recommend that the FBI consider whether (a) it is appropriately educating employees about both its media contact policy and the Department's ethics rules pertaining to the acceptance of gifts, and (b) its disciplinary provisions and penalties are sufficient to deter such improper conduct.

- We recommend that Department ethics officials include the review of campaign donations for possible conflict issues when Department employees or their spouses run for public office.

TABLE OF CONTENTS

PAGE LEFT INTENTIONALLY

BLANK

CHAPTER ONE:
INTRODUCTION

I.   Background

The Department of Justice (Department) Office of the Inspector General (OIG) undertook this review of various actions by the Federal Bureau of Investigation (FBI) and Department in connection with the investigation into the use of a private email server by former Secretary of State Hillary Clinton. Clinton served as Secretary of State from January 21, 2009, until February 1, 2013, and during that time used private email servers hosting the @clintonemail.com domain to conduct official Department of State (State Department) business.

In 2014, in response to a request from the State Department to Clinton for "copies of any Federal records in [her] possession, such as emails sent or received on a personal email account while serving as Secretary of State," Clinton produced to the State Department 30,490 emails from her private server that her attorneys determined were work-related. Clinton and her attorneys did not produce to the State Department approximately 31,830 emails because, they stated, they were personal in nature, and these emails subsequently were deleted from the laptop computers that the attorneys used to review them.

In 2015, at the State Department's request, the Office of the Inspector General of the Intelligence Community (IC IG) reviewed emails from Clinton's private email server that she had produced to the State Department and identified a potential compromise of classified information. The IC IG subsequently referred this information to the FBI.

The FBI opened an investigation, known as "Midyear Exam" (MYE or Midyear), into the storage and transmission of classified information on Clinton's unclassified private servers in July 2015. Over the course of the next year, FBI agents and analysts and Department prosecutors conducted the investigation. Their activities included obtaining and analyzing servers and devices used by Clinton, contents of private email accounts for certain senior aides, and computers and email accounts used to back up, process, or transfer Clinton's emails. The investigative team interviewed numerous witnesses, including current and former State Department employees.

On June 27, 2016, while the Midyear investigation was nearing completion, then Attorney General (AG) Loretta Lynch and former President Bill Clinton had an unscheduled meeting while their planes were parked on the tarmac at Phoenix's Sky Harbor Airport. Former President Clinton boarded Lynch's plane, and Lynch, Lynch's husband, and the former President met for approximately 20 to 30 minutes. Following the meeting, Lynch publicly denied having any conversation about the Midyear investigation or any other substantive matter pending before the Department. Nevertheless, the meeting created significant controversy. On July 1, 2016, Lynch publicly announced that she would accept the recommendation of the

1

Midyear investigative and prosecutorial team regarding whether to charge former Secretary Clinton.

The following day, Saturday, July 2, 2016, the FBI and Department prosecutors interviewed former Secretary Clinton at the FBI's Headquarters building. Then, on July 5, 2016, without coordinating with the Department and with very brief notice to it, then FBI Director James Comey publicly delivered a statement that criticized Clinton, characterized her and her senior aides as "extremely careless" in their handling of classified information, and asserted that it was possible hostile actors gained access to Clinton's personal email account. Comey concluded, however, that the investigation should be closed because "no reasonable prosecutor" would prosecute Clinton or others, citing the strength of the evidence and the lack of precedent for bringing a case on these facts. The following day, July 6, 2016, Lynch was briefed by the prosecutors and formally accepted their recommendation to decline prosecution.

On October 28, 2016, 11 days before the presidential election, Comey sent a letter to Congress announcing the discovery of emails that "appear[ed] to be pertinent" to the Midyear investigation. Comey's letter was referring to the FBI's discovery of a large quantity of emails during the search of a laptop computer obtained in an unrelated investigation of Anthony Weiner, the husband of Clinton's former Deputy Chief of Staff and personal assistant, Huma Abedin.

The FBI obtained a search warrant to review the emails 2 days later, on October 30, 2016. Over the next 6 days, the FBI processed and reviewed a large volume of emails. On November 6, 2016, 2 days before the election, Comey sent a second letter to Congress stating that the review of the emails on the laptop had not changed the FBI's earlier conclusions with respect to Clinton.

The OIG initiated this review on January 12, 2017, in response to requests from numerous Chairmen and Ranking Members of Congressional oversight committees, various organizations, and members of the public to investigate various decisions made in the Midyear investigation. The OIG announced that it would review the following issues:

- Allegations that Department or FBI policies or procedures were not followed in connection with, or in actions leading up to or related to, Comey's public announcement on July 5, 2016, and Comey's letters to Congress on October 28 and November 6, 2016, and that certain underlying investigative decisions were based on improper considerations;

- Allegations that then FBI Deputy Director Andrew McCabe should have been recused from participating in certain investigative matters;

- Allegations that then Assistant Attorney General for the Department's Office of Legislative Affairs, Peter Kadzik, improperly disclosed non-public information to the Clinton campaign and/or should have been recused from participating in certain matters;

- Allegations that Department and FBI employees improperly disclosed non-public information; and

- Allegations that decisions regarding the timing of the FBI's release of certain Freedom of Information Act (FOIA) documents on October 30 and November 1, 2016, and the use of a Twitter account to publicize the same, were influenced by improper considerations.

The OIG announcement added that "if circumstances warrant, the OIG will consider including other issues that may arise during the course of the review." One such issue that the OIG added to the scope of this review arose from the discovery of text messages and instant messages between some FBI employees on the investigative team, conducted using FBI mobile devices and computers, that expressed statements of hostility toward then candidate Donald Trump and statements of support for then candidate Clinton, as well as comments about the handling of the Midyear investigation. We addressed whether these communications evidencing a potential bias affected investigative decisions in the Midyear investigation.

This review is separate from the review the OIG announced on March 28, 2018, concerning the Department's and FBI's compliance with legal requirements, and with applicable Department and FBI policies and procedures, in applications filed with the U.S. Foreign Intelligence Surveillance Court (FISC) relating to a certain U.S. person. We will issue a separate report relating to those issues when our investigative work is complete at a future date.

II.   Methodology

During the course of this investigation, the OIG interviewed more than 100 witnesses, several on more than one occasion. These included former Director Comey, former AG Lynch, former Deputy Attorney General (DAG) Sally Yates, members of the former AG's and DAG's staffs, FBI agents and supervisors and Department attorneys and supervisors who conducted the Midyear investigation, personnel from the FBI's New York Field Office (NYO) and the U.S. Attorney's Office for the Southern District of New York (SDNY) involved in the Anthony Weiner investigation, former and current members of the FBI's senior executive leadership, and former President Clinton.

All of the former Department and FBI officials we contacted to request interviews related to the Midyear investigation agreed to be interviewed. However, two witnesses with whom we requested interviews in connection with our review of whether Peter Kadzik, the former Assistant Attorney General for the Department's Office of Legislative Affairs (OLA), should have been recused from certain matters declined our request for an interview or were unable to schedule an interview.

We also reviewed significantly more than 1.2 million documents. Among these were FBI documents from the Midyear investigation, including electronic communications (EC) and interview reports (FD-302s), agent notes from witness interviews, draft and final versions of the letterhead memorandum (LHM) summarizing the Midyear investigation, drafts of Comey's public statement and letters to Congress, and contemporaneous notes from agents and supervisors involved in meetings about the statement and letters to Congress. We also obtained documents from prosecutors and supervisors in the Department's National Security Division (NSD) and the U.S. Attorney's Office for the Eastern District of Virginia (EDVA), as well as the Office of the Deputy Attorney General (ODAG) and the Office of the Attorney General (OAG). Importantly, among these documents were contemporaneous notes from the prosecutors and supervisors involved in the investigation.

In connection with our efforts to investigate the circumstances surrounding the FBI's discovery of Midyear-related emails on Anthony Weiner's laptop computer and Comey's notification to Congress on October 28, 2016, we obtained documents from NYO and SDNY personnel. These documents included forensic logs from processing of the Weiner laptop by NYO Computer Analysis and Recovery Team (CART) personnel, NYO and SDNY communications about the discovery of the emails, and other documents.

We obtained communications between and among agents, prosecutors, supervisors, and FBI and Department officials to understand what happened during the investigation and identify the contemporaneous factors considered in making investigative decisions. In addition to a large volume of emails, we obtained and reviewed well in excess of 100,000 text messages and instant messages to or from FBI personnel who worked on the investigation.

Our review also included the examination of highly classified information. We were given broad access to relevant materials by the Department and the FBI, including the sensitive compartmented information (SCI) discussed in the classified appendix to this report and emails and instant messages from both the FBI's Top Secret SCINet system and Secret FBINet system. Several of the State Department emails between Secretary Clinton and her staff from the underlying Midyear investigation included information relevant to a tightly-held Special Access Program (SAP), and we did not seek or obtain the required read-ins for that program. Based on our review of emails containing redacted SAP and the FBI's explanation of the program, we determined that this information was not needed for us to make the findings in this report.

Finally, and as discussed in more detail below, our review included information obtained in the Midyear investigation and the Anthony Weiner child exploitation investigation pursuant to grand jury subpoenas and sealed search warrants. At the Inspector General's request, the Department sought court orders authorizing the release of sealed information that does not otherwise affect individual privacy interests so that we can include relevant information in this report. This information is included in the report where appropriate.

III. Analytical Construct

As noted above, the OIG undertook this review to determine, among other things, whether "certain investigative decisions [taken in connection with the Midyear investigation] were based on improper considerations," including political bias or concerns for personal gain. In conducting this portion of our review, it was necessary to select particular investigative decisions for focused attention. It would not have been possible to recreate and analyze every decision made in a year-long complex investigation. We therefore identified particular case decisions or other incidents which were the subject of controversy. These included the use of consent agreements and voluntary interviews to obtain evidence; grants of immunity to witnesses; and the decision to allow Cheryl Mills and Heather Samuelson, two of former Secretary Clinton's attorneys, to attend her interview.

During our investigation, we looked for direct evidence of improper considerations, such as contemporaneous statements in emails, memoranda, or other documents explicitly linking political or other improper considerations to specific investigative decisions. We likewise questioned witnesses about whether they had direct evidence of improper considerations affecting decisionmaking. As noted above, we reviewed significantly more than 1.2 million emails, text messages, and internal documents relating to the investigation, and interviewed more than 100 witnesses who were involved in the matter.

We also analyzed the justifications offered for the investigative decisions we selected for focused review (including contemporaneous justifications and those offered after the fact) to determine whether they were a pretext for improper, but unstated, considerations. We conducted this assessment with appreciation for the fact that Department and FBI officials were required to make numerous decisions involving complex matters daily, under the unusual pressures and challenges present in the Midyear investigation.

In the January 12, 2017 memorandum announcing this review, we stated, "Our review will not substitute the OIG's judgment for the judgments made by the FBI or the Department regarding the substantive merits of investigative or prosecutive decisions." Consistent with this statement, we do not criticize particular decisions or infer that they were influenced by improper considerations merely because we might have recommended a different investigative strategy or tactic based on the facts learned during our investigation. The question we considered was not whether a particular investigative decision was perfect or ideal or one that we believed could have been handled more effectively, but whether the circumstances surrounding the decision indicated that it was based on considerations other than the merits of the investigation. If the explanations that we were given for a particular decision were consistent with a rational investigative strategy and not unreasonable, we did not conclude that the decision was based on improper considerations in the absence of evidence to the contrary. We took this approach because our role as an OIG is not to second-guess valid discretionary judgments made during the course of an investigation, and this approach is consistent with the OIG's handling of such questions in past reviews.

We applied this same standard as we reviewed and considered the Department's declination decision, the letterhead memorandum (LHM) summarizing the investigation, and contemporaneous emails and notes reflecting analysis and discussion of legal research conducted by the prosecutors.

IV.   Structure of the Report

This report is divided into sixteen chapters. Following this introduction, Chapter Two summarizes the relevant Department policies governing the release of information to the public and to Congress and the conduct of criminal investigations, as well as the relevant statutes regarding the mishandling of classified information that provided the legal framework for the Midyear investigation.

In Chapter Three, we provide an overview of the Midyear investigation, including decisions about staffing and investigative strategy. In Chapter Four, we discuss the decision to publicly acknowledge the Midyear investigation and former President Obama's statements about the Midyear investigation. In Chapter Five, we discuss the conduct of the investigation, focusing on the significant investigative decisions that were subject to criticism by Congress and the public after the fact. In Chapters Six and Seven, we describe the events leading to former Director Comey's July 5 statement and the Department's decision to decline prosecution of former Secretary Clinton. Chapters Eight through Eleven provide a chronology of events between the FBI's discovery of Clinton-related emails on the Weiner laptop in late September 2016 and Comey's letter to Congress on October 28, 2016, and describe the FBI's analysis of those emails and letter to Congress on November 6, 2016.

Chapter Twelve describes the text messages and instant messages expressing political views we obtained between certain FBI employees involved in the Midyear investigation and provides the employees' explanations for those messages. It also briefly discusses the use of personal email by several FBI employees, and provides an update on the status of the OIG's leak investigations.

Chapters Thirteen and Fourteen address allegations that then Deputy Director Andrew McCabe and then Assistant Attorney General Peter Kadzik should have been recused from participating in certain matters, or violated the terms of their recusals.

Chapter Fifteen addresses allegations that the timing of the FBI's release of FOIA documents and its use of Twitter to publicize the release were influenced by improper considerations or were otherwise improper.

Chapter Sixteen includes our conclusions and recommendations.

We also include a non-public classified appendix, which discusses highly classified information relevant to the Midyear investigation (Appendix One), and a non-public Law Enforcement Sensitive (LES) appendix containing the complete, unmodified version of Chapter Thirteen (Appendix Two).

We are providing copies of our unclassified report and the classified appendix to Congress, and are publicly releasing our report without these appendices. We also are providing copies of our unclassified report to the Office of Special Counsel (OSC) for its consideration.

PAGE LEFT INTENTIONALLY

BLANK

CHAPTER TWO:
APPLICABLE LAWS AND DEPARTMENT POLICIES

In this chapter, we describe the applicable laws, regulations, policies, and practices that govern the conduct of the Midyear investigation and are relevant to the analysis in the report. We identify specific Department and FBI policies related to investigative steps taken during the Midyear investigation, overt investigative activities in advance of an election, and the disclosure of information to the media and to Congress. We also describe the Department regulations governing the appointment of a special counsel.

Finally, we summarize the criminal statutes relevant to the Midyear investigation. These statutes provide the legal framework for our discussion of the investigative strategy and the FBI's and Department's assessment of the evidence in subsequent chapters.

I.   Policies and Laws Governing Criminal Investigations

Under federal law, investigators and prosecutors are given substantial authority and discretion in conducting criminal investigations. To navigate challenges and issues that they may face during these investigations, and to assist them in exercising their authority and discretion appropriately, the Department maintains the United States Attorneys Manual (USAM) as a "comprehensive…quick and ready reference for…attorneys responsible for the prosecution of violations of federal law." USAM 1-1.2000, 1-1.1000. In reviewing investigative decisions made during the Midyear investigation, we identified several provisions of the USAM of potential relevance.

The principles guiding the exercise of decisions related to federal prosecutorial discretion and those relevant to criminal prosecutions can be found within USAM Title 9-27.000, the Principles of Federal Prosecution. There the Department lays out guidance for federal prosecutors with the intent of "ensuring the fair and effective exercise of prosecutorial discretion and responsibility by attorneys for the government, and promoting confidence on the part of the public and individual defendants that important prosecutorial decisions will be made rationally and objectively on the merits of the facts and circumstances of each case." USAM 9-27.001. USAM Section 9-27.220 specifies grounds for commencing or declining prosecution, stating that an attorney for the government should commence or recommend federal prosecution if he or she believes that the person's conduct constitutes a federal offense, and that the admissible evidence will probably be sufficient to obtain and sustain a conviction, unless the prosecution would serve no substantial federal interest, the person is subject to effective prosecution in another jurisdiction, or there exists an adequate non-criminal alternative to prosecution. This section also states, "[B]oth as a matter of fundamental fairness and in the interest of the efficient administration of justice, no prosecution should be initiated against any person unless the attorney for the government believes that the admissible evidence is sufficient to obtain and sustain a guilty verdict by an unbiased trier of fact."

A.   Grand Jury Subpoenas

A federal grand jury is a group of sixteen to twenty-three eligible citizens, empaneled by a federal court that considers evidence in order to decide if there has been a violation of federal law. Fed. R. Crim. P. 6(a)(1). It is the responsibility of federal prosecutors "to advise the grand jury on the law and to present evidence for its consideration." USAM 9-11.010.

Grand jury subpoenas are one tool frequently used by federal prosecutors to collect evidence to present to a grand jury. USAM 9-11.120, Fed. R. Crim. P. 17. There are two types of grand jury subpoenas: (1) a grand jury subpoena *ad testificandum* which compels an individual to testify before the grand jury; and (2) a grand jury subpoena *duces tecum* which compels an individual or entity, such as a business, to produce documents, records, tangible objects, or other physical evidence to the grand jury. G.J. Manual § 5.2; Fed. R. Crim. P. 17.[1]

Federal prosecutors have "considerable latitude in issuing [grand jury] subpoenas." G.J. Manual § 5.4 (*quoting Doe* v. *DiGenova*, 779 F.2d 74, 80 (D.C. Cir. 1985)). Nonetheless, "the powers of the grand jury are not unlimited." G.J. Manual § 5.1 (*quoting Branzburg* v. *Hayes*, 408 U.S. 665, 688 (1972)). A court may quash a grand jury subpoena, upon motion, "if compliance would be unreasonable or oppressive." Fed. R. Crim. P. 17. In addition, a grand jury subpoena cannot override the invocation of a valid "constitutional, common-law, or statutory privilege" and cannot be used when "a federal statute requires the use of a search warrant or other court order." G.J. Manual § 5.1 (*quoting Branzburg*, 408 U.S. at 688) and §§ 5.6, 5.26. These limitations are discussed, insofar as they are relevant to this review, in subparts I.B., I.C., and 1.E. of this chapter.

There are also policy limitations governing the use of grand jury subpoenas. For example, the USAM provides guidelines for issuing grand jury subpoenas to attorneys regarding their representation of clients.[2] USAM 9-13.410. These guidelines are discussed in subpart I.B. of this chapter. In addition, the USAM generally advises prosecutors to consider alternatives to grand jury subpoenas, such as obtaining testimony and other evidence by consent, in light of the requirement that the government maintain the secrecy of any testimony or evidence accessed through the grand jury. USAM 9-11.254(1).

B.   Search Warrants and 2703(d) Orders

The Fourth Amendment protects individuals from unlawful searches and seizures of their property. Generally, the government must obtain a search warrant

---

[1] *Federal Grand Jury Practice,* Office of Legal Education (October 2008), *available at* https://dojnet.doj.gov/usao/eousa/ole/usabook/gjma/index.htm.

[2] The USAM also provides guidelines for the use of grand jury subpoenas to obtain testimony from targets or subjects of an investigation. "Target" means a "person as to whom the prosecutor or the grand jury has substantial evidence linking him or her to the commission of a crime and who, in the judgment of the prosecutor, is a putative defendant," while "subject" means a "person whose conduct is within the scope of the grand jury's investigation." USAM 9-11.151.

before searching a person's property in which the person retains a reasonable expectation of privacy. *United States* v. *Ross*, 456 U.S. 798, 822-23 (1982). Courts have held that individuals retain a reasonable expectation of privacy in data held within electronic storage devices, such as computers and cellular telephones. *E.g., Riley v. California*, 134 S. Ct. 2473, 2485 (2014); *Trulock v. Freeh*, 275 F.3d 391, 403 (4th Cir. 2001). To obtain a search warrant pursuant to Federal Rule of Criminal Procedure 41 (Rule 41 search warrant), the government must make a showing of facts under oath demonstrating probable cause to believe that the property to be searched contains evidence of a crime. Thus, while the government may issue a grand jury subpoena to obtain an electronic device, such as a computer or cellular telephone, the government generally will only be able to search the electronic device if it can demonstrate probable cause to believe the device contains evidence of a crime.

In addition, as discussed above, a grand jury subpoena cannot be used when "a federal statute requires the use of a search warrant or other court order." The Stored Communications Act provides that the government must obtain a search warrant in order to require a "provider of electronic communication service" to produce the contents of a subscriber's electronic communication that have been in electronic storage for 180 days or less. *See* 18 U.S.C. § 2703(a). For the content of electronic communications that have been in electronic storage for more than 180 days, the government must usually either obtain a search warrant or provide prior notice to the subscriber or customer and obtain a court order or subpoena.[3] *See* 18 U.S.C. § 2703(b). Thus, except for specific circumstances, in order to obtain the contents of an individual's email communications that are older than 180 days from a communications service provider such as Yahoo! or Google (Gmail) without notifying the subscriber in advance, the government must first obtain a Rule 41 search warrant upon a showing of probable cause that the stored emails in possession of the provider contain evidence of a crime.

Independent of whether the government can make the requisite probable cause showing to warrant a Rule 41 search warrant, the government may be able to obtain a court order pursuant to 18 U.S.C. § 2703(d) (2703(d) order). A 2703(d) order requires a communications service provider to produce information related to an individual's email account other than the content of the individual's emails, such as subscriber information and email header information. A court will issue a 2703(d) order if the government "offers specific and articulable facts showing that there are reasonable grounds to believe that...the records or other information sought, are relevant and material to an ongoing criminal investigation." 18 U.S.C. § 2703(d).

---

[3] Under 18 U.S.C. § 2703(b)(1)(b)(ii), the court may permit delays in noticing a subscriber/customer for up to 90 days to avoid the adverse results listed at 18 U.S.C. § 2705. Those adverse results include: (A) endangering the life or physical safety of an individual; (B) flight from prosecution; (C) destruction of or tampering with evidence; (D) intimidation of potential witnesses; or (E) otherwise seriously jeopardizing an investigation or unduly delaying a trial.

C.   Evidence Collection Related to Attorney-Client Relationships

The USAM contains guidelines for the use of subpoenas and search warrants to obtain information from attorneys related to their representation of clients.

When a subpoena issued to an attorney may relate to information concerning the attorney's representation of a client, the USAM mandates additional process. USAM 9-13.410. As a preliminary matter, all reasonable attempts must be made to obtain the information from alternative sources (specifically including by consent) before issuing the subpoena to the attorney, unless such efforts would compromise the investigation. The Department thereafter exercises "close control" over the issuance of such a subpoena. Before seeking such a subpoena, it "must first be authorized by the Assistant Attorney General or a DAAG [Deputy Assistant Attorney General] for the Criminal Division" except in unusual circumstances. Before the Department official can authorize the subpoena, several principles must be examined regarding the submitted draft subpoena, including:

- All reasonable attempts to obtain the information from alternative sources shall have proved unsuccessful;

- The information sought is reasonably needed for the successful completion of the investigation;

- In a criminal investigation, there must be reasonable grounds to believe that a crime has been or is being committed, and that the information sought is reasonably needed for the successful completion of the investigation or prosecution; and

- The need for the information must outweigh the potential adverse effects upon the attorney-client relationship.

USAM 9-13.410.C.

The intent behind this additional process is to strike a "balance between an individual's right to the effective assistance of counsel and the public's interest in the fair administration of justice and effective law enforcement." USAM 9-13.410.B.

The Department similarly exercises "close control" when law enforcement seeks the issuance of a search warrant for "the premises of an attorney who is a subject of an investigation, and who also is or may be engaged in the practice of law on behalf of clients." USAM 9-13.420. Such a search has the potential to "effect...legitimate attorney-client relationships" or uncover material "protected by a legitimate claim of privilege[.]" *Id.* Therefore, prosecutors "are expected to take the least intrusive approach consistent with vigorous and effective law enforcement when evidence is sought from an attorney actively engaged in the practice of law." USAM 9-13.420.A. Unless it would compromise an investigation, the USAM advises that consideration be given to obtaining needed information from other sources or through the use of consent or a subpoena, rather than issuing such a search warrant. USAM 9-13.420.A. Consultation with the Criminal Division and approval from an Assistant Attorney General or U.S. Attorney are required as well. USAM 9-13.420.B-C.

The use of process to recover materials from "disinterested third parties," including disinterested third party attorneys, requires consideration of additional guidance under 28 C.F.R. § 59.1 and USAM 9-19.220. Pursuant to 28 C.F.R. § 59.1(b), "It is the responsibility of federal officers and employees to...protect against unnecessary intrusions. Generally, when documentary materials are held by a disinterested third party, a subpoena, administrative summons, or governmental request will be an effective alternative to the use of a search warrant and will be considerably less intrusive." Similarly, USAM 9-19.220 provides, "As with other disinterested third parties, a search warrant should normally not be used to obtain...confidential materials" from a disinterested third party attorney.

D.   Use of Classified Evidence Before A Grand Jury

The classification of information and evidence can be another significant challenge for a federal prosecutor advising a grand jury. *See* USAM 9-90.230. Because jurors lack security clearances, the disclosure of such information "may only be done with the approval of the agency responsible for classifying the information[.]" USAM 9-90.230. Though the Department offers measures to "increase the likelihood" a classifying agency will approve the use of such information, the Department encourages prosecutors to consider several alternatives to seeking such disclosures. *Id.* A significant number of limitations and high-level Department approvals make seeking approval from the classifying agency complex, and inevitably such approval takes additional time. *See* USAM 9-90.200, 210.

E.   Immunity Agreements

When a witness invokes their Fifth Amendment right against self-incrimination, the government must either forgo the witness's incriminating testimony or offer the witness protection from prosecution resulting from such testimony, a protection known as "use immunity." 28 C.F.R. § 0.175(a), Crim. Resource Manual 716. The term "use immunity" encompasses several degrees of legal protections for a witness: transactional immunity, formal use immunity, letter immunity, and "Queen for a Day" agreements. Crim. Resource Manual 719.

1.   Transactional Immunity

Transactional immunity offers the highest level of legal protection to a compelled witness, protecting the witness from actual prosecution for the offense(s) involved in the Grand Jury proceeding. Crim. Resource Manual 717. For decades prior to 1972, the Supreme Court only recognized transactional immunity as the government vehicle to compel testimony from a witness invoking their Fifth Amendment rights. *See Kastigar* v. *United States*, 406 U.S. 441, 449-52 (1972).

13

2.   Formal Use Immunity

In 1970, Congress created a framework for the Department to grant formal "use immunity" for a witness offering testimony in a federal criminal investigation. 18 U.S.C. § 6002; Crim. Resource Manual 716. Unlike transactional immunity, use immunity only protects the witness against the government's use of the immunized testimony in a subsequent prosecution of the witness, except for perjury or giving a false statement. Crim. Resource Manual 717. However, the Supreme Court subsequently found that the statutory framework creating formal use immunity also prohibits the government from using immunized testimony to discover new evidence that is then used to prosecute the witness. *Kastigar*, 406 U.S. at 453. This additional protection is known as "derivative use immunity." Crim. Resource Manual 718. Thus, the government retains the ability to prosecute a witness given formal use immunity, but only with evidence obtained independently of the witness's immunized testimony. Crim. Resource Manual 717-18. In order to do so, the government must overcome a "heavy, albeit not insurmountable burden, by a preponderance of the evidence" to demonstrate wholly independent discovery of such evidence. *United States* v. *Allen*, 864 F.3d 63, 92 (2d Cir. 2017) (*citing Kastigar*, 406 U.S. at 460).

To obtain formal, court-ordered use immunity, a U.S. Attorney, after obtaining the approval of the Attorney General or her designee and the Criminal Division, seeks a court order to compel testimony of a witness appearing before the grand jury. 18 U.S.C. § 6003(b); USAM 9-23.130. Such compelled testimony should be sought when the witness's testimony, in the judgment of the U.S. Attorney, is necessary for the public interest and the witness is likely to invoke (or has invoked) their Fifth Amendment privilege against self-incrimination.[4] *Id.* The decision to grant immunity by a designated Department division ultimately requires final approval from the Department's Criminal Division. Crim. Resource Manual 720. Once the U.S. Attorney receives Department approval, he or she submits a motion to the judge overseeing the grand jury requesting the order to compel testimony from the witness. *Id.* at 723.

3.   Letter Immunity and "Queen for a Day" Agreements

In contrast with transactional and formal use immunity, a witness receiving either letter immunity or a "Queen for a Day" agreement is provided legal protections by the prosecutor pursuant to an agreement in exchange for the witness's agreement to provide testimony. Crim. Resource Manual 719. The legal

---

[4] The USAM offers a non-exhaustive list of factors that should be weighed in judging the public interest: (1) the importance of the investigation or prosecution to effective enforcement of the criminal laws; (2) the value of the person's testimony or information to the investigation or prosecution; (3) the likelihood of prompt and full compliance with a compulsion order, and the effectiveness of available sanctions if there is no such compliance; (4) the person's relative culpability in connection with the offense or offenses being investigated or prosecuted, and his or her criminal history; (5) the possibility of successfully prosecuting the person prior to compelling his or her testimony; and (6) the likelihood of adverse collateral consequences to the person if he or she testifies under a compulsion order. USAM 9-23.210.

protections the witness receives for voluntary testimony result from the type of agreement the witness makes with the prosecutor. *Id.*

Letter immunity describes an agreement between the prosecuting office and the witness that results in a letter from the prosecuting office to the witness authorizing the grant of legal protections.[5] *Id.* While the provisions of the agreement can vary, as a general matter letter immunity, like formal immunity, only protects the witness against the government's use of the immunized testimony in a subsequent prosecution of the witness, except for perjury or giving a false statement. Crim. Resource Manual 717; *see United States* v. *Pelletier*, 898 F.2d 297, 301 (2d Cir. 1990). Depending on the provisions of the agreement, the government may retain the ability to prosecute the witness with evidence obtained independently of the witness's immunized testimony, but as with formal use immunity, the government bears a considerable burden in such a prosecution. Crim. Resource Manual 717-18; *see also Pelletier*, 88 F.2d at 303.

In a "Queen for a Day" agreement, often referred to as a "proffer" agreement, a witness "proffers" or informs prosecutors of what the witness would state under oath if called to testify and, in exchange, the federal prosecutor agrees to limited legal protection for the witness conditioned on the witness's truthful testimony. Crim. Resource Manual 719. In a standard "Queen for a Day" agreement, the government agrees not to use any statements made by the witness pursuant to the proffer agreement against the witness in its case-in-chief in any subsequent prosecution of the witness, or in connection with the sentencing of the witness if the witness is subsequently prosecuted and convicted. However, unlike with formal use immunity or letter use immunity, the government typically may use leads obtained from the witness's statements to develop evidence against the witness and may use the witness's statements to cross-examine the witness in any future prosecution of the witness. *United States* v. *Stein*, 440 F. Supp. 2d 315, 322 (S.D.N.Y. 2006); *see also* Richard B. Zabel and James J. Benjamin, Jr., *"Queen for a Day" or "Courtesan for a Day": The Sixth Amendment Limits to Proffer Agreements*, 15 No. 9 White–Collar Crime Rep. 1 (2001).

4. Act of Production Immunity

Act of production or "Doe" immunity describes a distinct type of immunity applying to a witness's production of records, instead of witness testimony. USAM 9-23.250; *United States* v. *Doe*, 465 U.S. 605 (1984). The production of records by a witness in response to a grand jury subpoena potentially implicates the right against self-incrimination if the fact that the witness produced the records could be used against the witness in a future prosecution as an admission of the existence and possession of the records. USAM 9-23.250. The Department uses the same procedure to grant act of production immunity as it does for formal use immunity, producing a formal letter authorizing the U.S. Attorney to make a motion for a judicial order to compel the production of specifically enumerated records in

---

[5] The reach of the legal protections offered in such a letter may vary, with some instances of letter immunity being restricted to the jurisdiction of a particular U.S. Attorney and others applying in multiple districts or extending nationwide, typically with the agreement of the other prosecutors.

exchange for not using the witness' act of production against the witness in a subsequent prosecution of the witness. *Id.*; Crim. Resource Manual 722. Alternatively, the prosecutor can enter into a letter agreement with the individuals. In either situation, the act of production immunity does not provide any protection for the witness from a future prosecution.

II. Department Policies and Practices Governing Investigative Activities in Advance of an Election

Department policies require all Department officials to "enforce the laws...in a neutral and impartial manner" and to remain "particularly sensitive to safeguarding the Department's reputation for fairness, neutrality, and nonpartisanship."[6] Various policies also address investigative activities timed to affect an election and require that prosecutors and agents consult with the Criminal Division's Public Integrity Section (PIN) before taking overt investigative steps in advance of a primary or general election. No Department policy contains a specific prohibition on overt investigative steps within a particular period before an election. Nevertheless, various witnesses testified that the Department has a longstanding unwritten practice to avoid overt law enforcement and prosecutorial activities close to an election, typically within 60 or 90 days of Election Day. We discuss relevant Department policies and practices below.

A. Election Year Sensitivities Policy

In 2008, 2012, and 2016, the then Attorney General issued a memorandum "to remind [all Department employees] of the Department's existing policies with respect to political activities."[7] These memoranda are substantially similar. Each memorandum contains two sections, one addressing the investigation and prosecution of election crimes and the other describing restrictions imposed on Department employees by the Hatch Act.[8] In its election crimes section, the 2016 memorandum requires consultation with PIN at "various stages of all criminal matters that focus on violations of federal and state campaign-finance laws, federal patronage laws and corruption of the election process."[9] However, the memorandum also states the following:

> Simply put, politics must play no role in the decisions of federal investigators or prosecutors regarding any investigations or criminal

---

[6] *See* Loretta Lynch, Attorney General, U.S. Department of Justice, Memorandum for all Department Employees, Election Year Sensitivities, April 11, 2016, 1.

[7] Lynch, Memorandum for Department Employees, 1; Eric Holder, Attorney General, U.S. Department of Justice, Memorandum for all Department Employees, Election Year Sensitivities, March 9, 2012, 1; Michael Mukasey, Attorney General, U.S. Department of Justice, Memorandum for all Department Employees, Election Year Sensitivities, March 5, 2008, 1.

[8] The Hatch Act prohibits Department employees from engaging in partisan political activity while on duty, in a federal facility, or using federal property, including using the Internet at work for political activities. *See* 5 U.S.C. §§ 7321-7326 (2017).

[9] Lynch, Memorandum for Department Employees, 1.

16

charges. Law enforcement officers and prosecutors may never select the timing of investigative steps or criminal charges for the purpose of affecting any election, or for the purpose of giving an advantage or disadvantage to any candidate or political party. Such a purpose is inconsistent with the Department's mission and with the Principles of Federal Prosecution.

Likewise, the 2016 memorandum recommends that all Department employees consult with PIN whenever an employee is "faced with a question regarding the timing of charges or overt investigative steps near the time of a primary or general election," without regard to the type or category of crime at issue.[10] Ray Hulser, the former Section Chief of PIN who currently is a DAAG in the Criminal Division, told us that this policy does not impose a "mandatory consult" with PIN, but rather encourages prosecutors to call if they have questions about investigative steps or criminal charges before an election.

B.   The Unwritten 60-Day Rule

After the FBI released its October 28, 2016 letter to Congress informing them that the FBI had learned of the existence of additional emails and planned to take investigative steps to review them, contemporaneous emails between Department personnel highlighted editorials authored by former Department officials discussing a longstanding Department practice of delaying overt investigative steps or disclosures that could impact an election. These former officials cited the so-called "60-Day Rule," under which prosecutors avoid public disclosure of investigative steps related to electoral matters or the return of indictments against a candidate for office within 60 days of a primary or general election.[11]

The 60-Day Rule is not written or described in any Department policy or regulation. Nevertheless, high-ranking Department and FBI officials acknowledged the existence of a general practice that informs Department decisions. Former Director Comey characterized the practice during his OIG testimony as "a very important norm which is...we avoid taking any action in the run up to an election, if we can avoid it." Preet Bharara, the former U.S. Attorney for the Southern District of New York, told us that the Department's most explicit policy is about crimes that affect the integrity of an election, such as voter fraud, but that there is generalized, unwritten guidance that prosecutors do not indict political candidates or use overt investigative methods in the weeks before an election.

---

[10] During late 2016, Department personnel also considered guidance in *The Federal Prosecution of Election Offenses* prohibiting overt investigative steps before an election. U.S. Department of Justice, *The Federal Prosecution of Election Offenses*, 7th edition (May 2007). However, this publication explicitly applies to election crimes, not to criminal investigations that involve candidates in an election. *See id*. at 91-93.

[11] *See* Eric Holder, *James Comey Is A Good Man, But He Made A Serious Mistake*, WASH. POST, Oct. 30, 2016; Jamie Gorelick and Larry Thompson, *James Comey is Damaging Our Democracy*, WASH. POST, Oct. 29, 2016; Jane Chong, *Pre-Election Disclosures: How Does, and Should, DOJ Analyze Edge Cases*, LAWFARE BLOG (Nov. 8, 2016), https://www.lawfareblog.com/pre-election-disclosures-how-does-and-should-doj-analyze-edge-cases (accessed May 8, 2018).

Several Department officials described a general principle of avoiding interference in elections rather than a specific time period before an election during which overt investigative steps are prohibited. Former AG Lynch told the OIG, "[I]n general, the practice has been not to take actions that might have an impact on an election, even if it's not an election case or something like that." Former DAG Yates stated, "I look at it sort of differently than 60 days. To me if it were 90 days off, and you think it has a significant chance of impacting an election, unless there's a reason you need to take that action now you don't do it." Former Principal Associate Deputy Attorney General Matt Axelrod stated, "...DOJ has policies and procedures on...how you're supposed to handle this. And remember...those policies and procedures apply to...every election at whatever level.... They apply, you know, months before.... [P]eople sometimes have a misimpression there's a magic 60-day rule or 90-day rule. There isn't. But...the closer you get to the election the more fraught it is."

Hulser told the OIG that there was "a sense, there still is, that there is a rule out there, that there is some specific place where it says 60 days or 90 days back from a primary or general [election], that you can't indict or do specific investigative steps." He said that there is not any such specific rule, and there never has been, but that there is a general admonition that politics should play no role in investigative decisions, and that taking investigative steps to impact an election is inconsistent with the Department's mission and violates the principles of federal prosecution.

Hulser said that while working on the Election Year Sensitivities memorandum, they considered codifying the substance of the 60-Day Rule, but that they rejected that approach as unworkable, and instead included the general admonition described above. Citing PIN guidance, Hulser told OIG that a prosecutor should look to the needs of the case and significant investigative steps should be taken "when the case is ready, not earlier or later."[12]

III. Public Allegations of Wrongdoing Against Uncharged Individuals and Disclosure of Information in a Criminal Investigation

The USAM instructs prosecutors that "[i]n all public filings and proceedings, federal prosecutors should remain sensitive to the privacy and reputation interests of uncharged third-parties" and that there is ordinarily no legitimate governmental interest in the public allegation of wrongdoing by an uncharged party. USAM 9-27.760. Accordingly, even where prosecutors have concluded that an uncharged individual committed a crime, Department policies generally prohibit the naming of unindicted individuals (as well as co-conspirators) because their privacy and reputational interests merit significant consideration and protection. *See* USAM 9-11.130, 9-16.500, 9-27.760.

---

[12] Hulser produced an excerpt of a publication, written by a former Deputy Chief of PIN, discussing the issues involved in choosing the timing for charging a public corruption case. U.S. Department of Justice, *Prosecution of Public Corruption Cases* (February 1988), 214-15.

Department regulations governing interactions with the media recognize that "[t]he availability to news media of information in criminal and civil cases is a matter which has become increasingly a subject of concern in the administration of justice." 28 C.F.R. § 50.2(a)(1). Addressing this concern, the FBI issued a Media Relations Policy Guide for FBI personnel. The FBI Media Relations Policy Guide recognizes that the regulations found at 28 C.F.R. § 50.2 lay out specific and controlling guidelines addressing the release of information to the media from Department authorities as well as from subordinate law enforcement components, including the FBI. *Id.*; *see also* 28 C.F.R. § 0.1. The FBI Media Relations Policy Guide also recognizes that the USAM offers further specific guidance consistent with federal regulations in its Media Policy section "governing the release of information...by all components (FBI...and DOJ divisions) and personnel of the Department of Justice." USAM 1-7.001. The Department's policy and regulations forbid the confirmation or denial and any discussion of active investigations, except in limited, specified circumstances. USAM 1-7.530. Taken together, these documents offer an understanding of Department operations related to the media, particularly publicity around FBI investigations.

A. FBI Media Relations Policy

In October 2015, the FBI issued the version of its *Media Relations at FBI Headquarters (HQ) and in Field Offices Policy Guide* ("FBI Media Policy Guide") pertinent to this review.[13] The FBI Media Policy Guide recognizes that the FBI Office of Public Affairs (FBI OPA) "works to enhance the public's trust and confidence in the FBI by releasing and promoting information about the FBI's responsibilities, operations, accomplishments, policies, and values." The FBI Media Policy Guide confirms that FBI OPA "operations are governed by DOJ-OPA's instructions, located at Title 28 Code of Federal Regulations (C.F.R.) § 50.2, and by the *United States Attorneys' Manual* [USAM], Title 1-7.000, 'Media Relations.'" As such, where the guidance in the FBI Media Policy Guide conflicts with the USAM or 28 C.F.R. § 50.2, the USAM and Code of Federal Regulations control FBI media practices.

In its provisions governing disclosure of information to the media from FBI Headquarters in Washington, the FBI Media Policy Guide states "the [FBI] Director, [FBI] deputy director (DD), associate deputy director (ADD), [Assistant Director] for [FBI] OPA, and [FBI] OPA personnel designated by the [OPA Assistant Director] are authorized to speak to the media." However "[a]ll releases of information by...any FBI personnel...authorized to speak to the media must conform with all applicable laws and regulations, as well as policies issued by DOJ," which includes specific reference to the USAM, among other Department legal authorities. The FBI Media Policy Guide itself constrains authorized disclosures, explaining "[d]isclosures

---

[13] The October 2015 FBI Media Policy Guide is available online in the FBI records vault. *See* FBI Office of Public Affairs, *Media Relations at FBIHQ and in Field Offices Policy Guide*, October 13, 2015, https://go.usa.gov/xQNXQ (accessed May 7, 2018). On November 14, 2017, the FBI released a significantly revised guidance for media relations entitled *Public Affairs Policy Guide: Media Relations, External Communications, and Personal Use of Social Media*.

must not prejudice an adjudicative proceeding and...must not address an ongoing investigation" except in specified circumstances.[14] The FBI Media Policy Guide offers limited justifications to release information regarding an ongoing investigation, specifying the need "to assure the public that an investigation is in progress[,]...to protect the public interest, welfare, or safety,...[or] to solicit information from the public that might be relevant to an investigation." Any such release requires "prior approval of FBIHQ entities...[and] the careful supervision of OPA."

The FBI Media Policy Guide specifies that when releasing information to the media via a press conference, FBI OPA personnel "must request approval...in advance from DOJ-OPA for any case or investigation that may result in an indictment." Further, FBI personnel "must coordinate with DOJ OPA on any materials, quotes, or information to be released in the press conference."

B.   28 C.F.R. § 50.2

In all criminal matters, federal regulations bar Department personnel from "furnish[ing] any statement or information...if such a statement or information may reasonably be expected to influence the outcome of...a future trial." 28 C.F.R. § 50.2(b)(2). The regulation also provides that "where information relating to the circumstances of...an investigation would be highly prejudicial or where the release thereof would serve no law enforcement function, such information should not be made public." 28 C.F.R. § 50.2(b)(3).

The regulations permit, subject to limitations, some facts to be released publicly, including a defendant's name, age, and similar background information, the substance of the charges at issue, specified details regarding an investigation, and the circumstances surrounding an arrest. *See* 28 C.F.R. § 50.2(b)(3). But while permitting this limited release, the regulation specifies that the Department personnel making the public "disclosures should include only incontrovertible, factual matters, and should not include subjective observations." *Id.* These strict limitations "shall apply to the release of information to news media from the time a person is the subject of a criminal investigation until any proceeding resulting from such an investigation has been terminated by trial or otherwise." 28 C.F.R. § 50.2(b)(1). A Department official explained to the OIG that "otherwise" included criminal actions ended when the Department declines to prosecute.

The regulations do provide for exceptions, acknowledging situations in which the regulations "limit the release of information which would not be prejudicial under the particular circumstances." 28 C.F.R. § 50.2(b)(9). When a Department official believes that "in the interest of the fair administration of justice and the law enforcement process information beyond these guidelines should be released, in a particular case, he shall request the permission of the Attorney General or the Deputy Attorney General to do so." *Id.*

---

[14] When FBI officials make a public comment, the FBI Office of General Counsel "must advise FBI OPA on the potential impact of public comment on...proposed and pending litigation."

C.   USAM Media Relations Guidance

The Attorney General's central role to information disclosures to the media is also recognized in the USAM's Media Relations policy.[15] *See* USAM 1-7.210. The USAM makes clear that "[f]inal responsibility for all matters involving the news media and the [Department] is vested in the Director of the Office of Public Affairs (OPA)" and, without exception, the "Attorney General is to be kept fully informed of appropriate matters at all times." USAM 1-7.210.

The USAM's Media Relations section offers several provisions governing how information disclosure to the media may permissibly take place. Overall, the USAM 1-701(E) requires "any public communication by any…investigative agency about pending matters or investigations that may result in a case, or about pending cases or final dispositions, must be approved by the appropriate Assistant Attorney General, the United States Attorney, or other designate responsible for the case." Reinforcing a general principle of non-disclosure, the USAM declares "[a]t no time shall any component or personnel of the Department of Justice furnish any statement or information that he or she knows or reasonably should know will have a substantial likelihood of materially prejudicing an adjudicative proceeding." USAM 1-7.500.

In keeping with that principle, USAM 1-7.530 instructs Department personnel that, except in unusual circumstances, they "shall not respond to questions about the existence of an ongoing investigation or comment on its nature or progress, including such things as the issuance or serving of a subpoena, prior to the public filing of the document." Those unusual circumstances where comment may be appropriate included "matters that have already received substantial publicity, or about which the community needs to be reassured that the appropriate law enforcement agency is investigating the incident, or where release of information is necessary to protect the public interest, safety, or welfare[.]" USAM 1-7.530. But in any such circumstances, "the involved investigative agency will consult and obtain approval from the…Department Division handling the matter prior to disseminating any information to the media." *Id.*

USAM 1-7.401 addresses specifically press conferences, emphasizing a preference for written press releases as the "usual method to release public information…by investigative agencies." While permissible, press conferences "should be held only for the most significant and newsworthy actions, or if a particularly important deterrent or law enforcement purpose would be served. Prudence and caution should be exercised in the conduct of any press conference[.]" USAM 1-7.401. Repeatedly the USAM states that before holding a

---

[15] The Department significantly revised the USAM Media Relations provisions in November 2017, retitling them under "Confidentiality and Media Contacts Policy." This report primarily addresses the USAM Media Relations provisions in effect at the time of the events within the scope of this review. We consider the revised USAM provisions related to the media in Chapter Six of this report.

press conference "prior coordination with OPA is required" for information "of national significance." USAM 1-7.330(B), 1-7.401(B).

IV.   Release of Information to Congress

The provision of information from the Department and the FBI to Congress is governed by Department policy guidance, the USAM, and FBI rules.[16]

A.   USAM Congressional Relations Guidance

Under the USAM Title 1-8.000, and consistent with 28 C.F.R. § 0.27, communications between Congress and the Department are the responsibility of the Assistant Attorney General, Office of Legislative Affairs (OLA).[17] As written, the USAM 1-8.000 generally addresses personnel within the staff of the various United States Attorneys' Offices. However, USAM 1-8.000 explicitly applies to Department components and several provisions of the USAM guidance regarding the Department's congressional relations bind all Department personnel.[18]

One such provision is USAM 1-8.030 requiring coordination of a Department response when Congress seeks information that is not public. USAM 1-8.030 states "[a]ll Congressional requests for information (other than public information), meetings of any type, or assistance must immediately be referred to the...OLA[.]" The USAM lists the following examples of congressional requests requiring referral to OLA: "requests for non-public documents or information; discussion of or requests for briefings on cases;...[and] suggestions or comments on case disposition or other treatment[.]" USAM 1-8.030. These standards apply "in both open and closed cases" and the USAM highlights a specific bar on "provid[ing] information on (1) pending investigations;...(3) matters that involve grand jury, tax, or other restricted information; (4) matters that would reveal...sensitive investigative techniques, deliberative processes, the reasoning behind the exercise

---

[16] We note that the policies and rules described herein do not restrict lawful whistleblowing, protections for which were recognized by Attorney General Sessions in a recent memorandum reiterating the Department's "commit[ment] to protecting the rights of whistleblowers (*i.e.*, those employees or applicants who have made a lawfully protected disclosure to Congress)." Jefferson B. Sessions, Attorney General, U.S. Department of Justice, Memorandum for All Heads of Department Components, Communications with Congress, May 2, 2018, 2.

[17] According to the Code of Federal Regulations, "[t]he following-described matters are assigned to, and shall be conducted, handled, or supervised by, the Assistant Attorney General, Office of Legislative and Intergovernmental Affairs: (a) Maintaining liaison between the Department and the Congress." 28 C.F.R. § 0.27.

[18] While the AAG of OLA "is responsible for communications between Congress and the Department under the authority of the Attorney General" per the USAM, that authority does not override statutory reporting requirements to Congress, such as those required for the OIG found at 5 U.S.C. App. 4(a)(5).

of prosecutorial discretion, or the identity of individuals who may have been investigated but not indicted."[19] *Id.*

B. FBI Guidance on Information Sharing with Congress

The FBI's status as the primary investigative agency of the federal government makes its sharing of information with Congress of special concern. Relevant guidance is provided in *The Attorney General's Guidelines for Domestic FBI Operations* ("AGG-Dom") and the FBI's Domestic Investigations and Operations Guide ("DIOG"). The AGG-Dom directs that the FBI may "disseminate information obtained or produced" through its domestic investigations "to congressional committees as authorized by the Department of Justice Office of Legislative Affairs."[20] AGG-Dom § VI.B.1(c). This direction is reinforced in the DIOG's section on the retention and sharing of information, which states "that the FBI may disseminate information obtained or produced through activities under the AGG-Dom...[t]o Congress or to congressional committees in coordination with the FBI Office of Congressional Affairs (OCA) and the DOJ Office of Legislative Affairs." DIOG § 14.3.1(D). Notably, both the AGG-DOM and DIOG anticipate circumstances requiring departure from their rules. DIOG §§ 2.6-2.7. The DIOG spells out how such departures may occur, usually involving high-level FBI approval, coordination with the FBI Office of General Counsel, and notice and/or approval at the highest levels of the Department of Justice. *Id.*

C. Current Department Policy on Communication of Investigative Information to Congress

While the USAM, AGG-Dom, and DIOG lay out the consistent institutional relationships in the Department and its components for Congressional information flow, the Department also uses policy memoranda and other communications to provide guidance on how communication should be handled with Congress in sensitive, investigation-related circumstances. Among these are two memoranda governing Department communications with Congress and a letter addressing the principles of Department communications with Congress on ongoing investigations.

---

[19] On its face, this portion of USAM 1-8.030 addresses U.S. Attorney's Offices specifically. But the provision thereafter offers broader guidance that "[a]ll requests for these types of information should be referred to OLA[.]" USAM 1-8.030. Moreover, a Department official with long-term experience in OLA explained that he viewed the entirety of the USAM guidance on Congressional Relations as helping to understand "the playing field on which we operate in terms of a sensitivity of congressional contacts."

[20] The FBI is required to coordinate with OLA before sending formal communications to Congress regarding substantive matters that impact the Department. According to a Department official with long-term experience in OLA, the FBI can sometimes speak to Congress more informally by email or phone about certain types of matters like procedural matters, without first obtaining OLA approval.

1. Policy Memoranda on Department Communications with Congress

On May 11, 2009, then Attorney General Holder issued a policy memorandum for all Department components (including the FBI) entitled *Communications with Congress and the White House* ("May 2009 Memo"). In addressing pending criminal investigations and cases, the May 2009 Memo explained that the heads of investigative agencies, tasked with the primary duty of initiating and supervising cases, "must be insulated from influences that should not affect decisions in particular criminal...cases." The May 2009 Memo continues that for communications with Congress, consistent with "policies, laws, regulations, or professional ethical obligations...and consistent with the need to avoid publicity that may undermine a particular investigation," congressional inquiries related to pending criminal investigations and cases "should be directed to the Attorney General or [DAG]."[21]

On August 17, 2009, then Attorney General Holder issued an updated memo ("August 2009 Memo") entitled *Communications with Congress.* The August 2009 Memo clarified that all inquiries from congressional officials should be directed to DOJ OLA. The August 2009 Memo also spelled out that "all communications between the Department and Congress...should be managed by OLA to ensure that relevant Department interests and other Executive Branch interests are protected." "[C]omponents should not communicate with members, committees, or congressional staff without advance coordination with OLA." The August 2009 Memo concluded with direction for component heads to contact DOJ OLA for any questions on the policy.[22]

2. The Linder Letter

In a January 2000 letter from the Department's AAG for OLA to then Congressman John Linder ("Linder letter"), the Department described in detail the principles that guide OLA and the Department in their decision to disclose or withhold information from Congress. The letter remains a reference guide for OLA.

The Linder letter lays out "governing principles" to foster "improved communications and sensitivity between the Executive and Legislative Branches regarding our respective institutional needs and interests." After discussing the general tension between the interests of the two branches, the Linder letter

---

[21] The May 2009 Memo exempts congressional hearing communications and communications internal to an investigation from this requirement. The August 2009 Memo does not include any exemption for congressional hearing communications.

[22] On January 29 and May 2, 2018, Attorney General Sessions released memoranda also entitled *Communications with Congress* that reiterated and expanded direction to Department and component personnel regarding coordination with OLA "[c]onsistent with past policy and practice[.]" Among other changes, the May 2018 memorandum states "communications between the Department and Congress...will be managed or coordinated by [OLA] to ensure that relevant Department and Executive Branch interests are fully protected." In addition, the May 2018 memorandum states that "OLA will review prior to transmittal all Department written communications to Congress, including letters...and any other materials intended for submission or presentation on Capitol Hill."

examines the "inherent threat to the integrity of the Department's law enforcement and litigation functions" that comes from congressional inquiries during pending investigations. The letter noted that this concern was "especially significant with respect to ongoing law enforcement investigations." It then described the Department's longstanding policy, "dating back to the beginning of the 20th Century," to decline to provide congressional committees with access to open law enforcement files. One risk, according to the letter, is the possible public perception that such congressional inquiries amount to pressure resulting in "undue political and Congressional influence over law enforcement and litigation decisions." Another risk is the "severe[] damage" to the reputations of those mentioned in disclosure of information on open matters, "even though the case might ultimately not warrant prosecution or other legal action."

Finally, even when an investigation results in a declination, the Linder letter explains that the disclosure of information contained in such a declination memorandum "would implicate significant individual privacy interests as well." Such information "often contain[s] unflattering personal information as well as assessments of witness credibility and legal positions. The disclosure of the contents of these documents could be devastating to the individuals they discuss."

V.   Special Counsel Regulations

Since the 1999 lapse of the Independent Counsel Reauthorization Act, Department regulations govern the process of appointing a special counsel. 28 U.S.C. §§ 591-599, 64 Fed. Reg. 37,038 (1999). According to 28 C.F.R. § 600.1, the Attorney General (or Acting Attorney General) may appoint a special counsel for the criminal investigation of a person or matter when it would be in the public interest and there exists a Department conflict of interest or other extraordinary circumstance.

The regulations provide that the Attorney General need not appoint a special counsel immediately when a possible conflict emerges. Instead, the Attorney General may authorize further investigation or mitigation efforts, such as recusal. *See* 28 C.F.R. § 600.2. The special counsel must come from outside the government.[23] *See* 28 C.F.R. § 600.3. The Attorney General sets the criminal jurisdiction of the special counsel through a "specific factual statement of the matter to be investigated," though the Attorney General may authorize the

---

[23] In 2003, then Deputy Attorney General James Comey, who was the Acting Attorney General after the recusal of then Attorney General John Ashcroft, appointed a U.S. Attorney as special counsel in a letter citing 28 U.S.C. §§ 509, 510, 515, which describe the delegation authority of the Attorney General's office. *See United States* v. *Scooter Libby*, 429 F.Supp. 27, 40 (D.D.C. 2006). This method of appointing a special counsel did not rely on Department regulations, eliminating restrictions on who may be appointed special counsel and removing guidance setting the Attorney General's supervisory role over the office. *See* 28 C.F.R. §§ 600.2, 600.7.

additional areas of investigation.[24] 28 C.F.R. §§ 600.3-600.4. Day to day, the special counsel is not subject to Department supervision, but the Attorney General maintains the ability to review and overrule special counsel decisions in certain circumstances. 28 C.F.R. § 600.7.

VI. Criminal Statutes Relevant to the Midyear Investigation

Four statutes governing the handling and retention of classified information are relevant to the Midyear investigation: 18 U.S.C. §§ 793(d), 793(e), 793(f), and 1924.[25] Section 793(f)(1), which prohibits the grossly negligent removal of "national defense information," became a central focus of the investigation and of subsequent prosecutive decisions. In addition to the mishandling and retention statutes, prosecutors also considered whether former Secretary Clinton or others violated 18 U.S.C. § 2071, a criminal statute prohibiting the willful concealment, removal, or destruction of federal records, in connection with the deletion of emails. We discuss the Department's analysis of these statutes in Chapter Seven.

A. Mishandling and Retention of Classified Information

1. 18 U.S.C. §§ 793(d) and (e)

Sections 793(d) and (e) are felony statutes that apply to the willful mishandling and retention of classified information. Section 793(d) governs the mishandling of classified documents or information by individuals who are authorized to possess it — that is, who have the appropriate security clearance and require access to the specific classified information to perform or assist in a lawful and authorized governmental function ("need to know").[26] Section 793(d) provides:

> Whoever, lawfully having possession of, access to, control over, or being entrusted with any document, writing, code book, signal book, sketch, photograph, photographic negative, blueprint, plan, map, model, instrument, appliance, or note relating to the national defense, or information relating to the national defense which information the possessor has reason to believe could be used to the injury of the United States or to the advantage of any foreign nation, willfully communicates, delivers, transmits or causes to be communicated, delivered, or transmitted or attempts to communicate, deliver, transmit or cause to be communicated, delivered or transmitted the same to any person not entitled to receive it, or willfully retains the

---

[24] A special counsel's jurisdiction also covers "federal crimes committed in the course of, and with the intent to interfere with, the Special Counsel's investigation, such as perjury, obstruction of justice, destruction of evidence, and intimidation of witnesses." 28 C.F.R. § 600.4.

[25] Under the USAM, the Department's National Security Division (NSD) must expressly approve any prosecution involving these statutory provisions. *See* USAM 9-90.020.

[26] *See* Exec. Order 13526 §§ 4.1(a)(1)-(3), 6.1(dd) (Dec. 29, 2009); *see also United States* v. *Truong Dinh Hung*, 629 F.2d 908, 919 n.10 (4th Cir. 1980).

same and fails to deliver it on demand to the officer or employee of the United States entitled to receive it...[is subject to a criminal fine or imprisonment].

Thus, to prove a violation of Section 793(d), the government must establish the following:

- The individual lawfully had possession of documents or "information relating to the national defense;"

- If information, he or she had reason to believe that the information could be used to the injury of the United States or to the advantage of a foreign nation; and

- The individual willfully communicated, delivered, or transmitted the document or information to a person not entitled to receive it, or willfully retained the document or information and failed to deliver it to the officer or employee of the United States entitled to receive it.

Section 793(e) addresses the possession and transmission of classified information by persons who are not authorized to possess it, either because they lacked the requisite security clearance and need to know, or because they exceeded the scope of their authorization by removing classified materials from a secure facility.[27] Apart from this distinction, Sections 793(d) and 793(e) are substantially identical.

Information Relating to the National Defense

Both 793(d) and 793(e) apply to individuals who possess documents or "information relating to the national defense." This term is not defined in the statute. Courts have not limited this phrase to any specific subject matter, but the Fourth Circuit has held that the government must establish first that the information is "closely held by the government," and second, that its "disclosure would be potentially damaging to the United States or useful to an enemy of the United States." *United States* v. *Rosen*, 445 F. Supp. 2d 602, 618, 620-21 (E.D. Va. 2006) (*Rosen I*) (*citing Gorin* v. *United States*, 312 U.S. 19 (1941)); *United States* v. *Morison*, 844 F.2d 1057, 1073 (4th Cir. 1988); *United States* v. *Truong*, 629 F.2d 908, 918-19 (4th Cir. 1980); *United States* v. *Heine*, 151 F.2d 813, 817 (2d Cir. 1945).

The classification level of information may be "highly probative of whether the information at issue is 'information relating to the national defense' and whether the person to whom they disclosed the information was 'entitled to receive'

---

[27] *See, e.g., United States* v. *Hitselberger*, 991 F. Supp. 2d 101, 104 (D.D.C. 2013) (Navy linguist who printed and removed Secret documents indicted under 793(e)); *United States* v. *Chattin*, 33 M.J. 802, 803 (1991) (Navy seaman who stuffed classified document down his pants and walked out of a secure facility charged under 793(e)).

[it]."[28] However, classification level does not conclusively establish that a document or information is "information relating to the national defense." In *United States* v. *Rosen*, 599 F. Supp. 2d 690, 694-95 (E.D. Va. 2009) (*Rosen II*), the court stated that the term "information relating to the national defense" is not synonymous with classified information. While the classification level of information may serve as evidence that the government intended that it be closely held, the defendant can rebut the conclusion by showing that the government in fact failed to hold it closely. The court also stated that the classification level could not be introduced to show that unauthorized disclosure of the information might potentially damage the United States or aid an enemy of the United States.[29]

Willfulness

Sections 793(d) and (e) both require that the prohibited act be done "willfully." Courts have interpreted "willfully" to mean an act done "intentionally and purposely and with the intent to do something the law forbids, that is, with the bad purpose to disobey or to disregard the law."[30]

In *Rosen I*, the court held that to prove that the defendants "willfully" committed the conduct prohibited under Sections 793(d) and (e), the government is required to prove beyond a reasonable doubt:

> [T]hat the defendants knew the information was NDI [information relating to the national defense], *i.e.*, that the information was closely held by the United States and that disclosure of this information might potentially harm the United States, and that the persons to whom the defendants communicated the information were not entitled under the classification regulations to receive the information. Further the government must prove beyond a reasonable doubt that the defendants communicated the information they had received from their government sources with "a bad purpose either to disobey or to disregard the law." It follows, therefore, that if the defendants, or

---

[28] *Rosen I*, 445 F. Supp. 2d at 623; *see also Hitselberger*, 991 F. Supp. 2d at 106 (document marked "Secret" was "information relating to the national defense" because the classification level indicated that it would cause serious damage to the security of the United States if lost, and defendant's training placed him on notice that the government considers information in classified documents important to national security); *United States* v. *Kiriakou*, 2012 WL 3263854, at *6 (E.D. Va. 2012) (unreported decision) (rejecting defendant's argument that 793(d) is unconstitutionally vague because courts have relied on the classified status of information to determine whether it is closely held by the government and harmful to the United States); *United States* v. *Kim*, 808 F. Supp. 2d 44, 53 (D.D.C. 2011) ("Defendant's vagueness challenge is particularly unpersuasive in light of the fact that he is charged with disclosing the contents of an intelligence report...which was marked TOP SECRET/SENSITIVE COMPARTMENTED INFORMATION....").

[29] Several weeks before trial was scheduled to begin, prosecutors moved to dismiss the indictment based on the "unexpectedly higher evidentiary threshold" required to prevail at trial. *See* Motion to Dismiss, *United States* v. *Rosen*, Crim. No. 1:05CR225 (E.D. Va. filed May 1, 2009).

[30] *Bryan* v. *United States*, 524 U.S. 184, 190 (1998) (*cited in Hitselberger*, 991 F. Supp. 2d at 107-08); *see also Morison*, 844 F.2d at 1071; *United States* v. *Truong*, 629 F.2d 908, 918-19 (4th Cir. 1980).

either of them, were truly unaware that the information they are alleged to have received and disclosed was classified, or if they were truly ignorant of the classification scheme governing who is entitled to receive the information, they cannot be held to have violated the statute.[31]

Additional Burden of Proof for Disclosures of Intangible Information

Courts have held that Sections 793(d) and (e) contain a "heightened" or "additional" *mens rea* requirement where the transmission of intangible information (as contrasted with the retention or transmission of classified documents) is involved.[32] In addition to showing that an individual acted willfully, the government must prove beyond a reasonable doubt that he or she possessed "reason to believe that the information could be used to the injury of the United States or to the advantage of a foreign nation."[33]

Vagueness Challenges

The term "information relating to the national defense" in Sections 793(d) and (e) repeatedly has been challenged as unconstitutionally vague. Courts have rejected such challenges because the statute requires the government to prove that an individual "willfully" committed the prohibited conduct, a requirement that "eliminat[es] any genuine risk of holding a person 'criminally responsible for conduct which he could not reasonably understand to be proscribed.'"[34]

2.   18 U.S.C. § 793(f)

Section 793(f)(1), known as the gross negligence provision, became a central focus in the controversy over the decision not to recommend prosecution of former Secretary Clinton or her senior aides, and former Director Comey's public statement on July 5, 2016. Below we discuss the statutory requirements under Section 793(f), the Midyear prosecutors' interpretation of Section 793(f)(1), and previous cases in which prosecution was declined under the gross negligence provision.

a.   Statutory Requirements

Section 793(f) provides as follows:

---

[31] *Rosen I*, 445 F. Supp. 2d at 625 (internal citation omitted).

[32] *See Hitselberger*, 991 F. Supp. 2d at 105; *Drake*, 818 F. Supp. 2d 909, 916-17 (D. Md.); *see also United States* v. *Leung*, No. 03-CR-434 (C.D. Cal. Jul. 14, 2003).

[33] *See Rosen I*, 445 F. Supp. 2d at 643; *see also* Memorandum Opinion, *United States* v. *Sterling*, No. 1:10-CR-00485-LHB (filed Jun. 28, 2011) (government asserted that it must prove that the defendant acted willfully and had reason to believe the information would harm the United States where he is alleged to have disclosed classified information).

[34] *Id.* at 625; *Morison*, 844 F.2d at 1073; *Truong*, 629 F.2d at 918-19 (4th Cir. 1980); *see also Gorin* v. *United States*, 312 U.S. 19 (1941) (holding that information "connected with" or "relating to" the national defense used in the predecessor to a related Espionage Act statute was not unconstitutionally vague because the statute included a scienter requirement).

Whoever, being entrusted with or having lawful possession or control of any document, writing, code book, signal book, sketch, photograph, photographic negative, blueprint, plan, map, model, instrument, appliance, note, or information, relating to the national defense, (1) through gross negligence permits the same to be removed from its proper place of custody or delivered to anyone in violation of his trust, or to be lost, stolen, abstracted, or destroyed, or (2) having knowledge that the same has been illegally removed from its proper place of custody or delivered to anyone in violation of its trust, or lost, or stolen, abstracted, or destroyed, and fails to make prompt report of such loss, theft, abstraction, or destruction to his superior officer...[is subject to a criminal fine or imprisonment].

Section 793(f)(1) addresses the removal, delivery, loss, theft, abstraction, or destruction of any document or "information relating to the national defense" through gross negligence, while Section 793(f)(2) penalizes the failure to report the removal, loss, theft, abstraction, or destruction of any document or "information relating to the national defense," if an individual has knowledge that it has been removed from its proper place of custody.

Section 793(f), like sections 793(d) and (e), requires that the information in question be "information relating to the national defense." In *United States* v. *Dedeyan*, 584 F.2d 36, 39 (4th Cir. 1978), the Fourth Circuit upheld jury instructions in a Section 793(f)(2) case that required the government to prove that "disclosure of information in the document would be potentially damaging to the national defense, or that information in the document disclosed might be useful to an enemy of the United States."

b. Prosecutors' Interpretation of the "Gross Negligence" Provision in Section 793(f)(1)

Section 793(f)(1) does not define what constitutes "gross negligence," nor have any federal court decisions interpreted this specific provision of the statute. However, the prosecutors analyzed the legislative history of Section 793(f)(1) and identified statements made during the 1917 congressional debate indicating that the state of mind required for a violation of Section 793(f)(1) is "so gross as to almost suggest deliberate intention," criminally reckless, or "something that falls just a little short of being willful." The prosecutors cited a statement by Congressman Andrew Volstead during the 1917 debate about the predecessor to Section 793(f)(1):

I want to call attention to the fact that the information that is covered by this section may be, and probably would be, of the very highest importance to the Government.... It is not an unusual provision at all. It occurs in a great many criminal statutes. Men are convicted for gross negligence, but it has to be so gross as almost to suggest deliberate intention before a jury will convict. For instance, a person is killed by a man running an automobile recklessly on a crowded street. He may, and under the laws of most States would be, adjudged guilty of manslaughter, and can be sent to State prison.... We have, as I have already stated, a number of statutes of that kind. This provision is not revolutionary. It is the ordinary practice to apply such statutes to cases where lack of care occasions the death or serious injury of persons. This section should be, and probably would be, applied only in those cases where something of real consequence ought to be guarded with extreme care and caution.[35]

Given the absence of a definition of "gross negligence" in Section 793(f), the prosecutors researched state manslaughter statutes in effect at the time of the 1917 congressional debate, and determined that gross negligence was interpreted in that context to require wantonness or recklessness that was equivalent to criminal intent. However, the prosecutors also identified contemporaneous state court decisions interpreting other criminal statutes using "gross negligence" to require proof that ranged from something more than civil negligence to willful, intentional conduct.

The Midyear prosecutors did not find any court cases addressing the state of mind required for a violation of Section 793(f)(1). However, the prosecutors analyzed *United States* v. *Dedeyan*, 584 F.2d 36, 39 (4th Cir. 1978), a Fourth Circuit decision interpreting Section 793(f)(2). This case involved a civilian employee who completed a military vulnerability analysis and marked it "Secret," then took a copy of it home to proofread. While at home, his cousin secretly photographed part of the analysis with a camera provided by the Soviet Union. When the defendant later learned that his cousin had taken these photos, he accepted $1,000 as a "payment for remaining silent" rather than reporting that the information had been compromised. Upholding the statute against a challenge that it was unconstitutionally vague, the court held that Section 793(f)(2) requires the government to prove that the defendant knew that the document had been illegally abstracted, and that this knowledge requirement was sufficient to save the statute from vagueness.

In addition, the Midyear prosecutors reviewed previous prosecutions under Section 793(f)(1) in federal or military courts and concluded that these cases involved either a defendant who knowingly removed classified information from a secure facility, or inadvertently removed classified information from a secure facility and, upon learning of its removal, failed to report its "loss, theft, abstraction, or destruction."[36] The prosecutors concluded that based on case law and the

---

[35] 65 Cong. Rec. H1762-63 (daily ed. May 3, 1917).

[36] *See* Indictment, *United States* v. *Smith*, No. 03-CR-429 (C.D. Cal filed Feb. 24, 2004); *see also United States* v. *Courpalais*, No. ACM 35571, 2005 WL 486145 (A.F. Ct. Crim. App. Feb. 10, 2005) (defendant removed four classified photographs and took them home); *United States* v. *Roller*, 37 M.J. 1093 (1993) (defendant inadvertently placed two classified documents in his gym bag and took them home, and left the documents in his garage when he later discovered them); *United States* v. *Chattin*, 33 M.J. 802 (1991) (defendant stuffed classified documents down his pants and took them home); *United States* v. *Gaffney*, 17 M.J. 565 (1983) (defendant was supposed to destroy classified material but instead took it home and put it in a neighborhood dumpster); *United States* v. *Gonzalez*, 12 M.J. 747 (1981) (defendant intermingled two classified messages with personal mail he was

Department's prior interpretation of the statute, charging a violation of Section 793(f) likely required evidence that the individuals who sent emails containing classified information "knowingly" included the classified information or transferred classified information onto unclassified systems (Section 793(f)(1)), or learned that classified information had been transferred to unclassified systems and failed to report it (Section 793(f)(2)). Thus, the Midyear prosecutors interpreted the "gross negligence" provision of Section 793(f)(1) to require proof that an individual acted with knowledge that the information in question was classified.[37]

As noted above, sections 793(d) and (e) have survived constitutional vagueness challenges because of the existence of a scienter requirement in the form of the requirement to prove "willfulness." Such a challenge has not yet been raised in a Section 793(f)(1) "gross negligence" case. The Midyear prosecutors stated:

> [T]he government would likely face a colorable constitutional challenge to the statute if it prosecuted an individual for committing gross negligence who was both unaware he had removed classified information at the time of the removal and never became aware he had done so.... Moreover, in bringing a vagueness challenge, defense counsel would also likely point to the significant disagreement as to the meaning of "gross negligence."

c.   Previous Section 793(f)(1) Declinations

The Midyear prosecutors also reviewed at least two previous investigations where prosecution was declined under the gross negligence provision in Section 793(f)(1). The Midyear prosecutors told us that these declinations informed their understanding of the Department's historical approach to Section 793(f)(1). We discuss these previous declinations below.

Gonzales Declination Decision

One of these previous cases involved an OIG investigation into the mishandling of documents containing highly classified, compartmented information about a National Security Agency (NSA) surveillance program by former White House Counsel and Attorney General Alberto Gonzales. In 2004, while Gonzales

---

carrying to a friend in Alaska, then put the message in a desk drawer in the friend's room and forgot them); *cf. United States* v. *Oxfort*, 44 M.J. 337 (1996) (defendant removed classified messages from a Sensitive Compartmented Information Facility (SCIF) in Japan with the intention of passing them along to individuals who were not entitled to receive them; although the opinion states the defendant was charged under 793(e), prosecutors found documents referencing charges filed under Section 793(f)(1) based on the same facts); *United States* v. *McGuinness*, 33 M.J. 781 (1991) (defendant took home numerous classified items from previous assignments and was charged under Section 793(e), but a Section 793(f)(1) conviction was set aside for statute of limitation reasons).

[37] Proof of such knowledge would also be necessary to establish a violation of Sections 793(d) or (e), which required proof of "willfulness." Accordingly, as detailed below and in subsequent chapters, the investigative team focused significant attention on determining whether Clinton, her senior aides, and senders of emails that contained classified information had actual knowledge of the classified status of the information.

was the White House Counsel, he took handwritten notes memorializing a meeting about the legality of the NSA program. The notes included operational details about the program, including its compartmented codeword. Although Gonzales did not mark the notes as classified, he said that he used two envelopes to double-wrap the notes and may have written an abbreviation for the codeword on the inner envelope. On the outer envelope, Gonzales said that he wrote "AG – EYES ONLY – TOP SECRET." He stored these notes in a safe in the West Wing of the White House and said that he took them with him when he became the Attorney General in February 2005. Gonzales said that he did not recall where he stored the notes after removing them from the White House, but that he may have taken them home. Gonzales also stored the notes and several other documents containing TS//SCI classification markings in a safe in the Attorney General's office that was not approved to hold such materials.

The OIG referred investigative findings to NSD for a prosecutive decision. According to information reviewed by the OIG, on August 19, 2008, NSD analyzed Gonzales' handling of the notes under the gross negligence provision in section 793(f)(1). NSD concluded that prosecutors likely could show that the documents were removed from their proper place of custody, but that the question was whether that removal constituted "gross negligence." After discussing the legislative history of Section 793(f)(1), NSD stated that the government likely would have to prove that Gonzales' conduct was "criminally reckless" to establish that he acted with gross negligence under Section 793(f)(1). NSD concluded that Gonzales' inability to recall precisely where he stored the notes detracted from prosecutors' ability to "show a state of mind approaching 'deliberate intention' to remove classified documents from a secure location."

AUSA Declination Decision

The Midyear prosecutors also reviewed another 2008 case in which prosecution was declined under Section 793(f)(1). This case involved an AUSA who sent numerous boxes of documents to his personal residence in the United States following an overseas tour as a legal attaché. According to the prosecutors' analysis, the boxes contained a large number of documents that were classified at the Secret and Confidential levels. Many of these documents were organized haphazardly or were improperly marked. The AUSA testified that he did not purposely ship classified documents to his house, but acknowledged that it was highly likely that the documents he shipped included some classified materials.

Interpreting section 793(f)(1), NSD stated that prosecutors likely would be required to prove that the AUSA's conduct was "criminally reckless." NSD identified factors suggesting that the AUSA's conduct did not rise to the level of gross negligence, including that he testified that he did not purposely ship classified documents to his house, and thus he did not deliberately intend to remove the classified documents from a secure location. In addition, the documents were not separated into classified and unclassified categories, and they did not contain proper classification markings in that the first few pages of certain documents were not marked but later pages in the same document contained classification markings. Based on these and other factors, NSD concluded that prosecution was not warranted.

3. 18 U.S.C. § 1924

Section 1924 is a misdemeanor statute that prohibits the "knowing" removal of documents or materials containing classified information without authority and with the "intent to retain" such documents or materials at an unauthorized location. To establish a violation of this statute, the government must show that an individual knowingly removed classified materials without authority and intended to store these materials at an unauthorized location. To remove "without authority" means that the classified materials were removed from the controlling agency's premises without permission.[38] Although no reported cases interpret this provision, the Midyear prosecutors concluded that Section 1924 requires the government to show beyond a reasonable doubt that the defendant had knowledge that the location where he or she intended to store classified material was an "unauthorized" or "unlawful" place to retain it, citing the legislative history, the Petraeus case we describe below, and other previous prosecutions under this provision.

High profile cases considered by the Midyear prosecutors and by FBI leadership involving plea agreements under Section 1924 include former Central Intelligence Agency (CIA) Director David Petraeus, former National Security Advisor Samuel "Sandy" Berger, and former CIA Director John Deutch. In each of these cases, the defendants knew the information at issue was classified or took actions reflecting knowledge that their handling or storage of it was improper.

Petraeus, a retired U.S. Army General, served as the Commander of the International Security Assistance Force in Afghanistan from July 2010 to July 2011, and as the Director of the CIA from September 2011 to November 2012. While in Afghanistan, Petraeus kept notes in black notebooks that included information about the identities of covert officers, war strategy, intelligence capabilities and mechanisms, diplomatic discussions, quotes and deliberative discussions from high-level National Security Council meetings, and discussions with the President. Petraeus retained these notebooks when he returned from Afghanistan and later shared them with his biographer, Paula Broadwell, admitting to her in a recorded conversation that the notebooks were "highly classified" and contained "code word stuff." He also stored them in an unlocked desk drawer in his home office. During a subsequent investigation into his mishandling and retention of classified information, Petraeus falsely told the FBI that he never provided or facilitated the provision of classified information to Broadwell. In March 2015, Petraeus pled guilty to one count under 18 U.S.C. § 1924, and was sentenced to 2 years of probation, a $25 special assessment, and a $100,000 fine.[39]

---

[38] *See* Exec. Order 13526, § 4.1(d).

[39] *See* Plea Agreement and Factual Basis, *United States* v. *Petraeus*, Crim. No. 3:15-CR-47 (W.D.N.C. filed Mar. 3, 2015); Information, *Petraeus*, 2015 WL 1884065 (W.D.N.C. filed Mar. 3, 2015) (charging Petraeus with knowingly removing classified documents "without authority and with the

Sandy Berger, the National Security Advisor under former President Bill Clinton, visited the National Archives and Records Administration to review documents for production to the 9/11 Commission. During his visits, Berger concealed and removed documents by folding the documents in his clothes, walking out of the National Archives building, and placing them under a nearby construction trailer for later retrieval.[40] Berger removed a total of five copies of classified documents, stored them in his office, and later destroyed three of them by cutting them into small pieces and discarding them. All of these documents were marked classified. Berger also created and removed handwritten notes of classified material that he had reviewed, and was aware that he removed these notes from the National Archives without authorization. Berger pled guilty to a criminal information charging one count of 18 U.S.C. § 1924.[41] He was sentenced to 2 years of probation, a $56,905.52 fine, a $25 special assessment, and 100 hours of community service, and was precluded from accessing classified information for 5 years.

Former CIA Director John Deutch was investigated for using unclassified, Internet-connected computer systems to create and process classified documents and storing classified memory cards in his personal residence. During an investigation by the CIA Inspector General (CIA IG), investigators recovered files from a computer at Deutch's residence that were labeled as unclassified but contained words indicating that the information was "Secret" or "Top Secret Codeword," or was otherwise highly sensitive. For example, recovered documents included reports on covert operations, communications intelligence, memoranda to then President Bill Clinton, and classified CIA budget information. The CIA IG report states that Deutch told investigators that he "fell into the habit" of using the unclassified system "in an inappropriate fashion," and admitted that he had intentionally created highly sensitive documents on unclassified computers. In addition, witnesses testified that Deutch was considered to be an "expert" or "fairly advanced" computer user. Following a criminal investigation, Deutch agreed to plead guilty to one count under 18 U.S.C. § 1924, but was pardoned by President Clinton on January 19, 2001, before the plea was consummated.

Examples of conduct prosecuted under Section 1924 include a former government employee who stored boxes of marked classified documents in his personal residence; a contractor who downloaded classified information from a secure network to a thumb drive, transferred the information to an unclassified computer, and shared it with others; and a government employee who concealed and removed highly classified documents from a Sensitive Compartmented

---

intent to retain such documents and materials at unauthorized locations, aware that these locations were unauthorized for the storage and retention of such classified documents").

[40] *See* National Archives, *Notable Thefts from the National Archives*, *at* https://www.archives.gov/research/recover/notable-thefts.html (accessed Mar. 1, 2018).

[41] *See* Factual Basis for Plea, *United States* v. *Berger*, Crim. No. 1:05-MJ-00175-DAR (D.D.C. filed Apr. 1, 2005).

Information Facility (SCIF) where he worked and stored the documents in his vehicle and house.

B.   18 U.S.C. § 2071(a)

Section 2071(a) is a felony statute criminalizing the concealment, removal, or mutilation of government records filed in any public office. To establish a violation of this provision, the government must prove the following beyond a reasonable doubt:

- An individual concealed, removed, or destroyed a record, or attempted to do so, or took and carried away a record with the intent to do so:

- The record was filed or deposited in a public office of the United States; and

- The individual acted willfully and unlawfully.

The purpose of this statute is to prohibit conduct that deprives the government of the use of its documents, such as by removing and altering or destroying them.[42] The Midyear prosecutors concluded that every prosecution under Section 2071 has involved the removal or destruction of documents that had already been filed or deposited in a public office of the United States (*i.e.*, physical removal of a document). In addition, to fulfill the requirement that the individual acted "willfully and unlawfully," Section 2071 requires the government to show that he or she acted intentionally, with knowledge that he or she was breaching the statute.[43]

---

[42] *See United States* v. *Hitselberger*, 991 F. Supp. 2d 108, 124 (D.D.C. 2014) (*See United States* v. *Rosner*, 352 F.Supp. 915, 919-20 (S.D.N.Y. 1972); *United States* v. *North*, 716 F.Supp. 644, 647 (D.D.C. 1989).

[43] *See United States* v. *Moylan*, 417 F.2d 1002, 1004 (4th Cir. 1969).

CHAPTER THREE:
OVERVIEW OF THE MIDYEAR INVESTIGATION

In this chapter, we provide an overview of the Midyear investigation. More specifically, we describe the referral and opening of the investigation, the staffing of the investigation by the Department and the FBI, and the investigative strategy.

I.   Referral and Opening of the Investigation

A.   Background

1.   Clinton's Use of Private Email Servers

Hillary Clinton served as Secretary of State from January 21, 2009, until February 1, 2013. During that time, she used private email servers hosting the @clintonemail.com domain to conduct official State Department business.[44] According to FBI documents, former Secretary Clinton and her husband, former President Bill Clinton, had a private email server in their house in Chappaqua, N.Y., beginning in approximately 2008 (before Clinton's tenure as Secretary of State) for use by former President Clinton's staff. Former Secretary Clinton told the FBI that, in or around January 2009, she "directed aides...to create the clintonemail.com account," and that this was done "as a matter of convenience."

According to the FBI letterhead memorandum (LHM) summarizing the Midyear investigation, Clinton used her clintonemail.com account and personal mobile devices linked to that account for both personal and official business throughout her tenure as Secretary of State. The LHM states that Clinton "decided to use a personal device to avoid carrying multiple devices." Clinton never personally used an official State Department email account or State Department-issued handheld device during her tenure, although there were official State Department email accounts from which emails were sent on her behalf.

2.   Production of Emails from the Private Email Servers to the State Department and Subsequent Deletion of Emails by Clinton's Staff

On September 11 and 12, 2012, terrorists attacked the U.S. Temporary Mission Facility and a Central Intelligence Agency (CIA) Annex in Benghazi, Libya, killing four Americans.[45] On May 8, 2014, the U.S. House Select Committee on Benghazi (House Benghazi Committee) was established to investigate the Benghazi attack and, thereafter, sought documents from the State Department as part of its

---

[44] As described in Chapter Five, the FBI discovered three servers that for different periods stored work-related emails sent or received by Clinton during her tenure as Secretary of State.

[45] *See* U.S. Senate Select Committee on Intelligence, *Review of the Terrorist Attacks on U.S. Facilities in Benghazi, Libya, September 11-12, 2012*, 113th Cong, 2d sess., 2014, S. Rept. 113-134, https://www.intelligence.senate.gov/sites/default/files/publications/113134.pdf (accessed May 7, 2018).

investigation. In the summer of 2014, State Department officials contacted Cheryl Mills, who had served as former Secretary Clinton's Chief of Staff and Counselor, concerning the State Department's inability to locate Clinton's and other former Secretaries' emails to respond to Congressional requests. Mills later told the FBI that she suggested that the State Department officials search State Department systems for Clinton's clintonemail.com email address. In addition, Mills told the FBI that State Department officials requested that she produce former Secretary Clinton's emails and advised her that it was Clinton's or Mills's "obligation to filter out personal emails from what was provided to State."

Former Secretary Clinton asked Mills and Clinton's personal attorney, David Kendall, to oversee the process of providing her emails to the State Department. In late summer 2014, Mills contacted Paul Combetta, an employee of the company that administered Clinton's private server at the time, and requested that he transfer copies of Clinton's emails onto Mills's laptop and a laptop belonging to Heather Samuelson, a lawyer who had served in the State Department as Secretary Clinton's White House Liaison. Mills, Samuelson, and Kendall then developed a methodology for Samuelson to "cull" former Secretary Clinton's work-related emails from her personal emails, to produce her work-related emails to the State Department.

In October and November 2014, the State Department sent letters to four former Secretaries of State, including Clinton, requesting that they "make available copies of any Federal records in their possession, such as emails sent or received on a personal email account while serving as Secretary of State."[46] In December 2014, former Secretary Clinton produced to the State Department "from her personal email account approximately 55,000 hard-copy pages, representing approximately 30,000 emails that she believed related to official business."[47] After receiving these documents, the State Department, in addition to responding to the House Benghazi Committee's document request, reviewed Clinton's emails for potential public release in response to Freedom of Information Act (FOIA) requests.

As described in Chapter Five, Mills, Samuelson, and Combetta told the FBI that in late 2014 or early 2015 Mills and Samuelson asked Combetta to remove former Secretary Clinton's emails from their laptops. Combetta then used the commercial software "BleachBit" to permanently remove or wipe former Secretary Clinton's emails from Mills's and Samuelson's laptops.[48] Mills told the FBI that at some point between November 2014 and January 2015, Clinton decided she no longer wished to retain on her server emails that were older than 60 days and Mills

---

[46] *See* U.S. Department of State Office of the Inspector General (State IG), *Office of the Secretary: Evaluation of Email Records Management and Cybersecurity Requirements*, ESP-16-03 (May 2016), https://oig.state.gov/system/files/esp-16-03.pdf (accessed May 7, 2018), 3.

[47] *See* State IG, *Office of the Secretary*, 4.

[48] According to documents we reviewed, BleachBit is a "freely available software that advertises the ability to 'shred' files. 'Shredding' is designed to prevent recovery of a file by overwriting the content."

instructed Combetta to change Clinton's email retention policy accordingly. Combetta, however, failed to do so until late March 2015.

On March 3, 2015, the House Benghazi Committee sent preservation orders requiring former Secretary Clinton to preserve emails on her servers.[49] As described in more detail in Chapter Five, Combetta told the FBI that later in March 2015 he realized that he had neglected to make the change to former Secretary Clinton's email retention policy earlier that year, had an "oh shit" moment, and, without consulting Mills, used BleachBit to permanently remove Clinton's emails from her server. These included emails that had been transferred from a prior server. According to FBI documents, former Secretary Clinton's attorneys advised Combetta about the congressional preservation order before he made the deletions. As a result of Combetta's actions, 31,830 emails that former Secretary Clinton's attorneys had deemed personal in nature were deleted from three locations on which they had previously been stored—Mills's and Samuelson's laptops and the Clinton server.

B.   State Department Inspector General and IC IG Review of Clinton's Emails and Subsequent 811 Referral

On March 12, 2015, three Members of Congress requested that the State Department Inspector General (State IG) conduct a review regarding State Department employees' use of personal email for official purposes. The Members of Congress requested that the State IG coordinate with the Office of the Intelligence Community Inspector General (IC IG) to determine whether classified information was transmitted or received by State Department employees over personal systems. Following this request, the IC IG reviewed 296 of the 30,490 emails that former Secretary Clinton's attorneys had provided to the State Department and determined that at least two of these emails contained classified information. The 296 emails, including the two determined to contain classified information, had already been publicly released by State Department FOIA officials.

In a June 24, 2015 letter, Kendall told the State IG and the IC IG that a copy of the 30,490 emails provided by former Secretary Clinton to the State Department was stored on a thumb drive in his law office and that her personal server was in the custody of the company "Platte River Networks" ("PRN"). Based on this information, the IC IG concluded that "the thumb drive and personal server contain classified information and are not currently in the Government's possession."

On July 6, 2015, the IC IG made a referral to the FBI pursuant to Section 811(c) of the Intelligence Authorization Act of Fiscal Year 1995 (811 referral). This provision requires Executive Branch departments and agencies to advise the FBI "immediately of any information, regardless of its origin, which indicates that

---

[49] *See* U.S. House of Representatives, Select Committee on the Events Surrounding the 2012 Terrorist Attack in Benghazi, *Final Report of the Select Committee on the Events Surrounding the 2012 Terrorist Attack in Benghazi*, 114th Cong., 2d sess., 2016, H. Rept. 114-848, https://www.congress.gov/congressional-report/114th-congress/house-report/848/1 (accessed May 7, 2018).

classified information is being, or may have been, disclosed in an unauthorized manner to a foreign power or an agent of a foreign power," and is typically used to refer to the FBI a loss or unauthorized disclosure of classified information. The IC IG referred the matter to the FBI "for any action you deem appropriate."

C.   FBI's Decision to Open a Criminal Investigation

On July 10, 2015, the FBI Counterintelligence Division opened a criminal investigation in response to the 811 referral from the IC IG. Although only a small percentage of 811 referrals result in criminal investigations, witnesses told the OIG that a criminal investigation was necessary to determine the extent of classified information on former Secretary Clinton's private server, who was responsible for introducing the information into an unclassified system, and why it was placed there. The FBI gave the investigation the code name "Midyear Exam," choosing it from a list of randomly generated names.

The FBI predicated the opening of the investigation on the possible compromise of highly sensitive classified secure compartmented information (SCI). One of the Midyear case agents told us that the Midyear investigative team was focused at the outset on the "potential unauthorized storage of classified information on an unauthorized system and then where it might have gotten [sic] from there." A Department prosecutor assigned to the investigation similarly described the scope of the investigation as "related to the email systems used by Secretary Clinton, and whether on her private email server there are individuals who improperly retained or transmitted classified information."

The FBI designated the Midyear investigation as a Sensitive Investigative Matter (SIM). According to the DIOG, a SIM includes "an investigative matter involving the activities of a domestic public official or domestic political candidate (involving corruption or a threat to the national security)" as well as "any other matter which, in the judgment of the official authorizing an Assessment, should be brought to the attention of FBI [Headquarters] and other DOJ officials." FBI witnesses told us that the SIM designation is typically given to investigations involving sensitive categories of persons such as attorneys, judges, clergy, journalists, and politicians, and that that SIM investigations are overseen more closely by FBI management and the FBI Office of General Counsel than other investigations.

The Midyear investigation was opened with an "Unknown Subject(s) (UNSUB)," and at no time during the investigation was any individual identified by the FBI as a subject or target of the investigation, including former Secretary Clinton. FBI witnesses told us that the "UNSUB" designation is common and means that the FBI has not identified a specific target or subject at the outset of an investigation. According to FBI witnesses, this allowed the FBI to expand the focus of the investigation based on the evidence without being "locked into a particular subject." With respect to the Midyear investigation, witnesses told the OIG that the FBI did not identify anyone as a subject or target during the investigation because it was unclear how the classified material had been introduced to the server and who was responsible for improperly placing it there.

Despite the UNSUB designation, witnesses told us that a primary focus of the Midyear investigation was on former Secretary Clinton's intent in setting up and using her private email server. An FBI OGC attorney assigned to the Midyear team (FBI Attorney 1) told the OIG, "We certainly started looking more closely at the Secretary because they were her emails." Randall Coleman, the former Assistant Director of the Counterintelligence Division, stated, "I don't know [why] that was the case, why it was UNSUB. I'm really shocked that it would have stayed that way because certainly the investigation started really kind of getting more focused."

In his OIG interview, Comey described former Secretary Clinton as the subject of the Midyear investigation and stated that he was unaware that the investigation had an UNSUB designation. Similarly, in his book, Comey referred to former Secretary Clinton as the subject of the Midyear investigation, stating that one question the investigation sought to answer was what Clinton was thinking "when she mishandled that classified information."[50]

D. Initial Briefing for the Department

On July 23, 2015, Coleman and then Deputy Director Mark as' met with Deputy Attorney General (DAG) Sally Yates and Principal Associate Deputy Attorney General (PADAG) Matt Axelrod to brief them on the opening of the Midyear investigation. According to Coleman, he and Giuliano told Yates and Axelrod why the Midyear investigation was opened and laid out their vision of how the investigation would be conducted, including that the FBI planned to run the investigation out of headquarters.

Yates recalled being briefed by Giuliano and Coleman at the beginning of the Midyear investigation, but said that she did not recall having concerns about the information they presented at the meeting or remembering anything significant about it. Axelrod told the OIG that Giuliano and Coleman showed them a copy of the 811 referral that the FBI had received, and either showed them or told them about some of the emails that had been identified as potentially classified. Axelrod stated:

> That, my recollection is that the way they explained it was that review of the certain emails contained on the personal server that Secretary Clinton had been using showed that some of those emails contained classified information. And so that, and that they, one of the things that was sort of standard practice when there was classified information on non-classified systems was that a review needed to be done to sort of contain the, I think the word they use in the [intelligence] community is a spill.... The spill of classified information out into sort of [a] non-classified arena. And so that they needed to, this was a referral so that the Bureau could help contain the spill and identify if there was classified information on non-classified systems so that that classified information could be contained and either, you

---

[50] JAMES COMEY, A HIGHER LOYALTY: TRUTH, LIES, AND LEADERSHIP at 162 (Amy Einhorn, ed., 1st ed. 2018).

know, destroyed or returned to proper information handling mechanisms.

Asked whether he considered the Midyear investigation to be criminal as of the date of this initial briefing, Axelrod replied, "Not in my view." According to Axelrod, "it was some time...before I, at least I understood that it had morphed into a criminal investigation."

The prosecutors and career Department staff assigned to the Midyear investigation told us that they considered it a criminal investigation from early on. Deputy Assistant Attorney General (DAAG) George Toscas, who was the most senior career Department official involved in the daily supervision of the investigation, told us that he approached it as a criminal investigation from the beginning of NSD's involvement. Prosecutors 1 and 2, both of whom were assigned to the investigation by late July 2015, understood that it was a criminal investigation from very early in the investigation. Prosecutor 1 told us, "I mean, pretty quickly this seemed like a, a criminal investigation.... [I]t looked, looked and it smelled like a criminal investigation to me."

II.   Staffing the Midyear Investigation

A.   FBI Staffing

The Midyear investigation was conducted by the FBI's Counterintelligence Division. For the first few weeks, the investigation was staffed by FBI Headquarters personnel and temporary duty assignment (TDY) FBI agents. Thereafter, FBI management decided to run the investigation as a "special" out of FBI Headquarters. This meant that the investigation was staffed by counterintelligence agents and analysts from the FBI Washington Field Office (WFO) who were temporarily located to headquarters and received support from headquarters personnel. FBI management selected WFO personnel based on WFO's geographic proximity to headquarters and its experience conducting sensitive counterintelligence investigations. FBI witnesses told us that previous sensitive investigations also had been run as "specials," and that this allowed FBI senior executives to exercise tighter control over the investigation.

There were approximately 15 agents, analysts, computer specialists, and forensic accountants assigned on a full-time basis to the Midyear team, as well as other FBI staff who provided periodic support. Four WFO agents served as the Midyear case agents and reported to a WFO Supervisory Special Agent ("SSA"). Several FBI witnesses described the SSA as an experienced and aggressive agent, and the SSA told us that he selected the "four strongest agents" from his WFO squad to be on the Midyear team.

The SSA reported to Peter Strzok, who was then an Assistant Special Agent in Charge (ASAC) at WFO.[51] Comey and Coleman told us that Strzok was selected to lead the Midyear investigative team because he was one of the most experienced and highly-regarded counterintelligence investigators within the FBI.

There were also several analysts on the Midyear team. Some analysts assigned to Midyear were on the review team, which reviewed and analyzed former Secretary Clinton's emails. These analysts reported to a Supervisory Intelligence Analyst, who in turn reported to the Lead Analyst. FBI witnesses, including Coleman, told us that the Lead Analyst was highly regarded within the FBI and very experienced in counterintelligence investigations. Other analysts were on the investigative team, which assisted the agents with interview preparation and performed other investigative tasks. These analysts reported to the SSA and Strzok, in addition to reporting directly to the Lead Analyst. Several analysts were on both the review and investigative teams.

Until approximately the end of 2015, the Lead Analyst and Strzok both reported to a Section Chief in the Counterintelligence Division, who in turn reported to Coleman for purposes of the Midyear investigation.[52] The remainder of the reporting chain was as follows: Coleman to John Giacalone, who was Executive Assistant Director (EAD) of the National Security Branch; Giacalone to DD Giuliano; and DD Giuliano to Director Comey.

During the course of the investigation, some FBI officials involved with the Midyear investigation retired or changed positions. In late 2015, Coleman became the EAD of the FBI Criminal, Cyber, Response, and Services Branch and was no longer involved in the Midyear investigation. At the same time, E.W. ("Bill") Priestap replaced Coleman as AD of the Counterintelligence Division. EAD Giacalone and DD Giuliano retired from the FBI in early 2016 and were replaced by Michael Steinbach and Andrew McCabe, respectively.

In addition, Lisa Page, who was Special Counsel to McCabe, became involved in the Midyear investigation after McCabe became the Deputy Director in February 2016. Page told the OIG that part of her function was to serve as a liaison between the Midyear team and McCabe. Page acknowledged that her role upset senior FBI officials, but told the OIG that McCabe relied on her to ensure that he had the information he needed to make decisions, without it being filtered through multiple layers of management. Several witnesses told the OIG that Page circumvented the official chain of command, and that Strzok communicated important Midyear case information to her, and thus to McCabe, without Priestap's or Steinbach's knowledge. McCabe said that he was aware of complaints about Page, and that he valued her ability to "spot issues" and bring them to his attention when others did not do so.

---

[51] Strzok was promoted to a Section Chief in the Counterintelligence Division in February 2016, and to Deputy Assistant Director (DAD) in the fall of 2016.

[52] A Deputy Assistant Director in the Counterintelligence Division was between the Section Chief and Coleman in the reporting chain but had limited involvement in the Midyear investigation.

The FBI Office of General Counsel (OGC) assigned FBI Attorney 1, who was a supervisory attorney in the National Security and Cyber Law Branch (NSCLB), to provide legal support to the Midyear team. A second, more junior attorney (FBI Attorney 2) also was assigned to the Midyear team. FBI Attorney 1 reported to Deputy General Counsel Trisha Anderson, who in turn reported to then General Counsel James Baker.[53]

Figure 3.1 describes the FBI chain of command for the Midyear investigation. This figure does not include intervening supervisors who had limited involvement in the investigation.

---

[53] Anderson now is the Principal Deputy General Counsel.

Figure 3.1: FBI Chain of Command for the Midyear Investigation

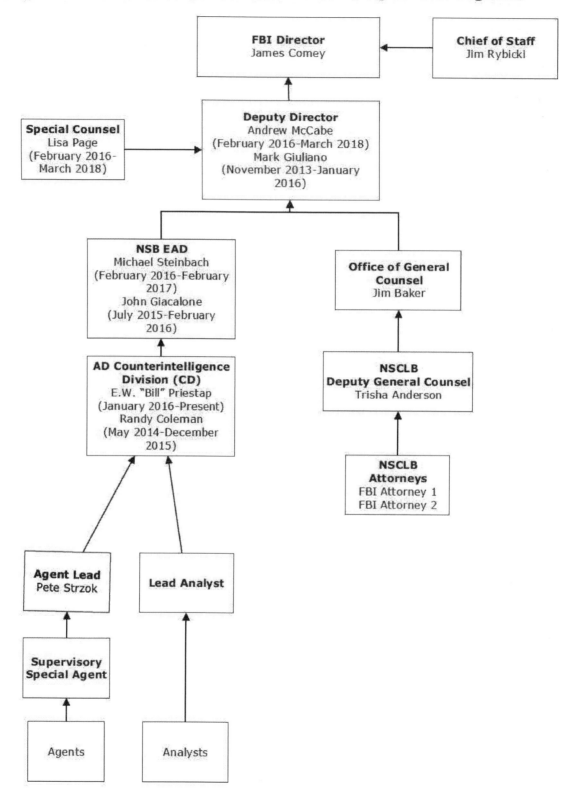

FBI Director
James Comey

Chief of Staff
Jim Rybicki

Special Counsel
Lisa Page
(February 2016-
March 2018)

Deputy Director
Andrew McCabe
(February 2016-March 2018)
Mark Giuliano
(November 2013-January
2016)

NSB EAD
Michael Steinbach
(February 2016-February
2017)
John Giacalone
(July 2015-February
2016)

Office of General Counsel
Jim Baker

AD Counterintelligence Division (CD)
E.W. "Bill" Priestap
(January 2016-Present)
Randy Coleman
(May 2014-December
2015)

NSCLB Deputy General Counsel
Trisha Anderson

NSCLB Attorneys
FBI Attorney 1
FBI Attorney 2

Agent Lead
Pete Strzok

Lead Analyst

Supervisory Special Agent

Agents

Analysts

45

B.   Department Staffing

Within the Department, the Midyear investigation was primarily handled by the Counterintelligence and Export Control Section (CES) of the National Security Division (NSD), with support from two prosecutors in the United States Attorney's Office for the Eastern District of Virginia (EDVA). All of the prosecutors assigned to the Midyear team had significant experience handling national security investigations or white collar criminal cases.

The lead prosecutor (Prosecutor 1) was a supervisory attorney in CES. Prosecutor 1 told us that he selected the "best" nonsupervisory line attorney within CES (Prosecutor 2) to handle the Midyear investigation with him. The two CES prosecutors reported directly to the Chief of CES, David Laufman, who in turn reported to DAAG George Toscas. Toscas was the highest level career Department employee involved in the Midyear investigation, and the prosecutors and supervisors below him who were involved in the Midyear investigation were also career employees. As described in more detail below, Department officials above Toscas, including then Assistant Attorney General (AAG) John Carlin, Axelrod, Yates, and Lynch, received briefings about the Midyear investigation but were not involved in its day-to-day management.

In August 2015, EDVA was brought into the Midyear investigation. EDVA assigned two supervisory attorneys to work with the CES prosecutors: Prosecutor 3 and Prosecutor 4. The role of the EDVA prosecutors initially was to facilitate the issuance of legal process, including grand jury subpoenas, search warrants, and 2703(d) orders. However, the NSD prosecutors told the OIG that ultimately they consulted and worked closely with the EDVA prosecutors on many issues and decisions throughout the course of the Midyear investigation. Prosecutor 3 similarly told us that as the investigation progressed, he and Prosecutor 4 were considered "equal partners" with the NSD prosecutors.

EDVA senior leadership, including then U.S. Attorney Dana Boente, received briefings on the Midyear investigation from the EDVA prosecutors and were informed of significant developments, but they were not involved in investigative decisions. Axelrod told the OIG that he recalled that he spoke to Boente early in the Midyear investigation and "let[] them know that this was NSD's investigation." Axelrod stated:

> [S]ometimes when you have a U.S. Attorney's office and a Main
> Justice component, you know, things have to go up two chains
> and...that's cumbersome.... [I]n...an investigation like this we figured
> it was easier just to have everything centralized in NSD. There's a
> reason why NSD has the ticket on, you know, all these matters, right?
> They're the subject matter experts[.]

Axelrod explained that NSD has primary responsibility for counterterrorism and counterintelligence cases not only because it has subject matter expertise in those areas, but also because those cases are nationwide. He stated that there are certain areas of law where it is important to ensure nationwide consistency in how

46

the law is applied, because if "one district does something really different than another district it can have very bad...ramifications or consequences." As noted previously, the USAM requires NSD to expressly approve in advance charges involving certain national security statutes, including those that were considered in this investigation.

Prosecutor 2 stated that NSD's typical role varies from case to case, and depends on the resources and experience of the specific U.S. Attorney's Office. This prosecutor told the OIG that NSD typically "drives" counterintelligence cases, but that its role "runs the gamut" from taking the lead on cases to playing a supporting role. Prosecutor 2 stated that EDVA has been more willing to allow NSD attorneys to play an active role in charged cases and is "very open to [NSD's] partnership and support."

Prosecutor 3 similarly told the OIG that EDVA's supporting role in the Midyear investigation was unusual, but he attributed this to logistics. This prosecutor stated, "[Prosecutors 1 and 2] were right across the street from FBI Headquarters.... [I]t was pretty work intensive, more so for them because they would have to go over there at the drop of a hat for meetings. You know, we were always kept in the loop of what was going on. But [the] FBI kept a pretty tight hold of the classified documents." Prosecutor 3 also said that running the case out of NSD, supervised by Toscas, allowed the Department to keep "one central location of control by a career person over the investigation."

Several witnesses told us that the FBI was frustrated at the perceived slow pace of bringing a U.S. Attorney's Office into the Midyear investigation. However, Toscas told us that it is not unusual for a U.S. Attorney's Office not to be involved in the beginning of an investigation, and that it took some time to determine the proper venue and select the most appropriate U.S. Attorney's Office. Prosecutor 1 told us that although the U.S. Attorney's Office for the District of Columbia also was considered, EDVA was selected in part based on the good historical working relationship between NSD and EDVA.

Boente told the OIG that he expressed concerns that EDVA was not the appropriate district given that former Secretary Clinton lived in New York. He said that they potentially could establish venue through an email server or victim agency server located in EDVA, but that it would be unusual to select venue to prosecute a high-profile public figure on that basis. Boente said that while no one explained why the Department chose EDVA, he assumed that it was because "we move quicker and do things a lot quicker than some districts can."

III. Role of Senior FBI and Department Leadership in the Investigation

A. FBI Leadership

The Midyear investigation was closely supervised by FBI leadership from the outset. Comey told the OIG that he received frequent briefings on the Midyear investigation:

And then once it got underway, either in July or maybe in August [2015], I told them I wanted to be briefed on it on a much more frequent basis then I would normally on a case because I was keen to make sure that they had the resources they need and that there was no—that I could both support them if they needed additional things and protect them in the event anybody outside of the investigative team tried to monkey with them in any way or exert any pressure on them or anything like that. Because I could see immediately how significant the matter was.... So I think they got into a rhythm of briefing me maybe every couple of weeks.

Comey said that briefings took place roughly every two to three weeks at the beginning of the investigation, and occurred on a weekly basis as the investigation progressed.

Comey said that the Midyear briefings typically were attended by a core team of senior officials:

- The Deputy Director (Giuliano, then McCabe);
- Comey's Chief of Staff, James Rybicki;
- FBI OGC personnel including Baker, Anderson, and FBI Attorney 1;
- The EAD of the National Security Branch (Giacalone, then Steinbach);
- The AD of the Counterintelligence Division (Coleman, then Priestap);
- Deputy Director McCabe's counsel, Lisa Page (beginning in February 2016); and
- Strzok and the Lead Analyst.

Other FBI officials periodically attended these briefings, including then Associate Deputy Director (ADD) David Bowdich after his appointment in April 2016, but witnesses told us that briefings were carefully controlled and limited to a select group of senior FBI managers.

Comey said that the Midyear team typically produced a biweekly or weekly written summary of their progress in the investigation, and that briefings generally focused on what the team had completed and what needed to be done. Comey stated, "[T]he way it tended to break down is [the Lead Analyst] would talk about exploitation of media and sorting through emails and things. And Pete [Strzok] would focus on investigative steps, interviews, things like that." Comey told the OIG:

[I]t would typically be here in the [Director's] conference room at the table and they would give me a progress report on where they were and I would typically ask the questions that were rooted in my interest in it to begin with which is— do you have the resources you need? Any problems that I can help you with? I just felt the need to stay close to it[.]

As described in more detail in Chapter Six, the same officials were involved in discussions about whether to do a public statement announcing the closing of the Midyear investigation. Comey characterized these discussions as "great family conversations," stating that he was a great believer in oppositional argument and encouraged people to bring up different points of view.

In addition to the Midyear-specific meetings, Comey and the Deputy Director (first Giuliano, then McCabe) had daily morning and late afternoon meetings about significant developments or issues that were impacting the FBI. The Midyear investigation was sometimes discussed immediately following these meetings in "sidebar" meetings involving a smaller group of participants due to the sensitivity of the investigation.[54]

As the result of these frequent briefings, Comey and McCabe knew about and were involved in significant investigative decisions. McCabe stated:

> [Comey] relied on me for kind of my advice and recommendation on those decisions. But he was very involved in the decisions on Midyear.... Not decisions like what time is the interview with John Jones going to take place tomorrow, but...we think we should serve a subpoena on so-and-so for these records, and the Department of Justice is saying no, we want to try to work it out with a letter. And so...as that conflict was brewing, he would learn about it and weigh in on it and not necessarily decide it. But he was up-to-speed on all of the kind of significant things that were happening in the case.

McCabe told the OIG that although Strzok and Priestap made the day-to-day investigative decisions, he and Comey were informed about any problems that arose during the investigation, as well as any significant information that the team discovered.

As described in more detail in Chapter Five, our review found examples where Comey or McCabe approved or directed specific investigation decisions. These included directing the Midyear agents to deliver a preamble at the first interview of Cheryl Mills about the need to answer questions about the process used to cull former Secretary Clinton's personal and work-related emails, without informing the prosecutors; authorizing Baker to contact Beth Wilkinson, counsel to Mills and Samuelson, again without telling the prosecutors; approving the consent and immunity agreements used to obtain the Mills and Samuelson laptops; and not prohibiting Mills and Samuelson from attending the interview of former Secretary Clinton as her counsel.

---

[54] Other senior FBI officials involved in the Midyear investigation received additional briefings as needed. The Deputy Director, EAD, and AD met on a daily basis regarding significant matters affecting the Counterintelligence Division, and these meetings at times included significant developments in the Midyear investigation. McCabe said he was briefed when issues arose. In addition, the Lead Analyst and Strzok briefed Giacalone on the Midyear investigation on a weekly basis.

B.   Department Leadership

Unlike the FBI's senior leadership, senior Department officials played a more limited role in the Midyear investigation. Although Lynch, Yates, Axelrod, and Carlin described making a conscious decision to allow the career staff to handle the Midyear investigation with minimal involvement by political appointees, they also told us that their involvement was consistent with their normal role in criminal investigations.

Lynch

Lynch told the OIG that she received limited briefings on the Midyear investigation. She explained that the Midyear investigation was not discussed at her morning meetings or staff meetings because it was a sensitive matter and involved potentially classified information. Lynch said that she had a monthly meeting with NSD, and that although the Midyear investigation was too sensitive to discuss during that meeting, afterward the meeting would "skinny down" to discuss sensitive cases among a smaller group of people that included Yates, Axelrod, Carlin, Toscas, and sometimes members of her staff. She said that the cases discussed among this smaller group included not only the Midyear investigation, but also other sensitive counterterrorism and classified cases.

Lynch said that she understood that there were political sensitivities inherent in the Midyear investigation, and she wanted to protect the Midyear team from perceived pressure from Department leadership. She stated:

> Because we knew that it was going to be scrutinized, we wanted to make sure that not only was the team supported, but they also were insulated from a lot of people talking about it and just discussing it in general throughout the office.... And so, my view was that unless you need me for something, you know, I don't want to be on top of the team for this. They, they should work as they always work. They should know that [they have] whatever they need to have, whatever resources they need to get. But the Front Office is not, you know, breathing down their neck on this.

Asked whether there was ever a conscious decision by the political appointees to step back and allow the career employees to handle the investigation, Lynch replied:

> Certainly it was my view, and I can't recall having discussions about that. But that was how I viewed the setup, was that we wanted to make sure that this was always handled by the career people, and that essentially even though they would need input, and certainly toward the end of anything you'd have to make certain decisions. But not to have, at least certainly from...the fifth floor level where I was, not to have that kind of input early on. Although I typically wouldn't have had input...in the inner workings of an investigation.

Lynch said that Toscas was the most senior career Department official involved in making decisions about the Midyear investigation, and that she had faith and confidence in his ability to handle the case.

Lynch explained that she was not involved in the day-to-day investigative decisions about how to staff the investigation, what witnesses to interview, or any of the other "things that [she] used to do as a line [Assistant U.S. Attorney (AUSA)]." Nor did she intervene in conflicts between the prosecutors and agents. She told the OIG that this was not unique to the Midyear investigation but rather represented her standard practice, stating:

> [M]y view is that...whoever is, is leading the team needs to deal with that initially because they've got to keep working with each other. And based on my experience as an AUSA, if you can resolve it at that level first, you will have a team that is, is, is more solid and can work together more easily. If not, then I think the, the next level supervisor has got to be involved in that.... [M]y view is that the chain of command is set up is there for that reason.

> But I wouldn't, if someone said to me the agents want to interview this person, and the prosecutors don't, my first question before I got involved would be to say what do the supervisors think? Because if, if I as AG, or even as U.S. Attorney immediately step in and make that decision, then what I've done is I may have solved a problem, but I've cut the knees off of every supervisor in between me and them. And, and that creates bigger problems down the road.

Lynch said her view was that problems or conflicts should not be elevated to the Attorney General unless the parties had exhausted all other remedies.

Yates and Axelrod

Yates told the OIG that although Department leadership understood the significance of the Midyear investigation, they agreed that it should be handled like any other case. She said that the role of Department leadership in the Midyear investigation represented their normal approach to criminal investigations, stating:

> [L]ook, we got the sensitivity of this matter obviously even from the beginning. And I remember we wanted to make certain that NSD had all the resources that they needed, that they were on top of it. That we stayed briefed on what was going on but from the very beginning it was important to us for this to be handled like any other case would be handled. That we wanted to make sure that the line prosecutors and lawyers who were doing this didn't feel like they had the leadership office breathing down their neck because that's going to put a layer of pressure on them that is not appropriate we felt like here. So it was important to us for NSD to be handling the day to day aspects of this. But at the same time we wanted to make sure that they were getting what they needed. And that we were staying apprised of significant developments in it....

Not only doing it the right way but making sure that we did this, that it had the appearance of doing it the right way too. And public confidence was going to be important. We knew that from the very beginning. And that we wanted to make sure that we had a process in place that was going to be the right process. And that would be for NSD to handle the day to day aspects of it. And so we had [that] conversation. You know, the DAG's office is really sort of more the operational one between the two leadership offices. And so I certainly had conversations with the AG about how we set this up and we're running it. But again, there was no real dispute with anybody about this. This seemed like the natural and right way to do things....

Asked whether her role in the Midyear investigation differed at all from her usual process, Yates replied:

Every other case is not on the radar screen of...[the] DAG, obviously. But this was a significant matter for the Department that was one of those small handful of cases that how you do it can be defining for the Department of Justice.... And we were very aware of that from the very beginning. So when I say we were handling it like any other case what I mean is that we wanted to ensure that the factors that went into a decision about how we should proceed in that matter and how, the kind of latitude that the line people were handling had to do it in that matter, that that should be done like any other case. Nobody should get any special treatment. Nobody should be treated more harshly...because of who they were. That's what I mean it should be like any other case. But we weren't stupid. I mean, we recognized that the profile and import of this matter was such that we needed to make sure that things were done correctly.

Yates explained that the DAG typically gets involved in an investigation from a decisionmaking standpoint if there is disagreement between one of the Department's litigating components and another government agency, or between a Department component and a U.S. Attorney's Office, or if there is "real uncertainty" about whether to take a potential investigative step. She stated, "Normally the DAG's office is not running an investigation and we weren't running this one."

Yates told the OIG that she received more frequent updates on the Midyear investigation than she did on other cases, attributing this to the profile and time sensitivity of the investigation. Yates told the OIG that it was hard to generalize how frequently she received updates, but that she had regular meetings with NSD every other week. Although the Midyear investigation was not discussed with the larger group present during these meetings, afterward they would "skinny down" to a smaller group to discuss sensitive matters, including the Midyear investigation. This smaller group included Carlin, Toscas, and Mary McCord, who was at the time the Principal DAAG in NSD. Yates said that she also participated in Lynch's regular meetings with NSD, which would similarly "skinny down" at the end.

The NSD and EDVA prosecutors told the OIG that they were concerned at various points during the Midyear investigation that there was a disparity between the involvement of Department and FBI leadership in discussions about investigative steps. For example, while McCabe (the second in command at the FBI) attended meetings at which the Midyear agents and prosecutors debated whether and how to obtain the Mills and Samuelson laptops, the highest ranking official representing the Department's position at those meetings was Toscas. Asked whether she was informed of these concerns, Yates told the OIG that she was not. She said that she was not aware that McCabe attended meetings with the Midyear prosecutors, nor did she know that Comey was closely involved in the investigation. Yates stated that she spoke to McCabe regularly about various issues, and that she thought he was "relaxed enough" with her to tell her that she needed to be at any meetings. Yates said that any disparity resulted from the unusually high level of involvement by FBI leadership, not a decreased role by Department leadership.

Axelrod similarly told the OIG that at the outset of the Midyear investigation, senior Department officials "made efforts to...set up a structure that would maintain the integrity of this matter." He explained that they were aware that no matter how the investigation turned out, there was likely to be criticism at the end. As a result, he said that they considered it "extra important to make sure things were...done...by the book, following procedures. Making sure that when people criticize[d] whatever the outcome was that we'd be able to say no, this was done straight down the middle on the facts and on the law."

Axelrod said that he met with Toscas at the outset of the investigation and explained that Toscas would be the primary supervisor over the investigation. Axelrod stated:

> [W]e were going to have sort of a lighter touch from the leadership offices than we might on a sort of high profile case. In other words, we were there for him for whatever he needed. But we weren't going to be sort of checking in day to day or week to week for updates or briefings. When...something significant happened...that we needed to know about he would let us know....

> And I, when I say a lighter touch I don't mean that folks weren't engaged or paying attention. I, not at all. I just mean we wanted to give them the space they needed to do whatever they thought necessary in the investigation. So that at the end...I just wanted to make sure that any allegation that there was some sort of political interference with this investigation wouldn't hold water.

Axelrod told the OIG that the difference between the role of Department leadership in the Midyear investigation and the typical high-profile investigation was "just a matter of degree." He said that he and Yates relied on Toscas to bring issues to their attention at "skinny down" sessions following the biweekly meetings with NSD, but that "it wasn't us saying okay, and what's the latest on the email investigation?"

Carlin

Carlin told the OIG that NSD's standard practice is for cases to be handled by the career staff, supervised by a DAAG. He said that at the beginning of the Midyear investigation, he held a meeting with McCord, Toscas, and the NSD prosecutors in which he emphasized the need to "go more by the book" and to follow the normal procedure. Carlin said that he wanted one person in the NSD Front Office to be in charge of the Midyear investigation, and that he chose Toscas based on his historical expertise with investigations involving "espionage, the straight-up a spy [cases], and the leak mishandling type portfolio."

Carlin said that he preferred having one person who was clearly accountable and in charge. He stated:

> I tend to like that as former career person...I knew what it felt like when you're in one of those spots. So, in general, I prefer that type of structure. In this case, I knew, as well, at the end of the day, whatever decision was made in the case, it was going to be a high-profile controversial decision. And so...you might need to explain later what process do we follow at the Department. And so, I wanted to make that clear, internally and to our partners, that this was the process we were following...at the National Security Division.
>
> And just, seeing some other cases in my career that were, they were high profile. They were handled in a way than was different than the norm. More people got involved in trying to make the day-to-day decisions. I didn't think that that redounded to the benefit of the case. Not just for appearance purposes, but...it also just created confusion and frustration among the relevant teams. And kind of, inconsistencies in how they were staffed, sometimes, when someone had a great idea later, and came in over the top, and changed the way they were approaching the case. So, right from the beginning, I wanted to, to set it up, and structure...it that way. I felt pretty strongly about it.

Carlin said that he discussed this with Lynch and Yates and made it clear to them that the team had the authority to make investigative and prosecutorial decisions. Carlin said that he told Lynch and Yates that "like other sensitive matters, we would periodically update them." According to Carlin, Lynch and Yates knew that this was how Carlin was handling the investigation and supported this structure. Carlin said that he also explicitly communicated this to the FBI, explaining it to both Giacalone and McCabe.

IV. Investigative Strategy

The Midyear team sought to determine whether any individuals were criminally liable under the laws prohibiting the mishandling of classified information, which are summarized in Chapter Two. To do so, the team employed an investigative strategy that included three primary lines of inquiry: collection and examination of the emails that traversed former Secretary Clinton's servers and other relevant evidence, interviews of relevant witnesses, and analysis of whether classified information was compromised by hostile cyber intrusions.[55]

A. Collection and Examination of Emails that Traversed Clinton's Servers and Other Relevant Evidence

The Midyear team sought to collect and review any emails that traversed Clinton's servers during her tenure as Secretary of State, as well as other evidence that would be helpful to understand classified information contained in those emails. This included a review of the 30,490 work-related emails and attachments to those emails that former Secretary Clinton's attorneys had produced to the State Department.

The team also attempted to recover or reconstruct the remaining 31,830 emails that Clinton's attorneys determined were personal and did not produce to the State Department. As described above and in Chapter Five, before the Midyear investigation began, these emails had been deleted and "wiped" from former Secretary Clinton's then current server. The Midyear team also believed that some work-related emails could have been deleted from Clinton's servers before her attorneys reviewed them for production to the State Department.

The Midyear investigators sought to recover and review deleted emails by obtaining and forensically analyzing, among other things, Clinton's servers and related equipment; other devices used by Clinton, such as Blackberries and cellular telephones; laptops and other devices that had been used to backup Clinton's emails from the server; and the laptops used by Clinton's attorneys to cull her personal emails from her work-related emails. The team also obtained email content or other information from the official government or private email accounts of certain individuals who communicated with Clinton by email, originated the classified email chains that were ultimately forwarded to Clinton, or transferred Clinton's emails to other locations.

As described in Chapter Five, the Midyear team did not seek to obtain every device or the contents of every email account that it had reason to believe a classified email traversed. Rather, the team focused the investigation on obtaining Clinton's servers and devices. Witnesses stated that, due to what they perceived to be systemic problems with handling classified information at the State Department, to expand the investigation beyond former Secretary Clinton's server systems and devices would have prolonged the investigation for years. They further stated that the State Department was the more appropriate agency to remediate classified spills by its own employees.

Analysts examined both the original 30,490 emails produced by former Secretary Clinton to the State Department and the emails recovered through other

---

[55] This section does not contain an exhaustive list of investigative efforts in the Midyear investigation, but rather is intended to be an overview of the Midyear team's investigative strategy. We discuss the specific investigative steps used during the Midyear investigation in Chapter Five.

means to identify potentially classified information. Once the analysts identified information that they suspected to be classified, the team sought formal classification review from government agencies with equities in the information. The analysts also examined the emails for evidence of criminal intent. For example, they searched for:

- Classification markings to assess whether participants in classified email chains were on notice that the information contained in them was classified;

- Statements by former Secretary Clinton or others indicating whether Clinton used private servers for the purpose of evading laws regarding the proper handling of federal records or classified information;

- Statements by former Secretary Clinton or others indicating whether they knew that emails contained information that was classified—even if they were not clearly marked—when they sent or received them on unauthorized systems;

- Evidence as to whether former Secretary Clinton or others forwarded classified information to persons without proper clearances or without the need to know about it; and

- Documentation showing whether originators of classified emails had received classified information in properly marked documents before transferring the information to unclassified systems without markings.

B.   Witness Interviews

The Midyear team told us that witness interviews covered several areas of investigative interest. First, the team interviewed individuals involved with setting up and administering former Secretary Clinton's servers to understand her intent in using private servers and to assess what measures they used to protect the servers from intrusion. These witnesses also helped FBI analysts understand the server structures to inform subsequent analyses. Additionally, they helped FBI investigators identify additional sources of evidence, such as devices containing backups of Clinton's emails.

Second, the Midyear team interviewed individuals who introduced, transmitted, or received information on unauthorized systems, including the originators of classified information, Clinton's aides who forwarded the originators' emails to her, and Clinton herself. The originators included State Department employees and employees of other government agencies. The team interviewed these witnesses to, among other things, assess: (1) whether they believed the information contained in the emails was classified; (2) how or from where they originally received the classified information (and whether based on those circumstances they should have known that the information contained in the emails was classified); and (3) why they sent the information on unclassified systems.

Third, the Midyear team interviewed individuals with knowledge of how and why 31,830 of former Secretary Clinton's emails were deleted from her servers and other locations. The team sought to assess whether Clinton or her attorneys deleted or directed the deletion of emails for an improper purpose, such as to avoid FOIA or Federal Records Act (FRA) requirements.

Fourth, the Midyear team interviewed State Department employees with knowledge of the State Department's policies and practices regarding federal records retention. The team sought to determine whether Clinton's use of a private server was sanctioned by the State Department, as well as what measures the State Department put in place to protect Clinton's private server from intrusion.

C.   Intrusion Analysis

The FBI also conducted intrusion analyses to determine whether any classified information had been compromised by domestic hostile actors or foreign adversaries. Agents and analysts specializing in forensics examined the servers, devices, and other evidence to assess whether unauthorized actors had attempted to log into, scan, or otherwise gain access to the email accounts on the servers and, if so, whether their efforts had been successful. They also examined various FBI datasets to assess whether emails containing classified information had been compromised.

PAGE LEFT INTENTIONALLY

BLANK

CHAPTER FOUR:
DECISION TO PUBLICLY ACKNOWLEDGE THE MIDYEAR INVESTIGATION AND REACTION TO WHITE HOUSE STATEMENTS ABOUT THE INVESTIGATION

In this chapter, we address the decision of the FBI and the Department to publicly acknowledge an investigation following the public referral from IC IG, including the allegation that former Lynch instructed former Director Comey to refer to the Midyear investigation as a "matter." We also discuss public statements by former President Barack Obama about the Midyear investigation, which raised concerns about White House influence on the investigation.

As we describe in Chapter Six, Comey cited the events set forth in this chapter as two of the factors that influenced his decision to deliver a public statement announcing the closing of the Midyear investigation on July 5, 2016, without coordinating with the Department.

I. Public Acknowledgement of the Investigation

A. Statements about the Investigation in Department and FBI Letters to Congress in August and September 2015

Following the public referral to the FBI from the IC IG in July 2015, the Department and the FBI received questions from the media and Congress asking whether they had opened a criminal investigation of former Secretary Clinton. According to emails exchanged in late August 2015, there was a significant disagreement between ODAG and FBI officials regarding whether to acknowledge that a criminal investigation had been opened. FBI officials, according to the emails, wanted to acknowledge "open[ing] an investigation into the matter," while ODAG officials approved language "neither confirm[ing] nor deny[ing] the existence of any ongoing investigation," based on longstanding Department policy. FBI and Department letters sent to Congress on August 27 and September 22, 2015, and a letter sent by the FBI General Counsel to the State Department on September 22, 2015, used the "neither confirm nor deny" language.

Contemporaneous emails show that former Director Comey disagreed with this approach. In an August 27, 2015 email to Deputy Director (DD) Giuliano, Chief of Staff James Rybicki, and FBI Office of Public Affairs (OPA) Assistant Director (AD) Mike Kortan, he stated, "I'm thinking it a bit silly to say we 'can't confirm or deny an investigation' when there are public statements by former [S]ecretary Clinton and others about the production of materials to us. I would rather be in a place where we say we 'don't comment on our investigations.'" Rybicki told the OIG that Comey thought that the Department and FBI needed to say more about the investigation because the IC IG referral was made publicly, and refusing to acknowledge an investigation would "stretch...any credibility the Department has."

B. September 28, 2015 Meeting between Attorney General Lynch and Director Comey

In late September and early October 2015, Comey and Lynch each had upcoming media and congressional appearances. Anticipating that they would be asked whether the Department and FBI had opened an investigation into former Secretary Clinton, Comey asked to meet with Lynch to coordinate what they would say. Comey told the OIG that it was the first time the two of them would be asked questions about the investigation publicly, and he wanted to discuss how they should talk about it given that there had been news coverage of the referral and "a lot of public discussion about that the FBI is already looking [into] this."

The meeting was held on September 28, 2015, and lasted approximately 15 minutes. Participants in the meeting included Lynch, Axelrod, and Toscas from the Department, and Comey, Rybicki, and then DD Giuliano from the FBI.

1. Comey's Account of the Meeting

Comey told the OIG that during this meeting AG Lynch agreed they needed to confirm the existence of the investigation, but she said not to use the word "investigation," and instead to call it a "matter." Comey said that Lynch seemed slightly irritated at him when she said this, and that he took it as a direction. Comey stated:

> And I remember saying, "Well, what should I call it?" And she said, "Call it a matter." And I said, "Why would I do that?" And she said, "I just want you to do that and so I would very much appreciate it if you would not refer to it as an investigation." And the reason that gave me pause is, it was during a period of time which lasted, where I knew from the open source that the Clinton campaign was keen not to use the word investigation.... [A]nd so that one concerned me and I remember getting a lump in my stomach and deciding at that moment should I fight on this or not.

Comey told the OIG that he decided not to fight this instruction from the AG, but that it "made [his] spider sense tingle" and caused him to "worry...that she's carrying water for the [Clinton] campaign[.]" As described in Chapter Six, Comey told the OIG and testified before Congress that this instruction from Lynch was one of the factors that influenced his unilateral decision to make a public statement on July 5, 2016, without coordinating with the Department.[56] However, Comey also said to us that he had no other reason to question Lynch's motives at that time, stating, "[I]n fact my experience with her has always been very good and independent, and she always struck me as an independent-minded person[.]"

---

[56] *See* U.S. Senate, Select Committee on Intelligence, *Open Hearing with Former FBI Director James Comey*, 115th Cong., 1st sess., June 8, 2017, https://www.intelligence.senate.gov/hearings/open-hearing-former-fbi-director-james-comey# (accessed May 8, 2018).

Comey stated that one of the reasons he remembered this meeting so well was that Toscas made a comment after the meeting about the "Federal Bureau of Matters," indicating to Comey that Toscas "had the same reaction I did to it." He said that Toscas did not say explicitly that he shared Comey's concerns about the meeting, but was "signaling" agreement to him through "body language and humor."

Rybicki and Giuliano did not specifically recall the discussion that took place at the meeting, other than that AG Lynch told Comey to refer to the investigation as a "matter." Giuliano stated, "I don't remember that specific [meeting]. I do remember the topic. And I do remember thinking that (A) it's ridiculous, and (B) quite honestly, I didn't care what they called it.... It wasn't going to change what we did." He recalled discussions with the Midyear team after the meeting with Lynch, telling the OIG that "a lot of people got wrapped around the axle" about the issue and "thought that that was kind of getting into the politics of the investigation." He also stated that Comey was "definitely troubled by it."

However, Rybicki said that he did not recall Comey being troubled by the meeting or expressing concern that the instruction from Lynch was an effort to coordinate with the Clinton campaign. Rybicki also said that he personally did not come away from the meeting with the view that Lynch was biased. Rybicki did recall Toscas joking about the "Federal Bureau of Matters."

2.   Lynch's Recollection of the Meeting

Lynch told the OIG that Comey expressed concern during the meeting about how to comply with the Department's longstanding policy of neither confirming nor denying ongoing criminal investigations in the face of direct questions about the number of agents assigned to the case and the resources dedicated to it, because answering those questions implicitly would acknowledge that there was an open investigation. Lynch said that providing testimony about the allocation of resources or the way that the Department works a case is a normal practice, but that in her view, they were not ready to publicly confirm an investigation.

Lynch stated that her discussion with Comey was framed in terms of how they could testify about the resources dedicated to the investigation without breaking Department policy. Lynch said that Comey was seeking guidance on how to handle those issues, particularly given that the referral was public, and that detailed information about the investigation had been discussed in the press.

Lynch said that she was aware of numerous letters from Members of Congress requesting information about the investigation, and that her meeting with Comey took place around the same time as a telephone call she had with Senator Charles Grassley, who wanted to discuss the Department's handling of Bryan Pagliano, a State Department employee who set up one of Clinton's servers, in order to inform Congress's decision as to whether to grant him immunity to compel his testimony before Congress.[57] Lynch told the OIG:

> Senator Grassley was asking me literally will I confirm that there is a criminal investigation of Secretary Clinton, who are the other targets, who are the subjects, has a grand jury been impaneled, has this young man [Pagliano] been given immunity, would I give him a copy of the immunity order, and all the things that, that Oversight typically asks for.
>
> So I knew, and I certainly had the view, that we had to be clear and open with Oversight. You know, whether it's me or the Director. But consistent with our law enforcement obligations, there are some doors that we do not open. And I did not think that we were ready to open that door on the Hill at that time.

Lynch said that her concerns about opening the door to detailed questions about the investigation informed her view that the Department should not confirm that there was an investigation. She said that she recalled stating at the meeting with Comey, "[T]hey don't need us to tell them that there is an investigation. They need us to confirm that there is an investigation. And there is a difference." She explained:

> And once we confirm it publicly, either by saying yes there is an investigation, or by talking about it in a way that confirms it, the next series of questions is going to be is it criminal. And it's all going to be about is the Secretary a subject or a target. And there were others involved as well. There are other people beyond her who may or may not be named, but, you know, you start having these discussions. When will it be over? What are you finding? All those things that in fact Grassley did ask.

The OIG asked Lynch if she instructed or told Comey, "I want you to call it a matter." Lynch said that she did not and would not have, because that was not how she spoke to people. She told the OIG that she remembered saying the following at the meeting:

> Well I, I do remember saying, you know, we typically say we have enough resources to handle the matter.... I don't know if I used other words like the case, you know, the inquiry, or something like that. But I do remember saying that, and I think I may have been saying that because, again, I was always careful not to talk about an investigation.

---

[57] Based on notes and Department emails, the OIG determined that Lynch's call with Senator Grassley was scheduled for later that same day, September 28, 2015. According to talking points prepared for this call, Lynch intended to tell Senator Grassley that the Department could neither confirm nor deny the existence of any ongoing investigation or persons or entities under investigation, consistent with longstanding Department policy. The talking points stated, "This policy, which has been applied across Administrations, is designed to protect the integrity of our investigations and to avoid any appearance of political influence."

I was getting questioned about the referral...and is it going to lead to an investigation and, you know, we have it, we acknowledge it, we're going to handle it. And that's all I can say kind of thing.

And so I know that in addition to saying...yes, everyone knows there's an investigation. They don't need us to tell them that. They need us to confirm it, and we don't do that. And here's why we don't do that. I remember making those statements. And I remember saying but of course you've got to...respond. And one way to respond is just to say...you've got what you need to handle the matter.

Lynch said that she thought that there had been agreement at the meeting about what to say. Her takeaway was that they were going to take steps not to confirm that there was an official investigation open and would be careful not to do so in how they discussed it. Lynch stated, "[I]t wasn't a long meeting. It was that, it wasn't contentious. Nobody seemed upset. So it was more of a discussion." She said that she did not recall Comey or anyone else expressing disagreement, or Comey asking, "Why on earth would I do that?"

Lynch said that the decision to avoid confirming an investigation was not made with any political motive in mind, and that she did not coordinate messaging with the Clinton campaign. Lynch told the OIG that she was surprised to learn from Comey's later congressional testimony that he interpreted the discussion at this meeting as evidence of potential political bias. She stated:

I was surprised. I was disappointed, somewhat angry. And mostly surprised that he had never raised it either at the time or later, that if it was a concern—I was surprised that if he thought that it was a problem, he was okay also handling things in that way. I just had never viewed him as someone who was reluctant to raise issues or concerns, given that I had known him for, for some time [.]

Lynch recalled Toscas making a joke about the "Federal Bureau of Matters" to one of the agents who was sitting beside him, and people laughing. She said that she took this as a joke, as good-natured "ribbing" or "teasing," and that the laughter told her that others in attendance also took it as a joke.

Axelrod told us that the discussion about whether to acknowledge an "investigation" was just one small part of that meeting. He said that Lynch suggested using the term "matter" as a way of "thread[ing] the needle" to avoid violating Department policy while also not appearing evasive. According to Axelrod, no one from the FBI raised objections during the meeting, and the tone of the discussion was collegial. He said that he thought that Comey and Lynch had reached a "mutual agreement that using the term 'matter' was the best way to thread the needle." Axelrod told the OIG that he was surprised to hear Comey's later congressional testimony that he (Comey) felt uncomfortable with the discussion, which Axelrod said was not consistent with his recollection of Comey's reaction in the room, and did not "square with...[his] recollection of the facts."

3.   Toscas's Notes and Recollection of the Meeting

Toscas took detailed notes at the September 28 meeting, which he provided to the OIG. Toscas said that his notes were unusually lengthy for such a brief meeting because AAG Carlin was out of town and he was asked to attend in Carlin's place, and he wanted to be able to tell Carlin what happened.

Referencing his notes, Toscas testified to the OIG at length about what took place during the meeting. According to Toscas, Comey told Lynch that he planned to acknowledge at a House Permanent Select Committee on Intelligence (HPSCI) roundtable that the FBI had received the referral from the IC IG and that it was being properly staffed and receiving all necessary resources. Comey stated that he planned to say that the FBI does not comment on its investigations per longstanding policy, but that all of its investigations are done professionally and timely. Toscas said that Comey assured Lynch that he would not say that they had opened an investigation, but that this would be implicit in what he said, and there would be news reports afterwards saying that there was an investigation.

According to Toscas, Lynch replied that she preferred "to discuss it in terms of a matter.... [T]his is the way I do it and then it avoids this issue because we should neither confirm nor deny." Toscas said that he interpreted Lynch's statement as expressing her preference rather than telling Comey what he should do. Toscas stated he did not recall Lynch instructing Comey to call it a matter, and he thought he would have remembered that if it had occurred. He also said that he did not interpret Lynch's comment as her "trying to shade [the investigation] into something it wasn't for some particular reason." However, he acknowledged that he was not the FBI Director, and that Comey may have had a different perspective.

Toscas said that after Lynch's comment, Axelrod stated that they needed to coordinate what to say with a letter sent by the FBI General Counsel to the State Department the previous week and attached to a public filing in FOIA litigation, in which the FBI took "great pains to not call this an investigation, so as not to confirm the existence of an investigation." According to Toscas, the Department and the FBI had used the same language in other letters to Congress, and Lynch had a call scheduled later that day with Senator Charles Grassley in which she planned to tell him that it would be premature to acknowledge or share information about any investigation.

Toscas said that Axelrod's statement led to a back and forth between Comey and Axelrod, during which Comey proposed modifying the letters to Congress to acknowledge that the FBI had opened an investigation. Toscas said that he was not sure if Comey was "toying with [Axelrod] at that point because I don't think we would ever reissue letters that...clearly state normal positions." Toscas said that Comey then asked Axelrod directly, "Why not use the word, you know we're trying to treat it like any other case and would we do that ordinarily?" In response, Axelrod again mentioned the need to be consistent with the letters that were sent the previous week.

Toscas told the OIG that he mentioned at the meeting that the Department opens only a small fraction of the referrals it receives from the intelligence community as criminal investigations, and that the Department may not want to publicly acknowledge an investigation into former Secretary Clinton because it could serve as precedent for other referrals. Toscas said he also made clear to the group that Midyear was a criminal investigation, and that the prosecutors had referred to it as an investigation in letters to counsel and in search warrant applications.

Toscas said that Comey concluded the meeting by agreeing to call it a matter, stating, "OK, I think that will work." This statement also appeared in Toscas's contemporaneous notes. Toscas told the OIG that there was no indication at the time that Comey was concerned about the meeting or that the meeting had led him to question Lynch's impartiality.

Asked whether he made a comment to Comey about the "Federal Bureau of Matters," Toscas said that he did not specifically recall doing so but may have. He said that, if he did, he intended it as a joke rather than as a criticism of Lynch. He told the OIG:

> I don't know if I ribbed [Comey] walking out. You know he's a friend of mine.... In any event, maybe I said that, maybe I didn't. It wouldn't faze me if I did, because it was in line with what I was saying to them [about "investigation" being part of the FBI's name]. But it makes it appear as though I was sort of knocking the AG [Lynch] in the way they reported it, which is obviously why some goofball felt that they should talk about that to the newspapers....[58]

C.   October 1, 2015 Comey Meeting with Media

In a "pen and pad" with reporters on October 1, 2015, Comey used the term "matter" in response to questions about whether the FBI had opened an investigation. According to a transcript of the appearance, Comey told reporters that he recently had a closed session with HPSCI and would say publicly what he told the committee: that the FBI had received a referral involving former Secretary Clinton's use of a private email account and the possible exposure of classified information through that account, but that he was limited in what he could say because the FBI does not talk about its ongoing work. Comey stated, "I am following this very closely and I get briefed on it regularly.... I am confident that we have the resources and the personnel assigned to the matter, as we do all our work, so we're able to do it as we do all our work in a professional, prompt and independent way." Asked about the timeline for completing any investigation, Comey stated, "Again, I'm not going to talk about this particular matter.... Part of doing our work well is we don't talk about it while we do it."

---

[58] *See* Matt Apuzzo et al., *In Trying to Avoid Politics, Comey Shaped an Election*, N.Y. Times, Apr. 23, 2017, at A1 (referencing two sources who reportedly heard Toscas state, "I guess you're the Federal Bureau of Matters now.").

Following Comey's appearance, various news articles reported that Comey had acknowledged the existence of an investigation into former Secretary Clinton's use of a private email server.[59] Comey received an email containing news clips summarizing several of these articles and forwarded it to Rybicki, stating, "Will leave it to you to tell DOJ that I never used the word investigation." Rybicki replied, "Already covered. I read back your statement to them and told them this is exactly the type of confusion we were concerned about as we were crafting."

II.   Reaction to White House Statements about the Midyear Investigation

On Sunday, October 11, 2015, an interview of then President Barack Obama was aired on the CBS show 60 Minutes. During this interview, Obama characterized former Secretary Clinton's use of a private email server as a "mistake," but stated that it did not "pose[] a national security problem" and was "not a situation in which America's national security was endangered." Obama also stated that the issue had been "ginned up" because of the presidential race. Two days later, on October 13, 2015, Obama's Press Secretary, Josh Earnest, was asked whether Obama's comments "should be read as an attempt to steer the direction of the FBI investigation." Earnest replied that Obama made his comments based on public information, and they were not intended to influence an independent investigation.

Former President Obama's comments caused concern among FBI officials about the potential impact on the investigation. Former EAD John Giacalone told the OIG, "[W]e open up criminal investigations. And you have the President of the United States saying this is just a mistake.... That's a problem, right?" Former AD Randy Coleman expressed the same concern, stating, "[The FBI had] a group of guys in here, professionals, that are conducting an investigation. And the...President of the United States just came out and said there's no there there." Coleman said that he would have expected someone in FBI or Department leadership to contact one of Obama's national security officials, and "tell [him or her], hey knock it off." Michael Steinbach, the former EAD for the National Security Branch, told the OIG that the comments generated "controversy" within the FBI. Steinbach stated, "[Y]ou're prejudging the results of an investigation before they really even have been started.... That's...hugely problematic for us."

Department prosecutors also were concerned. Responding to an email from Laufman about Obama's 60 Minutes interview, Toscas stated, "Saw this. And as [one of the prosecutors] and I discussed last week, of course it had no—and will never have any—effect whatsoever on our work and our independent judgment." Prosecutor 4 told the OIG that Obama's statement was the genesis of the FBI's suspicions that the Department's leadership was politically biased. This prosecutor stated, "I know that the FBI considered those [statements] inappropriate. And that it...[generated] a suspicion that there was a political bias...going on from the Executive Branch."

---

[59] *See, e.g.*, Pete Williams, *FBI Director Acknowledges Agency Looking Into Clinton Emails*, NBC News, Oct. 1, 2015, http://nbcnews.to/1LmHuMM (accessed Jan. 18, 2018).

Asked about former President Obama's statements, Lynch stated, "I never spoke to the President directly about it, because I never spoke to him about any case or investigation. He didn't speak to me about it either." She told the OIG that she did not think the President should have made the comment on 60 Minutes. She stated, "I don't know where it came from. And I don't know, I don't know why he would have thought that either, to be honest with you. Because, to me, anyone looking at this case would have seen a national security component to it. So I don't, I truly do not know where he got that from."

Former President Obama's Press Secretary, Josh Earnest, made additional comments about the Midyear investigation during a press conference in early 2016. On January 29, 2016, in response to a question about whether the White House thought that former Secretary Clinton would be indicted, Earnest stated:

> That will be a decision that is made by the Department of Justice and prosecutors over there. What I know that some officials over there have said is that she is not a target of the investigation. So that does not seem to be the direction that it's trending, but I'm certainly not going to weigh in on a decision or in that process in any way. That is a decision to be made solely by independent prosecutors. But, again, based on what we know from the Department of Justice, it does not seem to be headed in that direction.

After this press conference, Melanie Newman, the Director of the Department's Office of Public Affairs (OPA), received a transcript of Earnest's statements about the investigation and forwarded it to Axelrod and three other Department officials. Newman stated in the email to these officials, "I've spoken to the [White House] and asked that they clarify this, to make clear they have no insight into this investigation. And if they don't correct it, I will. I'm waiting to hear back." This email also was forwarded to Lynch.

Asked about this email, Newman said that she spoke to Earnest that day. Newman said that Earnest told her that he had based his comments on what he had read in news stories, not conversations with anyone in the Department. She said that no one in the White House ever reached out to her about the Midyear investigation, nor was she aware of White House staff reaching out to anyone else in the Department, noting, "They were very, very, very careful about engaging with us on that topic." Axelrod similarly told the OIG that Earnest's comments implied that the White House had received a briefing on the Midyear investigation, which he said "never happened."

Lynch's Chief of Staff stated that Department officials were "very upset" about Earnest's statement, because "as far as we knew, no one at Department of Justice had spoken to anyone in the White House about it." The Chief of Staff told the OIG that they were particularly concerned by Earnest's statement that former Secretary Clinton was not a target. The Chief of Staff said that she spoke to officials in the White House Counsel's Office to tell them that the Department did not know where Earnest was getting his information, and to ask them to talk to Earnest. The Chief of Staff did not specifically recall Lynch's reaction to this statement, but said that she was "[p]robably very upset.... [A]nytime there was ever any suggestion that the White House, or that DOJ had improperly done something in an investigation, or discussed something of...a political nature, she would not be happy about it."

Prosecutors again were concerned by these comments. On January 29, 2016, Toscas sent the following email to Laufman, seeking to assure the team that the investigation would not be influenced by White House statements:

> As discussed, I spoke with ODAG and they are not aware of anybody from DOJ sharing any such information or assessment with the White House, as the below statements appear to suggest. I want to reiterate what I've told you and the team throughout our work on this investigation—the explicit direction we received from the AG and DAG on multiple occasions is that they have total confidence in the team of prosecutors who are working on this case and they have instructed us to proceed with this matter as we would any other, without interference of any kind, and with the independence we have in all of our cases. They have never wavered from that and have never said or done anything to send or suggest a contrary message. With respect to the below statements that erroneously imply that the Department has shared information about, or an assessment of, this matter with the White House, we should not and will not allow such irresponsible statements to have any effect at all on our work. We will continue to thoroughly and professionally investigate this matter as we would any other—and, as always—and as you, John [Carlin], and I have said repeatedly—we will follow the facts wherever they lead. Thanks.

Toscas emailed Laufman a second time, stating, "Please feel free to share this with the whole team (if you haven't already)." During his interview with the OIG, Toscas described Earnest's statements as "goofy" and "ridiculous," expressing frustration that he had to address comments by the White House when preparing Lynch to testify before Congress because of the perception of political bias that they created.

Asked about Earnest's statements, prosecutors told the OIG that the only interactions they had with the White House concerning the investigation were with the White House Counsel's Office to obtain a classification review of documents in a Special Access Program (SAP) controlled by the White House and to interview a National Security Council staffer. Prosecutor 1 told the OIG that he was not aware of contacts between Department leadership and the White House Counsel's Office or White House staff. Notes taken by Laufman indicate that on January 30, 2016, one of the prosecutors reached out to their point of contact in the White House Counsel's Office and asked about Earnest's comments. According to these notes, this prosecutor was told that the content of the discussions between the White House Counsel's Office and the Midyear team about the classification review and the interview of the staffer was limited to a small group of people in the White House Counsel's Office, and that nothing that the prosecutors had discussed with the White House Counsel's Office would be known to Earnest.

Lynch testified before the Senate Judiciary Committee on March 9, 2016. Asked about the investigation, Lynch stated that she had never discussed the investigation with former President Obama or anyone in the White House. Lynch stated, "[I]t's my hope that when it comes to ongoing investigations that we all would stay silent. And I can assure you that neither I nor anyone from the Department has briefed to Mr. Earnest or anyone at the White House about this matter or other law enforcement matters.... I'm simply not aware of the source of his information."[60]

Lynch told the OIG that she recalled that Newman spoke with the White House Communications Office after Earnest's comments and was clear that they were inappropriate and needed to be corrected. Asked whether she perceived these comments as an effort to direct where the investigation was going or felt influenced by them, she said that she did not. Lynch said that she also had a discussion with the White House Counsel after she testified, and that during this discussion he acknowledged that the comments should not have happened.

However, former President Obama again made public comments about the Midyear investigation in an interview with FOX News Sunday on April 10, 2016. Obama stated that while former Secretary Clinton had been "careless" in managing her emails while she was Secretary of State, she would never intentionally do anything to endanger the security of the United States with her emails. He also stated that he would not interfere in the FBI's investigation into her private email server. Obama stated, "I guarantee that there is no political influence in any investigation conducted by the Justice Department, or the F.B.I.—not just in this case, but in any case."[61]

---

[60] U.S. Senate, Committee on the Judiciary, *Oversight of the U.S. Department of Justice*, 114th Cong., 2d sess., March 9, 2016, https://www.judiciary.senate.gov/meetings/oversight-of-the-us-department-of-justice.

[61] *See* Transcript, *President Barack Obama on FOX News Sunday*, Apr. 10, 2016, *at* http://www.foxnews.com/transcript/2016/04/10/exclusive-president-barack-obama-on-fox-news-sunday.html (accessed Mar. 22, 2018).

PAGE LEFT INTENTIONALLY

BLANK

CHAPTER FIVE:
INVESTIGATIVE METHODS USED IN THE INVESTIGATION

The Midyear team used several types of investigative methods and made various strategic decisions during the course of its investigation. Some of these decisions have been the subject of criticism and allegations that they were based on improper considerations.

In this chapter, we describe the following investigative methods and decisions made by the Midyear team: efforts to identify relevant sources of physical evidence; efforts to understand and access Clinton's servers; use of criminal process, including subpoenas, 2703(d) orders, and search warrants to obtain physical evidence; use of consent to obtain physical evidence; efforts to obtain evidence related to Clinton's senior aides; use of voluntary interviews; decisions to grant certain witnesses use immunity; strategies employed to secure voluntary interviews and voluntary production of evidence from Cheryl Mills and Heather Samuelson; and investigative decisions surrounding the voluntary interview of Hillary Clinton. We describe the reasons given for these decisions, disagreements among members of the Midyear team about them, especially between the FBI and the prosecutors, and the impact of these decisions on the investigation's access to relevant information and the completeness of the investigation. We also describe an internal file review of the Midyear investigation conducted by the FBI's Inspection Division (INSD) in September and October 2017 following our discovery of concerning text messages between Strzok and Page.

In addition, we discuss instant messages in which Agent 1 expressed concerns about the quality of the Midyear investigation. We considered these messages as part of our analysis of whether the Midyear team conducted a thorough and impartial investigation.

In the analysis section of this chapter, we assess whether the evidence supports a conclusion that any of the investigative decisions we reviewed were based on improper considerations, consistent with the analytical construct described in Chapter One.

I.   FBI's Efforts to Identify and Review Relevant Sources of Evidence

The Midyear team began its investigation by reviewing the 30,490 emails that Clinton had produced to the State Department. They reviewed them to identify emails that appeared to contain classified information and evidence of intent to mishandle classified information.[62] Witnesses told us that to search for evidence of intent, the analysts looked for, among other things, classification markings on the documents, statements indicating that email participants knew

---

[62] The Midyear Supervisory Special Agent told us that the State Department provided these emails to the FBI in paper form. According to the LHM, on August 6, 2015, Clinton's attorneys voluntarily provided the FBI thumb drives containing the same emails.

information was classified, and statements indicating that Clinton decided to use a private server for an improper purpose, such as to avoid FOIA or other laws. One analyst told us that there were at least six analysts consistently involved with reviewing these emails, and, at times, there were as many as fifteen or sixteen analysts doing so. Once the team identified emails that appeared to contain classified information, they sent them to other agencies within the U.S. Intelligence Community ("USIC agencies") with equities in them for formal classification review.

FBI agents and Department prosecutors told us that, thereafter, a large focus of the investigation was locating the remaining 31,830 emails that made up the entire 62,320 emails that Clinton's attorneys had reportedly reviewed before producing her work-related emails to the State Department. Clinton's attorneys did not produce those 31,830 emails to the State Department because, they stated, they were personal in nature; instead, the attorneys instructed Paul Combetta of Platte River Networks ("PRN")—the company that managed Clinton's server— to remove the emails from their own laptops and modify the server's email retention period so that emails older than 60 days would not be retained. In March 2015, Combetta removed the emails from Clinton's server using BleachBit after realizing he had failed to implement the new email retention period several months earlier. The FBI team wanted to review these emails, if possible, to determine whether any were work-related or contained classified information, and to search for evidence of Clinton's intent in using a private server.

FBI agents and analysts, including the Supervisory Special Agent (SSA) assigned to the Midyear investigation, told us that to find the missing 31,830 emails, the team attempted to identify and obtain access to any server or device— "whether it was a BlackBerry, iPad, PC [or] phone"—Clinton used during her tenure, as well as devices used to back up her emails. The FBI also sought email content or header information from the official U.S. government and private email accounts of certain individuals who were known to communicate directly with Clinton by email or who were involved in email chains that ultimately resulted in classified information being forwarded to Clinton. However, as discussed in Section V.C of this chapter, the FBI did not seek to obtain the personal devices of State Department employees, besides Clinton, who sometimes used private email for State Department work and who used those devices to communicate with Clinton while she was Secretary of State.

Based on our review, the FBI sent preservation requests to the State Department for nearly one-thousand official State Department email accounts. One analyst told us that the State Department was unable to supply many of the email records the FBI requested due to, among other things, limitations in the State Department's recordkeeping systems. However, the FBI obtained records from the official State Department email accounts of certain employees, including the three senior aides with whom Clinton had the most email contact. The FBI also made requests of other government agencies, including the CIA, the Defense Intelligence Agency (DIA), the Department of Defense (DOD), and the Executive Office of the President (EOP), to search their official email systems for emails to or from email accounts on the clintonemail.com domain. In addition, as discussed in Sections III and V below, the Midyear team used compulsory process to obtain email records from certain private email accounts.

The FBI also requested the State-Department-issued computers and handheld devices used by certain employees during their State Department tenure. However, with the exception of a desktop computer used by Bryan Pagliano (a State Department employee who set up Clinton's second server), the State Department told the FBI that it either did not preserve or could not locate those devices.

FBI witnesses told us that both FBI agents and analysts were involved in determining what devices and other evidence to obtain. Based on our review of the evidence, the FBI obtained more than 30 devices; received consent to search Clinton-related communications on most of these devices; and identified numerous work-related emails that were not part of the 30,490 emails produced by Clinton's attorneys to the State Department, many of which they sent to other agencies for classification review. The thirty devices included two of Clinton's servers, each of which consisted of multiple devices; storage devices used alongside Clinton's servers; numerous devices that were used to back up Clinton's emails during her tenure; some of Clinton's handheld devices; Pagliano's State Department desktop computer; several flash drives and laptop computers that contained copies of the 30,490 emails that Clinton's attorneys produced to the State Department; and the two laptops used by Clinton's attorneys to cull her emails for production to the State Department. Once the FBI received consent to review a device, staff from the FBI's Operational Technology Division (OTD) generally imaged the device and prepared the image for a filter team to remove material that was privileged or otherwise not subject to search pursuant to the terms of a consent agreement. OTD then uploaded the emails and other data from the device for FBI analysts to review. OTD also attempted to de-duplicate emails. The analysts reviewed the emails recovered from each device for the same purposes as they reviewed the initial 30,490—to identify both suspected classified information and evidence of intent to mishandle classified information.

The Midyear team also sought and obtained a wide range of other information relevant to the investigation, such as Clinton's cable, telephone, and Internet subscriber and service information; financial information for certain witnesses; business records pertaining to the services provided by the companies that supported Clinton's servers; records related to security services protecting Clinton's servers; and information from mail carriers related to the delivery of a laptop that at one time stored Clinton's archived emails. Prosecutor 1 told us that the team sought records from at least three different companies in an effort to find the Blackberry emails from the beginning of Clinton's tenure as Secretary of State.[63] Analysts told us that they reviewed these materials to search for, among

---

[63] Based on the LHM, the 30,490 emails provided by Clinton's attorneys to the State Department contained no emails sent or received by Clinton during the first two months of her tenure, January 21, 2009, through March 18, 2009, and the FBI investigative team was unable to locate the BlackBerry device she used during that time. Witnesses, including former Director Comey, told us

other things, evidence of mishandling classified information and additional leads for information. For example, one analyst stated that through records obtained from various phone companies, he was able to identify the 13 devices that were associated with two telephone numbers that Clinton used.

According to the LHM, the FBI found and reviewed "approximately 17,448 unique work-related and personal emails from Clinton's tenure" containing her email address that were not part of the original 30,490 that Clinton's lawyers had produced to the State Department. Comey stated in his July 5, 2016, press conference that the FBI found "several thousand" work-related emails that were not part of the 30,490 emails. However, one analyst told us, and documentation we reviewed showed, that the FBI did not conduct its review in such a way that it could calculate the precise amount of work-related emails discovered by the FBI that had not been produced to the State Department. Instead, as described below, they focused on identifying the number of classified emails that both were and were not included in the 30,490.

None of the emails, including those that were found to contain classified information, included a header or footer with classification markings. As we discuss further in Chapter Seven, this absence of clear classification markings played a significant role in the decision by the Midyear prosecutors to recommend to Attorney General Lynch in July 2016 that the investigation should be closed without prosecution. According to the LHM, the FBI, with the assistance of other USIC agencies, identified "81 email chains containing approximately 193 individual emails that were classified from the CONFIDENTIAL to TOP SECRET levels at the time the emails were drafted on UNCLASSIFIED systems and sent to or from Clinton's personal server." In other words, the USIC agencies determined that these 81 email chains, although not marked classified, contained information classified at the time the emails were sent and should have been so marked. Twelve of the 81 classified email chains were not among the 30,490 that Clinton's lawyers had produced to the State Department, and these were all classified at the Secret or Confidential levels. Seven of the 81 email chains contained information associated with a Special Access Program ("SAP"), which witnesses told us is considered particularly sensitive. The emails containing Top Secret and SAP information were included in the 30,490 provided to the State Department.

In June 2016, near the end of the investigation, investigators found three email chains, consisting of eight individual emails, that "contained at least one paragraph marked '(C),' a marking ostensibly indicating the presence of information classified at the CONFIDENTIAL level." According to a June 13, 2016 text message exchange between Strzok and Page, the emails containing the "(C)" portion markings were part of the 30,490 that Clinton's attorneys had provided to the State Department in 2014 but the FBI did not notice them until June 2016 after the IC IG discovered them. By that point in time, as discussed in Chapter Six below, Comey had been drafting his statement announcing the closing of the investigation. Strzok

---

that they believed these missing emails could contain important evidence regarding Clinton's intent in setting up a private email server.

wrote to Page that "DoJ was Very Concerned about this.... Because they're worried, holy cow, if the fbi missed this, what else was missed?" Strzok further wrote, "No one noticed. And while minor, it cuts against 'I never send or received anything marked classified.'"[64] According to the prosecutors, Mills, Abedin, and Jake Sullivan were each parties to at least one email in the chains with the (C) markings. However, none of them were ever asked about the emails, because the FBI had not discovered the markings before their interviews and did not seek to reinterview them.[65]

Witnesses told us that although the FBI found work-related emails, including classified emails, that were not part of the 30,490 produced to the State Department by Clinton's lawyers, they were not able to determine whether these emails were part of the original 62,320 reviewed by Clinton's attorneys. This is because some of the emails they found through other sources could have been deleted from Clinton's account or "overwritten in the ordinary course" before Clinton's attorneys reviewed her emails for production to the State Department. Thus, they also were unable to determine how many of the 31,830 deleted emails were never recovered.

The FBI also conducted "intrusion analyses" on each of the devices and other evidence to determine whether any classified information had been compromised. An FBI agent assigned to the Midyear team to conduct intrusion and other forensic analysis ("Forensics Agent") described the team's efforts in this regard as exhaustive. He stated that these efforts included (1) examining the servers and others devices to identify suspicious logins or other activity, and (2) searching numerous datasets to determine whether foreign adversaries or known hostile domestic actors had accessed emails that the Midyear team had confirmed to contain classified information.

Comey stated the following in his July 5, 2016, press conference regarding possible cyber intrusion of Clinton's email servers:

> With respect to potential computer intrusion by hostile actors, we did not find direct evidence that Secretary Clinton's personal email domain, in its various configurations since 2009, was successfully hacked. But, given the nature of the system and of the actors potentially involved, we assess that we would be unlikely to see such direct evidence. We do assess that hostile actors gained access to the private commercial email accounts of people with whom Secretary Clinton was in regular contact from her personal account. We also assess that Secretary Clinton's use of a personal email domain was

---

[64] Strzok told us that in this text message he was referring to the fact that "Secretary Clinton had always said [she] never received anything marked classified," and that the new discovery of the emails with the (C) markings was inconsistent with that claim. The emails with the (C) markings, Clinton's statements about them during her FBI interview, and the Midyear team's assessment of her credibility are discussed in Section IX.C of this chapter.

[65] Sullivan was Clinton's Deputy Chief of Staff for Policy from January 2009 to February 2011 and Director of Policy and Planning at the State Department from February 2011 to January 2013.

both known by a large number of people and readily apparent. She also used her personal email extensively while outside the United States, including sending and receiving work-related emails in the territory of sophisticated adversaries. Given that combination of factors, we assess it is possible that hostile actors gained access to Secretary Clinton's personal email account.

The LHM stated, "FBI investigation and forensic analysis did not find evidence confirming that Clinton's email server systems were compromised by cyber means." However, the LHM also stated that the FBI identified one successful compromise of an account belonging to one of former President Clinton's staffers on a different domain within the same server former Secretary Clinton used during her tenure. The FBI was unable to identify the individual responsible for the compromise, but confirmed that the individual had logged in to the former staffer's account and "browsed email folders and attachments." According to evidence we reviewed, the FBI also confirmed compromises to email accounts belonging to certain individuals who communicated with Clinton by email, such as Jake Sullivan and Sidney Blumenthal.[66]

The LHM stated that the FBI was limited in its intrusion analysis due to the "FBI's inability to recover all server equipment and the lack of complete server data for the relevant time period." According to the LHM, the FBI also identified vulnerabilities in Clinton's server systems and found that there had been numerous unsuccessful attempts by potential malicious actors to exploit those vulnerabilities. Nonetheless, the FBI Forensics Agent told the OIG that, although he did not believe there was "any way of determining...100%" whether Clinton's servers had been compromised, he felt "fairly confident that there wasn't an intrusion." When asked whether a sophisticated foreign adversary was likely to be able to cover its tracks, he stated, "They could. Yeah. But I, I felt as if we coordinated with the right units at headquarters...for those specific adversaries.... And the information that was returned back to me was that there was no indication of a compromise."

II. The Midyear Team's Efforts to Understand and Access Clinton's Servers

Prosecutor 1 told us that it took the Midyear team time to understand the setup and sequence of the various servers Clinton used. This prosecutor stated that an understanding of the server setup was a necessary foundation for the Midyear team's investigation. According to the LHM, the FBI discovered three servers that for different periods stored work-related emails sent or received by Clinton during her tenure as Secretary of State. Collectively, we refer to these three servers as the "Clinton servers."

The first server was set up in 2008 by Justin Cooper, a former aide to former President Clinton, and is referred to in the LHM as the "Apple Server." Based on

---

[66] Clinton told the FBI that Blumenthal was a "longtime friend" who "frequently sent information he thought would be useful" to her as Secretary of State.

evidence we reviewed, the Apple Server was primarily set up for former President Clinton's staff, but Secretary Clinton also used it for her work purposes from January 2009 until approximately March 18, 2009, about two months into her tenure. During this time, Clinton primarily used a personally acquired BlackBerry device that was connected to the Apple Server.

The LHM indicates that the second server, referred to in the LHM as the Pagliano Server, was used from March 2009 through June 2013. Cooper told the FBI that "in or around January 2009 the decision was made to move to another server because the Apple Server was antiquated and users were experiencing problems with email delivery on their Blackberry devices." Cooper contacted Bryan Pagliano, an information technology specialist who worked on Hillary Clinton's presidential campaign, to help him set up the Pagliano server. Numerous individuals had email accounts on the Pagliano Server, including former President Clinton, former President Clinton's staff, Huma Abedin—who was Clinton's Deputy Chief of Staff at the State Department—and Clinton herself. Clinton and Abedin were the only State Department employees with accounts on the @clintonemail.com domain on the Pagliano Server.

The third server, which is referred to in the LHM as the "PRN server," was active after Clinton's tenure as Secretary of State ended, from approximately June 2013 through October 2015. The LHM stated that in early 2013, staff for Clinton and former President Clinton discussed transitioning to a new vendor for email services, "due to user limitations and reliability concerns regarding the Pagliano Server." The staff chose the "Denver-based information technology firm Platte River Networks (PRN)" for this purpose. According to the LHM, PRN employee Paul Combetta migrated the email accounts from the Pagliano Server to the PRN server. Following the migration, the Pagliano Server was stored in a data center in New Jersey, although it no longer hosted email services and Microsoft Exchange was uninstalled from it on December 3, 2013.

According to the LHM, the FBI learned through witness interviews that the Apple Server, in use from 2007 to March 2009, was ultimately discarded and, thus, the FBI was never able to access it for review. However, based on evidence we reviewed, the Midyear team obtained access to certain back-up data from the Apple Server held on Cooper's personal laptops through consent agreements with Cooper's attorney. The Midyear team obtained both the Pagliano and PRN servers through consent agreements with David Kendall and Clinton's other attorneys at Williams and Connolly.

The FBI's ability to review emails on both the Pagliano and PRN servers was limited. With respect to the Pagliano Server, most of the emails that remained on the Pagliano server following the transition to the PRN server were in the "unallocated space" due to the removal of Microsoft Exchange in December 2013. FBI analysts told us that emails in the unallocated space were often fragmented and difficult to reconstruct. With respect to the PRN server, the FBI discovered through forensic analysis and witness interviews that Combetta had transferred most of Clinton's archived emails from her tenure as Secretary of State to the PRN server, but subsequently deleted and "wiped" them from the server using "BleachBit."

Based on the LHM, FD-302s, and PRN documents collected by the FBI, the transfer of emails to the PRN server and subsequent wiping of the PRN server occurred as described in the paragraphs below.

At around the time of the transition to the PRN server in the spring of 2013, Clinton's former aide, Monica Hanley, created two archives of Clinton's emails from the Pagliano Server, one on a thumb drive (Archive Thumb Drive) and one on a laptop computer (Archive Laptop).[67] In early 2014, Hanley mailed the Archive Laptop to Combetta to transfer Clinton's archived emails to the PRN server. She further directed him to "wipe" the Archive Laptop and mail it to Clinton's office assistant at the Clinton Foundation after he completed the transfer. Combetta used a "dummy" email account to transfer Clinton's archived emails into a mailbox entitled "HRC archive" on the PRN server.[68] Combetta told the FBI that he then, per Hanley's instructions, deleted the emails from the Archive Laptop and mailed the Archive Laptop to Clinton's office assistant, but did not "wipe" the laptop. Email records obtained by the FBI showed that Clinton's office assistant sent emails to Combetta in both March and April 2014 asking when she should expect to receive the "wiped laptop;" however, Clinton's office assistant told the FBI that she did not recall ever receiving it.

An analyst told us and FBI records show that the team sought and obtained records from multiple mail carriers in an effort to locate the Archive Laptop. Based on these records, the FBI was able to confirm that the laptop was delivered to Paul Combetta on February 24, 2014; however, the FBI found no records showing that Combetta mailed the Archive Laptop to Clinton's office assistant as requested. The FBI also attempted to obtain the Archive Thumb Drive from Hanley, but she stated she could not recall what happened to it.

According to the LHM, FD-302s from Combetta's, Mills's, and Samuelson's interviews, and PRN documents collected by the FBI, in the summer of 2014, Combetta uploaded .pst files of Clinton's archived emails to Mills's and Samuelson's laptops to enable them to review Clinton's emails and produce her work-related emails to the State Department. In late 2014 or early 2015, after Clinton produced her work-related emails to the State Department, Mills and Samuelson requested that Combetta remove Clinton's emails from their laptops, and he did so using BleachBit. At around the same time, Mills directed Combetta to change the email retention policy on Clinton's clintonemail.com account to 60 days, because Clinton had decided that she no longer needed access to her personal emails that were older than 60 days. Combetta told the FBI that he mistakenly neglected to make the change at the time and realized his mistake in March 2015. He stated that, despite the intervening issuance of a congressional preservation order on March 3,

---

[67] According to Hanley's FD-302, she told the FBI that the archives were created because Clinton "did not want to lose her old emails when she changed her email address." She further told the FBI that PRN advised Clinton to change her email address after Sidney Blumenthal's email account was compromised.

[68] As discussed in Section III of this chapter, the Midyear team obtained a search warrant for the dummy email account and recovered some of Clinton's work-related emails from that account.

2015, he "had an 'oh shit' moment" and wiped the HRC archive mailbox from the PRN server using BleachBit sometime between March 25 and March 31, 2015.

Despite the use of BleachBit, the FBI was able to recover some of Clinton's archived emails from both the PRN server and the laptops used by Mills and Samuelson to cull Clinton's emails. The FBI also recovered some of Clinton's archived emails from a search of the dummy email account that Combetta used to transfer Clinton's emails from the Archive Laptop to the PRN server and, as discussed in Section I of this chapter, from various other sources.

III. Use of Criminal Process to Obtain Documentary and Digital Evidence

Despite the public perception that the Midyear investigation did not use a grand jury, and instead relied exclusively on consent, we found that agents and prosecutors did use grand jury subpoenas and other compulsory process to gain access to documentary and digital evidence. According to documents we reviewed, at least 56 grand jury subpoenas were issued, five court orders were obtained pursuant to 18 U.S.C. § 2703(d) (2703(d) orders), and three search warrants were granted. The Midyear team also sent numerous preservation letters to various entities, including Internet Service Providers, former Secretary Clinton's attorneys, and U.S. government agencies. We were told that FBI agents generally worked directly with the EDVA prosecutors to obtain subpoenas and 2703(d) orders, without seeking approval from the CES prosecutors, Laufman, Toscas, or any higher level Department officials. Toscas told us that he was the highest level Department official that approved search warrant affidavits, and that he provided general information about search warrants that were being sought in briefings to Carlin, Yates, and Lynch.

The FBI served 2703(d) orders on commercial email service providers, such as Google (Gmail) and Yahoo!, for information maintained on their servers associated with the private email accounts used by Huma Abedin, Paul Combetta, Cheryl Mills, and two other individuals.[69] The FBI sought 2703(d) orders for these

---

[69] According to documentation we reviewed, the first individual was a senior State Department official who sometimes used a private email account to communicate with Clinton. The FBI sought a 2703(d) order for this individual's private email account after discovering an email sent from his private email account that the FBI determined was classified at the SECRET//NOFORN level. The abbreviation "NOFORN" means that the information may not be released to foreign governments, foreign nationals, foreign organizations, or non-U.S. citizens without the permission of the originator. According to Strzok's and the Lead Analyst's notes from early June 2016, the FBI received the returns from this 2703(d) order and determined that, as of that time, the email containing classified information no longer resided in this individual's account.

According to the 2703(d) order for the second individual's account, an email containing information that the FBI determined to be classified at the SECRET//NOFORN level was originated from his private email account and forwarded, after traversing two other private email accounts, to Mills's private Gmail account. This individual was not a State Department employee and was not a witness in the FBI's investigation. Rather, the 2703(d) order stated that the FBI believed this individual resided in Japan based on his phone number and address and that "[a] search of relevant databases reveal[ed] no U.S. Government security clearances" for him. According to Strzok's and the

individuals after discovering from other sources that emails containing classified information were sent from or received by their accounts. FBI witnesses told us that the purposes of obtaining the 2703(d) orders were to determine whether the known classified emails continued to reside in the unauthorized email accounts and whether they were forwarded to other unauthorized locations, thus posing risks to national security. If they confirmed that the known classified emails continued to reside in the email accounts, they would then consider seeking search warrants for email content within the same accounts.

Based on the 2703(d) results, the FBI was able to confirm that classified information continued to reside in just one of these five accounts—the account belonging to Combetta. Thus, on June 20, 2016, the FBI sought a search warrant for this account. According to the search warrant, the FBI initially sought the 2703(d) order for Combetta's account after observing numerous emails containing metadata for Combetta's dummy email account in the original 30,490 emails provided to the State Department and determining that many of these emails contained classified information. Combetta told the FBI that he created the dummy email account to transfer Clinton's archived emails from the Archive Laptop to the PRN Server. Based on the results of the 2703(d) order, the FBI determined that 820 of Clinton's emails, dated between October 25, 2010, and December 31, 2010, remained in the dummy email account. The Midyear team obtained a search warrant to view the content of these emails and search for other emails relevant to the investigation.

Prosecutor 2 told us that the Midyear team sought compulsory process when evidence could not be obtained through consent or when "the terms of the consent were such that additional process needed to be sought." For example, on August 28, 2015, the Midyear team obtained a search warrant for the Pagliano Server even though Clinton's attorneys had voluntarily produced and provided consent for the FBI to search it. According to the search warrant application, upon conducting a preliminary examination of the Pagliano server, the FBI discovered that it contained three domains—two besides the clintonemail.com domain—and email accounts of numerous individuals unrelated to the FBI's investigation, such as former President Clinton's staff. The FBI further discovered that Microsoft Exchange had been uninstalled from the Pagliano Server in December 2013. As a result, the three different domains were commingled in the server's unallocated space and the FBI could not segregate the accounts without "a complete forensic analysis of the Pagliano Server." Because Clinton's attorneys were only able to provide consent to

---

Lead Analyst's notes from early June 2016, the FBI received the returns from this 2703(d) order and, as of that time, the email containing classified information no longer resided in his account.

The Midyear team did not seek 2703(d) orders for information related to Clinton's private email accounts. Instead, as described later in this section and in Section IV of this chapter, the team reviewed the contents of Clinton's emails on the Pagliano and PRN servers through a combination of consent agreements and a search warrant. The team also sought records from three different companies in an effort to track down emails Clinton sent or received on her Blackberry account in early 2009, before she began using the clintonemail.com domain. However, witnesses told us that these companies no longer maintained Clinton's emails on their servers.

search Clinton's email accounts on the server, the FBI obtained a search warrant to examine the unallocated space.

IV.   Use of Consent to Obtain Physical Evidence

A.   Debate over the Use of Consent

Based on the evidence we reviewed, although the Midyear team used compulsory process on multiple occasions as described above, the prosecutors sought to obtain digital and documentary evidence by consent whenever possible. Witnesses told us that this caused frustration within the FBI, which preferred obtaining evidence with search warrants or subpoenas. The witnesses generally agreed that this debate is common among prosecutors and agents and was not unique to Midyear. To the extent the disagreement about the use of criminal process was more pronounced in Midyear, witnesses stated that they believed this was due to Midyear being a high-profile investigation. The Lead Analyst explained that "everyone [was] under intense pressure," which enhanced the "magnitude" of this disagreement.

Numerous Department and FBI witnesses told us that the debate over how to obtain evidence was mostly about efficiency—the prosecutors believed they could obtain evidence faster through consent and the FBI believed that criminal process was more efficient. The prosecutors stated that, in their view, consent is more efficient than process when witnesses are cooperative and, as Prosecutor 4 noted, when there is no concern that evidence will be destroyed to obstruct an investigation. Based on the evidence we reviewed, Clinton's attorneys contacted Department prosecutors numerous times to express Clinton's willingness to cooperate by being interviewed and providing evidence voluntarily. Prosecutor 4 told us it was his view that the risk of destruction of evidence, in response to a voluntary production request, is less likely in cases where parties are represented by experienced attorneys, such as "firms like Williams and Connolly" (which represented Clinton), because the attorneys are aware of the risks associated with destroying evidence. Prosecutor 4 stated, "I'm not saying that they're more ethical. I'm just saying they're smarter." The prosecutors stated that seeking evidence through consent also saved time by allowing the government to avoid motions to quash subpoenas based on privilege or lack of probable cause.

A few FBI witnesses told us that they believed the prosecutors in CES were generally more "risk averse" in their handling of cases than prosecutors in other parts of the Department. Prosecutor 1 explained that there are reasons to be especially cautious in the types of cases CES handles, including protecting the sensitive and classified information involved in those cases. This prosecutor told us that CES prosecutors must consider questions such as whether the intelligence community will permit the use of classified information in their cases, whether moving a "case forward" is worth the risk that the "use of information gathered by a human source could...identify sources and methods," and whether "the criminal prosecution of someone [is] more valuable than the continued collection[.]"

Laufman and Prosecutor 4 told us that the use of criminal process tends to increase the risk of leaks and public disclosures. Prosecutor 4 told us that leaks undermine investigations and that "unfair leaks" were an "added" consideration in the Midyear investigation. Laufman told us that the Midyear prosecution team's goal was to make sure that no stone was left unturned, while also being mindful that leaks "could be used by political actors in furtherance of political agendas." Agent 3 told us that when he sought process from the prosecutors, they responded that they would try to obtain the evidence by consent because the witnesses "don't want this to get in the paper." Comey told us that he believed the prosecutors were more hesitant to use criminal process in the Midyear investigation than normal because they wanted to keep "as low a profile as possible."

FBI team members told us that they believed they could have obtained evidence faster with process, especially after instances when, they believed, Clinton's attorneys had not been forthcoming about the existence of potential sources of evidence. For example, after Clinton's attorneys voluntarily provided the FBI the Pagliano Server pursuant to an August 7, 2015 consent agreement, the FBI discovered through its own investigation that there was a successor server—the PRN server. According to documentation we reviewed, the prosecutors and the FBI were frustrated that Clinton's attorneys had not been forthcoming about the PRN server, and Prosecutor 1 wrote a letter to Kendall expressing this frustration. The SSA told us that situations like this caused him to question whether consent was the best course. However, Prosecutor 1 stated that resorting to compulsory process for the PRN server would have been complicated, because, among other things, the server was "running tons of people's email accounts on it that were totally separate from...the former Secretary, including people working in the...former President's office." The Midyear team ultimately secured the PRN server through a September 30, 2015 consent agreement with Clinton's attorneys.

Some witnesses told us that they were concerned about certain devices that the FBI was never able to locate. For example, as described above in Section II of this chapter, the Midyear team was never able to locate the Archive Laptop and Archive Thumb Drive, both of which, according to Hanley and others, contained a complete copy of Clinton's archived emails. In addition, according to the LHM, the FBI's investigation identified a total of 13 mobile devices associated with Clinton's two known telephone numbers "which potentially were used to send emails using Clinton's clintonemail.com email addresses." The Midyear team asked Clinton's attorneys for these devices, but they stated they were "unable to locate" them.[70] According to the LHM and FD-302s, Cooper and Hanley told the FBI that they wiped or destroyed Clinton's devices once she transitioned to new devices. One FBI analyst told us that he was "frustrated" by the claim by Clinton's attorneys that they could not find her 13 devices. However, he stated that he "guess[ed]" the agency did not have probable cause to assert that the missing devices were in

---

[70] The attorneys produced two other Blackberry devices that they stated might contain relevant emails, but, according to the LHM, "FBI forensic analysis found no evidence to indicate either of the[se] devices...were connected to one of Clinton's personal servers or contained emails from her personal accounts during her tenure." The FBI also obtained three of Clinton's iPads, one of which contained three emails from her tenure.

Clinton's home such that a search warrant could be issued, given the testimony that her old devices had been destroyed before she transitioned to new devices. He further stated that his frustration was with Clinton and her attorneys, not the prosecutors.

We questioned whether the use of a subpoena or search warrant might have encouraged Clinton, her lawyers, Combetta, or others to search harder for the missing devices, or ensured that they were being honest that they could not find them. Prosecutor 2 told us that the prosecutors believed that Clinton's attorneys were dealing with them "in good faith" and had "no reason to think that they were lying" about their inability to find Clinton's mobile devices. Prosecutor 2 further stated that the team did not believe that Combetta still had the Archive Laptop in his possession, because "there would have been no reason for him to keep it." Similarly, the Lead Analyst told us that he did not know of any evidence to suggest that Clinton's attorneys were being dishonest about the evidence they could not locate, and compulsory process would not have made a difference in situations where Clinton's attorneys represented that they could not find a device.

Agents 1 and 2 told us that there were six laptops that Clinton's attorneys had provided the FBI early in the investigation with consent to store, but not search, and that they would have liked to search these laptops. Agent 2 stated that he believed that these laptops may have been used to review Clinton's emails before Clinton's attorneys produced her work-related emails to the State Department. Agent 1 told us that he believed these laptops were used by Clinton's Williams and Connolly attorneys to do the "QC of the 30,000 emails after they were culled by Mills and Samuelson."

Our review of the relevant FD-302s and other documents revealed the following regarding the six laptops: On August 6, 2015, Katherine Turner, one of Clinton's attorneys, voluntarily produced to the FBI three thumb drives and a laptop computer belonging to Williams and Connolly that contained identical copies of the 30,490 emails Clinton's attorneys had produced to the State Department, and signed a consent form for the FBI to search these devices. In addition, Turner told the two FBI agents that Williams and Connolly had six additional laptops containing identical copies of the 30,490 emails, but that these laptops also contained unrelated privileged information. Turner agreed to voluntarily produce the additional six laptops to the FBI so that the FBI could secure the classified information contained on them, but declined to provide consent to search the laptops because she "wished to ensure that privileged communications on the laptops would remain confidential." According to a FD-302 dated August 17, 2015, Turner told the FBI that one of the six laptops was in the custody of Mills's and Samuelson's attorneys at Paul, Weiss, Rifkind, Wharton, and Garrison, LLP ("Paul Weiss"). On August 21, 2015, FBI Attorney 1 wrote in a letter to Turner and a Paul Weiss attorney:

> It is the FBI's understanding that the six laptop computers may contain privileged materials. Therefore, the FBI will maintain the six laptop computers in a secure location separate from other materials that have been provided voluntarily to the FBI in conjunction with this

matter. The FBI will not access any material or information on the six laptops without further consultation with you or obtaining appropriate legal process.

Upon completion of this matter, the FBI will notify all parties and discuss the appropriate disposition of the material in a manner consistent with applicable laws and policies.

Although the Midyear team left open the possibility of obtaining process to search the six laptops, the team ultimately never sought a search warrant. Prosecutor 2 explained that the Midyear team originally believed that the six laptops included the laptops that Mills and Samuelson used to cull Clinton's emails. However, during a proffer session on March 19, 2016, Beth Wilkinson (attorney for Mills and Samuelson) told the prosecutors that the six laptops Clinton's attorneys had produced to the FBI did not include the culling laptops and, in fact, the culling laptops were still in Mills's and Samuelson's possession. Prosecutor 2 told us that, following the proffer, Mills and Samuelson turned the actual culling laptops over to Wilkinson, who agreed to disconnect the laptops from the Internet and place them in a safe in her office, until privilege issues could be resolved. As described in Section VIII.D of this chapter, the Midyear team ultimately received consent to search the culling laptops through an agreement with Wilkinson. Agent 2 told us that, despite his desire to search the content of the six laptops, the FBI might not have had sufficient probable cause to assert that the laptops contained emails that the FBI did not already have in its possession. He further told us that it was "completely logical" that Clinton's attorneys would not consent to the FBI's review of the laptops given that the laptops contained privileged information related to the attorneys' representation of other clients. FBI Attorney 1 told us that she believed, based on the representations of Clinton's counsel, that the six laptops never contained the full 62,320 emails and that they only contained copies of the 30,490 emails that had been produced to the State Department. She stated that, as a result, she did not believe that it was necessary to review the six laptops, especially given the privilege concerns.

There were points in the investigation when the debate about the use of consent versus compulsory process was particularly pronounced. Based on the evidence we reviewed, in or about March 2016, Page asked Strzok, on behalf of McCabe, to create a list of tasks that the Department had either refused to undertake or "asked to let them negotiate with counsel," even if the FBI ultimately agreed with the outcome. Page told us that McCabe suggested the list after she told him that Strzok and FBI Attorney 1 were "increasingly growing concerned about...the little things that are being left on the cutting room floor and...the deference to" the line prosecutors on how best to obtain evidence. On March 24, 2016, Strzok wrote to FBI Attorney 1 and the Lead Analyst describing the proposed list.[71] In the email, Strzok provided a rough list of the items he was considering

---

[71] In the March 24, 2016 email, Strzok stated that he had asked the SSA to work on the list. Strzok blind-copied Page on this email, who responded to Strzok later that day to explain that McCabe wanted the list to be "done quietly" and Strzok should tell the SSA to "stand down and just say you'll handle it." Page told us that McCabe wanted the list done quietly because it would not be "well-

including and wrote, "Problem is it's been death by a thousand cuts."[72] Strzok told us that at the time he wrote this email, he was "aggravated by the limitations" that the prosecutors were placing on the FBI's ability to obtain evidence and felt that "if you add up this delta over a bunch of decisions, all of a sudden it becomes substantive." Strzok and Page told us that they did not believe a list was ever finalized.

Despite this debate, the agents, analysts, prosecutors, and supervisors on the Midyear team generally told us that, aside from devices that had been destroyed or that could not be located, they ultimately obtained and reviewed all of the devices necessary to complete the investigation. For example, Strzok stated that once he was able to "step back towards the end of the investigation," he realized that "maybe we gave a little where we didn't need to give, and maybe we actually got lucky here. But is there anything that we ultimately are missing to make kind of an authoritative, accurate conclusion? No." McCabe stated that the team "drew some red lines around things that we absolutely insisted we had to do," such as obtaining the laptops Mills and Samuelson used to cull Clinton's emails, and that those items ultimately were attained. The SSA, who was described to us by several witnesses as an experienced and aggressive agent, stated that he "had a lot of hoops to jump through at times," but "no matter what the obstacles were, we moved through them." Similarly, Anderson told us, "At various points...as the investigation progressed...we were very anxious to...seek aggressively different materials.... [B]ut at the end of the day, I do believe everybody felt that we had obtained everything that we needed to obtain in order to assess criminality."

B.   Limits of Consent Agreements

The SSA told us that the terms of the consent agreements were primarily created through negotiations between the two line NSD prosecutors, on one side, and the attorneys for Clinton and other witnesses, on the other. For the most part, the consent agreements were limited such that the FBI was able to search only for emails sent or received by Clinton during her tenure as Secretary of State and for evidence of intrusion. These were generally the same limitations that were included in the subpoenas, search warrants, and 2703(d) orders obtained during the course of the investigation.

---

received" by the Department. Strzok stated that his understanding was that McCabe wanted to discuss the items in the list with Toscas during a "sidebar," rather than in a "big, official meeting."

[72] The items in the rough list were:

1) getting process .. at the beginning (the fight about opening a case, about assigning a field office and a usao for process)
2) a) media (consent vs SWs for all the servers and devices and games opposing counsel played), There is a ton here, from everything we have vs the stuff we didnt get ~ eg, apple server at Chappaqua, computer at Whitehaven, plethora of ipads, lack of blackberries, b) scoping and negotiating of what we've been able to search for
3) email accounts (thinking Mills Gmail account)
4) interviews (v FGJ compellence) and scoping of interviews. - I think that largely applies to PRN and the big four+Samuelson, right? Anyone else?

An FBI analyst told us that limiting the search time period to Clinton's tenure as Secretary was not controversial. The analyst explained, "[T]he reason it was scoped to the tenure is because...that is of course when she would have had access to the classified information." We questioned both Department and FBI witnesses as to whether emails from after Clinton's tenure could have shed light on whether Clinton instructed her staff to delete emails for an improper purpose. They told us that any relevant emails following Clinton's tenure mostly would consist of communications with her attorneys regarding the sort process, and such communications would be protected by attorney-client privilege.

The consent agreements and search warrants also were limited such that the FBI could not search emails sent or received by other accountholders on Clinton's servers—such as Abedin and former President Clinton and his staff—unless Clinton was also a party to those emails. One analyst told us that he would have liked to be able to look at emails to which Clinton was not a party. For example, he told us that he would have liked to review emails between Abedin and Cooper regarding what Clinton may have said about the server. We questioned the prosecutors as to why the consent agreements were not scoped such that they could search for any work-related or classified emails within Abedin's clintonemail.com account, especially since FBI witnesses told us that Clinton's server, not Clinton herself, was the subject of the investigation. This is addressed in Section V.D of this chapter below.

The consent agreements and search warrants incorporated provisions requiring the use of a filter team to ensure that the Midyear team did not review emails protected by privileges, including attorney-client, medical, and marital privileges. One analyst told us that the filter process was cumbersome and that some interpretations of the privileges were unusual. For example, because former President Clinton did not use email, one of his employees received former President Clinton's emails and then printed them for him. The privilege team considered the emails that Clinton sent to her husband through this employee as privileged, although this may not have been legally required. The Lead Analyst told us that he, too, was often frustrated by the cumbersome filter process. However, he stated that he agreed with the team's "conservative" approach to interpreting what was privileged, because it was important for the FBI to handle its mission and the materials in its possession "responsibly" and to not unnecessarily be looking "into the lives of the Clintons."

There were at least two consent agreements that did not incorporate the use of a filter team, but instead allowed the attorney for the owner of the devices to delete personal information before voluntary production to the FBI. These were the consent agreements that the Department negotiated with Justin Cooper's attorney to obtain Cooper's personal laptops that the team hoped contained, among other things, back-ups from the BlackBerry devices Clinton used during the first two months of her tenure.[73] According to the FD-302 from Cooper's September 2, 2015

---

[73] As noted in footnote 64 of this report, the 30,490 emails provided by Clinton's attorneys to the State Department contained no emails sent or received by Clinton during the first two months of

interview, Cooper's attorney told the FBI that Cooper's laptops contained "files related to the upgrade of former Secretary of State Hillary Clinton's Blackberry," as well as emails Cooper exchanged with Clinton. In a letter dated September 10, 2015, Cooper's attorney wrote to Prosecutor 1, "As we discussed and as the government has agreed, before providing Mr. Cooper's computer hardware to the FBI, we will remove and securely delete Mr. Cooper's personal and business files." In a letter dated September 24, 2015, Cooper's attorney wrote to Prosecutor 1 that he was voluntarily providing the FBI Cooper's Mac Book Air laptop computer and further wrote, "[a]s agreed, we have securely deleted from the Mac Book Air Mr. Cooper's personal and business files, and we have overwritten its unallocated space with zeros."

We asked some FBI and Department witnesses why they did not use a filter team instead of allowing Cooper to delete his personal files. FBI witnesses told us that they were not concerned by the limitations in the consent agreements for the Cooper laptops, because Cooper was particularly cooperative and the materials he voluntarily provided to the FBI turned out to be fruitful.[74] Indeed, according to the FD-302 from Cooper's interview, Cooper's attorney told the FBI about the back-ups on Cooper's laptop without prompting. In addition, FBI Attorney 1 and Agent 1 told us that they considered Cooper's devices to be different from other devices they reviewed, because there was no evidence that Cooper was the sender or recipient of classified information and Cooper was more of an aide to former President Clinton than to former Secretary Clinton. Strzok told us that the team was not certain that it could establish probable cause that there was classified information or other evidence of a crime on the Cooper laptops.

Some FBI witnesses told us, consistent with text message exchanges between Strzok and Page, that the FBI was concerned that the line NSD prosecutors were intimidated by the high-powered attorneys representing Clinton and her senior aides and, as a result, did not negotiate aggressively with them. Strzok told us that Prosecutor 1, who handled most of the negotiations with counsel, is "extraordinarily competent," but he believed more senior government officials should have been involved with deciding "how hard [to] push counsel." Nevertheless, the FBI witnesses generally told us that they were satisfied that the limitations of the consent agreements did not impair the investigation. Agent 2 stated regarding the limitations in consent agreements, "I think generally...we were able to get what we were looking for. It maybe was more complicated, time-consuming, and cumbersome." The Lead Analyst told us that "every single consent arrangement constrained what we did...to some degree." However, he, Strzok, and FBI Attorney 1 all told us that they believed the team might have actually obtained

_____

her tenure, and Midyear officials believed these missing emails could contain important evidence regarding Clinton's intent in setting up a private email server.

[74] For example, one analyst told us that within the Blackberry back-ups on the Cooper laptop, the FBI team found an email from former Secretary of State Colin Powell to Clinton on January 23, 2009, in which Powell warned Clinton that if it became "public" that she used a Blackberry to "do business," her emails could become "official record[s] and subject to the law." In the email, Powell further warned Clinton, "Be very careful. I got around it all by not saying much and not using systems that captured the data."

more through the consent agreements in some instances than they would have obtained through compulsory process. Strzok explained that for some devices they were not certain that the team could establish sufficient probable cause to convince a judge to issue a search warrant or allow a search that was as broad as what was agreed upon through a consent agreement. He provided as an example the Cooper laptops described above. Similarly, Prosecutor 2 told us that the Midyear team was able to search certain items through consent agreements, despite privilege issues that may have caused a subpoena or search warrant to be quashed.

In addition, based on our review, we determined that Department and FBI members of the Midyear team worked together to determine the scope of the review of the evidence and, in turn, the limitations to be included in consent agreements and search warrants. For example, in a September 23, 2015 email exchange among a WFO Computer Analysis and Recovery Team forensic examiner ("CART Examiner"), Strzok, the Lead Analyst, the four line prosecutors, three FBI OGC attorneys, and two case agents, Prosecutor 2 wrote that she assumed the consent agreement for the PRN server would be scoped such that the FBI would not review the content of any emails in domains other than the clintonemail.com domain. Strzok wrote back with a more expansive approach than that suggested by Prosecutor 2: "I think we would ask to search the other domains for any emails to/from the @clintonemail.com domain in the event those emails were deleted from whichever clintonemail.com account and no longer available there." The final consent agreement followed Strzok's more expansive approach, allowing the FBI to search the entire server, including the unallocated space and domains other than the clintonemail.com domain, for any emails to or from Clinton.

None of the witnesses we interviewed could point to specific examples of anyone involved in the investigation allowing political or other improper considerations to impact the decisions on how best to obtain evidence.

V.   Efforts to Obtain Email Content from the Private Accounts of Clinton's Senior Aides

In this section, we address the Midyear team's efforts to obtain email content from the accounts of the three senior aides that had the most email communication with Clinton—Jake Sullivan, Cheryl Mills, and Huma Abedin. Sullivan was Clinton's Deputy Chief of Staff for Policy from January 2009 to February 2011 and Director of Policy and Planning at the State Department from February 2011 to January 2013; Mills served as, among other things, Clinton's Chief of Staff during Clinton's tenure as Secretary; and Abedin served as Clinton's Deputy Chief of Staff during Clinton's tenure. According to the LHM, the FBI discovered through its review of emails from various sources that only 13 individuals had direct email contact with Clinton, and that Sullivan, Abedin, and Mills "accounted for 68 percent of the emails sent directly to Clinton."[75] State Department employees told the FBI that they considered emailing Sullivan, Mills, or Abedin the equivalent of emailing Clinton directly.

In addition to examining emails to or from these senior aides within the original 30,490 emails produced to the State Department, the investigators obtained emails from the State Department for each of their official State classified and unclassified email accounts. Based on a review of these emails and other evidence, the investigators determined that, in addition to their official State email accounts, Sullivan and Mills used personal Gmail accounts and Abedin used a personal Yahoo! account and her clintonemail.com account to conduct government business. Sullivan, Mills, and Abedin told the FBI that they used their private email accounts for official business occasionally, including on occasions when the official State email system was not functioning properly. Sullivan stated that he had the most difficulty using the official State system when he was traveling and on the weekends.

The investigators further determined that all three of these senior aides either sent or received classified information on their private email accounts and forwarded emails containing classified information to Clinton, although none of the emails the FBI discovered contained classification markings. The three aides provided the following explanations to the FBI for their conduct: they did not believe the information contained in their emails was classified; they tried to talk around classified information in situations where there was an urgent need to convey information and they did not have access to classified systems; some of the information they were discussing had already appeared in news reports; and they relied on the originators of the emails to properly mark them. These explanations were consistent with those provided to the FBI by both the originators of the emails containing classified information and Clinton. Based in part on these explanations, the prosecutors determined that no one "within the scope of the investigation," including the three senior aides, "committed any criminal offenses."

Nonetheless, the investigators considered obtaining additional information from or about the private email accounts of all three senior aides. Emails sent to or from the private email accounts were potentially relevant to: (1) further reconstructing the full collection of work-related emails and emails containing classified information that were sent to or from Clinton's servers; (2) finding additional emails containing classified information that were transmitted and stored on unclassified systems other than the Clinton's servers; (3) finding evidence of knowledge or intent on the part of Clinton, the senior aides, and possibly others regarding the transmission or storage of classified information on unclassified

---

[75] FBI analysts and Prosecutor 2 told us that former President Barack Obama was one of the 13 individuals with whom Clinton had direct contact using her clintonemail.com account. Obama, like other high level government officials, used a pseudonym for his username on his official government email account. The analysts told us that they questioned whether Obama's email address (combined with salutations that revealed that the emails were being exchanged with Obama) or other information contained in the emails were classified and, thus, sent the emails to relevant USIC agencies for classification review. However, they stated that the USIC agencies determined that none of the emails contained classified information.

systems; (4) controlling the spill of classified information in unauthorized locations; and (5) assessing whether there had been a compromise of classified information by hostile actors through intrusion analysis.

The Midyear team obtained 2703(d) orders for noncontent information in Mills's Gmail account and Abedin's Yahoo! account and a search warrant for Sullivan's personal Gmail account. However, the Midyear team did not obtain search warrants to examine the content of emails in Mills's or Abedin's private email accounts and did not seek to obtain any of the senior aides' personal devices.[76]

A.   Section 2703(d) Orders for Non-Content Information for Mills's and Abedin's Private Email Accounts

On February 18, 2016, the FBI obtained a 2703(d) order for Abedin's personal Yahoo! account. According to the government's application for the 2703(d) order, the FBI discovered that on October 4, 2009, an email attaching a Word document without classification markings was forwarded from Abedin's unclassified State Department email account to her Yahoo! account. The application stated that the next day, "the text from this Word document, with slight edits and reformatted to State Department letterhead, was sent from a State Department employee on SIPRNet, a classified email system, to Cheryl Mills" with a classification marking of SECRET//NOFORN. As a basis for the 2703(d) order, the application stated that a review of the 2703(d) returns would "help the FBI determine if the aforementioned email, containing a classified Word document, still resides within the Subject Account maintained by Huma Abedin and whether there are other records connecting email accounts associated with the improper transmission and storage of classified information."

Similarly, on May 31, 2016, the FBI sought and obtained a 2703(d) order for Mills's personal Gmail account. According to the government's application for the 2703(d) order, the FBI discovered that Mills sent or received at least 911 work-related emails to or from her Gmail account during the time she was employed at the State Department. The application stated that the FBI identified seven emails containing confirmed classified information and an additional 208 emails containing suspected classified information that had not yet undergone formal classification review. The application provided as an example one email that was determined to be classified at the level of SECRET//NOFORN at the time the email was sent. None of the emails contained classification markings.

We were told by an analyst who focused on handling legal process, and the notes of Strzok and the Lead Analyst from late May and early June 2016 confirmed, that the returns from the 2703(d) orders for Mills's and Abedin's accounts revealed that neither the confirmed classified emails nor any emails to or from Clinton continued to reside in Mills's or Abedin's personal accounts as of the date Google and Yahoo! searched their servers. According to Strzok's and the Lead Analyst's

---

[76] The senior aides' personal devices were potential sources of work-related emails or remnants of work-related emails that the senior aides had deleted and were not preserved on the commercial providers' servers.

notes, Abedin's email account contained less than 100 emails from Clinton's tenure as Secretary of State, while Mills's account contained numerous emails from Clinton's tenure as Secretary of State. Prosecutor 2 and one FBI analyst told us that these results provided no basis to conclude that Mills or Abedin had deleted emails to or from Clinton for an improper purpose, because there are various factors that could contribute to the preservation of emails in a personal email account.[77]

B. Decisions Regarding Search Warrants for Private Email Accounts

The Midyear team obtained a search warrant for Sullivan's Gmail account, on September 17, 2015. According to the search warrant, in reviewing the 30,490 emails provided by Clinton's attorneys to the State Department, the FBI found Sullivan's electronic business card, which identified him as an employee of the State Department and listed his private Gmail address. The search warrant stated that the FBI also had identified, among the 30,490 emails produced to the State Department, an unmarked email determined to contain information classified at the TOP SECRET level at the time it was forwarded by another State Department employee to Sullivan's Gmail account. The search warrant further stated that the FBI had identified an additional 496 emails from Sullivan's personal Gmail account that it suspected contained classified information, but had not yet submitted for formal classification review. One analyst told us that unlike the emails found on Clinton's servers, which often were derived from the unallocated space, emails from Sullivan's Gmail account were helpful because they clearly revealed important metadata, such as senders, recipients, and dates.

Given the significant roles of Mills and Abedin, and the usefulness of the material from Sullivan's personal account, we asked why the investigators did not seek search warrants for the private accounts of Mills or Abedin. We learned that the SSA initially drafted a search warrant affidavit for Mills's personal Gmail account, but it was never filed. In an email to FBI Attorney 1 and the Lead Analyst dated March 25, 2016, Strzok listed "email accounts (thinking Mills Gmail account)" as an item that the FBI unsuccessfully sought from the prosecutors. Strzok, the SSA, and Agent 3 told us that Strzok advocated in favor of applying for the search warrant, but that the prosecutors rejected the affidavit in favor of a 2703(d) order, based on insufficient probable cause and privilege concerns. The SSA stated that he disagreed with the prosecutors' position that there was insufficient probable cause for a search warrant, because there was evidence that Mills's Gmail account was used for official business and contained classified information.

Nevertheless, Prosecutor 2 told us that the FBI never made a follow-up request for a search warrant after receiving the 2703(d) returns. As discussed above, according to Strzok's and the Lead Analyst's notes and other evidence, the Midyear team received the 2703(d) returns in late May and early June 2016 and

---

[77] According to records we reviewed, the Midyear team also served preservation orders on Google and Yahoo! in relation to Mills's and Abedin's personal email accounts.

learned that neither the classified emails nor any emails to or from Clinton continued to reside in either account. Prosecutors 1 and 2 told us that, based on the facts developed at that point, there was likely no probable cause to seek a search warrant. Strzok stated about the proposed search warrant for Mills's Gmail account, "I remember we did not get it, and my general recollection is, if we thought it was important, and...we could have gotten probable cause, we would have done it. I think we just couldn't establish PC [probable cause]."

Some FBI witnesses told us that there were reasons to promptly seek a search warrant for Sullivan's Gmail account, instead of beginning with a 2703(d) order like they did with the private email accounts belonging to Mills and Abedin. They stated that unlike Sullivan, Mills and Abedin had not, based on the evidence they had reviewed, sent or received TS-SAP emails on their personal accounts, and these were the most sensitive emails discovered during the investigation. One analyst stated that Clinton's email exchanges with Sullivan were more substantive than her email exchanges with both Abedin and Mills. In addition, witnesses told us, consistent with the FD-302s we reviewed, that Sullivan was a more regular user of personal email for conducting State business, in part because he traveled overseas more often than the others.

Prosecutor 2 told us that Sullivan was treated differently from Mills and Abedin, because the information contained in the Top Secret email sent to Sullivan more clearly constituted classified information and NDI ("national defense information") than the information contained in the emails sent or received by Mills and Abedin.[78] Prosecutor 2 stated, "[T]here was a fundamental difference in the nature of information that we knew was in Jake Sullivan's account, versus the information that was in Abedin's account and Mills's accounts." In addition, Prosecutor 2 told us that the prosecutors would have had to obtain Criminal Division approval to obtain a search warrant for Mills's Gmail account, given that she was an attorney. Prosecutor 2 told us that, while they would have sought the approval if they believed it was "appropriate," this was among the factors they considered in "deciding what process to use."

C. Access to Personal Devices for Clinton's Senior Aides

Another potential means to obtain emails to or from the private accounts of Clinton's senior aides would be to obtain access to their personal devices, such as laptops or cellular telephones, on which copies of such emails might reside. Such access could possibly have been obtained by consent or via search warrant.[79] As

---

[78] As described in Chapter Two, 18 U.S.C. §§ 793(d), 793(e), and 793(f) require the information that is alleged to be mishandled to be "information relating to the national defense." This is also referred to as "national defense information" or NDI, and is not synonymous with classified information.

[79] As noted previously, while the government could also have issued a subpoena for any laptops or cellular telephones, it would not have been able to search the electronic communications within such a device without a search warrant. *See, e.g., Trulock v. Freeh*, 275 F.3d 391, 403 (4th Cir. 2001).

described in Section VIII.D of this chapter, the Midyear team obtained, through consent agreements with Beth Wilkinson, the laptops that Mills and Samuelson used to cull Clinton's emails for production of her work-related emails to the State Department. However, the investigators did not seek access to the private devices used by Sullivan, Mills, or Abedin during Clinton's tenure at State.[80]

Witnesses told us that the team's focus was on Clinton and obtaining her devices, such as her servers, computers, and hand-held devices. Prosecutor 2 stated, "[T]he scope of the investigation really related to the email systems used by Secretary Clinton, and whether on her private email server there are individuals who improperly retained or transmitted classified information." According to one analyst, there were generally two types of devices that the team sought: devices that Clinton used and devices to which her emails were transferred.

We asked several witnesses why they did not obtain devices used by Sullivan, Mills, and Abedin, both as a means of searching for evidence of the mishandling of classified information by Clinton and her aides and to prevent a further compromise of classified information. Both Strzok and Anderson told us that, at the outset of the investigation, former Deputy Director Giuliano generally advised the team that the purpose of the investigation was not to follow every potential lead of classified information. Strzok stated that Giuliano told the team, "[T]his is not going to become some octopus.... The focus of the investigation [is] the appearance of classified information on [Clinton's] personal emails and that server during the time she was Secretary of State." Strzok further stated that the FBI's "purpose and mission" was not to pursue "spilled [classified] information to the ends of the earth" and that the task of cleaning up classified spills by State Department employees was referred back to the State Department. He told us that the FBI's focus was whether there was a "violation of federal law." Prosecutors 1 and 2 similarly told us that the Department was not conducting a spill investigation, and that the State Department was the better entity for that role. Prosecutor 1 stated, "At a certain point, you have to decide what's your criminal investigation, and what is like a spill investigation.... [W]e could spend like a decade tracking emails...wherever they went." The SSA told us that the Midyear team engaged in several conversations with the State Department regarding the spill of classified information, and the State Department officials expressed concern about the problem and were receptive to resolving it. Generally the witnesses told us that they could not remember anyone within the team arguing that more should have been done to obtain the senior aides' devices.

We specifically questioned why the team did not attempt to obtain any personal devices used by Huma Abedin, given the team's finding that numerous

---

[80] FBI Attorney 1 told us that she believed the personal laptop that Mills had used to cull Clinton's emails was the same personal laptop she had used during her tenure at State. As described in Section VIII.D of this chapter, the FBI ultimately obtained Mills's culling laptop and the laptop did contain some emails from Clinton's State Department tenure. We were unable to determine whether this was in fact the personal device Mills used during her tenure at State and, if so, if she also used other personal devices.

work-related and classified email exchanges between Abedin and Clinton that the Midyear team found through various sources were absent from the 30,490 emails produced to the State Department by Clinton's lawyers. Witnesses told us that they believed there was a flaw in the culling process, which resulted in the exclusion of most of Abedin's clintonemail.com emails from the State Department production.[81] We also questioned (1) the failure to obtain Abedin's devices despite that, according to Abedin's FD-302, Abedin told the FBI that she turned both her personal laptop and her personal Blackberry over to her attorneys to be reviewed for production of work-related emails to the State Department; and (2) the inconsistency between the decision not to seek Abedin's devices before the July declination and the decision to obtain a search warrant for email on the laptop belonging to her husband, Anthony Weiner, in October 2016.

In response to the OIG's questions regarding the Midyear team's decision not to obtain the senior aides' devices, Prosecutor 1 told us that he did not remember any "meaningful discussion" before October 2016 about obtaining the senior aides' devices, aside from the laptops used by Mills and Samuelson to cull Clinton's emails for production of her work-related emails to the State Department. The SSA told us that in the beginning of the investigation, the Midyear team wanted to obtain every device that touched the server, but that over time the team realized that this would not be "fruitful." He stated that OTD personnel told the team that "it was not likely that there would be anything on the devices" themselves. Some FBI witnesses told us that they asked the senior aides during their Midyear interviews about any personal devices they used for State Department work, and the Midyear team relied on their responses to determine what devices to obtain. Agent 3 told us that the Midyear team asked Abedin whether she backed up her clintonemail.com emails and she responded that her email was "cloud-based" and she did not "know how to back up her archives." He stated that based on this testimony, the team assessed that finding helpful evidence on Abedin's devices was unlikely.

Both Strzok and Prosecutor 2 told us that the decision not to obtain the senior aides' devices was a joint decision. Prosecutors 1 and 2 and Strzok further told us that the team did not obtain Abedin's personal laptop and Blackberry that she used during her employment at the State Department, even after she told the FBI that she gave those devices to her attorneys, because the State Department provided to the FBI Abedin's work-related emails that her attorneys produced from those devices. Strzok stated that Abedin's attorneys told the Midyear team that they erred on the side of overproducing Abedin's emails to the State Department and that, unlike the sort process for Clinton's emails by Mills and Samuelson, there was no reason to believe Abedin's attorneys' sort process was flawed. Prosecutor 2

---

[81] According to a report prepared by one analyst, the team had found through various sources 1,716 work-related emails between Clinton's and Abedin's clintonemail.com accounts that had not been produced to the State Department by Clinton's lawyers, and that 90 of these emails contained classified information. The analyst who prepared the report told us that only approximately 32 email exchanges between Abedin and Clinton were included in the production, which was surprising to the FBI given Abedin's prominent role on Clinton's staff. According to the written analysis he prepared, the problem was likely that Clinton's attorneys only considered Clinton's exchanges with Abedin's clintonemail.com account to be work-related if they were also sent to a .gov account or contained a specific work-related key term.

told us, consistent with notes this prosecutor took at a meeting on October 27, 2016, that the only reason the FBI later obtained the Weiner laptop was because "it had ended up in our laps." We describe this issue further in Chapters Nine, Ten, and Eleven.

Several witnesses told us that tracking down Clinton's devices alone was very challenging. They stated that the investigation would have taken years if the team attempted to seek every possible device that might contain Clinton's emails or classified material. For example, Prosecutor 2 stated:

> I think the idea was that, that this investigation had to be somewhat focused, otherwise it could spin off into a million different directions. And this investigation could take different forms for years and years and years to come. So, you know, the, the focus of the investigation was, was really the private email system.

Agent 3 told us that the team focused on Clinton's devices because they were the most likely to have the full tranche of missing emails from Clinton's servers, whereas the devices of any one person would only have a "fraction" of them.

Midyear team members further told us that they placed limits on their investigation based on practical considerations, including what they observed to be systemic problems with handling classified information at the State Department. They stated that they discovered persistent practices of State Department employees, including both political and career employees, discussing classified information on both unclassified government email accounts and personal email accounts, and that this culture predated Clinton's tenure as Secretary of State. In addition, FBI Attorney 1 told us that the emails containing classified information that were forwarded to Clinton often originally copied numerous State Department and other government agency employees, some of whom could have forwarded them to other unclassified locations besides the chain that ultimately led to Clinton's server. Witnesses told us that these factors made it impractical for them to search every email account or device that classified emails may have traversed.

D. Review of Abedin's Emails on the Clinton Server

Abedin was the only State Department employee, besides Clinton, with an account on the clintonemail.com domain on Clinton's server. Witnesses told us and documents we reviewed showed that the Midyear team did not review all of Abedin's clintonemail.com emails on the server; rather, they limited their searches to her email exchanges with Clinton. We questioned why this limitation was put in place, given that the purpose of the investigation was to generally assess any mishandling of classified information in relation to Clinton's server.[82]

---

[82] As we discuss in Chapter Eleven, in October 2016, when the Midyear team was drafting the search warrant affidavit for the Weiner laptop, Baker questioned why the team was not seeking to review all of Abedin's emails on Weiner's laptop. He wrote, "I'm still concerned we are viewing the PC too narrowly. There is PC to believe that Huma used her email accounts to mishandle classified

Several witnesses told us that they did not seek to review all of Abedin's emails because her role was administrative in nature. While witnesses told us that Abedin had possibly the most contact with Clinton and sometimes forwarded or printed substantive work-related emails to or for Clinton, she was never an originator of classified materials, she did not typically use classified systems, she did not receive or forward the particularly sensitive information, and she did not comment substantively on classified information that was contained in the emails she forwarded. Prosecutor 1 explained that the team was not "as concerned that [Abedin] was taking stuff off the classified systems and dumping it down." These factors also contributed to the decision not to obtain a search warrant for content from Abedin's Yahoo! account.

However, during a review of the Weiner laptop in October and November 2016, the FBI discovered unmarked classified emails that Abedin had forwarded to Weiner. During an FBI interview on January 6, 2017, Abedin acknowledged that she "occasionally" forwarded work-related emails to her husband for printing.

E.   Decision Not to Seek Access to Certain Highly Classified Information

As detailed in the classified appendix to this report, the OIG learned late in our review that the FBI considered seeking access to certain highly classified materials that may have included information potentially relevant to the Midyear investigation, but ultimately did not do so.[83] In late May 2016, FBI Attorney 1 drafted a memorandum stating that review of the classified materials was necessary to complete the Midyear investigation and requesting permission to review them.

The FBI never finalized the May 2016 memorandum or received access to these classified materials for purposes of the Midyear investigation.[84] FBI witnesses told us that this was for various reasons, including that they believed that the classified materials were unlikely to include information from the beginning of former Secretary Clinton's tenure, and thus would not have a material impact on the investigation. However, other FBI witnesses including Strzok, the Lead Analyst, and the SSA told us that reviewing the materials would have been a logical investigative step.

---

information. I just don't understand why that us [sic] not enough to look at all her emails." Baker told us that he believed the team had probable cause to look at all of Abedin's clintonemail.com and Yahoo! emails, based on the evidence that classified information had traversed both private email accounts.

[83] The OIG also has not reviewed the highly classified information.

[84] As we describe in the classified appendix, the FBI sent a memorandum to the Department on June 1, 2018, requesting permission to review these classified materials for foreign intelligence purposes unrelated to the Midyear investigation.

The classified appendix describes in more detail the highly classified information, its potential relevance to the Midyear investigation, and the FBI's reasons for not seeking access to it.

VI.   Voluntary Interviews

According to documents we reviewed, the Midyear team conducted 72 witness interviews. The witnesses included individuals involved with setting up and administering Clinton's private servers, State Department employees, and other individuals with suspected knowledge of Clinton's email servers, the transmission of classified information on the servers, or her intent. Based on our review, we determined that all witnesses were interviewed voluntarily or pursuant to immunity agreements and, consistent with the FBI's normal procedures, none of the witnesses were placed under oath or recorded.[85] No witnesses testified before the grand jury.

The FBI and Department witnesses we interviewed told us that the Midyear team, including agents, analysts, the SSA, Strzok, the Lead Analyst, and line prosecutors worked together to decide whom to interview and the sequencing of witness interviews, without seeking approval from higher level Department or FBI officials. Agent 1 stated that the initial strategizing on whom to interview generally occurred at the level of the SSA and below. The SSA and most of the case agents told us that they did not recall any significant disputes over whom to interview and that they were never told by higher level managers, including Strzok, or Department employees, including the prosecutors, not to interview particular witnesses that they believed were essential to the investigation. Similarly, the prosecutors told us that their chain of command did not seek to influence the team's decisions on whom to interview. Toscas told us that the prosecutors made him aware of upcoming important interviews and he briefed that information up the chain, but he and higher level Department officials were not involved in deciding whom to interview.

FBI witnesses told us that the agents and analysts worked together to determine what questions to ask to witnesses, and that the analysts prepared packets of documents to use as exhibits. The SSA and the case agents told us that their supervisors were involved in strategy sessions before interviews and in editing and suggesting potential questions, but did not dictate the process and never forbade them from asking particular questions. They also told us that for more significant witnesses, the line prosecutors reviewed their interview outlines and suggested eliminating questions based on privilege, relevance, or a scope that had been agreed upon with the witness's counsel. The SSA stated that the prosecutors' review of the questions did not cause "friction" and that the process was "fairly seamless." The prosecutors told us that higher level Department officials were not involved in deciding what questions to ask witnesses.

---

[85] See DIOG § 18.5.6 (recording of noncustodial interviews is optional; no requirement that witnesses be placed under oath during voluntary interviews).

Witnesses told us and the FD-302s indicated that the case agents led the interviews, and prosecutors and supervisors only attended when witnesses were represented by counsel or particularly significant. According to documents we reviewed, Strzok attended the interviews of five key witnesses—Abedin, Mills, Samuelson, Sullivan, and Clinton. He stated that he only attended these interviews because Laufman insisted on attending them, and he believed that as Laufman's counterpart at the FBI he should attend them as well. Laufman told us that he attended the interviews that he believed were "potentially the most consequential," because of the "enormous implications" and "potential consequences" of the Midyear investigation and to ensure that no one involved in the investigation went "off in a direction that wasn't consistent with a purely independent, investigative, impartial approach." He further told us that he wanted to be involved in key interviews in order to make his own assessment of the witnesses' credibility and gain a full picture of the investigation, so that he could make an informed judgment at the end of the investigation as to whether to accept the FBI's and prosecutors' recommendations. Prosecutor 1 told us that the Midyear agents were "very, very diligent and most of them were very good interpersonally," and that the prosecutors only interjected occasionally during interviews.

We were told that the decision to conduct voluntary interviews rather than subpoenaing witnesses before the grand jury was not controversial or unusual. FBI agents and prosecutors told us that their usual practice is to interview witnesses voluntarily and only resort to grand jury if witnesses are uncooperative or not credible. They further told us that the Midyear witnesses were mostly cooperative and credible and that using the grand jury would have been complicated given the sensitive, classified information involved. Prosecutors 1 and 2 and Agent 1 told us that not calling any witnesses before the grand jury was common in mishandling investigations, because doing so would typically require grand jurors to learn about classified information. Before introducing classified information to the grand jury, prosecutors must obtain approval from the USIC agency that was responsible for classifying the information.[86] Prosecutor 1 explained that although "[y]ou can put classified information in front of the grand jury[,] [y]ou really would like to avoid that because you're basically exposing people that aren't going to be cleared to the information." Agent 1 stated that he had specialized in investigations concerning the loss of classified information since approximately 2008 and during that time he had only been involved in one or two investigations where witnesses were subpoenaed to testify before the grand jury. Agent 4 told us that voluntary interviews are better than the grand jury for "rapport-building" and obtaining information.

Prosecutor 1 told us that the prosecutors were prepared to issue grand jury subpoenas for any witnesses that refused to voluntarily submit to interviews, for situations where they believed witnesses were untruthful, or for situations where witnesses provided statements that would be helpful in a later prosecution and the team wanted to "lock them in." While all witnesses ultimately submitted to voluntary interviews, the team issued a grand jury subpoena for Paul Combetta. As

---

[86] See USAM 9-90.230.

discussed in Section VII.B of this chapter, ultimately the Midyear team decided that it was unnecessary to question Combetta before the grand jury.

VII. Use Immunity Agreements

The Department entered into letter use or "Queen for a Day" immunity agreements with three witnesses in the Midyear investigation: Bryan Pagliano, Paul Combetta, and John Bentel. These immunity agreements and the specific reasons for them are described in Sections A through C below. The Department also entered into two act-of-production immunity agreements in relation to the personal laptops used by Cheryl Mills and Heather Samuelson to cull Clinton's emails. These are discussed in Section VIII.D.3 of this Chapter. The Department did not enter into any transactional immunity agreements.

The prosecutors told us that, in deciding whether to grant use immunity to a witness, they considered whether the witness had criminal "exposure" (i.e., whether there were crimes for which the witness could be prosecuted), the witness's degree of culpability, the value of the witness's expected testimony, whether there were other sources of the same information, and whether the grant of immunity would help or hinder the investigation. Numerous Department and FBI witnesses told us that they did not oppose the immunity agreements. Some witnesses stated that there was nothing unusual or troubling about the nature or quantity of immunity agreements used in the Midyear investigation, especially since so many witnesses were represented by counsel. Witnesses also told us that the immunity agreements were approved within the Department through the level of DAAG Toscas, and that higher level Department and FBI officials were not involved in negotiating or approving the immunity agreements. Yates told us that she was briefed about immunity agreements, but, since she was not made aware of any disagreements related to them, she did not consider overruling them. Lynch told us that she generally was not briefed or otherwise involved in immunity issues.[87]

A. Pagliano

As previously noted, Bryan Pagliano was an information technology specialist who worked on Hillary Clinton's presidential campaign and later set up the Pagliano server, which was the second of the Clinton Servers. The Midyear team entered into two immunity agreements with Pagliano: a "Queen for a Day" use immunity agreement on December 22, 2015, and a letter use immunity agreement on December 28, 2015. Based on our review, the immunity was granted in response to a request by Pagliano's counsel and resulted in at least two voluntary interviews that helped inform the FBI's investigation.

Witnesses told us that Pagliano was a critical witness because he set up the server that Clinton used during her tenure. According to Prosecutor 2, Pagliano

---

[87] As described in Chapter Four, Lynch told us that she received a memorandum regarding congressional immunity issues for Pagliano, but only because Senator Charles Grassley had requested a phone call with her regarding Pagliano.

was "uniquely positioned" to describe to the FBI the "setup" and "mechanics" of Clinton's server, as well as to answer questions regarding possible cyber intrusion. On August 10, 2015, Pagliano's counsel emailed an FBI agent that he was "not prepared to have Mr. Pagliano participate in an interview with the FBI- particularly in the absence of any explanation as to the focus or scope of your prospective questions." According to an August 27, 2015 email among the prosecutors, Strzok, the Lead Analyst, and the SSA, Pagliano's attorney had spoken with Prosecutor 1 and was "insistent on immunity for his client even though it was explained to him that Pagliano is a witness and not a target." Prosecutor 3 wrote to the Midyear team, in response to the request of Pagliano's lawyer, "We're probably going to see this a lot with any witness who is facing having to be interviewed or testify on the Hill. We should all sit down and prioritize witnesses to be interviewed and decide who it's safe to immunize."

According to documents we reviewed, on or about September 4, 2015, Pagliano's attorneys told the Senate Judiciary Committee and the Senate Committee on Homeland Security and Governmental Affairs that he would exercise his Fifth Amendment rights in response to any questions by the Committees about his role in setting up Clinton's private email server. The next day, the Washington Post reported that the Clintons personally paid Pagliano to support Clinton's private email server while he was employed at the State Department.[88] According to emails we reviewed, within days of these allegations the Midyear team took steps to obtain financial information related to Pagliano from several sources. In addition, the Midyear prosecutors contacted the Criminal Division's Public Integrity Section (PIN) to consider whether Pagliano should be prosecuted under 18 U.S.C. § 209 for receiving outside compensation for government work or for improperly failing to report outside income on financial disclosure paperwork. On or about September 9, 2015, Pagliano pleaded his Fifth Amendment right against self-incrimination in response to questions about the set-up of Clinton's email server before the House Benghazi Committee.

On December 11, 2015, Prosecutor 2 wrote an email to the other line prosecutors notifying them that PIN had declined charges against Pagliano. Then PIN Chief Ray Hulser told us that PIN declined charges because the PIN prosecutors determined that (1) Pagliano's outside compensation was for work for the Clintons (primarily former President Clinton), not for State Department work;[89] and (2) Pagliano reported his compensation from the Clintons on federal financial disclosure reports before he was told by the State Department that this was not necessary. Hulser further told us that PIN's decision to decline charges against Pagliano was

---

[88] Rosalind S. Helderman and Carol D. Leonnig, *Clintons Personally Paid State Department Staffer to Maintain Server*, WASH. POST, Sept. 5, 2015.

[89] According to the FD-302 of Pagliano's subsequent interview pursuant to the immunity agreement, Pagliano told the FBI that at the time he built the Pagliano server he did not know Clinton would be Secretary of State or would have an account on the server. Rather, he told the FBI that he "believed the email server he was building would be used for private email exchange with Bill Clinton aides."

not influenced by the Midyear team's desire to interview Pagliano and that PIN was never pressured by anyone within the FBI or the Department to decline charges.

Prosecutor 1 told us that around the same time as PIN's declination, the team received a proffer from Pagliano's attorney, through which the team confirmed that Pagliano had important information to provide. Thus, on December 22, 2015, the Department entered into a "Queen for a Day" proffer letter with Pagliano. The "Queen for a Day" letter provided that Pagliano would "answer all questions completely and truthfully, and...provide all information, documents, and records" within his custody or control, related to the substance of his interview. In exchange, the Department agreed that any statements made during his proffer would not be admitted during the government's case-in-chief or at sentencing during any future prosecution of Pagliano. The Department would, though, be able to "make derivative use of, and pursue any leads suggested by" Pagliano; use his statements for appropriate cross examination and rebuttal; and prosecute Pagliano for statements or information that were "false, misleading, or designed to obstruct justice." The prosecutors told us that they wanted to ensure that Pagliano was a credible witness and that his statements would be consistent with his attorney's proffer before offering him the broader letter use immunity.

Two FBI case agents interviewed Pagliano for the proffer on December 22, 2015, in the presence of all four prosecutors, the CART examiner, and Pagliano's attorneys. Among other things, Pagliano described the set-up of the Pagliano server and related equipment, as well as the transition to the PRN server, to help inform later OTD analysis of those devices. In addition, Pagliano told the FBI about a late 2009 or early 2010 conversation with Mills in which he conveyed a concern raised by a State Department Information Technology Specialist that Clinton's use of a private email server could violate federal records retention laws. Pagliano told the FBI that Mills responded that former Secretaries of State, including Colin Powell, had done the same thing. The FBI relied on this testimony in subsequent interviews, including a later interview of Mills.[90]

The prosecutors and Agent 1 told us that they met afterwards and everyone agreed that Pagliano was credible and helpful. Prosecutor 1 told us that "everyone assessed that [Pagliano] was scared but truthful," and that Pagliano might have been even more nervous and less forthcoming had he been required to testify in the grand jury, outside the presence of his attorney. They also agreed that there were some follow-up questions that would need to be asked. Thus, on December 28, 2015, the Department offered Pagliano "use immunity coextensive with that granted under 18 U.S.C. § 6001" in exchange for future truthful court testimony, grand jury testimony, or voluntary interviews related to the Midyear matter, pursuant to a letter use immunity agreement. The letter provided that the government would not use any information directly or indirectly derived from Pagliano's truthful statements or testimony against him in a future prosecution,

---

[90] Mills told the FBI that she did not recall the conversation with Pagliano.

"except a prosecution for perjury, giving a false statement, or any other offense that may be prosecuted consistent with 18 U.S.C. § 6001."

According to a FD-302 and contemporaneous agent notes, the Midyear team interviewed Pagliano again on June 21, 2016, and he answered questions to clarify answers provided during the proffer. For example, Pagliano told the FBI that he decided not to "implement Transport Layer Security (TLS) between the Clinton email server and State server," because at the time he "understood the Clinton email server to be a personal email server and did not see a reason for encryption." He also told the FBI about "failed log-in attempt[s]" on the Clinton email server in January 2011, which Pagliano described as a "brute force attack (BFA)" that was not "abnormal." According to the LHM, "[T]he FBI's review of available Internet Information Services (IIS) web logs showed scanning attempts from external IP addressees over the course of Pagliano's administration of the server, though only one appear[ed] to have resulted in a successful compromise of an email account on the server." As described in Section I of this chapter, the one confirmed successful compromise was of an account belonging to one of President Clinton's aides.

Both Department and FBI witnesses told us that no one opposed the decision to grant Pagliano immunity. The SSA told us that the FBI did not consider him a subject or someone they would prosecute in connection with Midyear, the FBI believed his testimony was very important, and providing immunity was an effective way to secure his testimony. Prosecutor 4 told us that the way Pagliano was handled was "standard operating procedure." In addition, witnesses told us that Pagliano pleading the Fifth Amendment and refusing to testify before Congress gave the Department no choice but to offer Pagliano immunity.

B.   Combetta

As previously noted, Paul Combetta was the employee of PRN who migrated the email accounts from the Pagliano server to the PRN server in 2013, transferred Clinton's archived emails to the PRN server in 2014, and later wiped emails from the PRN server in March of 2015. The Department entered into a letter use immunity agreement with Combetta on May 3, 2016. Midyear team members told us that Combetta was an important witness for several reasons, including his involvement with the culling process and the deletion of emails and his interactions with several people that worked for Clinton. Several Midyear team members stated that after conducting two voluntary interviews of Combetta, they believed that Combetta had not been forthcoming about, among other things, his role in deleting emails from the PRN server following the issuance of a Congressional preservation order. The witnesses further stated that Combetta's truthful testimony was essential for assessing criminal intent for Clinton and other individuals, because he would be able to tell them whether Clinton's attorneys—Mills, Samuelson, or Kendall—had instructed him to delete emails.

Combetta was first interviewed on September 17, 2015, by two case agents, in the presence of Prosecutor 2 and Combetta's counsel. The interview was voluntary and there was no immunity agreement. According to the FD-302 and contemporaneous agent notes, Combetta provided information regarding the set-up of the PRN server, the roles of other PRN employees in the management of the PRN server, his role in transferring emails from the Archive Laptop to the PRN server, and his role in creating .pst files of Clinton's archived emails to be transferred to the laptops used by Mills and Samuelson to cull Clinton's emails ("culling laptops"). However, he denied that PRN "deleted or purged" Clinton's emails from the PRN server or from back-ups of the server and stated that Clinton's staff never requested that PRN do so.

On February 18, 2016, the same two agents interviewed Combetta again, this time in the presence of the CART examiner, the Forensics Agent, Prosecutor 2, and Combetta's counsel. Once again, the interview was voluntary and there was no immunity agreement. According to the FD-302 and contemporaneous agent notes, Combetta continued to deny deleting the HRC Archive Mailbox from the server and stated that "he believed the HRC Archive mailbox should still be on the Server in the possession of the FBI," despite documentation showing that the mailbox was no longer on the server as of January 7, 2015. Combetta stated that only he and one other administrator had the ability to delete a mailbox from the server. When the agents showed him documentation indicating that an administrator had manually deleted backup files and used BleachBit on March 31, 2015, he stated that he did not recall deleting backup files, he did not recall anyone asking him to delete backup files, any PRN employee had the ability to delete backup files, he believed he used BleachBit "for the removal of .pst files related to the various exports of Clinton's email" to Mills's and Samuelson's laptops, and he used BleachBit for this purpose "of his own accord based on his normal practices as an engineer." He further stated that he did not recall a March 9, 2015 email in which Mills reminded him of his obligation to preserve emails pursuant to a preservation order. The FD-302 and contemporaneous notes indicate that the agents attempted to ask Combetta about documents related to a conference call with Kendall and Mills on March 25, 2015, just before the deletions and use of BleachBit, but his attorney advised him not to answer based on the Fifth Amendment.

During the February 18, 2016 interview, the agents also showed Combetta an email dated December 11, 2014, in which he wrote to a PRN colleague, "I am stuck on the phone with CESC [Clinton's staff] again.... Its [sic] all part of the Hilary [sic] coverup [sic] operation ☺ I'll have to tell you about it at the party." Combetta told the agents that the reference to the "Hilary [sic] coverup [sic] operation" was "probably due to the recently requested change to a 60 day email retention policy and the comment was a joke."[91] Department and FBI witnesses told us that Combetta's explanation for this email seemed credible to them, given

---

[91] According to the FD-302, contemporaneous notes, and exhibits, the agents also asked Combetta about a July 24, 2014 email to Pagliano regarding using a "text expression editor." Combetta told the agents that Mills was concerned that Clinton's then current email address would be "disclosed publicly" when her archived emails were provided to the State IG, because "when a user changes his or her email address, Outlook updates the old email address with the new email address." We found that this might explain later media reports that Combetta posted on Reddit on or about July 24, 2014, "I may be facing a very interesting situation where I need to strip out a VIP's (VERY VIP) email address from a bunch of archived email...." *See, e.g.,* Caitlin Dewey, *Hillary Clinton's IT Guy Asked Reddit for Help Altering Emails, A Twitter Sleuth Claims,* WASH. POST, Sept. 20, 2016.

his personality and the way the email was written, and they did not discuss interviewing Combetta's colleague regarding the email.

The SSA told us that he believed Combetta should have been charged with false statements for lying multiple times; however, the SSA also stated that he was ultimately satisfied that Combetta's later immunized testimony was truthful and that he was "fine" with the immunity agreement. Prosecutor 2, Agent 2, and the Forensics Agent indicated that, while they believed that Combetta had not been forthcoming during the first two interviews, they were not certain that they had sufficient evidence to charge him with obstruction or false statements. According to documents we reviewed, the forensic evidence showed that Clinton's emails had been deleted and wiped from the server, but did not definitively link Combetta with those actions. Agent 2 explained that the team "felt pretty strongly that maybe he had deleted information off of Secretary Clinton's server," but that interpreting computer forensics and precisely what they mean can be "kind of messy." Similarly, the Forensics Agent stated that, based on the forensic evidence alone, it was "very difficult" to be certain that Combetta conducted the deletions; however, based on the Midyear team's assessments of the credibility of Combetta and the other administrator, the team was more "focused on" Combetta. Prosecutor 2 told us that using the forensic evidence in combination with witness testimony, the team "probably could have established" that Combetta conducted the deletions; however, Prosecutor 2 stated that there was insufficient evidence, after the first two interviews, to prove that Combetta understood his obligation to preserve Clinton's emails and deliberately violated the Congressional preservation order.

In addition, members of the Midyear team told us, consistent with their contemporaneous emails, that they believed Combetta's failure to be forthcoming during the first two interviews was largely due to a lack of sophistication and poor legal representation, rather than an intent to hide truth. For example, Prosecutor 2 wrote in an email on March 29, 2016, to the other line prosecutors, "It's really hard to tell whether Paul [Combetta] is trying to hide something, or we are simply experiencing the effects of really bad (no) attorney prep and/or an attorney that has counseled him to say 'I don't remember' if he doesn't have a specific recollection of taking a specific action on a specific date." Prosecutor 2 expressed the same sentiments during OIG interviews. Agent 2 stated, "We just felt like we weren't getting the whole story or maybe he was holding back a little." Prosecutor 1 stated, "[W]e didn't assess his exposure to be terribly significant." However, Prosecutor 1 also stated:

> There were certainly discussions about whether he had, had [18 U.S.C. §] 1001 exposure [for making false statements].... He was clearly not being forthright with us.... And I think, my, my guess is if we couldn't have gotten him to come in and, and he was messing around with us on the immunity, we probably would have had to charge him. But, I think we were more interested in understanding what had happened.... And the most expedient way to, to do that, I think we assessed, was just to, to immunize him and keep moving.

Both prosecutors and agents also told us that Combetta was not someone the government was interested in prosecuting given his role in the case. Agent 1 told us that the absence of evidence that Combetta knew anything about the content of the emails on Clinton's server minimized the FBI's interest in prosecuting him. Prosecutor 4 stated:

> I was concerned that we would end up with obstruction cases against some poor schmuck on the down, that, that had a crappy attorney who didn't really, you know, if I was his attorney, he wouldn't have gone in and been, you know, hiding the ball in the first place. And so at the end of the day, I was like, look, let's immunize him. We've got to get from Point A to Point B. Point B is to make a prosecution decision about Hillary Clinton and her senior staff well before the election if possible. And this guy with his dumb attorney doing some half-assed obstruction did not interest me. So I was totally in favor of giving him immunity.

Prosecutor 2 told us that Combetta's counsel was "concerned" that the Midyear team would "want to charge somebody...to show we had done something" and "go after some low-level person like Combetta to make a point." Prosecutor 2 stated, "that was never our intention" and "it was in our interest to...make him and his counsel feel comfortable enough that they were going to give us the facts that we needed to figure out what happened in this case."

In the March 29, 2016 email exchange, the four line prosecutors weighed two approaches to dealing with Combetta: (1) offering letter use immunity and only issuing a grand jury subpoena if Combetta did not comply or was untruthful during an immunized interview; versus (2) issuing a grand jury subpoena first and withdrawing the subpoena if Combetta was cooperative and truthful during a voluntary, immunized interview the morning before a scheduled grand jury appearance. In support of the second approach, Prosecutor 4 sent an email stating that it was "common for witnesses to play games early in high profile investigations as they try to figure out the lay of the land" and noting that a grand jury subpoena was a "powerful" tool in this situation.

On April 8, 2016, the Department subpoenaed Combetta to appear before the grand jury on May 3, 2016. Along with the subpoena, Prosecutor 3 wrote an email to Combetta's attorney that the FBI intended to "continue its interview of [Combetta] and go over any relevant documents with him" on May 3 and that "[i]n the event he needs to appear before the GJ, that would likely occur" the following morning. The prosecutors and agents explained to us that the plan was to interview Combetta on May 3, and place him in the grand jury on May 4 if they assessed that he was still uncooperative or untruthful.

On the evening of May 2, Prosecutor 3 wrote to the other prosecutors that that they would need to discuss whether to put Combetta in the grand jury on May 4. He further wrote, "Regardless as to how he answers the questions, I could see the FBI advocating that we put him in the GJ." Prosecutor 4 responded, "I would prefer that we not put him in the GJ without a clear articulable reason for doing so, but we can discuss." Prosecutor 4 told the OIG:

> Generally, I think people overestimate the value of the grand jury to get people that are lying to tell the truth. My experience, I've had the best luck with working with defense counsel or having very aggressive interviews with them personally, one-on-one, which I would typically not want to do in the grand jury. You know, if I'm going to beat somebody up to get them to tell the truth, I don't want 23 grand jurors sitting around while I'm yelling at somebody.

The prosecutors told us that Combetta's attorney had informed them in advance of the May 3 meeting that Combetta would plead the Fifth Amendment in the grand jury. They further told us they believed they had no real choice but to grant Combetta immunity.[92] They stated that they did not consider charging Combetta with a crime and then seeking his cooperation against other witnesses, because they did not believe he had significant criminal exposure. In addition, Prosecutor 1 explained that if the Department had dropped or lowered charges against Combetta in exchange for his cooperation, a defense attorney would have used the cooperation agreement to impeach Combetta's credibility at a subsequent trial.

Accordingly, on May 3, 2016, the Department entered into a standard letter use immunity agreement with Combetta. The terms of this agreement were identical to the terms incorporated into the Pagliano letter use immunity agreement. Specifically, in exchange for Combetta providing truthful information during FBI interviews as well as truthful testimony during any grand jury or court appearances, the Department agreed that it would not use his statement or testimony, or any information derived from it, during a subsequent criminal prosecution, "except for a prosecution for perjury, giving a false statement, or any other offense that may be prosecuted consistent with 18 U.S.C. § 6002."[93] Both the prosecutors and the FBI agents involved with Combetta's interview told us that the decision to grant Combetta use immunity was not controversial and that everyone agreed that it was the most effective way to obtain the information they needed from him.

During a speech at an FBI conference for Special Agents in Charge in October 2016, Comey indicated that he agreed with the decision to enter into a use immunity agreement with Combetta in order to obtain potentially valuable information concerning any role that Clinton played in the deletion of emails from

---

[92] The Midyear team did not first conduct a Queen for a Day proffer with Combetta, as they did with Pagliano. Prosecutors typically enter Queen for a Day immunity agreements before offering letter use immunity, because Queen for a Day agreements allow the government to assess the usefulness and reliability of the witness's expected testimony before agreeing not to use leads obtained from the testimony to develop evidence against the witness.

[93] This language meant that Combetta could be prosecuted for lying during his May 3 immunized interview. However, the government could not use Combetta's statements on May 3 to prosecute him for lying in the past, including during the previous two Midyear interviews.

her server. Responding to the complaint that the Midyear team "handed out immunity like candy," he stated:

> I hope you also notice our subject here was Hillary Clinton. We wanted to see[,] this very aggressive investigative team wanted to see can we make a case on Hillary Clinton. To make that case they worked up from the bottom. The guy who set up her server, the guy who panicked and deleted emails, he is really not our interest. Out interest is trying to figure out did he give us anything against her.

Combetta was interviewed subject to the terms of the immunity agreement on May 3, 2016, by the same two FBI case agents, this time in the presence of the SSA, the CART examiner, all four line prosecutors, and Combetta's attorneys. According to the FD-302 and contemporaneous notes of the two agents and the CART Examiner, Combetta provided the FBI additional detail regarding his removal of emails from the culling laptops, stating that Mills had requested that he "securely delete the .pst files" in November or December 2014 but had not specifically requested that he use "deletion software." He told the FBI that he was the one who recommended the use of "BleachBit" because he had used it for other clients. He also acknowledged removing the HRC Archive mailbox from the PRN server between March 25, 2015, and March 31, 2015, and using BleachBit to "shred" any remaining copies of Clinton's email on the server, despite his awareness of Congress's preservation order and his understanding that the order meant that "he should not disturb Clinton's email data on the PRN server." According to the FD-302 and contemporaneous notes, Combetta told the FBI that he had an "oh shit" moment upon realizing that he had failed to comply with Mills's request in late 2014 or early 2015 to "change the retention policy for Clinton's and Abedin's existing and ongoing mail to 60 days." He further told the FBI that Mills had contacted him on or about March 8, 2015, to assess what was still on the servers, including whether there were any "old back up data or copies of mailboxes hanging out there on old equipment." However, he stated that he did not tell Mills that he subsequently realized the archived emails were still on the PRN server or that he deleted them in late March. In addition, he stated that he "could not recall the content" of the March 25, 2015, call with Kendall and Mills. In sum, Combetta took responsibility for the deletions, without implicating Clinton or her attorneys.

We interviewed seven Midyear team members who attended Combetta's May 3, 2016, interview, all of whom told us that they conferred immediately following Combetta's interview and agreed that Combetta's testimony finally "made sense," that he had been truthful and forthcoming, and that he did not implicate anyone in criminal activity such that there was a need to "lock in" his testimony in the grand jury. Prosecutor 1 told us that Combetta's testimony finally "squared with the forensic evidence," and also corroborated the testimony of other witnesses, including Mills and Samuelson, that they were unaware of the March deletions by Combetta.

C.   Bentel

As noted previously, John Bentel worked at the State Department for 39 years, the last four of which he served as Director of the Executive Secretariat Information Resource Management (S/ES-IRM), before he retired in 2012. As detailed below, the investigators had received evidence that Bentel had information relating to the State Department's possible sanctioning of Clinton's use of a private email server.

According to documentation we reviewed, the Department entered into a "Queen for a Day" agreement with Bentel on June 10, 2016. The terms of this agreement were similar to those offered to Pagliano. Prosecutor 2 told us that the team did not subsequently grant Bentel the broader letter use immunity granted to Pagliano and Combetta, nor did his counsel ask for it. The witnesses we interviewed told us that the decision to enter into a Queen for a Day agreement with Bentel was not controversial. Prosecutors 1 and 2 stated that Bentel's attorney sought use immunity because he thought that Bentel was portrayed poorly in the State IG report. They further stated that the team granted Bentel immunity because he was a necessary witness, who did not, to their knowledge, face any criminal "exposure." Prosecutor 2 described the Bentel interview as a "check-the-box type interview." The SSA told us that he did not oppose immunity for Bentel, because the FBI had no intentions of seeking that Bentel be prosecuted.

The agents asked Bentel about allegations by two S/ES-IRM staff members that they had raised concerns about Clinton's use of personal email to him during separate meetings. According to the State IG report, one of the staff members told the State IG that Bentel told the staff member that "the mission of S/ES-IRM is to support the Secretary" and instructed the staff member to "never speak of the Secretary's personal email system again."[94] According to the FD-302 and agent notes, the agents showed Bentel documents that suggested that he was aware that Clinton had a private email server that she used for official business during their joint tenure. One of the agents explained that the purpose of asking Bentel about his knowledge of the server was to assess whether Clinton's use of the server was sanctioned by the State Department. However, Bentel maintained that he was unaware that Clinton used personal email to conduct official business until it was reported in the news and denied that anyone had raised concerns about it to him.

Both agents who interviewed Bentel told us that he was uncooperative and the interview was unproductive; however, they attributed these problems to nervousness and fear of being found culpable. Agent 3 told us that he did not believe that immunity for Bentel was necessary and that it did not help the investigation because Bentel was not forthcoming during his interview. However, he did not believe that Bentel had any criminal exposure and therefore the immunity agreement did not harm the investigation.

---

[94] Department of State Office of Inspector General, Office of the Secretary: Evaluation of Email Records Management and Cybersecurity Requirements (May 2016), Evaluations and Special Projects Report ES-16-03, https://oig.state.gov/system/files/esp-16-03.pdf (accessed May 7, 2018).

VIII. Use of Consent and Act of Production Immunity to Obtain Mills and Samuelson Testimony and Laptops

In this section we examine decisions made by the FBI and the Department regarding whether to interview Mills and Samuelson regarding the process they used to cull Clinton's emails in connection with providing emails to the State Department in 2014, as well as whether and how to obtain and review the personal laptops used by Mills and Samuelson for this culling process ("culling laptops"). The investigators told us that access to these laptops was particularly important to ensure the completeness of the investigation. All 62,320 emails pulled from the Clinton servers were stored at one time on these laptops, so access to the laptops offered the possibility of reconstructing a large number of the deleted emails through digital forensics.[95] Moreover, the deletion of emails by Mills and Samuelson from these laptops had become a matter of great public controversy, including allegations that they had been deleted for improper purposes, increasing the importance of attempting to recover as many of them as possible. Ultimately, both Mills and Samuelson submitted to voluntary interviews regarding the culling process and voluntarily provided the culling laptops to the FBI after receiving "act of production" immunity.

In the subsections below we discuss: privilege claims raised by Mills and Samuelson; the debate between the FBI and the Department; the events that led to the Department securing voluntary interviews of Mills and Samuelson; the steps that were taken to secure and search the culling laptops, including the decision to grant Mills and Samuelson "act of production" immunity and the consent agreements for the culling laptops; the involvement of senior Department and FBI officials; and a discussion of the motivations behind the Mills and Samuelson dispute.

A.   Privilege Claims Raised by Mills and Samuelson

As noted previously, in response to a State Department request in 2014, Mills and Samuelson, neither of whom were still employed by the State Department, worked together on behalf of Clinton to produce Clinton's State work-related emails that were on the PRN server by crafting a process to cull what they believed to be Clinton's personal emails from her work-related emails. Samuelson, under Mills's supervision, reviewed the emails that had been placed on the culling laptops and, following completion of this culling process, Clinton produced 30,490 work-related emails to the State Department. Thereafter, Mills and Samuelson asked Combetta to securely delete the .pst files from the culling laptops, which, as described above, he did using BleachBit. Mills and Samuelson then continued to use the culling laptops for work related to their legal representation of other clients.

---

[95] By comparison, personal devices used by other persons who might have sent or received emails to or from addresses on the Clinton servers would only contain the emails sent or received by that person.

While the Midyear team was interested in speaking with Mills and Samuelson about this culling process, they also were interested in interviewing Mills concerning her time at the State Department with Clinton, due to evidence that Mills frequently communicated directly with Clinton and that she received and forwarded classified information on both her unclassified State email and personal Gmail accounts.[96] During Clinton's tenure as Secretary of State, Mills served as, among other things, Clinton's Chief of Staff and Samuelson served as a senior advisor to Clinton and White House Liaison.

According to documents we reviewed, Mills and Samuelson told the FBI and Wilkinson told the prosecutors that Mills and Samuelson had attorney-client relationships with Clinton for purposes of their work culling Clinton's emails in 2014. According to internal memoranda and emails, the prosecutors began asking Wilkinson to provide her clients for voluntary interviews regarding the culling process in December 2015, but Wilkinson raised objections. Specifically, Wilkinson argued that any interview questions regarding the culling process "would require answers revealing privileged information," and she suggested that the Department obtain the information through an attorney proffer by Wilkinson instead.[97] Prosecutor 2 told us, and contemporaneous notes show, that the prosecutors also asked Wilkinson to voluntarily turn over the culling laptops in March 2016, after Wilkinson informed them that the laptops were still in her clients' possession. However, Wilkinson refused to voluntarily turn over the culling laptops, arguing that the laptops contained privileged information related to both Clinton and Mills's and Samuelson's other clients. Wilkinson told the prosecutors that she would instead take possession of the culling laptops from her clients, disconnect them from the Internet, and secure them in a safe in her office.

B.   Debate over Interviewing Mills and Samuelson Regarding the Culling Process and Obtaining the Culling Laptops

FBI case agents and the SSA told us, and contemporaneous emails show, that they believed that interviewing Mills and Samuelson regarding the culling process and searching the culling laptops were essential investigative steps. They stated that they hoped to be able to find the full 62,320 emails that were originally reviewed by Mills and Samuelson to determine whether any additional emails— beyond those that Clinton's attorneys provided to the State Department and those that the FBI found through other sources—contained classified information. They further stated that they believed the culling process might have been flawed,

---

[96] Prosecutor 1 told us that the Midyear team did not have an investigative need to interview Samuelson concerning her time at State.

[97] Wilkinson also represented two other witnesses, a former senior State Department official and Jake Sullivan. According to emails we reviewed, Wilkinson agreed to provide the former senior State Department official for an interview, but at first refused to provide Sullivan, although she acknowledged that Sullivan never had an attorney-client relationship with Clinton. On January 14, 2016, the prosecutors prepared a memorandum requesting authorization to notify Wilkinson that the Department was prepared to issue a grand jury subpoena for Sullivan's testimony, as well as authorization to issue the grand jury subpoena if Wilkinson continued to object. On January 18, 2016, Toscas emailed Laufman approving both requests. Wilkinson ultimately agreed to provide Sullivan for a voluntary interview, which took place on February 27, 2016.

because their other reconstruction efforts had revealed a significant number of work related emails to or from Clinton that had not been included in the State Department production. Strzok told us that the FBI investigators hoped that asking questions about the culling process and reviewing the culling laptops would help determine why this was the case and whether there was a nefarious purpose. For example, several FBI witnesses stated that they believed that asking questions about the culling process might help them determine why Abedin's emails were underrepresented in the State IG production.

FBI witnesses told us that once Wilkinson refused to voluntarily provide her clients for interviews and the culling laptops, they believed it was appropriate and in the interest of efficiency to subpoena Mills and Samuelson before the grand jury and seek a search warrant to seize the culling laptops from Wilkinson's office. The FBI witnesses stated that even if a judge ultimately were to quash a subpoena or decide that there was no probable cause to issue a search warrant, it was the FBI's obligation to at least try to obtain what they believed to be critical potential sources of evidence.

The line prosecutors and Laufman told us, and contemporaneous emails and internal memoranda show, that they agreed that it would be helpful to interview Mills and Samuelson regarding the culling process and obtain the culling laptops. However, they had several concerns about using compulsory process to do so. First, they were concerned that at least certain questions regarding the culling process would seek information protected by attorney-client privilege and the attorney work product doctrine. Second, they were concerned that the culling laptops contained privileged material relating to both Clinton and Mills's and Samuelson's other clients. Third, they raised questions about establishing probable cause to search the culling laptops given evidence that they had been wiped of the emails relevant to the Midyear investigation. Fourth, based on conversations with Wilkinson, they believed she would file a motion to quash any search warrant or subpoena and that this would lead to protracted litigation that would delay the investigation. Finally, they stated that they were required to follow the procedures set forth in the Department policy for obtaining physical evidence and testimony from an attorney regarding the attorney's representation of a client. They stated that, at a minimum, 28 C.F.R. § 59.4 and USAM 9-19.220 and 9-13.420 did not permit them to execute a search warrant on Wilkinson's office under these circumstances.

The prosecutors told the OIG that the FBI did not appreciate the complexity involved with obtaining the culling testimony and laptops. Prosecutor 4, whom several witnesses told us was known for being an experienced prosecutor with significant experience handling privilege issues, explained that he was frustrated that the FBI was "willing to litigate to the death issues that [he] thought would be very close calls and could delay the investigation for two years without a strong belief that it would actually change the results" of the investigation.

111

C. Events Leading to Voluntary Interviews of Mills and Samuelson Regarding the Culling Process

1. Attorney Proffer on March 19, 2016

On February 1, 2016, Toscas received from the NSD prosecutors their proposed investigative steps for Mills and Samuelson. The prosecutors proposed pursuing a grand jury subpoena to question Mills concerning her State Department tenure (where there were no attorney-client privilege issues), but seeking attorney proffers before considering grand jury subpoenas for Mills's and Samuelson's testimony about the culling process. They provided two reasons for this approach.

First, they indicated that, pursuant to the USAM, to obtain Criminal Division authorization for a subpoena to an attorney regarding the attorney's representation of a client they must show that the information sought is not protected by a valid claim of privilege and that "[a]ll reasonable attempts to obtain the information from alternative sources shall have proved to be unsuccessful." USAM 9-13.410(C). The prosecutors described how they would tailor their questions about the culling process to avoid seeking information protected by attorney client privilege.[98] However, they indicated that they could not represent that all reasonable attempts had been made to obtain the information from alternative sources without first attempting to obtain the information through an attorney proffer.

Second, they indicated that they were concerned that issuing subpoenas for testimony regarding the culling process could result in protracted litigation with an uncertain outcome. They indicated that, despite extensive legal research, the team had been unable to find clear authority indicating that a court should allow an attorney to be questioned about actions taken on behalf of a client, even if describing those actions would not implicate confidential communications between the client and attorney.

In February 2016, Wilkinson agreed to both an attorney proffer by Wilkinson regarding the culling process and a voluntary interview of Mills regarding her State Department tenure. On February 8, 2016, the prosecutors emailed Wilkinson a short list of broad topics for the attorney proffer and the proffer was scheduled for March 19, 2016. Separately, Mills's interview regarding her State Department tenure was set for April 9, 2016.

According to Prosecutor 2's notes of the March 19 attorney proffer, the proffer was attended by all four line prosecutors, Beth Wilkinson, and two other attorneys from Wilkinson's firm. Mills's and Samuelson's attorneys told the prosecutors, consistent with a State IG Report described above, that Mills and Samuelson initiated the culling process after the State Department requested Clinton's assistance reconstructing her work-related emails. The attorneys further

---

[98] Specifically, they indicated that they intended to ask Mills and Samuelson questions falling into three categories: "(1) receipt of emails from PRN; (2) general questions about the culling process that do not implicate the attorney-client privilege; and (3) handling of the emails, which have been confirmed to contain classified information."

stated that the State Department had told Mills that "it was HRC's responsibility to determine" what was personal and what was work-related, because this would be "too burdensome for State." The attorneys described the manner in which Mills and Samuelson obtained the emails from Combetta and generally how they conducted their review. The attorneys told the prosecutors that Mills asked Combetta to remove the .pst files from Mills's and Samuelson's laptops after Clinton's work-related emails were produced to the State Department; however, the attorneys stated that they "never heard of BleachBit." According to the notes, the attorneys confirmed that Clinton had changed her email retention policy to 60 days in early 2015, but would not "say reason for changing policy – either [privilege] or HRC's question to answer."

2.   Midyear Team Meeting on March 28, 2016

After the March 19 attorney proffer, the FBI team took the position that it was still essential to interview Mills and Samuelson regarding the culling process. On March 28, 2016, the Midyear team held a meeting to decide the best way forward. McCabe and Toscas were the highest level FBI and Department officials, respectively, at the meeting. Witnesses told the OIG and contemporaneous emails show that this meeting was contentious and that the FBI insisted that the team either interview Mills regarding the culling process during the scheduled interview on April 9, 2016, or inform Wilkinson before April 9 of its intent to do so at a future date. The FBI witnesses stated that they believed if they did not do this, Mills would only give the FBI one "bite at the apple"—that she would assert publicly that she cooperated with the FBI without an incentive to return for another interview.

Based on a review of emails and text message exchanges, we determined that Page was one of the more outspoken FBI personnel at the March 28 meeting in favor of interviewing Mills and Samuelson about the culling process and countering the Department's privilege concerns. In a March 29, 2016 email exchange, Strzok asked Prosecutor 4, "[H]ow are you doing? You seemed none too pleased at times on Monday [March 28]." Prosecutor 4 replied with an email about Page:

> I am fine. I don't like "former prosecutors" [Page] giving their opinions from the cheap seats. I have been known throughout my career by the agents I work with as the most aggressive prosecutor that they have ever seen. During my last five jury trials I have forced no fewer than a dozen lawyers to testify against their former clients. It is easy for FBI attorneys to second guess our opinions when they haven't ever had to actually stand before a judge and defend their opinion.[99]

In response, Strzok defended Page and wrote, "Best I can tell is I think everyone in the room's motives were (are) pure." Prosecutor 4 then wrote:

---

[99] Page told us that she had been a prosecutor in the Department's Organized Crime and Racketeering Section before joining the FBI.

113

I am stuck in the middle of pushing NSD along and trying to get FBI to be realistic. The investigation is degenerating into everyone trying to figure out what the congressional testimony looks like in the future. My job is to put criminals in jail, period.

Following the March 28 meeting, Strzok drafted an email to send to the prosecutors to memorialize the FBI's understanding of the decision made at the meeting regarding Mills and Samuelson. The email was approved by FBI OGC, Steinbach, and McCabe. Strzok sent the email on March 29, 2016, to the four line prosecutors and copied Toscas and several FBI employees. In the email, Strzok wrote that the prosecutors had agreed to "inform Wilkinson of DOJ's and FBI's intention to interview Mills and Samuelson about the sort process." In addition, Strzok wrote that the prosecutors had agreed to contact the Department's Professional Responsibility Advisory Office (PRAO) regarding whether they could seek a waiver of attorney-client privilege from Clinton through Kendall.

According to emails we reviewed, the line prosecutors and Laufman agreed with reaching out to PRAO for advice on seeking a waiver from Kendall and did so on March 31, 2016. In addition, in early April, 2016, they sought guidance from the Criminal Division as to whether seeking the waiver was permissible under Department policy. On April 12, 2016, three days after the Mills interview, a Criminal Division official told NSD that he was "not aware of any DOJ policy that would prevent [CES] from seeking the waiver."

As far as Strzok's assertion that the prosecutors had agreed to notify Wilkinson that the FBI intended to interview her clients regarding the culling process, Prosecutors 1 and 2 indicated in an email exchange on March 30, 2016, that this was not correct. According to the March 30 email exchange, the prosecutors were concerned that certain issues had not yet been resolved, including obtaining necessary approvals from the Criminal Division. Also on March 30, 2016, Prosecutor 1 wrote to Prosecutor 2 and Laufman that he did not want to take a position with Wilkinson that they would be unable to "stand behind" and thus be accused of "dealing with her in bad faith." Prosecutor 1 told us, "It's not smart to make demands when you don't understand what kind of leverage you have." Thus, Prosecutor 2 told us, and documents showed, that before the April 9 interview the prosecutors told Wilkinson that the FBI "had not foreclosed" the possibility of interviewing her clients regarding the culling process, but not that the FBI insisted on doing so.

3. FBI Call to Wilkinson on April 8 About Mills and Samuelson Interviews Without Informing Prosecutors

On April 8, 2016, the day before the Mills interview, FBI GC Baker contacted Wilkinson, without notifying the line prosecutors or higher Department officials in advance, to convince her to consent to the FBI's demands for the culling testimony and culling laptops.[100] The prosecutors learned of Baker's call to Wilkinson the following day, when Wilkinson told the prosecutors at the Mills interview she had been contacted by a "senior FBI official" regarding interviews of her clients.

Comey told us that he approved Baker's call to Wilkinson and that he "must have known [Baker] was not going to tell DOJ." In addition, Laufman's notes of a meeting following the Mills interview indicate that McCabe was aware of the call beforehand. Baker told us that he reached out to Wilkinson because he believed the line prosecutors had not been sufficiently aggressive. Laufman stated that he took "great offense" to Baker's assertion that the prosecutors had not been aggressive with Wilkinson, "because we were accomplishing and had accomplished great things through creative troubleshooting of extraordinarily sensitive issues with counsel to obtain the media and devices whose review was the foundation of this investigation." Prosecutors 1 and 2 told us that Baker's efforts were not effective, because Wilkinson continued to refuse to provide consent.

4.   FBI Surprise Statement at Outset of April 9 Mills Interview

On April 9, 2016, Mills appeared with Wilkinson for a voluntary interview concerning Mills's tenure at State. According to a FBI memorandum ("Mills Interview Memorandum"), shortly before the interview Strzok advised the prosecutors and Laufman that the agent conducting the interview would be making a statement at the start of the interview "concerning the scope of [the] interview, the FBI's view of the importance of the email sorting process, and the expectation of a follow-up interview once legal issues had been resolved." Witnesses referred to this statement as "the preamble."

Comey told the OIG that he approved of the preamble but did not suggest it, and McCabe stated that he "authorized" the preamble. McCabe told us that he directed the FBI team not to discuss the preamble with the prosecutors before the day of the interview because he was "concerned that if we raised another issue with DOJ, we would spend another two weeks arguing over the drafting of the preamble to the interview, which I just was not prepared to do."

The prosecutors told us that they were surprised and upset because the preamble was inconsistent with their prior representations to Wilkinson and they believed it was strategically ill-advised. The Mills Interview Memorandum states that the prosecutors objected to the preamble but that they were told that "the FBI's position was not subject to further discussion."

According to the Mills Interview Memorandum, the interviewing agents delivered the preamble at the outset of the interview as planned. Witnesses told us

---

[100] Baker told us that he had known Wilkinson for many years, and documents show that she had previously reached out to him in Midyear as part of a broad effort to speak with senior Department and FBI officials, up to and including Attorney General Lynch. Lynch and other high level Department officials told us that they did not speak with Wilkinson during the course of the investigation.

that Wilkinson was visibly angered by the preamble and that she and Mills stepped outside the interview room after the agent delivered it. The prosecutors stated that they convinced Wilkinson and Mills to return for the remainder of the scheduled interview concerning Mills's tenure. However, according to Prosecutor 1, Mills was "on edge the whole time."[101]

According to notes of the interview, the prosecutors told Wilkinson that they were "sandbagged" by the FBI and that they did not know in advance about the preamble. Additionally, according to the notes, Wilkinson informed the prosecutors of the call the previous day from a "senior FBI official."

Prosecutors and FBI agents told us that the events surrounding the April 9 Mills interview, including both the preamble and Baker phone call that were planned without Department coordination, caused significant strife and mistrust between the line prosecutors and the FBI. AAG Carlin told us that the prosecution team asked him to call McCabe and "deliver a message that this is just not an acceptable way to run an investigation." Carlin told us that he delivered this message to McCabe and also briefed Lynch and Yates on the issues.

Witnesses told us that the strife between the prosecutors and the FBI team culminated in a contentious meeting chaired by McCabe a few days later. On the Department side, this meeting was attended by the line prosecutors, Laufman, and Toscas. Prosecutor 2 told us that during this meeting the prosecutors explained that they were trying to be "careful" in their handling of complicated issues, and that McCabe responded that they should "be careful faster." Laufman stated that McCabe's comment "undervalued what we had been able to accomplish to date investigatively through negotiating consent agreements." According to Laufman's notes, McCabe agreed that Baker's unilateral contacts with Wilkinson should not have happened, and Baker agreed not to have further contact with Wilkinson. With respect to the preamble, however, the prosecutors told us that McCabe stated that he would "do it again."

5.   Mills and Samuelson Agree to Voluntary Interviews Regarding the Culling Process

In May 2016, Wilkinson agreed to allow Mills and Samuelson to be voluntarily interviewed regarding the culling process, provided the questions asked during the interviews did not seek information that was considered "opinion work product."[102]

---

[101] During the interview, according to the FD-302, Mills told the FBI that she "did not learn Clinton was using a private server until after Clinton's [State Department] tenure." The FD-302 further states, "Mills stated she was not even sure she knew what a server was at the time." Abedin similarly told the FBI that she "did not know that Clinton had a private server until...it became public knowledge." The prosecutors told us that they found it credible that Mills and Abedin did not understand that Clinton had a "private server," even though Mills and Abedin knew Clinton had an email account on the clintonemail.com domain. They further stated that Mills's and Abedin's statements were consistent with what the prosecutors understood to be Mills's and Abedin's limited technical knowledge and abilities.

[102] Opinion work product is attorney work product that involves "mental impressions, conclusions, opinions, or legal theories" concerning litigation and, like communications protected by

The prosecutors told us that this meant that the agents could ask questions regarding the "mechanics" of the culling process, including how Mills and Samuelson obtained and reviewed the emails for production to the State Department. However, they told us that they could not put a particular email in front of Mills or Samuelson and ask why the call was made to consider it work-related or personal. The prosecutors explained that, based upon their research and Prosecutor 4's experience with privilege, they believed they would not likely be successful convincing a judge that such questions were permissible.

Samuelson and Mills were interviewed regarding the culling process on May 24, 2016, and May 28, 2016, respectively, which was before the Midyear team obtained access to the culling laptops. Witnesses told us and contemporaneous documents show that the agents prepared outlines in advance of the interviews and the prosecutors reviewed them to ensure they were consistent with the agreed upon parameters. For example, based on witness testimony and the outline we reviewed, the prosecutors eliminated a question that asked for the "exact" search terms that were used during the culling process. Prosecutor 2 told us that during

---

the attorney-client privilege, is generally protected from discovery. Strzok told us that the Midyear team considered whether questions regarding how Mills and Samuelson made decisions to exclude particular emails could have been asked based on the "crime-fraud" exception to the attorney-work product doctrine. In the Fourth Circuit (which includes EDVA), in order to invoke the crime-fraud exception, the government "must make a prima facie showing that (1) the client was engaged in or planning a criminal or fraudulent scheme when he sought the advice of counsel to further the scheme, and (2) the documents containing the privileged materials bear a close relationship to the client's existing or future scheme to commit a crime or fraud." In order to apply the crime-fraud exception to an attorney's opinion work product, the government must also "make a prima facie showing that the attorney in question was aware of or a knowing participant in the criminal conduct." *In re Grand Jury Proceedings No. 5,* 401 F.3d 247, 251-52 (4th Cir. 2005).

While we did not ask the prosecutors about the crime-fraud exception directly, it appeared, based on their answers to other questions, that that they did not believe that they could show that Mills or Samuelson were "engaged in or planning a criminal or fraudulent scheme" when they culled Clinton's emails for production to the State IG. Prosecutor 2 stated that the Midyear team had not uncovered evidence during the course of the investigation that Mills or Samuelson had a criminal "motive" when they conducted the culling process. Prosecutor 2 explained, "[T]here was nothing that was different in the type of emails that were produced and the types of emails that were found elsewhere to indicate to us that there was any sort of...nefarious intent." Similarly, Prosecutor 1 stated that the notion that Mills or Samuelson had criminal mens rea when they conducted the sort process was contradicted by the fact that the production to the State Department contained numerous classified emails. This prosecutor stated, "[L]ots of classified stuff got turned over in FOIA, so the notion that they would have been deleting the classified didn't make a lot of sense to us at this point in the investigation, because [they] probably would have done a better job of getting rid of it." The Lead Analyst told us that "he had no evidence to suggest that" there was "some sort of willful arrangement to...remove and otherwise sideline material that would, you know, reflect criminal activity." He further stated, "We didn't see anything else to suggest that there [are] these like willful criminal arrangements with attorneys."

Prosecutor 2 told us, and contemporaneous documents show, that the Midyear team also considered whether there was a waiver of privilege, due to either (1) the publication of certain information regarding the culling process on the Clinton campaign website; or (2) Mills's testimony about aspects of the culling process before the House Benghazi Committee. Prosecutor 2 stated, "[W]e thought we had pretty good arguments to argue waiver on fact work product but not opinion work product, which is kind of like...the way I differentiate it, asking about the mechanics versus asking about why substantive decisions were made."

the interviews "there were a couple of assertions of privilege," but overall the interviews went well.

One of the case agents who led Mills's and Samuelson's interviews told us that he believed the interviews regarding the culling process were not as productive as he would have liked, because Mills and Samuelson were "so well-rehearsed." He attributed this to a number of factors, including that they were interviewed late in the investigation, Wilkinson was aware of the scope of the interview in advance from discussions with the prosecutors, and Mills was a "highly-trained professional" with an "excellent" attorney. He further stated that the limited scope of the questioning "took away some of our tools that we would have had going into that interview." Other FBI witnesses, however, told us that while there was some debate over the scope of the interviews beforehand, the team was ultimately satisfied with the information that was obtained. Prosecutor 2 told us that "nobody ever expressed a concern following the interviews that there was something that we needed that we didn't get."

D.   Steps Taken to Obtain and Search the Culling Laptops

As noted above, the investigators wanted access to the laptops primarily because such access promised the possibility of reconstructing the emails that had been deleted in the culling process. However, because Mills and Samuelson were both attorneys, the issue of obtaining access to the laptops implicated questions regarding how to protect any privileged information residing on them.

1.   Internal Strategizing and Call with Clinton's Counsel

Documents we reviewed reflected that the prosecutors spent significant time and effort conducting research, analyzing relevant legal, policy, and ethical issues, and strategizing how to best handle the issue of the culling laptops. Contemporaneous emails and text message exchanges we reviewed show that Strzok and Page challenged the prosecutors' laptop privilege concerns and were two of the most outspoken proponents of using compulsory process to obtain the culling laptops. Page explained to the OIG why she did not agree that the emails on the laptops were privileged:

> These are materials, these are the State Department's records. And if the Secretary in the first place had actually followed normal protocol, every single one of these emails, whether personal or work-related would have been in the State Department's possession, and there would be no attorney-client discussions happening with respect to the sort of this material.

In addition, Page stated that any other privileged material on the laptops could be handled by the Midyear team's already established filter team.

On May 18, 2016, Toscas, McCabe, Page, and Prosecutor 1 had a telephone conference with DAAG Paul O'Brien of the Department's Criminal Division regarding the likelihood of Department approval for search warrants or subpoenas to obtain the culling laptops. O'Brien told the OIG, and Page's and Toscas's

118

contemporaneous notes show, that during this call McCabe advocated in favor of a search warrant, but O'Brien stated that a search warrant was "a nonstarter." O'Brien stated that he explained to McCabe that a search warrant for Beth Wilkinson's office was inconsistent with the USAM and 28 C.F.R. § 59.1. He further stated that he told McCabe that a judge was likely to question why the government was seeking a search warrant to seize the laptops from Wilkinson's office, when a subpoena would suffice to obtain them (and a search warrant could be sought later to review their contents).[103] O'Brien told the OIG that even with a filter team, "any time you issue a search warrant for an attorney's office, you run the potential and the possibility that you can be inadvertently coming across protected client, sensitive attorney-client information." He further told us that he believed a subpoena was more appropriate, because it would be less intrusive and "there was no thought that Beth Wilkinson was going to destroy the evidence." According to Page's notes, O'Brien stated on the call that he had never seen the Department seek a search warrant in similar circumstances.[104]

On May 23, 2016, Toscas, McCabe, Page, and Prosecutor 1 spoke with Kendall based on the approval previously received from the Criminal Division. During the call, they described to Kendall the difficulty the team was having obtaining the culling laptops and told him that they would not interview Clinton before obtaining the laptops. Prosecutor 1 stated that the team assumed Kendall and Wilkinson were speaking with one another and that a conversation with Kendall might ultimately lead to Wilkinson voluntarily providing the laptops.

2.   Approval to Subpoena the Culling Laptops

On May 31, 2016, after hearing nothing further from Kendall, the Midyear team submitted applications for the approval of subpoenas for the culling laptops to the Criminal Division through O'Brien. The applications were signed by EDVA U.S. Attorney Boente. The team also prepared and submitted to O'Brien search warrant

---

[103] O'Brien told us that even if the laptops were still in the possession of Mills and Samuelson, "we still would have looked to determine whether we could obtain the materials with a subpoena rather than doing a search warrant," as required by the USAM.

28 C.F.R. § 59.1 and USAM 9-19.220 apply to the use of process against "distinterested third parties." Pursuant to 28 C.F.R. § 59.1, "It is the responsibility of federal officers and employees to...protect against unnecessary intrusions. Generally, when documentary materials are held by a disinterested third party, a subpoena, administrative summons, or governmental request will be an effective alternative to the use of a search warrant and will be considerably less intrusive." Similarly, USAM 9-19.220 provides, "As with other disinterested third parties, a search warrant should normally not be used to obtain...confidential materials" from a disinterested third party attorney."

USAM 9-13.420 applies to searches of the premises of an attorney that is a "suspect, subject or target" of an investigation and provides: "In order to avoid impinging on valid attorney-client relationships, prosecutors are expected to take the least intrusive approach consistent with vigorous and effective law enforcement when evidence is sought from an attorney actively engaged in the practice of law."

[104] The policies set forth in the USAM are binding on both FBI and Department employees.

applications for reviewing the content of the culling laptops, to submit to a court once the laptops were obtained.

In a letter to Toscas dated June 3, 2016, O'Brien authorized the issuance of the proposed subpoenas. He further wrote that the team "had satisfied the requirement, pursuant to USAM 9-13.420(C), to consult the Criminal Division before applying for a warrant to search the laptop computers."[105] Toscas told us, and contemporaneous emails show, that he proposed applying to the court for an "anticipatory search warrant." An anticipatory search warrant is one that is approved by the court for use once a triggering event occurs, in this case the FBI securing the laptops by subpoena. Toscas stated that he was in favor of the anticipatory search warrant because he thought it might help persuade a judge to side with the government when litigating a possible later motion to quash the subpoena. However, he said that Boente and the prosecutors in EDVA did not agree because anticipatory search warrants were not typically used in that fashion in their jurisdiction.

On June 4, 2016, Prosecutor 1 wrote to Wilkinson:

> I had wanted to speak to you personally today to discuss next steps. Since we were unable to connect, in the interest of time, I am advising you that DOJ has authorized subpoenas for both laptops, which we intend to serve by COB Monday. It is important that we speak on the phone as soon as possible tomorrow.

The prosecutors had a series of phone calls with Wilkinson over the next two days, ultimately resulting in four letters dated June 10, 2016: two from the Department (one for Mills and one for Samuelson) granting Wilkinson's clients "act of production" immunity in exchange for voluntarily providing the culling laptops and two from Wilkinson (one for Mills and one for Samuelson) granting the Department consent to review the culling laptops, with certain restrictions. Witnesses told us that McCabe and Toscas were the highest level FBI and Department officials, respectively, to approve these agreements.

3.   Act of Production Immunity for Mills and Samuelson

The Department entered into "act of production" immunity agreements with both Mills and Samuelson on June 10, 2016. The immunity agreements provided that the government would "not...use any information directly obtained from" the culling laptops in any prosecution of either witness "for the mishandling of classified information and/or the removal or destruction of records," pursuant to "18 U.S.C. § 793(e) and/or (f); 18 U.S.C. § 1924; and/or 18 U.S.C. § 2071." Therefore, Prosecutors 1 and 2 told us it was their view that the government would have been free to use in any future prosecution of Mills and Samuelson leads developed as a result of the FBI's review of the information on the culling laptops, as well as information provided by Mills and Samuelson during their voluntary interviews.

---

[105] The USAM did not require Criminal Division approval for the search warrant, just consultation once the request for had been approved by a U.S. Attorney (here that was Boente). USAM 9-13.420(C)

FBI and Department witnesses told us that no one within the team disagreed with the decision to enter into these immunity agreement with Mills and Samuelson in exchange for obtaining the culling laptops. We also were told by FBI and Department witnesses that, based on the evidence they had gathered at that point in the investigation, they did not expect to uncover anything on the culling laptops that would be incriminating to Mills or Samuelson. The prosecutors told us that that Mills and Samuelson had included in the State Department production numerous emails containing classified information, including emails containing SAP information which was the most sensitive material identified during the Midyear investigation. They also had included the emails with the (C) portion markings, which were the only emails containing classification markings that were discovered during the investigation. According to Prosecutor 2, "[T]here was nothing that was different in the type of emails that were produced and the types of emails that were found elsewhere to indicate to us that there was any sort of motive" or "nefarious intent."

In addition, Prosecutor 1 stated that, even after the prosecutors had approval to obtain the laptops by subpoena, they believed that obtaining them through consent was preferable, because they expected a motion to quash and time lost through subsequent litigation. Similarly, FBI agents and supervisors told us that they did not object to the immunity agreements because the protection offered by them was limited and allowed the team to obtain needed sources of potential evidence without inhibiting the investigation.

Comey explained in a speech at an FBI conference for Special Agents in Charge in October 2016 that there were "huge concerns" about attorney-client privilege and attorney work product on the culling laptops that warranted entering into the immunity agreements with Mills and Samuelson in order to secure them. He stated:

> You can also imagine given that you're experienced people the challenge in trying to get a lawyer to give you their laptop that you use for all of their legal work. Huge concerns there about attorney-client privilege, attorney work product. We had a few options there. One was to serve them with a Grand Jury subpoena and then litigate the work product protection and the attorney-client protections for probably the next five years, or reach some agreement with them to voluntarily produce it and give them some sort of assurance as to how the information will be used on that laptop.... Department of Justice reached an agreement at the request of the lawyer for these two lawyers that for act of production of immunity is the way I understand it in my career that is you give this laptop, we will not use anything on the laptop against you personally in a prosecution for mishandling of classified information or anything else related to classified information. Reasonable to ask for a lawyer to ask to give us the laptops and enabled us to short circuit the months and months of litigation that would've come otherwise. I was actually surprised they agree[d] to give us the laptops.

4.   Limitations in the Consents to Search the Culling Laptops

In addition to the immunity agreements, which the Department entered into to obtain possession of the culling laptops, the Department entered into consent agreements with both Mills and Samuelson in order to enable the FBI to search the laptops with certain limitations. The consent agreements provided that the "sole purposes of the search" were:

> "[T]o search for any .pst files, or .ost files, or compressed files containing .pst or .ost files, that were created by Platte River Networks ("PRN") after June 1, 2014 and before February 1, 2015, in response to requests for former Secretary Clinton's email from her tenure as Secretary of State;"

> "[T]o attempt to identify any emails from, or remnants of, the PRN Files that could potentially be present on the Device;"

> "[T]o identify any emails resident on the Device sent to or received from" Hillary Clinton's known email accounts, "for the period of January 21, 2009 through February 1, 2013;" and

> "[T]o conduct a forensic analysis of the device to determine whether the Device was subject to intrusions or otherwise compromised."

The consent agreements described in detail a two-phase process the FBI would use to search the devices for the listed purposes. In the first phase, OTD would search the allocated space of the devices for the .pst files created by Combetta. If the intact .pst files were found, OTD would not move on to the second phase. If not, OTD would go on to the second phase, which would entail searching both the allocated and unallocated space for "any emails, fragments of emails, files, or fragments of files" that could "clearly be identified as having been sent to or received by" one of Clinton's email accounts during her tenure.[106]

Witnesses told us, and contemporaneous text and instant message exchanges among FBI employees show, that negotiating the consent agreements was a difficult process and, at least at the outset, Strzok and others at the FBI believed that the prosecutors were giving Wilkinson too much control.[107] However,

---

[106] The consent agreements also each provided: "As soon as the investigation is completed, and to the extent consistent with all FBI policies and applicable laws, including the Federal Records Act, the FBI will dispose of the Device and any printed or electronic materials resulting from your search." According to talking points drafted by members of the Midyear team in October 2016, the FBI had agreed to destroy the laptops because the laptops contained classified information and, as such, could not be returned to the attorneys following compliance with FOIA and Federal Records Act obligations. The draft talking points stated that as of October 2016 the laptops had not been destroyed, because the FBI was still "under a legal obligation to preserve the laptops and other electronic media due to numerous pending FOIA requests." On June 11, 2018, the FBI informed the OIG that the FBI still had in its possession the culling laptops and all other evidence collected during the Midyear investigation.

[107] FBI employees have the ability to communicate internally via Microsoft Lync instant messages when logged on to their FBI workstation. We discovered several Lync messages that were relevant to our review, and we discuss these in Section XI of this chapter and in Chapter Twelve.

when we interviewed Strzok, he told us that he no longer could remember what his specific concerns were at the time and, in the end, "we got what we needed to credibly come to the resolution that we did in the investigation." He further stated that some of the sentiments he expressed over text message to Page about the prosecutors' handling of the issue reflected only the heat of the moment and his opinions at the time.

Agent 1 told us that the phases outlined in the consent agreements were overly complicated and that he did not agree that the FBI should not have been able to review the unallocated space if the analysts found the .pst files in phase 1. Contemporaneous instant messages show that the Lead Analyst, FBI Attorney 1, and FBI Attorney 2 shared this concern. However, this concern became moot when OTD was unable to find the .pst files in phase 1 and ultimately went on to phase 2 and searched the unallocated space.

FBI Attorney 1 exchanged instant messages with the Lead Analyst and FBI Attorney 2 in which she expressed frustration during the drafting of the consent agreements. For example, on June 8, 2016, she wrote to the Lead Analyst, "The fact that Pete [Strzok] met with [Prosecutor 1] and hashed all this out and capitulated really pisses me off." Also on June 8, 2016, she wrote to FBI Attorney 2, "OMG. I'm so defeated. Why do I bother?" FBI Attorney 1 told us, in an interview before viewing these instant messages, that she had concerns with the filter process set forth in the consent agreements, which limited the filter team to "two attorneys, one FBI agent, and one FBI analyst, none of whom are members of the investigative team." The agreements stated that OTD would provide the emails from its search to the filter team, which would then "review those results to identify and remove: (1) any privileged material; (2) any material that, upon further review, is determined not to be an e-mail sent to, or received by, the Relevant Accounts during the Relevant Period; and (3) any material that, upon further review, is determined not to be a work-related e-mail sent to, or received by," Clinton's relevant email account. FBI Attorney 1 stated that she opposed this language because it differed from the filter process that had been used for other devices, wherein the filter team, with the assistance of OTD, relied more heavily on search terms to eliminate material that was beyond the scope of review or privileged. She stated that her concern was that the filter process would be too time-consuming. However, she told us that in the end the filter team was able to "get it done in a timely manner" and that resolved her concerns.

In a follow up interview after viewing the instant messages, FBI Attorney 1 told us that the June 8, 2016 instant messages were exchanged during a lengthy telephone conference with Prosecutors 1 and 2, Strzok, the Lead Analyst, FBI Attorney 2, and OTD technicians. She stated that the frustrations expressed in her instant messages related to her concerns about the filter process discussed during her first interview. She further stated that her complaints about Strzok had to do with him not including her in certain conversations with the prosecutors. However, she told us that she did not believe that Strzok was failing to represent the FBI's interests in those conversations. She also reiterated that she was ultimately satisfied with the terms of the consent agreements. On June 28, 2016, FBI Attorney 1 sent an instant message to the lead filter team attorney offering to provide the filter team with additional resources to review the culling laptops. The filter attorney responded, "Just got data from OTD and we seem to be in a good place with our current filter resources."

Agent 3 told us he was concerned by the requirement in Phase 2 that the emails be "clearly identifiable" as having been sent to or from one of Clinton's email accounts during her tenure, because sometimes the metadata in the unallocated space was unclear. However, he told us that he did not express this concern to the prosecutors at the time the consent agreements were being negotiated and that he was not sure that he had sufficient "technical basis" to do so. We asked Prosecutors 1 and 2 about this concern and they stated that the language was developed with input from the investigative team and OTD to ensure that they were able to access what they needed to access in order to adequately review the laptops. Prosecutor 2 stated, "We came to the conclusion that the procedures that were in this letter would allow us to look at the material that we thought was critical to look at, and yet protect the attorney-client privilege in a way we thought we were required to do."

Other FBI employees told us that they would have preferred to be able to search for emails sent or received just before or after Clinton's tenure, in the hope of identifying Clinton's intent in setting up the email server or the intent behind the later deletions of emails. The Lead Analyst told us that he would have liked to have been able to search Mills's and Samuelson's own emails on the culling laptops, to determine what instructions were provided to Samuelson regarding how to conduct the culling process and to see if there was any evidence regarding why later deletions occurred. He stated that this information would have helped the FBI determine whether Mills and Samuelson "willfully" did something "illegal or inappropriate" during the sort process or whether there were "serious flaws" in the process. However, he stated he had "no evidence to suggest" that Clinton or her attorneys had a criminal purpose in the way they conducted the sort process or in the deletion of emails. He further stated, "We didn't see anything anywhere else to suggest that there is these like willful criminal arrangements with attorneys. Like, there's nothing to suggest that that's the case. It's just, you know, it's the curious part of the investigator in all of us that thinks about that."

The prosecutors and some of the agents told us that the consent agreements were date restricted, because the primary purpose of reviewing the culling laptops was to find the .pst files of Clinton's emails that were transferred by Combetta, in order to reconstruct, to the extent possible, the deleted emails. They further told us that the attorneys' own communications following Clinton's tenure, with either Clinton or other clients, would mostly consist of items protected by privilege, and that they had already obtained records of communications between Clinton's attorneys and PRN staff from PRN.[108] Similarly, the Lead Analyst acknowledged that he might not have been able to view such emails even with legal process due to privilege and probable cause concerns. He stated, "[T]his was not a snap

---

[108] As noted in Section V of this chapter, the Midyear team also did not seek a search warrant of Mills's personal Gmail account for email exchanges following Clinton's tenure, when she had an attorney-client relationship with Clinton.

decision. This decision was made, and this was the best and most effective way to...obtain this content. And there's going to be trade-offs involved in that."

Most of the Department and FBI witnesses we interviewed told us that they were ultimately satisfied with the consent agreements to search the Mills and Samuelson laptops and did not feel that the consent agreements unduly limited their investigation. In addition, some witnesses told us that in the end they believed that the FBI obtained more through the consent agreements than it would have obtained through a subpoena or search warrant. For example, Prosecutor 4 stated that that he told the FBI "repeatedly in no uncertain terms that I thought that the probability of success on a grand jury subpoena for the laptops [because of a motion to quash] was, that they would get some things, but the vast majority of what they wanted, they would not get." Similarly, the Lead Analyst told us that he eventually learned that sometimes consent allows the FBI to obtain "a broader swath of material."

5. Review of the Laptops

The FBI and Department witnesses told us that they ultimately did not identify evidence on the Mills or Samuelson laptops that changed the outcome of the investigation. According to documents we reviewed, the team recovered 9,000 emails on Mills's laptop, which were mostly duplicates of the emails included within the 30,490 produced to the State Department, and they found no new classified emails. The team was able to recover "approximately 112 files" from Samuelson's laptop, but the analysts did not believe these files contained "work-related material."

E. Involvement of Senior Department and FBI Officials

Witnesses told us, and documents show, that the issues surrounding the culling laptops and testimony was one of the few issues in the Midyear investigation that was briefed to high-level Department officials. The highest level Department official involved in substantive decisionmaking regarding the culling testimony and laptops, including the decision to grant immunity, was Toscas. Toscas told us that while he agreed with the prosecutors that there were complicated privilege concerns, he also agreed with the FBI that the culling laptops had to be reviewed and that the prosecutors had more leverage than they realized in negotiating with Wilkinson.

Toscas told the OIG that he briefed Lynch on the negotiations with Wilkinson because of the potential for litigation, and because Wilkinson had stated that she planned to contact Department leadership. He stated that Lynch responded that she knew Wilkinson and was familiar with her aggressive style. He stated that Lynch told him, "[P]ursue whatever you want to do, she's going to be that way. That is her reputation.... Tell the team to get what they need done." Based on that guidance, Toscas told us that he conveyed to the line prosecutors to "be civil" but "be just as aggressive back" to Wilkinson.

Lynch told us that she did not recall Toscas bringing to her attention the prosecutors' difficulties negotiating with Wilkinson or conflict with the FBI. However, she stated that in the spring of 2016 Toscas briefed her and Yates that "additional laptops were found" and that "because the people who owned the laptops were lawyers, in addition to having had a connection with Secretary Clinton's team, there were issues of privilege." She stated that the only reason this issue was brought to her attention was because it "raised the possibility of litigation." She further told us that the team was able to "resolve" the issues without litigation, but she did not "know the specifics." In addition, Lynch stated that she and Wilkinson had been "prosecutors together in Brooklyn" and that, based on that experience, she described Wilkinson's "aggressive" style to Toscas. Yates and Carlin similarly told us that they were briefed on the Mills and Samuelson issues, but could not remember many details. Carlin stated that at one point he reached out to McCabe to discuss the issues and that he "fully agreed" with the recommendation of the prosecutors that "trying to do an adversarial search warrant on a lawyer's office" would result in the case being "tied up in litigation for a period of time."

On the FBI side, Comey, McCabe, and Baker were all substantively involved with the debate with the prosecutors over whether and how to obtain the culling testimony and laptops. McCabe stated, "I was very clear about this with the Director, that we could not conclude this investigation in a credible way until we had done everything humanly possible to look at those laptops, fully realizing that it likely, there may not be anything on them." He stated he also made this point clear to "Carlin, Toscas, and others." Comey told the OIG that he agreed with the FBI team that the culling laptops were "critically important." He stated:

> I believe we could not credibly complete this investigation without getting access to those laptops, and that I was not going to agree to complete this investigation until we had access to those laptops because...we just couldn't credibly say we had done all we could do, if we didn't do everything possible to see, is there a forensic trace of emails that were deleted and can we tell whether there was obstructive intent.

Comey, Baker, and other FBI witnesses told us that they believed the prosecutors were overly cautious about obtaining the laptops, because they were intimidated by high-powered defense counsel like Wilkinson. Referencing the prosecutors' concerns about obtaining the laptops, Comey stated:

> And I remember a general concern that...there was a sense that [the prosecutors] didn't want to do things that were too overt or too aggressive and I don't know whether that extended to the use of a grand jury or not....

> But there was a sense that there was a general lack of aggressiveness and willingness to take steps that would roil the waters. In my judgment honestly, was that that wasn't politically motivated that's just the normal cowardice...this is the normal fear and conservatism

126

and the higher profile the matter, the more afraid sometimes the prosecutors are.

And so I didn't attribute that to a political motive....

Lynch and Yates told us that they were unaware of any complaints that the prosecutors were not sufficiently aggressive, or that they were believed by the FBI to be intimidated by high-powered defense counsel. Lynch stated, "I don't remember that being conveyed to me. You know, agents always think that prosecutors aren't aggressive enough. But they don't know the discussions and decisions that go behind the decisions as to...what steps you're going to take[.]" She said that she would have viewed any such complaints as part of the normal dialogue that often occurs between prosecutors and agents unless someone had brought the complaints to her as a "catalogue" of specific decisions that were problematic.

Comey told us that he addressed the laptop issue with Yates, because he was concerned that higher level Department officials needed to be involved. He stated:

> I think I had the sense that there's nobody home. That the grownups aren't home at Justice because they've, they're stepping away from this. And so to be fair to myself, I think the laying over this was this sense that, in a way Carlin and above has abdicated responsibility for this.

However, despite his testimony that the prosecutors were not aggressive enough with Wilkinson and that higher level Department officials were not engaged, Comey told us that he did not discuss his concerns with the Department, ask the Department to assign new prosecutors, or seek the appointment of a special counsel.[109] As discussed in Section II.A.2 of Chapter Six of this report, Comey told the OIG that he told Yates in April 2016 that the closer they got to the political conventions, the more likely he would be to insist that a special counsel be appointed. Comey said that his comment to Yates was motivated in part by his frustration that it was taking the Midyear prosecutors too long to obtain the Mills and Samuelson laptops. However, as explained in Section VII of Chapter Six, we did not find evidence that Comey ever seriously considered seeking the appointment of a special counsel. His reasons for not seeking the appointment of a special counsel or even seeking the assignment of new prosecutors were that he had the "A-team" working on the investigation on the FBI side and it was "too late in the game" at that point. In addition, Comey stated that he believed Yates "must have done something" in response to his discussion with her, "because the team perceived an adrenaline injection into the DOJ's side that we had not seen before" and secured the culling testimony and laptops. Comey indicated to the OIG that he was satisfied with this result, stating, "We got access, we negotiated access to the

---

[109] Comey also told us that he was not "troubled or struck" by the Department's decision to have NSD run the investigation.

laptops and interviews of the lawyers, so the team got what the investigators thought they needed."

F.   Motivations behind the Culling Testimony and Laptop Dispute

Several FBI officials told us that they perceived that the prosecutors were reluctant to obtain the culling laptops and testimony, but they did not believe that such reluctance was motivated by bias or political considerations. Comey stated, "There was serious concern about the reluctance to pursue the laptops...I had no reason to believe that was driven by an improper consideration."

Based on the evidence we reviewed, Comey and others at the FBI were primarily motivated in the debate over obtaining the culling testimony and laptops by a desire to credibly complete the investigation and to do so sufficiently in advance of the election to not be perceived as political. Indeed, witnesses told us, and contemporaneous notes show, that by the time the Midyear team was debating how to handle Mills and Samuelson, the team generally agreed that the investigation was headed toward a declination and did not believe that it was likely that anything found on the culling laptops would change that outcome. For example, according to Laufman's notes from May 11, 2016, Strzok told Laufman that although he did not believe that finding something on the culling laptops that would change the outcome of the investigation was likely, it was nonetheless important to secure them from an "investigative standpoint."

In addition, the notes of both Department and FBI employees show that beginning as early as May 2016, Comey conveyed to his employees a sense of urgency to complete the Midyear investigation. For example, Page wrote in her notes from a meeting on May 9, 2016, "Need to act with incredible urgency." In the same notes, she included a reminder to herself to "call John [Carlin]" and ask, "do your people know D's urgency?" The next day, an analyst wrote in her notes:

> [The Lead Analyst] and Pete
> Meeting with Director
> Sense of urgency

Similarly, Laufman's May 11, 2016 notes state:

> Director Comey...
> - Extraordinary sense of urgency...
> - As get closer to election would be more difficult to close
> - Risk of perception that won't be credible, be seen as partisan...
> FBI desires to wrap up in weeks, not months.

Moreover, as described in Chapter Six, Comey shared with Baker, McCabe, Rybicki, Priestap, Strzok, the Lead Analyst, and Page his first draft of a public statement recommending that no charges be pressed against Clinton in early May 2016, before the Midyear team interviewed Mills and Samuelson or obtained the culling laptops.

128

As described above, Strzok and Page were two of the strongest advocates of obtaining the culling testimony and laptops by compulsory process. On May 4, 2016, a few weeks before Mills and Samuelson were voluntarily interviewed regarding the culling process and a little over a month before the FBI obtained the culling laptops, Strzok and Page exchanged the following text messages. The sender of each message is identified after the timestamp.

> 8:40 p.m., Page: "And holy shit Cruz just dropped out of the race. It's going to be a Clinton Trump race. Unbelievable."
>
> 8:41 p.m., Strzok: "What?!?!??"
>
> 8:41 p.m., Page: "You heard that right my friend."
>
> 8:41 p.m., Strzok: "I saw trump won, figured it would be a bit."
>
> 8:41 p.m., Strzok: "Now the pressure really starts to finish MYE..."
>
> 8:42 p.m., Page: "It sure does. We need to talk about follow up call tomorrow. We still never have."

The same day, at 8:48 p.m., Strzok sent a similar text message to the Lead Analyst. However, the Lead Analyst responded, "Did he? We need to finish it well and promptly, but it's more important that we do it well. A wise man once said that." The Lead Analyst told us that the "wise man" referenced in his text message was Comey.

Both Strzok and Page told us that the May 4, 2016 text message exchange was not an example of them allowing their political viewpoints to impact their work on the Midyear investigation. Rather, they told us that Comey had expressed a desire complete the investigation as far in advance of the elections as possible to avoid impacting the political process, and the fact that the presidential race was down to two candidates was a milestone that enhanced that sense of urgency. They both told us that their desire to move quickly to finish Midyear was not impacted by Donald Trump, in particular, securing the nomination over the other Republican candidates.

IX.   Interview of Former Secretary Clinton

The interview of Hillary Clinton took place on Saturday, July 2, 2016. Comey provided a few reasons for conducting the interview on a Saturday, including to complete the interview as soon as possible after the team finished all other investigative steps, to accommodate Clinton's schedule, and to "keep very low visibility." Comey told us that he received a briefing before the interview regarding general parameters, including when the interview would take place and who would be conducting it. However, he stated that he was not involved in formulating the questions for the interview.

We reviewed several issues related to the Clinton interview, including: the decision to conduct her interview last; a debate over the number of FBI agents and Department employees who would attend her interview and whether there were any efforts to adjust that number for political reasons; the conduct of the interview; the decision to allow Mills and Samuelson to attend the interview as Clinton's attorneys even though they were also witnesses in the investigation; and the decision to conduct a voluntary interview rather than subpoena Clinton before the grand jury.

A.   Decision to Conduct Clinton's Interview Last

Witnesses told us that interviewing Clinton at the end of the investigation was logical. Prosecutor 3 told us that generally if investigators want to determine whether someone "at the top" is culpable, they first want to see what "lower level people have to say." Prosecutor 3 told us that none of the prosecutors or agents disagreed with the decision to interview Clinton last.

Witnesses told us that in the Midyear case in particular it made sense to start at the bottom, because lower level people generally originated the emails containing classified information on unclassified systems and sent them to Clinton's closer aides who, in turn, forwarded them to Clinton. Prosecutor 1 explained:

> [T]he natural thing to do was work your way up the chain. And I say chain, but I also mean email chain.... And just get to the, get to the end. The Secretary's email system was obviously the sort of foundation of all of this and why it became an issue. So we needed to understand the thinking in, in setting that up. So we naturally wanted to do her last. Also, doing interviews in that order in my experience allows you not to have to come back in serial fashion to the higher-level people who it's harder to get time with them.

Toscas stated that the team wanted to ask the lower level employees who originated the emails that turned out to be classified why they wrote the emails on unclassified systems, before asking the same questions of Clinton's aides and Clinton herself. Comey told us that one of the strategies behind interviewing Clinton last was that the interviewing agents would know enough information from other witnesses that they could test Clinton's credibility by asking her questions to which they already knew the answers.

B.   Number of People Attending ("Loaded for Bear" Text Message)

Witnesses told us that there were disagreements within the Midyear team regarding who should attend the interviews of certain key players in the investigation. They stated that Laufman insisted on attending certain interviews, including Clinton's interview, although he normally did not attend interviews. The FBI took the position that if Laufman would be at an interview, Strzok, who was roughly his counterpart at the FBI, should also be at the same interview.

Strzok and Page told us, and contemporaneous emails and notes show, that they and other members of the Midyear team, including the line prosecutors, were concerned about the number of people attending Clinton's interview and Laufman's insistence on attending. These discussions started well before Clinton's July 2 interview.[110] On February 24, 2016, Strzok emailed Priestap that Laufman had called him earlier stating that he "felt strongly about DoJ bringing four attorneys ([Laufman] + 3), and that he was going to raise it up his chain." Strzok further wrote that he told Laufman that raising the issue up the chain would be "necessary because the DD had indicated the group should be 2-2," meaning two agents and two prosecutors. Strzok forwarded this email to Page and another employee, who was also an advisor to McCabe, two minutes later. Strzok told us, and the email chain that followed shows, that Strzok agreed with McCabe that two agents and two prosecutors would be ideal, but he was amenable to three agents and three prosecutors as a compromise. However, both McCabe and Strzok were opposed to allowing four prosecutors to attend the interview.

Later that evening, Strzok and Page exchanged several text messages about the dilemma over how many people should attend Clinton's interview. Based on a review of this exchange, Strzok was concerned that if only two agents and two prosecutors attended the interview and Laufman insisted on being one of the prosecutors, it would be difficult for Strzok to decide whether to send two case agents or himself and one case agent. The following text messages were part of this exchange. The sender of each message is identified after the timestamp.

> 10:32 p.m., Page: "Do you or Bill [Priestap] fundamentally believe that 3 and 3 is the RIGHT thing for the case? If the answer is no, then you call [McCabe's advisor] back and say we're good as is. You have never wavered from saying 2 and 2 is best. I don't get what the hesitation is now."

> 10:52 p.m., Page: "One more thing: she might be our next president. The last thing you need us going in there loaded for bear. You think she's going to remember or care that it was more doj than fbi?"

> 10:56 p.m., Strzok: "Agreed."

Page sent a similar text message to an advisor to McCabe a few minutes after her text message to Strzok, and later to McCabe himself. With McCabe's advisor, she had the following exchange.

> 10:56 p.m., Page: "Hey, if you have one opportunity to discuss further with andy, please convey the following: She might be our next president. The last thing we need is us going in there loaded for bear, when it is not operationally necessary. You think she's going to remember or care that it was more doj than fbi? This is as much about reputational protection as anything."

> 11:00 p.m., Advisor: "I'll catch him before the morning brief to give him this nugget....

---

[110] Both FBI and Department witnesses, including Comey, told us that the Midyear team had originally planned to interview Clinton much earlier, but the interview was delayed because other tasks took longer than expected to complete.

The next morning, on February 25, 2016, this exchange continued as follows.

> 4:10 a.m., Page: "Hey I'll just text andy this morning with my thought."

> 4:11 a.m., Advisor: "Sounds good."

The text message to McCabe was on February 25, 2016, at 7:41 a.m.:

> Page: "Hey, you've surely already considered this, but in my view our best reason to hold the line at 2 and 2 is: She might be our next president. The last thing we need is us going in there loaded for bear, when it is not operationally necessary. You think she's going to remember or care that it was more doj than fbi? This is as much about reputational protection as anything."

The next text message exchange between McCabe and Page was in the evening on February 25, 2016:

> 9:16 p.m., Page: "Hey I'm sorry. It's just wildly aggravating how much churn has gone on this. Have a good night."

> 9:50 p.m., McCabe: "Agree. Strongly."

Page told us that the term "loaded for bear" in her mind meant "a ton of people," such that the FBI was "trying to intimidate." She stated that the message she was trying to send in her text message was not that Clinton should be treated differently, but that she should be handled the same as any other witness the FBI interviews. She further stated that as a former prosecutor her "personal preference" would be to not have too many people in an interview, because "[t]hat's just sort of not conducive to both rapport-building and also just...what it looks like...just pure optics." In addition, she told us that she believed the additional interviewers were "unnecessary" and "if there is no value to be added, then we should do things the way we always do things, which is with a smaller, more discrete footprint." She further told us that, while "it's irrelevant whether or not [Clinton]...would or would not become president...if she did become president, I don't want her left with a feeling that...the FBI marched in with an army of 50 in order to interview me." In other words, Page stated that her concern had to do with the "reputational risk" to the FBI.

McCabe's advisor told us that he was not substantively involved in the Midyear investigation but, as an advisor to McCabe, he was sometimes present when Midyear was discussed at meetings and copied on emails in which Midyear was discussed. He stated that he believed that he was involved in the late February conversations regarding how many Midyear team members should attend Clinton's interview, because he was filling in for Page at one point during the conversations. McCabe's advisor told us that he did not recall the above text message exchange with Page, likely because he was not substantively involved with the issues and was distracted at the time he received it. McCabe's advisor stated that he "did not know that the fact that [Clinton] might be our next President might be one of those motivating factors in Pete's or in Lisa's mind in determining the size of the interview team." After reviewing the text message exchange during his OIG interview he stated:

> My reaction to that is that that should not be a consideration in, in determining the right investigative step to take in the investigation, in determining the size of the team, the interview team. That...should have no bearing on it. What's right for the case is right for the case, and that's how we should make our decisions.

However, Strzok told us that he did not take Page's comment to mean that "we need to treat her differently because she's the next president." He further told us, "I am certain I made no decision based on anything [Clinton] might be or become." Strzok stated that strategically, to obtain "the best answer" it is "always ideal" to conduct an interview with "two agents and the subject." He went on: "Now, if they want counsel, fine. If you have a DOJ attorney, fine. But ideally...my experience is the smaller the setting, the more effective the interview." Strzok told us that the only relevance of her being the next president was that "you don't want the president thinking you're a bunch of clowns."

Similarly, McCabe stated that the "typical" way to run an interview is with two agents and one attorney, and "one of the reasons for doing that is to kind of keep the interviewees...defenses a little bit lower and not make people so concerned." He stated that he understood Page to be saying in her text message that she would not want the future president to think the FBI was "a bunch of...brutes." In addition, McCabe told us that when he wrote that he "agree[d] strongly" with Page, he was agreeing that it was "ridiculous that we're still talking about who is going to what interview from which side," not that the team should not go into Clinton's interview too aggressively.

Several other FBI and Department witnesses we interviewed corroborated Page's, Strzok's, and McCabe's testimony that typically the FBI limits the number of interviewers in an interview for strategic investigative purposes, and that Laufman's insistence on attending certain interviews caused frustration within the FBI. For example, Agent 2 stated, "when the room gets too big...it's hard as the interviewer to try to build that connection with the person you're interviewing...to get a good interview." AAG Carlin told us that disputes regarding which prosecutors and agents will attend an interview are common. He further told us that "to do an effective interview you don't want to have 50 people in the room." As noted in Section VI of this chapter, Laufman told us that he attended the interviews of Clinton and other key witnesses to ensure that those interviews were handled properly and to ensure that he had a complete picture of the investigation before accepting the FBI's and the prosecutors' recommendations.

Ultimately, Clinton's interview was attended by Agents 1 and 2, Strzok, Laufman, and all four line prosecutors. McCabe stated that the number of people that ultimately attended Clinton's interview shows that investigative steps were not influenced by a desire to go easy on Clinton. In addition, multiple witnesses told us that they never heard anyone discussing the need to go easy on Clinton in light of her candidacy for president and that any such discussions would have been inappropriate. Carlin stated that such discussions would have been "thoroughly unacceptable and no one on our team would have done that."

C.   Conduct of Clinton's Interview

Both agents and prosecutors told us that by the time of Clinton's interview they did not believe criminal charges were likely because they had conducted all other investigative steps and, absent a confession from Clinton, they had concluded that there was insufficient evidence of intent. Comey told us that by early May 2016 (when he circulated a first draft of a public statement recommending that the Midyear investigation be closed without prosecution), the team had not "found anything that seemed to the team or to me as a case that DOJ would prosecute" and he had a "reasonable confidence read at this point that barring something else, this looks like it's on a path" toward declination. However, he stated that if Clinton had "lied to us in a way that we thought we could prove, that would have changed everything." Prosecutor 1 stated that there were important topics the team wanted to cover with Clinton, including whether she was aware that classified information was present in her emails, her understanding of the highly classified SAP material contained in some of her emails, why she used a private email account on a private server, and security measures she took when emailing overseas.

Agents 1 and 2 were the case agents that conducted Clinton's interview, in the presence of all four prosecutors, Laufman, Strzok, and Clinton's attorneys. Witnesses told us that Agent 2 focused on questioning Clinton regarding her involvement in emails that the FBI determined to contain classified information, while Agent 1 questioned her regarding her server and the production of emails to the State Department by her attorneys.

As discussed in Chapter Twelve, we identified instant messages from Agent 1 that raised concerns about potential bias. This included an instant message exchange on November 8, 2016 (Election Day), between Agent 1 and Agent 5 (who were in a relationship at the time and are now married), in which Agent 1 messaged, "You should know;…. that I'm…. with her."[111] (Punctuation in original). Additionally, we observed instant messages in which Agent 1 expressed concerns about the quality of the Midyear investigation, as described in Section XI of this chapter. Two of the instant message exchanges we identified occurred close in time to the Clinton interview.

On June 28, 2016, four days before the Clinton interview, Agent 1 sent an instant message complaining about the numerous people involved in preparing for the Clinton interview. Agent 1 messaged, "…very aggravating making this flow with 20+ voices for disparate information anyway. We have nothing – shouldn't [sic] even be interviewing. Today, someone said we really need to call out that she had two phones when her excuse not to have a state bb [State Department Blackberry] in the first place was because she didnt [sic] want to carry two phones." Agent 1 sent a series of messages that continued, "My god…. I'm

---

[111] "I'm with her" was one of the Clinton campaign slogans.

actually starting to have embarrassment sprinkled on my disappointment.... Ever been forced to do something you adamantly opposed."

We asked Agent 1 about this instant message exchange. He told us that when he wrote "20+ voices" he was referring to the number of FBI and Department employees involved in the Clinton interview preparation. He stated that Agent 2 and he were "working together well," and they "just kept saying to each other when are we going to actually have time to prepare for this other than prepare everyone else for it?" He stated that the frustration expressed in the instant message exchange was related to his sense that Midyear was not the "normal" case where the FBI "culminate[s]" with an interview of a subject who introduced classified information onto an unclassified system, unlike Clinton who mostly received classified material from others. We asked Agent 1 if he thought that the Clinton interview was unnecessary. Agent 1 told us he thought the interview was necessary and stated:

> I think we needed to get statements from the Secretary about what she knew this information to be, she was the Secretary of State, so if you thought this was classified, why did you not, if you had an impression it was classified, why did you not stop it, or why did you not say to the people that were underneath you that you should handle this better? What did you know about where it was? How do you understand a server to, to work, and do you know that a copy resides there? Those types of things, to include a couple that we found. I don't, I don't want to make it sound like there was no reason to interview her. That, including, including a couple of emails we found where there were portion markings, what we thought to be portion markings inside of the email. And she had made statements before that...there were no emails that were marked classified.

Agent 1 told us that he did not know what he meant by "forced to do something you adamantly opposed." Agent 1 stated that this may have been a reference to not being able to prevent Mills and Samuelson from attending the Clinton interview.

On July 6, 2016, four days after Clinton's interview, Agent 1 sent an instant message in which he stated that he was "done interviewing the President," referring to Clinton. We asked Agent 1 if he thought of Clinton as the next president while conducting the Midyear investigation. Agent 1 stated, "I think my impression going into the election in that personal realm is that all of the polls were favoring Hillary Clinton." We asked Agent 1 if he treated Clinton differently because of this assumption. Agent 1 stated, "Absolutely not. I think the message they said that our leadership told us and our actions were to find whatever was there and whatever, whatever that means is what it means."

We interviewed all eight of the FBI and Department officials that attended Clinton's interview, and none of the witnesses we interviewed expressed concerns about the way the case agents handled the interview. Prosecutor 1 told us that Prosecutors 1 and 2 and the case agents did "most of the talking during the interview," which was "led by the agents." Prosecutor 1 further told us that

135

generally "agents would lead [the interviews], and attorneys would interject as needed, and we'd pause after different, as we transitioned to make sure things were covered." In addition, Prosecutor 1 stated that, "The agents had a good rapport with [Clinton]." Prosecutor 1 further stated, generally, that the agents did a "good job" in interviews and that he did not have concerns about the agents not "pushing hard enough."

Based on a review of the FD-302 and contemporaneous notes from Clinton's interview, Clinton told the Midyear team that she chose to use a personal Blackberry connected to her personal email account for official communications for convenience, and she denied using personal email or a personal server to avoid FOIA or Federal Records Act requirements. Clinton further told the FBI that during her tenure she received classified information through secure briefings, secure calls, classified hard documents, and classified faxes, and she "did not recall receiving any emails she thought should not be on an unclassified system." According to the FD-302, Clinton stated that she was aware that her email was supported by a private server, but she did not know the details of the different server systems she used. The FD-302 indicated that the interviewers showed Clinton numerous unmarked emails she had received containing information that was determined to have been classified. Clinton responded with respect to each email that she did not believe the information contained in the email was classified or that she relied on the State Department employees who worked for her to use their judgment in determining whether information was classified and appropriate to send on unclassified systems. Agent 1 told us that the interviewers asked "probing questions" with respect to each of Clinton's responses. Prosecutor 1 told us, and our review of other FD-302s showed, that Clinton's responses to these questions were consistent with the testimony of other witnesses on the email chains, including Clinton's senior aides who forwarded classified information to her.

The FD-302 and contemporaneous notes indicate that the interviewers asked Clinton about her understanding of her record keeping obligations, the culling process that was used to provide her work-related emails to the State Department, and the deletion of emails from her server. According to the FD-302, Clinton told the FBI, among other things, that she did not recall being asked to turn over her email records upon her departure from State and that she believed her work-related emails were "captured by her practice of sending them to state.gov email addresses of her staff." She stated that, upon receiving a request from the State Department in 2014, she "expected" her attorneys to turn over any emails that were "work-related or arguably work-related," but she did not otherwise participate in developing the culling process. Agent 1 told us, consistent with the FD-302, that he pressed her on her lack of involvement in the State Department production, by showing her a work-related email that was not produced as part of the 30,490. Clinton responded that she agreed that the email was work-related and did not know why it was not included in the State Department production. Clinton told the FBI that in December 2014, after the production of her work-related emails to the State Department, her staff asked her what she wanted to do with her personal emails and she responded that she "did not need them anymore." The FD-302 states that "Clinton never deleted, nor did she instruct anyone to delete, her email

136

to avoid complying with Federal Records Act, FOIA, or State or FBI requests for information" and that she "trusted her legal team" would comply with the March 3, 2015 Congressional preservation request.

In addition, the interviewers asked Clinton about an email that contained a parenthetical with a "(C)" at the beginning. According to the prosecutors, Clinton received three email chains during her State Department tenure that contained at least one paragraph that began with a '(C),' a classification marking used to denote information classified at the Confidential level. The prosecutors stated that these were the only emails containing classification markings that the FBI identified during its investigation, the emails did not contain any markings other than the one or two paragraphs in each email beginning with a "(C)," and as of July 6, 2016, the State Department had not responded to the FBI's request for a determination as to as to whether the information in these three emails was classified at the time the emails were sent. The prosecutors further stated that the State Department had determined through the FOIA process that only one of the three emails contained information that was classified as of July 6, 2016, and that this email was classified at the Confidential level. According to the FD-302 from Clinton's interview, Clinton told the FBI that she did not know what the "(C)" meant and "speculated it was a reference to paragraphs ranked in alphabetical order." The FD-302 indicates that the FBI had added a classification marking of "Confidential" to the top of the document and that, upon noticing this marking, Clinton asked if the "(C)" meant Confidential. Clinton told the interviewers that she did not agree that the information contained in the email was classified, because it described information that was already in the press. Witnesses told us, and contemporaneous emails show, that the FBI and Department officials who attended Clinton's interview found that her claim that she did not understand the significance of the "(C)" marking strained credulity. Agent 1 stated, "I filed that in the bucket of hard to impossible to believe." Agent 1 further stated that he and the other interviewers asked Clinton about her understanding of the "(C)" markings four or five times, but she did not change her answer. He told us, "I also don't know at that point in the interview what else we could have done besides all the different ways that we asked it."

Comey told us that one of the purposes of interviewing Clinton was to see if she would be truthful. However, he stated that the agents that conducted the interview found her credible and were surprised at how "technically illiterate" she was. While Comey did not specifically comment on the team's reactions to Clinton's testimony regarding the "(C)" portion markings, he stated, "By her demeanor, she was credible and open and all that kind of stuff, but—so I can't sit here and tell you I believed her. I can only tell you, in no particular could we prove that she was being untruthful to us." The prosecutors similarly indicated that the team did not believe it could prove that Clinton had been dishonest during her interview or that she knew that the document with the "(C)" marking was classified. The prosecutors stated that the "(C)" markings were somewhat ambiguous given their placement in the email chains and the fact that the classification marking 'Confidential' was not spelled out anywhere in the email, let alone in a readily apparent manner. They further stated that Clinton's statement regarding her knowledge of the "(C)" marking was not one that could be affirmatively disproved.

D. Decision to Allow Mills and Samuelson to Attend Clinton Interview

According to the FD-302 for Clinton's interview, Mills and Samuelson attended the interview as Clinton's counsel, in addition to Clinton's three attorneys from the Williams and Connolly law firm. Numerous FBI and Department witnesses told us that they were opposed to Mills and Samuelson attending Clinton's interview, because Mills and Samuelson were also witnesses in the investigation. They stated that they were concerned both that Mills and Samuelson could influence Clinton's testimony and that their presence would be bad from an "optics" standpoint.

Prosecutor 1 told us that the prosecutors first learned that Mills and Samuelson planned to attend Clinton's interview less than a week before the interview took place. Witnesses told us that the prosecutors contacted Kendall to discuss their concerns about Mills and Samuelson attending, but that Kendall "pushed back." Several Midyear team members stated, and contemporaneous notes show, that after the call with Kendall the Midyear team conferred more than once and that everyone agreed that, although they were not comfortable with the situation, they could not prevent Clinton from bringing her counsel of choice to a voluntary interview. Laufman stated, "We gave careful thought to whether we had any grounds to bar admission to Mills and Samuelson from the interview of Secretary Clinton. And we determined we did not have a legal or bar rule-slash-ethics based premise to do so." Several witnesses also told us that they were more concerned with the "optics" of Mills and Samuelson attending than them influencing Clinton's testimony, because they were confident that Clinton had already been well prepared by her attorneys and had probably conferred with Mills and Samuelson in advance of the interview in any event (which the investigators could not prevent).

Based on the evidence we reviewed, the issue of Mills's and Samuelson's attendance was raised up the chain within the FBI through former Director Comey and within NSD through Toscas. According to FBI Attorney 1, the issue was discussed at a meeting she attended that included Comey, McCabe, Baker, Rybicki, Deputy General Counsel Anderson, EAD Steinbach, AD Priestap, Strzok, Page, and the Lead Analyst. FBI Attorney 1 stated that the lawyers in the meeting, including Comey, all agreed that there was no legal basis to exclude Mills and Samuelson from the interview. Comey told us that he could not remember the specifics of his conversations regarding Mills and Samuelson attending the Clinton interview; however, he stated that he believed "it was a fairly brief discussion because our judgment was it's an essential interview, we've washed them out. We've looked at their conduct pretty carefully and so those two things together, so we don't really have a basis for excluding...either of them from the interview."

Lynch and Yates both told us they did not recall being briefed on Mills and Samuelson attending Clinton's interview. Carlin told us, "I don't remember [Mills's and Samuelson's attendance] being a major issue so I'm assuming they worked that out without, I kind of more was just briefed that that was occurring rather than that there was some dispute over it."

The prosecutors told us that the team put a plan in place to prevent Mills or Samuelson from influencing Clinton's testimony: if Mills or Samuelson "actively involved themselves in the interview" they would address the issue further at that time, possibly through a "side bar" with Kendall. The prosecutors and agents that attended the interview all told us that ultimately Mills and Samuelson did not interfere or object, engage in side-bars with Clinton, or speak substantively during the interview. Rather, Prosecutor 1 told us that Clinton's Williams and Connolly attorneys did the "actual...lawyering, such that there was any there."

Prosecutor 1 stated that they did not consult PRAO regarding the ethical implications of Mills's and Samuelson's attendance. We asked the prosecutors whether they spoke to Wilkinson about their concerns or suggested to Wilkinson that her clients' attendance could violate their own ethical duties, given that at the time of the culling testimony and laptop dispute Wilkinson had indicated that her client's interests were different from Clinton's in the Midyear investigation.[112] They told us they had not done so, and Laufman stated he did not recall considering those ethical concerns. However, Laufman and FBI Attorney 1 both told us that if there was such a conflict, Clinton could waive it. In addition, Prosecutor 1 stated that the team did not question at the time of the Clinton interview whether Mills and Samuelson in fact had ongoing attorney-client relationships with Clinton, because the prosecutors had already concluded there were ongoing attorney-client relationships when they sought subpoenas for the culling laptops.[113]

E.   Consideration of Subpoenaing Clinton before the Grand Jury

We asked several witnesses whether they considered subpoenaing Clinton before the grand jury in order to avoid Mills's and Samuelson's presence at the interview. We also asked whether they considered simply refusing to interview Clinton if she insisted on having Mills and Samuelson present, given the pressure on Clinton to cooperate with the investigation—in other words, whether the Midyear team underestimated its strategic position against Clinton's attorneys.

Some witnesses told us that use of the grand jury was the only way to legally prevent Mills and Samuelson from attending, but that the team did not seriously consider that option. Prosecutor 4 stated:

---

[112] In the March 31, 2016 PRAO request seeking advice on whether the prosecutors could seek a waiver of attorney-client privilege from Kendall, Laufman wrote that Wilkinson had represented that her clients' interests "may differ from, or conflict with" Clinton's interests.

[113] As part of the application for the subpoenas for the laptops, the prosecutors had to answer whether Mills and Samuelson had ongoing attorney client relationships with Clinton and whether the subpoenas would have any potential adverse effects on those relationships. The prosecutors wrote in the applications that Wilkinson had represented that Mills and Samuelson continued to have attorney-client relationships with Clinton, but that "the nature and scope of that representation is unclear given that the former Secretary has separate counsel (David Kendall) representing her during this investigation." They further wrote, "Even if [Mills and Samuelson are] representing Clinton in conjunction with this matter, it is highly unlikely that issuance of the subpoena would result in Mills being disqualified from representing the former Secretary."

I thought Mills being present was idiotic. And I believe that [Prosecutor 1] and I talked about it. And I said, well, look, we cannot exclude her as a legal matter unless we are willing to threaten to throw Hillary in the grand jury, at which point I'm fairly confident that they will fold. And [Prosecutor 1] and I discussed it. And I don't know if he ever raised that possibility. But it was obvious to me that nobody was willing to, to threaten, to threaten Hillary in the grand jury.

However, Prosecutor 4 stated that his concern about Mills and Samuelson attending Clinton's interview was "from an optics standpoint" and that "from my vantage point, the cost-benefit analysis of trying to go through and get somebody to authorize me to threaten to throw Hillary in the grand jury was not worth getting the, the interview done at that point." Prosecutor 3 told us that if the Midyear team insisted that Mills and Samuelson not attend, Clinton likely would have relented because of her desire to say publicly that she cooperated with the investigation. Other FBI and Department witnesses we interviewed told us that they simply did not consider these options.

The SSA told us that it would have been anomalous to subpoena Clinton before the grand jury given that no other witnesses had testified before the grand jury and Clinton, like the other witnesses, was cooperating. Strzok told us that the team decided against subpoenaing Clinton to testify before the grand jury because "the expectation of the information we would get from her in either setting was not substantively different," given that she had "extraordinary counsel" preparing her.

Toscas told us that if Clinton had been required to testify before the grand jury, members of the FBI team would not have been able to participate in the interview. In addition, Laufman, Prosecutor 1, and FBI Attorney 1 told us that admitting classified information before the grand jury would have involved an uncertain and lengthy process of obtaining approvals from the various government agencies that owned the classified information. Prosecutor 1 stated that, even if the approvals could be obtained, it is better to avoid sharing classified information with the grand jury, if possible.

Laufman stated that subpoenaing Clinton to testify before the grand jury would have been "a grossly disproportionate course of action in relation to what we were dealing with and [out of] step with how we had previously been conducting the investigation throughout its course." He further stated, "[W]e did not think this was worth blowing up the investigation, and, and creating what almost certainly would have become a matter of public knowledge that we had suddenly issued a grand jury subpoena to the Secretary at this stage of the national electoral process." He explained that throughout the investigation the team was attempting to avoid "extrinsic information" from the investigation being publicly disclosed and used for political purposes, and this was no exception.

Witnesses told us that at the point of Clinton's interview, they had conducted all other investigative steps and knew that there was insufficient evidence to prosecute Clinton unless she incriminated herself. Laufman told us that because the prosecutors did not believe a subsequent trial was likely, they were not concerned that Mills's or Samuelson's later testimony would be influenced by being privy to Clinton's interview. Prosecutor 4 told us that if he had the investigation to do over again, the one thing he would have done differently was "insist that Mills not attend the Hillary interview." However, he also stated that at that point he agreed with the rest of the team that there was no prosecutable case and the main reason to have put her in the grand jury was to avoid subjecting the investigation to criticism.[114]

Comey told us that he did not remember discussing with anyone the possibility of subpoenaing Clinton before the grand jury. However, he stated:

> At that point, I really didn't think there was a there there, and the question was, is she going to lie to us? She'd be as likely to lie to us in a grand jury or in an interview. And I just suppose in the grand jury is you've got the transcript, but we've got a bunch of agents taking notes, so I don't think it would've mattered much to me at that point.

X.   FBI Inspection Division Internal File Review of the Midyear Investigation

In September and October 2017, the FBI assigned three SSAs (File Review SSAs) from the Boston Field Office to the FBI's Inspection Division (INSD) to conduct a special review of the Midyear investigation (File Review).[115] Baker told us that he proposed the File Review after being informed of the OIG's discovery of text messages between Strzok and Page expressing political views. He stated that once he learned of the text messages, he suggested to EAD Carl Ghattas and possibly other senior FBI officials that a review team be brought in to "look at the case and all the decisions that were made in a quiet way." Baker further stated that the purposes of the File Review were to "make sure that [Strzok, Page,] or others did not make decisions in the case based on improper political considerations, including failing to taken actions they should have," and to "make sure that, from a management perspective, if other steps needed to be taken, we should find that out quickly and take those steps, including reopening the investigation." He told us that they decided that the File Review team would not interview witnesses, because they did not want to interfere with the ongoing OIG review. Baker stated that Ghattas took the lead on the review.

Two of the SSAs who conducted the File Review had experience in the FBI's Criminal Investigative Division (CID) while the third SSA had experience in the FBI's Counterintelligence Division (CD). The File Review SSAs told us that Ghattas requested that they do the File Review, and that they met with Ghattas in FBI

---

[114] Prosecutor 4 stated that once he realized there was no prosecutable case, he had two goals in the investigation: "One was to conduct the investigation quickly to get it resolved before the election, as soon before the election as possible. And the second was to do it in a way that would engender public trust to the maximum extent possible."

[115] Due to fact that the OIG's review was ongoing at the time, the FBI sought and obtained permission from the OIG to conduct the File Review.

Headquarters at the start of their review. They stated that they were instructed not to discuss their review with other FBI employees. The File Review SSAs also told us that they were not told about the text messages between Strzok and Page before the start of the review. Baker told us he was unaware that the File Review SSAs were not told about the text messages before the start of the File Review.

File Review SSAs 2 and 3 told us that they understood the purpose of the review to be to assess what the Midyear investigators appeared to have done well, what investigative steps were missed, and what lessons could be learned from the investigation. File Review SSA 2 stated that the File Review was not intended to be a reinvestigation. The File Review SSAs told us that their review was limited, by design, to the official FBI Midyear file. They did not interview any witnesses nor did they review any documents that were not included in the official file, such as handwritten notes taken by Midyear team members during meetings, emails or text messages sent or received by Midyear team members, or materials maintained by the prosecutors or others Department officials. They also did not review SAP material. File Review SSA 2 told us that the team did not "intend [for the file review] necessarily to be a...final...judgment or indictment on the FBI or on WFO or the case agents. It was more just...here are our observations, and here are some questions...should anyone else...take a look at this...take this into consideration. That's kind of all we intended by it."

The File Review SSAs told us, consistent with their File Review Report, that they conducted their review over the course of six days, between September 5 and September 8, 2017, and between October 3 and 4, 2017; however, the first day was mostly spent meeting with Ghattas and locating the records to review. They stated that thereafter they spent approximately 12 hours per day reviewing records in the official file, discussing items they came across that caused them concern, and recording information in spreadsheets. File Review SSAs 2 and 3 told us that each File Review SSA focused on a different portion of the file, and none of them individually reviewed the entire file. During the course of their review, in addition to reviewing and discussing the records, the File Review SSAs completed a first draft of the File Review Report, which File Review SSA 1 finalized with minor edits thereafter. The File Review SSAs told us that they all approved the final File Review Report.

Under the heading "FBI Investigative Actions," the File Review Report stated:

The [File] Review Team's analysis of the MIDYEAR EXAM investigation did not find substantial or significant areas of investigative oversight based on the stated goals of the investigation. In contrast, [the File Review Team] assessed [that] the [Midyear] investigative team conducted a thorough investigation within the constraints imposed by DOJ. Appropriate witnesses were interviewed, records preserved, information and computer devices obtained, and necessary business records were subpoenaed to meet the goals of the investigation. FBI resources such as [Computer Analysis and Recovery Team (CART) personnel], Intelligence personnel, communication analysis, and Cyber Agents were skillfully and successfully utilized to review and fully

142

exploit substantial amounts of data in support of the investigation....
The efforts of the case Agents and case team should be commended.

Nonetheless, the File Review Report also contained criticisms of the Midyear investigation. Generally, the File Review Report assessed that it would have been better to run the Midyear investigation as a traditional criminal investigation out of a Criminal Investigative Division (CID) field office, rather than as a counterintelligence investigation out of CD. The File Review SSAs expressed concern that treating the investigation as a CD investigation with NSD oversight resulted in more limited use of compulsory process such as grand jury subpoenas and search warrants. However, the File Review SSAs told the OIG that they were not aware of any precedent for handling a counterintelligence investigation out of CID. File Review SSA 2 stated that counterintelligence investigations "are always run out of the Counterintelligence Division."[116]

The File Review SSAs identified specific concerns with the Midyear investigation, although we found that many of these concerns were the result of the fact that the File Review SSAs had incomplete information. For example, the File Review Report states, "No immunity in exchange for testimony was observed in the investigation," and "[o]ne instance of a proffer letter was observed," referring to the limited use immunity agreement between the Department and John Bentel. The File Review SSAs told us that they were unaware that the Midyear prosecutors also entered into letter use immunity agreements with Combetta and Pagliano.[117]

The File Review SSAs told us, consistent with the File Review Report, that they believed the Midyear agents relied too heavily on outlines during interviews and did not ask sufficient follow-up questions. However, they stated that they based this assessment only on their review of the FD-302s. The Midyear SSA and Agent 1 told us that the CD Division does not draft FD-302s in such a way that a reader would know what follow-up questions were asked of witnesses; instead, the FD-302s generally set forth each witness's ultimate statements in response to series of questions.

In addition, the File Review SSAs told us that they considered the DIOG, but did not consider any Department policies, such as the USAM, regarding guidelines for obtaining evidence relevant to the Midyear investigation. For example, they

---

[116] The File Review Report also described a concern that the Midyear Team was "directly supervised by CD-4 personnel [in FBIHQ] as opposed to an SSA and ASAC as found during field office investigations." In fact, at the time the Midyear investigation began, Strzok was an ASAC in the FBI's Washington Field Office (WFO) and the Midyear SSA was an SSA in WFO.

[117] Additionally, the File Review Report expressed a concern regarding the timing of the Pagliano declination letter, but we found that this concern was based on incomplete information. The report stated, "It was unclear to the [file] review team the need for such an expedited prosecution declination." However, the File Review SSAs told us they were unaware that the declination concerned only Pagliano's compensation from the Clintons (for which PIN ultimately determined he faced no criminal exposure), and not the mishandling of classified information or destruction of federal records.

stated they did not consult the USAM provisions regarding obtaining evidence from attorneys concerning their representation of clients.

Based on these findings, the report concluded:

INSD assessed the FBI Midyear Exam investigation successfully determined classified information was improperly stored and transmitted on Clinton's email server, and classified information was compromised by unauthorized individuals, to include foreign government's or intelligence services, via cyber intrusion or other means [referring to compromises of email accounts associated with certain individuals who communicated with Clinton's server, such as Blumenthal]. However, the structure of the investigation and prosecution team, as prescribed in the CD PG, and treatment of the investigation as a traditional espionage matter rather than a criminal investigation significantly hindered the ability of the investigative team to obtain full, accurate and timely information.

XI. Instant Messages Relating to the Conduct of the Midyear Investigation

FBI employees have the ability to communicate internally via Microsoft Lync instant messages when logged on to their FBI workstation. As part of our review, the OIG identified contemporaneous instant messages in which Agent 1 expressed concerns about the quality of the Midyear investigation. These messages were sent to numerous FBI employees, including an agent assigned to the Midyear filter team (Agent 5). Agent 1 and Agent 5, who are now married, were in a relationship for the entirety of the Midyear investigation. We identified additional instant messages sent by Agent 1 and Agent 5 that raised concerns about potential bias. We discuss these messages and others in Chapter Twelve.

The Midyear filter team was responsible for conducting an initial review of evidence obtained during the investigation and ensuring that nothing that was either beyond the scope of the FBI's authority to review or protected by a valid privilege was provided to the investigative team. We found that Agent 1 and Agent 5 exchanged numerous instant messages about the Midyear investigation. However, we identified no instances where Agent 5 provided Midyear-related information to Agent 1 that should have been withheld from the investigative team. Agent 1 and Agent 5 told us that their Midyear supervisors were aware of their relationship by the end of 2015 at the latest and it was never identified as a concern.

We asked Agent 1 generally about his use of instant messaging on his FBI workstation. Agent 1 told us that he believed that instant messages were not retained by the FBI and therefore used less caution with those communications than he would have with other types of communications, such as email or text messages. Agent 1 also repeatedly emphasized that the instant messages served as a type of emotional release for him. Agent 1 stated:

I took that [instant messaging] as an informal, akin to a conversation almost, almost, you know, water cooler style. I think in there....
There is personal and emotional communications between my then girlfriend, now wife. There is some jocularity there. There is, you know, I think, I think some outlet, stress outlet....

You know, guys, I just, I think this was primarily used as a personal conversation venting mode for me. I'm embarrassed for it. I don't think that it affected my actions.

Agent 1 told us that the nature of his workspace also contributed to his use of instant messaging. Agent 1 explained that for the Midyear investigation he was relocated to FBI Headquarters and placed inside a SCIF with others on the Midyear team. Due to this, he was effectively unable to use his personal electronic devices at work and was also in a small space with his coworkers and supervisors, thereby preventing phone communication. Agent 1 emphasized that these were not excuses for the substance of his instant messages, but explanations for why he used them as an outlet for "stress relief" about frustrations he encountered at work. Agent 1 described his instant messages with Agent 5 as personal communications with his significant other that they used for mutual support and complaints. Similarly, Agent 1 stated his instant messages with FBI personnel not assigned to the Midyear investigations were typically communications with friends. He also noted that many of these communications were initiated by FBI personnel seeking information on the Midyear investigation. Agent 5 echoed many of Agent 1's explanations, stating that she considered instant messaging to be a private channel to communicate with Agent 1. Agent 5 told us that Agent 1 was her outlet at work for "emotional outbursts" and "relief of stress."

Agent 1 sent instant messages in the initial months of the Midyear investigation commenting on the investigation. Some of these messages are listed below, along with the date sent and the recipient.

September 2, 2015, to Agent 5: "Have a really bad feeling about this...this case...situation.... No control and horrible decisions and chaos on the most meaningless thing I've ever done with people acting like fucking 9/11."

September 25, 2015, to an FBI employee: "...I dont care about it. I think its continued waste of resources and time and focus...."

October 26, 2015, to Agent 5: "Its just so obvious how pointless this exercise is. And everyone is so into it...."

We asked Agent 1 about these messages. Agent 1 told us that prior to Midyear he had worked on other high-profile cases and part of the sentiment he expressed in these messages was a reluctance to be involved in another high-profile investigation. Agent 1 stated that he knew from prior experience that decisions in such investigation were typically made at higher levels. Agent 1 described the comment about the investigation being "meaningless" as "a little exaggerated" and explained that "maybe the intense scrutiny didn't seem commensurate to what we had to do." Agent 1 explained, "The FBI absolutely needs to investigate why classified information is in a place where it should not be. I just, it would, this is more probably an emotional comment on how scrutinized and how focused and how continued, there's a continued focus on it to this day."

Agent 1 also sent numerous messages that referenced "political" considerations in the context of the Midyear investigation. We list examples of these messages below with the date sent and the content of the message along with context where necessary. Unless otherwise identified, the recipients of the messages are FBI employees not involved in the Midyear investigation.

> January 15, 2016: Responding to a question of when the investigation would be finished, Agent 1 stated, "[M]y guess is March. Doesnt matter what we have, political winds will want to beat the Primarys."

> January 28, 2016: "...The case is the same is all of them. Alot of work and bullshit for a political exercise."

> February 1, 2016: "...Its primary season – so we're being dictated to now...."

> February 1, 2016: "This is the biggest political shit show of them all. No substance. Up at dawn – pride swallowing seige. No headset and hermetically sealed in SIOC."

> February 2, 2016: Responding to a question about how the investigation was going, "Going well.... Busy, and sometimes I feel for naught (political exercise), but I feel good...."

> May 6, 2016, to Agent 5: "pretty bad news today...someone has breathed some political urgency into this.... Everyday DD brief and once a week D brief from now on."

We asked Agent 1 about these messages. Agent 1 stated that he hoped these messages "would just directly reflect upon me and not anybody else that worked the case." He explained that these messages simply reflect the fact that he wanted to work on something besides Midyear. We asked Agent 1 whether these messages indicated that the Midyear investigation was simply an exercise in "going through the motions." Agent 1 responded, "No. I think this investigation needed to be worked." He later continued, "I think if classified information is found in a place that it shouldn't be, there should be an investigation." Agent 1 added that he felt the scrutiny and attention that Midyear received was not "commensurate" with the nature of the violation the team was investigating. As to the messages about timing, Agent 1 told us that at some point in the investigation the "pace" increased and, although the team was never given a "finish by" date, there was "a sense that things were picking up."

On February 9, 2016, Agent 5 sent Agent 1 an instant message complaining about a meeting the filter team had with a Department attorney and the frustrating review task she was assigned. Agent 1 responded:

Yeah, I hear you. You guys have a shitty task, in a shitty environment. To look for something conjured in a place where you cant find it, for a case that doesnt matter and is predestined. All you ask for is acknowledgment of that and clear guidance. But no. DOJ comes in there every once in awhile and takes a wishy-washy, political, cowardice stance. Salt meets wound. That is the environment love. Can't sugar coat it. Now, what? What can you do? What can you control? Work hard, do the best you can, and try to keep others motivated.

After reading this message during his OIG interview, Agent 1 stated:

I have no information that it was a pre-determined outcome by anyone. I had, I had no statement from anyone that I can tell you that I worked with that said this is where we're going.... I think even the leadership that stopped by in the, in the, in our space always said that as well. Whatever you find, you know, is what it is. You know, just, just find what it was, and, you know, don't worry about anything else, the outside noise.

All I can tell you is this is probably, I mean, it's a little overwhelming to see all [these messages] at once, as probably somebody who was, who wanted to do something else, I think.

Agent 1 stated that he could not recall anything specific to add to this exchange.

In another exchange on February 4, 2016, Agent 1 and an FBI employee who was not assigned to the Midyear investigation discussed Agent 1's interview with a witness who assisted the Clintons at their Chappaqua residence. Part of this exchange follows.

FBI Employee: "boom...how did the [witness] go"

Agent 1: "Awesome. Lied his ass off. Went from never inside the scif [sensitive compartmented information facility] at res, to looked in when it was being constructed, to removed the trash twice, to troubleshot the secure fax with HRC a couple times, to everytime there was a secure fax i did it with HRC. Ridic,"

FBI Employee: "would be funny if he was the only guy charged n this deal"

Agent 1: "I know. For 1001. Even if he said the truth and didnt have a clearance when handling the secure fax – aint noone gonna do shit"

We asked Agent 1 about the implication in this message that no one would be charged irrespective of what the team found. Agent 1 stated:

Yeah, I, I don't think I can say there's a specific person that I worked with in this case that wouldn't charge him for that. I think it's a general complaint of, you know, of FBI agents that are kind of, kind of being emotional and, and complaining that no one is going to do something about, about something.... But there's nothing specific that I, that I can tell you.

Agent 1 told us he did not recall any discussion about whether this witness should be charged with a crime.

In a January 19, 2016 message to Agent 4, Agent 1 stated, "What we want to do and what we're going to be allowed to do are two different things." Agent 1 told us that he did not remember this exchange and did not know what he was referring to in this message. However, he stated that he appears "to be venting a little bit" to Agent 4.

XII. Analysis of Investigative Decisions

In this part, we provide our analysis of whether the investigative decisions taken in connection with the Midyear investigation that we reviewed were based on improper considerations, including political bias. As described in the Analytical Construct set forth in Chapter One of this report, we selected for examination particular case decisions that were the subject of public or internal controversy. For each decision, we analyzed whether there was evidence of improper considerations or evidence that the justifications offered for the decision were a pretext for improper, but unstated, considerations. If a choice made by the investigative team was among two or more reasonable alternatives, we did not find that it was improper even if we believed an alternative decision would have been more effective. Thus, a determination by the OIG that a decision was not unreasonable does not mean that the OIG has endorsed the decision or concluded that the decision was the most effective among the options considered. We took this analytical approach because our role as an OIG is not to second-guess valid discretionary judgments made during the course of an investigation, and this approach is consistent with the OIG's handling of such questions in past reviews.

In undertaking this analysis, our task was made significantly more difficult because of the text messages we discovered between Strzok and Page, given the critical roles they played in most of the decisions made by the FBI; the instant messages of Agent 1, who was one of four Midyear case agents; and the instant messages of FBI Attorney 2, who was one of the FBI attorneys assigned to the investigation.[118] That these employees used an FBI system or device to express political views about individuals affected by ongoing investigations for which they were responsible was particularly disappointing in comparison to their colleagues on the Midyear investigative team who, based on the emails, notes, memoranda, and

---

[118] As we describe in this chapter and in Chapter Twelve, many of those messages reflected hostility toward then candidate Trump and statements of support for candidate Clinton, and some of them mixed political commentary with discussions regarding the Midyear investigation.

other materials we reviewed, conducted themselves with professionalism during a difficult and high-pressure investigation.[119]

We were cognizant of and considered these messages in reaching the conclusions regarding the specific investigative decisions discussed below. In particular, we were concerned about text messages exchanged by Strzok and Page that potentially indicated or created the appearance that investigative decisions were impacted by bias or improper considerations. As we describe in Chapter Twelve, most of the text messages raising such questions pertained to the Russia investigation. Nonetheless, the implication in certain Russia-related text messages that Strzok might be willing to take official action to impact presidential candidate Trump's electoral prospects—for example, the August 8, 2016 text exchange in which Page asked Strzok "[Trump's] not ever going to become president, right? Right?!" and Strzok replied "No. No he won't. We'll stop it"—caused us to question the earlier Midyear investigative decisions in which he was involved, and whether he took specific actions in the Midyear investigation based on his political views.[120] As we describe in this chapter, we found that Strzok was not the sole decisionmaker for any of the specific investigative decisions examined in this chapter. We further found evidence that in some instances Strzok and Page advocated for more aggressive investigative measures than did others on the Midyear team, such as the use of grand jury subpoenas and search warrants to obtain evidence.

There were clearly tensions and disagreements in a number of important areas between Midyear agents and prosecutors. However, we did not find documentary or testimonial evidence that improper considerations, including political bias, directly affected the specific investigative decisions discussed below, or that the justifications offered for these decisions were pretextual. We recognize that these text and instant messages cast a cloud over the FBI's handling of the Midyear investigation and the investigation's credibility. But our review did not find documentary or testimonial evidence that these political views directly affected the specific investigative decisions that we reviewed in this chapter. The broader impact of these text and instant messages, including on such matters as the public perception of the FBI and the Midyear investigation, are discussed in Chapter Twelve.

---

[119] As discussed in Section X of this chapter, FBI INSD conducted a File Review of the Midyear investigation. We found that the File Review's ability to assess the Midyear investigation was limited based on the narrow scope of the review and the limited information available to them. We also found that, as a result of the limited information available to the File Review SSAs, a number of the factual statements in the File Review report were inaccurate. Accordingly, the assessments and recommendations of the File Review did not significantly influence the analysis of the OIG, which had a far more developed record, including extensive interviews, as discussed in our report.

[120] As we describe in Chapter Nine, these text messages also caused us to assess Strzok's decision in October 2016 to prioritize the Russia investigation over following up on the Midyear-related investigative lead discovered on the Weiner laptop. We concluded that we did not have confidence that this decision by Strzok was free from bias.

A.   Preference for Consent Rather than Compulsory Process to Obtain Evidence

At the outset we note that, contrary to public perception, the Midyear team used compulsory process in the Midyear investigation. This included grand jury subpoenas, search warrants, and 2703(d) orders. Nonetheless, the Midyear prosecutors told us that they obtained evidence through consent whenever possible. We found no evidence that the use of consent to obtain evidence in the Midyear investigation was based on improper considerations. The decisions regarding how to obtain particular pieces of evidence were primarily made by the career prosecutors, for whom we identified no evidence of political or other bias, and we found that the reasons they provided for those decisions were not unreasonable.

The FBI investigators, attorneys, and supervisors involved with the Midyear investigation—including individuals for whom we identified electronic messages expressing political opinions—advocated for greater use of compulsory process and for more aggressive investigative methods, including the use of search warrants. However, the prosecutors told us that they often chose consent over compulsory process or court orders based on the following considerations: (1) avoiding delay that could result from motions to quash subpoenas or search warrants; (2) complying with Department policies; (3) protecting classified and other sensitive information; (4) avoiding media leaks and public disclosures that could harm the investigation; (5) the perceived obstacles to establishing probable cause; and (6) the risk of improperly accessing privileged information. We found these explanations to be supported by Department and FBI policy and practice, and that the disputes between the agents and the prosecutors about how aggressively to pursue certain evidence were good faith disagreements.

It was not unreasonable for Department prosecutors to consider the delay that could result from motions to quash subpoenas and search warrants. Both Department and FBI witnesses told us that they hoped to complete the investigation well in advance of the election, if possible, to avoid influencing the political process. Indeed, Comey pressed in early May for the prompt completion of the investigation. However, in seeking to avoid delay, prosecutors were required to balance the need for timely completion of an investigation against the need to ensure a thorough and complete investigation. We did not identify bias or improper considerations affecting that judgment call by the prosecutors.

Both Department and FBI policies generally support the use of consent agreements to obtain evidence. The USAM advises prosecutors to consider alternatives to grand jury subpoenas when practicable, such as obtaining testimony and other evidence by consent, in light of the requirement that the government maintain the secrecy of any testimony or evidence accessed through the grand jury. USAM 9-11.254(1). Had the prosecutors not used consent agreements to obtain most of the evidence in the Midyear investigation, the FBI likely would not have been able to be as transparent as it was in response to FOIA and Congressional requests following the conclusion of the investigation.

The Attorney General's Guidelines for Domestic Operations (AGG-Dom) and the FBI's Domestic Investigations and Operations Guide (DIOG) require the FBI, when choosing among two or more operationally sound and effective methods for obtaining evidence or intelligence, to strongly consider using the one that is "least intrusive" with respect to "such factors as the effect on the privacy and civil liberties of individuals and potential damage to reputation." AGG-Dom § I.C.2; DIOG §§ 4.1.1, 4.4, 5.3, 18.2. The DIOG specifically identifies search warrants as a method that is "very intrusive." DIOG § 4.4.3 The DIOG's guidance regarding choosing the least intrusive method is emphasized in relation to Sensitive Investigative Matters (SIMs), such as the Midyear investigation. The DIOG states, "In the context of a SIM, particular care should be taken when considering whether the planned course of action is the least intrusive method if reasonable based upon the circumstances of the investigation." DIOG § 10.1.3. Assessing which investigative options to use, and whether various options are operationally sound and effective, are judgment calls. Accordingly, the Midyear team's use of consent agreements, after their evaluation of the circumstances, was an approach to gathering evidence that complied with Department policies. Likewise, had the prosecutors and agents agreed to pursue a more aggressive course after evaluating the circumstances and determining that it would have been a more effective method, it also would have been a rational approach to gathering evidence.

Under FBI policy, it also was appropriate for the Midyear team to consider how the use of compulsory process or more intrusive evidence collection methods might result in the public disclosure of information about the investigation—particularly public disclosure that had the potential to negatively impact the investigation. The DIOG states that in deciding the least intrusive method necessary for effectively obtaining information, the FBI should consider the "risk of public exposure" and the potential that public exposure will be used to an individual's "detriment and/or embarrassment." DIOG §§ 4.4.3(E), 5.3. Witnesses told us that there is a need to be particularly cautious with respect to the use of process in national security cases, due to the risk of classified information being leaked.

It was, of course, proper for the prosecutors to consider whether they could demonstrate probable cause before using criminal process. The Fourth Amendment protects individuals from unlawful searches and seizures of their property, and courts have held that individuals have privacy interests in their electronic communications. *See Ross*, 456 U.S. at 822-23; *Riley*, 134 S. Ct. at 2485; *Trulock*, 275 F.3d at 403. Generally, the government must obtain a search warrant before searching data contained in an individual's electronic storage devices, such as computers and cellular telephones. *Id.*; *Riley*, 134 S. Ct. at 2485. To obtain such a search warrant, the government must make a showing of facts under oath demonstrating probable cause to believe that a device to be searched contains evidence of a crime. *See* Fed. R. Crim. P. 41. Both Department and FBI witnesses told us that, in some circumstances, they were not certain they could make such a showing.

It was also proper for the prosecutors to consider privilege issues. By law, prosecutors cannot use compulsory process to override privileges, such as attorney-client or marital privilege. G.J. Manual § 5.1 (*quoting Branzburg*, 408 U.S. at 688); G.J. Manual §§ 5.6, 5.26. While a filter team may be used to cull privileged material from seized evidence before an investigative team reviews that evidence, there are also Department policies that apply to seizing evidence that may contain privileged information. For example, under USAM 9-13.410, prosecutors can only issue a subpoena to an attorney for information or evidence related to the representation of clients if the prosecutors first obtain approval from the AAG or DAAG of the Criminal Division. The AAG or DAAG will only provide such approval if the prosecutors make reasonable efforts to first obtain the evidence through alternative sources, including consent, unless such efforts would compromise the investigation. USAM 9-13.410. Similarly, the DIOG provides that, "It is less intrusive to obtain information from existing government sources...or from publicly-available data in commercial data bases, than to obtain the same information from a third party (usually through legal process) that has a confidential relationship with the subject." DIOG § 4.4.3(D).

We questioned why the Midyear team did not serve subpoenas on or seek to obtain search warrants related to the last known persons to possess devices that the team was never able to locate. These included Combetta for the missing Archive Laptop and Clinton or her attorneys for Clinton's handheld devices. Both FBI and Department witnesses told us that they believed Combetta and Clinton's attorneys were being truthful that they could not locate these devices and therefore subpoenas would not have made a difference in these situations. This was a judgment call made by the prosecutors and agents, and we did not identify evidence that it was infected by bias or improper considerations.

We also found no evidence that the particular limitations contained in the consent agreements were based on improper considerations or bias. For example, the prosecutors told us that the scope of consent was often limited to the time period of Clinton's tenure as Secretary of State, because that is when she had access to classified information. Although email communications among Clinton, her attorneys, and PRN staff following Clinton's tenure may have been relevant to Clinton's production of work-related emails to the State Department and the subsequent deletions of emails her attorneys deemed personal, the prosecutors told us that (1) most of these communications would have been protected by attorney-client privilege; and (2) the FBI obtained communications between Clinton's staff, including her attorneys, and PRN staff from PRN. In determining that these and other limitations in the consent agreements were not unreasonable, we considered the Department and FBI policies cited above.

B.   Decisions Not to Obtain or Seek to Review Certain Evidence

The Midyear team did not obtain or review some evidence that we found might have been useful to the investigation. The team's reasons for not doing so appear to have been based on limitations they imposed on the scope of their investigation, the desire to complete the investigation well before the election, and their belief that the foregone evidence was likely of limited value. Those reasons were, in part, in tension with Comey's reaction and response in October 2016 to the discovery of emails between Clinton and Abedin on the Weiner laptop. However, we found no evidence that the decisions not to obtain this evidence were based on improper considerations or bias. We concluded that these were judgment calls made by the prosecutors and agents.

We asked members of the Midyear team why they did not seek to obtain the personal devices that Clinton's senior aides used during their tenure at the State Department, given that these devices were both (1) potential sources of Clinton's work-related or classified emails; and (2) unauthorized locations where classified emails were potentially being stored. In addition, we inquired about the decision not to obtain Huma Abedin's personal devices given (1) that she stated during her interview that she had given them to her attorneys for production of her work-related emails to the State Department; and (2) the decision to seek a search warrant in October 2016 in order to search the Weiner laptop. Witnesses also told us they believed there was a flaw in the culling process that resulted in the exclusion of most of Abedin's clintonemail.com emails from the State Department production.

We found that the FBI team and the prosecutors decided together to generally limit the devices they sought to those that either belonged to Clinton or were used to back-up or cull Clinton's emails. The team provided, among others, the following reasons for placing this limitation on the scope of the investigation: (1) the culture of mishandling classified information at the State Department which made the quantity of potential sources of evidence particularly vast; (2) the belief that Clinton's own devices and the laptops used to cull her emails were the most likely places to find the complete collection of her emails from her tenure as Secretary of State; and (3) the belief that the State Department was the better entity to conduct a "spill investigation." With respect to the first rationale, we note that it fails to acknowledge that the team was not required to take an all-or-nothing approach. For example, a middle ground existed where those devices belonging to Clinton's three top aides—which the team determined accounted for approximately 68 percent of Clinton's email exchanges—would have been reviewed, but devices belonging to other State Department employees would not.

Regarding Abedin's devices, witnesses told us that Abedin played largely an administrative role on Clinton's staff and, as such, they did not believe her emails were likely to be significant to the investigation. Yet, as referenced above, this view was in tension with Comey's approach in late October 2016, discussed in detail in Chapters Nine and Ten. Comey described the discovery on the Weiner laptop in October as being the potentially "golden emails" based on what we concluded was very little information about the possible contents of the emails—a stark contrast to the Midyear team's assessment that the potential emails on Abedin's devices, including exchanges with Clinton, were unlikely to be significant. The team distinguished their approach with the Weiner laptop based mostly on the fact that it happened to be in the government's possession.

We recognize that reasonable minds differ on investigative approaches. We concluded that, in deciding not to seek the devices of Clinton's top aides, the Midyear team members weighed what they believed to be the limited evidentiary value of the senior aides' devices against their concerns about how pursuing them would add time to and increase the scope of the investigation. Ultimately, Department prosecutors have discretion with respect to "when, whom, how and even whether to prosecute for apparent violations of federal criminal law," provided that discretion is exercised without reliance on improper considerations, such as political bias or concerns for personal gain, and otherwise consistent with their oath of office and Department policy. *See* USAM 9-27.110 (comment) (*citing* U.S. Const. Art. II § 3; *United States* v. *LaBonte,* 520 U.S. 751, 762 (1997); *Nader* v. *Saxbe,* 497 F.2d 676, 679 n. 18 (D.C. Cir. 1974); *Oyler* v. *Boles,* 368 U.S. 448 (1962); *United States* v. *Fokker Servs. B.V.,* 818 F.3d 733, 741 (D.C. Cir. 2016); *Newman* v. *United States,* 382 F.2d 479 (D.C. Cir. 1967); *Powell* v. *Ratzenbach,* 359 F.2d 234 (D.C. Cir. 1965)); 5 U.S.C. § 3331 (oath of office). We did not find evidence that the decisions not to obtain the senior aides' devices were based on improper considerations, nor did we find that the reasons provided were a pretext for improper considerations. We also did not find that the decisions regarding the scoping of the investigation were inconsistent with any Department polices. Accordingly, these were judgment calls that were within the discretion of the Midyear agents and prosecutors to make.

In addition, as we describe in the classified appendix to this report, the OIG learned near the end of our review that the FBI had considered obtaining permission from the Department to review certain classified materials that may have included information potentially relevant to the Midyear investigation. Although the Midyear team drafted a memorandum to the Deputy Attorney General in late May 2016 stating that review of the highly classified materials was necessary to complete the investigation and requesting permission to access them, the FBI never sent this request to the Department. FBI witnesses told us that they did not seek access to these classified materials for various reasons, including that they believed this information would not materially impact the conclusion. The classified appendix describes in more detail the highly classified information, its potential relevance to the Midyear investigation, the FBI's reasons for not seeking access to it, and our analysis.

C.   Voluntary Interviews

The Midyear investigation did not use the grand jury for the purpose of collecting testimony from witnesses. FBI and Department witnesses told us that through voluntary interviews they were able to establish better rapport with witnesses and avoid risks associated with exposing grand jurors to classified information. We found no evidence that the use of voluntary interviews instead of grand jury testimony was based on improper considerations or influenced by bias. Rather, we concluded that these were judgment calls made by the prosecutors and agents.

As with the use of consent to obtain documentary and physical evidence, the use of voluntary interviews instead of grand jury testimony was consistent with the DIOG's preference for the "least intrusive" method. In addition, due to grand jury secrecy the use of voluntary interviews contributed to the FBI's ability to be transparent in response to FOIA requests and Congressional inquiries. The preference for voluntary interviews also was consistent with Department policy regarding the use of classified information before the grand jury. Before classified information can be utilized before the grand jury, the USAM requires prosecutors to seek approval from the agency responsible for classifying the information. USAM 9-90.230. Witnesses told us that this can be a lengthy process. In addition, the USAM cautions that questioning grand jury witnesses regarding classified information poses a risk that the witness will disclose more classified information than expected or permitted. *Id.* Even if the Midyear team could have obtained the necessary approvals to use classified information in the grand jury, the prosecutors told us that there are concerns with exposing grand jurors to classified information—the more individuals that are exposed to classified information, the greater the risk of compromise.

The Midyear prosecutors told us they kept open the possibility of subpoenaing witnesses before the grand jury, especially witnesses like Paul Combetta, whose testimony would not likely require the disclosure of classified information. The Midyear team subpoenaed Combetta to appear before the grand jury. However, Department prosecutors and FBI agents ultimately decided that questioning him before the grand jury was unnecessary because (1) they perceived him to be credible during his third interview; and (2) he did not implicate anyone else in criminal conduct such that it would have been helpful to "lock in" his testimony for a future trial. We did not find evidence that this decision was motivated by an improper consideration.

D. Use Immunity Agreements

Prosecutors have wide latitude in deciding to whom to give immunity, and the Department entered into "letter use" or "Queen for a Day" immunity agreements with three witnesses in the Midyear investigation: Pagliano, Combetta, and Bentel. We found no evidence that the decisions to enter into these immunity agreements were based on improper considerations. The factors that the Midyear prosecutors told us they considered in deciding to grant immunity were consistent with the factors Department policy required them to consider, including:

- "The value of the person's testimony or information to the investigation or prosecution;"

- "The person's relative culpability in connection with the offense or offenses being investigated or prosecuted;" and

- "The possibility of successfully prosecuting the person prior to compelling his or her testimony."

See USAM 9-23.210.

With respect to Pagliano, the prosecutors told us that they entered into a letter use immunity agreement because they believed the information he could provide regarding the set-up and maintenance of Clinton's servers was critical to the Midyear investigation and they determined that he faced no criminal exposure. Based on a review of his FD-302s (as described in Section VII.A of this chapter) and the fact that PIN considered and declined criminal charges against Pagliano, we found that the prosecutors' assessments regarding Pagliano were not unreasonable or motivated by improper considerations or bias.

With respect to Bentel, the only immunity agreement was a Queen for a Day proffer agreement. This agreement prevented the Department from using any statements made by Bentel pursuant to the agreement against him in its case-in-chief in any subsequent prosecution, but did not prevent the Department from using leads obtained from Bentel's statements or using Bentel's statements to cross-examine him in any future prosecution. *See* Chapter Two, Section I.E.3. The prosecutors assessed that interviewing Bentel was a necessary investigative step, and that he faced no criminal exposure. Based on our review of Bentel's FD-302 and the limited nature of the Queen for a Day immunity agreement, we found that the prosecutors' decision to grant Bentel immunity was not unreasonable or based on improper considerations or bias.

With respect to Combetta, we found his actions in deleting Clinton's emails in violation of a Congressional subpoena and preservation order and then lying about it to the FBI to be particularly serious. We asked the prosecutors why they chose to grant him immunity instead of charging him with obstruction of justice, in violation of 18 U.S.C. § 1505, or making false statements, in violation of 18 U.S.C. § 1001.

Department policy provides that, when considering whether to pursue criminal charges against an individual:

> The attorney for the government should commence or recommend federal prosecution if he/she believes that the person's conduct constitutes a federal offense, and that the admissible evidence will probably be sufficient to obtain and sustain a conviction, unless (1) the prosecution would serve no substantial federal interest; (2) the person is subject to effective prosecution in another jurisdiction; or (3) there exists an adequate non-criminal alternative to prosecution.

USAM 9-27.220. In determining whether the prosecution would serve a federal interest, the Department should "weigh all relevant considerations," including:

- "The nature and seriousness of the offense;"
- "The person's culpability in connection with the offense;" and
- "The person's willingness to cooperate in the investigation or prosecution of others."

USAM 9-27.230.

We received mixed testimony from Department and FBI witnesses regarding the strength of the evidence that Combetta committed obstruction or made false statements following his first two interviews. The prosecutors and agents we interviewed indicated that, even assuming that "the admissible evidence [was] probably...sufficient to obtain and sustain a conviction" after Combetta's first two interviews—an assumption the prosecutors indicated was not necessarily true—they believed prosecuting Combetta would not "serve a federal interest." The reasons they provided to us for reaching this conclusion included: (1) relevant to the nature and seriousness of the offense, there was no evidence that Combetta knew anything about the content of the emails on Clinton's server or that they were classified when he deleted them; (2) relevant to Combetta's culpability, they believed Combetta's failure to be forthcoming had been primarily due to poor representation rather than a motive to mislead the investigators; and (3) relevant to his willingness to cooperate, Combetta was willing to cooperate with immunity. Prosecutor 1 told us that the team would have considered pursuing charges against Combetta if he refused to cooperate with immunity, but that granting immunity was "the most expedient way" to obtain truthful information from him.

The prosecutors told us they believed granting Combetta use immunity was the best available option. They told us that they could not forgo Combetta's testimony, because they believed his truthful testimony regarding his role and the roles of others in the March deletions was essential to the investigation. Moreover, they said they had no means other than immunity to gain his testimony, because he had stated that he would invoke his Fifth Amendment privilege against self-incrimination. The prosecutors told us they did not charge Combetta and then pursue his cooperation in exchange for a guilty plea to reduced charges or a sentencing reduction because of, as discussed above, concerns about the strength of the admissible evidence and because they did not believe criminal charges were in the federal interest given his willingness to cooperate with immunity. The decision to choose a use immunity agreement over a non-prosecution agreement is supported by the USAM, which provides that immunity is (1) appropriate when "the testimony or other information that is expected to be obtained from the witness may be necessary to the public interest;" and (2) preferable to a nonprosecution agreement in exchange for cooperation because immunity "at least leave[s] open the possibility of prosecuting [the witness] on the basis of independently obtained evidence." USAM 9-23.210; 9-27.600 (comment).

We did not find evidence that the judgments made by the prosecutors in entering into these immunity agreements were inconsistent with Department policy, or based on improper considerations or bias. Ultimately, assessing the strength of the evidence and applying the provisions of the U.S. Attorney's Manual in determining whether to pursue federal criminal charges is a matter within the discretion and judgment of the prosecutors.

E.   Mills and Samuelson

The issues surrounding obtaining Mills's and Samuelson's testimony regarding the culling process and searching the culling laptops consumed a significant amount of the Midyear team's time and attention and caused significant strife between the FBI and Department prosecutors. Several members of the FBI Midyear team, including Comey, expressed concerns that the prosecutors had not been sufficiently aggressive. Ultimately, Mills and Samuelson submitted to voluntary interviews—albeit with limitations that prevented the investigators from soliciting privileged information—and the laptops were secured through consent agreements and act-of-production immunity. Both the prosecutors and the FBI told us that the team obtained what it needed from Mills and Samuelson to conduct a thorough investigation. Comey himself, during a speech at an October 2016 FBI conference for Special Agents in Charge, which we describe below in Chapter Eight, acknowledged the complex issues involved with obtaining the culling laptops from Mills and Samuelson. He further stated that the decision to obtain the culling laptops by consent was "reasonable...to short circuit the months and months of litigation that would've come otherwise" and that he was "actually surprised they agree[d] to give us the laptops."

We noted that these decisions concerning the laptops were occurring at a time when Comey and the Midyear team had already concluded that there was likely no prosecutable case and believed it was unlikely the culling laptops would change the outcome of the investigation. Moreover, as we describe in Chapter Six, at the time of the deliberations regarding the Mills and Samuelson issues, Comey was motivated by a desire to "credibly" complete the investigation sufficiently in advance of the election to not be perceived as political. Consistent with this motivation, Comey told us that one of the reasons he raised the possibility of a Special Counsel with Yates in April 2016 was to push the Department to move more quickly to obtain the culling laptops. Comey also pressed the Midyear investigators in early May for the prompt completion of the investigation.

The Mills and Samuelson issues were somewhat complicated. Not only were Mills and Samuelson both fact witnesses, Mills had numerous classified emails pass through her unclassified government and personal email addresses while working at the State Department under Secretary Clinton; both Mills and Samuelson acted as attorneys for Clinton after they departed from the State Department; and both were represented by their own (and the same) counsel, Beth Wilkinson, while former Secretary Clinton was represented by separate counsel, David Kendall, in connection with the Midyear investigation. These different layers of conduct and representation made obtaining evidence from Mills and Samuelson complex, whether the prosecutors sought to obtain the evidence by consent or compulsory process. In seeking evidence by consent, they had to consider whose consent was necessary—Wilkinsons's on behalf of Mills and Samuelson, Kendall's on behalf of Clinton, or both. They had to be cognizant of attorney-client privilege and attorney-work product with respect to Mills's and Samuelson's relationship to Clinton, Kendall's relationship to Clinton, Wilkinson's relationship to Mills and Samuelson, and information on the laptops related to Mills's and Samuelson's representation of other clients. They had to consider the implications of the fact that Wilkinson represented both Mills and Samuelson, as well as two other witnesses in the Midyear investigation. They also had to consider the policy restrictions set forth in the USAM, ethical issues, strategic issues (such as whether issuing criminal process might jeopardize the testimony that Mills consented to provide regarding her tenure at the State Department), and the concern that using criminal process could delay the investigation. Based on the evidence we reviewed, the Department prosecutors extensively considered all of these issues, analyzed the relevant law and policy, and ultimately made judgment calls with respect to Mills and Samuelson that were within their exercise of prosecutorial discretion and we found were not unreasonable.

We likewise found no evidence that bias impacted the decision to obtain testimony and evidence from Mills and Samuelson by consent agreement and with act-of-production immunity. Indeed, individuals for whom we had concerns about potential bias due to the content of their electronic messages advocated for the use of aggressive investigative measures with respect to Mills and Samuelson. For example, Strzok and Page both urged the Department to issue grand jury subpoenas for Mills's and Samuelson's testimony regarding the culling process and to seek a search warrant to seize the culling laptops from Wilkinson's office.

The prosecutors told us that they followed the procedures set forth in Department policy for obtaining testimony and evidence from attorneys related to their representation of clients. Based on our review of the relevant Department policy and privilege law, we found that the prosecutors' interpretations of the relevant Department policy were not unreasonable and we found no evidence that they were motivated by improper considerations. In accordance with 28 C.F.R. § 59.4, USAM 9-19.220, and USAM 9-13.420, the prosecutors correctly determined that, in the absence of evidence that such efforts would compromise the investigation, they could not seek a search warrant to seize the culling laptops from Wilkinson's office without first attempting to obtain the culling laptops through consent and, if that was unsuccessful, a grand jury subpoena. Under the circumstances, and in accordance with USAM 9-13.410, they determined that they could not issue a subpoena for the culling laptops without first taking several preliminary steps, including: (1) assessing whether the laptops were reasonably needed for the successful completion of the investigation, (2) attempting to first obtain the laptops by consent, and (3) seeking approval from the AAG or DAAG of the Criminal Division. Also in accordance with USAM 9-13.410, they determined that they could not issue subpoenas for Mills's and Samuelson's testimony regarding the culling process without first seeking their testimony by consent and tailoring their questions such that they did not seek information that was "protected by a valid claim of privilege."

In accordance with these policies, the prosecutors conducted voluntary interviews with Mills and Samuelson, obtained Criminal Division approval to issue subpoenas for the culling laptops, and ultimately obtained the culling laptops through consent agreements and act-of-production immunity agreements rather than subpoena. They told us that, even with the approval for subpoenas, they believed securing the laptops through consent was preferable to avoid the uncertainty and delays of a potential motion to quash the subpoenas. The act-of-production immunity agreements prevented the Department from using information obtained from the laptops in a criminal prosecution against Mills or Samuelson for violations of 18 U.S.C. §§ 793(e) and (f) (felony mishandling of classified information), 18 U.S.C. § 1924 (misdemeanor mishandling of classified information), and 18 U.S.C. § 2071 (destruction of federal records). The immunity agreements did not prevent the Department from: (1) using information obtained from the laptops to prosecute Mills or Samuelson for other crimes, such as obstructing a Congressional or FBI investigation or lying to federal investigators;

(2) using evidence obtained from other sources, including their voluntary interviews, to prosecute Mills and Samuelson for mishandling classified information, destroying federal records, or any other offenses; (3) using information obtained from the laptops to prosecute other individuals, including Clinton, for mishandling classified information, destroying federal records, or any other offenses; or (4) using leads developed as a result of the FBI's review of the information on the culling laptops.

Ultimately, these decisions were judgment calls made by, and within the discretion of, the prosecutors, much like the decisions discussed above regarding use immunity agreements. We found no evidence that these decisions were the result of improper considerations or were influenced by bias.

F.   Handling of Clinton's Interview

By the time of Clinton's interview on July 2, we found that the Midyear agents and prosecutors, along with Comey, had decided that absent a confession or false statements by Clinton, the investigation would be closed without charges. We further found that this conclusion was based on the prosecutors' view that there was insufficient evidence of Clinton's knowledge and intent to support criminal charges, which we discuss in detail in Chapter Seven.

We did not find evidence that decisions regarding the timing or scoping of Clinton's interview were based on improper considerations or influenced by bias. In addition, based on our review of the FD-302 and contemporaneous notes, the investigators appeared to ask appropriate questions of Clinton and made use of documents to challenge Clinton's testimony and assess her credibility during the interview.[121] However, we had three primary concerns related to the Clinton interview: (1) text messages sent by Page to Strzok, McCabe, and another FBI employee that appeared to suggest that the team limit the number of attendees at Clinton's interview because she might be the next President and it could leave her upset at the FBI; (2) certain instant messages sent by Agent 1, who was one of the case agents that handled Clinton's interview; and (3) the presence of Mills and Samuelson at Clinton's interview, despite that they were also witnesses in the investigation.

With regard to the number of attendees, Page sent the following text message in support of fewer agents and prosecutors attending Clinton's interview: "[S]he might be our next president. The last thing you need us going in there loaded for bear. You think she's going to remember or care that it was more doj

---

[121] For example, based on the FD-302 from Clinton's interview, Clinton told the interviewing agents that she "expected her team to provide any work-related or arguably work-related emails to State." The interviewing agents then challenged this statement by showing Clinton a work-related email that was not produced to the State Department. Clinton acknowledged that the email was work-related and stated that she did not know why her team did not produce it.

than fbi?"[122] The text messages and contemporaneous emails reflect that Page was particularly concerned with the Department's request that four prosecutors attend the interview. Ultimately, eight people attended Clinton's interview from the Department and FBI, including five prosecutors. Therefore, we concluded that Page's suggestion of limiting the number of attendees to four or six did not in fact occur. Moreover, based on witness testimony, we found that the approach Page was advocating—keeping the number of interviewers down to a lower number—was consistent with legitimate investigative strategy.

Nevertheless, we found that Page's statement, on its face, consisted of a recommendation that the Midyear team consider how Clinton would treat the FBI if she were to become President in deciding how to handle Clinton's interview. Suggesting that investigative decisions be based on this consideration was inappropriate and created an appearance of bias.

We also were concerned that Agent 1 was one of the two agents who questioned Clinton during the interview given certain instant messages that we identified from Agent 1, including some that expressed support for Clinton and hostility toward Trump. We interviewed each of the seven other FBI and Department attendees at Clinton's interview, and none of them expressed concerns regarding the conduct of the interview. We also did not find, based on our review of the interview outline prepared in advance of the interview as well as the FD-302 and contemporaneous notes of the interview, evidence that bias or improper considerations influenced the conduct of the interview. We took note of the fact that, because the Midyear team and Comey had concluded prior to the interview that the evidence did not support criminal charges (absent a confession or false statement by Clinton during the interview), the interview had little effect on the outcome of the investigation. Nonetheless, as discussed above, we found Agent 1's messages to be troubling and in Chapter Twelve, we discuss the impact of these instant messages on such matters as the public perception of the handling of the Midyear investigation and the FBI.

Finally, we questioned why the Department and FBI allowed Mills and Samuelson, two percipient witnesses (one of whom, Mills, herself had classified information transit through her unclassified personal email account) attend Clinton's interview, even if they had also both served as lawyers for Clinton after they left the State Department. The FBI and Department employees we interviewed all agreed that the attendance of Mills and Samuelson at Clinton's interview posed potential evidentiary problems, was unusual, and was unhelpful from an "optics" perspective. Witnesses also told us that the only way they could have excluded Mills and Samuelson was by subpoenaing Clinton before the grand jury, but that the team did not seriously consider that option. If the team had issued a grand jury subpoena, Clinton either would have been required to testify before the grand jury without her attorneys in the room or she might have agreed to a voluntary interview outside the presence of Mills and Samuelson to avoid having to appear

---

[122] From the context of this message in the series of text messages that day, we determined that the text message was focused on the number of Midyear team members attending and not on the nature of the questioning.

before the grand jury, given that a grand jury appearance would have delayed the investigation.

We did not find evidence that bias played a role in the decision to proceed with the Clinton interview with Mills and Samuelson in attendance. Rather, we concluded that it was largely based on four factors. First, the Midyear prosecutors were concerned about interviewing Clinton before the grand jury because of the challenges of presenting classified information before the grand jury. Second, the Midyear team had decided by the time of Clinton's interview that the case was headed toward a declination absent a confession or false statement by Clinton. Third, had Clinton been required to testify before the grand jury, the FBI would not have been able to participate in the interview. Fourth, the team planned to pause the interview and conduct a sidebar with Kendall if Mills or Samuelson interfered during the interview.

Ultimately, witnesses told us that Mills and Samuelson did not interfere, object, or speak substantively during the interview. Moreover, Clinton's interview did not result in any change in the conclusion of the Midyear team and Comey that a declination decision was warranted. Accordingly, we found no persuasive evidence that Mills's or Samuelson's presence influenced Clinton's interview, or that the outcome of the investigation would have been different had Clinton been subpoenaed before the grand jury.

Nevertheless, we found the decision to allow the Clinton interview to proceed in the presence of two fact witnesses, who also were serving as Clinton's counsel, was inconsistent with typical investigative strategy and gave rise to accusations of bias and preferential treatment.[123] Moreover, there are serious potential ramifications when one witness attends another witness's interview. The Midyear team could have developed information during the Clinton interview that led the team to reconsider its conclusion that the investigation was headed towards a declination, or led the team to believe that Clinton made a false statement during the interview. In either case, the presence of two fact witnesses at the interview could have negatively impacted subsequent FBI investigative efforts or a subsequent trial. We believe that it would have been useful for the Midyear team to have had guidance to consider in this situation. Thus, we recommend that the Department and the FBI consider developing guidance consider developing practice guidance that would assist investigators and prosecutors in identifying the general risks with and alternatives to permitting a witness to attend a voluntary interview of another witness, in particular when the witness is serving as counsel for the other witness.

---

[123] We recognize that, as a general matter, a witness is free to consult with counsel of the witness's choice. However, the government is not required to agree to conduct an interview of a witness in the presence of counsel who is also a witness.

CHAPTER SIX:
"ENDGAME" DISCUSSIONS AND FORMER DIRECTOR COMEY'S
PUBLIC STATEMENT

Our review found that the Midyear team concluded beginning in early 2016 that evidence supporting a prosecution of former Secretary Clinton or her senior aides was likely lacking. This conclusion was based on the fact that the Midyear team had not found evidence that former Secretary Clinton or her senior aides knowingly transmitted classified information on unclassified systems because (1) classified information exchanged in unclassified emails was not clearly or properly marked, and (2) State Department staff introducing classified information into emails made an effort to "talk around" it. Although the Midyear team continued its investigation, taking the investigative steps described in Chapter Five and looking for evidence that could change their assessment, they also began discussing what witnesses referred to as the "endgame" for the investigation—ways for the Department and FBI to credibly announce the closing of the investigation.

In this chapter, we discuss the factors that led the Midyear team to conclude that the investigation likely would result in a declination. We then describe the discussions among Comey, Rybicki, Yates, and Axelrod beginning in April 2016 about how to announce the closing of the Midyear investigation, including Comey's mention of a special counsel and Lynch's knowledge of these discussions. We also describe the origins of Comey's decision to hold a press conference without coordinating with or informing the Department in advance, the various drafts of his public statement, and the Department's reactions to the statement after he delivered it on July 5, 2016. In addition, we describe the tarmac meeting between Lynch and former President Bill Clinton on June 27, 2016, and its impact on the Midyear investigation. Finally, we describe Comey's congressional testimony about the reasons for his public statement.

I.   Evidence that the Case Was Headed toward a Declination

As described above, both Department and FBI witnesses said that the central question in the Midyear investigation was whether there was evidence that former Secretary Clinton and her aides acted with knowledge that the information transmitted was classified or transmitted with criminal intent. Various witnesses told the OIG that the investigation focused on identifying what classified information transited former Secretary Clinton's server, who introduced it, and why. The investigative team looked for evidence that individuals who sent emails containing classified information did so with knowledge that the information was classified—for example, took information from documents that were marked with classification headers and stripped off the header information—or that former Secretary Clinton's private server was set up to circumvent classification requirements.

From early in the investigation, the investigative team said they knew that proving intent would be a challenge.[124] Prosecutor 1 told the OIG:

> [T]his whole case turned on mens rea [guilty state of mind].... I've run a lot of mishandling cases. The issue is usually that people are taking things home or they're communicating them to someone for, to set up a business outside or to do something that's like, what we don't tend to prosecute criminally anyway are people who are communicating things for work purposes.... Usually to people who are already cleared. So, those are the kinds of things that when we're talking about mens rea, were sort of instructive for us....

This prosecutor explained that Secretary Clinton and her staff did not display any of the counterintelligence indicators that prosecutors typically see in mishandling cases, such as unreported foreign contacts or "weird" meetings with foreigners. This prosecutor said that evidence of intent was lacking for other reasons as well, including that numerous witnesses testified that the State Department had terrible information technology (IT) systems and that its remote email system did not work when employees were traveling and sending emails in different time zones. As a result, the investigative team said they could not infer bad intent from the use of personal email accounts as they might in other cases.

Prosecutor 2 similarly stated that mishandling cases generally involve "people who have an intent to give classified information to others, people who have an intent to...take documents home and...do nefarious things with them, or sometimes hoarders of classified information." This prosecutor told the OIG that, unlike the typical mishandling case, the State Department employees who introduced classified information into the unclassified system were trying to "talk around" it in the course of doing their jobs. This prosecutor stated, "And looking in terms of some of the times when the classified information appeared on [un]classified systems in this case, we see, we see problems, you know, late at night, weekends, the time between Christmas and New Year's when no one is in the office."

FBI officials agreed with the prosecutors that the need to prove intent was problematic from the outset. In his recent book, Comey stated:

> ...Hillary Clinton's case, at least as far as we knew at the start, did not appear to come anywhere near General Petraeus's in the volume and classification level of the information mishandled. Although she seemed to be using an unclassified system for some classified topics,

---

[124] The legal framework for the Midyear investigation and the basis for the decision not to recommend or pursue prosecution of former Secretary Clinton or her staff are described in Chapters Two and Seven, respectively. Even though Section 793(f)(1) does not require intent, prosecutors told us that the Department has interpreted the provision to require that the person accused of having removed or delivered classified information in violation of this provision possess knowledge that the information is classified. In addition, based on the legislative history of Section 793(f)(1), the prosecutors determined that conduct must be "so gross as to almost suggest deliberate intention," be "criminally reckless," or fall "just a little short of willful" to meet the "gross negligence" standard.

everyone she emailed appeared to have both the appropriate clearance and a legitimate need to know the information. So although we were not going to prejudge the result, we started the Clinton investigation aware that it was unlikely to be a case that career prosecutors at the Department of Justice would prosecute. That might change, of course, if we could find a smoking-gun email where someone in government told Secretary Clinton not to do what she was doing, or if we could prove she obstructed justice, or if she, like Petraeus, lied to us in an interview. It would all turn on what we could prove beyond a reasonable doubt[.][125]

As described in more detail below, Comey said that by early May 2016, when he wrote the first draft of his public statement, the Midyear team was aware that evidence of intent was lacking.

Others on the Midyear team agreed. FBI Attorney 1 stated, "I have cases where there [are] people with thousands of classified documents in their home and we don't prosecute them.... [T]his is not something we prosecute lightly or we do regularly. There needs to be, usually, some either nefarious intent or some...actual harm that has happened because of it." Agent 2 told the OIG:

[F]rom like my level looking at it...you were hard-pressed to find the intent of anyone to put classified information on that server. And again, sloppy security practices, for sure. Right? But, and, and preventable? Yes. But somebody intentionally putting classified on it, we just never found clear-cut evidence of somebody intending to do that.

As early as September 2015, FBI and Department officials realized that they were unlikely to find evidence of intent. Prosecutor 2 stated that within a month of first obtaining criminal process, they had seen no evidence of intent. This prosecutor told the OIG that the team realized that the case likely would lead to a declination after they had reviewed the classified information in former Secretary Clinton's emails and heard the explanations for including that information in unclassified emails. Prosecutor 2 said that there were a number of other investigative steps they needed to take to complete their due diligence, but that by September 2015 they knew that they would need a "game changer" to be able to prove intent.

Notes obtained by the OIG from a meeting between Toscas and then EAD John Giacalone on December 4, 2015, confirm that the lack of intent was the subject of ongoing discussions. According to the notes, Giacalone asked the team, "Still [do not] have much on the intent side, right?" The notes show that the team members present at the meeting agreed with him. Giacalone, who retired from the FBI in February 2016, said that there were "no smoking guns" showing intent when he left.

---

[125] COMEY, *supra*, at 164-65.

Similarly, other notes show that prosecutors met with NSD supervisors on January 29, 2016, to discuss the lack of evidence supporting prosecution. The notes state:

Don't see prosecutable case at this point.

A lot of stuff done from Ops Center [lower level State Department staff] —> up. HRC is receiving.

Want to insulate DOJ from criticism about how we did this work.

No daylight [between] FBI management and investigative team agents re: view of criminal liability.

Asked what led the team to conclude by January 2016 that there would not be a prosecutable case, Laufman said that there was not a fixed point in time or organized discussion that produced this realization. He said that every time the team concluded "another consequential investigative step, and no additional information emerged that...pointed in the direction of potential criminal liability, then the...foundation of facts emerged that was not likely to support a recommendation to charge."

Asked whether there was a particular piece of evidence or an interview that led to the realization that the case would result in a declination, Prosecutor 3 stated that it became apparent once the team had interviewed all of former Secretary Clinton's senior staff members, including Jake Sullivan and Cheryl Mills, and heard the same explanation for what they believed to be an innocuous transmission of emails containing classified information. Other witnesses described the team's realization that the investigation would not result in a prosecutable case as "iterative" or "emerging over time" based on the cumulative lack of intent evidence over the course of the entire investigation. In any event, various witnesses agreed that the team had come to the conclusion that there likely was not a prosecutable case by the Spring of 2016.

Baker told the OIG that he thought that the conduct of former Secretary Clinton and her senior aides was "appalling with respect to how they handled the classified information...[and] arrogant in terms of their knowledge and understanding of these matters." He stated that he was concerned about former Secretary Clinton's level of knowledge and intent, and thought that she should have recognized the sensitivity of information in the emails sent to her. Baker said that he "debated and argued" with Comey and the Midyear team about former Secretary Clinton's criminal liability, but ultimately came to the conclusion that declining prosecution was the correct decision after reviewing a binder of her emails. Baker said that he recognized there was a lack of evidence establishing knowledge or criminal intent, and that based on "the volume of...communications coming at [Clinton] at all times, day and night, given the heavy responsibilities that a Secretary of State has, isn't she entitled to rely on [the classification determinations by] her folks?" Baker stated that he "did not like it.... I eventually agreed with it, but I did not like it."

Yates told the OIG that she had been getting updates regularly from Carlin and Toscas about where the investigation was going. In Spring 2016, Carlin or Toscas told her that if the investigation continued in the same direction it was going, they expected that the prosecutors and the agents would be recommending a declination. Yates told us that this assessment of the case was based on evidence indicating that the people transmitting classified information did not have a "bad purpose." She pointed to a variety of factors, including that emails were sent by State Department employees to other State Department employees, and usually contained time-sensitive logistical information that former Secretary Clinton needed to receive. She said that the information was not marked classified, with the exception of three paragraphs that were portion marked as "Confidential," and that there were even disputes within the originating agencies as to whether the information should be classified at all.

Yates said that Department leadership began talking internally in the Spring of 2016 about how to convey a declination decision because they knew that it would be controversial, and that they were all of the view that it needed to be clear that the decision was supported by both the FBI and the Department. Yates said that these discussions always proceeded with the "great big caveat" that former Secretary Clinton could lie during her interview, but that they could not wait until after the interview to begin preparing for a declination due, in part, to the proximity of the election. Discussions between the FBI and the Department about the "endgame" for concluding the Midyear investigation began around this same time, and are described in more detail below.

II.   Discussions between FBI and Department Leadership about How to Credibly Announce a Declination (Spring 2016)

As noted above, Comey said that the Midyear team was aware from the outset that the investigation was unlikely to result in a prosecutable case, absent a "smoking-gun" email. Comey told the OIG that he realized sometime in March or April 2016 that the evidence obtained in the Midyear investigation likely would not support a prosecution. Asked what led him to that conclusion at that time, Comey stated:

> [T]he picture that was fairly clear at that point, [was] that Hillary Clinton had used a private email...to conduct her State Department business. And in the course of conduct [of] her State Department business, she discussed classified topics on eight occasions TS, dozens of occasions SECRET, and there was no indication that we had found that she knew that was improper, unlawful, that someone had said don't do that, that will violate 18 U.S.C. [the federal criminal code], but that there was no evidence of intent and it's looking, despite the fact of the prominence of it, like an unusual, but in a way fairly typical spill and that there was no fricking way that the Department of Justice in a million years was going to prosecute that.

167

And because Counterintelligence Division of the FBI was involved in all the other spill cases and it collected for me the history of them, no way, there's no way, unless we find something else in May and June or we get [18 U.S.C. §] 1001 [false statements] handed to us during her interview.

Comey said that, as he came to this realization, he became concerned that the Department would be unable to announce the closing of the investigation in a way that the public would find credible and objective. Comey said he was concerned that having the Department's political leadership announce a declination would expose it to a "corrosive doubt about whether you did [the investigation] in a credible way." He said that this concern "dominated [his] thinking...for most of 2016, but especially from the spring on." According to Comey, his concern was based on the appearance or perception created by the Department's leadership declining prosecution of the presumptive Democratic nominee, because they were political appointees; it was not based on evidence that Lynch or Yates were interfering in the investigation or were politically biased.

A.   Initial Discussion between Comey and Yates in April 2016

1.   Options Discussed at the Meeting

Comey said that beginning in March or April 2016, he began to think of ways to announce a declination. Comey said that during this time he had a meeting with Rybicki, Yates, and Axelrod to discuss how the FBI and Department could credibly close the investigation. Based on Yates's description of the circumstances of the meeting (described below) and FBI emails, we determined that this meeting likely took place on Tuesday, April 12, 2016.

According to Comey, he told Yates and Axelrod during the meeting that they needed to begin thinking about the how to announce the end of the investigation. Comey said that he told Yates, "[M]y sense of this, and I'm not done, but my sense of this is this is heading for a declination and how do you credibly decline this? And what can you say to people to support the credibility of the work that's been done?"

Comey said that he urged Yates and Axelrod to consider the most transparent options available for announcing a declination. Comey told the OIG:

> [M]y view was, still is, that the more information you are able to supply, the higher the credibility of the investigation and the conclusion. And that especially in a poisonous political atmosphere, where all kinds of nonsense is said, the more you can fill that space with actual facts, the more reliable, believable, credible the conclusion is.

He stated, "People are still going to disagree. They are still going to fight, but at least there will be facts in the public square that show...[we] did this in a good way, thought about it in a good way and here is our reasoning as to why we think there is no there there."

Comey told the OIG that they did not discuss or consider specific options, but that he simply said to Yates, "[Y]ou need to get smart people working on what are the range of possibilities...what is possible under the law, I remember mentioning the Privacy Act, what is possible and what are the vehicles for transparency, what are the outer boundaries.... I think I just teed up the issue and said, hope you will get smart people thinking about this." Asked whether he was ever involved in discussions about a joint appearance with Attorney General Lynch, Comey said that he did not recall any discussions about that option.

Yates recalled this discussion with Comey differently. Yates said that she had a regular monthly meeting with Comey, and that the day before one of these meetings, Axelrod received a call from Rybicki suggesting that they meet to discuss how to conclude the case. She did not recall precisely when this meeting took place or what had happened in the investigation leading up to it, but she described the investigation at that time as "wrapping up."

Yates said that the meeting took place in her office. She said that they talked about the investigation and agreed that public confidence in its resolution was important. She said that everyone was of the same view that there was not a criminal case based on the evidence to date, and that it was not going to be sufficient to announce the conclusion by saying, "We looked at it...case closed." She said that the four of them agreed that people needed to have confidence that there had been a thorough look at the facts, and that a declination was the right decision.

Yates told the OIG that any discussion about how to announce a declination always proceeded with "great big caveat on it" that former Secretary Clinton could lie during her interview. Yates stated, "This is if things continue to go that way. Because you don't want to be like planning the declination that you don't really know is a declination yet. Because I mean, if she lied for example. There's about, that could change things entirely if she wasn't truthful in the interview."

According to Yates, one of the options they considered was a written memorandum released to the public, which would give some level of facts about the investigation. Yates stated that they all agreed that if they released a written memorandum, they also would need to hold a press conference to allow them to "look the [American] people in the eye" and say that there was not a criminal case, rather than "hiding behind a behind a [press] release or a writing that...would not be sufficient to convey the earnestness of that decision." She said that no one committed to a decision at this meeting, but rather they were "thinking out loud."

We asked Axelrod about these discussions between Yates and Comey. He said they focused on whether the FBI would be part of any announcement at the conclusion of the investigation. Axelrod said that they discussed preparing a letterhead memorandum (LHM) that could at least be provided to Congress, along with some form of a public announcement.

Axelrod said that one of the options they discussed was a joint announcement involving Lynch and Comey. Axelrod told the OIG that "the view from the Department was it would be important for the Bureau to be part of that." He stated, "[Comey] hadn't committed to it but was...comfortable with it being some sort of joint thing." Asked why he thought it was important to have Comey participate in an announcement, Axelrod said that it was important for the Department and the FBI to display a "unified front...having both organizations together saying the truth, which was this was done by the book and this was the result."

Axelrod said that they never discussed the idea of Comey being the one to announce a declination because it was never raised, but that he was "not sure that would have been rejected out of hand." He stated, "[T]here would have been some advantages to that having been coordinated and planned that way. And some disadvantages, too.... [T]he thing...that I knew that the Department felt strongly about was that Bureau had to be part of that [announcement]."

Rybicki said that he did not recall any specific discussions, stating, "I just remember all ideas sort of being, you know, people talking about, you know, press conferences and, and, and ways of closing and things like that. I don't remember specific conversations."

2.   Comey Mentions a Special Counsel at April Meeting with Yates

Comey's Testimony

Comey told the OIG that during the April meeting with Yates and Axelrod, he told Yates that the closer they got to the political conventions, the more likely he would be to insist that a special counsel be appointed, because there was no way the Department could credibly finish the investigation once former Secretary Clinton was the Democratic Party nominee. Comey said that his comment to Yates was motivated in part by his frustration that it was taking the Midyear prosecutors too long to obtain the Mills and Samuelson laptops (discussed above in Chapter Five). He said that he emphasized to Yates that the team needed to obtain the laptops to be able to finish the investigation. According to Comey, Yates reacted to his comment about the possible need for a special counsel with concern, and that he responded, "[L]ook I'm not saying we have to do it, but the deeper we get into this summer, the more likely it's going to be that I'll feel that way. And I was saying it in part to get them to just move—to move, to get us this thing [the laptops]."

As part of this discussion, Comey said he recounted his experience when he was the DAG appointing then U.S. Attorney Patrick Fitzgerald as the special counsel to investigate the leak of the name of a covert CIA operative, Valerie Plame.[126] He said he explained to Yates that the investigation focused in part on whether Karl

---

[126] Comey served as the DAG from December 9, 2003, to August 15, 2005, under President George W. Bush. On July 14, 2003, the Washington Post published Plame's name, sourced to unidentified senior administration officials. On December 30, 2003, then Attorney General Ashcroft recused himself from the investigation. Comey became the Acting Attorney General for purposes of the investigation and appointed Fitzgerald to oversee it.

Rove, then President George W. Bush's senior political advisor, had leaked the information, and that he (Comey) was concerned about the appearance of a conflict of interest between Rove and then Attorney General John Ashcroft because Rove had managed one of Ashcroft's Senate campaigns. He told the OIG that he mentioned this to Yates because he saw similarities between the Plame leak case and the Midyear investigation: namely, that in the Plame case there was no basis to prosecute Rove, and he did not think the Bush Administration could have announced a declination in a way that assured the public the investigation was done objectively.

Comey said that his comment to Yates about appointing a special counsel also was motivated by concerns about the appearance of political bias in the Department. He said that these concerns were based on the overall political environment—given then President Obama's comments about the investigation, he did not think the Department leadership could credibly complete the investigation without charges.[127]

Comey said that he also was concerned about an issue specific to Lynch. As discussed in more detail in the classified appendix to this report, Comey told the OIG that the FBI had obtained highly classified information in March 2016 that included allegations of partisan bias or attempts to impede the Midyear investigation by Lynch. Numerous witnesses we interviewed—including Comey—said that the FBI assessed that these allegations were not credible based on various factors, including that some of the information was objectively false. For example, the information also suggested that Comey was attempting to influence the investigation by extending it to help Republicans win the election, which witnesses said the FBI knew was not true. By mid-June 2016, the FBI had obtained no information corroborating the Lynch-related allegations.

When asked about this information, Comey stated that he knew it was not credible on its face because it was not consistent with his personal experience with Lynch. Comey stated, "I saw no, I'll say this again, I saw no reality of Loretta Lynch interfering in this investigation." However, Comey said that he became concerned that the information about Lynch would taint the public's perception of the Midyear investigation if it leaked, particularly after DCLeaks and Guccifer 2.0 began releasing hacked emails in mid-June 2016.

Despite these concerns, Comey told the OIG that it did not occur to him to request a special counsel in late 2015, after Lynch's instruction to use the term "matter" or former President Obama's public comments about the investigation (discussed in Chapter Four), because Comey was satisfied with the nature and the quality of the investigation being conducted by the FBI. Comey emphasized that

---

[127] As discussed in Chapter Four, former President Obama made comments about the investigation in October 2015 and April 2016, while White House Press Secretary Josh Earnest made statements in January 2016 suggesting that the Midyear investigation was not headed toward an indictment.

the FBI had its "A team" working on the investigation, and that he was closely involved to ensure that the team was protected from political or other influence.

As we describe in more detail in the classified appendix, Yates and Axelrod told us that the FBI mentioned this information to them sometime in the Spring of 2016 and provided a defensive briefing on it on July 12, 2016.[128] Yates said that the FBI told her that the information was not deemed credible and did not show her the relevant documents. After being shown the documents in her OIG interview, Yates expressed frustration and said that, had she been informed that the FBI had concerns about the information, she would have engaged Comey in discussions about the impact on the Midyear investigation. The FBI also did not provide Lynch with a defensive briefing about the information until August 2016, more than a month after investigative activity in Midyear was concluded, and she also was told that the information was not credible. Lynch said that until Comey's public testimony in 2017, she was never told that the information played a role in his unilateral decision to make a public statement about the Midyear investigation or concerns about whether a special counsel was necessary.

However, Comey said that he became increasingly concerned and began thinking about the possible need for a special counsel when he realized in March or April 2016 that the case likely would result in a declination, and that the declination might not happen until after the political conventions. He explained that the Department's leadership could not credibly announce a declination around or after the nominating convention, because "the confluence of a decision on a case and a key political event" would cause "grievous" damage to the Department's and the FBI's reputation.[129]

Yates's and Axelrod's Testimony

Yates told us that she recalled Comey raising the possibility of a special counsel at the April meeting. She told the OIG that Comey commented that they may need a special counsel to announce the closing of the Midyear investigation if the investigation ran past the convention and former Secretary Clinton was formally the Democratic Party's nominee.[130] According to Yates, Comey added that there was no reason to request a special counsel because the investigation would be

---

[128] A defensive briefing is intended to warn government officials of specific security concerns or risks. As we describe in the classified appendix to this report, the Department discussed this information with career Department officials in March 2016, and later provided defensive briefings to Yates and Lynch on July 12, 2016 and August 10, 2016, respectively.

[129] In Section VI.C below, we describe Comey's testimony before the Senate Select Committee on Intelligence on June 8, 2017. During that testimony, Comey was asked whether Lynch had an appearance of a conflict of interest in the Midyear investigation. Comey replied, "I think that's fair. I didn't believe she could credibly decline that investigation—at least, not without grievous damage to the Department of Justice and to the FBI."

[130] The Democratic National Convention was held from July 25 to 28, 2016. Clinton was formally nominated to be the Democratic Party's Presidential nominee on July 26, and accepted the nomination on July 28, 2016. However, she secured a majority of delegates and became the presumptive nominee several weeks earlier, on June 6, 2016.

completed before the convention. She said that she did not interpret Comey's comment as a line drawn in the sand, but more of a "musing."

Yates characterized Comey's suggestion as a "weird thing" that he raised "out of the blue," and said that she did not understand why the convention was a bright line for him. She stated, "Because if you were concerned about an appearance that [Clinton is] the Democratic nominee and you have a Democratic Attorney General, well, you got that before the convention. You've kind of had that for quite some time now." Yates said that she may have mentioned to Comey that Clinton had been the presumptive Democratic Party nominee for some time and that using the convention as a dividing line seemed "really artificial."

Yates also said that she was taken aback by Comey's comments, because the investigation had been going on for some time and he had never mentioned the need for a special counsel. She said that his concern was based on the perception created by a Democratic-appointed Attorney General announcing that the Democratic Party's Presidential nominee would not be prosecuted. Yates said that she understood that this was "all for appearance reasons." She stated, "Jim [Comey] never, ever, raised any concern about Attorney General Lynch having any kind of actual conflict or even an appearance of a conflict before we got to the tarmac. Never, ever. Nor did anyone else at the FBI ever raise any concern about that that I'm aware of."

Asked whether Comey at any time raised concerns about the involvement of Lynch in either the investigation or the announcement, Yates stated:

> No...I mean, this is where, and when I am so emphatic about that it's because I read articles and testimony later that frankly, shocked me. Because I thought, this was not the only discussion that I had with former Director Comey about how we would roll it out. And I thought...I read and I have no way of knowing if this is true, but I think Director Comey's testimony indicated that he had been thinking for quite some time that he felt like he needed to go in alone in making the announcement. And not only did I never hear that, I'm not aware of anybody, I mean, maybe somebody else at DOJ had heard that and it never made its way to me. But I'm not aware of anybody else at DOJ hearing that.
>
> In fact, that's just the opposite of what our discussions were. I would have thought when...we're talking about a joint press conference, et cetera, that if he harbored either (A), any reservations about whether Attorney General Lynch had a conflict or appeared to have a conflict he would have said something. I don't know how you have a discussion about that and have those feelings and not say anything about it. And then (B), if he was actually planning on doing it on his own I don't know how he didn't tell me that.

Yates said that she would have expected Comey to discuss any concerns he had about Lynch or the Department with her, and said that Comey had not been shy or hesitant to give his opinion in discussions with her. However, she said that Comey "kept FBI's information very tight," and that she "sometimes...felt like [she] had to pry information out of him."

Axelrod gave a similar account of Comey's mention of a special counsel. He said that Comey was concerned with the dates of the national political conventions, particularly the Democratic National Convention, because he thought that it would not be tenable for the Department's leadership to continue to oversee the investigation or announce a declination once former Secretary Clinton was the Democratic Party's nominee. Axelrod said that he perceived Comey's concern as "purely calendar-driven." He told the OIG that he did not know if Comey appreciated the way that the appointment of a special counsel would be perceived by the outside world, or whether it was "some sort of gambit to sort of say hey, if you guys don't pick up the pace, right, this is going to get really ugly." Axelrod said that at the time he interpreted the suggestion as Comey thinking through how to "navigate this in such a way that it gets accepted by, again, not by everyone but at least by some chunk of the public, the reasonable center, as having been done on the level."

Rybicki told the OIG that he did not recall any discussions between Comey and Yates about the need to appoint a special counsel.

3. Lynch's Knowledge of the April Meeting

Asked about her knowledge of the meeting between Yates and Comey, Lynch said that Yates told her that she met with Comey, and that Comey indicated that he was not sure there was a "there there" with respect to the Midyear investigation. According to Lynch, Yates said that Comey mentioned that he should be the one to make any announcement about the resolution of the case, because this would be best for the independence of the Department. Lynch said that Yates and she both thought that any discussion about an announcement was "very premature."

Lynch said that she did not think about the option to have Comey make any eventual announcement in terms of a "decision tree" because it was so premature. She stated that she was not aware of any other options that Comey and Yates discussed, but that she did not see a basis for the Department to "have the investigative arm announce a prosecutive decision." Asked whether there was anything about the case that in her view would warrant deviating from the standard practice of having prosecutors announcing a prosecutorial decision, Lynch responded that there was not.

Lynch told the OIG that she understood from Yates that Comey wanted to complete the investigation before the political conventions. However, she said she did not recall being told that Comey had mentioned the possibility of requesting a special counsel if the investigation continued beyond that point. She said that, other than letters from Members of Congress requesting a special counsel to handle

174

the investigation, no one ever mentioned that a special counsel might be necessary or might be requested if the investigation took too long.[131]

Lynch said that she had looked at the special counsel regulation at one point because that is "a decision that the AG has to make," but had not taken steps to have anyone look into it or research it. She said that she was convinced that the team handling the investigation could come to a conclusion. She stated, "I was convinced that if, for example, they thought that someone should be charged, they were not going to hesitate to recommend that."

As we discuss in Section IV.B below, Lynch received an ethics opinion following the tarmac meeting with former President Bill Clinton on June 27, 2016, that she was not required to recuse herself from the Midyear investigation. She decided not to voluntarily recuse herself for a variety of reasons, including that she did not have a personal relationship with either former President Clinton or former Secretary Clinton.

B.   Subsequent Discussions Between Comey and Yates

Yates said that sometime after her initial meeting with Comey, she received a phone call from him in which he said that he had been talking to "his people," and they had decided that the FBI would not make a recommendation at all. Yates said that Comey told her that the FBI instead would "just give DOJ the facts and DOJ would make the decision and [the FBI] wouldn't make a recommendation." According to Yates, Comey described this as the way the FBI and the Department "normally do it."

Yates said that she asked Comey what he was talking about, because the FBI always makes recommendations about charging decisions. According to Yates, she recalled saying the following to Comey:

> Jim, I thought we had talked about it the last meeting.... That we were all going to hold hands and jump off the bridge together. Because that's kind of how I viewed this was that this was going to be a tough thing here. That a lot of people were not going to like our decision but that's our job. And that we were going to, you know, we were all going to stand there together. We were going to announce it together.

Yates said that Comey was non-committal after she made this statement.

---

[131] On October 28, 2015, 44 Members of the House of Representatives sent a letter to Lynch requesting the appointment of a special counsel in the Midyear investigation, citing former President Obama's comments about the investigation on 60 Minutes as evidence that he had prejudged the investigation. The letter stated that a special counsel was warranted to ensure that the investigation was conducted free of undue bias from the White House. In addition, Senator Charles Grassley sent a letter to former Director Comey on May 17, 2016, asking various questions, including whether Comey believed that a special counsel was necessary.

Yates said that she remembered sitting at her desk after this call and thinking, "What?" She said that she spoke to Axelrod and Carlin after hanging up the phone, saying, "Holy cow. I mean, what is this business of now they're not even going to make a recommendation?"

Yates said that when she thought back to every major announcement she had done throughout her career, the lead investigative agency was always involved. She said that by that point it was "really clear that from the line agents all the way up they were all of the view that this shouldn't be a criminal prosecution." She said that given that agents and prosecutors agreed there was no basis to prosecute former Secretary Clinton, it was important to present a unified view of the investigation.

Comey told the OIG that he did not recall discussions about the end of the investigation with the Department other than his initial April meeting with Yates and Axelrod, and he did not recall any discussions with them about a joint Director-Attorney General announcement. Rybicki also said he did not recall any discussions about the end of the investigation.

Axelrod said he recalled that the FBI "went back and forth on whether...they wanted to be, whether they were willing or the Director was going to be willing to be part of...sort of some sort of joint roll out." Lynch also told the OIG that she recalled Yates mentioning that at some point that she had had another discussion with Comey, and that Comey was no longer sure that he should be the person making the announcement.

Yates said that after this call with Comey, there were other discussions with him where they were "back on track" and "all holding hands and jumping off the bridge together." Yates said she did not recall whether these subsequent discussions took place face-to-face or on the phone, or whether anyone else from the FBI was there. She said that they never made a final decision about how they would announce the declination, but that it was likely to be with a press conference where they laid out the facts supporting a conclusion that there was not a crime to be prosecuted. Yates said she had anticipated that Lynch would speak, but that they had not determined whether there would be other speakers. She said that they also planned to release a written document.

Yates told the OIG that she did not recall identifying a target date for making the announcement, but that they understood it would be a "matter of days" after the interview of former Secretary Clinton on Saturday, July 2, 2016. Yates stated, "And we were trying to be careful not to plan this too much, again, because we hadn't made the final decision yet. This is where we thought it was going to go but you don't know until that interview is concluded." Axelrod also told us that plans for an announcement were not "solidified because we weren't quite at the end."

C.   Other Discussions within the FBI and Department

1.   Discussions between McCabe and Carlin

Axelrod said that the discussions between Yates and Comey about the conclusion of the case were not the only ones that took place between the Department and the FBI. He said that during the Spring of 2016, Toscas, Carlin, Rybicki, and McCabe also were involved in discussions about how to credibly conclude and announce the conclusion of the investigation.

We asked various witnesses about these discussions but were unable to develop a precise timeline for them or a specific recollection of what was discussed. Carlin told the OIG that he may have talked about how to credibly announce a declination with McCabe "once or twice." He said that they discussed the "incredible scrutiny" that the case would receive and the need to memorialize in writing any disagreements between the team. He said they also discussed the need for a written description recounting the steps that were taken in the investigation. Carlin stated:

> And then what made this a little unusual for me anyway was that it came over as an IG, an 811 referral matter. And so one thing we had discussed was doing some closeout [summary of] facts to the IG.... If there were no criminal charges that doesn't mean there's not more to be done for the IG and lessons that they can learn from what we did in terms of the steps that they apparently felt they couldn't take...for things that were outside Government servers. And so I'd always thought at the end that some version of just the facts, not our thinking as to whether or not you bring a criminal charge, should go back to the IG in a closeout form. So then they could continue with whatever they were going to do, either administratively because there may be bad practices, or the set. Substantively it was clear to me from the investigation that there could be improvements made in terms of how the State Department was giving guidance and handling potentially classified information.

Carlin said that he did not know if Comey ever approved the idea of a referral back to IC IG, "But at the Deputy [McCabe] level I thought there was some agreement by a meeting of the minds that that was the likely way we were going to proceed." He said that he did not want to overstate it or give the impression that everyone had "signed off on" the idea, but that when he "raised that as a potential course it seemed like people thought that was reasonable." Carlin said that he did not recall discussing a joint press appearance by Lynch and Comey.

McCabe told the OIG that he recalled talking to Carlin about how to credibly conclude the investigation during lunch together in May or June 2016. McCabe said that neither of them had a "very well-formed idea" about what the end of the investigation looked like at that point, but that Carlin felt strongly that Comey should have a "very active and prominent role" in any public announcement.

McCabe said that they discussed various options, including a written memorandum or a joint press conference.

Asked about his involvement in discussions with the FBI about how to announce the conclusion of the case, Toscas said that he did not have a specific recollection of any such discussions. He stated:

> I very much wanted the Bureau [to be] part of the discussion and I know that there was some discussion of making sure that—or to try to have a joint AG/FBI Director statement, whether in front of cameras or an issued written statement, and I remember thinking, and I may have even talked to our team you know specifically about this, like we want—like we want the FBI Director talking about this, right. We want there to be—the American public to know that DOJ and FBI are together on this and that we've run it down and we've concluded the investigation.

Toscas also said that he thought that Department leadership separately was involved in discussions with the FBI about how to announce a declination, and that he vaguely recalled a discussion the week before the interview of former Secretary Clinton about what a joint appearance or statement would look like.

2. Discussions among Prosecutors and NSD Supervisors

On March 30, 2016, Prosecutor 1 sent an email to Prosecutor 2 stating, "Read the Ruth Marcus column in the [Washington] Post if you haven't yet."[132] The column referenced in the email discussed the public skepticism that would result from a decision not to indict former Secretary Clinton and recommended that the Department consider releasing a detailed investigative summary. It included a hyperlink to a public report released by the Department in 2010 that summarized the investigation into the 2001 anthrax letter attacks. The column also highlighted the need for a credible government official to provide the public with information about the investigation, noting, "Senior Justice officials will be mistrusted whatever they say, but what about FBI Director James B. Comey, who served in the Justice Department under George W. Bush?" Apparently after reading this column, Prosecutor 2 replied, "It is not dissimilar from some of the thoughts running through my head in the middle of the night...or what I tried expressing at that disastrous meeting we called with Toscas a couple months ago."

Prosecutor 2 told the OIG that they had a meeting with Toscas in or around February 2016 focused on what the end of the investigation should look like. According to Prosecutor 2, Toscas said at this meeting that the prosecutors would provide their legal analysis and conclusions to Carlin, through Toscas, and that there was some "vague idea" that Comey or McCabe would release a statement. This prosecutor told the OIG that the Department's involvement in any FBI statement was uncertain, and it was unclear at that point whether the statement would be written or oral. This prosecutor described this meeting as "contentious,"

---

[132] See Ruth Marcus, *What If Clinton Isn't Indicted?*, WASH. POST, Mar. 30, 2016, A17.

and said that NSD supervisors seemed to wonder what the line prosecutors wanted from them. This prosecutor said they brought up the issue of how to announce the end of the investigation because they were searching for assurances from their management that high-level Department officials would be involved. Prosecutor 2 stated:

> [I]f the statement is made, who is making that statement? Is it Comey? Will DOJ be standing by his side? If DOJ is standing by his side, is that going to be the Attorney General, or is that going to be [Prosecutor 1] and [Prosecutor 2]? Because [Prosecutor 1] and [Prosecutor 2] are driving this investigation for DOJ.

Prosecutor 1 did not recall when the meeting with Toscas took place, but estimated that it was sometime in early 2016. Prosecutor 1 stated that the plan discussed at that meeting was for them to finalize their legal analysis and conclusions and provide it to the NSD chain of command. Prosecutor 1 said that he also expected that there would be a public announcement of some sort given the high-profile nature of the investigation. As described in Section II.C.4 below, Prosecutor 1 said that as the investigation moved toward completion, he understood that Comey likely would be the official publicly announcing a declination.

Prosecutors 3 and 4 said that the team thought that the FBI would be involved in announcing the conclusion of the investigation, but they did not know what the plans were. Prosecutor 3 stated, "We speculated...that it would be some FBI report, like maybe a classified report of findings, and then a public report...because it was a high-profile investigation.... And no one really knew what, what the FBI was going to do." Prosecutor 4 told the OIG that he did not care how announcing a declination was handled, other than he wanted Comey to participate in it. This prosecutor stated:

> And from my vantage point, I didn't care other than the fact that I wanted Comey up there on a podium. I didn't care whether the AG was sitting next to, standing next to him or not. But I wanted Comey to make the announcement that, that the investigation was closed and that in FBI's viewpoint that there was not a prosecutable case....

> Because Comey was a Republican, or [had] a Republican background. He'd been a Republican-appointed U.S. Attorney. He had been a Republican-appointed DAG. I know Comey from his EDVA days. I think, thought he was widely respected on both sides of the aisle, before this case especially. And I thought that he had the gravitas, that no matter what he did, it was going to be questioned, but that it would be, that there would be an air of legitimacy to what I thought was a legitimate investigation if he made the announcement, and especially after the tarmac meeting.

This prosecutor told the OIG that Laufman had tried on several occasions to raise the issue of planning for a joint announcement at meetings with the FBI, and that Strzok was "always really squirrely about that." He said that Strzok would say that they should wait to see how everything worked out, or that the decision was "above [his] pay grade."

3. Additional Special Counsel Discussions

FBI Attorney 1 told us that the FBI Midyear team discussed whether they needed a special counsel at the beginning of the investigation in 2015. She said that at that time they had a legal intern research the statute, which expired and was replaced by regulations requiring appointment by the Attorney General.[133] She said that the discussion among the FBI Midyear team was, "[D]o we need one? When would we need one? How does this work sort of questions.... Was it necessary? And I, and I think we kind of thought we could handle this without the special counsel."

FBI Attorney 1 stated that the idea of a special counsel came up again at various points during the investigation, but that "[t]here was not any really significant discussion about it." She said that the team thought that they could complete the investigation, and they saw no signs of a conflict of interest on the part of the NSD lawyers.

Discussions about requesting a special counsel resurfaced within the Midyear team in mid-March 2016, following the discovery of the highly classified information, and occurred at various points through at least mid-May 2016. Text messages between Page and Strzok on March 18, 2016, indicate that the two of them discussed requesting a special counsel to oversee the investigation:

> 7:31 a.m., Strzok: "Thought of the perfect person D[irector Comey] can bounce this off of."
>
> 7:31 a.m., Page: "Who?"
>
> 7:37 a.m., Strzok: "Pat [Fitzgerald]. You gotta give me credit if we go with him. And delay briefing him on until I can get back and do it. Late next week or later."
>
> 7:38 a.m., Page: "We talked about him last night, not for this, but how great he is. He's in private practice though, right? Suppose you could still bring him back. And yes, I'll hold."
>
> 7:57 a.m., Strzok: "Yes, he's at Skadden in Chicago. I haven't talked to him for a year or two. Don't forget that D[AG] Comey appointed

---

[133] As discussed in Chapter Two, Department regulations at 28 C.F.R. § 600.1 provide that the Attorney General, or in cases in which the Attorney General is recused, the Acting Attorney General, will appoint a Special Counsel when he or she determines that criminal investigation of a person or matter is warranted and (a) that investigation or prosecution of that person or matter by a United States Attorney's Office or litigating Division of the Department of Justice would present a conflict of interest for the Department or other extraordinary circumstances; and (b) that under the circumstances, it would be in the public interest to appoint an outside Special Counsel to assume responsibility for the matter.

him as special counsel in the Plame matter, and that he was there for Comey's investiture."

7:58 a.m., Strzok: "I could work with him again. And damn we'd get sh*t DONE."

7:58 a.m., Page: "I know. Like I said, we discussed boss and him yesterday."

Based on the date of this exchange, Page told the OIG that the discovery of classified information relating to Lynch likely prompted her discussion with Strzok, but that she did not recall the idea of appointing Fitzgerald to be the special counsel for the Midyear investigation being discussed with FBI leadership. After reviewing a draft of the report, Page stated that she and Strzok had discussed consulting Fitzgerald about the classified information relating to Lynch, not about serving as a special counsel. Strzok said that he did not recall what led to this discussion, but he speculated that it may have been motivated by concerns about the information discussed in the classified appendix to this report. Strzok told the OIG that discussions about a special counsel reflected a genuine concern about the Department's ability to credibly close the investigation, denying that the idea was intended to get the Department to move more quickly on the Mills and Samuelson laptops.

Although witnesses denied that there was a specific deadline for completing the Midyear investigation, witnesses told us that Comey and other senior FBI officials strongly encouraged the team to finish the investigation as quickly as possible to avoid impacting the 2016 election. Notes reviewed by the OIG reflect that Comey increasingly was concerned by the timetable for completing the investigation as the debate about obtaining the laptops continued into May 2016. According to these notes, on May 9, 2016, Comey met with the FBI's Midyear team and told them that there "will come a point when DOJ can't credibly close this, and will need a special prosecutor." On May 11, 2016, other notes indicate that Comey told agents and prosecutors at a Midyear briefing that there was an "extraordinary sense of urgency" to complete the investigation, and that there was the risk that a declination would be perceived as partisan the closer they got to the election.

The next day, May 12, 2016, Strzok raised the possibility of a special counsel during a meeting with Laufman. Notes indicate that there was a lengthy discussion about Comey's timetable for completing the investigation and the need to obtain the Mills and Samuelson laptops, and that Strzok mentioned the possibility of requesting a special counsel if they got closer to the election. Laufman said that he viewed Strzok's comment as a "veiled threat" to make it clear that the FBI was dissatisfied with how NSD was handling the laptop issue and would proceed how it wanted. Laufman said he did not recall other instances where anyone from the FBI mentioned the possibility of requesting a special counsel.

4.   NSD Notes Reflecting Plans for an Announcement

As the team progressed toward the end of the investigation, information obtained by the OIG indicates that prosecutors and NSD supervisors were aware that Comey was planning to participate in an announcement. On May 16, 2016, Priestap sent an email to Toscas stating:

> I wanted you to be aware that Director Comey would like to see a list of all cases charged in the last 20 years where the gravam[e]n of the charge was mishandling classified information. He requested the information in chart form with: (1) case name, (2) a short summary for context (3) charges brought, and (4) charge of conviction.

Toscas forwarded the email to Laufman, who replied, "What is the meaning of this request? Have no problem sharing data we have amassed, but am concerned that it signifies an expectation by Bureau to play a larger role in DOJ charging decision than usual." Toscas replied, "We will all continue to work together with the Bu[reau] on all aspects of this, including with respect to any such decisions, so we should plan for and expect that our usual close collaboration with the Bureau will continue all the way through to the conclusion, including any such decisions."

Toscas also asked Laufman to call him. Notes memorializing a telephone call that day indicate that Toscas told Laufman, "Bureau may simply close this.... Don't think this is an insane request. Thinks Comey wants to see cases because he wants to be able to say why outcome not [out] of line. Everyone knows where we are going to end up."

NSD prosecutors prepared a chart of cases indicted since 2000 under various provisions prohibiting the mishandling and improper retention of classified information. Toscas emailed McCabe and Rybicki about the chart on May 23, 2016, and hand-delivered a copy to them at his routine morning meeting. The email sent by Toscas included the following caveats distinguishing the charged cases from the Midyear investigation:

> While it is not noted specifically in the chart, the vast majority of the listed cases involved documents or electronic files with classification markings on them. The few examples of charged cases where no markings were present involved photographs taken by the defendant (e.g., a case involving photos inside sensitive areas of a nuclear submarine) or handwritten notes where there were clear indications of knowledge of the sensitive nature of the materials (e.g., a case in which there was a recording of the defendant speaking about the classified nature of information in his hand-written notebooks).

> The "charging/plea information" column should make it clear, but the mishandling noted in the chart often occurred in conjunction with other criminal activity, including espionage, export control violations, and false statements, among others.

The chart did not include any examples of cases charged under Section 793(f).

Asked whether he thought Comey's request signaled a plan for greater involvement by the FBI, Laufman told the OIG that he viewed it as part of Comey's desire to make as knowledgeable a decision as possible about whether to charge Secretary Clinton or her senior aides. He stated, "And that's a conversation prosecutors always have with the agent, right?... So, I didn't have any problem arming him with the legal precedents that we thought informed our judgment, which we expected to be somewhat controversial, especially on the gross negligence statute."

Notes reviewed by the OIG indicate that Laufman had, or was told about by Toscas, discussions with the FBI regarding plans to announce a declination as the interview of former Secretary Clinton approached. In early June, the FBI and NSD began working jointly on an LHM outlining the facts developed in the investigation. The prosecutors began developing the legal framework for their analysis around the same time, but did not finalize any charging recommendations until after the interview.

On June 19, 2016, Laufman had a telephone conversation with Strzok about Comey's plans to make a statement about the investigation. Laufman's notes from this conversation listed the following topics for discussion:

(1) July 2 -----> Director's statement.

    Q: How many days later?

    Q: Content?

    E.g., is he planning on saying anything about DOJ's conclusions?

(2) Do you foresee any investigative activity after July 2?

The notes do not indicate what Strzok's responses were about Comey's plans for a statement. However, according to the notes, Strzok told Laufman that Comey wanted the investigation to be completed as soon as feasible, and thought it could be "largely done" other than classification reviews that were "unlikely to change [our] view" by July 2.

Laufman's notes from a telephone call with Toscas on June 24, 2016 indicate that the two of them discussed plans for a coordinated statement with Comey. The notes state:

"Good news/bad news"

Sounds like greater sense of "ownership" than expected – coming to realization that better if Dir[ector] is person who announces it; and seems like Dir[ector] will be up front explaining thoroughness, conclusion, not proceeding with any case. Voice of joint investigation.

But don't know what form this will take.

Bureau's exploitation of computers: by July 2 completed ---> goal.

Soon after interview, all will be put into motion.

Director will be champing at bit to make announcement....

Want team to sit down w[ith] DAG and AG, before Dir[ector] speaks.

183

On June 27, 2016, Laufman provided this information to Prosecutor 1 and another NSD supervisor. Laufman's notes from this date state, "Director will want to wrap up and make announcement quickly after interview.... Will be withering pressure after interview...expect to be very little that occurs at interview pertinent to mens rea determinations." These notes discuss the need to complete the joint LHM and the prosecutors' legal analysis and conclusions as quickly as possible.

Other notes obtained by the OIG indicate that prosecutors expected an announcement by Comey by Friday, July 8, 2016. On June 30, 2016, Laufman was told by another NSD supervisor, "Expect that FBI wants to announce by next Friday.... Wed or Thurs: briefing for DOJ leadership." On July 1, 2016, Laufman received a telephone call from Toscas stating that Toscas had spoken to McCabe and was told they were "still on track for Friday and FBI statement that day." Laufman met with Prosecutors 1 and 2 later that day and told them, "No change in known timetable for next week ---> Friday, July 8 announcement by Bureau. Details not known yet. Expect briefing of DAG + AG before (Thursday?)" The notes indicate that the team proposed staying at the FBI after the Clinton interview to "hash out differences" and finalize the closing LHM.

Asked whether these notes reflected advance knowledge by NSD supervisors and prosecutors about former Director Comey's plans for a public statement, Laufman said they did not. He told the OIG that discussions about how to announce the closing of the case intensified as the interview of former Secretary Clinton approached. He said that they understood that Comey was going to make some kind of a statement, but that anything he was going to say would be closely coordinated with the Department. He said he had no knowledge of and was not privy to discussions about plans for a joint statement by Comey and Lynch. Asked what he thought would happen as of July 1, 2016, he stated:

> I expected that we would complete the Clinton interview. The Bureau would complete its LHM. We would complete our [legal analysis]. Discussions would take place within DOJ, between DOJ and the Bureau, there would be a closely-coordinated endgame, like there is in the disposition of many matters in the Department where a bunch of people stand up...in front of a bunch of flags and carefully orchestrated, well thought through set of statements about a matter.... And we were going to be briefing the AG and the DAG before that.

Laufman also recalled Toscas telling him on several occasions that there was value in having Comey out front on the investigation, given the accusations by "political actors" that the Department could not be trusted to conduct a fair and balanced or complete investigation.

Strzok told the OIG that he participated in discussions with prosecutors about how to announce the closing of the investigation, including some discussions with Toscas. Strzok said they discussed whether there would be a press conference, who would participate in a press conference, and what level of detail any statement would provide, but he characterized these discussions as "preliminary." Anderson similarly told the OIG, "So, I think at some point, DOJ began pressing us to start talking about the end game. But we, within the Bureau, were already pretty far along in terms of our own thinking about what we thought the end game should be, such that we didn't really engage that meaningfully with DOJ on the issue at the line level."

However, notes indicate that FBI agents, lawyers, and senior officials were aware that the Department expected to make a joint announcement with the FBI at the end of the investigation. According to FBI Attorney 1's notes from a Midyear update meeting with Comey on June 27, 2016, the FBI discussed this expectation, stating, "Laufman saying pros memo + joint statement one week after HRC interview." Page's notes from the June 27 meeting indicate that FBI leadership told the Midyear team what to say to NSD about an announcement: "[Clinton] Interview Sat[urday]; LHM Tues[day], and our leadership will be talking to yours, & what you expect a final announcement will look like."

The next day, June 28, 2016, Laufman's notes reflect that an attorney in NSD's Front Office asked him to call Strzok and find out when the FBI planned to close the investigation. The notes read, "If not w/in short order after July 2 – if not by next week – Why not?! What's the plan...?" The notes indicate that Laufman spoke to Strzok, and Strzok told him that the FBI would finalize the LHM by the following Tuesday. The notes indicate that Laufman asked what Comey's goal was for announcing the closing of the investigation, and Strzok told Laufman he was not sure how soon it would be. That same day, Strzok and Page exchanged the following text messages:

> 12:43 p.m., Strzok: "God I am getting GRILLED by Laufman right now."
>
> 12:46 p.m., Page: "You've got your answer to give him...."
>
> 12:52 p.m., Strzok: "I do...Still going...."

III. Drafting of Former Director Comey's Public Statement

A. Original Draft Statement

Former Director Comey told the OIG that after his initial meeting with Yates and Axelrod in April 2016, he began thinking about the "outer boundaries" for announcing the conclusion of the investigation. He explained that a one-line press release by the Department stating that the case was closed was one outer boundary, and an FBI-only press conference providing a detailed statement about the investigation was the other. Comey said that the team from Strzok and the Lead Analyst on up discussed every option in between these two "outer boundaries." Comey told the OIG that he considered what options would be best calculated to minimize the reputational damage to the Department that might result from a declination decision given the partisan political environment in the country at that time.

Comey said that the possibility of the FBI doing a statement separate from the Department occurred to him around that time. He stated:

> I mean to my mind it was a crazy idea, but we were in a [500]-year flood, as you all have now investigated enough and lived enough to know, that this is a circumstance that has never happened before. We're criminally investigating one of the candidates for president of the United States.... [P]resident [Obama']s comments obviously weighed on me as well. You've got the President who has already said there's no there there.... And so all of that creates a situation where how do we get out of this without grievous damage to the institution?

Comey told us that, in addition to preserving the credibility and integrity of the Department and the FBI, his concern was protecting "a sense of justice more broadly in the country—that things are fair not fixed, and they're done independently."

McCabe told the OIG that he recalled that Comey first mentioned the idea of doing an independent statement as "an aside, at either the beginning or the end of a meeting that we had...in his conference room." McCabe said that Baker and Rybicki also were present, and that the group had been discussing where the investigation was going and what the end would look like "if we end up with nothing." He said that Comey asked them, "[W]hat do you think about the prospect of just like me doing something solo?" McCabe stated:

> And I remember when he said it kind of looking at Rybicki. And the both of us are just kind of like, oh my God, you know? And I, I mean honestly I, I, at first blush I was like, whew, wow, that's, that could go really wrong.... Because for, you know, for the obvious reason. It's just so not what we do. And we thought...that would be a huge break with...protocol...and everything else.

McCabe said that he may have told Comey that he was concerned that an independent statement would be a "complete departure" from Department protocol and could set a "potentially dangerous precedent" for the FBI. McCabe said that Comey was "very aware" that there were many reasons he should not do a statement on his own, and that "conventional wisdom might mitigate against it." He said that in late April and early May 2016, Comey was "not anywhere close to having decided to do it that way."

Comey told the OIG that he sat down one weekend and typed out a draft statement. He told the OIG that he did so from memory, explaining that it helps him to write when he is struggling with an idea. Comey described the draft statement as a "straw person," and told the OIG that he did this with the intention of giving the draft to the team and asking, "What do you think?"

On May 2, 2016, Comey sent an email to McCabe, Baker, and Rybicki including the text of the draft "straw person." He stated at the beginning of the email:

I've been trying to imagine what it would look like if I decided to do an FBI only press event to close out our work and hand the matter to DOJ. To help shape our discussions of whether that, or something different, makes sense, I have spent some time crafting what I would say, which follows. In my imagination, I don't see me taking any questions. Here is what it might look like.

Comey sent a four-page draft statement outlining what the Midyear team did and found by email, which we have provided as Attachment C to this report. The May 2 draft was substantially similar to Comey's final version, but with several notable exceptions. In particular, the May 2 draft statement used the statutory language from Section 793(f)(1), describing former Secretary Clinton's handling of classified information as "grossly negligent." It also concluded that there was evidence of potential violations of this provision and the misdemeanor removal statute, Section 1924. The draft stated:

> There is evidence to support a conclusion that Secretary Clinton, and others, used the private email server in a manner that was grossly negligent with respect to the handling of classified information.... There is evidence to support a conclusion that any reasonable person in Secretary Clinton's position, or in the position of those government employees with whom she was corresponding about these matters, should have known that an unclassified system was no place for such an email conversation. Although we did not find clear evidence that Secretary Clinton or her colleagues intended to violate laws governing the handling of classified information, there is evidence that they were extremely careless in their handling of very sensitive, highly classified information.

> Similarly, the sheer volume of information that was properly classified as Secret at the time it was discussed on email (that is, excluding the "up classified" emails) supports an inference that the participants were grossly negligent in their handling of that information....

> Finally, with respect to our recommendation to the Department of Justice. In our system, the prosecutors make the decisions about whether charges are appropriate based on evidence the FBI has helped collect. Although we don't normally make public our recommendations to the prosecutors, we frequently make recommendations and engage in productive conversations with prosecutors about what resolution may be appropriate, given the evidence. In this case, given the importance of the matter, I think unusual transparency is in order.

> Although there is evidence of potential violations of the statute proscribing gross negligence in the handling of classified information and of the statute proscribing misdemeanor mishandling, my judgment is that no reasonable prosecutor would bring such a case. At the outset, we are not aware of a case where anyone has been charged solely based on the gross negligence prohibition in the statute. All charged cases of which we are aware have involved the accusation

that a government employee intentionally mishandled classified information. In looking back at our investigations in similar circumstances, we cannot find a case that would support bringing criminal charges on these facts. All the cases prosecuted involved some combination of: (1) clearly intentional misconduct; (2) vast quantities of materials exposed in such a way as to support an inference of intentional misconduct; (3) indications of disloyalty to the United States; or (4) efforts to obstruct justice. We see none of that here.

As described in more detail below, the language characterizing former Secretary Clinton's conduct as "grossly negligent," the inference of gross negligence from the volume of classified email, and the reference to the misdemeanor mishandling statute were omitted from the final version delivered by Comey on July 5, 2016.

We asked Comey about the date of this initial draft and whether it indicated that he had predecided the outcome of the investigation even before the interview of former Secretary Clinton. Comey stated:

[I]f you were in my position after nine months you're incompetent if you don't know where this is going. Now the notion that I committed perjury by saying the decision wasn't made by then. The decision was not made by then. But it was a high probability...this was going to end in a certain way that would be really, really hard, which is the declination, so we better get to work thinking about that. Now if we find something else, great, or if...Hillary Clinton either gives us [18 U.S.C. §] 1001 [false statements] during the interview or the team says you know what, we've got to dig into some more stuff because she might have lied to us, wants to pursue additional investigative steps, you either recommend the 1001 or you say you know what, we've got more work to do here.... But in May, unless those things happen, I can see where this is headed and we've got to start to think carefully because you cannot be thinking about this on the weekend before the case ends. That's my reaction.

Comey also told the OIG that when he wrote the May 2 draft, he thought the investigation would be completed by June. As described in more detail below, Comey said he did not recall that his original draft used the term "gross negligence," and did not recall discussions about that issue.

On May 6, 2016, Comey emailed Rybicki and McCabe, stating, "Think maybe you should share my straw person announcement with Priestap, [Strzok], and [the Lead Analyst]. Close hold to the three of them but might be good to get them thinking." That afternoon, McCabe forwarded the draft statement to Priestap, Strzok, and the Lead Analyst, as well as Page. In the email, McCabe stated:

The Director composed the below straw man in an effort to compose what a "final" statement might look like in the context of a press conference. This was really more of an exercise for him to get his thoughts on the matter in order, and not any kind of decision about venue, strategy, product, etc.

The Director asked me to share this with you four, <u>but not any further</u>. The only additional people who have seen this draft are Jim Rybicki and Jim Baker. Please do not disseminate or discuss any further. (Emphasis in original).

McCabe's email noted that Comey might want to discuss the draft at the update meeting the following Monday, May 9, 2016. Strzok replied, "Understood and will do." McCabe then replied to Comey, "Spoke to Bill [Priestap] and passed the email on the red side to Bill, Pete and [the Lead Analyst]. Also took the liberty of including Lisa [Page] – I hope that was ok."

On May 6, 2016, shortly after receiving the draft, Priestap sent McCabe his initial comments. Priestap stated, "The piece is superb," and made several suggestions for minor changes. Priestap also noted that the draft contained information indicating that former Secretary Clinton did not comply with federal record requirements, suggesting that Comey have someone study the impact such a statement could have on administrative inquiries related to federal record obligations. McCabe sent these comments to Comey the following week.

On May 16, 2016, Rybicki sent the original draft to a larger group of people that included Anderson, FBI Attorney 1, and Bowdich, stating, "Please send me any comments on this statement so we may roll into a master doc for discussion with the Director at a future date." The draft statement also was discussed at a meeting that day that was attended by Comey, Rybicki, Bowdich, Steinbach, Priestap, Strzok, the Lead Analyst, Baker, Anderson, FBI Attorney 1, and Page. According to notes from this meeting, one of the items discussed was, "Do we agree w[ith] gross negligence assessment??"

Later that same day, the Lead Analyst provided comments to Strzok for incorporation into a "team response." The Lead Analyst characterized his comments as technical corrections, including one in which he recommended highlighting that some of the emails were found to contain classified information when sent, not just after the fact. The Lead Analyst stated, "All of this to emphasize that it is not true that this is all a matter of classification after-the-fact and that the people sending these emails should have known better."

Strzok included these comments and added his and Page's to an email that he sent to Rybicki, McCabe, and Priestap on behalf of the team on May 17, 2016. This email provided "overarching observations" about the draft, stating that they would provide additional comments and fact checking as Comey narrowed down what he wanted to say. Among the specific recommendations provided were suggestions that the statement include the number of emails containing information that was determined to be classified at the time they were sent to "more directly counter the continuous characterization by Hillary Clinton describing the emails involved in this investigation as having been classified after the fact."

The May 17 comments also noted the need to distinguish between prior high-profile mishandling prosecutions and the Midyear investigation. Strzok stated:

> We'd draw the distinction in noting that we have no evidence classified information was ever shared with an unauthorized party, i.e., notwithstanding the server set up, we have not seen classified information shared with a member of the media, an agent of a foreign power, a lover, etc. Additionally, it's important to note that had these same emails been sent on a state.gov system rather than a private one, it's not clear that the FBI would currently have an open investigation.

The May 17 email also commented on language in the initial draft that it was "reasonably likely that hostile actors gained access to Secretary Clinton's private email account." Strzok stated:

> It is more accurate to say we know foreign actors obtained access to some of her emails (including at least one Secret one) via compromises of the private email accounts of some of her staffers. It's also accurate to say that a sophisticated foreign actor would likely have known about her private email domain, and would be competent enough not to leave a trace if they gained access. But we have seen no direct evidence they did.

Finally, the May 17 comments listed "whether her conduct rises to the legal definition of gross negligence" as a topic for further discussion.

Responding to Strzok's email, Priestap provided additional comments on the draft the following day, May 18, 2016. Priestap suggested that the statement should more fully describe the FBI's role in recommending or not recommending that charges be brought in criminal cases, and why Comey was recommending that charges not be brought against former Secretary Clinton, stating:

> I believe it's equally important for the Director to more fully explain why the FBI can, in good faith, recommend to DOJ that they not charge someone who has committed a crime (as defined by the letter of the law). It's important the Director explain our recommendation from the FBI perspective and not from the DOJ/prosecutorial perspective. The FBI is recommending that charges not be brought in this instance, not only because "no reasonable prosecutor would bring such a case," but because the FBI believes it's the right thing to do based on.... (Emphasis and ellipses in original).

Priestap also suggested that Comey had the option of not making a charging recommendation at all, but that this would undermine the FBI's position with the Department in future cases. He suggested that Comey could emphasize privately to the Department that it should take the FBI's charging recommendations seriously, stating, "DOJ can't just stand with us when it's easy for them to do so." Priestap's comments also stated, "While I was initially wary of having the Director provide an investigative update, I'm beginning to warm to the idea...if we don't soon shape the narrative with the facts, the narrative will be shaped by others, potentially harming the FBI."

According to a meeting log prepared by FBI OGC, on May 24, 2016, Comey met with Page, Strzok, Baker, Anderson, FBI Attorney 1, and others to discuss the statement. Page's notes from the meeting indicate that the group discussed adding language highlighting how well the Midyear investigation was done and that there had been no political interference. The notes also state that they planned to "have another conversation about the strategy at all [sic]."

B.   The Decision to Omit "Gross Negligence"

Comey again met with Rybicki, Bowdich, Steinbach, Priestap, Strzok, the Lead Analyst, Baker, Anderson, FBI Attorney 1, and Page to discuss the statement on May 31, 2016. Notes from this meeting indicate that the discussion included "Lisa [Page]/[FBI Attorney 1] legal thinking." According to Page, she raised concerns about the use of "grossly negligent" in the draft statement at one of the meetings with Comey (likely the May 31 meeting) before making edits to the statement. Page told us:

> I believe that I raised with [Comey] the concern...with the use of gross negligence in particular because I was concerned that it would be confusing if we used a...term that has a legal definition...if we say she's grossly negligent, that despite the fact that we, we and the Department had a good reason to not charge her with gross negligence, given the fact that they thought it was unconstitutionally vague, and it had never been done, and, you know, sort of all of the concomitant defenses that would also follow from, from her conduct, that it would just be overly confusing.

Page further stated, "If the purpose of this is sort of clarity, and the purpose of this is to sort of try to explain to the American populace what happened and what we think about it, that to use a term that had an actual legal definition would be confusing." She said that the team discussed the need to find some other way to characterize former Secretary Clinton's conduct.

FBI Attorney 1 told the OIG that she remembered sitting down with Rybicki, Strzok, the Lead Analyst, and Page to discuss the language of the statute and whether to use "grossly negligent" wording in the draft statement. Based on a meeting log prepared by FBI OGC, we determined that this meeting took place on June 6, 2016. Rybicki said that he did not recall the substance of discussions about removing "grossly negligent" from the draft, but that there was "a lot of discussion" among the FBI OGC lawyers about the statute." He said he primarily input changes made by others and described his role in revising the statement as "scribe detail."

After this meeting, Strzok, the Lead Analyst, Page, and FBI Attorney 1 met to edit the statement. Page told the OIG that the four of them edited the document together at Strzok's computer. Metadata from a version of the statement indicates that Strzok modified the draft on June 6, 2016.[134]

The next day, June 7, 2016, Strzok emailed an electronic copy of the revised draft to Page, and Page sent it to Rybicki, stating in the email, "Our thoughts, for the Director's consideration." The revised draft attached to Page's email was entitled "MYE thoughts 06-07-16" and included a number of changes from Comey's original draft. Among the changes in the revised draft was the removal of the conclusion that there was evidence that former Secretary Clinton and her staff were "grossly negligent" in their handling of classified information. Instead, the June 7 draft moved language from the end of the same paragraph in Comey's original version to the beginning of that paragraph, stating:

> Although we did not find evidence that Secretary Clinton or her colleagues intended to violate laws governing the handling of classified information, there is evidence that they were extremely careless in their handling of very sensitive, highly classified information.... There is evidence to support a conclusion that any reasonable person in Secretary Clinton's position, or in the position of those government employees with whom she was corresponding about these matters, should have known that an unclassified system was no place for such an email conversation.

Page told us that FBI Attorney 1 was the one who moved "extremely careless" to the beginning of the paragraph. FBI Attorney 1 agreed that she likely was the one who suggested this edit given that she had the most familiarity with the statute. This change was included in the final version of the statement.

The draft also removed a reference to evidence of potential violations of the misdemeanor mishandling statute.[135] The draft instead concluded that there was evidence of potential violations of statutes regarding the handling of classified information, and used the language from Comey's original draft that no reasonable prosecutor would bring such a case.

The June 7 draft included two other significant changes. It removed the statement that the sheer volume of information classified as Secret supported an inference of gross negligence, replacing it with a statement that the Secret information they discovered was "especially concerning because all of these emails

---

[134] Separately, on June 6, 2016, Priestap sent an email to McCabe and other providing input on the draft statement. In this email, he stated, "In my opinion, due to the election, this matter warrants the Director providing the American public an update. Ideally, this update would be provided as many weeks in advance of the National Conventions as is possible." When asked about this email, Priestap told the OIG that in his view the investigation had been politicized, and that former Secretary Clinton engendered strong feelings of support or dislike in some. He explained that he viewed it as the FBI's obligation to "let people know what was and was not found."

[135] As set forth in Chapter Two, 18 U.S.C. § 1924 prohibits the knowing removal of documents or materials containing classified information without authority and with the intent to retain such documents or materials at an unauthorized location.

were housed on servers not supported by full-time staff." The draft also stated that it was "possible," rather than "reasonably likely," that hostile actors gained access to former Secretary Clinton's server.[136]

Comey told the OIG that he did not recall that his initial draft used "grossly negligent," and did not specifically recall what discussions led to this change. He said that the group that met to discuss the drafts of his statement—which included Rybicki, Bowdich, Steinbach, Priestap, Strzok, the Lead Analyst, Baker, Anderson, FBI Attorney 1, and Page—struggled to figure out what term to use to describe former Secretary Clinton's conduct, because "it was more than your ordinary somebody left a document in a unprotected place or had a single conversation." According to Comey, they tried to capture the sense that her use of the private server was "really sloppy, but it doesn't rise to the level of prosecution." He speculated during his OIG interview that the team advised him that it was unwise to track the statutory language because the "grossly negligent" conduct required by Section 793(f) is something just short of willful or reckless.

Comey told the OIG that nothing the FBI learned between May 2 and July 5 changed their view of whether former Secretary Clinton's conduct met the definition of "gross negligence." Comey said that it was his understanding based on the statute's legislative history that Congress intended for there to be some level of willfulness present even to prove a "gross negligence" violation. When asked whether he believed at any time in the process that former Secretary Clinton was grossly negligent within the meaning of Section 793(f), Comey said, "No." Comey explained:

> There was no evidence to establish anything close to willfulness which I take as a conscious disregard of a non-legal duty and that the closest to there to me was, it's just really sloppy. A reasonable person in her position should have known, but what I understood 793(f) to be about is something closer to actual knowledge, but I think that it was this is obviously wildly distorted, but I think that's what we were grappling with....

> I'm trying to find a way to credibly describe what we think she did and our sense was, frankly mere negligence didn't get it because it was not just ordinary sloppiness, it was sloppiness across a multiyear period and so there was, I had in my head some sense that to be credible, we have to capture that and what words do we use to capture it—and

---

[136] As described in Chapter Five, the LHM summarizing the Midyear investigation stated, "FBI investigation and forensic analysis did not find evidence confirming that Clinton's email server systems were compromised by cyber means." The LHM noted that the FBI identified one successful compromise of an account belonging to one of former President Clinton's staffers on a different domain within the same server that former Secretary Clinton used during her tenure, as well as compromises to email accounts belonging to certain people who communicated with Clinton by email, such as Jake Sullivan and Sidney Blumenthal. The FBI Forensics Agent who conducted the intrusion analysis told the OIG that, although he did not believe there was "any way of determining...100%" whether Clinton's servers had been compromised, he felt "fairly confident that there wasn't an intrusion."

that's where we found the formulation extremely careless. Now if I had to do it over again, I might have tried to find another term because this, we sort of walked into this entire side show about 793(f), but I haven't thought of another term since then.

Comey said that he thought that the June 7 edits "track[ed] [his] formulation" by moving the "extremely careless" language from the end of the paragraph in his original draft to the beginning.

After reviewing a draft of the report, Anderson told the OIG that she raised concerns about the use of the phrase "extremely careless" to describe former Secretary Clinton's conduct, as being unnecessary to the statement and also likely to raise questions as to why the conduct did not constitute gross negligence. Anderson said that she recalled that others voiced the same concern, but that she did not recall precisely who raised this issue or what was said. She said that she recalled that Comey felt strongly that former Secretary Clinton's behavior was "extremely careless," and thought that this was the most accurate phrase to describe Clinton's conduct notwithstanding concerns about criticizing her uncharged conduct or the potential for confusion.

C.   Comey's Edits to the Statement

On June 10, 2016, Rybicki emailed a revised draft of the statement to Comey. Two days later, on June 12, 2016, Comey emailed additional revisions to Rybicki. Comey stated in his email, "Here is my near final [draft]. Please have the team review it. I have saved as PDF so the team reads it fresh and not as a track-change."

Comey's June 12 draft incorporated the "extremely careless" language from the previous revisions:

> Although we did not find clear evidence that Secretary Clinton or her colleagues intended to violate laws governing the handling of classified information, there is evidence that they were extremely careless in their handling of very sensitive, highly classified information.

> For example, seven email chains concern matters that were classified at the Top Secret/Special Access Program level when they were sent and received. These chains involved Secretary Clinton both sending emails about those matters and receiving emails from others about the same matters. There is evidence to support a conclusion that any reasonable person in Secretary Clinton's position, or in the position of those government employees with whom she was corresponding about these matters, should have known that an unclassified system was no place for that conversation. In addition to this highly sensitive information, we also found information that was properly classified as Secret by the U.S. Intelligence Community at the time it was discussed on email (that is, excluding the later "upclassified" emails).

Comey's June 12 draft added new language that stated, "Separately, it is important to point out that even if information is not marked 'classified' in an email, participants who know or should know that the subject matter is classified are still obligated to protect it." This language was included in a revised form in the final statement delivered by Comey.

The revisions by Comey and Rybicki included new language about the factors that a "reasonable prosecutor" would consider in declining to prosecute a case. Comey's June 12 draft stated:

> Although there is evidence of potential violations of the statutes regarding the handling of classified information, our judgment is that no reasonable prosecutor would bring such a case. Prosecutors necessarily weigh a number of factors before bringing charges. There are obvious considerations, like the strength of the evidence, especially about intent. Responsible decisions also consider the context of a person's actions, and how similar situations have been handled in the past.

> In looking back at our investigations into mishandling or removal of classified information, we cannot find a case that would support bringing criminal charges on these facts. All the cases prosecuted involved some combination of: clearly intentional and willful mishandling of classified information; or vast quantities of materials exposed in such a way as to support an inference of intentional misconduct; or indications of disloyalty to the United States; or efforts to obstruct justice. We do not see those things here.

> To be clear, this is not to suggest that in similar circumstances, a person who engaged in this activity would face no consequences. To the contrary, those individuals are often subject to security or administrative sanctions. But that is not what we are deciding now.

Following these revisions, discussions about the draft statement continued. Meetings took place on June 13, 14, and 15 to discuss various issues related to the draft. Documents provide little information about the substance of these meetings, and witnesses did not have a specific recollection of them.

Comey and Rybicki also continued to refine the draft statement, exchanging revised versions on June 25, 26, and 30, and July 1, 2, and 4. Two significant changes appeared in the statement during this time period.

A June 25 draft added a sentence to a paragraph that summarized the factors that led the FBI to conclude that it was possible that hostile actors accessed former Secretary Clinton's private server. This new sentence stated, "She also used her personal email extensively while outside the United States, including from the territory of sophisticated adversaries. That use included an email exchange with the President while Secretary Clinton was on [sic] the territory of such an adversary." On June 30, Rybicki circulated another version that changed the second sentence to remove the reference to the President, replacing it with "another senior government official."[137] The final version of the statement omitted this reference altogether and instead read, "She also used her personal email extensively while outside the United States, including sending and receiving work-related emails in the territory of sophisticated adversaries." FBI emails indicate that the decision to remove this sentence was based on concerns about litigation risk under the Privacy Act.

In addition, on the morning of June 30, Comey added the following paragraph to the statement introduction:

> This will be an unusual statement in at least a couple ways. First, I am going to include more detail than I ordinarily would, because I think the American people deserve those details in a case of intense public interest. Second, I have not coordinated or reviewed this statement in any way with the Department of Justice or any other part of the government. They do not know what I am about to say.

This paragraph was included in the final version of the statement that Comey publicly delivered on July 5, 2016. While we did not ask Comey if he added this paragraph in response to the tarmac meeting between Lynch and former President Clinton, as described below in Section IV.D, Comey told us that this meeting "tipped the scales" in terms of his decision to deliver his statement "separate and apart" from the Department.[138]

---

[137] After reviewing a draft of this report, Rybicki explained that, although he circulated the new version of the draft statement, he did not suggest or make this specific edit.

[138] Text messages between Page and Strzok on July 1, 2016, the day Lynch announced she would accept the recommendations of career prosecutors and agents, speculated that the tarmac meeting was the reason for inserting the "no coordination" language:

> 5:34 p.m., Strzok: "Holy cow...nyt breaking Apuzzo, Lync[h] will accept whatever rec D and career prosecutors make. No political appointee input."

> 5:41 p.m., Strzok: "Lynch. Timing not great, but whatever. Wonder if that's why the no coordination language added[.]"

> 7:29 p.m., Strzok: "Timing looks like hell. Will appear choreographed. All major news networks literally leading with 'AG to accept FBI D's recommendation.'"

> 7:30 p.m., Page: "Yeah, that is awful timing. Nothing we can do about it."

> 7:31 p.m., Strzok: "What I meant was, did DOJ tell us yesterday they were doing this, so D added that language[?]"

> 7:31 p.m., Strzok: "Yep. I told Bill the same thing. Delaying just makes it worse."

> 7:35 p.m., Page: "And yes. I think we had some warning of it. I know they sent some statement to rybicki, bc he called andy."

> 7:35 p.m., Page: "And yeah, it's a real profile in courag[e], since she knows no charges will be brought."

D. FBI Analysis of Legal and Policy Issues Implicated by the Draft Statement

Comey told the OIG that he included criticism of former Secretary Clinton's uncharged conduct because "unusual transparency…was necessary for an unprecedented situation," and that such transparency "was the best chance we had of having the American people have confidence that the justice system works[.]" He said that that he asked Baker and FBI OGC to "scrub" his draft statement and "think about it through all possible policy, legal lenses." He said that his recollection was that "the only [issue] they thought that was worthy of discussion was the Privacy Act, and they had their Privacy Act czar d[o] a memo for me laying out how—why they thought it was fine under the Privacy Act."[139] Comey said that Baker's advice to him was that "there w[ere] no policy or legal issues created by you doing this." Baker told the OIG that he and other FBI OGC attorneys did see numerous legal and policy issues associated with the statement, but that they could not find a clear legal prohibition that would have prevented Comey from issuing the statement.

Comey cited as precedent for his statement the press conference he gave in June 2004, when he was the Deputy Attorney General, summarizing the evidence against José Padilla, a U.S. citizen who had been designated as an enemy combatant due to his support for al Qaeda.[140] He stated:

> I mean it wasn't a case, but I actually remember when I was DAG providing extraordinary transparency to the public around José Padilla which was a subject of great concern and controversy at the time and I remember commissioning the drafting of a very transparent statement about everything we knew about him and then pushing to get it declassified, get it reviewed for Privacy Act compliance which we

---

[139] The Privacy Act of 1974, 5 U.S.C. § 552a, prohibits an agency from disclosing a record about an individual to a person, or to another government agency, from a "system of records" absent the written consent of the individual, unless the disclosure is pursuant to a statutory exception. A system of records is a group of records under the control of an agency from which information is retrieved by the name of the individual or some other personal identifier assigned to the individual. Relevant information about an individual may be disclosed without consent under 12 statutory exceptions set forth in the Privacy Act, including one permitting "routine use" by the agency. See 5 U.S.C. § 552a(b)(3). One of the "routine uses" adopted by the FBI permits disclosure to "members of the general public in furtherance of a legitimate law enforcement or public safety function as determined by the FBI," for example, "to provide notification of arrests…or to keep the public appropriately informed of other law enforcement or FBI matters or other matters of legitimate public interest where disclosure could not reasonably be expected to constitute an unwarranted invasion of personal privacy." This includes the disclosure of information under 28 C.F.R. § 50.2, which governs the release of information about criminal and civil proceedings by Department personnel (including the FBI).

[140] See Transcript, Press Conference of James Comey, CNN, June 1, 2004, http://www.cnn.com/2004/LAW/06/01/comey.padilla.transcript (accessed May 1, 2018). Padilla was initially arrested on a material witness warrant in May 2002 but was then declared an enemy combatant by President Bush in June 2002 and transferred to military custody. Padilla was subsequently prosecuted by the Department in the civilian court system and in August 2007 a federal jury found him guilty of conspiring to commit murder and fund terrorism.

also did here and then getting that out, so I remembered that pretty well.

Comey also cited the Department's letter to Congress summarizing the results of the criminal investigation into Internal Revenue Service (IRS) officials, including Lois Lerner.[141] Comey said that the Lerner letter, which criticized IRS officials for "mismanagement, poor judgment, and institutional inertia" that did not amount to criminal conduct, supported his decision to criticize former Secretary Clinton's handling of classified information even in the absence of sufficient evidence to establish her criminal liability.[142]

Witnesses told us that the Privacy Act concerns stemmed largely from Comey's criticism of former Secretary Clinton's conduct in his draft statement, but that they believed including such criticism served a legitimate law enforcement function (and thus was permitted). According to FBI Attorney 1, the high public interest in the case, the particular individual involved, and the need to deter others provided justifications for including the information:

> So it wasn't just that we weren't prosecuting her, but you didn't want to leave the impression with...the rest of the community that she's getting away with something or...that this is okay to do this. And so I think there was that, that balance. And that's why I don't think I thought so hard about the, the fact that we were talking about uncharged conduct of her. I was thinking more in terms of well we need to kind of balance this so that people understand that we're not

---

[141] On October 23, 2015, the Department's Office of Legislative Affairs (OLA) sent a letter to Congress summarizing the results of a criminal investigation conducted by the Criminal and Civil Rights Divisions, in conjunction with the FBI and the Treasury Inspector General for Tax Administration, into whether any IRS official targeted tax-exempt organizations for scrutiny based on their ideological views. The letter stated that the investigation uncovered "substantial evidence of mismanagement, poor judgment, and institutional inertia," but "no evidence that any IRS official acted based on political, discriminatory, corrupt, or other inappropriate motives that would support a criminal prosecution." Regarding Lois Lerner, the former Director of the IRS Exempt Organizations Division, the letter stated that the investigation had focused on her criminal culpability given her oversight role and emails discovered in which she "expressed her personal political views and, in one case, hostility toward conservative radio personalities." The letter concluded that Lerner "exercised poor judgment in using her IRS email account to exchange personal messages that reflected her political views," but that prosecutors could not "show that these messages related to her official duties and actions[.]" Peter Kadzik, Assistant Attorney General, U.S. Department of Justice, letter to The Honorable Bob Goodlatte and John Conyers, Jr., October 23, 2015, *at* http://online.wsj.com/public/resources/documents/IRS1023.pdf.

[142] Comey told the OIG that "a friend of [his who] is a law professor" had a law student compile a chart showing cases in which the Department made a public statement announcing the closing of an investigation. The chart was created in January 2017, and included 31 cases since February 2010 in which such statements were made by Department leadership or a U.S. Attorney's Office. Although the chart noted one case in which an FBI agent spoke at a press conference with the U.S. Attorney, every case listed in the chart involved a public statement coordinated with or made by the prosecutors. The OIG determined that the "law professor" referenced by Comey was Dan Richman, a professor at Columbia Law School who was also a special government employee (SGE) for the FBI from June 2015 to February 2017.

giving her a clean bill of health, you know, and that people can do this kind of activity.

Anderson told the OIG that she expressed concerns about criticizing uncharged conduct during discussions with Comey in June 2016. She said that the decision to include such criticism "was a signal that...we weren't just letting her off the hook.... [O]ur conclusions were going to be viewed as less assailable...at the end of the day if this kind of content was included."

Baker told the OIG that "there were multiple audiences" for the criticism of former Secretary Clinton in Comey's statement. He recounted hearing that FBI employees not involved in the Midyear investigation hated former Secretary Clinton and had made comments such as, "[Y]ou guys are finally going to get that bitch," and, "[W]e're rooting for you." Baker stated, "And if we're not going to get her on these facts and circumstances, then we'd better explain that now." Related to this idea, notes taken by Strzok at a May 12, 2016 meeting involving the Midyear team state, "Messaging thoughts: Workforce Qs: (1) If I did this, I'd be prosecuted; (2) Petraeus, Berger, etc. were charged; (3) Overwhelming conservative outlook."

FBI Attorney 1 told the OIG that she also considered whether the July 5 statement would violate the Department's Election Year Sensitivities Policy. As described in Chapter Two, that policy requires approval from the Public Integrity Section of the Criminal Division before filing charges or taking overt investigative steps near the time of a primary or general election. However, the policy applies only to election crimes cases. FBI Attorney 1 told us, "Someone mentioned [the policy] at that time. And I looked into it, and...it's not specific to this kind of case. And that's kind of the problem, I think, with the policy."

Baker told the OIG that the FBI took into account and complied with the requirement that Department personnel obtain the approval of the Attorney General or the Deputy Attorney General for the public release of certain information.[143] Baker said that Comey's call to Lynch and Yates on the morning of his July 5 press conference (described below) telling them that he planned to hold a press conference later that morning, and their failure to instruct him not to do so, constituted "permission" under Department regulations. Baker said that this was so even though Comey called Lynch and Yates only after calling the press and he had refused to tell Lynch and Yates what he planned to say. When pressed by the OIG about this interpretation of the regulation, Baker acknowledged that it was "aggressive." In comments to the draft report, Baker further explained that because Comey did call Yates and Lynch on July 5:

> They could have demanded to know what he was going to say, and/or could have told him not to do it without a full discussion with them. They did not. One is the AG, the other the DAG. They had an

---

[143] Under 28 C.F.R. § 50.2(b)(9), the permission of the Attorney General or the Deputy Attorney General is required "if a representative of the Department believes that in the interest of the fair administration of justice and the law enforcement process information beyond these guidelines should be released."

opportunity to say "no" or "stop" to the FBI Director. For whatever reasons, they did not. That is on them.

E.   Concerns about a Public Statement

Numerous witnesses told the OIG that, while they did not recall any significant disagreement within the FBI about whether Comey should do a public statement, there was concern about whether he should do one on his own, without advance notification to or coordination with the Department. McCabe's initial reaction to the idea was that it would breach Department protocol and create "dangerous precedent" for the FBI, among "a million other possible things" that could go wrong. However, McCabe told the OIG, "[U]ltimately I was convinced that, that he was doing what he thought was right and that what was right for the case."

Baker told the OIG that he raised similar concerns in various one-on-one discussions with Comey over an extended time period. Baker said he did so because he "viewed it as my obligation to push back aggressively with respect to whatever [Comey] said if I thought it was wrong," to make sure that all legal, policy, and ethical issues were fully evaluated, and to "think about how others would think about things" from different perspectives and at different times. Baker said that he and Comey discussed a range of options for announcing a declination and thought through the benefits and drawbacks of each, "tr[ying] to find some door other than the doors that led to hell."

Comey also sought input from his former FBI Chief of Staff, Chuck Rosenberg, who at the time was the Acting Administrator of the Drug Enforcement Administration. Comey told the OIG that in May and June 2016 he spoke to Rosenberg and "sounded him out" about the possibility of doing an FBI-only press announcement to close the investigation. According to Comey, Rosenberg was concerned that doing a statement would be unprecedented, expose Comey to "extraordinary fire," and create an irreparable breach with the Department. Comey said that Rosenberg thought that doing the statement was a "close call, but on balance, it's the right call."

Rosenberg told the OIG that he spoke to Comey three times about the draft statement. He said that Comey first reached out to him in late April or early May 2016, before there was a draft statement and well before the tarmac meeting between Lynch and former President Clinton. Rosenberg said that Comey was seeking guidance on whether he should make a public statement to announce the FBI was closing the Midyear investigation, or should do a referral to the Department. Rosenberg described Comey as "wrestling" with the decision and trying to figure out the right thing to do.

Rosenberg said that Comey showed him a hard copy of the May 2 draft statement, and told him that he planned to do the statement on his own, without coordinating with the Department. Rosenberg said that Comey thought he could more credibly announce a declination without the Department because of the "politics" of having an Attorney General appointed by a Democratic President close an investigation into the Democratic presidential nominee without charges. Asked whether Comey discussed concerns about Lynch based on her instruction to him to call the investigation a "matter" or classified issues reflecting potential bias by her, Rosenberg said that he did not recall Comey mentioning those to him.

Rosenberg said that he had two competing reactions to the statement. He said that on one hand, it was "outside the norm" and inconsistent with the Department's practice, and that had the FBI publicly announced a recommendation when he was a U.S. Attorney instead of giving it to him privately, he would not have been happy. On the other hand, he thought that Comey was a "compelling and credible public servant," and he said he understood why Comey thought he could "do this and do it well." Rosenberg said that he did not tell Comey that it was a good or bad idea, but instead raised questions about what other options were available and the potential ramifications of an FBI Director giving a public declination. Rosenberg said that he recalled telling Comey it was a "52-48 call," but that he went back and forth on whether the "52" weighed in favor of or against doing the statement.

F.   Comey's Decision Not to Inform the Department

As described above, documents and testimony indicate that Comey planned to do the statement independently without advance notice to the Department even before the tarmac meeting between Lynch and former President Bill Clinton. Comey acknowledged that he made a conscious decision not to tell Department leadership about his plans to independently announce a declination because he was concerned that they would instruct him not to do it, and that he made this decision when he first conceived of the idea to do the statement. He stated:

> The, come May, and I'm trying to figure out how the endgame should work, to preserve the option that I ended up concluding was best suited to protect the institutions, I couldn't tell them that I was considering that. Because if I told them that one of the—in my mind I drew this spectrum—at one end of the spectrum is I'm going to announce separate from you what the FBI thinks about this and very practical about it they, I remember thinking this, if I surface that with them, they might well say, I order you not to do that and then I would abide that, I wouldn't do that.

> And so I remember saying to the Midyear team when I circulated in May my first draft I said what would the most, one end of the spectrum, what would that option look like? I said keep this close hold, I mean you can have conversations with the Department of Justice about the endgame, but don't tell them I'm considering this because then that option is going from us. Because if I were the DAG, maybe they wouldn't have, but what I was thinking was, if I'm the DAG I say, just to be clear, I order you not to make any statements on this case without coordinating it with us. And so to be honest, I would lose that option.

201

Asked whether he owed it to Department leadership to inform them of what he was thinking so that they could make a decision on behalf of the Department, Comey stated, "In a normal circumstance, sure." He explained that the Midyear investigation was not a normal circumstance:

> [T]o my mind, the peril to the Department, including the FBI, was so extraordinary, the potential for damage to the institution, that I needed to preserve that option.... And so look I, everything about this is unprecedented and God willing no Director will ever face this circumstance, but I thought that to protect the institution I care about so much, I have to preserve that option. Of course, in a normal circumstance it's the right of the Attorney General and Deputy Attorney General to make those decisions and the FBI Director should tell them, but this was not the normal circumstance.

Comey told the OIG that he did not credibly think that Lynch and Yates were going to stop him when he informed them about his plans on the morning of his press conference, and that he wrestled with whether to tell them at all.

IV. June 27, 2016 Tarmac Meeting and Aftermath

A. Meeting between Lynch and Former President Clinton

1. How the Meeting Came About

On June 27, 2016, Lynch flew to Phoenix as the first stop in a week-long community policing tour.[144] Traveling with her were her husband, her Deputy Chief of Staff, a senior counselor to the AG (Senior Counselor), a supervisor in the Department's Office of Public Affairs (OPA Supervisor), and another Department official. Lynch told the OIG that her plane landed several hours late, and they arrived in Phoenix around 7 p.m. local time. According to Department witnesses, Lynch's staff left the plane first and boarded the staff van. Lynch remained on the plane with her husband and the head of her security detail, and waited to get off the plane until her motorcade was ready. The OPA Supervisor explained that this practice is standard FBI protocol and is intended to leave the Attorney General "out in the open for the least amount of time."

Approximately 20 to 30 yards from Lynch's plane was a private plane with former President Bill Clinton on it. Former President Clinton had been in Phoenix for several campaign events, including a roundtable discussion with Latino leaders and a campaign fundraiser, and his plane was preparing to depart. Former President Clinton said that he did not know in advance that Lynch was in Phoenix and was not aware that her plane was close to his until his staff told him. Asked

---

[144] The Attorney General is required to travel on government aircraft for communications and security reasons, and used FBI and Department aircraft to do so.

about news reports that he purposely delayed his takeoff to speak to Lynch, former President Clinton stated:

> It's absolutely not true. I literally didn't know she was there until somebody told me she was there. And we looked out the window and it was really close and all of her staff was unloading, so I thought she's about to get off and I'll just go shake hands with her when she gets off. I don't want her to think I'm afraid to shake hands with her because she's the Attorney General.

He said that he discussed with his Chief of Staff whether he should say hello to Lynch, and that they debated whether he should do it because of "all the hoopla" in the campaign. He stated, "I just wanted to say hello to her and I thought it would look really crazy if we were living in [a] world [where] I couldn't shake hands with the Attorney General you know when she was right there."

Former President Clinton said that he did not consider that meeting with Lynch might impact the investigation into his wife's use of a private email server. He stated, "Well what I didn't want to do is to look like I was having some big huddle-up session with her you know.... [B]ecause it was a paranoid time, but...I knew what I believed to be the truth of that whole thing. It was after all my server and the FBI knew it was there and the Secret Service approved it coming in and she just used what was mine." As a result, he said that he never thought the investigation "amounted to much frankly so I didn't probably take it as seriously as maybe I might have in this unusual period[.]"

Former President Clinton said that he recalled walking toward Lynch's plane with his Chief of Staff, and that Lynch and her staff were "getting off the airplane." He said that he greeted Lynch, who was on the plane, and Lynch stated, "[L]ook it's a 100 degrees out there, come up and we'll talk about our grandkids."

The Senior Counselor told the OIG that she was waiting in the van with the three other Department employees on the trip, and she saw two people walking toward Lynch's plane. She said that as the two people went up the stairs to the plane, she realized that one of them was former President Clinton. The Senior Counselor said that she saw the head of Lynch's security detail turn away the second person at the door and allow former President Clinton to board the plane. Other witnesses recalled that former President Clinton had additional staff members with him, and that these people did not board the plane.

The Deputy Chief of Staff said that she had "zero knowledge" that former President Clinton was there before she saw him approach the plane. She stated, "And if I had knowledge, I would not have been in that van. I would've...stayed on the plane and got everybody off.... No heads up or anything." The Senior Counselor said she asked everyone in the van if they knew that former President Clinton was going to be there, and they all said no. The OPA Supervisor said that he later learned that former President Clinton's Secret Service detail had contacted Lynch's FBI security detail and let them know that the former President wanted to meet with Lynch. Although Lynch's staff was supposed to receive notice of such requests, witnesses told us that they were not informed of the request from former President Clinton.[145]

Lynch said that she was on the plane with her husband and the head of her security detail, and that they were preparing to leave when she learned that former President Clinton had asked to speak to her. She stated:

> [W]e were walking toward the front door, and then...the head of my detail stopped and spoke to someone outside the plane, turned around and said former President Clinton is here, and he wants to say hello to you. And I think my initial reaction was the profound statement, what? Something like that. And he repeated that. And he spoke again to someone outside the plane. And we were, we were about to walk off the plane. We were going to go down the stairs and get into the motorcade and go on, and...the head of my detail said...can he come on and say hello to you? And I said, yes, he can come on the plane and say hello. And he was literally there. So I don't know if he was talking to President Clinton or somebody else. I don't know who was on the steps.

Lynch said that former President Clinton boarded the plane in a matter of seconds, suggesting that he was in the stairwell near the door to the plane. Lynch said that she was very surprised that he wanted to meet with her because they did not have a social relationship, and she was also surprised to see him "right there in the doorway so quickly."

Lynch said that she had "never really had a conversation" with former President Clinton before this meeting, or with former Secretary Clinton at any time. She said that "years ago" when she was the U.S. Attorney for the Eastern District of New York, she saw former Secretary Clinton at a 9/11 event and said hello.[146] She said that she also saw both of them at the funeral for former Vice President Joe Biden's son, Beau Biden, which was held on June 6, 2015. She said that she recalled that during that conversation former President Clinton congratulated her on the FIFA corruption case. Lynch told the OIG that she did not have a social

---

[145] On July 2, 2016, the head of Lynch's security detail sent an email to another agent in the FBI Security Division, stating, "I will explain the details later, but you know, we [are] not the final word as to who comes in or out of the AG's space. Her staff dropped the ball in a big way, and we were the easy scapegoats! I'm pretty pissed about the way things went down and how they were handled afterwards, needless to say I will be making some changes as to how much interaction we will have with this staff going forward." The OIG considered but decided not to interview the head of Lynch's FBI security detail because of concerns that requiring a member of the Attorney General's security detail to testify about what he observed in the course of conducting his official duties could impair the protective relationship and because the security concerns raised by the head of the security detail in his email were not a focus of this review. Further, we believed it was unlikely that the head of the security detail would have been in a position to be able to overhear the conversation between Lynch and former President Clinton.

[146] Lynch was nominated by former President Clinton to be the U.S. Attorney for the Eastern District of New York, and served from June 2, 1999 to May 2, 2001. Lynch served in the same position from May 8, 2010 to April 27, 2015.

relationship or socialize with either former President Clinton or former Secretary Clinton.

However, Lynch said that public officials often stopped her to say hello when she traveled, and that as a result she was not initially concerned when former President Clinton wanted to say hello. For example, Lynch told us that Ohio Governor John Kasich, who was a candidate in the 2016 Republican presidential primary, stopped her one time to say hello in an airport, and they had a 10-minute conversation even though they had never met before. The OPA Supervisor told the OIG, "It wouldn't be uncommon for [Lynch] to...match courtesy with courtesy regardless of [whether the person was] Republican, Democrat, whatever."

2.   Discussion between Former President Clinton and Lynch

During our review, we found no contemporaneous evidence, such as notes, documenting the substance of the discussion between Lynch and former President Clinton. The only documentary evidence we identified that summarized the meeting were "talking points" created by Lynch's staff after the meeting became a subject of controversy, as discussed in Section IV.B.

Former President Clinton and Lynch denied that they discussed the Midyear investigation, the upcoming interview of former Secretary Clinton, any other Department investigation, or plans for Lynch to serve in some capacity in a Hillary Clinton administration. We summarize below what they told us about their discussion.

Former President Clinton's Testimony

Former President Clinton told us that he congratulated Lynch on being named Attorney General and mentioned several things that she had done that he thought were good policy, such as continuing with criminal justice reforms that were implemented by former Attorney General Eric Holder. He said that they then talked about their grandchildren, his recent visit to see former Attorney General Janet Reno, and his golf game.

We asked former President Clinton if he had discussed Brexit or West Virginia coal policy with Lynch. He said he did not recall Brexit coming up, but acknowledged that he probably did discuss it with her because he was very worried that it would disrupt the Irish peace process.[147] When asked whether his comments included the potential implications of the Brexit vote and the rise of populism for the U.S. election, he stated that he did not remember discussing that, but that one of his "automatic responses" during the campaign was to describe how the press had underestimated the reaction to globalization and the resulting identity crisis, and how Brexit was simply a manifestation of that. As a result, he said he could not rule out that he said something similar to Lynch. Former President Clinton also said that he did not recall mentioning West Virginia coal policy to Lynch, but that he

---

[147] On June 23, 2016, voters in the United Kingdom approved a referendum to leave the European Union, a decision known as Brexit.

would not be shocked if he had done so because he thought a lot about it, and he frequently talked about the issue.

Former President Clinton said he did not recall telling Lynch that she was doing a great job, but told us he probably did so because "the Justice Department...when President Obama was there, I thought they did a lot of good things that needed doing, especially in criminal justice." However, he denied that his comments were motivated by an intent to influence the investigation. He told us that he did not recall telling Lynch that she was his favorite cabinet member, and he did not think it was likely that he would have made such a comment. He stated, "I like her, but I'm very close to Tom Vilsack and was very close to a couple of the others, so I couldn't have said that, but I do like her a lot."

Former President Clinton said he only mentioned former Secretary Clinton once during the discussion, and that concerned how happy she was to be a grandmother. He said he told Lynch:

> [T]hat she was a happy grandmother and an ardent one and that we were very lucky because our daughter and her husband and our grandchildren live in New York, so they are about an hour from us in a decent traffic day. And I told her that before the campaign was underway Hillary and I tried to see our grandkids every week and in the best weeks, she would see them once when she was down there. Then I would see them once and then we'd see them once together and I was down, and I remember talking about every now and then we got them up in Chappaqua where we live and it was quite bracing trying to keep up with them and how much fun it was and that's really what we talked about.

> I do remember saying that grandparents typically say it's better than being a parent because it's all the fun and none of the responsibilities, and I told Chelsea once after [her daughter] was born that she would never hear me say that, that I still thought being her father was the best gig I ever had.

When asked whether they discussed former Secretary Clinton's upcoming interview with the FBI, Clinton replied, "Absolutely not.... [I]t wouldn't have been appropriate for me to talk to her about any of that and I didn't." He said that they also did not discuss the Midyear investigation, the Clinton Foundation matter, any other Department investigation, the Benghazi hearings held by Congress, or then FBI Director Comey.

We asked former President Clinton whether he discussed the possibility of Lynch serving as Attorney General or in another position in a future Hillary Clinton administration, or a possible judicial nomination. He stated:

> No. Not even with anybody else. Not with Hillary. Not with anybody.... We didn't discuss that because...I'm very superstitious. I never discuss anything like that. I want everybody to focus on the

matter at hand and I thought the environment was much more volatile than a lot of people did.

Former President Clinton also said that he was a little surprised by the criticism after his tarmac meeting with Lynch. He stated:

> [T]he mainstream media wasn't as bad on that as they were on a lot of things, I thought, I think the ones that were criticizing me, I thought you know, I don't know whether I'm more offended that they think I'm crooked or that they think I'm stupid. I've got an idea, I'll do all these things they accuse me of doing in broad daylight in an airport in Phoenix when the whole world can see it in front of an Air Force One crew and I believe one of her security guards. It was an interesting proposition, but no we did not.

Lynch's Testimony

As described above, Lynch said the head of her security detail told her that former President Clinton wanted to speak to her, and she said that he could come on the plane and say hello. Lynch told the OIG that she thought that she and former President Clinton would briefly exchange greetings, and then she would get off the plane. She described what happened after he boarded the plane:

> Well first we're...standing in the...the cabin of the plane because, again, he's saying he wanted to say hello. I introduce him to my husband. We were standing up, because I thought we were going to stand up, say hello, and then keep walking. There were two members of the flight crew in the back section of the plane. So, President Clinton shook hands with the head of my detail, with my husband, with me. He went back and spoke to the two members of the flight crew, and he stayed back there for a few minutes, like five minutes maybe, because he spoke individually to each of them for a few minutes.... And they were very excited, you know.... [H]e was very gracious to them.

Lynch said that former President Clinton then returned to the front of the plane where she and her husband were standing and began talking to her husband. She said they had a brief discussion about Lynch's trip to Phoenix, Clinton's new grandchild, and various family issues including how to deal with sibling rivalry. She said they were still standing during this discussion, but that former President Clinton sat down after a few minutes:

> At some point, after two or three minutes, President Clinton turned around. I had my tote bags on the bench seat of the plane, because I had put them there when he came on board. I had been holding them. I put them down. He picked up my tote bags and moved them, and then he sat down. So he sat down, and my husband and I were still standing in front of him having the discussion. And...he sort of sat heavily, and...I didn't know...how he felt, so I can't say one way or the

other. But he sat down and started talking about, you know, the grandkids and how they introduced them to each other. And so, and ultimately, because this went on for a little but, my husband and I sat down also, and, you know, had that discussion about his family and the kids[.]

She said that after this, the discussion continued, with former President Clinton doing most of the talking. She stated:

Well, after he was sharing with us his story about how...they introduced the two grandchildren to each other, which involved a toy...and that was green, and just, again, the family issues, he said what brings you to Phoenix. And I said I'm here on a police tour, and I'm doing a lot about the law enforcement community relations. And I said, you know, how did you find Phoenix? And he mentioned that he had been there for several meetings, he had played golf. I made a reference to the heat, because it was still incredibly hot while we landed, which was why we were still on the plane.

And he made a comment about playing golf, and you can manage the heat. Just, he was talking a lot about the golfing issue was well, but nothing of substance about that. And he asked about my travels, and I said that I had been recently traveling to China. I had to come back for the Pulse Nightclub [shooting]. I had been to Alaska and met with Native youth. I then said...you know, that was an issue of great importance to [former Attorney General Janet] Reno. Have you talked with her lately and do you know about her health? And he said, yes, I've seen her. I visited her along with Donna Shalala, I visited her, and he told me when. And I said because she's not doing well. We talked about that for a few minutes.

And I remember at that point saying, well, you know, thank you very much kind of thing, and he sort of continued chatting and, and said, and made a comment about his travels he was headed on. And I said, well, we've got to get going to the hotel. And I said I'm sure you've got somewhere to, to go. And he said yes. And I forget where he told me he was going. He was flying somewhere, but...I've forgotten where. He said I'm going to wherever I'm off to. And then he made some comment about West Virginia. And I do not know if he was headed to West Virginia. I just don't know...if that was the reference to it. And he made a...comment about West Virginia and coal issues and how their problems really stem from policies that were set forth in 1932. And he talked about those policies for a while. And, and I said, okay, well.

According to Lynch, Clinton discussed West Virginia coal policy as an historical issue, not in connection with the campaign. She said that he discussed Brexit in a similar context, talking about the cultural issues that led to the decision and whether "people in the UK viewed themselves as citizens of the world or the country or whatever."

In response to specific questions asked by the OIG, Lynch said that she and former President Clinton did not discuss the Midyear investigation or any other Department investigation, James Comey, Donald Trump, or the upcoming Presidential election. She said that they also did not discuss possible positions for her in a future Hillary Clinton administration, a potential nomination to the Supreme Court, or her future plans after President Obama left office.

Lynch said that Clinton told her that she was "doing a great job as a cabinet member or...words to that effect." She said that she thought that he was flattering her and "would have said that to every cabinet member at that time. No, I, I viewed it as...him being jovial, honestly, and being genial."

Lynch estimated that she talked to former President Clinton for approximately 20 minutes before a member of her staff came back onto the plane, as we describe below. She said that she became increasingly concerned as the meeting "went on and on." Lynch said that when she thought about it later that evening and discussed it with her staff about in the context of the case, she concluded "that it was just too long a conversation to have had. It...went beyond hi, how are you, shake hands, move on sort of thing. It went beyond the discussions I've had with other people in public life, even in political life, it went beyond that [in terms of length]."

3. Intervention by Lynch's Staff

While former President Clinton was on the plane, Lynch's staff were waiting in the staff van. The Deputy Chief of Staff said that they quickly realized that the meeting was problematic, because Clinton was not just the former President but was also the husband of someone who was under investigation. The Deputy Chief of Staff said that she felt "shocked," and that they all "just felt completely...blindsided." The Senior Counselor said that they immediately were aware that the meeting was ill-advised and that the "optics were not great."

The OPA Supervisor said that he waited approximately 5 minutes, and then he left the van. He said he went over to one of the other agents on Lynch's security detail, who was waiting in the vehicle that was going to carry Lynch. The OPA Supervisor said that he asked the agent what was going on, whether there had been any notice that former President Clinton wanted to say hello, and how long he was supposed to be on the plane. The OPA Supervisor said that the agent did not know. According to the OPA Supervisor, he asked the agent to tell the head of Lynch's security detail that Lynch needed to end the meeting. The OPA Supervisor stated, "And I don't know that [the head of Lynch's security detail] thought it was appropriate to [ask her to] wrap it up because I guess that's his boss too."

The OPA Supervisor said that there was a photographer outside, and he recalled telling the photographer that Lynch would not be taking pictures. The OPA Supervisor said that he remembered telling the photographer that he (the photographer) needed to go back in his car. The OPA Supervisor stated, "I'm going back in my car. Like, no one is hanging out. I like President Clinton, too. I'm not hanging out for a photo." The OPA Supervisor said that he then got back in the staff van.[148]

By this time, former President Clinton had been on the plane for approximately 10 to 15 minutes. The Deputy Chief of Staff said that they were discussing the need for someone to go back on the plane when the Senior Counselor, who led the Phoenix portion of the trip and therefore was seated in the front of the van closest to the door, told the group that she was going to go and jumped out of the van. The Deputy Chief of Staff said, "And then [the Senior Counselor] was just running upstairs. And so, that's how—that's when we decided...to do something." The Senior Counselor described her thinking at the time: "And I don't know what's going on up there, but I should at least go up to intervene or help her if she needs help.... I think...it was part uncertainty and part kind of like this is a bad idea."

The Senior Counselor said that when she tried to go back on the plane, she was stopped by the head of Lynch's security detail, who was at the door of the plane. The Senior Counselor said that she told him that Lynch's meeting with former President Clinton was not a good idea, and that she needed to get back on the plane, but he still would not let her on. The Senior Counselor said that she then asked him to convey to Lynch that she was advising that the meeting was a bad idea. According to the Senior Counselor, he told her, "All right, why don't you tell her yourself," and finally allowed her to board.

The Senior Counselor said that when she got on the plane, she saw Lynch, Lynch's husband, and former President Clinton sitting down and "chatting...in a casual way." The Senior Counselor said that she walked up to the three of them and stood there hoping that her presence would break up the meeting. She said that Lynch saw her and introduced her to former President Clinton, and she shook his hand. The Senior Counselor said that she hoped this would get everyone moving, but then former President Clinton sat back down. The Senior Counselor stated, "So then...I kind of didn't know what to do because...it was a little bit unusual to be in a room with...a former president and say...you need to leave.... So...I think I stared at them for a little bit longer, and then went back to where [the head of Lynch's security detail] was standing." The Senior Counselor said that she considered whether she should go get someone else or go back over to Lynch and tell her, "Look, ma'am, we have to go." She said she then went and stood in front of the group again.

The Senior Counselor said that her presence prompted Lynch to tell former President Clinton that the reason she (the Senior Counselor) was standing there was that she was too polite to tell Lynch that they had to go. The Senior Counselor said that Lynch told former President Clinton, "And we do have to go. You know...we have a pretty busy schedule." The Senior Counselor said that she could not recall what Lynch and former President Clinton were discussing, but that her

---

[148] We asked Lynch about news reports that her security detail did not allow photos to be taken of the meeting. Lynch said that she did not recall any such discussions, but that it was her standard practice not to take photos with anyone involved in a campaign around an election.

impression was that Lynch was "uncomfortable and wanted the meeting to be done."

Lynch said that after the Senior Counselor got back on the plane, former President Clinton commented, "Oh, she's mad at me, because I'd been on the plane too long. And she's come to get you." Lynch said that she replied to him, "[W]ell, we do have to go. And then he kept talking about something else." She said that he kept talking for "a good 5 minutes" after the Senior Counselor got back on the plane. Lynch said that she finally stood up and said, "[Y]ou know, it was very nice of you to come. Thank you so much. And just...thank you again for stopping by." She said that they said goodbye several times, and her husband shook former President Clinton's hand again. Former President Clinton then left the plane.

The Senior Counselor said she went to talk to Lynch after former President Clinton left. She stated, "And I kind of looked at her and...I think I said...something like that was not great, or...something like that. And she's like, yeah." She described Lynch as "look[ing] kind of...gray and, you know, not pleased." The Senior Counselor said that after they left the plane, she got into the staff van, Lynch got into her vehicle, and they went to the hotel. She said that they did not talk to Lynch about what happened until the next day.

The Deputy Chief of Staff told the OIG that they did not attempt to get information from the head of Lynch's security detail about the conversation that took place on the plane. She explained:

> And my only conversation with [the head of Lynch's security detail] was a rare, fairly admonishing one...just saying, this is not okay, this shouldn't be the protocol; you didn't contact me; you could've radioed your FBI guy in the van to say, send someone up. So...my conversation was not a very pleasant one by the time I talked to [the head of Lynch's security detail]. So I didn't ask questions like, oh, what did you hear. I was just like, we need to figure this out, and this never needs to happen again.

The Deputy Chief of Staff said that the security protocol was changed almost immediately as the result of what happened. Under the revised protocol, the senior counselor (*i.e.*, the staff member in charge of the trip) was required to remain on the plane with Lynch and the head of her security detail, and to escort her at other times.

B.   Responding to Media Questions about the Tarmac Meeting

Melanie Newman, the Director of OPA, said that the OPA Supervisor called her from the van and "sounded the alarm," telling her that he just saw former President Clinton board Lynch's plane. According to Newman, she asked the OPA Supervisor a number of questions, including why former President Clinton was there and whether he had a press pool with them, which he could not answer. Newman said that she asked the OPA Supervisor to get out of the van and figure out what was going on. Newman said that she was not just concerned that there was a press event going on that they did not know about, but that the potential implications for the investigation were obvious to everyone "except apparently the FBI agents on the Attorney General's detail."

Newman said that the OPA Supervisor called her back approximately 30 minutes later, after the Senior Counselor had returned to the van. According to Newman, the OPA Supervisor told her that there was no press pool, but that former President Clinton had his own photographer there. Newman said that the OPA Supervisor told her that former President Clinton had asked Lynch's FBI detail if he could go on Lynch's plane, and no one had communicated this to her staff. Newman stated, "No one talks to the AG without staff saying they can talk to the AG. But they didn't do this because he's a former President."[149]

Newman said she spoke to Lynch and the staff traveling with her by phone the next day, June 28, 2016. According to Newman, during this call Lynch described how the meeting with former President Clinton happened, what they discussed, and how she had tried to end the discussion. Newman characterized Lynch as "devastated" about the tarmac meeting. She stated:

> [Lynch] doesn't take mistakes lightly, and she felt like she had made...an incredible...mistake in judgment by saying yes instead of no, that he could come on the plane. But also, she's like the most polite, Southern person alive. I, I don't know in what circumstances she would have said no, or what would have happened if she had said no.... I would have much preferred a story that the Attorney General turned a former President of the United States away on the tarmac, but...she doesn't make mistakes, and she was not pleased with herself for making this kind of high-stakes mistake.

Newman said that they discussed the best way to respond to any press questions about the meeting. She said that Lynch had a press conference scheduled in Phoenix, so she (Newman) wanted to have talking points prepared in case someone asked about the meeting with former President Clinton.

At approximately 1:15 p.m. EDT, Newman received an email from an ABC News reporter asking about the meeting between Lynch and former President Clinton, based on information from its Phoenix affiliate. Newman said that this inquiry confirmed that the meeting would come up at Lynch's press conference, and she sped up the process to develop talking points. Newman forwarded the inquiry to the OPA Supervisor and Lynch's Acting Chief of Staff stating, "We need to talk."

The Acting Chief of Staff arranged a conference call, and added Matt Axelrod, the Deputy Chief of Staff, and the Senior Counselor to the list of invitees. However, the OPA Supervisor and the Senior Counselor were waiting for an event in Phoenix to begin and could not join the call. Following the call, Newman emailed a short

---

[149] After reviewing draft of the OIG's report, Newman clarified that "typically" no one talks to the AG without staff approval, and that she "assumed" that this typical practice was not followed because Clinton was a former president.

draft statement to the Senior Counselor and the Deputy Chief of Staff, copying Axelrod, the Acting Chief of Staff, the OPA Supervisor, and Peter Kadzik, the AAG for the Office of Legislative Affairs (OLA). A number of additional emails and phone calls followed as the draft statement was expanded and edited to include talking points about the topics Lynch and former President Clinton discussed. Newman then emailed the statement to Lynch and her staff.

During Lynch's Phoenix press conference, a local reporter asked Lynch about her meeting with former President Clinton and whether Benghazi was discussed. She answered the question based on the talking points and draft statement:

> No. Actually, while I was landing at the airport, I did see President Clinton at the Phoenix airport as I was leaving, and he spoke to myself and my husband on the plane. Our conversation was a great deal about his grandchildren. It was primarily social and about our travels. He mentioned the golf he played in Phoenix, and he mentioned travels he'd had in West Virginia. We talked about former Attorney General Janet Reno, for example, whom we both know, but there was no discussion of any matter pending before the Department or any matter pending before any other body. There was no discussion of Benghazi, no discussion of the State Department emails, by way of example. I would say the current news of the day was the Brexit decision, and what that might mean. And again, the Department's not involved in that or implicated in that.

Lynch did not receive any follow up questions from either the reporter who asked the question or from the other reporters in attendance.

Based on the lack of follow up questions, Newman decided not to release a statement about Lynch's meeting with former President Clinton. However, by the following afternoon, several media organizations had begun picking up coverage of the meeting.

On June 29, 2016, Newman emailed Lynch's statement at her Phoenix press conference and the Department's talking points to two officials in the FBI's Office of Public Affairs (OPA), stating, "I want to flag a story that is gaining some traction tonight...about a casual, unscheduled meeting between former [P]resident Bill Clinton and the AG." The FBI OPA officials forwarded the talking points to McCabe, Rybicki, and Comey. We discuss the impact of the tarmac meeting on Comey's decision not to tell the Department about his decision to do a public statement in Section IV.E below.

C.   Discussions about Possible Recusal

1.   Departmental Ethics Opinion

Lynch told the OIG that she began discussing whether she needed to recuse herself from the Midyear investigation on June 28, 2016, the morning after the tarmac incident. Lynch said that she called her Acting Chief of Staff, who was back in Washington, D.C., and asked her to contact the Departmental Ethics Office to find out if the ethics regulations required recusal. Lynch said (and the Acting Chief of Staff confirmed) that she obtained an oral ethics opinion that there was no legal requirement to recuse herself.

Janice Rodgers, the former Director of the Departmental Ethics Office, said that she remembered receiving a call from someone on Lynch's staff, although she did not remember who it was. Rodgers said that she spoke to Lynch's staff member over the phone, and after hearing what happened, concluded that the ethics regulations did not require recusal. Rodgers explained her understanding of the facts:

> [T]he fact that the subject's spouse had, I don't know what the right word is. You know, sort of created, engineered a, you know, contact with the AG, which was apparently, you know, completely non-substantive, and in my view. And also in circumstances that made it very difficult for the AG to decline or avoid contact.

Rodgers said that the question was "more of...a capital-P political issue...meaning people were going to make hay of it," and that Department leadership would have to weigh the amount of heat they were willing to take versus the importance of Lynch's participation in the matter. She stated, "There was nothing about that that required recusal.... [W]hether the AG chose to recuse based on sort of the more...global considerations was...out of my bailiwick."

2.   Discussions about Voluntary Recusal

Lynch said that she then considered whether she should recuse voluntarily based on appearance concerns—*i.e.*, concerns that the meeting created the appearance that former President Clinton was influencing the Midyear investigation through her, or that she was influencing it by having a connection to him. Lynch said she wanted to be able to make a statement about her plans for remaining involved in the Midyear investigation during an interview with a Washington Post reporter at the Aspen Ideas Festival, which was scheduled for the last day of her trip, July 1, 2016.

Lynch said she held a number of calls that involved Yates, Axelrod, Newman, the Acting Chief of Staff, and other Department officials, and that these calls likely took place on the Wednesday or Thursday of that week. She said she also discussed the issue with the staff members who were traveling with her. Lynch said that she did not recall anyone expressing the view that she should recuse herself; she said that her staff raised issues and concerns for discussion, but no one presented her with a conclusion that she should recuse.

Discussions Involving Yates, Axelrod, and Other Department Officials

Yates told the OIG that the group participating in these calls quickly dismissed the idea of recusal because they knew that the Department was going to announce what they expected to be a declination "in a matter of days." She stated:

> And the fear [was] that this is going to look really artificial...if you've spent over a year with [Lynch] at the helm of this investigating it, and then this tarmac thing happens and she recuses.... That's going to look really artificial then if all of a sudden somebody else is announcing it and we're saying oh, there's no problem with the tarmac because she's recused. When really that decision had been all but made...while she was AG.

Axelrod expressed a similar opinion, and stated that other factors weighed against recusal as well. In particular, he said that he understood that Lynch had not discussed anything improper with former President Clinton, and for her to recuse would have made it look like she had. He said he also thought that the people calling for her recusal would not be satisfied by it:

> I thought that for folks who had already, again, for...political reasons been calling for a special counsel I wasn't sure that a recusal...would be sufficient. That it would end there with...the AG stepping aside and the DAG taking over. I thought calls would increase for Department leadership to step out altogether. Which again, I didn't think was good for the integrity of the investigation. And that was my goal was to protect the integrity of the investigation.

Axelrod told the OIG that he did not specifically recall having a discussion with Rybicki or McCabe about the tarmac incident, but said that he was "sure [he] did have conversations.... [T]his would be a big thing not to have a conversation about[.]" Rybicki told us that Axelrod called him early in the week to tell him that the tarmac meeting had happened. McCabe said that he also spoke to Axelrod a day or two after the tarmac meeting, and that Axelrod told him that Lynch likely would not recuse herself from the Midyear investigation.

Toscas said he was on vacation the week of the tarmac meeting, and Axelrod contacted him by phone to tell him about it. Toscas said that he contacted Laufman, and that both he and Laufman thought that recusal was unwise. Toscas stated, "I thought that a recusal would make it look like, oh this person who is doing inappropriate things has been overseeing this thing for a long time now, so that means the whole thing is tainted by it.... [T]hat would actually probably be more harmful to our investigation and the appearance to the public of our investigation."

Lynch's Decision Not to Recuse

Lynch said that she decided not to recuse herself from the Midyear investigation. In making this decision, Lynch said she considered whether her meeting with former President Clinton would cause people not to have faith in the judgment or decisions of the Department. She said she weighed this against the concern that stepping aside would create a misimpression that she and former President Clinton had discussed inappropriate topics, or that her role in the case somehow was greater than it was.

She explained that other considerations informed her decision:

> And I, and I also had the view that, you know, when you create a situation, as I felt I did by sitting down with, with the President, it's, yes, it can be almost a relief in some ways to say, you know what? I'm going to recuse myself and get out of it and not take, not take the hits. And then you're just asking someone else to step up and endure all the hits the Department will take for the case for the result, whatever it is.
>
> And, you know, I thought about it from that, that angle as well. You're just asking someone else to step up and do your job for you. And if I did not think it rose to the level of recusal, then I did not want to do something out of a desire to protect myself sort of personally from embarrassment also because that's not the way to make somebody else take on that responsibility.

Lynch said that she took into account that NSD did not think recusal was necessary. She said she conveyed her regrets to the Midyear prosecutors for putting them in the position of having people outside the Department look at their work and think that it would be influenced by anything improper.

Planning for the Aspen Interview

Axelrod told the OIG that the "game plan" that emerged from these discussions was for Lynch to explain publicly how the Midyear investigation had been handled all along:

- It was handled by career agents and prosecutors;
- The career agents and prosecutors had been the ones doing the work for more than a year;
- When the career agents and prosecutors finished their work, they would make a recommendation to Department leadership; and
- When Lynch received that recommendation, she fully expected to accept it, but she ultimately was the decider.

Axelrod said it was "definitely not the game plan" for Lynch to convey that she would accept the recommendation of the career staff no matter what they brought her, or that she would take herself out of the decisionmaking process but not

216

formally recuse herself. However, he acknowledged that the different ways she described this process in her interview with the Washington Post reporter (discussed below) led to some confusion.

Carlin spoke at the Aspen Ideas Festival before Lynch arrived and said he was scheduled to return to Washington, D.C., with her. Carlin said that he met with Lynch, her husband, and her staff in person before her interview with the Washington Post reporter, and Carlin conveyed to her that NSD was not making a request that she recuse herself. Carlin said they also discussed what Lynch planned to say in her interview. Like Axelrod, Carlin told us that Lynch intended to provide more insight than she normally would into the investigative process, not to communicate that something had changed because of the tarmac incident.

Melanie Newman told the OIG that she made it known that she disagreed with this approach from a messaging perspective. Newman said that she thought recusal was appropriate because public statements and actions "need to be clear-cut." Newman stated:

> [W]e tried to have it both ways.... [W]e said that she would accept the recommendation of the senior career prosecutors and investigators on the case. Well, usually that is what the Attorney General does anyway. That means literally nothing....

> This is the Attorney General, I mean, I'm not aware of, there may be disputes [in other cases] between the [FBI and the prosecutors] that the Attorney General is sort of the deciding vote. But generally speaking, in charging decisions, the Attorney General accepts the recommendation of those people who know the evidence most intimately. I think in the rare instance that there are disagreements, the Attorney General may, may accept the recommendation of one over the other, for example. But that's, that's sort of what they do.

Newman said that Lynch was doing the same thing that she usually does, except that "she was saying before the conclusion of the investigation that this was how she was going to handle it. That was the difference."

D.   Lynch's July 1 Aspen Institute Statement

During the interview with the Washington Post reporter, Lynch acknowledged that her meeting with former President Clinton raised questions about her role in the Midyear investigation. Addressing how that investigation would be resolved, Lynch stated:

> But I think the issue is, again, what is my role in how that matter is going to be resolved? And so let me be clear on how that is going to be resolved. I've gotten that question a lot also over time and we usually don't go into those deliberations, but I do think it's important that people see what that process is like.

As I have always indicated, the matter is being handled by career agents and investigators with the Department of Justice. They've had it since the beginning. They are independent.... It predates my tenure as Attorney General. It is the same team and they are acting independently. They follow the law, they follow the facts. That team will make findings. That is to say they will come up with a chronology of what happened, the factual scenario. They will make recommendations as to how to resolve what those facts lead to. Those—the recommendations will be reviewed by career supervisors in the Department of Justice and in the FBI and by the FBI Director. And then, as is the common process, they present it to me and I fully expect to accept their recommendations.

Lynch then responded to a question about a news article that morning reporting that she planned to recuse herself from the Midyear investigation. She stated, "Well, a recusal would mean that I wouldn't even be briefed on what the findings were or what the actions going forward would be. And while I don't have a role in those findings and coming up with those findings or making those recommendations as to how to go forward, I'll be briefed on it and I will be accepting their recommendations."

As the discussion continued, Lynch responded to additional questions about her continued role in Midyear. Asked about a news report that she had made the decision in April 2016 to accept the recommendations of the career staff, Lynch replied:

Yes, I had already determined that that would be the process.... And as I've said on occasions as to why we don't talk about ongoing investigations in terms of what's being discussed and who's being interviewed, is to preserve the integrity of that investigation. We also typically don't talk about the process by which we make decisions, and I have provided that response too.

But in this situation, you know, because I did have that meeting, it has raised concerns, I feel, and I feel that while I can certainly say this matter's going to be handled like any other, as it has always been, it's going to be resolved like any other, as it was always going to be. I think people need the information about exactly how that resolution will come about in order to know what that means and really accept that and have faith in the ultimate decision of the Department of Justice.

Lynch's comments about the status of her continuing involvement in the Midyear investigation created considerable confusion. After her appearance, various new articles reported that she had decided to defer to the recommendations of the FBI or had effected a "non-recusal recusal."[150] Lynch said she participated in a follow-up interview with the Washington Post reporter during which she attempted to clarify her statement. The resulting article quoted her as follows:

> I can certainly say this matter is going to be handled like any other as it has always been. It's going to be resolved like any other, as it was always going to be.... I've always said that this matter will be handled by the career people who are independent. They live from administration to administration. Their role is to follow the facts and follow the law and make a determination as to what happened and what those next steps should be.... This team is dedicated and professional. So I can't imagine a circumstance in which I would not be accepting their recommendations.[151]

Lynch told us that her role in oversight of the Midyear investigation did not change. She stated:

> [A]s I said to, to the reporter at the time, that the team is going to continue and, and do what they needed to do in terms of interviews, forensics, all the investigative steps that they would take that were not influenced by me. They would look at all the facts, all the evidence, and come up with a recommendation that was going to be vetted through supervisors on both sides of the house, the legal side of the house, the investigative side of the house, and they would make a recommendation to me.

Lynch continued:

> [T]hey are going to present me with a recommendation, that I expect to accept, which I always expected that I would accept given the people involved in the process, then there is really no need for me to step aside from this because I'm, I'm listening to their recommendation. I'm doing what I'm supposed to do in terms of discharging my duties in running the Department, in, in managing the Department in what is an important case and a sensitive case. And, and essentially, there won't be a change.

E.   Impact of the Tarmac Meeting on Comey's Decision to Make a Public Statement

As described above, Comey began drafting a public statement announcing the conclusion of the Midyear investigation in early May 2016, well before the tarmac meeting, and told the OIG that he planned not to inform the Department. Comey told us that he had struggled with the decision, and that "in a way the

---

[150] *See, e.g.*, Mark Landler *et al.*, *Loretta Lynch to Accept F.B.I. Recommendations in Clinton Email Inquiry*, N.Y. Times, Jul. 1, 2016; Joel B. Pollak, *Loretta Lynch's Non-Recusal Recusal*, Breitbart, Jul. 1, 2016.

[151] Jonathan Capehart, *This Is What Loretta Lynch is Thinking Now*, Wash. Post, Jul. 5, 2016.

tarmac thing made it easy for me" and "tipped the scales" towards making his mind up to go forward with an independent announcement. He stated, "I think I was nearly there. That I have to do this separate and apart.... And so I would say I was 90 percent there, like highly likely going to do it anyway, and [the tarmac meeting] capped it."

Comey said that Lynch's decision not to recuse herself and to defer to his recommendation impacted his decision. He stated:

> [I]f you believe the nature, the circumstance, 500-year flood, if you believe that it's officially unusual that you can't participate meaningfully in one of the most important investigations in here, in your organization, then I think your obligation is to find another way to discharge leadership responsibilities. Either appoint someone within the organization to be in charge of the case to make sure there is leadership to engage across the street with us, not to be this neither fish nor fowl, I'm still the Attorney General and really in an odd way, what she said explicitly was sort of the culture of the case before the tarmac thing [in that she was not closely involved in the investigation], which was I'm the Attorney General and that's not really my thing and then she made it explicit by saying, I'm still the Attorney General, but I'm going to accept what Jim Comey and the prosecutors say.

Comey also stated:

> Had Loretta said, I'm stepping out of this [after the tarmac meeting]. I'm making Sally Yates the acting Attorney General and had I gone and sat down with Sally and heard her vision for it, maybe we would have ended up in a different place. I don't know. It's possible we'd end up in the same place, but it's hard to relive different, imaginary lives.

As described in more detail in Chapter Eight, on October 13, 2016, Comey gave a speech at the SAC Conference in which he spoke at length about the Midyear investigation. Comey stated the following regarding the tarmac meeting in explaining his decision to deliver a unilateral public statement:

> At the end of [the investigation], [the team's] view of it was there isn't anything that anybody could prosecute. My view was the same. Everybody between me and the people who worked this case felt the same way about it. It was not a prosecutable case.... The decision there was not a prosecutable case here was not a hard one. The hard one, as I've told you, was how do we communicate about it. I decided to do something unprecedented that I was very nervous about at the time, and I've asked myself a thousand times since was it the right decision. I still believe it was.
>
> Here was the thinking. Especially after the Attorney General met with former President Clinton on that airplane the week before we [interviewed] Hillary Clinton.... The hard part in the wake of the

Attorney General's meeting was what would happen to the FBI if we did the normal thing? The normal thing would be send over an LHM even if we didn't write it. Go talk to them. Tell them what we think, tell them whether we think there's something here or whether we think a declination makes sense, but all of that would be done privately.

What I said to myself at the time, we talked about it as a leadership team a lot and all believed that this was the right course, try to imagine what will happen to the FBI if we do the normal thing. Then what will happen to us is the Department of Justice will screw around it for Lord knows how long, issue probably a one sentence declination, and then the world will catch on fire, and then the cry in the public will be where on the earth is the FBI, how could the FBI be part of some corrupt political bargain like this, there's no transparency whatsoever, where is the FBI, where is the FBI. Then, after a period of many weeks where a corrosive doubt about us leaks into the public's square, then I'd have to testify in exactly the way I did before. Our view of it would be dragged out in that way, in a way I think would've hugely damaging to us, and frankly, to the Justice Department more broadly and for the sense of justice in the country more broadly.

V.   July 5, 2016 Press Conference

A.   Notifications to Department Leadership

On July 1, 2016, Comey emailed Rybicki a script containing what he planned to say to Lynch and Yates on the morning of July 5. Entitled "What I will say Tuesday on phone," the script stated:

> I wanted to let you know that I am doing a press conference this morning announcing the completion of our Midyear investigation and referral of the matter to DOJ. I'm not going to tell you anything about what I will say, for reasons I hope you understand. I think it is very important that I not have coordinated my statement outside the FBI. I'm not going to take questions at the press conference. When it is over, my staff will be available to work with your team.

Rybicki told the OIG that Comey wanted to be "very careful" about what he said on the phone to avoid substantive discussion before the actual press conference, and that was why he wrote out what he planned to say. Rybicki said that Comey did not deliver this script verbatim during his calls to Lynch and Yates, but that it was close to what he actually said.

Comey and Rybicki also developed a timeline for notifying the media, the Department, and Congress about the press conference. After notifying the press pool and sending out a media advisory by 8:00 a.m., Comey planned to call Yates at 8:30 a.m. and Lynch at 8:35 a.m. After those calls took place, McCabe, Rybicki, and, Strzok were assigned to call Toscas, Axelrod, and Laufman, respectively, beginning at 8:30 a.m. The timeline is set forth below in Figure 4.1.

Figure 6.1: FBI Timeline for Notifications on July 5, 2016

0700-0730:	☐	Pool notified. [AD Kortan]
0800:	☐	Media Advisory sent out [AD Kortan]
0830:	☐	DAG notified [Director]
	☐	NSD/DAAG Toscas notified [DD]
	☐	PADAG Axelrod notified [COS]
	☐	CES notified [SC Strzok]
0835:	☐	AG notified [Director]
1000:	☐	House and Senate Judiciary and Intel Chair and RM staff notified that D would like to speak to members after noon [AD Kelly]
1050:	☐	E-mail sent out to workforce
1100:		Press Conference in Webster

After Press Conference Notifications:

- ☐ ICIG [SC Strzok]
- ☐ DNI [Director or DD]
- ☐ USA/EDVA [DD]
- ☐ SJC Chair Grassley [Director]
- ☐ SJC RM Leahy [Director]
- ☐ SSCI Chair Burr [Director]
- ☐ SSCI Vice Chair Feinstein [Director]
- ☐ HJC Chair Goodlatte [Director]
- ☐ HJC RM Conyers [Director]
- ☐ HPSCI Chair Nunes [Director]
- ☐ HPSCI RM Schiff [Director]

Emails indicate that the Department first learned about Comey's press conference as the result of the media notifications on the morning of July 5, not from Comey or Rybicki. At 8:08 a.m., Melanie Newman sent an email to Lynch's Acting Chief of Staff, Axelrod, and Lynch's Deputy Chief of Staff entitled "FBI presser at 11 a.m." This email stated, "Just heard that the Director is having a press briefing today at 11 a.m. I have not heard anything but have asked for guidance." Axelrod replied at 8:15 a.m., "I'll call Rybicki." At 8:16 a.m., apparently after talking to the FBI Office of Public Affairs (OPA), Newman stated, "[The FBI OPA Section Chief] says the Director has called the DAG." Axelrod replied at 8:18 a.m., "Nope." At 8:31 a.m., Axelrod replied again and stated, "They just spoke. He's going to call the AG too."

Newman emailed Axelrod and Lynch's Acting Chief of Staff with additional information at 8:33 and 8:43 a.m. She stated in the first email, "For the record, these notifications [to Lynch and Yates] are happening AFTER they notified press. I learned from a reporter that they were requesting pool coverage—which means they want live TV." In the second email she stated, "They are also doing an off the record call this morning."

Newman told the OIG that in the weeks leading up to July 5, she had been "clamoring" for information from Axelrod about the conclusion of the investigation so that she could get some sense of the timeline. She said she had been "hearing from reporters that [the investigation] was, it was coming to an end and the FBI was likely to announce something." She said that Axelrod assured her that the FBI would not announce a conclusion without the Department, that they were not at the point where they were ready to announce anything, and that he would tell her when they were. Newman told the OIG that she did not doubt that Axelrod "believed this to be true."

Newman said that on the morning of July 5, after she found out from a reporter that the FBI would hold a press conference that day, she called the FBI OPA Section Chief to inquire about it and was told, "I can't tell you what this is about...but I'm sure you can guess." According to Newman, the Department's OPA had longstanding problems getting information from FBI OPA, but this was "unprecedented" and "absolutely ridiculous."

1. Call to Yates

Comey said that when he spoke with Yates, he told her he was about to make a public press statement about the email investigation, including that the FBI had finished it and was sending it to the Department with its recommendation. Comey told the OIG that Yates did not say anything except "thanks for letting me know." According to contemporaneous emails, both Yates and Axelrod were notified by the FBI by 8:28 a.m.

Yates told us that she remembered Comey saying that he was going to hold a press conference that morning. She said that she did not recall if Comey said that it would be about the Clinton investigation, but that she knew it would be. She stated, "And I remember thinking sort of, what the heck is this? And hanging up immediately and calling Matt [Axelrod] to find out more of what he knew, because if there's ever anybody who's going to know what's going on it's going to be Matt." She said that Comey's tone during the call was "very emphatic, I'm not going to tell you what it is," and that made her determined to find some other way to find out what Comey planned to say.

Yates said that she and Axelrod assumed that Comey would deliver a very brief statement that the FBI had concluded the Clinton investigation and had reached a determination, and possibly would state what the FBI's recommendation to the Department was going to be. She said that based on her knowledge of the investigation, they expected that if Comey announced a recommendation it would be a declination. She stated, "But [we] certainly didn't expect what then

223

happened." She said that she viewed Comey's decision to do a press statement without coordinating with the Department as problematic, particularly the failure to coordinate on the content of the statement. We discuss Yates's reaction to the content of Comey's statement in more detail below.

Axelrod said that he was surprised that Comey had chosen to do an independent press statement. He said he thought that the statement should have been "coordinated and planned and discussed" with the Department. However, at the time, he did not view the fact that Comey was the one delivering the declination as the primary problem. He stated:

> I think it's important to think about Comey's press conference in two ways. One was the decision to do it. And then two was...what he said. I just, one was the decision to do it at all. And on the decision to do it at all, I mean, we're surprised. We were like completely taken aback. But you know, again, we had already wanted the FBI to at least be, even before the tarmac, be part of the public face of this.... Comey was...about to be the entire public face of it. You know, there were some upsides and downsides to that. But you know, it wasn't all bad.

As described in more detail below, Axelrod thought that the content of Comey's statement was misleading, and that the way Comey executed the press conference hurt the perception of the integrity of the investigation in a significant way.

Axelrod said that he and Yates did not discuss ordering Comey not to make the statement. Axelrod stated, "I don't recall that being discussed. Because I don't think that would have been tenable, right. The press was already coming. And...ordering the Director not to do something can be very fraught. And so I don't recall that being a discussion."

2.   Call to Lynch

At 8:24 a.m., Lynch's Acting Chief of Staff, after being told by Newman about the notice of the FBI press conference, sent an email to Axelrod, asking, "[P]lease call my cell when you are done with Rybicki." At 8:39 a.m., the Acting Chief of Staff sent the following email to Lynch: "AG: [Y]ou are about to receive a call from the director. Please give me a call on my cell, and I can fill you in as to what it's about. Alternatively I will be in the office in about 5 to 10 minutes and will stop by."

Comey said that he called Lynch that morning and told her that he was going to make a public press statement about the email investigation, and that the FBI had completed the investigation and was sending it to the Department with its recommendation. Comey stated that Lynch asked him, "Can you tell me what your recommendation is going to be?" He said that he replied, "I can't and I hope someday you'll understand why, but I can't answer any of your questions—I can't answer any questions. I'm not going to tell you what I'm going to say." Rybicki told us that Comey called from his (Rybicki's) office because of the "snafus" with connecting the calls and provided us with a similar account of what Comey said.

Lynch told the OIG that she was in her office when Comey called her. She said that he told her he was going to make a public statement "very soon," and that it would be about the email investigation. She described this call as follows:

> And I said, when are you proposing to do this? And he said, very soon, within a few moments. I don't recall if he said 10:00, but certainly it was a short time period. And then he said, and I am not going to discuss the contents with you because I think it's best if we say, if we, if we are able to say that we did not coordinate the statement. Then I said something, I had another question.... I don't recall whether I said, what is it about? I just don't recall my other question. And he said, it's about, it's going to be about the email investigation.

Lynch said that he gave her no further indication about the substance of his statement. She said that Comey told her he was not going to go over the statement with her so they both could say that it was not coordinated. Asked whether this language raised a red flag indicating that she should find out more or tell him to stop, Lynch said it did not because it did not occur to her that Comey would talk about the end of the investigation or the FBI's recommendation. She stated, "And certainly I did not, at that time...on that day, even though [I] knew that they had interviewed the Secretary, I don't think I had a view that [the investigation] was done at that point."

Lynch told the OIG that, had she known what Comey was going to do, she would have told him to stop. She said she also would have asked him, "Why would you want to do this?" She stated, "Ultimately, announcing the end of a matter, whether it's going to be...how will we resolve it, would not be something that I would ever think that the, that the investigative side would do, which is why that was not what I thought he was going to do."

3.   Notifications to NSD

At 8:28 a.m., McCabe and Strzok received notice that Axelrod and Yates had been notified, which served as the "green light" for them to contact Toscas and Laufman, respectively. At 8:33 a.m., McCabe sent an email to Toscas, stating:

> The Director just informed the DAG that at 1100 this morning he has convened a press conference to announce the completion of our investigation and the referral to DOJ. He will not tell her what he is going to say. It is important that he not coordinate his statement in any way. He will not take questions at the conference. His next call is to the AG.
>
> I wanted you to hear this from me. I understand that this will be troubling to the team and I very much regret that. I want to talk to

you after the [Principals Committee] and am happy to bring my folks over to DOJ this afternoon to discuss next steps.

McCabe said that he called Toscas, but Toscas was traveling, so he instead sent Toscas an email. At 8:53 a.m., Toscas sent an email to Carlin, Laufman, and Mary McCord, stating:

> I'm on hold to talk to the DD now. I received a message from him a few minutes ago saying that this morning the Director informed the DAG that he will have a press conference at 11am today to announce the completion of the FBI's investigation and the referral to DOJ. He will not take questions at the conference, but he is not coordinating his statement with us. I'll call when I get off the phone.

According to Laufman's notes, Toscas then held a conference call with McCord, Laufman, and Prosecutors 1 and 2. According to these notes, Toscas told the group that he had spoken with McCabe and learned that Comey planned to hold a press conference at 11:00 a.m. to announce the conclusion of the investigation and the FBI's recommendation to the Department. The notes stated, "Director has told AG + DAG. McCabe refused to convey substance. Director doesn't want statement to appear coordinated with DOJ."

Laufman's notes also stated that, even though McCabe said that he would not share the content of Comey's planned statement, McCabe told Toscas that Comey planned to talk for 10 to 15 minutes and would say what the FBI had done, what the FBI had found, and what the FBI's recommendation to the Attorney General and the Department would be. Finally, the notes indicate that Toscas spoke to Carlin, and Carlin "said not to discuss w/ OAG or ODAG in advance."

Other notes obtained by the OIG indicate that Laufman separately spoke to Strzok at 8:35 a.m. that morning. According to these notes, Strzok called Laufman and said that he was "told to call [him] and say" that Comey would hold a press conference at 11:00 a.m. that morning. These notes indicate that Laufman asked, "What exactly will he say," and that Strzok replied, "Midyear." The notes also indicate that the "7th floor has told AG/DAG."

B.   Reactions to the Statement

Comey held his press conference at 11:00 a.m. on July 5, 2016. He delivered the final version of his statement verbatim (provided as Attachment D to this report) and did not take any questions. In this section we describe reactions to his statement within the Department.

1.   Department and NSD Leadership

Lynch told the OIG that she watched Comey's statement on the television in her office. She described her thoughts as she watched Comey speak:

> [D]iscussing findings in something that was technically not closed was, I was a little stunned, actually.... I had no way to stop him at that

226

point, I mean, short of, you know, dashing across the street and unplugging something....

But, so, as he went further into the analysis of not only what they found but what they recommended, I just thought this was, this was done to protect the image of the FBI because of the perception that somehow the FBI was not going to be allowed to have their views known or their views expressed or their views respected within the process. Because that had, that in fact had been, for those of us who were inside the Department at the time, and I don't know how the FBI was taking it at the time, but certainly if you looked at criticism aimed at the Department, people said, oh yeah, you know, the AG was appointed by Bill Clinton to be U.S. Attorney.

But that was never the real, the real stated concern. It was that there was going to be, you know, these strong investigators who wanted to bring charges who would be somehow silenced or stepped on by the legal side of the house, whether it was the political side or the career side, they never really made much of a differentiation. Easy to attach it to the political side if you're talking to the AG. But that was really something that was, that was thrown around a lot in, in debate outside of the Department.

So I viewed it as him trying to make his recommendation clear so that, and from, and when he made the recommendation clear and said this is our recommendation, I remember wondering does the, does the team know that this is happening, you know, that the literal investigative team, both sides of it? Did George [Toscas] know this was going to happen? Who knew that this was going to occur? And why didn't we know in advance?... Meaning the fifth floor, myself, the DAG. Why weren't we informed in advance of this? So those are my thoughts during the, during, watching of the, of that particular press conference.

Lynch said that she thought that the strongest public concern about the Midyear investigation was not that she as the Attorney General was going to "kill it," but that the investigative side would want to charge somebody, and the legal side would say no for political reasons. She said that she viewed Comey's public statement as "basically saying...look...we're independent. We...aren't influenced by anybody. And now...no one is also silencing us." Lynch stated that she did not ascribe malicious intent to Comey, but that she thought that his statement was a "huge mistake."

Lynch told the OIG that she did not think that the FBI's recommendation should have been made public "because we don't make those things public. That's part of the discussion that we [agents and prosecutors] have. That's part of, you know, we can talk about it. We can argue about it. We can go back and forth about it."

Yates told the OIG that she had concerns about the substance of Comey's statement as she watched the press conference. She stated:

> And while I can't point to specific facts in Jim [Comey]'s description, you know, narrative description there that I would say were inaccurate, I also remember at the time thinking the facts as those are being laid out with much more censure than the facts as I understood them to be and how I had been briefed on this matter. Sort of by way of example, I don't recall Jim going through and explaining that there were no classification markings on the vast, vast, vast majority. We got three email chains with a, you know, the small C [indicating that the information was Confidential]. Not the Top Secret or anything on there. That it was all to people within the State Department....

> That were really, to me gave the most accurate picture of what the facts actually were there. And so I was stunned A, at the level of detail that he went into. B, that he then made judgments and said things like extremely careless and should have known that this material was. And every, anyone should know you shouldn't have it on a private server. That he gave the impression that, you know, the private server could have been hacked. We don't really know for sure.... That, you know, I thought wasn't really a balanced description of what the facts were here.

> And so, you know, there are a number of things that are concerning about that. One, that he sort of put that slant on it, that it was done without any consultation with folks at Main Justice. That it impugned someone we weren't charging. We don't trash people we're not charging. And we don't get to just make value or moral judgments about their conduct. And there were things in there that I thought were unnecessary from a factual, those, they were opinion as opposed to laying out, even if he were going to do this, what was a fair, evenhanded recitation of what the facts were. And I thought that was way out of order.

Asked what her reaction was when she looked back on the statement, Yates said that she was "even more stunned." She stated:

> At the time all of this is happening it's such a swirl. You know, the tarmac happens and trying to figure out what to happen. I mean, all of this is happening so quickly and in such a charged environment it's hard to fully, for it all to fully sink in like it does when you look at it then in the calm of day in, you know, in retrospect on that. And look, it was a difficult situation with the tarmac. But that's not something I think that was appropriate for the FBI Director to unilaterally then decide how he was going to handle that. I think that was a factor that we should consider in how we were going to publicly convey the results of the investigation. And certainly if he had views about how that ought to happen I think he should speak up and should convey those views. But to make the unilateral decision to do it is one thing.

And then to put out that level of detail without coordinating that with DOJ or, you know, DOJ agreeing with that, and then for it to be with a slant that I didn't think was accurate—and I'm not saying he did that intentionally. I don't know. I certainly wouldn't accuse anybody of that. But the way it was conveyed I didn't think gave the most accurate description. And then, as I said, impugning someone that we weren't charging with sort of personal judgments....

Yates said that she did agree with Comey's statement that no reasonable prosecutor would bring a case based on the facts developed in the investigation, but that she did not think that it was "the place of the FBI Director to be out telling the public what a prosecutor would do there."

Axelrod stated that he and Yates watched the press conference in her office. He said that he was "pretty confident" in what Comey was going to conclude based on what they had been led to believe about the investigation and did not fully process the content of the statement while Comey was delivering it. He said that he reacted more negatively to the statement after attending the briefing by prosecutors the next day:

I didn't know all the facts because we were giving George [Toscas] the space to tell us what we thought we needed to know. We were not in the weeds. And the next day when we got the briefing o[n] some of the stuff in the weeds there were important facts that the NSD guys briefed the AG on that were absent from Comey's statement. And so that was when I started to have a much more strongly negative reaction to what Comey had said.

Asked what facts were missing that he thought were important, Axelrod identified the following:

A couple. One, that according to the NSD guys and what I recall from their briefing is that if you look at the spectrum of cases that the Department has brought in the past historically in this area the Department has never brought a case where the classified information was shared between people who work for the Government. It was always someone sharing classified information with someone outside of the Government. That's a pretty important fact. That if you are laying out your reasons or reasons for recommending declining prosecution that's a, you know, to me a pretty important one. The other one I recall was that the NSD guys said that most of the emails were, I think whether it was all or most, the majority of the emails that turned out to be classified had been sent late at night or on the weekends. Which, you know, to me means it's people sort of trying to, you know, were not at their desks, right, where they have access to classified systems trying to talk about, you know, talk around or talk about issues. So I thought that was a really important fact. And again, just when you're talking about intent, right, that's an important thing that bears on intent.

Axelrod contrasted Comey's statement with the briefing by the prosecutors the following day, which he characterized as a "much more complete picture." He stated, "[W]hen [the prosecutors] were done talking the reaction was like oh, this is clearly a declination. When Comey was done talking, as I think you saw from the public reaction,...it was much more of a mixed bag."

Axelrod told the OIG that the way the press conference was executed hurt the perception of the integrity of the investigation in a significant way. He stated:

> Because if the goal, to do what he did the goal would need to be, and I would imagine his goal was that by the time he's done talking that even if people don't agree with the outcome they can see why, you know, understand his thinking and see like why he got to the place he got. And that it would sort of be like a closing argument or something, right. It would be, right, here's the rationale and I've [seen] the facts and here's why I'm coming out the way I'm coming out. And people again, on the, and for the partisans and people with political agendas, they're not going to be convinced. But that reasonable center would say like okay, yeah, we get it.

> That was not the reaction to the statement. Which I think just by its own terms means the execution failed. Because it raised a lot of questions. It, just it wasn't, it was much more of a, like I said, the difference in tone and emphasis between what he said and then what we heard in the AG's office the next morning was striking—to me. And I think if he had, you know, if the folks who gave the briefing the next [day] were the ones who, I mean, obviously not but that those words had been said at the press conference I think it would have been received quite differently.

Toscas told the OIG that his initial reaction to Comey's statement was, "[H]oly cow, like they [Axelrod and the FBI] were talking about doing a joint appearance or statement of some sort and he's just doing it all on his own." Toscas said that he had concerns about Comey's statement, both the substance of it and the fact that it deviated from Department practice. He stated:

> We don't say we're closing something, but let me tell you some bad stuff that we saw along the way, but it doesn't rise to the level of bringing a case. We just don't do it.... I don't know whether you can point back to a document some place, but after doing this for almost 24 years, somehow it's ingrained in me and it appears to be ingrained in everyone around me and everyone who does this whether they're new or veterans, it's just something you don't do, you do not.

> It's the same reason why, if you, for example, and we have these discussions in some cases, if you go get a search warrant and it's under seal and in the search warrant you're seeing Tom—there's probable cause that Tom committed, fill in the blank, whatever horrible crime you want or a lesser crime. You go do your search. There's no case. There's no prosecution. It never comes. You know it

230

never leads to a prosecutable case. You don't unseal that warrant and tell the public, hey, there's probable cause that Tom is, you know engages in child pornography or we suspect him of a bank robbery, you just don't do it.

And so it's the same type of principle. When you decide you're not proceeding, you say nothing more. I get that in some instances there's going to be a lot of public knowledge of the facts. A shooting, for example, where the public has seen what happened, so they already know of actual conduct whether it's criminal or not is different, so you could say, we're not bringing a charge, but still comment on what everyone has seen.

But that's not what this was and people could have tried to guess or you know surmise what the actual exchanges were in some instances or what the particular parts of the classified information were, but I just didn't see it as something that—it did not square with the way we would ordinarily operate.

Toscas said that Comey's decision to do the statement seemed "beyond strange" and "incredibly dangerous" considering the ongoing campaign and the proximity to the election.

Asked whether "extremely careless" was too similar to "gross negligence," Toscas said that it was. Toscas said that once Comey was getting "grilled about...gross negligence," it must have become obvious that they chose words that were so similar to the statutory language that they "created friction in being able to explain [his] ultimate decision." He told the OIG that he did not know how Comey's lawyers missed this issue, and that the statement would have benefitted from legal review by the prosecutors.

Toscas did not have a problem with Comey's statement that no "reasonable prosecutor" would bring a case. He stated:

[T]hat didn't bother me at all. This is a man who was the Deputy Attorney General of our country. He ran this Department. He was a lifelong prosecutor. I had no problem with that. I know other people do because they say, oh he's usurping authority and things like that, but I think he is a—he is perfectly qualified, and regardless of his position, even in private practice or as a citizen, a private citizen, he could say that and I think it has credibility.

However, Toscas expressed concerns about the downstream effects of Comey's deviation from Department practice in making a public statement in July, which he said then impacted Comey's decisions in October. We discuss those concerns in Chapter Ten.

2.   Prosecutors

As described above, Prosecutors 1 and 2 learned about Comey's plan to hold a press conference as the result of McCabe's call to Toscas and Strzok's call to Laufman. Strzok also spoke directly to Prosecutor 1 that morning. Prosecutor 1 said that he was "extremely angry" on the phone and pressed Strzok to tell him what Comey planned to say, but that Strzok flatly refused and said that he was not allowed to tell him. Following this call, Prosecutor 1 contacted Prosecutors 3 and 4 and informed them that Comey planned to hold a press conference that morning.

The prosecutors had varying reactions to the substance of Comey's statement. Prosecutor 4 told the OIG that he was surprised at how strong Comey's "no reasonable prosecutor" language was and by the inclusion of negative commentary about former Secretary Clinton's conduct, but that he did not recall hearing anything factually inaccurate in the statement.

Prosecutors 1, 2, and 3 identified substantive concerns with Comey's statement. Prosecutor 1 highlighted Comey's negative comments about former Secretary Clinton, characterizing them as "declining to prosecute someone and then sort of dirtying them up with facts that you develop along the way." Prosecutor 1 also said that the use of "extremely careless" to describe her conduct "begs questions about gross negligence" that could have been avoided if the statement were more carefully crafted. Prosecutor 2 thought that the statement was "totally unfair on many levels," particularly the discussion of uncharged conduct, and that the characterization of the evidence in the statement was "very skewed."

Prosecutors 3 and 4 said they had concerns about Comey's use of "extremely careless" to describe former Secretary Clinton's conduct in the statement. On July 6, 2016, Prosecutor 3 sent the following email to Prosecutors 1, 2, and 4:

> It's unfortunate that Comey didn't differentiate the standard of proof between 793(f) and the other statutes. He glossed over all with mention of the absence of intent and made no mention of the necessity of proving knowledge of classified [information] with regard to 793(f) and why that proof was deficient. By using the phrase "extremely careless" he lit up the talking heads last night, many of whom opined that such verbiage warranted a gross negligence charge and that Comey was giving Clinton an unwarranted pass. Even the so-called legal experts didn't seem to understand the elements of that statute and why it did not apply to the facts.

In his OIG interview, Prosecutor 3 said that he thought that Comey's remarks had a good assessment of the investigation, but that he should have better articulated the gross negligence provision "because that seemed to draw a lot of fire from the public." Prosecutor 3 said that Comey's statement did not explain well enough that under the gross negligence provision "you have to know...you're being careless with what is in fact classified information."

On August 2, 2016, Laufman sent an email to FBI Attorney 1 in connection with draft FBI responses to Congressional inquiries that had been made to Comey, and copied Toscas and the NSD prosecutors and supervisors on the email. Laufman stated the following about Comey's July 5 statement:

> We appreciate the Bureau sending us its draft response to the inquiries Director Comey received from Congress. We assume you have already considered and rejected simply responding to the letters (which were sent before the Director's congressional testimony) by referring the Committees to the Director's lengthy [congressional] testimony. As the Director has publicly stated, the Bureau did not coordinate the Director's public statements about this case (many of which are repeated in the Bureau's draft response) with the Justice Department, and we therefore did not have an opportunity to express our views about those statements in advance. As I'm sure you understand, some of the Director's statements went beyond the types of statements that we, as prosecutors, would typically make in a case where no charges were brought (e.g., characterizing uncharged conduct of individuals within the scope of the investigation). While we understand and respect the Director's reasons for departing from normal practice in this one instance, we, of course, have not departed from our practice of refraining from making such statements—and we do not want to be perceived as concurring in or adopting such statements.

VI.   Congressional Testimony Explaining the July 5 Statement

A.   July 7, 2016

Two days after his statement, on July 7, 2016, Comey testified for several hours before the House Committee on Oversight and Government Reform (HOGR).[152] During this hearing, Comey was asked numerous questions about the basis for the decision to recommend declining prosecution of former Secretary Clinton and whether there was evidence that former Secretary Clinton violated any criminal statutes, including the gross negligence provision in 18 U.S.C. § 793(f). He also was asked about the specific language used in his statement. In response to a question about the meaning of "extremely careless," Comey stated, "I intended it as a common sense term.... Somebody who is—should know better, someone who is demonstrating a lack of care that strikes me as—there's ordinary accidents, and then there's just real sloppiness. So I kind of think of that as real sloppiness."

Representative John Mica noted the proximity of the tarmac incident on June 27, Lynch's announcement that she would "defer to the FBI" on July 1, Comey's

---

[152] *See* U.S. House of Representatives, Committee on Oversight and Government Reform, *Oversight of the State Department*, 114th Cong., 2d sess., July 7, 2016, https://oversight.house.gov/wp-content/uploads/2016/07/7-7-2016-Oversight-of-the-State-Department.pdf (accessed May 8, 2018).

statement on the morning of July 5, and former Secretary Clinton's campaign appearance with then President Obama on the afternoon of July 5. In response to a series of questions about the circumstances of his statement, Comey responded, "Look me in the eye and listen to what I'm about to say. I did not coordinate [my statement] with anyone. The White House, the Department of Justice, nobody outside the FBI family had any idea what I was about to say. I say that under oath. I stand by that. There was no coordination." Comey also testified that there was no interference in or attempt to influence the investigation by then President Obama, the Clinton campaign, or former Secretary Clinton herself.

Comey also was asked questions about his reasons for doing an independent press conference. In response to a question about whether the system was "rigged," Comey stated:

> I get a 10-year term to ensure that I stay outside of politics, but in a way that it's easy. I lead an organization that is resolutely apolitical. We are tough aggressive people. If we can make a case, we'll make a case. We do not care what the person's stripes are or what their bank account looks like.

> And I worry very much when people doubt that. It's the reason I did the press conference 2 days ago. I care about the FBI's reputation, I care about the Justice Department. I care about the whole system deeply. And so I decided I'm going to do something no Director's ever done before. I'm not going to tell the Attorney General or anybody else what I'm going to say, or even that I'm going to say it. They did not know, nor did the media know, until I walked out what I was going to talk about.

> And then I offered extraordinary transparency, which I'm sure confused and bugged a lot of people.

Responding to another question about his statement, Comey stated:

> [E]verything I did would have been done privately in the normal course. We have great conversations between the FBI and prosecutors. We make recommendations. We argue back and forth. What I decided to do was offer transparency to the American people about the "whys" of that, what I was going to do because I thought it was very, very important for their confidence in the system of justice. And within that their confidence in the FBI.

> And I was very concerned that if I didn't show that transparency, that in that lack of transparency people would say, "Gee. What is going on here? Something—you know, something seems squirrely here?" So I said I would do something unprecedented because I think it is unprecedented situation.

> Now, the next Director who is criminally investigating one of the two candidates for President may find him or herself bound by my

precedent. Okay. So if that happens in the next 100 years they'll have to deal with what I did. So I decided it was worth doing.

B.   September 28, 2016

Comey also testified in an oversight hearing before the House Judiciary Committee on September 28, 2016, several weeks after the FBI released various materials from the Midyear investigation to Congress and in response to Freedom of Information Act (FOIA) requests.[153] During this hearing, Comey answered questions about the conduct of the Midyear investigation, including questions about the reliance on voluntary production of information, the destruction of devices used by former Secretary Clinton, decisions to grant immunity to witnesses, and the interpretation of the gross negligence provision.

Comey was asked again about the independence of the investigation. Representative Steve King asked about the interview of former Secretary Clinton and whether "Loretta Lynch had her people in there?" Comey responded, "There was no advice to me from the Attorney General or any of the lawyers working for her. My team formulated a recommendation that was communicated to me. And the FBI reached its conclusion as to what to do uncoordinated from the Department of Justice." Asked whether he was responsible for the decision to decline prosecution, Comey said that the decision to decline was made in the Department, but acknowledged that there was "virtually zero chance" that the Department would make a different decision once Comey had made his recommendation public. He stated, "But part of my decision was based on my prediction that there was no way the Department of Justice would prosecute on these facts in any event."

Importantly, at the September 28 hearing, Comey was asked, "Would you reopen the Clinton investigation if you discovered new information that was both relevant and substantial?" Comey answered, "It is hard for me to answer in the abstract. We would certainly look at any new and substantial information.... What we can say is...if people have new and substantial information, we would like to see it so we can make an evaluation."

C.   June 8, 2017

On June 8, 2017, following his firing as FBI Director, Comey testified about Russian interference in the 2016 presidential election before the Senate Select Committee on Intelligence (SSCI).[154] In an exchange with Committee Chairman Senator Richard Burr, Comey was asked about the Midyear investigation, including whether his decision to publicly report the results of the investigation was

---

[153] *See* U.S. House of Representatives, Committee on the Judiciary, *Oversight of the Federal Bureau of Investigation*, 114th Cong., 2d sess., September 28, 2016, https://judiciary.house.gov/wp-content/uploads/2016/09/114-91_22125.pdf (accessed May 8, 2018).

[154] *See* U.S. Senate, Select Committee on Intelligence, *Open Hearing with Former FBI Director James Comey*, 115th Cong., 1st sess., June 8, 2017, https://www.intelligence.senate.gov/hearings/open-hearing-former-fbi-director-james-comey# (accessed May 8, 2018).

influenced by the tarmac meeting between former Attorney General Lynch and former President Clinton. Comey replied, "Yes. In—in an ultimately conclusive way. That was the thing that capped it for me that I had to do something separately to protect the credibility of the investigation, which meant both the FBI and the Justice Department."

Senator Burr then asked whether there were other things that contributed to Comey's decision that he could describe in an open session. Comey stated:

> There were other things that contributed to that. One significant item I can't, I know the committee's been briefed on. There's been some public accounts of it, which are nonsense, but I understand the committee's been briefed on the classified facts.

> Probably the only other consideration that I guess I can talk about in an open setting is at one point the Attorney General had directed me not to call it an "investigation," but instead to call it a "matter," which confused me and concerned me. But that was one of the bricks in the load that led me to conclude I have to step away from the Department if we're to close this case credibly.

The classified facts indicating potential bias by the former Attorney General referenced in Comey's testimony are discussed in the classified appendix to this report. As described in more detail in that appendix, Comey had concerns about Lynch's ability to credibly announce the closure of the investigation, in part because of classified information learned by the FBI in March 2016 regarding alleged attempts to influence the Midyear investigation by Lynch, as well efforts by Comey to extend the investigation to impact the election. Although the FBI did not find these allegations credible, did not investigate the allegations, and did not inform Lynch about the information until August 2016, Comey was concerned that, if the allegations became known, it could affect the public's perception of Lynch's involvement in the investigation.

Comey was asked to provide additional details about Lynch's instruction to call the Midyear investigation a "matter" by Senator James Lankford. Comey stated:

> Well, it concerned me because we were at the point where we had refused to confirm the existence, as we typically do, of an investigation for months, and it was getting to a place where that looked silly, because the campaigns were talking about interacting with the FBI in the course of our work.

> The Clinton campaign at the time was using all kind of euphemisms—security review, matters, things like that—for what was going on. We were getting to a place where the Attorney General and I were both going to have to testify and talk publicly about [it]. And I wanted to know, was she going to authorize us to confirm we had an investigation?

And she said, "Yes," but don't call it that, call it a "matter." And I said, why would I do that? And she said, just call it a "matter."

And, again, you look back in hindsight, you think should I have resisted harder? I just said, all right, it isn't worth—this isn't a hill worth dying on and so I just said, okay, the press is going to completely ignore it. And that's what happened. When I said, we have opened a matter, they all reported the FBI has an investigation open.

And so that concerned me because that language tracked the way the campaign was talking about FBI's work and that's concerning.[155]

In response to a follow up question about this testimony, Comey stated:

And again, I don't know whether it was intentional or not, but it gave the impression that the Attorney General was looking to align the way we talked about our work with the way a political campaign was describing the same activity, which was inaccurate. We had a criminal investigation open with, as I said before, the Federal Bureau of Investigation. We had an investigation open at the time, and so that gave me a queasy feeling.

Comey also had an extended exchange with Senator John Cornyn about whether Lynch had an appearance of a conflict of interest requiring appointment of a special counsel.

SENATOR CORNYN: But it seems to me that you clearly believe that Loretta Lynch, the Attorney General, had an appearance of a conflict of interest on the Clinton email investigation. Is that correct?

COMEY: I think that's fair. I didn't believe she could credibly decline that investigation, at least not without grievous damage to the Department of Justice and to the FBI.

SENATOR CORNYN: And, under Department of Justice and FBI norms, wouldn't it have been appropriate for the Attorney General, or, if she had recused herself—which she did not do—for the Deputy Attorney General to appoint a special counsel? That's essentially what's happened now with Director Mueller. Would that have been an appropriate step in the Clinton email investigation in your opinion?

COMEY: Certainly a possible step, yes, sir.

---

[155] In an interview on September 8, 2015, former Secretary Clinton described the FBI's investigation as a "security investigation.... It's not, as has been confirmed, a criminal investigation." Interview with Hillary Clinton, ABC News (Sept. 8, 2015), https://abcnews.go.com/Politics/full-transcript-abcs-david-muir-interviews-hillary-clinton/story?id=33607656 (accessed June 1, 2018). Her campaign also referred to it as a "security review." See Eugene Kiely, More Spin on Clinton Emails, FactCheck.org (Sept. 8, 2015), https://www.factcheck.org/2015/09/more-spin-on-clinton-emails (accessed June 2, 2018).

SENATOR CORNYN: And were you aware that Ms. Lynch had been requested numerous times to appoint a special counsel and had refused?

COMEY: Yes, from—I think Congress had, members of Congress had repeatedly asked. Yes, sir.

SENATOR CORNYN: Yours truly did on multiple occasions. And that heightened your concerns about the appearance of a conflict of interest with the Department of Justice, which caused you to make what you have described as an incredibly painful decision to basically take the matter up yourself and led to that July press conference.

COMEY: Yes, sir. After President Clinton, former President Clinton, met on the plane with the Attorney General, I considered whether I should call for the appointment of a special counsel and had decided that that would be an unfair thing to do, because I knew there was no case there. We had investigated it very, very thoroughly.

I know this is a subject of passionate disagreement, but I knew there was no case there. And calling for the appointment of a special counsel would be brutally unfair because it would send the message, aha, there's something here. That was my judgment. Again, lots of people have different views of it. But that's how I thought about it.

SENATOR CORNYN: Well, if the special counsel had been appointed, they could've made that determination that there was nothing there and declined to pursue it, right?

COMEY: Sure, but it would've been many months later or a year later.

VII. Analysis

We found no evidence that Comey's public statement announcing the FBI's decision to close the investigation was the result of bias or an effort to influence the election. Instead, the documentary and testimonial evidence reviewed by the OIG reflected that Comey's decision was the result of his consideration of the evidence that the FBI had collected during the course of the investigation and his understanding of the proof required to pursue a prosecution under the relevant statutes. Nevertheless, we concluded that Comey's unilateral announcement was inconsistent with Department policy, usurped the authority of Attorney General, and did not accurately describe the legal position of the Department prosecutors.

Although we found no evidence that Lynch and former President Clinton discussed the Midyear investigation or engaged in other inappropriate discussion during their tarmac meeting on June 27, 2016, we also found that Lynch's failure to recognize the appearance problem created by former President Clinton's visit and to take action to cut the visit short was an error in judgment. We further concluded that her efforts to respond to the meeting by explaining what her role would be in the investigation going forward created public confusion and did not adequately address the situation. Finally, we found that Lynch, having decided not to recuse herself, retained authority over both the final prosecution decision and the Department's management of the Midyear investigation, including whether to respond to Comey's call to her on the morning of July 5 by instructing him to share his statement with her.

A.   Comey's Decision to Make a Unilateral Announcement

Beginning in early 2016, and certainly by late April 2016, the Midyear team reached a general consensus that the evidence would not support a prosecution, absent major unexpected developments in the form of newly discovered emails or testimony. This assessment was based on a lack of evidence showing that former Secretary Clinton, her senior aides, or other State Department officials knew that they were emailing unmarked classified information or intended to introduce classified information onto an unclassified system. Witnesses told us that, at the time, they understood the emails in question were sent by State Department employees to other State Department employees in the course of doing their jobs, and that both the senders and recipients had the appropriate clearances and the need to know the information. As described in Chapter Two, the prosecutors determined based on their legal research and review of past Department practice that evidence of knowledge or intent was necessary to charge any individual with violations of 18 U.S.C. §§ 793(d), 793(e), or 793(f)(1).

Comey understood and agreed with this assessment. He told us that, as he realized that the case likely would not result in charges, he became concerned that senior Department officials were unable to announce a declination in a way that the public would find credible and objective. Comey said that these concerns were based on the public perception created by an Attorney General appointed by a Democratic President announcing that the Democratic Presidential candidate would not be prosecuted, not on any actions by or concerns specific to Lynch or Yates; however, as discussed below, Comey also pointed to public comments made by then President Obama and his White House Press Secretary about the Midyear investigation, concerns that classified information referencing Lynch would be publicly released and would impact her credibility, Lynch's alleged admonition to him early on to refer to the FBI's investigation as a "matter," and Lynch's meeting with former President Clinton as contributing to his concerns about her.

In April 2016, Comey initiated discussions with Yates and Axelrod about how to credibly announce the conclusion of the investigation based on the likelihood that the case would result in a declination. During this discussion, Comey stated that he was likely to request the appointment of a special counsel "the deeper we get into summer" without concluding the investigation. Comey told the OIG that his reference to a special counsel was intended to induce the Department to move more quickly to obtain the Mills and Samuelson laptops. We did not find evidence that Comey at any time seriously considered requesting a special counsel.

Lynch told us that she was aware that Yates met with Comey, and that Comey indicated that he was not sure there was a "there there"—*i.e.*, it was not a prosecutable case. Lynch also was receiving periodic briefings about the Midyear investigation, and said that she thought that any discussions about announcing a declination were "very premature" at that time because there were remaining investigative steps to be taken. Lynch told us that she did not know that Comey mentioned requesting a special counsel during his discussion with Yates, and that no one in the Department or the FBI ever suggested to her that a special counsel was needed.

Discussions about a strategy for announcing a declination also took place within the FBI. Comey told the OIG that he considered every option for announcing a declination, from a one-line press release issued by the Department to an FBI-only press conference providing a detailed statement about the investigation. Comey said that foremost in his mind was the need to minimize the "reputational damage" to the Department and the FBI that would result from a declination, and to preserve the credibility and integrity of the institution.

In late April 2016, Comey raised the possibility of "doing something solo" in a meeting with Baker, McCabe, and Rybicki. He also began drafting a public statement that contemplated that he would act alone in announcing the declination, sending a first draft of this statement to Baker, McCabe, and Rybicki on May 2, 2016. Witnesses told us that Comey had not yet made a firm decision to deliver a public statement when he sent this draft, but that he wanted to discuss it as one possible option for announcing a declination.

According to various witnesses we interviewed, Comey and other senior FBI officials knew that delivering a separate public statement held substantial risk. McCabe said that he expressed concerns that such a statement would represent a "complete departure" from Department protocol and could set a "potentially dangerous precedent" for the FBI. Rosenberg said that in discussions with Comey, he raised the possibility that doing a separate statement would create an irreparable breach with the Department. Comey said that he knew it was a "crazy idea, but we were in a [500]-year flood."

Comey discussed the draft public statement in meetings with members of the Midyear team and with senior FBI officials at various times in May and June 2016. These discussions included whether to do a separate statement at all, in addition to the specific language revisions discussed in Section III.B and C above. Comey said that by June 27, 2016, the date of Lynch's tarmac meeting with former President Clinton, he was "90 percent there, like highly likely" in terms of deciding to deliver the statement.

Despite this, Comey and other senior FBI officials continued to engage their Department counterparts in discussions about how to credibly announce a declination. These discussions occurred at various levels: between Comey and Yates; between McCabe and Carlin; and between Strzok and Laufman. At no time did anyone from the FBI inform anyone from the Department that Comey was even considering making a statement on his own, let alone that he had already drafted such a statement. Department witnesses at all levels told us that they believed that shortly after the interview of former Secretary Clinton was completed, the Department and the FBI would work together to deliver some sort of coordinated statement, and that Comey would be involved. Yates told the OIG that her understanding was that they would be "all holding hands and jumping off the bridge together."

Comey said that from the time he first conceived of making a separate statement, he intended to deliver it without coordinating with the Department. He told the OIG that he made a conscious decision not to tell Department leadership about his plans to "go it alone" because he was concerned that they would instruct him not to do it. Comey admitted that he concealed his intentions from the Department until the morning of his press conference, and instructed his staff to do the same, to make it impracticable for Department leadership to prevent him from delivering his statement.

We found that it was extraordinary and insubordinate for Comey to conceal his intentions from his superiors, the Attorney General and Deputy Attorney General, for the admitted purpose of preventing them from telling him not to make the statement, and to instruct his subordinates in the FBI to do the same. Comey waited until the morning of his press conference to inform Lynch and Yates of his plans to hold one without them, and did so only after first notifying the press. As a result, Lynch's office learned about Comey's plans via press inquiries rather than from Comey. Moreover, when Comey spoke with Lynch he did not tell her what he intended to say in his statement.

Factors Cited by Comey as Influencing His Decision

Comey cited several factors that he said influenced his decision to make a statement on his own and without coordinating with the Department. In addition to public comments made by former President Obama and his White House Press Secretary about the Midyear investigation, Comey cited four things that he said caused him to be concerned that Lynch could not credibly participate in announcing a declination: her alleged instruction to call the Midyear investigation a "matter" in a meeting held on September 28, 2015, which Comey said "made [his] spider sense tingle" and caused him to "worry...that she's carrying water for the [Clinton] campaign"; concerns that highly classified information referencing Lynch would be publicly released and would impact her credibility; the tarmac meeting between Lynch and former President Bill Clinton; and the fact that Lynch was appointed by a President that was the same political party as former Secretary Clinton.

We found none of these reasons persuasive, either standing alone or considered together, as a basis for deviating from well-established Department policies and acting unilaterally in a way intentionally designed to avoid supervision by Department leadership over his actions.

Lynch's Reference to the Investigation as a "Matter." We found that the discussion between Lynch and Comey on September 28, 2015, was not generally viewed as a particularly significant event, other than by Comey. As described in Chapter Four, Department and FBI officials present at this meeting did not interpret Lynch's reference in the way Comey did, and contemporaneous notes indicate that the discussion at the meeting was focused on the need to track language in recent letters to Congress and the State Department. Lynch told us that her intent in suggesting that Comey refer to Midyear as a "matter" was to allow them to answer questions about staffing and resources while also complying with longstanding Department policy to refrain from confirming ongoing criminal investigations, not to downplay the significance of the investigation. Other Department witnesses present at this meeting interpreted Lynch's comment as a suggestion, not an instruction from Lynch. We found no evidence that this phrasing was intended to "track" the language used by the Clinton campaign or was an attempt to influence the investigation. Remarkably, Comey never told Lynch or Yates that this (or any other) incident raised questions about Lynch's impartiality in his mind, or that such concerns might influence his actions in handling the case.

Concerns about Future Leaks of Classified Information. As described in the classified appendix to this report, Comey told the OIG that he became concerned in mid-June 2016 that classified information suggesting that Lynch was exerting influence on the Midyear investigation would be publicly released, and that this would impact her ability to credibly announce a declination. However, by mid-June Comey was already very far along in his plans to make a unilateral statement. Moreover, witnesses told us that the FBI determined based on various factors that the allegations that Lynch had interfered with the investigation were not credible, describing the information as "objectively false."

Comey told the OIG that he never saw any actions by Lynch to interfere with the investigation, stating, "I'll say this again, I saw no reality of Loretta Lynch interfering in this investigation." Rather, Comey said he was concerned that leaks of this non-credible information about Lynch would undermine her credibility. The FBI did not inform Lynch about the allegation in the highly classified information until August 2016, more than a month after Comey's announcement, and then (according to Lynch) did so in a way that highlighted the FBI's assessment that the information lacked credibility.[156] At no time did Comey alert Lynch or Yates that the information raised concerns about Lynch's ability to participate credibly in the Midyear investigation or in any declination announcement. At no time did Comey consult with Lynch or Yates about how to deal with this false information to protect the credibility of the declination decision.

Finally, the OIG found that the same classified information also included an allegation, equally lacking in credibility, that Comey planned to delay the Midyear investigation to aid Republicans. Comey did not inform Lynch or Yates of this fact, let alone discuss with them whether this information might be leaked or whether, if it was, it might undermine his credibility as a spokesman.

Lynch's Tarmac Meeting with Former President Clinton. Comey told us that by the time the tarmac incident occurred on June 27, 2016, he was already "90 percent there" in terms of the decision to make a public statement, but that the tarmac meeting "tipped the scales" towards making his mind up to go forward with an independent announcement on the Midyear investigation. While Comey's

---

[156] As described in the classified appendix to this report, the FBI notified senior career Department officials about this information in March 2016, but did not convey that it raised concerns about Lynch's ability to credibly participate in announcing a declination in the Midyear investigation.

concerns about the impact of the meeting were legitimate, and warranted his informing Lynch of his concerns and providing her with any views he had on how it should be addressed, ultimately the decision whether Lynch should voluntarily recuse herself was Lynch's to make, not Comey's.

In his October 2016 SAC Conference speech, Comey emphasized the damage to the FBI that would result if he "did the normal thing" in the wake of the tarmac meeting. He stated that he was concerned that if the FBI made a private recommendation to Lynch, "the Department of Justice will screw around it for Lord knows how long, issue probably a one sentence declination, and then the world will catch on fire[.]" However, the stated concerns are inconsistent with what Comey had already discussed with the Department about the "endgame" of the investigation. Comey knew that the Department was well aware of his view that the Midyear investigation needed to be completed promptly. Comey had previously discussed with Yates the prospect of requesting a special counsel if the investigation continued past the nominating conventions, and Yates told us that she and Comey had made plans to "hold hands and jump off the bridge together" in announcing a declination. Moreover, notes from discussions of the Midyear team that occurred shortly before the Clinton interview on July 2 reflected that the prosecutors understood that Comey wanted to make the announcement by July 8 and therefore there would be "withering pressure" to complete the LHM and memorialize the Midyear prosecutors' conclusions immediately after the Clinton interview. There simply was no basis for Comey to believe that the Department would take weeks to act on the FBI's recommendation on such a consequential matter.

Moreover, Comey never raised his concerns about the tarmac meeting with Yates or requested that Lynch recuse herself. Instead, Comey viewed the tarmac meeting as a justification for proceeding with his existing plan to act alone. Comey admitted that had Lynch recused herself he might have reconsidered his decision to make a separate announcement, stating, "Had Loretta said, I'm stepping out of this. I'm making Sally Yates the Acting Attorney General and had I gone and sat down with Sally and heard her vision for it, maybe we would have ended up in a different place." While Comey indicated that he did not speak with Yates because Lynch had already made her announcement on July 1, we found that he still could and should have done so.

Lynch was Appointed by a Democratic President. Comey cited a general concern that Lynch was appointed by a President who was from the same political party as former Secretary Clinton. Yet that fact existed at the beginning of the Midyear investigation. At no time did Comey inform either Lynch or Yates that he viewed Lynch as having a "conflict of interest," or that he thought she should be recused from the investigation on the basis of party affiliation, or for any other reason. While Comey did mention the prospect of a special counsel in his April 2016 meeting with Yates, he did so seemingly as a bargaining chip to get the Department to move more quickly on the Mills and Samuelson laptops, and we found no evidence that he seriously pursued this option.

We found it troubling that Comey would have formed views about Lynch's inability to participate in or credibly decline prosecution of the Midyear investigation, yet never once raised them with Lynch or Yates. If Comey genuinely believed that Lynch could not credibly participate in the Midyear investigation or announce a declination, he should have raised these concerns with Yates or Lynch and requested that Lynch recuse herself. If he believed that neither Lynch nor Yates could credibly make a prosecutive decision, he should have discussed this with them at the beginning of the investigation and requested appointment of a special counsel. He did not.

Impact of Comey's Decision to Make a Unilateral Statement

Comey's decision to depart from longstanding Department practice and publicly announce the FBI's declination recommendation without coordinating with the Department was an unjustified usurpation of authority.[157] Although Comey was aware that the Midyear prosecutors and Department leadership viewed the case as a likely declination, Comey made the decision to announce the conclusion of the investigation before prosecutors had a chance to render their own formal prosecutorial decision. Comey's views on what a "reasonable prosecutor" would do—while informed by the prosecutors' views on the likely outcome of the case and the Department's research on past mishandling cases—were nonetheless made without consulting the Department in advance. Although Comey stated in his press conference that "the prosecutors make the decisions about whether charges are appropriate based on evidence the FBI has helped collect," by making this public announcement about the FBI's charging recommendation, and by stating his view that "no reasonable prosecutor" would bring charges, he effectively made the decision for the prosecutors because it would thereafter have been virtually impossible for them to make any other decision.

Even if Comey had every reason to believe that Lynch and Yates agreed with him, speaking unilaterally and publicly for the Department about a decision to decline prosecution is not a function granted to the Director. The authority to make such a statement had not been delegated to him by his superiors, the Attorney General and the Deputy Attorney General. Comey acknowledged this, but argued that "the potential for damage to the institution" outweighed the need to follow Department practice, stating, "[I]n a normal circumstance it's the right of the

---

[157] After reviewing a draft of the report, counsel for Comey stated that even before Lynch's July 1 statement that she would accept the recommendation of the career staff, the decision about whether to prosecute former Secretary Clinton was publicly framed as belonging to him, and Department leadership did not correct this impression. *See, e.g.,* Massimo Calabresi, *Inside the FBI Investigation of Hillary Clinton's Email*, TIME, Mar. 31, 2016 (noting that Lynch testified in February 2016 that she was waiting for a charging recommendation from Comey, and that some Republicans were referring to the investigation as the "Comey primary"). As a result, counsel said that Comey did not "usurp" the Attorney General's authority, but rather had the role of the Attorney General given to him by Department leadership. However, waiting for a charging recommendation from the FBI Director is substantially different than making a public announcement without any prior consultation with or approval from the Attorney General. Indeed, there would have been no need for Comey to have affirmatively concealed his plans for a public statement from Lynch if he believed Lynch had effectively ceded authority over the prosecution decision to him.

Attorney General and Deputy Attorney General to make those decisions and the FBI Director should tell them, but this was not the normal circumstance."

In our criminal justice system, the investigative and prosecutive functions are intentionally kept separate as a check on the government's power to bring criminal charges. While Comey's statement acknowledged those differing roles and responsibilities, his actions violated those separate authorities by arrogating to himself and the FBI the ability to make judgments about whether a case of the highest political consequence should be charged, and he did so by intentionally seeking to prevent Department leadership from being able to stop him based on concerns that he never even gave them an opportunity to consider. In making a statement announcing the conclusion of the Midyear investigation and opining on what the only possible prosecutorial decision could be, Comey made it virtually impossible for any prosecutor to make any other recommendation. He thereby effectively operated as not only the FBI Director, but also as the Attorney General. It is the Attorney General who is accountable to the public and to Congress for prosecutorial decisions made by the Department, not the head of the investigating law enforcement agency. Comey took that accountability away from Lynch and placed it on himself when he decided to deliver a unilateral statement.

Additionally, Comey's decision to make an announcement without consulting or obtaining approval from Department leadership violated the Department's media policy and also may have violated regulations regarding the public release of information. See 28 C.F.R. § 50.2(b)(9). Although Baker told the OIG that Comey's call to Lynch and Yates on the morning of his press conference constituted approval for purposes of this regulation, Comey's testimony that he concealed his plans from Lynch until the morning of July 5, only contacted her after the FBI had notified the press in order to make it impossible for her to stop him, and told Lynch when they did speak that he was not going to tell her what he intended to say in his statement, does not constitute consulting with or obtaining approval from Department leadership. In light of these events, we recommend that the Department consider making explicit in the USAM what we thought was obvious in light of Department policy and protocol—that an investigating agency cannot publicly announce its recommended charging decision in a criminal investigation prior to consulting with the Attorney General, Deputy Attorney General, U.S. Attorney, or his or her designee, and cannot proceed to publicly announce that decision prior to obtaining a final prosecution decision from one of these officials.[158]

B.   Content of Comey's Unilateral Announcement

We identified two significant substantive concerns with the content of Comey's July 5 statement. First, Comey included criticism of former Secretary Clinton's uncharged conduct, including calling her "extremely careless," thereby violating longstanding Department practice to avoid what others described as "trash[ing] people we're not charging." Second, having improperly decided to comment on what were prosecutorial decisions, Comey proceeded to inadequately

---

[158] Such a policy would necessarily need to include exceptions for certain situations where the law required or permitted disclosure.

and incompletely explain how the Department's prosecutors applied the relevant statutory provisions and why they believed the evidence was insufficient to support a prosecution. For example, Comey described former Secretary Clinton's handling of classified information as "extremely careless" but then asserted that such conduct did not amount to "gross negligence" under the relevant statute. In so doing, Comey failed to explain that, since at least 2008, it had been the Department's position that, before bringing a "gross negligence" case, prosecutors had to be able to prove that a defendant knew at the time that the information was gathered, transmitted, or lost that it was in fact classified information. As delivered, Comey's statement led to greater public confusion and second guessing, not greater public clarity.

Many of the problems with the statement resulted from Comey's failure to coordinate with Department officials. By deciding not to consult with the Midyear prosecutors about their assessment of the Department's historical approach to and interpretation of the "gross negligence" statute or their assessment of the evidence under the applicable legal standard, Comey lost the opportunity to hear the views of the career prosecutors responsible for prosecuting violations of the mishandling statutes. Based on our interviews, these prosecutors would likely have warned him about the substantive questions presented by his statement. In addition, Department witnesses told the OIG that the presentation of the case by the Midyear prosecutors at the briefing of the Attorney General on July 6, 2016, which is described in Chapter Six, differed significantly from Comey's statement, leading these witnesses to conclude that the presentation of the facts in Comey's statement was "very skewed" or delivered with a "slant."

Description of Uncharged Conduct

It is not unprecedented for the Department to announce the completion of an investigation without a prosecution. In fact, it happens frequently in high profile matters, including in many federal civil rights investigations. Such an announcement may serve several legitimate purposes, including allowing the public to know that the Department thoroughly investigated the matter and lifting the cloud over an individual known to have been under investigation. In limited instances, the Department has included criticism of individuals not charged with a crime. Comey cited as precedent for his July 5 public statement the June 2004 press conference by then DAG Comey summarizing the evidence against Jose Padilla, who was designated as an enemy combatant, and the Department's October 2015 letter to Congress summarizing the results of the criminal investigation into IRS officials, which did not result in criminal charges. However, in both of those instances, the *Department* was responsible for issuing the statement, not the FBI Director.

Moreover, Comey's announcement was unusual in that it concentrated in substantial part on criticizing former Secretary Clinton's uncharged conduct. This was contrary to longstanding Department practice and protocol. Witnesses told us that criticizing individuals for conduct that does not warrant prosecution is something that the Department simply does not do. For example, Toscas stated, "We don't say we're closing something, but let me tell you some bad stuff that we saw along the way, but it doesn't rise to the level of bringing a case. We just don't do it." Prosecutor 1 characterized the negative comments about former Secretary Clinton as "declining to prosecute someone and then sort of dirtying them up with facts that you develop along the way."

Department witnesses did not identify a specific regulation or USAM provision that required Comey to refrain from commenting on uncharged conduct, and we found none. Rather, witnesses described this as a practice that is "ingrained" in every Department prosecutor. This principle underlies other Department policies and practices that do not directly apply in these circumstances, but that are nonetheless salient. USAM 9-27.760 requires prosecutors to remain sensitive to the privacy and reputation interests of uncharged third parties—for example, by not identifying or causing a defendant to identify a third-party wrongdoer by name or description in public plea and sentencing proceedings, without the express approval of the U.S. Attorney and the appropriate Assistant Attorney General prior to the hearing absent exigent circumstances. USAM 9-27.760 states, "In other less predictable contexts, federal prosecutors should strive to avoid unnecessary public references to wrongdoing by uncharged third-parties."

Similarly, when a case is closed without charges being filed, the Department does not seek to unseal a search warrant for the purpose of revealing to the public that there was probable cause that someone engaged in criminal activity. In addition, where the Department has concluded that an uncharged individual was a participant in a criminal conspiracy, the Department's rules specifically prohibit prosecutors from naming the uncharged co-conspirator in an indictment or including sufficient detail in public filings that would allow the co-conspirator to be identified. See, e.g., USAM 9-11.130. The common principle underlying these policies is that neither the FBI nor Department prosecutors are permitted to insinuate or allege that an individual who has not been charged with a crime is nevertheless guilty of some wrongdoing. We see no reason why an unindicted co-conspirator should be afforded greater protection than a person who has been investigated and found not to be criminally liable. We therefore recommend that the Department and the FBI consider adopting a policy addressing the appropriateness of Department employees discussing uncharged conduct in public statements.

Several witnesses acknowledged that one major purpose of including negative comments about former Secretary Clinton was to send the message that the FBI was not condoning her conduct: essentially, to protect the FBI from criticism that it failed to recognize the seriousness of her conduct and was "letting her off the hook." We recognize that this investigation was subject to scrutiny not typical of the average criminal case, but that does not provide a basis for violating well-established Department norms and, essentially, "trashing" the subject of an investigation with uncharged misconduct that Comey, every agent, and every prosecutor agreed did not warrant prosecution. Such norms exist for important reasons and none of the justifications provided by witnesses for why such criticism was warranted in the Midyear investigation—including expressing disapproval of former Secretary Clinton's conduct to the FBI workforce, "counter[ing]" statements made on the campaign trail that the emails in question were classified after the fact, or informing the American people about the facts of the investigation—provided legitimate reasons to depart from normal and appropriate Department practice.

Substantive Issues with the Statement

Department witnesses told the OIG that they considered Comey's statement to be both factually and legally incomplete. These witnesses said that critical facts supporting the decision to decline prosecution were not included in Comey's statement. Axelrod told the OIG that Comey's most notable omission was the failure to explain that the Department has never prosecuted mishandling violations "where the classified information was shared between people who work for the Government.... That's a pretty important fact." Axelrod and other Department witnesses also noted that Comey did not include information explaining that "the majority of the emails that turned out to be classified had been sent late at night or on the weekends," suggesting that State Department employees sending the emails tried to "talk around" classified information in the course of doing their jobs. Department witnesses described the characterization of the evidence in Comey's statement as "very skewed" or unintentionally "slant[ed]."

Comey also included in his statement a comment that although the FBI did not find direct evidence that former Secretary Clinton's private email account was hacked, the FBI assessed that it was "possible" that hostile actors gained access to former Secretary Clinton's personal email account based on various factors. He added that the FBI assessed it would be unlikely to see such direct evidence given the nature of the system and the actors potentially involved in hostile intrusions, and that former Secretary Clinton had used her personal email in the territory of foreign adversaries. The statement thus insinuated that hostile foreign actors may have in fact gained access to former Secretary Clinton's private email account, based almost entirely on speculation and without any evidence from the Midyear investigation to support his claim. As described in Chapter Five, the FBI Midyear Forensics Agent told the OIG that, although he did not believe there was "any way of determining...100%" whether Clinton's servers had been compromised, he felt "fairly confident that there wasn't an intrusion." The LHM summarizing the Midyear investigation similarly stated, "FBI investigation and forensic analysis did not find evidence confirming that Clinton's email server systems were compromised by cyber means."

In addition, Comey's statement failed to describe accurately what the Midyear prosecutors deemed was essential to make out a violation of the "gross negligence" statute. As described in Chapters Two and Seven, the Midyear prosecutors took into account the legislative history of the statute, previous military prosecutions and indictments brought under it, and the Department's historical interpretation of the provision in declinations dating to at least 2008. Based on this authority, the Midyear prosecutors determined that a violation of Section 793(f)(1) requires (1) a state of mind that is "just a little short of being willful," "criminally reckless," or "so gross as to almost suggest deliberate intention," and (2) evidence that the individuals who sent emails containing classified information did so "knowingly." With respect to former Secretary Clinton, the Midyear prosecutors determined that in the absence of evidence showing that she knew that emails she received contained classified information, such as through obvious classification markings, Department practice and precedent required that they decline prosecution.

Comey told the OIG that he understood Section 793(f)(1) to require "something closer to actual knowledge." Yet nowhere in his statement did Comey say that the FBI concluded that former Secretary Clinton lacked knowledge that the information in question was classified, and that prosecutors determined that evidence of such knowledge was needed to bring charges under the "gross negligence" statute. On July 6, 2016, Prosecutor 3 sent an email to the other Midyear prosecutors highlighting this problem. He stated:

> It's unfortunate that Comey didn't differentiate the standard of proof between 793(f) and the other statutes. He glossed over all with mention of the absence of intent and made no mention of the necessity of proving knowledge of classified [information] with regard to 793(f) and why that proof was deficient. By using the phrase "extremely careless" he lit up the talking heads last night, many of whom opined that such verbiage warranted a gross negligence charge and that Comey was giving Clinton an unwarranted pass. Even the so-called legal experts didn't seem to understand the elements of that statute and why it did not apply to the facts.

By describing former Secretary Clinton's conduct as "extremely careless" while failing to explain what the Midyear team concluded was the lack of proof for the other requirements of Section 793(f)(1), Comey created confusion about the FBI's assessment of her culpability and the reasons for recommending that prosecution be declined. The focus on former Secretary Clinton's "extremely careless" handling of classified information foreseeably and predictably led the public to question why former Secretary Clinton was not being charged with "gross negligence."

The issue for the Midyear prosecutors was never whether former Secretary Clinton's conduct was "extremely careless," but whether her conduct met the requirements for charging a violation of Section 793(f)—*i.e.*, whether there was sufficient evidence to establish that she knowingly included classified information on her unclassified private email server, or learned that classified information was transferred to her unclassified server and failed to report it. The prosecutors concluded that there was not. As described in Chapter Seven below, the prosecutors found no evidence that former Secretary Clinton believed or was aware that the emails contained classified information, or had concerns about the information included in unclassified emails sent to her.

C.   Lynch's Decision Not to Recuse after the Tarmac Meeting

After the tarmac meeting with former President Clinton, Lynch obtained an opinion from the Departmental Ethics Office that she was not legally required to recuse herself from the Midyear investigation. Although the opinion was not memorialized in writing, former OAG staff and former officials in the Departmental

Ethics Office confirmed that Lynch obtained this opinion, and that the conclusion was that recusal was not required. Lynch was entitled to rely on that ethics opinion in the face of subsequent questions about her involvement in the Midyear investigation.

Lynch told the OIG that she considered voluntarily recusing herself. However, she thought that doing so would create the impression that something inappropriate had occurred during her conversation with former President Clinton. Lynch said that she felt a responsibility to remain involved in the Midyear investigation, because if she decided to recuse herself, she would be "asking someone else to step up and endure all the hits the Department will take for the case for the result, whatever it is."

Lynch said that she applied her usual process in the Midyear investigation, and that her role did not change after the tarmac meeting. Lynch told the OIG that the only thing that differed was that she decided to speak publicly about how the Department's process typically works. However, Lynch's July 1, 2016 statements at the Aspen Institute were confusing and created the impression that, while she would not formally recuse from the investigation, she also would not remain in a deciding role in the investigation (by stating "I will be accepting their recommendations"). In an effort to address the confusion, Lynch sought to clarify her remarks by providing the reporter with another formulation of her intentions, stating, "I can't imagine a circumstance in which I would not be accepting their recommendations." However, these statements continued to make it appear that Lynch would cede her decisionmaking authority to the career staff and the FBI Director in a way that was akin to some type of recusal.

In our view, Lynch should have either made it unambiguously clear that she did not believe there was a basis for recusal and that she was going to remain the final decisionmaker (thereby making her accountable for the final decision, not Comey), or recused herself and allowed Yates to serve as Acting Attorney General, or sought a special counsel appointment. Instead, Lynch took none of these actions, leaving it ambiguous to the public as to what her role would be. Ultimately, that left the public with the perception that the FBI Director, and not the Attorney General, was accountable for the declination decision.

D. Lynch's Response to Comey's Notification

As described above, Comey concealed his plans to make a public statement from senior Department officials, and instructed his subordinates to do the same. He did not inform Lynch and Yates of his plans to hold a press conference until the morning of July 5, 2016. Comey intentionally left Department leadership a short time to respond to his information, admitting that he did this to avoid having them tell him not to do it.

Comey notified Lynch and Yates of his plans only after first contacting the press. He did not tell Lynch what he planned to say when she asked. According to Lynch, Comey told her he would not go over his statement with her so they both could say that it was not coordinated. Department officials understandably had concerns about directing Comey to cancel the press conference after he had already announced his plans to hold one.

Lynch said while Comey told her that his statement would be about the Midyear investigation, it did not occur to her that Comey would announce the end of the investigation or the FBI's recommendation. She explained that while she knew that former Secretary Clinton had been interviewed, she was not aware that the investigation was considered complete. Lynch told the OIG that if she had known what Comey was planning to do, she would have told him to stop. However, Lynch said that she trusted him based on her long relationship with Comey and his comment to her that it would be better if they could both say that they did not coordinate his statement. Lynch told the OIG that she thought this was a reasonable decision, and that it was the right decision under the circumstances because the Comey she knew followed the rules. She said that once Comey started speaking and she realized what he was doing, she had "no way to stop him at that point, I mean, short of, you know, dashing across the street and unplugging something."

Nonetheless, we found that Lynch retained authority over both the final prosecutive decision and the Department's management of the Midyear investigation. This included the authority to insist that Comey share his statement with her and allow the Department to review and comment on it. Although we recognize that Comey made it impracticable for her to tell him not to make any statement given the FBI had already notified the press, there was time still available for her to review his proposed statement and to instruct him to make changes to it. Even if Lynch did not think that Comey was going to announce that the FBI was closing its Midyear investigation, Comey told her the statement was going to be about the Midyear investigation, a case over which she retained the authority and responsibility as the Attorney General. As such, we believe she should have instructed Comey to tell her what he intended to say beforehand, and should have discussed it with Comey.

PAGE LEFT INTENTIONALLY

BLANK

CHAPTER SEVEN:
THE DEPARTMENT'S DECISION NOT TO PROSECUTE

After former Director Comey's statement on July 5, 2016, the Midyear prosecutors finalized their analysis and conclusions under the relevant statutes, recommending that prosecution of former Secretary Clinton and others be declined. They then provided their conclusions to NSD supervisors.

On the afternoon of July 6, 2016, former AG Lynch held a briefing attended by Comey, McCabe, and other senior Department and FBI officials. The Midyear prosecutors briefed Lynch on the relevant evidence, the applicable statutes, and the basis for their recommendations. Following the briefing, the Department issued a brief statement announcing that Lynch had accepted the recommendation of the career prosecutors and agents who worked on the Midyear investigation.

In this chapter we discuss the prosecutors' conclusions and the July 6 briefing, focusing on issues that have been subject to public criticism. Consistent with the role of the OIG and our statement that we will not substitute the OIG's judgment for the judgments made by the Department or the FBI regarding the substantive merits of investigative or prosecutive decisions, we reviewed whether there was evidence that the Department's decision to decline prosecution was based on improper considerations or bias. As with our review of investigative decisions, our role was not to determine whether a prosecution should or should not have been brought but rather whether the Department's explanations for its declination decision were not unreasonable and whether there was evidence that the justifications offered for the decision were a pretext for improper, but unstated, considerations.

I.   The Declination Recommendation

As described above, prosecutors and NSD supervisors began to realize that the investigation could lead to a declination in early 2016. As the investigation continued into the Spring of 2016, the prosecutors began to consider how to summarize the investigation and memorialize their legal conclusions to provide to their supervisors and to Department leadership. The prosecutors told the OIG that they wanted to wait until the end of the investigation before making a charging recommendation.

The prosecutors planned to complete their legal analysis after former Secretary Clinton was interviewed on July 2, 2016. Following Comey's announcement on July 5, 2016, they realized they had a much shorter time period to do so and worked until almost midnight on July 5 to finish their legal analysis. They completed this process the following afternoon and provided their analysis and conclusions to Toscas.

The prosecutors' legal analysis referenced an FBI letterhead memorandum (LHM) summarizing the Midyear investigation.[159] In their analysis, the Midyear prosecutors categorized the witnesses that had been interviewed in the investigation into four categories:

- Originators of classified information (*i.e.*, individuals who introduced classified information into unclassified emails, including State Department Bureau of Public Affairs employees, an individual who regularly interfaced with State Department employees, State Department Operations Center employees, and other State Department employees responsible for conveying information to their superiors);

- U.S. government employees who had involvement with a specific Top Secret//Special Access Program ("TS//SAP");

- Senior aides to former Secretary Clinton, including Huma Abedin, Cheryl Mills, and Jake Sullivan; and

- Former Secretary Clinton herself.

The prosecutors referred to the first three categories of witnesses—the Originators, the officials involved with the TS//SAP, and former Secretary Clinton's senior aides—collectively as the "senders."

The prosecutors analyzed the conduct of former Secretary Clinton and the "senders" under five statutes:

- 18 U.S.C. §§ 793(d) and 793(e) (willful mishandling of documents or information relating to the national defense);

- 18 U.S.C. § 793(f) (removal, loss, theft, abstraction, or destruction of documents or information relating to the national defense through gross negligence, or failure to report such removal, loss, theft, abstraction, or destruction);

- 18 U.S.C. § 1924 (unauthorized removal and retention of classified documents or material by government employees); and

- 18 U.S.C. § 2071 (concealment, removal, or mutilation of government records).

The requirements of these statutes are described in more detail in Chapter Three.

As summarized below, the Midyear prosecutors concluded that there was not a basis to prosecute former Secretary Clinton, her senior aides, or others under any of these statutes. The prosecutors cited the following factual conclusions from the investigation as critical to its recommendation not to prosecute:

---

[159] A redacted version of the LHM is publicly available on the FBI's website. *See* FBI Records: The Vault, Hillary R. Clinton, Part 1, https://vault.fbi.gov/hillary-r.-clinton (accessed March 6, 2018).

- None of the emails contained clear classification markings as required under Executive Order 13526 and its predecessor. Only three email chains contained any classification markings of any kind. These email chains had one or two paragraphs that were marked "(C)" for "Confidential" but contained none of the other required markings, such as classification headers.

- There was no evidence that the senders or former Secretary Clinton believed or were aware at the time that the emails contained classified information. In the absence of clear classification markings, the prosecutors determined that it would be difficult to dispute the sincerity of these witnesses' stated beliefs that the material was not classified.

- The senders and former Secretary Clinton relied on the judgment of employees experienced in protecting sensitive information to properly handle classified information.

- The emails in question were sent to other government officials in furtherance of the senders' official duties. There was no evidence that the senders or former Secretary Clinton intended that classified information be sent to unauthorized recipients, or that they intentionally sought to store classified information on unauthorized systems.

- There was no evidence that former Secretary Clinton had any contemporaneous concerns about the classified status of the information that was conveyed on her unclassified systems, nor any evidence that any individual ever contemporaneously conveyed such concerns to her.

- Although some witnesses expressed concern or surprise when they saw some of the classified content in unclassified emails, the prosecutors concluded that the investigation did not reveal evidence that any U.S. government employees involved in the SAP willfully communicated the information to a person not entitled to receive it, or willfully retained the same.

- The senders used unclassified emails because of "operational tempo," that is, the need to get information quickly to senior State Department officials at times when the recipients lacked access to classified systems. To accomplish this, senders often refrained from using specific classified facts or terms in emails and worded emails carefully in an attempt to avoid transmitting classified information.

- There was no evidence that Clinton set up her servers or private email account with the intent of communicating or retaining classified information, or that she had knowledge that classified information would be communicated or retained on it.

In addition to these facts as described by the prosecutors, various witnesses told us that one reason it was difficult to establish intent was that the mishandling of classified information was a persistent practice at the State Department. These practices made it difficult for the Midyear team to conclude that particular individuals had the necessary criminal intent to mishandle classified materials. According to Prosecutor 4, "[T]he problem was the State Department was so screwed up in the way they treated classified information that if you wanted to prosecute Hillary Clinton, you would have had to prosecute 150 State Department people."

Based on facts evincing a lack of intent to communicate classified information on unclassified systems, the prosecutors concluded that there was no basis to recommend prosecution of former Secretary Clinton or the senders of classified information under Sections 793(d) or (e).

In addition, as described in Chapter Two, prosecutors reviewed the legislative history of the gross negligence provision in Section 793(f)(1) and court decisions impacting the interpretation of it. The prosecutors noted that the congressional debate at the time the predecessor to Section 793(f)(1) was passed indicated that conduct charged under the provision must be "so gross as to almost suggest deliberate intention," criminally reckless, or "something that falls just a little short of being willful." The prosecutors also reviewed military and federal court cases and previous prosecutions under Section 793(f)(1), and concluded that they involved either a defendant who knowingly removed classified information from a secure facility, or inadvertently removed classified information from a secure facility and, upon learning this, failed to report its "loss, theft, abstraction, or destruction." In addition, based on a review of constitutional vagueness challenges of Sections 793(d) and (e), the Midyear prosecutors observed that "the government would very likely face a colorable constitutional challenge to the statute if it prosecuted an individual for gross negligence who was both unaware he had removed classified information at the time of the removal and never became aware he had done so."

The prosecutors concluded that based on case law and the Department's prior interpretation of the statute, charging a violation of Section 793(f) likely required evidence that the individuals who sent emails containing classified information "knowingly" included the classified information or transferred classified information onto unclassified systems (Section 793(f)(1)), or learned that classified information had been transferred to unclassified systems and failed to report it (Section 793(f)(2)).

Applying this interpretation, the prosecutors concluded that there was no evidence that the senders of emails knew that classified information had been improperly transferred to an unclassified system, or that former Secretary Clinton acted in a grossly negligent manner with respect to receiving emails determined to contain classified information. According to information reviewed by the OIG, the prosecutors also considered whether the decision to conduct official business using a personal server could itself constitute gross negligence, but concluded that there was no evidence that former Secretary Clinton ever considered the possibility that classified information would be present in unclassified emails or on her private email server.

Distinguishing military prosecutions for "grossly negligent" mishandling, the prosecutors also noted that there was no evidence that classified emails were provided to or discovered by people who were unauthorized to receive them. The prosecutors stated, "[A]ll of the emails containing information subsequently determined to be classified were sent for work purposes and were delivered to State Department or other U.S. government officials."

Regarding Section 1924, the prosecutors stated that the statute requires proof that an individual knew of the removal of classified information and intended to retain that information in an unauthorized location, and that such proof was lacking. The prosecutors cited the absence of classification markings on the emails sent by the senders, with the exception of the three emails forwarded to Clinton containing paragraph markings denoting Confidential information, as well as the lack of evidence that the senders knowingly took classified information and sent it in unmarked emails over unclassified systems. The prosecutors similarly concluded that former Secretary Clinton did not recognize or have reason to believe that the information sent to her contained classified information. Prosecutors cited Clinton's reliance on the judgment of senior aides and other State Department staff, their attempts to talk around sensitive information in unclassified emails, and her testimony that she did not have reason to question their use of unclassified systems to send that information. The prosecutors concluded that the evidence was insufficient to charge former Secretary Clinton under Section 1924.

The prosecutors also concluded that there was insufficient evidence to support prosecution under 18 U.S.C. § 2071, which prohibits the willful concealment, removal, or destruction of federal records. They concluded that there was insufficient evidence to establish beyond a reasonable doubt that former Secretary Clinton or her senior aides intended to conceal records, citing testimony that these witnesses expected that any emails sent to a state.gov address would be preserved. The prosecutors acknowledged that this testimony was undercut by former Secretary Clinton's admission that she sometimes communicated with her senior aides using their personal email accounts, as well as an email she received from former Secretary of State Colin Powell at the beginning of her tenure outlining his use of personal email. However, the prosecutors noted that Section 2071 had "never been used to prosecute individuals for attempting to avoid Federal Records Act requirements by failing to ensure that government records are filed appropriately."

Finally, the prosecutors evaluated whether Mills and Samuelson intentionally deleted emails during the culling process used to separate former Secretary Clinton's "personal" and "work-related" emails for production to the State Department. They concluded that there was no evidence that emails intentionally were deleted by former Secretary Clinton's lawyers to conceal the presence of classified information on former Secretary Clinton's server, particularly because some of the emails produced as "work-related" later were determined to contain highly classified, compartmented information.

II.   The Attorney General Briefing

A briefing for Lynch and Yates on the prosecutors' recommendation was held in the Attorney General's Conference Room at 4 p.m. on July 6, 2016. According to the prosecutors, they learned about the briefing after they completed their legal analysis, and had only a short time to prepare. Prosecutors 1 and 2 said they quickly divided the topics and prepared bullet points for the presentation based on their legal analysis.

Attending the briefing were Lynch, Yates, Axelrod, and David Margolis, at the time the most senior career official in ODAG, as well as several OAG and ODAG staff members. Toscas and Laufman were present from NSD, while Carlin participated by phone. Present from the FBI were Comey, McCabe, Rybicki, Baker, FBI Attorney 1, and Strzok. All four prosecutors attended the briefing.

Toscas told the OIG that he gave a brief introduction at the meeting. Toscas prepared handwritten talking points that he used as a guide for his comments at the meeting, but he said that these did not end up being his "precise script." Toscas said that he "frontloaded" his comments with an acknowledgement that Lynch had stated publicly that she planned to accept the recommendation of the career staff, and that the prosecutors and the FBI were in agreement that no charges should be filed. According to Toscas's handwritten talking points, he stated, "[A]t the conclusion of the meeting you will have the unanimous recommendation of the FBI [and] DOJ team that this investigation should be closed [and] that charges should not be brought against anybody within the scope of the investigation in this matter."

The notes indicate that Toscas then praised the team and handed the briefing over to Laufman to introduce the prosecutors. Following their introduction, Prosecutors 1 and 2 walked through the various legal statutes and the facts developed in the investigation. Prosecutor 2 handled sections 793(d) and (e), while Prosecutor 1 handled discussion of the other statutes, including the gross negligence provision.

Lynch described the briefing as "very, very thorough." She said that it lasted about an hour-and-a-half, and included a "very specific, very dense" briefing of the case. Lynch told the OIG that the prosecutors showed her various documents, including some of the emails that were determined to contain classified information. She said that she asked questions about access to the classified emails and who saw them, as well as numerous questions that related to the issue of intent. Lynch described the prosecutors as "very responsive" to her questions.

Lynch told the OIG that the meeting included a briefing on key interviews, including the interview of former Secretary Clinton. Lynch said that the prosecutors provided a synopsis of her interview, her reaction when shown documents, and their opinions about what she said. Lynch said that she asked whether any of the witnesses, including former Secretary Clinton, had engaged in obstruction of justice, committed perjury, or made false statements, and she was told that they had not.

Prosecutor 1 told the OIG that the discussion with Lynch about Secretary Clinton's interview included whether Clinton was credible when she testified that (C) paragraph markings in an email could mean subparagraphs (A), (B), and (C), rather than that the paragraph contained information classified at the "Confidential" level. Prosecutor 1 stated that he told Lynch that Clinton's testimony "strained credulity a little bit because, well, if anyone knows Confidential, the State Department is the entity that uses Confidential information a lot." He said that they discussed with Lynch that their reaction to this explanation was skeptical, but that they also did not know what "people at the very highest levels" understood about classification markings.

Prosecutor 4 said that he recalled Yates also asking whether former Secretary Clinton was truthful in her interview, and that they all responded that she was. He said that this answer caused him some "consternation" but that he did not disagree.[160] Asked to explain this statement, Prosecutor 4 told the OIG that he did not think that former Secretary Clinton lied in a provable way, but that her responses to questions about paragraph markings for information designated as "Confidential" and her statement that the private server was set up for convenience were questionable. Prosecutor 4 stated, "My view was and still remains that the private email server was set up to avoid FOIA.... [I]f you look at Colin Powell's email, he pretty much was trying to avoid FOIA too."

Various witnesses told the OIG that the briefing included legal discussion of the gross negligence provision, and that prosecutors fielded questions from Comey and Baker about the provision. Prosecutor 2 stated:

> I think their attorneys hadn't really gotten him up to speed on the prior use of 793(f), and how it hadn't been used, and the Department's views on the statute. So I think it was kind of an opportunity for him and his team to figure out how Comey was going to explain the decision [to Congress] under 793(f). And following the briefing, questions from his team came our way, specifically about 793(f).

Prosecutor 1 similarly told the OIG that Comey was "very interested" in section 793(f), and that "a lot of notebooks came out from the Bureau" when Prosecutor 1

---

[160] On July 8, 2016, following Comey's congressional testimony about the Midyear investigation described in Chapter Six, Prosecutor 3 emailed Strzok and Prosecutors 1, 2, and 4 and stated the following:

> [O]ne thing that was apparent just from the highlights of the Committee hearings that I saw last night was the fact that the Director's statements about the number and levels of classified doc[ument]s found are being used by the Hill and others to claim that [Clinton] was lying when she has said in the past that she never sent or received classified info[rmation]. What undercuts the ability to prove intent in support of a false statement charge is that when [Clinton] made these statements she didn't have the benefit of later findings by those who did the classification reviews and of course there weren't the classification markings on the emails to put her on notice, and give us the ability to prove, that she was lying. This never seemed to get discussed or emphasized in the clips I saw last night.

began to talk about the provision. Prosecutor 1 stated that his briefing about section 793(f) included "[w]hat kind of factors we considered..., what gross negligence meant in the criminal context, what it meant in the statute, [and] how it had been applied in the [Uniform Code of Military Justice]."

Witnesses told the OIG that they did not discuss Comey's statement at the briefing. However, Yates said that she recalled thinking that "you'd kind of wonder if it's the same case" when she heard the facts as laid out by the prosecutors at the briefing and compared them to Comey's statement. She said that she recalled discussing with Axelrod, Lynch, and Carlin after the briefing whether the briefing impacted what Comey's thinking was about the case and how those facts were cast in his statement.

Witnesses said that at the end of the discussion, Lynch went around the room and asked for people's opinions to see if anyone objected to declining prosecution. According to several witnesses, Margolis responded that he did not see a prosecutable case, and that if the Department prosecuted former Secretary Clinton, it would be because she was a high-profile public official. Toscas, Baker, and Comey said that Margolis described this as "celebrity hunting." Lynch said that she recalled that Margolis then said, "[W]e at the Department don't do that.... We will bring cases when they should be brought. We don't when they shouldn't be brought."

Lynch told the OIG that after everyone had the opportunity to provide his or her opinion, she expressed her appreciation to the team and asked Comey and Strzok to convey her appreciation to the agents who had worked on the case. She said that she then told the group that she accepted the recommendation to decline prosecution, and that the Department would issue a statement reflecting the decision shortly. Lynch said that about half of the group stayed behind to talk about how to announce the declination, and that Toscas drafted a short statement. That afternoon, the Department released the following statement:

> Late this afternoon, I met with the FBI Director James Comey and career prosecutors and agents who conducted the investigation of Secretary Hillary Clinton's use of a personal email system during her time as Secretary of State. I received and accepted their unanimous recommendation that the thorough, year-long investigation be closed and that no charges be brought against any individuals within the scope of the investigation.

III. Analysis

We analyzed the Department's decision to decline to prosecute former Secretary Clinton or anyone else according to the same analytical standard that we applied to other decisions made during the investigation. We sought to determine whether the declination decision was based on improper considerations, including political bias. We both looked for direct evidence of improper considerations and analyzed the justifications offered for the decision to determine whether they were

260

a pretext for improper, but unstated, considerations. We did not substitute the OIG's judgment for the judgments made by the Department.

We found that the prosecutors' decision was based on their assessment of the facts, the law, and past Department practice in cases involving these statutes. We did not identify evidence of bias or improper considerations. Our analysis focuses substantially on 18 U.S.C. § 793(f)(1), the "gross negligence" statute that has been the focus of much criticism of the Department's decision. However, we first address the declination decision with respect to the other statutes that the Department considered.

We begin with 18 U.S.C. §§ 793(d) and (e), which prohibit the "willful" mishandling or retention of classified information. As detailed in Chapter Two, Courts have interpreted "willfully" to mean an act done "intentionally and purposely and with the intent to do something the law forbids, that is, with the bad purpose to disobey or to disregard the law." All of the prosecutors and agents we asked told us that they could not prove that Clinton had actual knowledge that the emails in question were classified or that Clinton used private servers and a private email account with the purpose or intent of receiving classified information on them. None of the emails Clinton received were properly marked to inform her of the classified status of the information.[161] Additionally, investigators found evidence of a conscious effort to avoid sending classified information by writing around the most sensitive material. The investigators did not find any emails in which the sender communicated information to someone not authorized to receive it. In brief, we found no evidence that the decision not to prosecute Clinton under these statutory provisions was tainted by bias or other improper considerations.

We reached a similar conclusion with respect to 18 U.S.C. § 1924, which, as described in Chapter Two, prohibits the "knowing" removal of classified information with "intent to retain" it in an unauthorized location. In determining that a Section 1924 prosecution was not viable, the prosecutors pointed to the same absence of evidence that Clinton had actual knowledge that any of the emails were classified or that she used private servers and a private email account with the purpose or intent of receiving classified information on them. The prosecutors distinguished the Petraeus case brought under this section (discussed in Chapter Two) on the basis that this case involved clear evidence that the defendant knew the information at issue was classified and took actions reflecting knowledge that his handling or storage of it was improper. This was precisely the evidence that the investigators told us was conspicuously absent in the Midyear case. We found no basis to conclude that the decision not to pursue a Section 1924 case was tainted by bias or other improper considerations.

The Department also determined that prosecution under 18 U.S.C. § 2071 was not viable. Section 2071 prohibits the concealment, removal, or destruction of a record filed in a public office. The prosecutors concluded that, as to emails on the

---

[161] As noted above, even the handful of emails in which some paragraphs were marked "(C)" did not bear the required classification headers or footers, and Clinton testified that she did not recognize these paragraph markings as denoting classified information.

Clinton servers that were sent to or from government email accounts, because they also existed on government systems there was no evidence that Clinton or anyone else took any actions to conceal, remove, or destroy them from the government systems on which they resided. As to the work-related emails that were not sent to or from any government system, the prosecutors concluded that such emails were never "filed within a public office." The prosecutors also noted that every prosecution under Section 2071 involved the removal or destruction of documents that had already been filed or deposited in a public office. Additionally, the prosecutors found no evidence that the laptop "culling" process involved the intentional destruction of government records in an effort to conceal them in violation of Section 2071. We did not identify any evidence to suggest that these determinations were based on bias or other improper considerations.

The statute that required the most complex analysis by the prosecutors was 18 U.S.C. § 793(f)(1), which criminalizes the removal, delivery, loss, theft, abstraction, or destruction of national defense information through "gross negligence." Due in part to Comey's July 5 statement criticizing Clinton for being "extremely careless," which many observers equated with being "grossly negligent," this provision became the focus of much of the questioning of the declination decision. As detailed above, the prosecutors identified statements in the legislative history of Section 793(f)(1) that they found indicated that the state of mind required for a violation of that section is "so gross as to almost suggest deliberate intention," criminally reckless, or "something that falls just short of being willful." In addition, based on a review of constitutional vagueness challenges of Sections 793(d) and (e), the Midyear prosecutors stated that "the government would very likely face a colorable constitutional challenge to the statute if it prosecuted an individual for gross negligence who was both unaware he had removed classified information at the time of the removal and never became aware he had done so." Based on all of these circumstances, and a review of the small number of prior civilian and military cases under Section 793(f), the prosecutors interpreted the "gross negligence" provision of Section 793(f)(1) to require proof that an individual acted with knowledge that the information in question was classified. The investigators and prosecutors told us that proof of such knowledge was lacking.

We found that the prosecutors' interpretation of the requirements of Section 793(f)(1) was consistent with prior Department declination decisions that the prosecutors considered and that we reviewed. As noted in Chapter Two, in 2008 the Department declined to prosecute former Attorney General Gonzales based on an interpretation that would have required them to prove that his state of mind was "criminally reckless," or that he had "a state of mind approaching 'deliberate intention' to remove classified documents from a secure location." The same year, the Department declined prosecution of an AUSA for mishandling classified information because of its inability to prove that he was "criminally reckless." Prosecutors told the OIG that they reviewed these declination decisions to see how the Department had construed Section 793(f)(1) in the past. These prior cases demonstrate that the interpretation of the gross negligence requirement of Section

793(f)(1) used as a basis to decline prosecution of former Secretary Clinton was consistent with interpretations applied in prior cases under different leadership.

We found no evidence that the conclusions by Department prosecutors were affected by bias or other improper considerations; rather, we concluded that they were based on the prosecutors' assessment of the facts, the law, and past Department practice. In reaching this conclusion, we recognize that much of the questioning of the Department's prosecutorial decision in this case has focused on whether the Department too narrowly interpreted the "gross negligence" provision of Section 793(f)(1) and should have pursued a prosecution because the FBI found Clinton to be "extremely careless." That, however, is a legal and policy judgment involving core prosecutorial discretion for the Department to make.

PAGE LEFT INTENTIONALLY

BLANK

CHAPTER EIGHT:
OCTOBER EFFORTS BY FBI LEADERSHIP TO RESPOND TO CRITICISM OF THE MIDYEAR INVESTIGATION

During October 2016, we found that FBI leadership devoted significant time and attention responding to both internal and external interest in, and criticism of, the Midyear investigation.[162] This included remarks by Comey about the Midyear investigation at the FBI's SAC Conference, the development of Midyear talking points for all FBI SACs, a Midyear briefing for the Society of Former Special Agents of the FBI, and continued monitoring of media discussion of the Midyear investigation.

As described in Chapter Nine, these events occurred immediately after FBI Headquarters and the FBI Midyear team were made aware of the potential significance of the Weiner laptop by the FBI's New York Field Office (NYO) on September 28 and 29. And as we further describe in Chapter Nine, at the same time that FBI leadership was taking the steps we describe in this chapter to defend its handling of the Midyear investigation as thorough and complete, it was taking no action in response to the notification by NYO regarding the Weiner laptop.

I.   SAC Conference (October 11 to 14)

The FBI held its annual SAC Conference in San Diego, California, from October 11 through October 14. The SAC Conference was immediately followed by the International Association of Chiefs of Police (IACP) Conference from October 15 through October 18. Almost the entire FBI executive workforce attends the SAC Conference and top leadership frequently stays for the IACP Conference as well. Comey and McCabe attended both of the conferences in San Diego.

On October 12, Comey spoke to the SAC Conference about a variety of topics. This speech included lengthy remarks about the Midyear investigation. In part, he stated:

> I do want to hit Hillary Clinton's emails which I never tire of talking about, as you know. Because I want to make sure that you are equipped especially to answer questions and comments from our formers who are out trapped in a Fox News bubble and are hearing all kinds of nonsense. I want to make sure you have the information you need to bat some of that stuff down....
>
> At the end of [the investigation], [the team's] view of it was there really isn't anything here that anybody would prosecute. My view was the same. Everybody between me and the people who worked this case felt the same way about it. It was not a cliffhanger. What

---

[162] For example, during the presidential debate on Sunday, October 9, 2016, and at a campaign rally two days later, then candidate Trump, among other things, criticized the outcome of the investigation of Clinton.

sometimes confuses our workforces, and I have gotten emails from some employees about this, who said if I did what Hillary Clinton did I'd be in huge trouble. My response is you bet your ass you'd be in huge trouble. If you used a personal email, Gmail or if you [had] the capabilities to set up your own email domain, if you used an unclassified personal email system to do our business in the course of doing our business even though you were communicating with people with clearances and doing work you discussed classified matters in that, in those communications, TS/SCI, special access programs, you would be in huge trouble in the FBI....

...Of that I am highly confident. I'm also highly confident, in fact, certain you would not be criminally prosecuted for that conduct....

...What I'm getting from the left is savage attacks for violating policy and law by talking publicly about somebody who wasn't indicted, by revealing facts that you should've been prescribed from revealing by decades of tradition. All of that's nonsense just as this is nonsense. It is a uniquely difficult time. I expect after the election, which is coming up I'm told, we will have probably more conversations about this....

We asked Comey in general about the SAC Conference and whether he recalled receiving criticism about the Midyear investigation while at the conference. Comey said he did not recall specific criticism, but noted that "given how prevalent the criticism was, I would have expected it to be talked about."

II.   Midyear Talking Points Distributed to FBI Field Offices (October 21)

On October 17, Page sent an email to Baker and Anderson entitled "MYE TPs (LCP)."[163] Strzok, the Lead Analyst, FBI Attorney 1, and FBI Attorney 2 were cc'd on the email. The email stated:

Last week, Jim Rybicki and Mike Kortan reached out to a couple of us to ask that we put together some detailed MYE information related to the topics SACs most frequently get asked about. I'm not 100% certain about the uses these talking points will be used to, (I think the current thinking is that they would be provided to SACs to use with formers, in Citizen's Academies, etc.), but attached is a very quick attempt at answering the specific questions requested by Jim and Mike. Could you both please take a look, and edit at will? Thanks.

The Midyear talking points were ultimately distributed to FBI SACs on October 21.

The talking points, which included a section on frequently asked questions, were nine pages and largely tracked Comey's July 5 statement and his July 7 testimony before Congress. At the top of the first page of the talking points was a

---

[163] After reviewing a draft of the report, Page asked the OIG to clarify that she did not draft the talking points, but was the conduit through which they were distributed.

note to FBI executives, the first sentence of which stated, "The purpose of these talking points is to provide FBI executive management with a factual basis by which to inform discussions with employees or interested parties in the community."

Comey described the talking points as "part of an effort to make sure that the workforce, given the prominence of the issue, understood why we had done what we did." Comey described this commitment to transparency as part of his management philosophy. When asked if he was concerned with essentially deputizing 56 different spokesmen for the Midyear investigation, Comey stated, "No, in fact I think it cuts the other way. They're all going to be talking about it anyway in lunchrooms, in town halls and sidebars, and so it makes sense to me to equip people who are going to be talking about it anyway with the actual facts and our actual perspective on it."

McCabe described the talking points as part of a broad effort "to keep the SACs particularly more well-informed about all the major issues" the FBI was dealing with. McCabe said that the SACs were being asked about Midyear frequently and this was an effort to "give them some information to work off of." McCabe also noted that the SACs requested this information from headquarters. When asked why the FBI did not just refer the SACs or anyone else to Comey's July 5 statement, McCabe stated that he believed the FBI did send Comey's statement to the field, but "maybe that didn't answer the mail."

Rybicki told us he agreed with the assessments given by Comey and McCabe and that SACs were contacting FBI Headquarters stating "that they weren't getting enough information from headquarters" about the Midyear investigation. Rybicki described the Midyear talking points as an effort by headquarters to arm SACs with information they could use to respond to questions they received.

Priestap attributed the revival of Midyear talking points in mid-October to the "churn" and the fact that "the issue [of Midyear] just didn't go away." Strzok agreed with this assessment, stating:

> [B]ecause SACs were still getting an extraordinary number of questions because it had become a campaign issue and that was still being batted around by the Hill and by then candidate Trump. And SACs were getting questions. The thought was, you know, give them enough information so they can at least accurately answer some of those questions rather than just saying, you know, I don't know, or here is what I've read.

III. Midyear Briefing for Retired FBI Special Agents (October 21)

On October 7, the President of the Society of Former Special Agents of the FBI (the "Society") sent an email to Bowdich entitled "Controversy over the Director/Clinton Email Situation." The Society's President stated, in part:

> I continue to hear negative comments about the Bureau's handling of the Clinton email controversy from former agents. This is after a

267

period where things seemed to quiet and comments mellowed. The renewed negative comments appeared to be timed with the release of additional emails in the Clinton situation and with the Director's recent congressional testimony.

I would like to offer a strategy which would possibly lower the rhetoric on this issue. My sense is there are probably 10-15 hard core issues that are at the heart of former agents' discontent. I know what those issues are based on the many emails and phone calls I've received.

My proposal is to have a small group of Society people meet with the Director and discuss those issues and formulate thorough in-depth answers, to be published in the Grapevine, or to be directly emailed to our members....

Bowdich replied that he would be "happy to discuss this weekend." Bowdich told us he recalled the Society wanting a sit-down with Comey, which Bowdich considered a bad idea, and we did not find evidence that the meeting with Comey occurred prior to the election.

However, on October 21, Strzok briefed a group of retired FBI personnel on the Midyear investigation during a conference call. This call was organized by Kortan, and Page also dialed into the call, although she did not speak. Strzok told us that the call was the idea of "the seventh floor," meaning top leadership at FBI Headquarters, and added, "Rybicki might have been the one whose idea it was." According to Strzok:

[O]ur Office of Public Affairs got a bunch of the former folks, like John Giacalone and other former EADs and Deputies and the head of the Society of Special Agents, to essentially say, okay, please sit down with them. And kind of walk through the investigation. And give a very fact-based pattern of, despite the huge turn of everything you're hearing and the allegations and people saying you gave immunity out like candy, and you didn't even issue subpoenas. Sit down to the extent you can and walk through, from the beginning to the end, what we did investigatively.... [S]it there and say...you know, we, we did a thorough job. This is what we did. This is what our mandate was. This is how we went about doing it. You know, here are, there are a lot of falsehoods and exaggerations being thrown around. This is the truth. And again, not giving out classified information, not giving the 6(e) information out. But to the extent that any of these folks, whether they are getting asked by CNN, whether they're appearing in front of a congressional committee, whether they are going to a Citizens Academy, that they have the facts.

We asked Page about this call and she told us:

[W]e got a ton of criticism from the formers about the, why we let her off the hook, and why she should have been prosecuted, and why if she had, if they had done this, they would have prosecuted, all those

268

sort of criticism that you have surely heard. And so Steinbach and Kortan, Mike Kortan, came up with the idea of well why don't we put Pete on, you know, kind of agent-to-agent to sort of, because we need to get the formers to stop sort of criticizing the, the case. And get them to understand actually the facts and why the facts led to not having a prosecution.

Page described her role on the call as "trying to like give advice along the way to sort of help them explain."

Comey told us that he is not sure he knew about Strzok's call beforehand, but "it rings true to me." We asked him if it was normal to have the agent who oversaw an investigation directly brief the retired agents on that case. Comey stated, "No...there's nothing normal at all about this, but it seemed a reasonable thing to do given the stakes which was the credibility of the organization."

Steinbach described a separate speech he gave to the Washington, D.C., chapter of the Society of Former Special Agents of the FBI in October 2016. A news article from October 31, 2016, reported on Steinbach's remarks and his comments on the Midyear investigation. Steinbach told us that his "intention" in giving the remarks was "to kind of level set that from one investigator to another former investigator. Say, hey look, you know, here is why we did it."

IV.   FBI Office of Public Affairs Research Project (October 14 to 31)

On October 14, Rybicki and Kortan assigned an FBI Office of Public Affairs (OPA) Public Affairs Advisor a "research project." The Public Affairs Advisor's initial email to Kortan and Rybicki on October 14 stated, "Per Mike [Kortan]'s suggestion, I'll compile a list of stories from the past 24 hours that I've found that revolve around the recent email story from Fox."[164] Rybicki responded that evening, "Thanks.... This is very helpful. I think the idea is that you would also track all email investigation stories each day and then we can figure out which ones are so inaccurate that we need to respond in some way." Consistent with this assignment, from October 14 and continuing through the end of October, we identified a series of almost daily emails from the Public Affairs Advisor to Kortan and Rybicki highlighting critical media coverage of the Clinton email server investigation. The emails typically included links to and summaries of the articles cited.

We identified October 13 notes from FBI Attorney 1 entitled "MYE—Fox article w/Rybicki + Kortan." The notes included the following entry:

• Special projects person—fact check news of the day

---

[164] Based on the content of emails and the timing, we believe "the recent email story from Fox" refers to an October 13, 2016 article on Fox News entitled, "FBI, DOJ roiled by Comey, Lynch decision to let Clinton slide by on emails, says insider." *See* Malia Zimmerman and Adam Housley, *FBI, DOJ Roiled by Comey, Lynch Decision to Let Clinton Slide by on Emails, Says Insider*, Fox News, Oct. 13, 2016.

to SACs

and maybe bkgd to reporters? √ OPA

or maybe reach out to people who wrote article

FBI Attorney 1 told us she did not remember this meeting and "had no idea" what the "special projects person" notation signified.

An October 22 email from the Public Affairs Advisor to Kortan and Rybicki provided some insight into his assignment. He stated, "I've done several searches on the topic we discussed today and yesterday, and I'm not seeing anything falling under the themes that we discussed (destruction of materials, dissention [sic], etc.) that is creeping into the main stream."

We asked Rybicki about the Public Affairs Advisor's assignment and showed him examples of the emails cited above. Rybicki did not recall giving the Public Affairs Advisor "any directive to look at specific outlets or anything like that." Rybicki did recall that "the Director had [the Public Affairs Advisor] tracking stories I think from back in, you know, early July, maybe even prior to that about the [Midyear] investigation." Similarly, Kortan told us, "I think the Director or the Director's Office actually asked him during some period of time there just to keep track of the reporting on everything to see how it was, how things were being reported."

The Public Affairs Advisor said he recalled very little about this research assignment "other than...if there was an article that had c[o]me out, and they said can you see if, find the other stories that, that were like this or had this similar narrative, and if it was being picked up." He told us that he "can't imagine [Rybicki] would ask me to track all email investigation stories. As there were a mountain, a flood of them." When we pointed out the specific guidance about "destruction of materials" and "dissention" in the October 22 email, the Public Affairs Adviser said that he assumed the destruction guidance related to an inaccurate story about the destruction of Clinton's server and he was unsure what the "dissention" guidance meant. Kortan told us that he thought the "dissention" reference referred to stories about "all kind of conflict within the [Midyear] team about...the conclusion of the [Midyear] investigation."

The Public Affairs Advisor said he was not sure why he was given this assignment in mid-October, but recalled more coverage of the Midyear investigation "popped up" at this time. The Public Affairs Advisor also could not recall if he was given similar research assignments during other time periods.

We asked Comey about the Public Affairs Advisor and the assignment. Comey told us that he first met the Public Affairs Advisor when Comey worked in EDVA. Comey stated that he recruited the Public Affairs Advisor to SDNY after he became the U.S. Attorney there. The Public Affairs Advisor then followed Comey to the Department when Comey was appointed DAG and later to the FBI after Comey became Director. We pointed out to Comey that almost all of the media coverage identified by the Public Affairs Advisor in the October time period was negative coverage of the FBI's handling of Midyear and asked if that was a particular focus of the FBI's efforts at the time. Comey stated that "knowing what critics are saying is very, very important." Comey added that this sometimes permitted the FBI to push back on inaccurate reporting.

We asked Comey more generally about the FBI's role in the run up to the election. Specifically, we cited several of the above examples—correcting inaccuracies in the media, issuing talking points to SACs, briefing former agents— and we asked Comey why the FBI was essentially inserting itself into the back and forth dialogue of two political campaigns. Comey replied:

> It's not our role, but it's our role to be believed by the American people. And you've heard me say this before, when we rise and say, I found this under the car seat or I heard this statement or I seized this document in the bureau drawer...we have to be believed. And so my worry was, actually I had a great sense of relief after the July 5th thing, like that's over and now what I need to worry about is making sure that I did what I did in July as we talked about a million times because I thought it was best calculated to preserve the institutions, now I need to do my absolute best to make sure that the poison that follows doesn't continue to undercut the credibility of the institution in American life. And so I could have just pulled back, but if I pulled back without any push back, a doubt about the FBI's political independence first would be pushed in from the right and then it would be pushed in from the left and then I'd be left after the election trying to un-ring a bell and a lot of what I was trying to avoid to start with would have crept in and then the FBI would have been, oh they're those people with the Clintons or fix-it, we need to, so I was with the Clintons, then I was with the Trumps, and if—and so it's not, the reason I disagree with your characterization, it's not pushing our way into a political campaign, all this is flowing out from the campaigns and lots of other[s] through the media at the FBI and its reputation with the American people; I have to worry about that in my view.

V.   FOIA and Congressional Requests in October

Throughout the month of October, the FBI responded to various Freedom of Information Act (FOIA) and congressional requests for information about the Midyear investigation. McCabe told us, "[T]he fact is, we were meeting about Midyear-related things constantly, like during [the October] time period. FOIA requests, Congressional requests." For example, McCabe, Rybicki, Anderson, Strzok, Page, FBI Attorney 1, Baker, and Priestap were invited to a meeting entitled "Mtg. w/DD RE Decision Points" at 2:30 p.m. on September 29. Contemporaneous notes from the meeting showed that this meeting involved a discussion of congressional requests for materials from the Midyear investigation. In another example, McCabe sent an email to Comey on October 17 to summarize the events of the day. Rybicki and Bowdich were copied on the email. The email stated, in part, "Lots of OPA action on the Midyear investigation email front with eh [sic]

271

release of the 302s. Nothing unexpected, will likely drive some additional committee requests...."

CHAPTER NINE:
DISCOVERY OF CLINTON EMAILS ON THE
WEINER LAPTOP AND REACTIVATION OF THE MIDYEAR
INVESTIGATION

In this chapter, we discuss the discovery of Clinton emails on the Weiner laptop and the eventual reactivation of the Midyear investigation. Section I details the discovery of these emails by the FBI's New York Field Office (NYO) and Section II discusses the numerous notifications of this fact to FBI Headquarters in late September and early October. Section III describes the initial response by FBI Headquarters and Midyear personnel to this discovery. Section IV discusses NYO's processing of the Weiner laptop. Section V details the ensuing inaction by FBI Headquarters and Midyear personnel, and the explanations we received from FBI leadership and Midyear personnel for this inactivity. In Section VI, we discuss the Weiner case agent's concerns about this inactivity and, in Section VII, we describe the actions taken by the U.S. Attorney's Office for the Southern District of New York (SDNY) as a result of these concerns. In Section VIII, we discuss the response by the Department and FBI to SDNY's notification about the Weiner laptop. Section IX examines the reengagement on this issue by FBI Headquarters and Midyear personnel. Section X describes the events that led to the decision to seek a search warrant for the Weiner laptop. We provide our analysis in Section XI.

I.   Discovery of Emails by the FBI's New York Field Office

A.   Seizure of Weiner Laptop and Devices

In September 2016, the FBI and the U.S. Attorney's Office for the Southern District of New York (SDNY) began investigating former Congressman Anthony Weiner for his online relationship with a minor. The FBI's New York Field Office (NYO) was in charge of the investigation. A federal search warrant was obtained on September 26, 2016, for Weiner's iPhone, iPad, and laptop computer. The FBI obtained these devices the same day. The search warrant authorized the government to search for evidence relating to the following crimes: transmitting obscene material to a minor, sexual exploitation of children, and activities related to child pornography.

B.   Emails and BlackBerry PIN Message Viewed by Case Agent

The case agent assigned to the Weiner investigation was certified as a Digital Extraction Technician and, as such, had the training and skills to extract digital evidence from electronic devices. The case agent told the OIG that he began processing Weiner's devices upon receipt on September 26. The case agent stated that he noticed "within hours" that there were "over 300,000 emails on the laptop."

The case agent told us that on either the evening of September 26 or the morning of September 27, he noticed the software program on his workstation was having trouble processing the data on the laptop.[165] The case agent stated that he went into the email folder on the laptop to see why the processing was "hung up." He explained that, because the laptop was still processing, he was only able to view the emails that were immediately visible in the window on his computer screen. The case agent told us that the first item he clicked on was "either an email between Hillary and Huma [Abedin] or a BlackBerry PIN message." The case agent stated that, in the window of items visible to him, he saw a "couple" of emails between Clinton and Abedin and at least one BlackBerry PIN message between Clinton and Abedin. The case agent told us that the BlackBerry PIN message in particular caught his attention because his "general understanding" was that those messages reside on a "BlackBerry proprietary-like backbone" and would not "leave much of a trace because it doesn't go through any external servers other than a BlackBerry server." When asked specifically how he identified this BlackBerry PIN message as being between Clinton and Abedin, the case agent stated that "it was obvious" from the domains, which were "something like HR15@BBM-dot-something, and HAbedin@BBM-dot." With respect to the emails he observed, the case agent said he recalled seeing emails associated with "about seven domains," such as yahoo.com, state.gov, clintonfoundation.org, clintonemail, and hillaryclinton.com.

The case agent told us that he asked another agent to take a quick look at his computer to "make sure, am I, am I seeing what I think I'm seeing?" The other agent told the OIG that he "vividly" recalled what he described as the "oh-shit moment" when the case agent said that Hillary Clinton's emails were on the laptop. The other agent stated that, while he did not view the content, he believed that he did see the domain portion of the emails and remembered thinking at the time that it was the same domain that had been associated with Clinton in news coverage. The other agent told the OIG that he and the case agent agreed that this information needed "to get reported up the chain" immediately.

C.   Reporting of Clinton-Related Emails to FBI NYO Supervisors

The case agent told us that, after speaking with the other agent, he immediately told his Supervisory Special Agent (SSA) what he had observed, including that he had seen "private BlackBerry messages, private messages between Hillary and Huma to which Anthony Weiner was not a party." The NYO SSA corroborated this account, stating that the case agent came into his office on September 27 and told him "he had discovered emails that could be tied to Hillary

---

[165] No electronic record exists of the case agent's initial review of the Weiner laptop. The case agent told us that at some point in mid-October 2016 the NYO ASAC instructed the case agent to wipe his work station. The case agent explained that the ASAC was concerned about the presence of potentially classified information on the case agent's work station, which was not authorized to process classified information. The case agent told us that he followed the ASAC's instructions, but that this request concerned him because the audit trail of his initial processing of the laptop would no longer be available. The case agent clarified that none of the evidence on the Weiner laptop was impacted by this, explaining that the FBI retained the Weiner laptop and only the image that had been copied onto his work station was deleted. The ASAC recalled that the case agent "worked through the security department to address the concern" of classified information on an unclassified system. He told us that he did not recall how the issue was resolved.

Clinton." The SSA told us that he specifically recalled the case agent mentioning domain names associated with Hillary Clinton, the Clinton Foundation, and possibly Clinton for President. The SSA also recalled the case agent telling him "early on" that there were "hundreds of thousands" of emails. The case agent and SSA told us that because the search warrant for the laptop was limited to child exploitation offenses, they agreed during this meeting that the emails were not covered under the search warrant and the case agent should not review those emails. The SSA and the case agent met with their Assistant Special Agent in Charge (ASAC) to make him aware of the emails. The ASAC told us that the SSA and case agent initially briefed him on September 28. The ASAC stated they reported that the laptop was still processing, but there were approximately 141,000 emails of interest at that moment. The ASAC further stated that the case agent and SSA identified seven different domains of interest. The ASAC's notes from the morning of September 28 corroborated this account. The notes included references to "imaging, processing ½ way through," "141k emails," and seven domains, which were @clinton.com/gov, @state.gov, @clintonemail.com, @AW.com, @clintonfoundation.org, @presidentclinton.com, and @hillaryclinton.com.

The ASAC told us that he immediately instructed the case agent and SSA to stay focused on the Weiner investigation and to "stay completely out of" the Clinton email case. The SSA and case agent stated that the ASAC told them to stop reviewing the emails pending further guidance from FBI Headquarters. The ASAC told us that he briefed the information that he received from the SSA and case agent to his immediate supervisor, the Acting SAC (A/SAC), that day. The A/SAC confirmed this account, stating that he was "told there were emails here related to Hillary Clinton and others."

According to both the A/SAC and NYO Assistant Director in Charge (ADIC) William Sweeney, the A/SAC relayed this information to Sweeney on September 28 immediately after the FBI's weekly 3:00 p.m. secure video teleconference (SVTC) for SACs, which is a SVTC held by the Director or, in his absence, the Deputy Director or another FBI senior executive. The weekly SAC SVTC is followed by another SVTC for FBI Assistant Directors (AD). Sweeney explained:

> Between those two SVTCs, so there's a pause so all the other offices
> bail out, and then they basically reset. Between that pause I think is
> the first time I hear about Clinton domain names on this thing. And
> that comes from [the A/SAC].... And so he tells me about this laptop.
> I don't know if he described [it as] a laptop, but I think he did. Hey,
> and there's a whole bunch of Clinton email domain names. I don't
> know if he described it as domain names, but, and I wrote them on an
> index card—which I can't find for the life of me right now. But it was
> like Clinton.com, state-dot—like, it was clearly it was her stuff. And
> that they had about 141,000.

The A/SAC told us that he and Sweeney both had concerns about not exceeding the scope of the Weiner search warrant. The A/SAC's notes from that meeting stated, "400 PM—Spoke w/Sweeney. Do not do anything with the emails [illegible] move forward with other agents."

D.   Reporting of Clinton-Related Emails to SDNY

On September 27, the case agent also began advising the two SDNY Assistant United States Attorneys (AUSA) assigned to the Weiner case about what he was finding on the Weiner laptop. Many of the case agent's communications with SDNY were captured in a timeline created by the two AUSAs detailing key events in the Weiner investigation in September and October 2016. This timeline was created in late October and AUSA 2 told us that she and AUSA 1 created the timeline because they thought that "at some point somebody is going to want to know sort of what was happening when, and [it's] better to piece this together now." That timeline showed, and the prosecutors confirmed during interviews, that the case agent first told the prosecutors about the presence of Abedin's emails on the Weiner laptop on September 27. Similar communication was also occurring between higher levels of NYO and SDNY. On September 27 at 3:30 p.m., the A/SAC and SDNY Deputy U.S. Attorney Joon Kim spoke by telephone. The A/SAC's notes stated, "Spoke with Joon Kim who advised we need to be very careful looking at that server because it is apparently a shared computer with Huma. SDNY will provide protocol and guidance." Similarly, Kim emailed prosecutors and supervisors at SDNY after the call, "I just got a call from [the A/SAC] about what to do with his computer in light of the facts that there are lots of emails, etc. including what appear to be [Abedin's]. We need to come up with a clear protocol."

The AUSAs provided written guidance to the case agent about how to handle review of the laptop. In a September 28 email to the case agent and the SSA, AUSA 1 advised that the case agent should review "only evidence of crimes related to the sexual exploitation of children, enticement, and obscenity" and instructed the case agent "that all emails and other communications between Anthony Weiner and Huma Abedin (even if there are other parties to the communication) should be sequestered and not reviewed at this time." The case agent agreed and responded that the "[o]nly emails I will review are those to/from Weiner accounts to which [Huma Abedin] is not party."

Later in the day on September 28, the AUSA-created timeline noted:

[The case agent] informed AUSAs that the header info previously described seen in plain view search revealed numerous emails between Abedin and HRC (on which Weiner was not a party) using potentially sensitive email addresses, which indicated that Abedin had used the laptop. [The case agent] said that his chain of command was aware of the information. AUSAs informed supervisors of these facts. Later that day, SDNY USAO and FBI NY leadership discussed situation and agreed that Rule 41 prevented any search in this case beyond scope of warrant, and that any emails outside that scope should be segregated and not reviewed in this case. Same day, FBI NY ASAC [] asked AUSA to forward him the guidance for conducting the search that the AUSA had sent to [the case agent] because FBI counsel was interested in issuing guidance for review and seeing what we had already said on this point.

This timeline entry was consistent with testimony by the case agent and AUSAs during their interviews with the OIG.

II. Reporting of Clinton-Related Emails to FBI Headquarters

A. AD Secure Video Teleconference on September 28

As noted above, ADIC Sweeney and the A/SAC both told us that, just before the start of the weekly AD SVTC on September 28, the A/SAC briefed Sweeney about the discovery of emails on the Weiner laptop that were potentially relevant to the Clinton email investigation. The AD SVTC typically includes the FBI Director, the Deputy Director (DD), the Associate Deputy Director (ADD), the General Counsel, all Executive Assistant Directors (EAD), all ADs, and the ADICs of the New York, Los Angeles, and Washington Field Offices. However, on September 28, Comey testified in front of the House Judiciary Committee until approximately 1 p.m. Comey and others told us that Comey was not present for the SVTC, and the SVTC was also not included on his calendar for September 28. Instead, the SVTC was chaired by then DD McCabe, which McCabe told us would be the typical practice in the absence of the Director. McCabe's calendar for September 28 included time for the weekly SVTC at 3 p.m. The FBI was unable to provide the OIG with a roster of attendees for the September 28 SVTC. However, based upon the leadership structure of the FBI at the time, there would have been approximately 39 FBI executives on the SVTC, including the DD, the ADD, 6 EADs, 28 ADs, and 3 ADICs. Any executive on leave or travel would have typically been replaced by a subordinate.

Sweeney stated that, during the September 28 AD SVTC, he reported that NYO agents involved in the Weiner investigation had discovered 141,000 emails on Weiner's laptop that were potentially relevant to the Clinton email investigation. Paul Abbate, then the ADIC for the Washington Field Office, recalled Sweeney stating that NYO had discovered "a large volume of emails that might be relevant to the Clinton email matter" on a computer in the Weiner investigation. Abbate told us that he believed Sweeney also provided specific numbers and added that Sweeney "very much emphasized the significance of what he thought they had there." Abbate described the moment as like "dropping a bomb in the middle of the meeting" and stated that "everybody realized the significance of this, like, potential trove of information."

Sweeney told the OIG that McCabe responded to his briefing by stating, "Hey, I'm going to Quantico. I'll call you en route." Abbate also recalled someone, possibly McCabe, telling Sweeney that they would "talk offline afterwards." McCabe's Outlook calendar for September 28 showed that he was scheduled to be at Quantico at 6:00 p.m. that evening.

McCabe told us that he did not remember Sweeney briefing the Weiner laptop issue on a SVTC, although he said it was possible that Sweeney had done so. McCabe explained that the reports by the ADICs on the SVTC are usually "like 10 seconds." We showed McCabe his notes from September 28, which contained the

277

following entry: "NY - … Weiner – atty took data off cloud – 2007 emails." McCabe told us the notes did not refresh his recollection but agreed that they "would be a pretty good indication" that he was made aware of the issue.

Other witnesses also provided recollections of this briefing. Counterintelligence Division AD Priestap (one of the 39 FBI executives who regularly participated in the weekly AD SVTC) told us he vaguely recalled Sweeney mentioning the discovery of emails on the Weiner laptop that were potentially relevant to the Midyear investigation in a forum similar to the AD SVTC. The Human Resources Division AD told us that he recalled Sweeney mentioning "emails relevant to the Clinton investigation" that had been discovered on a laptop associated with Anthony Weiner. He added, "I remember Bill saying like hey, we think there's some stuff on here you guys may not have seen."

Comey, who was not present for the SVTC, stated that he was unaware that Sweeney had reported the discovery of Clinton emails on the Weiner laptop during the September 28 AD SVTC. When asked if this was information he would have expected to have been told, he stated, "Yeah, I would think so," adding that he was surprised that he had not been informed.

B.   McCabe Post-SVTC Phone Call and Meeting on September 28

1.   Phone Call with Sweeney

Sweeney told us that he had not heard back from McCabe after the September 28 SVTC, so he called McCabe on his drive home that evening. Phone records show two calls from Sweeney to McCabe on September 28. The first occurred at 4:51 p.m. and lasted for 9 minutes and 50 seconds, and the second occurred at 5:03 p.m. and lasted for 56 seconds. In addition, Sweeney's Outlook calendar for that day contained the following entry at 5:00 p.m.: "Telcal w/DD re: Weiner invest & Garner." Sweeney stated that NYO personnel had continued processing the laptop in the time since the initial notification on the AD SVTC and he had been informed there were now 347,000 emails on the laptop. Sweeney told us that he informed McCabe that there were now 347,000 emails.

McCabe, who told us that his earliest recollection of learning about the Weiner laptop was in a telephone call with Sweeney in late September or early October, recalled Sweeney informing him that NYO had seized a laptop from Anthony Weiner "and they thought there would be Clinton stuff in it." When asked what Sweeney specifically told him, McCabe stated, "I just remember him saying we think, you know, like, we've got this laptop and we opened it up, and it looks like there's stuff on there from Clinton, and, you know. Oh, my gosh, what do we do kind of thing." McCabe also recalled that Sweeney made "very clear" that "it was a large volume" of emails. McCabe stated that he understood "large volume" to mean "like many thousands of emails." McCabe recalled telling Sweeney that Counterintelligence Division personnel and NYO personnel should connect "[t]o figure out, like, what do we have or what do we do with this?"

McCabe stated that shortly after this call he contacted Priestap and said, "[Y]ou need to get somebody up to New York right away to take a look at what they have because it might be Clinton emails." Priestap told us that he did not recall either this conversation or McCabe telling him to send a team to New York to examine the Weiner laptop. As described below, Priestap's emails on the evening of September 28 reflect that he spoke with Sweeney and then instructed Strzok to have someone from his team contact NYO regarding the information.

2.   Meeting with Strzok and Priestap

Our review of Strzok's text messages revealed that McCabe discussed the Weiner laptop with Strzok and Priestap on September 28. Later that same day, Strzok and Page discussed the meeting in a series of text messages. Their exchange is quoted below. The sender of each text message is identified after the timestamp.

> 7:25 p.m., Strzok: "Got called up to Andy's earlier...hundreds of thousands of emails turned over by Weiner's atty to sdny, includes a ton of material from spouse. Sending team up tomorrow to review...this will never end...."
>
> 7:27 p.m., Page: "Turned over to them why?"
>
> 7:28 p.m., Strzok: "Apparently one of his recent texting partners may not have been 18...don't have the details yet"
>
> 7:29 p.m., Page: "Yes, reported 15 in the news."
>
> 7:31 p.m., Strzok: "And funny. Bill [Priestap] and I were waiting outside his door. He was down with the director...."
>
> 7:51 p.m., Strzok: "So I kinda want to go up to NY tomorrw [sic], coordinate this, take a leisurely Acela back Friday...."

Strzok stated that he was sure that "got called up to Andy's" referred to McCabe's office, but he had no recollection of that meeting. Strzok could not recall who first told him about the Weiner laptop, only recalling that someone told him that some "Clinton-type emails" had been discovered in New York. Strzok's notes from September 28 stated, "NY invest Weiner sexting 15 y'o. Weiner atty produces copy of everything Weiner has on iCloud to SDNY. Significant email from Huma [NFI – their email vs. her independent email]? Relevance to MYE, Clinton Foundation? MYE go review." Strzok stated that he initially planned to send a team to New York to review the emails, but that a conference call with NYO was scheduled instead. (This conference call, which occurred on September 29, is discussed below.)

Strzok told us that he did not consider the new information all that noteworthy because "throughout the summer [we had] retired Foreign Service officers...any number of people coming and saying, hey, I've got, you know, a handful of emails related to, you know, the Secretary or Cheryl Mills or something. And so we would run if they, we thought they had potential merit. We would track them down." Strzok conceded that this lead was more credible since it came from an FBI field office and involved information obtained from Abedin's husband. He added, though, "[T]here is no inkling, there is not a shadow of the, you know, what's going to unfold a month later."

Page said she believed the September 28 text message from Strzok was the first time she heard about the emails on the Weiner laptop and told us that she knew little information about it. Page explained that she was "not really that involved" in "most of the October stuff." Page stated her lack of involvement was due in part to the FBI's Russia investigation. Page explained that the many of the supervisors on the Midyear team were also assigned to the Russia investigation and they were "super-occupied" with the Russia investigation during October. Page stated that most of her information about the Weiner laptop came from either Strzok or FBI Attorney 1.

We showed McCabe these text messages and he said he did not recall talking to Strzok about the Weiner laptop on September 28. McCabe also did not recall Sweeney describing the quantity of emails numerically, other than to say there were a "large volume." When asked about Strzok's text message that he was "sending [a] team up tomorrow to review," McCabe noted that the text message would be consistent with what McCabe told Priestap. McCabe told us that the issue of the Weiner laptop "kind of falls off my radar" at this point, but when he reengaged with the team at a later point (he could not recall the amount of time that had elapsed), he discovered, "that [the team] did go up, but there [was] a problem, a legal, you know, an access problem because what they want to look for [was] not covered within the warrant, and yada, yada, yada." McCabe could not recall who told him this information about the trip to New York, but speculated it was Priestap.

C.   Comey and McCabe Communications After AD SVTC on September 28

Phone records show two phone calls between McCabe and Comey on the evening of September 28. The first call was from McCabe to Comey at 7:34 p.m. for 1 minute and 31 seconds. The second call was from Comey to McCabe at 8:36 p.m. for 8 minutes and 13 seconds. McCabe told us he could not recall the content of either phone call. When asked specifically if they discussed the issue of the Clinton emails on the Weiner laptop, McCabe said he did not recall and noted that he would talk with Comey at the end of the day on an almost daily basis. Additionally, as noted above, Strzok's text message on September 28 reflected that, while Strzok was waiting outside McCabe's office to meet with him regarding the Weiner laptop emails, McCabe "was down with the director." McCabe told us that he did not recall that and noted that the text message did not "seem consistent" with McCabe's calendar, which showed that he was at Quantico the evening of September 28.

McCabe said he recalled talking to Comey about the Weiner laptop issue "right around the time [McCabe] found out about it." McCabe described it as a "fly-by," where the Weiner laptop was "like one in a list of things that we discussed." McCabe continued, "[A]nd it would have been like, hey, Bill Sweeney called. This is what he has. I'm going to have [the Counterintelligence Division] take a look at it. I'll let you know." McCabe stated that he would have told Comey about the importance of sending a team up the next day in order "to get eyes on this thing and figure out what we have." McCabe did not recall Comey "weighing in on it at all." Given the scrutiny of the Clinton email server investigation, we asked McCabe why he believed Comey did not have a stronger reaction to this information and whether this was considered a "big deal." McCabe responded:

> Well, it was a big deal to me. I can't tell you what he was thinking when I told him about it. But I, I represented to him that we were taking steps to figure out what we had and would come back with some sort of an assessment as to what we need to do. So, I mean, there's, I'm not sure that there's anything else that he would have said to do.

Comey told the OIG that he recalled first learning of the presence of the additional emails on the Weiner laptop at some point in early October 2016, although Comey said it was possible this could have occurred in late September. Comey explained:

> I was aware sometime in the first week or two of October that there was a laptop that a criminal squad had seized from Anthony Weiner in New York and someone said to me that—and I'm thinking it might have been Andrew McCabe, but someone said to me kind of in passing, they're trying to figure out whether it has any connection to the Midyear investigation. And the reason that's so vague in my head is I think—I never imagined that there might be something on a guy named Anthony Weiner's computer that might connect to the Hillary Clinton email investigation, so I kind of just put it out of my mind.

Comey described himself as having a "reasonably good memory" and speculated, "[T]he reason I didn't index it is, it was a passing thing that almost seemed like he might be kidding, and so I don't think I indexed it hard. And I think it was the beginning of October and then I think it disappears from my memory. And then I remember for certain when Andy emails me, I think it's the 27th [of October] saying, the Midyear team needs to meet with you urgently or right away or something."

We asked Comey to explain why this initial information about the Weiner laptop did not "index" with him given that Abedin was closely connected to Clinton. Comey stated, "I don't know that I knew that [Weiner] was married to Huma Abedin at the time." Comey told us that even if he had had known that Abedin was married to Weiner "it wouldn't have been [at the] top of [my] mind." Comey also stated that the manner in which he was informed of this information affected his reaction. Comey told us that he was "quite confident" that he was not told this information in a "sit down" briefing in his office. Instead, Comey thought it most likely that McCabe was "passing the office" and said, "hey Boss, I just want you to know that the criminal squad in New York has got Anthony Weiner['s] laptop and I think it may have some connect to Midyear." Comey said he knew that "if it's

281

important, Andy [McCabe] will make sure that I focus on it." Comey said that it "could be" that whoever told him about the Weiner laptop "understated the significance of the information." He said, "The notion that I knew something important was on that laptop and did what—concealed or hid it or something?—is crazy."

We asked Comey if McCabe told him that Sweeney had called McCabe about the emails on the Weiner laptop. Comey responded, "No." We also showed Comey the Strzok text messages and asked him if he recalled being briefed in person by McCabe on September 28. Comey said he did not recall that occurring. Comey stated that he would have expected to be briefed if NYO had discovered a large volume of Hillary Clinton's emails. However, if NYO had only discovered a large volume of Abedin's emails, he was not sure that information would be briefed to him since there would not necessarily be a connection to Midyear. He acknowledged, however, that it "would be significant" if the laptop contained Abedin's emails on a clintonemail.com domain.

We asked Comey, "[I]f [McCabe] had been told on September 28th that there were…at one point 141,000 and at another 347,000 emails related to the Clinton investigation and didn't tell you, would you be concerned by that?" Comey responded, "Sure, I'd want to know why, what the thinking was." Since Comey told us he did not recall being told this information, we asked for his reaction. Comey stated:

> I'm mystified. First of all doubting, worried that I'm crazy is my first instinct, but I don't think I'm crazy. You said and I think I would remember if I were being told, so the question is, why wouldn't you tell me. I always try and keep an open mind and maybe some explanation and one I can't see, but I'd want to know, why, what's the thinking. Why didn't the, given the Director is closely associated with this, why, what's the reasoning. Maybe there is one I can't see, but I certainly would want to ask.

As detailed in the next section, Sweeney told us he also called EAD Coleman, EAD Steinbach, and AD Priestap on September 28 regarding the Weiner laptop emails. We asked Comey if any of those officials or anyone else informed him at this time (late September) of Sweeney's report that Midyear-related information had been discovered on the Weiner laptop. Comey responded, "Unless I'm having a stroke, no. I don't remember any of that." We also asked Comey if he would have expected someone on his leadership team other than McCabe to bring this to his attention. Comey stated that he would "not necessarily" have expected this if "they were assuming that the Deputy Director is briefing the Director." He described the FBI as "a big chain of command place."

D. Sweeney Calls Other FBI Executives on September 28

In addition to the phone call with McCabe detailed above, Sweeney told us that on September 28 he also called Criminal EAD Randy Coleman, National Security Branch EAD Mike Steinbach, and Counterintelligence AD Bill Priestap with updates on the Weiner laptop. Sweeney stated that he told all three essentially the same thing that he told McCabe, that NYO had continued processing the laptop and the number of emails was now at 347,000.

1. Criminal EAD Coleman

Sweeney's phone records show several calls with EAD Coleman during the afternoon of September 28. Coleman said Sweeney told him that NYO had reviewed a computer belonging to Anthony Weiner and had found thousands of "emails that pertain to Clinton...[during] her time as the Secretary of State and to Huma that were connected with the Midyear investigation." Coleman stated that he told Sweeney to make sure "to let management and headquarters know" about this development.

Coleman drafted a "Memorandum for Record" on November 7, 2016, documenting his involvement in the discovery of Clinton emails on the Weiner laptop. Coleman's memorandum stated, in part:

> On 09/28/2016, EAD Randall Coleman received for [sic] call from AD Bill Sweeney indicating team of Agents investigating Anthony Weiner sexting case had discovered emails relevant to Clinton email investigation. AD Sweeney advised team had halted further review and would be requesting guidance from FBIHQ. EAD Coleman agreed and advised he would notify FBI General Counsel James Baker and DD Andrew McCabe. The call was concluded. On 09/28/2016, immediately after call with AD Sweeney, Coleman telephonically contacted DD McCabe at his office number to advise him of the circumstance described by AD Sweeney. DD McCabe advised he had already been made aware of matter.

Coleman told us that he called McCabe immediately because he "considered this important." Coleman stated that McCabe's secretary answered his call and he told the secretary to get McCabe on the phone because Coleman "need[ed] to talk to him." Coleman described his conversation with McCabe as "very short." Coleman stated, "I said, hey listen, I just got called by Sweeney. Here is what he told me. And I think Andy is like, yeah, I already know. I got it." After his conversation with McCabe, Coleman told us, "[T]here was no doubt in my mind when we finished that conversation that [McCabe] understood the, the gravity of what the find was."

McCabe told us he did not recall receiving a phone call from Coleman. He told us Coleman's memorandum did not refresh his memory, but that he had no reason to doubt Coleman's account.

2. National Security EAD Steinbach

Steinbach stated that he believed the discovery of Midyear-related material on the Weiner laptop was first discussed at a meeting that he was unable to attend. Steinbach recalled receiving a phone call from Sweeney "just to give me a heads up saying, hey, you weren't here but just FYI we may have found something."

Steinbach told us this conversation may have occurred in late September. Steinbach said he could not recall specifics and stated that he did not think NYO "knew exactly what they had" at the time, but added that he received "some indication that there may be some Clinton domain emails."

3. Counterintelligence AD Priestap

On September 28, at 7:04 p.m., Priestap sent an email to Strzok, with the Lead Analyst and the NYO A/SAC copied, that stated, "I spoke to Sweeney. Our agent and analyst should call [the NYO A/SAC].... Sweeney said [the A/SAC] will get them access to what they need." At 9:26 p.m. on September 28, Sweeney sent the following email to Priestap, "Bill, The NYO POC for the sensitive email issue is A/SAC [] (cc'd). He can coordinate for your team. Have a quiet night. – Bill."

Priestap told us he could not recall if he heard about the discovery of Midyear-related material on the Weiner laptop during the September 28 AD SVTC. However, Priestap stated that he thought Sweeney "mentioned something to that effect in one of those" forums. Priestap told us that believed that he first learned of this issue in a phone call with Sweeney. Priestap described what information he was provided, stating:

> When I first was told about it, if I'm recalling correctly, it was something to the effect of it's Anthony Weiner's laptop or computer.... His wife's emails are on it. And his wife has email communication with the former Secretary, or probably then Secretary. And that the time frame overlaps with some of the time frame we were interested in. In other words, it was explained like this is in...the Midyear lane. I don't remember getting into any volume then, although...one of my first questions, if not the first question is, I would ask is what's the volume.

Priestap told us that he "would have certainly talked" to his immediate supervisor, EAD Steinbach, about this information because "the bottom line is this was explosive." Priestap stated that he did not recall talking to McCabe directly, although he stated that he may have if Steinbach was out of the office that day. Priestap stated that either he or Steinbach would have advised McCabe of "something of this magnitude" very quickly. Priestap described the information he received from Sweeney about the Weiner laptop as "hot information" and stated, "[I]t's the type of thing where I don't need an appointment. I walk upstairs and just, I make sure they know that before they go home."

III. Initial Response of FBI Headquarters to Discovery of Midyear-Related Information on the Weiner Laptop

A. Phone Call between Sweeney and Priestap on September 29

On September 29 at 6:09 a.m., Sweeney sent the following email to Priestap, "Can you give me a call on the ride in? Not clear under what authorities we have. Thx." Sweeney told us that he conveyed to Priestap in the phone call that NYO did not have the legal authority to look at the Midyear-related material on the Weiner laptop. Priestap told us he could not recall this specific conversation, but noted that it would be standard practice to examine what legal authority was needed. At 8:12 a.m., the A/SAC forwarded to Sweeney the 7:04 p.m. email from Priestap the night before. The A/SAC stated, "FYI There is no way that they can just look at the emails. I even went over the guidance from SDNY. Not happening unless they have some authority I am in the dark on. Let me known [sic] if you want to discuss."

At 9:02 a.m. on September 29, Sweeney forwarded Priestap the September 28 email from SDNY AUSA 1 (detailed above) advising the Weiner case agent on the limited scope of the Weiner search warrant and instructing him not to review any communication to which Abedin was a party. Priestap forwarded the email to FBI Attorney 1 and commented, "Per our conversation." Priestap described FBI Attorney 1 as someone he typically relies on when legal issues arise. FBI Attorney 1 confirmed that Priestap told her about the issue with the Weiner laptop and asked her "to follow up on it." We asked FBI Attorney 1 what she understood this to mean. FBI Attorney 1 told us that she believed there was a question of whether the Midyear team should go to New York and review the Weiner laptop. FBI Attorney 1 continued, "And, you know, we had over the course of the investigation, we would have various means of people saying, we have all of Clinton's emails. And so this was just to follow up on that. This obviously is more, a more solid lead than some of the other things we had, but it was just to find out really what were the details of this. Should we send a team up there."

B.   Conference Call between NYO and Midyear Personnel on September 29

Early on September 29, the Midyear SSA called the NYO A/SAC supervising the Weiner investigation and, according to the A/SAC, informed the A/SAC that he was the supervisor of the Clinton email server investigation. The A/SAC and SSA both told us that they had a brief discussion about what NYO had found on the Weiner laptop. The A/SAC stated, "I'm sure I told him exactly what I'd been representing to others, that, look, there are a lot of emails. You may want to get a search warrant. We can't, we're not looking at anything. That's the normal stuff I would have said." The SSA stated that the A/SAC told him, "[W]e've got some Clinton emails here, explained what it was. And they weren't sure what to do with it in that it was outside the scope of what they were working on." The SSA stated that the A/SAC explained that NYO wanted to notify FBI Headquarters about what they had found and were also seeking "guidance on how to deal with this."

The A/SAC and SSA scheduled a conference call, also known as a Lync call, between NYO and Midyear personnel at 11:30 a.m. that morning. Nine people participated in this conference call. This included the NYO A/SAC, ASAC, and SSA supervising the Weiner investigation; a NYO SSA assigned to public corruption matters; and five members of the FBI Midyear team: the SSA, FBI Attorney 1, Agent 2, and two analysts. FBI Attorney 1 told us that she participated in the call at the request of Priestap. The Midyear SSA told us that he gave Strzok a "heads up" that the SSA was going to have a conference call with NYO about the Weiner laptop.

1. Testimony and Contemporaneous Notes from Call Participants

We interviewed all nine participants to the September 29 call and reviewed the contemporaneous notes taken by eight of them (one participant, the NYO SSA on the Weiner investigation, took no notes).

The NYO participants told us that they provided the Midyear team with an overview of what they had found on the Weiner laptop. This included the fact that the laptop contained "hundreds of thousands" of emails potentially relevant to the Midyear investigation. Both the ASAC and public corruption SSA recalled the number 141,000 being provided. Each of the NYO participants said that the connection to both Hillary Clinton and the Clinton email server investigation was made clear on the call. The ASAC and public corruption SSA told us that NYO reported that there were emails addresses that appeared to be "directly tied" to Abedin and Clinton. NYO personnel stated that they informed the Midyear team that the laptop was "still downloading." The public corruption SSA's notes from the call also included the notation "2007 present," which he explained was the timeline for "the span of information that they had seen to date on the laptop." Each of the NYO participants told us that the limited nature of Weiner search warrant was discussed. The ASAC stated, "I know that we said to them that the warrant didn't authorize us to look at these particular emails." He continued, "And [the Midyear personnel] understood that. There was no pushback from them on that." NYO personnel told us that they were given no tasks to complete after the call. The ASAC explained, "I had the feeling like the ball is down in somebody else's court. Because...we were done."

The Midyear SSA stated that he "knew right off the bat" that NYO had emails from Clinton's server and that they "appeared to be government in nature." As for volume, the Midyear SSA recalled that "it wasn't a one-off" and NYO had seen either "hundreds or thousands" of emails. Either way, the SSA described it as a "significant number." The Midyear SSA also told us that "content-wise" NYO "had only seen a couple" of emails because "they couldn't review content." He said he understood that NYO had seen more of Abedin's emails, but they had seen Clinton emails as well, including emails from the @clintonemail.com domain. The Midyear SSA told us that he asked NYO personnel why they thought these were Clinton's emails and NYO responded, "Well, because they're her initials", indicating that they had seen something beyond the domain name. The Midyear SSA stated that Midyear personnel were informed that the Weiner search warrant had a very limited scope. He stated that Midyear personnel knew that they "were going to need to get a warrant to review this." We asked the Midyear SSA if NYO had mentioned seeing BlackBerry domain emails on the Weiner laptop. The SSA responded, "Yeah.... [T]hey had looked from the forensic side, that they had determined that it appeared to be like an entire" file. The Midyear SSA described the conclusion of the call as follows:

> Well, from my standpoint, I said we were going to, we were going to address whether we had enough for a warrant. And that we would run this up the chain on our side. And...they agreed especially that they

would go back to SDNY and see what the exact parameters of what they could and couldn't do, because they were not going to cross a line that would compromise their case.

Agent 2, Analyst 1, and Analyst 2 told us that NYO reported a large volume of emails on the laptop and noted that they were still processing the laptop. Notes for each of these three referenced "350k items," with Agent 2's notes also stating, "350k items in messages tab." All three told us that NYO reported the presence of emails related to Clinton. Analyst 1 stated that NYO reported that they had seen metadata showing "what they were characterizing as like [Hillary Clinton's] email addresses." Analyst 1 stated that the Midyear team was trying to determine if these were Clinton's or were from the clintonemail.com domain. Analyst 2 stated that she had only a vague recollection of the call, but told us that she recalled that NYO had seen a large volume of emails between Clinton and Abedin. Agent 2 stated that NYO reported seeing emails from the clintonemail.com domain. Analyst 1's notes referenced the following domains: state.gov, clinton.com, hillary@clinton.com, clintonfoundation, and clintonemail.com. Analyst 2's notes included a reference to "2007 dates on PC." Each of the three also said that NYO emphasized the limited nature of the Weiner search warrant and the fact that the Midyear team was "going to need to get a warrant to review this." Agent 2's notes included the following references: "SDNY advised to avoid emails" and "not looked @ any content." Analyst 2's notes included the following references: "SDNY—said put them aside" and "Huma has not waived marrital [sic] priv." Analyst 2 described the limited nature of the Weiner search warrant as an "overarching theme" of the call.

FBI Attorney 1 provided a slightly different account of the call. She stated that NYO said on the call that it was still processing the evidence and they were not sure "whether or not it had anything to do with" Midyear. FBI Attorney 1 explained:

> We didn't know if it was the right timeframe. So, you know, Huma we knew, Huma had...worked for [Clinton] for a long time. So we weren't sure of exactly, one, what, how much of the information on this was Huma's versus Weiner's. Because we thought it was his laptop. And then, two, whether it would have been relevant to the right timeframe. We were looking for Clinton's emails, not Huma's emails. We also knew Huma had a clintonemail address, so she could have been using that for her own personal activities, so we just didn't know the full extent of what was on there.

When asked about volume, FBI Attorney 1 told us that she "knew that it was a large amount of data" and FBI Attorney 1's notes from the call referenced "over 350k items." However, FBI Attorney 1 added:

> We always got things that said the data was larger than, it always ended up getting narrowed down after we got more, got it processed more. It doesn't change for me though, even though the 350k that's what we think. Like, there was also all the talk about it hadn't been

fully processed. So, to me, that number was just sort of a preliminary number.

FBI Attorney 1 stated that NYO said it had seen either Clinton's emails or emails from the clintonemail.com domain. FBI Attorney 1 told us that NYO relayed that "SDNY was very concerned about staying within the scope of their warrant." FBI Attorney 1 stated that the Midyear team told NYO, "well when you get further clarity about what this laptop is, get back to us and let us know, and we'll try to figure out what to do from there." She told us that Midyear personnel specifically requested that NYO look for emails related to the clintonemail.com domain. When asked whether NYO was supposed to create an inventory or list for Midyear, FBI Attorney 1 stated that she "thought we talked about [the Weiner case agent] not being able to do that. Because of the instructions. I mean, because of how the warrant was drafted." FBI Attorney 1's notes were entitled "NYO Lync – MYE Emails" and included references to "image – not complete b/c so large," "SDNY told them to avoid emails," "over 350k items – including emails + IMs different addresses including state.gov Clinton.com," "not sure if they saw clintonemail.com," "WFO interest - @clintonemail.com @state.gov," and "2009-2013 time frame / early next week."

2.   Post-Call NYO Communications

Shortly after the call concluded, at 11:52 a.m., the NYO ASAC forwarded to the Midyear SSA and FBI Attorney 1 the September 28 email from AUSA 1 to the Weiner case agent (detailed above) outlining the limited scope of the Weiner search warrant and providing instructions for the case agent's search of the laptop. The ASAC told us that he forwarded this email to make sure "they understood the directives that we had from [SDNY] in terms of limitations and really kind of under what circumstances we would be able to look at anything that was attached to an email." Witnesses in NYO and SDNY told us that the case agent was told not to affirmatively search the emails for information unrelated to the Weiner child exploitation investigation. At 12:42 p.m. on September 29, the A/SAC informed Sweeney by email: "Just had the lync call with HQ/WFO. They were misinformed about the accessibility. All good for now. We can discuss further if you like."

The NYO A/SAC and ASAC told us they did not recall any tasking of NYO related to the material on the Weiner laptop that was potentially relevant to the Midyear investigation. The A/SAC told us, "I fully expected [the Midyear team] to reach back out to ask me for certain things, and, and for assistance of some sort. I know that's what I'd do." The NYO A/SAC, ASAC, and SSA told us they had no further contact with FBI Headquarters about the Clinton email issue until late October. The SSA told us that he felt like NYO had done its job reporting the information to FBI Headquarters and he "assumed they were doing something."

3.   Post-Call Midyear Team and FBI Headquarters Response

We asked members of the Midyear team what steps were taken immediately after the September 29 call. FBI Attorney 1 recalled discussing the September 29 call with both Strzok and Deputy General Counsel Trisha Anderson. FBI Attorney 1 stated that it was clear the Midyear team would need "additional process or consent" to be able to do anything with the laptop. Despite this, FBI Attorney 1 stated that she did not reach out to the AUSAs at SDNY at this time. FBI Attorney 1 explained, "[A]fter the SVTC, I thought, well I'm not sure we're that far along, and I think I get what, where New York is. And so I didn't feel the need to reach out to SDNY at that time." We asked FBI Attorney 1 whether NYO was supposed to follow up with the Midyear team or the Midyear team was supposed to follow up with NYO after the call. FBI Attorney 1 stated, "I don't have an answer to that. I don't think it was very clear. I would have expected New York to follow up because they were the one that had to process the computer...." We asked FBI Attorney 1 what she expected NYO to do as a result the call. FBI Attorney 1 stated:

> I would have expected that the computer would have been processed, New York would have been continuing their investigation, and to the extent that they saw more things that could have helped us—that would have been relevant to our case—they would have reached back out and told us like they did on [October] 26th or whatever that date was, on that Wednesday.... It just took three weeks to do that.

Strzok told us that either the Midyear SSA or FBI Attorney 1 briefed him on the call. In a 12:26 p.m. email to Strzok on September 29, the Midyear SSA stated, "No travel planned for tomorrow. [FBI Attorney 1] will brief you at 1 pm." FBI Attorney 1 told us she recalled this discussion with Strzok. She stated:

> ...Bill [Priestap] was wondering if we were going to send a team to New York, to go with them and review this material with them. And based on the call, I didn't think it was the right time yet. Obviously that's not my decision as counsel, but I did explain to Pete, like, we didn't know the volume. We didn't know if it was related to our material. The search warrant was about Weiner's activities, so there would be limited utility in sending a team to New York at this point.

Strzok's notes from September 29 stated, "NY: SW – Saw some @clintonemail.com, @state.gov." Strzok did not recall being briefed in any detail, but stated that he was told about the limited scope of the Weiner search warrant. Strzok told us his takeaway was:

> [T]hat there is material there.... [T]he upshot of what I recall is, you know, we need to, we need to kind of go down this route. It isn't a crank lead. It is something that we need to look into. There is work they've got to do. We're not there yet, but it isn't something we can just say, ah, let, there's nothing relevant there.

Strzok said the next step was for NYO to process the laptop and for NYO to look for the type of data on the laptop that the Midyear team would need. Strzok continued:

> [A]nd...when you're done with that, you know, call us back and let us know. And again...there is no sense of this is going to be huge and

horrible and the election is a month away, and God, are we going to say something, do we need to say something to Congress? This is just, oh, good lead and, you know, we'll get to the end of the year, next year. We'll get to it as they process through it.

Anderson told us she vaguely recalled a "preliminary conversation" with FBI Attorney 1 on this issue. At 10:27 a.m. on September 29, FBI Attorney 1 sent a message to Anderson on the FBI's Lync system that stated, "Sorry I missed the 10:15. I was meeting with [Priestap] about a new development in MYE. I believe he also reached out to you, but you were in a meeting. I can bring you up to speed when you have a minute." Anderson said she recalled a "very skeletal" overview of the facts, including that some Abedin materials may have been found on a laptop obtained in an investigation of Weiner. Anderson said that she was informed that it was unclear what was on the laptop at this point and NYO was going "to try to figure out as much as they could" consistent with the terms of their search warrant. When asked if FBI Attorney 1 would have been responsible for following up with NYO after the call, Anderson stated, "[I]t wouldn't have been [FBI Attorney 1's] job to call New York and say, hey, where are you guys on this? You know, as a lawyer, that's not what she would have been doing." Anderson said she thought it would have been the job of "the Midyear investigative team" to reach out to NYO to find out "where things stood." Anderson did not recall hearing about the Weiner laptop issue again until approximately October 27.

Priestap's notes from September 29 contained the following entry: "<u>Baker</u> Voluntarily provided emails from 2007 on (347,000 emails) – state.gov, - foundation.gov." Priestap explained that the "Baker" notation meant that either Priestap received this information from FBI GC Baker or Priestap felt that he needed to tell Baker this information. As noted below, Baker recalled first learning about the Weiner laptop issue from EAD Coleman on October 3. Priestap provided the following interpretation of his notes, "[M]y guess, I'm not positive, is that this was an indication, you know, we thought the time frame was roughly 2007 on, there were roughly this many emails [347,000], and that it included both" State Department and Clinton Foundation business. Priestap told us that he met with the Lead Analyst, Strzok, and FBI Attorney 1 on a nearly daily basis during this period and the information in his notes may have been provided by one of those individuals.

McCabe told us he could not recall if he learned about the September 29 call before or after it occurred.[166] He stated that the call was the Midyear team's way "of following through with my direction to them to kind of get their hands around this thing and let us know what do we have." We asked McCabe if anyone informed him of the limited scope of the Weiner search warrant at this time and he stated that he did not recall being told that until later. McCabe stated if he had been told

---

[166] As noted in Chapter Eight, McCabe held a meeting on the afternoon of September 29 entitled "Mtg. w/DD RE Decision Points" that Rybicki, Anderson, Strzok, Page, FBI Attorney 1, Baker, and Priestap were invited to attend. Contemporaneous notes from the meeting reflected a discussion of congressional requests for materials from the Midyear investigation. The notes did not reference the NYO call.

about the limited scope of NYO's search warrant on September 29, "I would have said well what do we have to do to get another warrant if that's the route we need to take."

C.   McCabe Call to NSD Leadership on October 3

NSD Principal Deputy Assistant Attorney General (DAAG) Mary McCord told us that on or about October 3, she received a phone call from McCabe. McCord stated that this was the first time she learned that there was a potential issue relating to emails in an iCloud account used by Abedin and Weiner. We found no evidence of any other contact between the FBI Midyear team and the Midyear prosecutors regarding any material obtained from Weiner until October 21, as discussed below.

McCord described their conversation as follows:

[W]hat he says to me is that there's this criminal case. New York is investigating Anthony Weiner. And his counsel...provided a copy of the content of his iCloud account. It includes a substantial number of emails from his wife's email account. And Andy [McCabe] said he was sending a Midyear agent up to look at what it is. You know, hopefully it's all duplicates and we don't have to, you know, worry about, about it. And at the time, he was, he was saying to me you may want to touch base with [SDNY U.S. Attorney] Preet [Bharara] to make sure he's not like charging ahead like doing some sort of process, like, that would bump up against the work of Midyear.

According to McCord, she and McCabe thought that these emails were likely duplicates given the "thorough scrub of everything" during Midyear. McCord told us that she did not think this was "a major thing," but agreed that they should "make sure that there's nothing new there."

McCord's notes from the call stated, "Andy McCabe. NY CRM investigating Anthony Weiner, his counsel provided copy of content of his i-cloud account – includes substantial # of emails from wife's email account. Andy sending mid-year agent up to look at what it is. Hopefully all duplicates. May want to touch base w/Preet to make sure doesn't charge ahead. Consent?" McCord stated that the "Consent?" entry was a thought about whether consent would have been "good enough" to allow a forensic review to determine if these were duplicate emails. After the conversation, McCord stated, "And then, honestly, I get busy with things. I don't really think much about this again until, and I did not call Preet. I just decided it wasn't" warranted at that time. McCord stated that she did not hear about the issue again until McCabe called a second time later in October. As we discuss below, we believe this call occurred on October 25.

McCabe only vaguely recalled a conversation with McCord. He told us that he believed that he contacted McCord, but he thought that the conversation occurred later in October.

NSD DAAG Toscas recalled being informed of McCabe's call to NSD in early October and stated that he thought it related to emails in an iCloud account used by Weiner and Abedin. Toscas did not remember the exact timing of the call and thought that McCabe called NSD AAG John Carlin instead of McCord. Nevertheless, the information provided by Toscas was similar to McCord's testimony. Toscas stated that he did not hear about this issue again until he received a phone call from SDNY Deputy U.S. Attorney Kim on October 21. We discuss that call below.

We also asked NSD AAG Carlin about an early October call between either McCabe and himself or McCabe and McCord related to the Weiner investigation. Carlin, who had announced on September 27, 2016, that he would resign as AAG effective October 15, 2016, told us he did not recall a conversation between McCabe and himself or McCabe and McCord.

D. FBI Headquarters Discussions on October 3 and 4

1. EAD Coleman October 3 Meeting with Baker and Bowdich

As noted previously, Coleman drafted a "Memorandum for Record" on November 7, 2016, documenting his involvement in the discovery of emails on the Weiner laptop that were potentially relevant to the Midyear investigation. The memorandum contained an entry for October 3 that stated, "On or about 10/03/2016, EAD Coleman verbally advised OGC Baker and Associate Deputy Director David Bowdich of the matter described by AD Sweeney in a 'sidebar' meeting after normal DD [Deputy Director] daily update meeting. OGC Baker advised he was not aware of the matter and would need to look into it further." Coleman told us that he believed McCabe was out of the office on October 3 and ADD Bowdich was leading the daily update meeting. McCabe was scheduled to travel to New York on October 3 to attend a symposium the following day.[167] Coleman told us that after a meeting on October 3, he informed Bowdich and Baker about the information he had received from Sweeney concerning the laptop. Bowdich told us that he did not "specifically remember" this discussion with Coleman, but had no reason to doubt the memorandum's accuracy.

We showed Baker the Coleman memorandum and Baker stated that Coleman's account "sounds about right." We asked Baker what he was told about the Weiner laptop. Baker stated:

> Pretty basic, but along the lines of we have this laptop in this other, unrelated case. And somehow they figured out that there were some additional emails on there that were outside the scope of the warrant, if I recall correctly, that they were working on, and that they needed to do more work to get access to them, and they would be...working on it to try to get access to it.

---

[167] In McCabe's absence, Bowdich as ADD would run the daily update meeting.

Coleman's memorandum stated that Baker planned to look into the issue further. We asked Baker about that and he stated he did not recall specifics, but he believed he asked "somebody on the Midyear team" about the issue.

In the Coleman memorandum's next and final paragraph, which is undated, it stated, "It was determined by DD McCabe and EAD Steinbach that any follow on investigative activity concerning the emails located on Anthony Weiner's laptop would be reviewed by the MIDYEAR investigative team." Coleman said he did not recall why this entry was undated and was unsure at what point this occurred. He told us that he shared an office with Steinbach and that this could have been a dialogue between himself and Steinbach at some point later in October.

2.   Email from Bowdich to Comey on October 3

On October 3, at 7:42 p.m., Bowdich sent an email to Comey and McCabe briefing them on items of interest from that day. Rybicki was cc'd on the email, which was entitled "Daily Report." After highlighting three unrelated items, Bowdich stated, "I asked Randy Coleman to stay behind tomorrow to quickly brief you on the Weiner matter which is growing more complicated, but it can wait until then." Bowdich told the OIG that he did not remember what was "growing more complicated" with the Weiner matter. Bowdich noted that when dealing with issues of this type he typically "would have pushed that up to Andy, and/or the Director, and Baker would have been right in the middle of it."

Comey told us he did not recall this email and also did not recall what was "growing more complicated" in the Weiner matter. Comey stated that he was "only dimly" aware of the Weiner child exploitation investigation at this point in time.

We also asked Rybicki about this email. Rybicki stated that he did not know what was meant by "the Weiner matter which is growing more complicated." Rybicki told us that he first recalled hearing about the issue of Clinton emails on the Weiner laptop on October "26th into the 27th." When asked if this email made Rybicki think that he and Comey were aware of the Weiner laptop issue earlier than he recalled, Rybicki responded, "I don't think so.... I remember on the 27th right when I heard about it thinking this is [unintelligible]. That would, that's my first recollection as well of hearing anything about it."

3.   Meeting between Comey and Coleman on October 4

Comey's Outlook calendar for October 4 contains an entry for "Morning Briefs" from 8:15 a.m. to 9:00 a.m. that is immediately followed by an entry for "Meeting w/EAD Coleman" from 9:00 a.m. to 9:30 a.m. Coleman told us that he could not recall this briefing with Comey. Coleman stated that staying behind to brief Comey would be consistent with normal practice, but added that he did not recall this specific instance. Coleman told us that it would be unusual to have a one-on-one meeting with Comey and told us someone else would typically be present at these briefings, such as the DD or ADD. While not remembering this meeting, Coleman speculated that this may have been a one-on-one meeting with Comey to discuss Coleman's upcoming retirement from the FBI in December 2016.

Coleman told us that he kept regularly took notes in a journal. Coleman's notes from October 4 contained the following entry:

(1) Anthony Wiener [sic]

(2) [Unrelated]

(3) Wiener [sic] – texting 15 yo – Sexually Explicit

     9/26 – Federal SW – IPhone/IPAD/Laptop

     Initial analysis of laptop – thousands emails

     Hillary Clinton & Foundation

     Crime Against Children

We asked Coleman about these notes and he told us that, given their placement in his notebook, the notes would most likely represent information he was briefed on first thing in the morning by his subordinates in the Criminal Investigative Division. Coleman stated that he may have passed this information to other FBI executives after the morning briefing with the Director, but he could not remember if that occurred here.

Comey told us that he did not recall the briefing by Coleman reflected in his calendar. We asked Comey if this briefing could have been the time in early October that he recalled being told about the connection between Midyear and the Weiner investigation. Comey stated:

> It's possible, possible this is what is knocking around in the back of my head, but I really, see I know the frailty of memory from having done a lot of this work, at least in my memory it's much more of an informal than a meeting about it, but it's possible.

We showed Coleman's notes from October 4 to Comey. Comey did not recall being briefed on the information contained in the notes. When asked about Coleman, Comey said he "thought very highly of him" and described him as a "straight shooter."

We asked Comey if this information was something that he likely would have "put out of his mind" after being informed of it in early October. Comey responded, "I don't think so unless, unless the way it was passed to me was with some, you don't need to do anything. We're doing, we're running it down or something. Something that pushed it down on my priority list."

When asked if he recalled this meeting between Coleman and Comey, Rybicki stated that he did not. Bowdich told us that it is possible that he would have been at this meeting between Comey and Coleman, but he had no recollection of it. McCabe continued to be on travel and was not in Washington, D.C., on October 4.

IV.   NYO Completes Processing of Weiner Laptop Around October 4

As noted previously, the Weiner case agent told us that he noticed on September 26 or 27 that the software program that he was using on the Weiner laptop was having trouble processing the data on it. The case agent told us that he reached out to a CART examiner for assistance and the CART examiner decided to process the laptop on the CART examiner's workstation. CART logs show that the CART examiner received the laptop on September 29 and imaged, or made an exact copy of, the laptop the same day. The CART examiner told us that he began using FBI software programs to analyze and categorize the contents of the laptop the next day and that was completed by around October 4. In total, there were approximately 675,000 emails on the laptop.

The CART examiner told us once the processing was completed he conducted a spot check of the results to ensure everything had processed completely. The CART examiner stated that the first file he clicked on was an image of a document marked "Sensitive But Unclassified" with the initials "HRC" written on it in a blue felt-tipped marker. The CART examiner stated that he immediately ceased his examination and reported this to the case agent and the CART supervisor. The case agent recalled the CART examiner showing him this document and told us that he commented, "We can't be looking at this."

V.   FBI Headquarters Inaction and Explanations for the Delay

After October 4, we found no evidence that anyone associated with the Midyear investigation, including the entire leadership team at FBI Headquarters, took any action on the Weiner laptop issue until the week of October 24, and then did so only after SDNY raised concerns about the lack of action. In this section, we detail the explanations given to us by FBI Headquarters and Midyear personnel about the reasons for this inaction.

When we asked McCabe about this period from late September until late October and the lack of activity on the Weiner laptop, he stated:

> During that period in between, you know, I expected that we were making progress on it. I probably met with some combination of the Midyear team every day of that month. Near to every single day on a whole kind of range of Midyear-related issues. And I would have expected that if they were having problems with that issue and not making progress on something that I had put on, on their radar as an important thing, that that would have come to my attention. And it didn't. So I don't, I can't sit here and tell you with perfect clarity why it didn't, whether they thought they had it under control but they didn't, or it was being ignored and not given the attention it, it needed, but it, it didn't come to me during that time.

McCabe stated that he was "absolutely" disappointed that the team had not found out more information about what was on the Weiner laptop during this period.

McCabe added, "So to find out that we didn't know the answers to any of those questions at the end of October was very concerning to me."

FBI Headquarters and Midyear personnel provided multiple explanations for the apparent inactivity on the Weiner laptop during this period. Explanations included claims of delay by NYO in processing the Weiner laptop, a lack of specific information about what had been discovered on the laptop, a focus on the Russia investigation, the fact that the Weiner laptop was not considered a priority during this period, and legal impediments to reviewing the materials on the laptop. We discuss each of these explanations below, recognizing that these explanations are interrelated and not mutually exclusive.

A.   Delays in Processing the Weiner Laptop

Numerous witnesses cited delays in processing the Weiner laptop by NYO personnel as a primary reason for the apparent inaction by FBI Headquarters and Midyear personnel. Strzok told us that, after the September 29 call, he understood that NYO was going to continue processing the laptop and then when they were "done with that, you know, call us back and let us know." FBI Attorney 1 also stated that the Midyear team was waiting on NYO to finish processing the laptop. When asked why it would take so long, FBI Attorney 1 stated that this "is not that long of a period of time for the Bureau to take to get something done." Rybicki told us that he learned after the fact that NYO had "technical issues" with the laptop, but he did not know "why it took a month." Comey recalled being told after the fact of a "technical delay" or "something about a glitch with getting a mirror image of the Weiner laptop," which ultimately "had to be sent to the Operational Technology Division."

Page stated that NYO was "having trouble" processing the Weiner laptop and "that gap represents the time that New York is getting a workable image of the Weiner laptop because it is so large." She noted that there was "no particular urgency" on this issue, however. Page explained, "[N]ot to say it's not an important case, but it's not, there's no specific reason why like all hands on deck need to be helping New York CART sort of get this thing loaded or whatever else." Later in the interview, Page again reiterated that NYO did not really know what they had "until they finally sort of have it up and imaged, and start doing their...forensic review." She continued:

> And the reality is, emails had been found lots of other places that
> ultimately weren't worth pursuing lots of other times. And so, until we
> understand that, that the volume of emails is not simply the volume
> with respect to Weiner, but that it represents Huma emails as well,
> you know, my understanding is, like, it's just not super-significant yet.

B.   Prioritization of Weiner Laptop and Russia Investigation

Priestap told us that the Weiner laptop was not his top priority at this time due to his involvement in the Russia investigation. Priestap explained:

[I]f you're wondering, you know, hey, this is a really big deal, and why aren't you asking about it every, every minute of every day type thing, whatever, it was the, we went from this thing to the Russia thing. And the Russia thing took them as much as my time as this thing before. And I don't want to say distracted, but yeah. My focus wasn't on Midyear anymore, even with this new, yes, we've got to review it. Yes, it may contain evidence we didn't know, but I'd be shocked if it's evidence that's going to change the outcome of the case because, again...aside from this, did we see enough information previously in which I felt confident that we had gotten to the bottom of the, of the issue? I did. And so, again, I would have been shocked if it was information that, and so the bottom line is, as important as this was, it was, some ways it was water under the bridge. The issue of the day was what's, what's going to be done to possibly interfere with the election.

In written comments provided to the OIG after reviewing the draft report, Priestap further explained:

With respect to the criticism that the FBI should have placed a higher priority on obtaining legal authority to access and review the potentially relevant emails on [the Weiner] laptop, I maintain that we made the correct judgments. In this regard, our work on [Midyear] was extensive and included the review of tens of thousands of emails, (over 7 million email fragments), and interviews of more than 70 individuals. We amassed and analyzed an enormous volume of information, reaching the recommendation in July 2016 that no prosecution be initiated. I sincerely doubted that the emails identified on [the Weiner] laptop were likely to alter our informed view of the matter, and therefore did not prioritize the follow-on work over higher priority matters.

Regarding these higher priority matters, Priestap stated that in late September 2016 Comey had tasked the Counterintelligence Division with a multifaceted effort to protect the 2016 election from foreign interference. This tasking included the implementation of "a national supply chain risk management effort to identify vulnerabilities in voting infrastructure," engaging state election officials about potential threats, the investigation of "whether foreign adversaries were attempting to interfere with or improperly influence the" 2016 election, and the investigation of certain U.S. persons' contacts with foreign adversaries. Priestap told the OIG that, as the AD of the Counterintelligence Division, he was in charge of all of these efforts. Priestap stated:

In sum, I do not believe that the Bureau made a conscious decision to specifically assign a lower priority to the review of [the Weiner] laptop, but rather—given the other extremely significant matters being handled by the Counterintelligence Division and the time typically associated with obtaining legal authority and processing data—it was not viewed as a mission critical activity. My team was prepared to pursue this matter in the normal course, recognizing that it might not be completed until after the presidential election.[168]

Strzok echoed this notion that the Weiner laptop was not initially his highest priority. He stated:

> This is just, you know a lead that likely is going to result in some investigation, maybe some data we're going to have to review, you know, January, February 2017, whenever it gets done. In my experience, it is not unusual at all for processing to crap out and have to get restarted, or to have problems with certain types of media.... This isn't a, a ticking terrorist bomb. This is a, you know, again, despite the high-profile nature of the client, a, and a very serious case, something where it goes in the queue and gets prioritized and they're going through it. So, if you were to ask me, you know, were there alarm bells going off in my head on October 15th that we haven't heard back? No, absolutely not. I didn't expect, it would not have surprised me to have heard back in early-November or to have heard back in early-December.

Strzok explained that he had no crystal ball that could have foreseen the events that ultimately occurred in late October and he thought it "a misplaced assumption and belief that there should have been some sense of urgency after September 29th, and we should have reprioritized everything we were doing to go after this. We did not know what was there." Strzok also cited his assignment to the Russia investigation as an explanation for why the Weiner laptop was not seen as his top priority. He stated:

> We were consumed by these ever-increasing allegations of [Russian] contacts and coordination and trying to get operations up, and following people.... Doing a lot of stuff that was extraordinarily consuming and concerning. So this pops up, and it's like...another thing to worry about. And it's important, and we need to do it. Okay, get it handled. Come back to us, and then back to this, you know, is the government of Russia trying to get somebody elected here in the United States?"

Likewise, Page stated that she and other members of the Midyear team were "super-focused" on the Russia investigation at this point.

We also asked Comey whether the fact that key members of the Midyear team, including Strzok, were also assigned to the Russia investigation contributed to the delay in reviewing the Weiner laptop. Comey told us that he remembered

---

[168] Priestap further explained his thought process at the time, noting that he considered the Weiner laptop to be an important issue when first informed about it on September 28 and made sure it received his immediate attention. However, Priestap told us that once he was informed of potential legal and technical issues regarding the laptop, he believed from past experience that those issues would take time to resolve and therefore expected no immediate update.

being told that the team assigned to the Russia investigation was "overwhelmed." Comey continued:

> It was Russia, Russia, Russia all the time.... Well not just Russia, Russia, Russia. [It was also] Midyear Congress, Midyear Congress – because they had, somebody had to review the documents that were going up to Congress and there was a constant demand for documents and briefings on Midyear and Russia at the same time.

We asked Comey if, in retrospect, the team should have been bigger. Comey responded, "Yeah maybe, yeah.... I think that's a reasonable question to ask and I'm sure in hindsight I needed another Strzok and maybe I needed two teams, and you always have in the Bureau, the challenge is the talent is not necessarily that deep when it comes to counterintelligence matters, people who can work this stuff."

C.   Lack of Specific Information

We were also told that FBI Headquarters and Midyear personnel were waiting on NYO to provide more specific information about what was on the Weiner laptop. FBI Attorney 1 explained:

> And you also have to remember too, like, throughout this whole investigation, we would randomly occasionally get someone that said, oh, I know where all the emails are. So...this was more certain than that. But it wasn't, it wasn't like, oh, I think we have the smoking gun on this laptop. We better hurry up and make sure we get it processed. It was like let's see what the process turns out to be. There may not be that much, you know, it may just be duplicative of what we already have.

When asked if she was receiving updates during this period, FBI Attorney 1 stated that she was not and did not know if anyone else was getting updates either. FBI Attorney 1's supervisor, Anderson, also told us that her understanding was that NYO was processing the materials and trying to figure out what they had during this time period.

Strzok discussed this issue of a lack of information as well, stating that only when NYO reported "the scope and content" of what was on the laptop did it become a significant development. Specifically, Strzok cited the facts that the Weiner laptop contained "a variety of backups from Huma's devices," it contained information she forwarded to Weiner, and, most importantly, had BlackBerry backups from "the missing three months."[169]

---

[169] As noted in Chapter Five, the 30,490 emails provided by Clinton's attorneys contained no emails sent or received by Clinton during the first two months of her tenure, January 21, 2009, through March 18, 2009, and the FBI investigative team was unable to locate the BlackBerry device she used during that time, although they were able to obtain some of the BlackBerry emails from other sources. Witnesses, including former Director Comey, told us that they believed these missing emails could contain important evidence regarding Clinton's intent in setting up a private email server.

The Midyear SSA told us that he believed NYO was able to provide more information on the volume of emails on the laptop later in October. When asked if there was any additional information provided beyond volume, the Midyear SSA stated that there may have been "something more specific too" that he could not recall at the time of our interview. The Midyear SSA told us:

> I remember walking away the first time thinking that...we probably had enough [probable cause to get a search warrant to review the emails]. But I understood why that discussion wanted to be made, is that, you know, well let's see what happens.... [T]hat lag in time was as a result of allowing [the Weiner] investigation to proceed. And then they contacted us when they felt that they had a lot more information that needed to be addressed by, by our team. And then we proceeded with moving forward.

The Midyear SSA stated that he did not seek an update from NYO in this period because it was "an [FBI] OGC [and] SDNY type thing."

D. Questions About Legal Authority

Another reason cited by McCabe, Baker, and Priestap for the inactivity during this period was the need to resolve questions about the legal authority. Priestap explained:

> [W]hat is our legal basis by which we can conduct the review? And again...it's not the first time, and...I run into this all the, all the time with trying to cross the T's, dot the I's on the legal end before we take activity. Now, again, why it took so long, should it have took so long? I don't know. But I saw it as a, let's, we don't have, I don't have knowledge that we have the legal authority to say go.

Baker stated that he thought the Midyear team was "struggling with trying to figure out" a way to access the material on the Weiner laptop since "it was beyond the scope of the original search warrant." Baker told us he thought that the FBI and SDNY "were continuing to work on" overcoming these "legal complications."

FBI Attorney 1 did not share this view. She told us that "it had already been concluded" on the September 29 call that the Midyear team would not be able to use the Weiner search warrant to review the laptop and, instead, the Midyear team "would need additional process or consent if we needed to do anything." The Midyear SSA agreed with this assessment, stating that there was a "consensus" on the September 29 call that the only way they would be able to review the Clinton emails on the Weiner laptop was with a new warrant.

E. Strzok Timeline

We asked Strzok about a document he subsequently created entitled "Weiner timeline" and included in an email he sent to Page on November 3, 2016. The document contained the following entries for the period from September 26 through October 21:

09/26/2016 – NYO obtains [search warrant] for Weiner laptop

09/28/2016 – ADIC NY notes potential MYE-related material following weekly SAC SVTC

09/29/2016 – Conference call between NYO and MYE team

– NYO notes processing is crashing system and not complete, but during troubleshooting observes material potentially related to MYE (clintonemail.com and state.gov domains) seen during course of review

– No numbers/volume available

– Discussion about ability to search for material determines such activity would be outside scope of warrant

– Request to NYO to gather basic facts (numbers, domains, etc) based on their review

Approx. 10/19/2016 – NYO completes carving

– NYO observes [Sensitive But Unclassified] attachment

10/21/2016 – 6:00 PM DOJ/NSD advised MYE leadership that SDNY informed them of MYE-related media on Weiner media

We asked Strzok why he created this timeline on November 3, which was days after Comey sent his letter to Congress informing it that the FBI had discovered additional emails. Strzok stated:

Because I think the, the question was, okay, here we are. We're having to reopen and it's right in the middle of, you know, the last week of the election. You know, potentially we would need to do this. And that people are going to come afterwards and say either you delayed to help Hillary, you delayed to help Trump, whatever it was. Let's, while it is fresh or as fresh as possible, let's kind of document out. And I, you know, again, I don't know if the political hue and cry had already begun of, you know, conspiracy. But I think the sense was, okay, let's kind of write down and while it's still sort of fresh, yeah.

Strzok told us he could not remember if he was directed to put together the timeline. He stated that he sent the timeline to Page for "her and Baker" and FBI executive leadership "consumption."

As for the contents of the timeline, we asked Strzok about the September 29 entry of "[n]o numbers/volume available" and how that squared with his September 28 text message to Page that stated there were "hundreds of thousands of emails" on the laptop. Strzok replied:

Because this is specific to the Huma Midyear stuff. I think when they gave that volume, and I don't know what, again, I wasn't there, my

301

read of that text is that New York said they had in total hundreds of thousands of emails, Anthony's, Huma's, who-knows-who. But that the sum total were hundreds of thousands. And within that, there was more than the de minimis amount of Huma stuff. And that is a result of the conference call, they were able to say we don't know how many we have.

We also asked Strzok about the October 19 entry and why he wrote that it was approximately October 19 when NYO had completed "carving" the laptop.[170] As noted in Section 9.IV above, processing of the Weiner laptop was, in fact, completed by NYO around October 4 and the Sensitive But Unclassified attachment was observed by NYO around the same time. Strzok stated, "It was roughly that time table. And I don't know how I arrived at the 19th, if there was a notation that clearly indicated that on or prior to that date, something had come in."

We asked Strzok to respond to the accusation that this inaction on the Weiner laptop was a politically motivated attempt to bury information that could negatively impact the chances of Hillary Clinton in the election. Strzok responded:

> No, I'd say quite the opposite.... I think every act was taken with an objective reason to say, okay, here is why we did it, and why it was prioritized the way it was.... [The Midyear SSA] and [FBI Attorney 1] were the ones engaging with New York. You had agents and AUSAs up in New York who were involved in pursuing it, that ultimately, you know, we sat there, and we decided when we found out what was there that we needed to get the case and reopen the case. And if you want to pitch in the conspiracy perspective, everything we pushed to do, the Clinton side is going to say, what you did absolutely killed my chances at the election. So, you know, pick it. Which is your conspiracy?... [I]t angers me because there is not, if there were bias, and there is not bias, if there were bias...it didn't result in actions which would be indicative of bias.

VI.   Concerns of Weiner Case Agent and Conversation with SDNY AUSAs on October 19

As early as October 3, the case agent assigned to the Weiner investigation expressed concern that no action appeared to be occurring with regard to the Clinton emails discovered on the Weiner laptop. He began documenting these concerns in contemporaneous emails and also discussed his concerns with his supervisor and the SDNY AUSAs assigned to the Weiner investigation. In an October 3 email, the case agent stated that a "significant number" of the emails on the Weiner laptop "appeared to be between Huma Abedin and Hillary Clinton (the latter who appears to have used a number of different email addresses)." The case agent also noted in that email that he was "obviously" unable to "review any emails

---

[170] "Data carving" is typically the last phase of processing an electronic device and involves recovering files and data that have been either deleted or no longer contain complete metadata.

to which Anthony Weiner is not a party (such as emails between Ms. Abedin and Mrs. Clinton)." The October 3 email was serialized and inserted into the Weiner case file in Sentinel, the FBI's case management system, on October 5.

The case agent told the OIG that no one had contacted him about the laptop and, as the case agent, "the only person who has the authority to release that laptop's image is me." The case agent explained his growing concern by stating:

> The crickets I was hearing was really making me uncomfortable because something was going to come crashing down.... And my understanding, which is uninformed because...I didn't work the Hillary Clinton matter. My understanding at the time was I am telling you people I have private Hillary Clinton emails, number one, and BlackBerry messages, number two. I'm telling you that we have potentially 10 times the volume that Director Comey said we had on the record. Why isn't anybody here? Like, if I'm the supervisor of any CI squad in Seattle and I hear about this, I'm getting on with headquarters and saying, hey, some agent working child porn here may have [Hillary Clinton] emails. Get your ass on the phone, call [the case agent], and get a copy of that drive, because that's how you should be. And that nobody reached out to me within, like, that night, I still to this day I don't understand what the hell went wrong.

The case agent told us that he scheduled a meeting on October 19 with the two SDNY AUSAs assigned to the Weiner investigation because he felt like he had nowhere else to turn. He described AUSA 1, the lead prosecutor, as a friend. He added, "I felt like if I went there and [AUSA 1] got the attention of Preet Bharara, maybe they'd kick some of these lazy FBI folks in the butt and get them moving." The case agent stated that he told the AUSAs in detail about the emails he had seen between Clinton and Abedin. He continued:

> And I told her, I'm a little scared here. I don't know what to do because I'm not political. Like I don't care who wins this election, but this is going to make us look really, really horrible. And it could ruin this case, too. And...I said the thing that also bothers me is that Comey's testimony is inaccurate. And as a big admirer of the guy, and I think he's a straight shooter, I wanted to, I felt like he needed to know, like, we got this. And I didn't know if he did.

The AUSAs both told us that the case agent appeared to be very stressed and worried that somehow he would be blamed in the end if no action was taken. AUSA 1 stated that the case agent worried that the information relating to the Clinton emails had not been provided to the right people and AUSA 2 observed that the case agent "was getting, for lack of a better word, paranoid that, like, somebody was not acting appropriately, somebody was trying to bury this."

VII. SDNY Response to Weiner Case Agent Concerns

A.   SDNY Internal Discussions on October 20

On October 20, 2016, the AUSAs met with their supervisors at SDNY and informed them of their conversation with the Weiner case agent. The AUSAs stated that they told their supervisors the substantive information reported by the case agent, the case agent's concerns that no one at the FBI had expressed interest in this information, and their concern that the case agent was stressed out and might act out in some way.

SDNY Deputy U.S. Attorney Joon Kim said that after being briefed on this issue and discussing it with U.S. Attorney Preet Bharara and other supervisors in the office, SDNY leadership made the decision to call the Office of the Deputy Attorney General (ODAG) about this information. As Kim told us, "I remember our discussing it and saying, look, it's not really our business. And, but maybe to be safe we should reach out and call."

Bharara also recalled being briefed on the case agent's concerns and being told that the discovery of the Clinton emails had been "reported up the chain of command at the FBI." He stated that SDNY recognized that they had no involvement in the Clinton email server case and "wanted to stay in our lane." Nevertheless, given the concerns and "agitation" of the case agent, Bharara said that he and the SDNY leadership team decided to contact ODAG in case "something had fallen through the cracks."

B.   SDNY Calls to ODAG and NSD on October 21

The following day, October 21, Kim reached out to ODAG about this issue. Kim told us that he was unsure about whom to call because SDNY did not know which office had handled the Clinton email server investigation. Kim called the Associate Deputy Attorney General (ADAG) who was SDNY's primary point of contact in ODAG. Kim stated that the ADAG told him to contact DAAG George Toscas in NSD. The ADAG told us that she vaguely recalled a conversation where she put Kim and Toscas in touch with each other to discuss an issue arising out of the Weiner case. The ADAG stated that PADAG Axelrod "wanted me to make sure that SDNY and George from NSD connected directly so that whatever it was that SDNY was doing would be coordinated with whatever it was NSD was doing." The ADAG told us that Axelrod "check[ed] in with me a number of times" to ensure Kim and Toscas had connected. At 7:08 p.m. that evening, the ADAG emailed Axelrod, "One last FYI—I also spoke with George [Toscas] earlier to give heads up and then to Joon [Kim]. They have since connected and will take it from there." Axelrod recalled that SDNY contacted the ADAG about the presence of Clinton emails on the Weiner laptop. Axelrod told us that this call "set off alarm bells" and he wanted to make sure the information was immediately provided to Toscas and NSD.[171]

---

[171] Axelrod also recalled hearing about the Weiner laptop issue at some point prior to this call. He told us that he thought SDNY had called the ADAG at an earlier point to inform ODAG that some of

Kim did not recall the specifics of his conversation with Toscas, but stated that he generally gave Toscas an overview of the Weiner investigation and told him he wanted to make sure those connected with the Clinton email server investigation were aware of the information the case agent had found. Toscas told us the information provided by Kim was much more substantive than the prior information that NSD had received from McCabe on October 3. Toscas described his call with Kim as "the first time that I actually got information like something you could actually think through and analyze." Toscas's notes from the call stated:

> 10/21/16, 3:50 p.m.: Anthony Weiner. N.C. 15 yr-old → asked her to send video/photos. Got his laptop/phone etc. + got SW for child exploitation → FBI following normal protocol (to/from images). Although its his laptop, his wife apparently used it. 100K's of her emails some to/from HRC.

> Told [NSD Prosecutor 1] to tell Pete [Strzok] + DHL [Laufman] 10/21 4:05 p.m.

According to Toscas, his notes represent in essence the entirety of the information he received from Kim. In our interview, Toscas specifically commented on the fact that he was told by Kim that there were hundreds of thousands of Abedin's emails on this laptop, some of which were to and from Clinton. Toscas stated that he immediately called NSD Prosecutor 1 and told him to contact Strzok and Laufman. Toscas explained that he meant Prosecutor 1 should tell them "that there's this issue and we're going to be getting together to talk…and get more information on it."

At 4:04 p.m. on October 21, Kim emailed the SDNY prosecutors and leadership to inform them that he had just spoken with Toscas. AUSA 2 then called the Weiner case agent to let him know that SDNY had raised this issue with Main Justice. The case agent emailed AUSA 2 that evening, "Thanks for the call. I feel much better about it. Not to sound sappy, but I appreciate you guys understanding how uneasy I felt about the situation." The case agent also emailed his SSA and another agent at 5:51 p.m.:

> Just got a call from SDNY. [The AUSAs] understood my concerns yesterday about the nature of the stuff I have on Weiner computer (ie, that I will be scapegoated if it comes out that the FBI had this stuff). They appreciated that I was in a tight spot and spoke to their chain of command who agreed.

> So they called down to DOJ, who will apparently now make a decision on what to do. This is a good thing according to SDNY because it means we (FBI C20) went above and beyond to make known that the material was of potential concern. It is out of my hands now so now I know I did the right thing by speaking up.

Abedin's emails had been found on Weiner's laptop. Axelrod stated that this information "didn't trigger any alarm bells."

SDNY probably will talk to crim management at NYO to inform them that DOJ is aware and handling. I feel much better about this now. But I wanted you to have a heads up in case [the ASAC] called you.

At 4:41 p.m. that same day, Kim called the A/SAC to inform him of the call to ODAG. The A/SAC's notes stated, "Joon Kim – Weiner – looking at the computer – ton of emails related to Huma that we are not looking at. SDNY reached out to DOJ and advised there are a lot of emails between Huma and Hillary and others but that we are doing nothing and have no basis to do that." The A/SAC told us that he was "glad" that Kim had made the call, explaining that "I've been an agent for 21 years, so I knew that this was something I would try to get probable cause for."

C.   SDNY Memo on October 21

On October 21, the SDNY Chief Counsel began drafting a memorandum summarizing SDNY's involvement with the issue of the Clinton emails on the Weiner laptop. Bharara told us that he instructed the Chief Counsel to write the memorandum in order to "put down, precisely, and with a hundred percent accuracy, you know, what we did, what the timeline was, and why we did what we did." Bharara told us that he decided to take this step because "things seemed unusual to" him and he anticipated that SDNY would be asked questions about this in the future. Kim provided a similar explanation for the memorandum, stating that SDNY leadership "concluded at this point that we should have something in the document, either email or memo, that laid out the chronology as, to make sure that if people did ask that, you know, we had it, we had it down on paper."

The memorandum was dated October 21, 2016, and the Chief Counsel emailed the memorandum to the relevant SDNY personnel on October 24. We have excerpted the portions most relevant to our review below:

> ...[The Weiner search warrant] did not provide authority to search for evidence of any other crimes [beyond the child exploitation offenses detailed above]. We advised the [Weiner] agents of the proper scope of the search warrant and they understood the scope.

> ...[The case agent's] search of emails stored on the computer apparently recovered in excess of 700,000 emails. In order to stay within the scope authorized by the warrant, [the case agent] sorted the emails recovered by sender. In performing that sort, we understand that header information for all of the emails was visible, and he noticed a very large number of emails that appear to be between Huma Abedin and Hillary Clinton. [The case agent] believes that, although Weiner's counsel provided the computer to us, the computer was used by both Anthony Weiner and Huma Abedin.

> We understand that the FBI agents in our case will not be reviewing the contents of the Abedin-Clinton emails because it would not be appropriate to do so under the search warrant issued in support of our child exploitation investigation. The agents, however, have reported

306

the existence of the emails up their chain of command at FBI to enable other agents to take any action that is appropriate for their cases.

Because we understand that another component of DOJ may be conducting an investigation related to Hillary Clinton's emails, we have advised ODAG and George Toscas at NSD, who we're told is the most senior career prosecutor involved in investigations of Hillary Clinton and the Clinton Foundation, of the existence of the emails so that they can take any steps that may be appropriate in their investigation, including, if proper, making an application for the content of potentially hundreds of thousands of emails that are outside the scope of the warrant in our case, which authorized a search only for evidence of child exploitation crimes.[172]

VIII. DOJ and FBI Response to SDNY Notification

As mentioned above, Toscas called Prosecutor 1 on October 21, after his phone call with Kim, and told Prosecutor 1 to notify Strzok and Laufman about the issue. Laufman stated that he could not recall the date he first heard about the Weiner laptop, but told us that he recalled Prosecutor 1 coming into his office and telling him that he had gotten a call from SDNY. Laufman said Prosecutor 1 stated that the prosecutors on the Weiner case told him that material on Weiner's laptop "appeared on its face potentially to relate to the Clinton investigation."

As discussed previously, until Prosecutor 1 called Strzok on October 21 to see if he was aware of the Weiner laptop issue, no one from the FBI had spoken with anyone from the Midyear prosecution team to inform them about the issue. The only contact that occurred prior to that regarding the laptop was the call previously described from McCabe to McCord on October 3.

A.   Prosecutor 1-Strzok Call on October 21

At 5:41 p.m. on October 21, Prosecutor 1 sent an email to Strzok entitled "Call." The email stated, "Pete, George Toscas called me and wanted me to pass along some information to you as soon as I could. Let me know if you have a couple of minutes to talk. I left a message on your cell. I am about to head out and can be reached on my cell. Thanks."

Strzok and Page exchanged the following text messages on the evening of October 21. The sender of each text message is identified after the timestamp.

> 6:49 p.m., Strzok: "Also, work-wise, [Prosecutor 1] called b/c Toscas now aware NY has hrc-huma emails via weiner invest. Told he [sic] we knew. Wanted to know our thoughts on getting it. George

---

[172] After reviewing a draft of the report, Toscas asked that the OIG clarify that he was not involved in the investigation of the Clinton Foundation.

[Toscas] wanted to ensure info got to Andy [McCabe]. I told Bill [Priestap]."

6:55 p.m., Page: "I'm sure Andy is aware, but whatever."

Strzok told us he had a conversation at some point with either Toscas or Prosecutor 1, and thought that the conversation with Prosecutor 1 referenced in the text message was likely that conversation. Strzok told us that he had not talked about the Weiner laptop issue with Prosecutor 1 previously and he believed this was his first discussion with the Midyear prosecutors about the Weiner laptop. Strzok stated that Prosecutor 1 asked if Strzok was aware of "the potential Huma stuff up in the Weiner laptop in New York." Strzok said that when he responded affirmatively, Prosecutor 1 asked, "And, you know, what are you doing about it, and, you know, kind of what do we need to do, and kind of the path forward on it." Page told us that she did not remember any of the specifics about this text message.

Prosecutor 1 stated that Toscas told him "the basic facts" about the Weiner laptop and told Prosecutor 1 to call Strzok. Prosecutor 1 stated that he did not "recall getting much detail" from Toscas. Prosecutor 1 told us that the October 21 phone call from Toscas was the first time he was informed of the potential presence of Midyear material on the Weiner laptop.

B.   FBI Leadership Knowledge of SDNY Notification on October 21

We asked other FBI officials about the call by SDNY to ODAG. McCabe, Priestap, and Rybicki told us that they were unaware of the call. McCabe also said he did not recall any discussion with Page about the Weiner laptop at this time. We asked McCabe if he we was aware of the fact that the Weiner case agent had expressed concern that nothing was happening with the Clinton emails discovered on the Weiner laptop. McCabe stated that he was not aware of that and told us he found it "disturbing."

Comey did not recall being briefed about either the SDNY call to ODAG or NSD contacting the FBI about the Weiner laptop issue. Comey told us, though, that the fact of these communications is not something that would necessarily need to be briefed to the Director. We asked Comey—looking only at the Strzok-Page text messages excerpted above—if he found it concerning that McCabe, Priestap, Strzok, Page, Toscas, and Prosecutor 1 were all apparently aware of the presence of "hrc-huma emails" on the Weiner laptop by October 21 and no one bothered to inform him. Comey replied:

> [T]he fact that who these people are doesn't matter, but if there's something that I found hugely significant on the 27th, if I was in a position to know that before then, then I should have been informed earlier. And like I said, honest to God I can't remember being informed before that.

C. Toscas Asks McCabe About Weiner Laptop on October 24[173]

McCabe told the OIG about a passing interaction with Toscas after a morning Attorney General briefing that he had "towards the end of October." McCabe stated:

> I wouldn't even characterize it as a discussion, but a comment, I think, that I think that George Toscas mentioned to me on the tail end of a morning AG brief, like hey, whatever, whatever happened to that thing with the laptop in New York or whatever. And I remember thinking, like, I got to, oh, I don't know. Let me find out. I've got to follow up on that.

McCabe also stated:

> I think he thought, like...you should ask about this. You should take a look at this thing. Like, or what, what are you guys thinking you want to do with this kind of thing was, was how he asked about it. And so he was clearly bringing it to my attention because he wanted to make sure that I was tracking it, and weighing in on it.

McCabe stated that this interaction with Toscas caused him to follow up with the team on the Weiner laptop issue and also to call Mary McCord at NSD. McCabe stated that all of this occurred "right around the same time" and "maybe even the same day." He stated that "this all is what compels me to talk to the Director and to tell him that we need to have a meeting about this." We discuss McCabe's call to McCord and his conversation with Comey in more detail below.

McCabe noted during our interview that briefings for the Attorney General were typically held three times a week on Mondays, Wednesdays, and Fridays. McCabe's calendar contained entries for an "AG/OGA Brief" at 9.a.m. on both Monday, October 24 and Wednesday, October 26. As noted above, Kim's call to Toscas occurred in the afternoon of Friday, October 21, and therefore after the usual time for the morning AG briefing. Also, as noted below, McCabe spoke to McCord on Tuesday, October 25. Based on this timing and McCabe's testimony that he spoke with Toscas prior to calling McCord, we believe the conversation with Toscas occurred on Monday, October 24.[174]

Toscas described this interaction as "just a passing comment at the end of our [Attorney General] briefing." Toscas stated that either he or someone else

---

[173] The day before, Sunday, October 23, the Wall Street Journal published online its story about McCabe's wife and her prior run for elective office in Virginia in 2015, including donations to her campaign by entities connected to then Governor McAuliffe. The story raised questions about McCabe's participation in Clinton-related investigations, which we discuss in detail in Chapter Thirteen.

[174] According to both Comey and McCabe's Outlook calendars, they met at 9:30 a.m. on Monday, October 24 for a "Weekly Update." Rybicki was also scheduled to attend this meeting. Their calendars showed that this meeting occurred immediately after the Monday morning briefing for the Attorney General where we believe Toscas and McCabe spoke. Neither Comey nor McCabe said that they recalled any discussion of the Weiner laptop at this 9:30 a.m. meeting.

asked McCabe, "[H]ey, what's happening...what's the next step with respect to these, you know, what we learned about the stuff on the laptop." According to Toscas, McCabe stated that "the [Midyear] team was going to be either sent or had been sent or tasked with doing that."

Page also told us about this interaction between McCabe and Toscas. She said that Toscas's comment prompted McCabe to ask, "[H]ey, where are we on the Weiner stuff?" Page described this a catalyst for the Midyear team to reengage on the issue of the Weiner laptop.

Strzok's contemporaneous notes from October 25 included a reference to this conversation between Toscas and McCabe on October 24. The notes stated, "Toscas saw Andy: What's the <u>Bureau</u> doing? DD spoke w/Mary McCord." (Emphasis in original). We asked Strzok about these notes. Strzok stated:

> [M]y recollection is that on this date, or whenever it was, at some point, Toscas runs into the Deputy and says, hey, there are, and I think this might have been, I heard there are potentially emails having to do with Clinton on the case up in New York. What are you guys doing? And then, so, and I don't know if the, if the Deputy then spoke to Mary [McCord] about it or not. But in any event, Toscas prompting Andy, then caused Andy to ask Bill [Priestap], hey, what's going on? Where are we with regard to that process? What are we, what do we need to do to look at it? Are you engaged, essentially? And get an update. And so Bill then brings that back down and relays that to me.

McCabe described himself as "concerned" when the Weiner laptop came to his attention again and said that he asked the team to explain why he had not been updated. McCabe stated:

> Ultimately, when I got the feedback on the status, what I was told was that when the team went up the first time because of their legal limitations they, they really weren't able to dig into the thing, to make an assessment of what was there. And so therefore they couldn't recommend to us what we should do with it. And so that some, they had to go back to the district, either get a new search warrant or modify the previous search warrant, and that's essentially what had taken place over the intervening time.

McCabe said he would have expected the team to report this information to him directly rather than getting asked about it by Department personnel. We asked McCabe who was responsible for following up on the Weiner laptop. McCabe told us his understanding was that Strzok "was actually doing it" and Priestap would have had an oversight role. In fact, as discussed previously, nobody on the FBI Midyear team had taken any steps to follow up on the laptop, including steps to obtain legal authority to review its contents, after they learned about it in late September.

D. Call between McCabe, Sweeney, and NYO Criminal SAC on October 24

NYO ADIC Sweeney's Outlook calendar contained the following entry for October 24: "7:30 pm-7:45 pm Telcal w/DD and [the incoming NYO Criminal SAC]." At the time of the call, the SAC was transitioning from an FBI job in Washington, D.C. to the Criminal SAC job in NYO. Although not reflected in his calendar entry, Sweeney told us he was "pretty sure" that during this call he mentioned to McCabe that SDNY had called Main Justice about the Weiner matter. Sweeney stated that he did not recall McCabe's response to this information.

The SAC told us that Sweeney called him at some point during the week of October 24 while McCabe was giving him a ride home. The SAC told us that he almost immediately put Sweeney on speaker phone and the three discussed several topics. The SAC continued, "I don't remember specifics. But I do remember talking about, it did come up regarding the Weiner laptop." The SAC stated that he also believed that it "wasn't a first impression," meaning it did not seem like the first time Sweeney and McCabe had discussed the Weiner laptop.

McCabe told us that he had no recollection of this phone call.

IX. Reengagement of FBI Headquarters and the Midyear Team on the Weiner Laptop

Beginning on October 25, both McCabe and the FBI Midyear team took a renewed interest in the issue of the Weiner laptop. We discuss this renewed interest below, including conversations by McCabe with both the Department and Comey about the laptop, and reengagement by the Midyear team.

A. McCabe Phone Call with McCord on October 25

McCabe and McCord both told us that they discussed the Weiner laptop in a phone call in late October, though neither could recall the specific date. McCord provided contemporaneous notes from the call, but they were undated. Page also provided notes that referenced this call and her notes suggest the conversation occurred on October 25. Given the timeline of other events, we believe October 25 is the date on which this conversation occurred.

McCabe stated that he wanted to update McCord on the status of the Weiner laptop and tell her that "we have a problem here that we need to deal with." McCabe said he thought that he would have asked McCord about "scope of the warrant issues," although he told us he did not remember many details about the conversation.

Page's contemporaneous notes from October 25 included McCord's name and phone number, and stated: "Anthony Weiner — ADIC NY – where are we on this? □ Not sure we can legally look at the material — Mary McCord ~~needs to~~ will find out where it is, status of the request."

311

McCord stated that McCabe told her that NYO had found "many hundreds of thousands of emails from Huma Abedin to Secretary Clinton" on the laptop. According to McCord, McCabe stated that the Midyear team had planned to review, but SDNY told them to hold off while they examined the legality of doing that under the Weiner search warrant. McCord's notes from the phone call included entries that stated, "mid-year team to try to determine if duplicative or new" and "Spoke to Sweeney last night." McCord told us that the entry about Sweeney referred to a conversation McCabe stated that he had with Sweeney the prior night.

McCord told us that she spoke with Toscas after the call with McCabe. According to McCord, Toscas stated that "SDNY had not shopped a search warrant on the laptop" and that the Midyear team was "getting together tomorrow to decide whether they want to search it and if they have probable cause to get a warrant." Toscas told us that he did not recall a conversation between McCabe and McCord, but added that "it seems like something that would be in the ordinary course of what happened and would not stand out to me." We also showed McCord's notes to Toscas. Toscas commented that he did not know what the word "shopped" could mean in this context.

B. Comey, McCabe, and Sweeney Discuss the Weiner Laptop on October 25

On October 25 from 2:30 p.m. to 4:30 p.m., numerous FBI executives participated in one of Director Comey's Quarterly Strategy Review sessions. According to Sweeney, who participated in the session by phone, at the conclusion of the discussions, McCabe asked him to stay on the line. Sweeney told us that only he, McCabe, and Comey remained.[175]

Sweeney's notes from the October 25 discussion stated:

4:15 to 4:30 p.m. – SVTC – Short discussion w/D/DD/ADD following main SVTC re: [Clinton Foundation] matter. Follow-up following Strategy Briefing. Brief update re: Weiner investigation; overt legal process and ability to get fed SW for computer. DD – need to move forward and request action consistent with DOJ guidelines/election.

Sweeney described the discussion:

And then when the room clears, [McCabe] starts talking about the Weiner laptop.... [I]t goes into an explanation of who Weiner is, Huma Abedin's husband. She's the chief of staff. This is how these emails would likely be there. And that gets into a conversation about authority, like we can't look at this stuff, and we're not doing.

According to Sweeney, the conversation then turned to the NYO Clinton Foundation investigation.

---

[175] Sweeney told us that he did not recall Bowdich participating in this discussion despite the "ADD" notation in his calendar. Bowdich likewise told us he did not recall this discussion.

Sweeney stated that he did not remember McCabe going into detail about what had been discovered. For example, Sweeney said that he did not recall McCabe providing the total number of emails on the laptop, although Sweeney stated McCabe may have mentioned that a large volume of emails had been discovered. According to Sweeney, McCabe stated that the Midyear team was "going to look at" the laptop and "get a search warrant." We asked Sweeney about Comey's reaction to the discussion of the Weiner laptop. Sweeney described Comey as "just absorbing the information."

That evening, according to Sweeney's notes, he made calls to the NYO A/SAC, incoming NYO Criminal SAC, the Criminal Investigative Division AD, and Rybicki. The notes also included an entry for a follow-up call to McCabe. Each of these entries noted a discussion related to Sweeney's earlier call with Comey and McCabe and the Clinton Foundation investigation. The entries for the calls with Rybicki and the Criminal Investigative Division AD also mentioned the Weiner investigation.

McCabe told us that he did not recall the discussion with Comey and Sweeney about the Weiner laptop and Clinton Foundation investigation. With regard to the Weiner laptop discussion, McCabe stated, "[T]he only conversation I recollect with the Director, it probably took place on the 26th, was telling him you need to have a meeting on this tomorrow. And as I said before, I remember that as being a one-on-one in his office." Comey said that he did not recall the discussion with McCabe and Sweeney about the Weiner laptop and Clinton Foundation.

C. Midyear Team Emails on October 25

Strzok and FBI Attorney 1 exchanged the followings emails on October 25. The subject line of the email was "Weiner Material" and the sender of each email is identified after the timestamp.

> 2:55 p.m., Strzok: "Sorry to bother you, DoJ called [McCabe] looking for status of our potential review of the huma-hrc emails. Where/with who is that decision now? What would we need to do to get a decision? Thanks, Pete".

> 3:31 p.m., FBI Attorney 1: "Is this the NY search warrant issue? We were waiting for NYO to get back to us about the volume of Huma related emails on the devices."

> 3:35 p.m., Strzok: "Yes. I thought they said thousands? But I have no idea who I heard that from. Who at NYO is supposed to tell us?"

> 3:38 p.m., FBI Attorney 1: "I'miss [sic] not sure. [The Midyear SSA] was working with the NYO SSA. Thousands? I hadn't heard any numbers."

> 3:45 p.m., Strzok: "OK I'll ask [the Midyear SSA]".

This exchange is immediately followed by an email exchange between Strzok, FBI Attorney 1, and the Midyear SSA entitled "Weiner emails." Again, the sender of each email is identified after the timestamp.

> 3:47 p.m., Strzok: "[H]ave you gotten an idea how many Huma-HRC emails are in the Weiner stuff? Has popped up on people's radars again".

> 4:34 p.m., Midyear SSA: "NY did not have an estimate of the number of emails during our lync call on 9/29/2016. I have not heard back from NY but can contact [the A/SAC] or ASAC...if needed for an update. [FBI Attorney 1] – do you know the status of the SW and whether we can review the emails?"

> 4:58 p.m., FBI Attorney 1: "They never did send me the actual SW, but based on they're [sic] representations, we won't be able to review the emails without additional process or consent."

> 5:00 p.m., Strzok: "Yes please contact NY for #s. Thanks".

We asked Strzok, FBI Attorney 1, and the SSA about this exchange. We told Strzok that this exchange suggested that nothing had happened since the September 29 call. Strzok replied, "That's right. That's my assumption I believe. Yep." FBI Attorney 1 stated that Strzok's email was the first time she recalled hearing about the Weiner laptop issue since September 29. The Midyear SSA agreed that this was probably his first contact about the issue since September 29.

We asked Strzok whether any action would have occurred without the Department notification to McCabe. Strzok stated:

> Probably not. I mean, at some point, yes. At some point, there would have been a, God, what happened to that follow-up.... [T]his caused that to happen. There certainly would have been action. Whether that was the 25th or November 8th, or whenever, I'm not sure when that would have occurred.

However, Strzok emphasized that, at this point, there "was no indication on anybody's radar that this was going to result in a notification to Congress." Instead, Strzok stated that this was something the Midyear team would have to pursue, but he did not think it had any relevance to the election.

The Midyear SSA told us that the reason this was "coming on people's radar again" was because NYO "was saying, hey, once again, we've got this stuff. What do you want us to do with it?" The Midyear SSA stated that he reached out to NYO after receiving this email. He recalled that "New York was somewhat frustrated."

X. Events Leading to the Decision to Seek a Search Warrant

In this section, we discuss the meetings, discussions, and emails that preceded the October 27 briefing where Comey authorized the Midyear team to seek a search warrant for the Weiner laptop.

314

A.   Midyear-NYO-SDNY Call on October 26

At 2:30 p.m. on October 26, Midyear FBI personnel, Midyear prosecutors, NYO, and SDNY participated in a conference call about the Weiner laptop. The highest ranking participants for each group on the call were Strzok, Toscas, the NYO A/SAC, and Kim.

The NYO A/SAC, ASAC, SSA, and Weiner case agent all participated in the call. This was the first time that the Weiner case agent had spoken directly with anyone associated with the Midyear investigation. The case agent told us that he felt he was asked questions about information that he had already reported up the chain of command in September. He stated:

> They were asking questions that I had already repeatedly answered in other calls. In other words, people were asking what domains are you seeing? How many emails are you seeing? What do you think you're seeing? Who are they to, who are they from? What are the domains? Oh, we have that domain? What years? Like, questions that we, I had been asked and either had answered preliminarily, and then we became uncomfortable legally searching for those answers. But these were things that were known to me and had been made known above me for weeks.

The Weiner case agent stated that "the only thing that was new" was that others on the call asked him to speculate on what he had seen. According to the case agent, he stated, "Based on the number of emails, we could have every email that Huma and Hillary ever sent each other. It's possible, given the pure volume, it's possible."

The NYO SSA described the call as "just basically discussions and information about...potentially what...was there, which we still didn't know because we hadn't looked at anything." The A/SAC thought the call was "matter-of-fact" and said it was the first time they were questioned by an NSD lawyer. According to the A/SAC's notes, NYO briefed that there were 675,000 emails on the laptop spanning a time period from 2006 to 2016, and stated that there "appears to be blackberry messages" on the laptop.

The FBI's Midyear team told us that they learned important new information on the call.[176] Strzok described it as "the triggering event" and FBI Attorney 1 stated that this was the "call where it was crystallized to me what was on the laptop." Strzok, FBI Attorney 1, and the Lead Analyst each cited two important pieces of information provided by NYO on the call.[177] First, the presence of a large

---

[176] Except for the September 29 call with NYO, the Midyear case agents and analysts had limited knowledge of and involvement with the Weiner laptop until after Comey's October 28 letter to Congress. Our references to the "FBI Midyear team" in this Chapter generally refer to the leadership of the team, including Strzok, the Midyear SSA, and FBI Attorney 1.

[177] In comments provided to the OIG after reviewing a draft of this report, the Lead Analyst stated that he believed the October 26 call "was the first time [he] had ever personally heard the details related to the" Weiner laptop.

volume of emails on the Weiner laptop, particularly the potential for a large number of @clintonemail.com emails. Second, the indication that the "missing emails," meaning emails from Clinton's first three months as Secretary of State, could be present on the laptop. Strzok explained that this was the most important factor and he did not believe that the Midyear team knew about the potential presence of the BlackBerry data earlier. Strzok added, "We need[ed] to try and get this because this is, potentially would alter, would change our understanding of the investigative conclusions that we arrived at in July."

We asked Strzok what he was specifically told about the BlackBerry backups and if he thought these might be Blackberry backups for Clinton. Strzok stated:

> [I]t wasn't Clinton's backups. It was the sense that it was Huma's backups, and that Huma was frequently used, my recollection, as kind of a proxy for the, for Secretary Clinton. So if people wanted to get something to Clinton, they'd email it to Huma and say please print for the Secretary. And she would, she was a gatekeeper in that way. And, you know, would print it out and then take it to the Secretary.

> I don't, my recollection is that we certainly saw the domain. And that, the domain, because I think it was, and again, I'm, if I'm wrong forgive me. Att.Blackberry.net I think was that domain they used for the first three months, and we saw that on there. I don't know if we had the granularity of detail to say Huma's account on that domain in that time frame. I don't know if we had that granularity. But I do know we had, I think, that domain in the span, coupling with the kind of overall volume that we thought there was a reasonable likelihood that, that it would be in there.

When asked how this information differed from the information presented on the September 29 call, Strzok, who did not participate in the September 29 call, stated that his understanding from the Midyear SSA and FBI Attorney 1, who were on that call, was that NYO did not have "the numbers" or "the volume of domains." Strzok said that he also thought that NYO had only provided preliminary data on the September call and "they weren't quite sure what they had yet." Strzok added that he knew NYO "couldn't review it because it was outside the scope of their warrant."

FBI Attorney 1 told us, "I don't...even think they discussed any of that stuff [on the September 29 call]. They certainly said there was some clintonemail.com, but again, like I said, that we were finding, people had clintonemail.com emails all over the place. There was nothing with this sort of certainty that this is what was on there." The Midyear SSA stated that NYO provided "numbers" on this call, which he believed had not been provided previously.

Page told us that as a result of the conference call "we now understand that the Huma emails are of a volume that it could be meaningful and that there could be meaningfully new evidence that we have not previously seen in other materials we had reviewed." She added that the "volume of emails" coupled with the presence of a "BlackBerry backup" were the two most important new facts that came out of this call. Page's notes from the call were entitled "Good news, in a bad news way (MYE)." She explained this heading by stating:

[M]y good news in a bad news way is a reflection of like, well, more evidence is always good news. It might either change our decision or outcome or further substantiate the outcome we reached. In a bad news way because, like, I cannot believe we are, we are here. We are doing this again on October 26th. Like, oh, my goodness.

FBI Attorney 1 told us that the decision to obtain a search warrant was made either on the call or shortly after it. FBI Attorney 1 noted that Toscas was on the call and "seemed to be on board" with the idea that the Midyear team needed to get the Weiner laptop. FBI Attorney 1 added that she was "surprised" that the Department left the call "talking about getting a search warrant." She explained that she was surprised because it "definitely was...more aggressive than they had been before," but thought this may have been due to "the time pressure."

Prosecutor 2 told us that this call was when she first learned about the Weiner laptop. Prosecutor 2 stated that the prosecutors asked numerous questions to NYO and SDNY personnel "to try to figure out what they knew about the emails and, and about the devices, so we knew what the scope of like what we could look at." Toscas stated that the information he learned in late October about the Weiner laptop, including information provided on this call, was markedly different than what he had been told McCabe had informed NSD about in early October. Toscas described the information provided earlier in October as "totally off base" and he told us that he attributed this discrepancy to a "garble," or miscommunication.

B.   Briefing of McCabe on October 26

Page told us that the team briefed McCabe about the information from the conference call on the evening of October 26. Page stated that McCabe indicated that "we're going to need to reopen. This, this is significant. Or we're going to need to at least seek a search warrant to sort of look at this material." Page stated, "We informed the Deputy Director, and he says, yeah, we've got to get this in front of the Director tomorrow. And so that gets scheduled for the next day...[to] tell him what we found and what the team thinks, which is certainly we need to go get a warrant for this information." On the morning of October 27, at 6:10 a.m., Baker sent Page an email entitled "Follow up" and asked her if she had talked to McCabe yet and whether "[McCabe] talked to [Comey]?" Page replied at 6:19 a.m., stating, "Yes I did talk to Andy, but he did not connect with [Comey]. Andy sent him an email this morning asking that he get a briefing from the MYE team." We describe McCabe's email and the events of October 27 below.

Strzok said that he thought that he and possibly the Lead Analyst and FBI Attorney 1 briefed McCabe after the conference call. Strzok stated that he explained the scope of what NYO possessed, why that was important, and why the Midyear team thought they should review the material. FBI Attorney 1 said that she recalled briefing "the executives" about what they had learned on the conference call and the need to "look into this" using process.

Priestap told us that he did not recall this briefing with McCabe, but stated that he would normally be present for such a briefing. Priestap stated, "Very rarely would my team be there if I wasn't there."

McCabe told us that he could not recall who informed him of the substance of the conference call with SDNY and NYO, but stated it would have been some combination of Strzok, Priestap, the Lead Analyst, Page, and FBI Attorney 1. When asked what he was told, McCabe stated:

> The only thing I remember is like we had at that point confirmed that, yes, there is no doubt what appears to be relevant email for us on this laptop. So the question then becomes like do we go full-bore into another round of exploitation along the lines of what we had already done in Midyear? How do we handle this thing? And then the implications of like notification and, and everything that they ended up struggling with the next day.

McCabe said that he did not recall any mention of seeing domains or emails associated with a BlackBerry device. We asked McCabe what was relayed that was not known in late September. McCabe replied:

> I think they had looked a little bit deeper than just the tos and froms and could actually say, like, you know, I seem to remember in the kind of legally restricted view it was just kind of a snapshot having looking, you know, at stuff and then determined they couldn't look further. That's how they had a sense of what was there. Now, at this point, we had done some sort of more extensive review to say, okay, yeah, it's like this number between these people, that sort of thing.

McCabe stated that he could not remember who had conducted this "more extensive review" and "was surprised" to learn that no one from the Midyear team reviewed the laptop until October 30. McCabe told us that he assumed someone on the Midyear team had reviewed the laptop "[b]ecause that's what I initially asked for." We asked McCabe if the fact that no one from Midyear had reviewed the laptop was an important fact that the team should have been brought to his attention. McCabe stated:

> I know that I asked them to go up there and look at it. And they had a...SVTC with the team I think the following day. I think at some point I learned that they had a SVTC early on in this. In this process rather than traveling up there. But I certainly expected that our folks would be in New York looking at what we had on that laptop.

We asked McCabe why this issue was coming back to the forefront on October 26 instead of sometime earlier. McCabe stated that it was "[b]ecause I started asking questions about it probably." We also asked McCabe what would have occurred if SDNY had not contacted ODAG and Toscas had not mentioned the

Weiner laptop to McCabe after the morning briefing. McCabe said he could not speculate on what would have happened if the facts were different, but stated that "it certainly is a good thing that George Toscas brought it to my attention." McCabe added, "Is it something that I should have been getting briefed upon as the month went on? Absolutely." McCabe told us that he had no idea why the topic of the Weiner laptop "wasn't making its way into the agenda for those regular meetings and interactions with [Page], [Strzok], Steinbach, the Director."

We also asked Baker why the Weiner laptop issue reemerged at this time. Baker stated:

> [M]y understanding, it was simply that senior managers thought that they had delegated this to the right people and that the issue was being worked. And that they would come back with a proposal about what to do, and that we took the, took our collective eyes off the ball, didn't pay attention to it, and when it came back and we were informed that it was not resolved, then it became a crisis. That's the best I can reconstruct for you.

C.   McCabe Recollection of Discussion with Comey on October 26

McCabe told us that he remembered mentioning the issue of the Weiner laptop to Comey twice. The first, as we described previously, McCabe stated was shortly after he learned of the laptop in late September. The second time McCabe stated was toward "the end of October"—McCabe estimated it was on October 26— when he sat down with Comey "one-on-one" in Comey's office. McCabe stated:

> I told him we need to have a meeting on this because now we have some, you know, some clarity on, on what's in this laptop. I specifically remember telling him, this is about that laptop we discussed a couple of weeks ago. I don't know if he remembered it.

McCabe stated that he did not remember Comey asking him about the Weiner laptop during the period between the two meetings. McCabe told us that he believed that second meeting with Comey "was truly the second time that we discussed it."

We asked McCabe to describe Comey's reaction to this second conversation about the Weiner laptop. McCabe stated:

> The best of my recollection it was just kind of an acknowledgement that, like, this was a very complicated issue that had a lot of problematic, you know, kind of downstream, there are all kinds of decision and issues that were related to this. It would be complicated and, and we need to figure it out.

McCabe said that he did not recall Comey mentioning the issue of congressional notification during this conversation.

319

As mentioned earlier, Comey told us that he dimly recalled being informed about the Weiner laptop in the "beginning of October." Comey stated that he did not remember hearing of the Weiner laptop again until McCabe emailed him on the morning of October 27.

D. McCabe Email to Comey on October 27

On October 27, at 5:20 a.m., McCabe sent an email to Comey entitled "MYR." Rybicki, Bowdich, and Page were cc'd on the email. It stated, "Boss, The MYR team has come across some additional actions they believe they need to take. I think we should probably gather today to discuss implications if you have any space on your calendar. I am happy to join by phone. Will push to Lisa and Jim to coordinate if you are good." At 7:13 a.m., Comey responded, "Copy."

McCabe told us that he felt the situation was "absolutely urgent" and that is why he proposed an October 27 meeting with Comey even though McCabe knew he would be out of town that day. When asked why it was urgent, McCabe stated that the situation was urgent because "it's been sitting around for three weeks," "it's important," and "it's getting closer to" the election. We questioned McCabe about the tone of the email, pointing out that phrases such as "we should probably gather today" and "if you have any space on your calendar" did not suggest urgency. McCabe disagreed, stating, "I mean, by me saying I think we should probably gather today, that's me saying this can't wait until tomorrow." McCabe told us that he assumed his second conversation with Comey, which he estimated was on October 26, "predated this email" and the email was simply the notification to Comey to set up the meeting.

We also asked Comey about the tone of McCabe's email and whether the phrasing suggested a lack of urgency. Comey replied:

> No, I didn't take it that way since he's emailing me at 5:20 a.m. I mean I took this, and the reason I remember it that way is, you don't send the Director a dawn email about it would be nice to get together to talk about how we're going to celebrate Arbor Day. I mean this is, the Midyear team has come across some additional actions they believe they need to take. And so I took it as, I believe what it intended is, we need to speak to you.

We asked Comey if knew what this email was about when he received it. He stated:

> I don't think so. I don't remember—when I got this, I don't remember, because my recollection is as I told you, is walking into the conference room with this grin on my face because they're all sitting in the same seats and sitting down and saying something like the band is back together, what's going on? And seeing these sort of dark faces, so I don't—at least to my recollection, this is the first time that this dawn email from Andy is we need to speak to you because the Midyear team has some additional actions they need to take and it didn't, I

don't remember this resonating context, resonating from this like, okay, let's do it.

Comey also told us that he did not initially recall that he had been previously notified about the Weiner laptop. He explained:

October 27th, Andy...sent me an email early in the morning saying that the Midyear Team needs to meet with you today. And I responded, of course. And I actually don't—I've thought about it since, I remember now, but I didn't focus on it at the time. I was aware sometime in the first week or two of October that there was a laptop that a criminal squad had seized from Anthony Weiner in New York and someone said to me...kind of in passing, they're trying to figure out whether it has any connection to the Midyear investigation.... And it's funny, when I was first reminded, I didn't even remember—by my staff saying, remember this is the laptop they mentioned to you. And I said, I don't remember being told about a laptop, but it definitely was sometime in early October.

E.   Midyear Team Communications Preceding Comey Briefing on October 27

On October 27, at 6:49 a.m., Page sent an email entitled "MYE" to Bowdich, Rybicki, Baker, Anderson, FBI Attorney 1, Strzok, the Lead Analyst, Priestap, McCabe, and Comey's administrative assistant. The email stated, "Team, The Deputy has asked that we convene today to inform the Director about what we know regarding the laptop in NY. Time is TBD, but I just wanted to alert you all now."

Strzok sent an email to the Lead Analyst a few minutes later about the briefing, stating, "I've got this. Will grab you and run down brief. Promise to make at least one sponsorship plug for William and Mary and one gratuitous yuck yuck joke about de-duping or getting the band back together." We asked Strzok about the tone of the email and his state of mind at the time. Strzok stated that it was a "here we go again" moment, meaning that he was thinking that "we've got to get the team back together and make sure all the systems are set up and figure out how we're going to get CART to do it." Strzok added that he was not thinking about a letter to Congress at this point. Strzok told us that the first time the issue of congressional notification came up is during the briefing with Comey.

At 6:55 a.m., Strzok sent an email to the Midyear SSA and FBI Attorney 1 asking "Would you please find out when NY got the [Weiner] laptop?" and to provide "a rough date [for] when you initially talked to them about their warrant." FBI Attorney 1 responded:

[The Midyear SSA] and I had a conference call with NYO on Sept 29. I believe they got the devices several days prior to that, but I'm sure [the Midyear SSA] can find the exact date. At the time of the call, due to the volume, the system doing the imaging had just crashed so they thought it would take into the next week to find out any specifics about the volume or email domains. We also discussed the fact that we received this via SW, not consent, so we really couldn't look at the other emails without additional process or consent. But we wanted to find out more about what was on the device before deciding what to do next....

F.   Comey Briefing on October 27

At 10:00 a.m. on October 27, the Midyear team briefed Comey on what NYO had discovered on the Weiner laptop. The following individuals were present for the briefing: Comey, Rybicki, Bowdich, Baker, Steinbach, Priestap, Strzok, Anderson, Page, FBI Attorney 1, and the Lead Analyst. McCabe was out of the office on October 27, but phoned in at the start of the briefing. However, shortly after phoning in, Comey asked McCabe to "drop off" the call, stating, "I don't need you on this call." Comey told us that he asked McCabe to leave the call because of the Wall Street Journal article on October 23 about then Governor McAuliffe's contributions to McCabe's wife's campaign in 2015. (The circumstances leading up to Comey's decision to exclude McCabe from this call and ultimately to McCabe's recusal are discussed in detail in Chapter Thirteen of this report.) Comey told us that from that point forward McCabe had no involvement in the Midyear investigation. Page also left the meeting once Comey asked McCabe to "drop off" the call.

Comey stated that he was told during the briefing:

[T]hat the criminal squad had gotten this laptop from—through a search warrant in New York. They had obtained it in some odd way from like Anthony Weiner's lawyers or something, but it came from Anthony Weiner who had been married to Huma Abedin for a number of years. And that the criminal squad had a search warrant, the scope of which they obviously were going to abide carefully, but that they had alerted—sometime in the previous couple of weeks, they had alerted the Midyear team that from the metadata they could see, there may be materials that the Midyear team would want to look at. And then they told me they had engaged in some sort of process where they got—I don't know what it was, but somehow technically they got the stuff transferred down here and figured out how they could—what they could look at properly without a warrant and had been able to look at an image of that computer and what they saw led them to believe that they needed to go get a search warrant.

And I said, well tell me what you see. And they said, we see evidence of many, many, many, thousands and thousands of emails from the period of Secretary Clinton's tenure as Secretary of State that—I forget how they said it, but basically that involved the Clinton email address domain. And they said that's one. Two, we see Verizon.Blackberry.net email metadata. We don't know what the content is, from the period of time when Secretary Clinton was using a Blackberry, Verizon.Blackberry.net account at the beginning of her tenure as Secretary of State. And I remember them telling me this specifically, we think this may be the missing three months of emails. And as we talked about earlier, the reason that would be so important is that could be germane to an evaluation of her intent which is a central part of our investigation. They said we think we may have found the missing emails. We see thousands and thousands of others and so we're highly confident that there are Secretary Clinton emails on there. Logic tells us that there will be classified emails on there because even if it's a dup[licate] of what she had elsewhere, those classified emails would be there and we think it may be the missing emails and so we have—we feel compelled to go get a search warrant.

Comey reiterated that "the volume of emails" and the presence of the BlackBerry emails were "two highly significant facts" and that the presence of the BlackBerry emails in particular "weighed very heavily on me."

Comey told us that the decision to authorize the Midyear team to seek a search warrant for the Weiner laptop "was an easy decision" and that there was no controversy over this decision. He noted that the Department agreed with the decision to seek the search warrant. Comey stated that "the harder decision [was] going to be what obligation do we have in the wake of that." We describe these discussions, which led to the October 28 letter to Congress, in more detail in Chapter Ten.

Others present for the briefing provided a similar account. Priestap told us that he recalled Comey asking if the Midyear team needed to review the Weiner laptop to be satisfied that they have "turned over the necessary stones" and "be comfortable with the decision we made." Priestap continued:

And I remember telling him, yes. We don't know with certainty what's in there. It could be information that we've not seen, you know, thus far, and so yes...in effect it's dereliction of duty to not, you know this thing is out here to pass it over. So yes, we've got to, we have to do it.

Strzok stated that Comey agreed "fairly quickly" with the team's suggestion to seek a search warrant. Strzok continued, "And then it very quickly turns to a, okay, so do we need to tell Congress? And that, I think, in my mind, my recollection the first time that kind of comes up...."

Anderson told us that Comey asked Strzok and the Lead Analyst:

[I]f we ignore this pool of material, you know, can we still stand behind the assertion that we've done everything that, that, that we should have done? And the answer that, you know, that Pete and [the Lead Analyst] gave...these are not quotes or anything like that. But this is sort of like generally the sense, was that, no, we have to pursue this material, because, you know, we, we would do it in any other case. And it is, you know, a pool of evidence that hypothetically, now understandably it's very speculative, but there is that possibility that it could change our outcome, because of that, you know, that possibility that it could contain something about intent.

Strzok also cited the missing emails, stating that if data from "that first three months" was present on the laptop it could be "substantively different from what we have recovered" to date.

Priestap provided a different perspective on the potential impact of the material on the Weiner laptop. He told us that he thought the review of the Weiner laptop was necessary even though he "would have been shocked" if they found anything on the laptop that changed the outcome of the Midyear investigation. Priestap explained:

> I felt that we had reviewed so much stuff that even if this was all stuff we hadn't reviewed, the chances that it was going to be some smoking gun in this subset of communications that didn't come up in all of this other stuff, again, would have been, would have shocked me. Could it have been possible? Absolutely. That's why we had to review it. But again, we had just done so much work and learned and seen so much else that to think there is going to be a sliver of, you know, information on nefarious activity that we weren't seeing other places, I, I just doubt it.

XI. Analysis

A. Failure of the FBI to Take Earlier Action on the Weiner Laptop

In this section we analyze the failure of the FBI to take any significant action to obtain access to the contents of the Weiner laptop for purposes of the Midyear investigation between late September, when NYO communicated the essential facts about the laptop to the Midyear team, and late October, when the FBI finally obtained a search warrant and began the accelerated process of analyzing the laptop's contents. As detailed below, we found most of the explanations offered for this delay to be unconvincing. Faster action could and should have been taken to review the laptop's emails.

By no later than September 29, the FBI had learned virtually every fact that was cited by the FBI in late October as justification for obtaining the search warrant for the Weiner laptop, including that the laptop contained:

- Over 340,000 emails, some of which were from domains associated with Clinton, including state.gov, clintonfoundation.org, clintonemail.com, and hillaryclinton.com;

- Numerous emails between Hillary Clinton and Huma Abedin;

- An unknown number of BlackBerry communications on the laptop, including one or more messages between Abedin and Clinton,

324

indicating the possibility that the laptop contained communications from the early months of Clinton's tenure;[178] and

- Emails dated beginning in 2007 and covering the entire period of Clinton's tenure as Secretary of State.

Much if not all of this information was communicated to FBI Headquarters and to the FBI Midyear team before the end of September. NYO ADIC Sweeney described facts about the laptop to senior headquarters personnel on a September 28 video teleconference. Testimony and documents show that Sweeney also briefed McCabe, Coleman, Steinbach, and Priestap individually on September 28. Of equal significance, NYO briefed the FBI Midyear team about the Weiner laptop in another conference call on September 29, including providing information that NYO lacked legal authority to review emails between Abedin and former Secretary Clinton under the existing search warrant. Witness interviews and contemporaneous notes show that most or all of the above information was known to the FBI Midyear team by late September.

The explanations given to the OIG for the FBI's failure to take immediate action on the Weiner laptop fell into four general categories:

1. The FBI Midyear team was waiting for additional information about the contents of the laptop from NYO, which was not provided until late October.

2. The FBI Midyear team could not review the emails without additional legal authority, such as consent or a new search warrant.

3. The FBI Midyear team and senior FBI officials did not believe that the information on the laptop was likely to be significant.

4. Key members of the FBI Midyear team had been reassigned to the investigation of Russian interference in the U.S. election, which was a higher priority.

We examine each of these explanations in turn below.

The FBI Midyear Team was awaiting further information from NYO:
Several members of the Midyear team offered this explanation, which we found unpersuasive. To begin with, all participants in the September 29 conference call knew that no one in the FBI could examine the contents of the emails of interest to the Midyear investigation without first obtaining either consent or a new search warrant, because the scope of the existing search warrant issued in the Anthony Weiner investigation was strictly limited. In addition, Sweeney informed Priestap of this fact on September 29. Although NYO was still processing the laptop as of

---

[178] Although Comey identified this fact as critical to his assessment of the potential significance of the emails on the Weiner laptop, the information was not included in the October 30 search warrant application for the Weiner laptop.

September 29, the completion of this task would not eliminate the need to obtain proper search authority. It was up to the Midyear team and the NSD prosecutors to obtain authority to review the emails, not NYO or SDNY. Yet the FBI Midyear team took no action to inform the prosecutors about the laptop or to obtain authority to search it.[179]

Even if the FBI Midyear team somehow misapprehended the intentions and ability of NYO to provide more information about the emails, no one from the Midyear team followed up when NYO provided no update in the weeks following the September 29 call. Had the Midyear team inquired, they would have learned that NYO completed processing the laptop by around October 4, but was taking no further actions to review any information, including emails, unrelated to the Weiner child exploitation investigation—a fact that had previously been briefed to the FBI Midyear team.

The FBI Midyear Team needed legal authority to review the emails: This explanation for the absence of action, which was given by several witnesses, is illogical. As described above, the lack of legal authority to search the laptop related to the investigative interests of the FBI Midyear team, not to those of the NYO Weiner team. Thus, the factual information necessary to establish probable cause to obtain a search warrant for the information that the Midyear team was seeking resided with the FBI Midyear team, not the NYO Weiner investigation team. Moreover, this lack of authority to review emails between Abedin and former Secretary Clinton was known to the FBI Midyear team by September 29. If anything, this explanation should have served as a rationale for the FBI Midyear team to take affirmative steps to obtain a new search warrant that provided them with authority to review the emails between Abedin and Clinton on the Weiner laptop. Instead, the FBI Midyear team took no action at all to solve this problem. Indeed, they did not even tell the Midyear prosecutors, who would have to be involved in any search warrant application process (as they were in late October), about the NYO discovery on the laptop.

The FBI Midyear Team did not believe the laptop evidence was likely to be significant: Strzok described his view of the Weiner laptop in late September as simply "a lead that likely is going to result in some investigation." Strzok stated that the suggestion that the matter should have been treated with more urgency was "misplaced" because "[w]e did not know what was there." He stated the team would have reviewed the emails at some point, perhaps in January or February 2017. Page also told us that the emails were not yet considered significant at that time because "emails had been found lots of other places that ultimately weren't worth pursuing lots of other times." Priestap similarly stated

---

[179] We found that McCabe called NSD Principal DAAG McCord on October 3 and flagged the issue of emails in an iCloud account shared by Abedin and Weiner. However, McCord told us, and her contemporaneous notes indicated, that McCabe provided minimal information about this issue, and did not mention the potential presence of emails between Abedin and Clinton on Weiner's laptop. We identified no other FBI Headquarters or Midyear personnel communications with the Department about the Weiner investigation—and no communications about the presence of Midyear-related emails on the Weiner laptop—until October 21.

that he did not expect any new information discovered on the laptop to "change the outcome of the case" because the team had seen enough information previously to make him "confident we had gotten to the bottom of the...issue." While the FBI ultimately concluded, after obtaining a search warrant and reviewing the Clinton-Abedin emails, that the Weiner laptop contained no significant new evidence, Comey had a very different view of its potential importance after being briefed on it on October 27.

The view that the Weiner laptop was unlikely to contain significant evidence arguably accorded with the FBI's investigative strategy in this matter, although this approach was inconsistent with what witnesses told us was a "leave no stone unturned" approach to the investigation. As detailed in Chapter Five, the FBI Midyear team had decided to obtain or exploit only those personal devices directly associated with Clinton or the servers hosting clintonemail.com. The FBI sought no personal devices used by any other individual to conduct State Department work, including Mills, Abedin, and Sullivan. This included a decision not to seek the devices and culled work-related emails in the possession of Abedin's attorney. Witnesses told us that the team's focus was on Clinton's conduct as opposed to the conduct of others, including Clinton's senior aides, and the team assessed that Clinton's devices and the laptops used to cull her emails were the most likely places to find the complete collection of emails from her tenure or evidence of Clinton's intent. In addition, witnesses told us that the Midyear team deemed Abedin's emails to be less likely to contain classified information given her role and the nature of her communications with Clinton.

We found the belief that the Weiner laptop was unlikely to contain significant evidence to be an insufficient justification for neglecting to take action on the Weiner laptop immediately after September 29. Unlike the personal devices that the FBI had previously decided not to attempt to acquire, the Weiner laptop was already in the FBI's custody and known to contain potentially relevant emails. Even those FBI officials who told us they did not expect to find new evidence agreed that it was a logical investigative step to seek to obtain a search warrant so that they could review the contents of the potentially relevant emails. In addition, and as we note below, the FBI developed little additional information about what was on the Weiner laptop between September 29 and October 27. However, Comey's reaction to the information he was presented on October 27—which was substantially similar to what FBI Midyear and Headquarters personnel knew on September 29—suggests that the Weiner laptop should have been viewed as a more significant discovery.

We hasten to add that not every witness described the Weiner laptop as being unlikely to contain significant evidence. In particular, McCabe said he thought that the discovery of the emails on the Weiner laptop was a "big deal" and that he understood that the FBI Midyear team was proceeding with obtaining authority to review the laptop contents during the period immediately after September 29. Yet McCabe took no action for weeks to obtain a progress report or otherwise ensure completion of the analysis and when he did finally do so it was in response to Toscas mentioning the laptop issue to him on October 24. McCabe also did not convey a much-needed sense of urgency about this matter to Comey. Instead, he told us he gave Comey a "fly-by" briefing about the discovery shortly after hearing about it on September 28. Comey told us he vaguely recalled hearing about the Weiner laptop around this time, but did not recall learning at that time any of the details that later caused him to announce the reactivation of the investigation on October 28. As the Deputy Director who was overseeing the Midyear investigation and who had been briefed by NYO on September 28 on the Weiner laptop discovery, McCabe should have demanded a progress report from the Midyear team and should have provided a full briefing to Comey well before October 27.[180]

The Russia investigation was a higher priority: On July 31, 2016, just weeks after the conclusion of the Midyear investigation, the FBI opened its investigation of Russian interference in the ongoing presidential election. Strzok and several others from the Midyear investigation were assigned to the Russia investigation, which we were told was extremely active during this September and October time period.[181] Several witnesses, including Priestap, Strzok, and Page,

---

[180] After reviewing a draft of the report, McCabe's counsel submitted a written response stating that McCabe shared all of the information he knew about the Weiner laptop with Comey soon after he first learned about it, and that any claim that McCabe "failed to fully inform Director Comey of what he initially knew about the Weiner laptop is inaccurate."

The submission also asserts that "[t]he OIG places inordinate weight on Mr. McCabe's apparent reference during his OIG interview to a 'fly by' briefing of Director Comey in late September or early October." However, as noted above, our primary concern was with McCabe's failure to take any action in the weeks prior to October 24, and then doing so only in response to Toscas mentioning the laptop issue to him on October 24.

McCabe also asserts in his written response that the "importance of exploring this collection of emails [on the Weiner laptop] was not immediately obvious" because the FBI had learned about various collections of allegedly relevant emails throughout the Midyear investigation, most of which turned out to be duplicative of previously examined emails or of marginal significance—a statement that we note is at odds with his description of the emails to us during his testimony as a "big deal." McCabe stated that it was "unfair and misleading" to place the blame squarely on him for failing to follow up on the Weiner laptop with sufficient urgency, "even though many people in both FBI Headquarters and the New York Office were responsible for pushing the matter forward and failed to do so." McCabe described the delays in reviewing the Weiner laptop as a "failure with many fathers, including many other FBI executives, and not a shortcoming attributable to Mr. McCabe alone." McCabe added, "And, while the OIG holds Mr. McCabe responsible for failing to demand progress reports, it is undeniable that Director Comey could have asked for updates based on what he had been told by Mr. McCabe, and he did not.... The OIG's exercise of hindsight that leads it to place blame on Mr. McCabe—and only Mr. McCabe—for the failure to more promptly 'demand a progress report,'...ignores the other FBI managers and executives who dropped the ball."

[181] We were surprised to learn that FBI leadership decided to assign many of the key members of the Midyear team, immediately after determining that no charges should be brought against then candidate Clinton, to the Russia investigation, which touched upon the campaign of then candidate Trump. This is particularly so given the questions being raised by candidate Trump and his supporters regarding the declination decision in the Midyear investigation. While we recognize that staffing decisions are for management to make, we question the judgment of assigning agents who had just determined that one candidate running in an election should not be prosecuted to an investigation that relates to the campaign of the other candidate in the election. The appearance problems created by such a staffing decision were exacerbated here due to the text messages expressing political opinions that we discuss later in this report. Surely, the FBI's Counterintelligence Division had talented agents who were not involved in the Midyear investigation who could have fully staffed the Russia investigation. Such a decision also would have eliminated the excuse we were

328

stated that the Russia investigation was a higher priority in October than reviewing the Weiner laptop. Priestap, in particular, provided convincing justifications for the prioritization decisions he made in light of his management responsibilities, including that Comey had tasked him with overseeing the FBI's multifaceted efforts to protect the 2016 election from foreign interference.

Nevertheless, from an institutional perspective, we found this explanation unpersuasive and concerning. Strzok and the other Midyear personnel reassigned to the Russia investigation were not the only agents in the FBI. Had the FBI considered the Weiner laptop significant, additional personnel could have been assigned to handle it. Moreover, not all of the Midyear personnel were assigned to Russia. This was a staffing choice, not an excuse for inaction.

This is even more evident when contrasted with the attention that the FBI gave to other activities in connection with the Midyear investigation during the same period. As detailed in Chapter Eight, these activities included the preparation of Comey's speech at the FBI's SAC Conference on October 12—a speech designed to help equip SACs to "bat down" misinformation about the July 5 declination decision; the preparation and distribution of detailed talking points to FBI SACs in mid-October in order, again, "to equip people who are going to be talking about it anyway with the actual facts and [the FBI's] actual perspective on [the declination]"; and a briefing for retired FBI agents conducted on October 21 for the purpose of describing the investigative decisions made during Midyear so as to arm former employees with facts so that they, too, might counter "falsehoods and exaggerations." Some of these discretionary activities required significant efforts by members of the Midyear team. Moreover, some of the claims made in those talking points and presentations concerning the thoroughness of the investigation were at odds with the approach that these Midyear team members were taking with regard to the Weiner laptop.

In assessing the decision to prioritize the Russia investigation over following up on the Midyear-related investigative lead discovered on the Weiner laptop, we considered the text messages that Strzok exchanged with Page expressing hostility for then candidate Trump and preference for a Clinton victory. We were particularly concerned about text messages sent by Strzok and Page that potentially indicated or created the appearance that investigative decisions they made were impacted by bias or improper considerations. Most of the text messages raising such questions pertained to the Russia investigation, and the implication in some of these text messages, particularly Strzok's August 8 text message ("we'll stop" candidate Trump from being elected), was that Strzok might be willing to take official action to impact a presidential candidate's electoral prospects. Under these circumstances, we did not have confidence that Strzok's decision to prioritize the Russia investigation over following up on the Midyear-related investigative lead discovered on the Weiner laptop was free from bias.

---

given here about the Russia investigation impacting the ability of agents to address the Weiner laptop issue.

329

We searched for evidence that the Weiner laptop was deliberately placed on the back-burner by others in the FBI to protect Clinton, but found no evidence in emails, text messages, instant messages, or documents that suggested an improper purpose. We also took note of the fact that numerous other FBI executives—including the approximately 39 who participated in the September 28 SVTC—were briefed on the potential existence of Midyear-related emails on the Weiner laptop. We also noted that the Russia investigation was under the supervision of Priestap—for whom we found no evidence of bias and who himself was aware of the Weiner laptop issue by September 29. However, we also did not identify a consistent or persuasive explanation for the FBI's failure to act for almost a month after learning of potential Midyear-related emails on the Weiner laptop.

In sum, we concluded that the explanations given for the failure of the FBI to take action on the Weiner laptop between September 29 and the end of October were unpersuasive. The FBI had all the information it needed on September 29 to obtain the search warrant that it did not seek until more than a month later. The FBI's neglect had potentially far-reaching consequences. Comey told the OIG that, had he known about the laptop in the beginning of October and thought the email review could have been completed before the election, it may have affected his decision to notify Congress. Comey told the OIG, "I don't know [if] it would have put us in a different place, but I would have wanted to have the opportunity."

B.   Decision to Seek Search Warrant on October 27

Several FBI witnesses told us that the reason the FBI decided to seek a search warrant on October 27 was because the Midyear team learned important new information about the contents of the Weiner laptop at around that time. We concluded, however, that this decision resulted not from the discovery of dramatic new information about the Weiner laptop, but rather as a result of inquiries from the Weiner case agent and prosecutors from the U.S. Attorney's Office for SDNY on October 21.

We begin by noting that every fact that would ultimately be included in the October 30 search warrant that the Midyear team obtained to review the Weiner laptop was known to the FBI in late September. As we discuss in Chapter Eleven, the October 30 search warrant included limited factual information about what the Weiner case agent had seen during his review of the laptop. The search warrant stated that the FBI had "information indicating that there are thousands of Abedin's emails on the [Weiner laptop] – including emails, during and around Abedin's tenure at the State Department, from Abedin's @clintonemail.com account as well as a Yahoo! Account appearing to belong to Abedin." As detailed above, these facts were not only known to FBI NYO, but had been communicated to FBI Headquarters and FBI Midyear personnel on multiple occasions in late September.

Moreover, the information known to the Midyear team on October 27 when it briefed Comey about the laptop was substantially similar to the information that NYO had made known to FBI leadership and the FBI Midyear team on September 28 and 29. This information is summarized in the bullet points in the prior section. There was a conference call on October 26 between NYO and the FBI Midyear team which involved some participants who had not participated in the September 29 conference call, including Strzok and the Weiner case agent. However, apart from an update on the total number of emails on the laptop, we found no evidence the October 26 call involved the communication of significantly more specific information about the nature of the messages on the laptop.

Witnesses, including Comey, cited two pieces of information from the October 26 call that they described as new and of particular importance in triggering the decision to reactivate the investigation. The first involved the total volume of emails on the Weiner laptop. Contemporaneous notes show that during the September 29 call NYO reported that there were approximately 350,000 emails on the Weiner laptop, that these included emails between Huma Abedin and former Secretary Clinton using various Clinton-related domain names, and that the laptop was still being processed. On the October 26 call, NYO reported approximately 675,000 emails were on the laptop. We found that the increased volume of emails on the Weiner laptop—from 350,000 to 675,000—to have little or no significance in the absence of additional information about the content or metadata of the emails.

The second piece of new information cited by witnesses was the presence of BlackBerry backups on the laptop. However, this information was not new. One of the first messages the Weiner case agent saw on the laptop in late September was a BlackBerry message between Clinton and Abedin. And the Midyear SSA told us that the presence of BlackBerry information on the laptop was mentioned during the September 29 call between Midyear and NYO personnel.

While Comey and other witnesses gave much significance to the BlackBerry data (the former describing them as the "golden emails"), very little specific information was known about those messages as of October 27. No specific information had been developed or provided regarding the volume or date range of the BlackBerry data. We found no evidence that NYO provided any more specific information about the BlackBerry data in late October than they had previously provided in late September. Indeed, this seems even more apparent given the fact that NYO was legally prohibited under the scope of the Weiner search warrant from reviewing any information unrelated to their child exploitation investigation.

We found that what changed between September 29 and October 27 that finally prompted the FBI to take action was not new information about what was on the Weiner laptop but rather the inquiries from the SDNY prosecutors and then from the Department. The only thing of significance that had changed was the calendar and the fact that people outside of the FBI were inquiring about the status of the Weiner laptop.

PAGE LEFT INTENTIONALLY

BLANK

CHAPTER TEN:
THE DECISION TO NOTIFY CONGRESS ON OCTOBER 28

In this Chapter we address Comey's decision to send a letter to Congress on October 28, 2016, about the emails discovered on the Weiner laptop. Comey made the decision to send the letter on October 27, following the briefing he received from the Midyear team that morning.

In Section I of this Chapter, we address various factors that Comey and others in the FBI said they considered with respect to the decision to make the disclosure. In Section II we compare the decision to notify Congress about the Midyear investigation with the way in which the Russia and Clinton Foundation investigations were handled. In Section III we discuss certain internal FBI messages about the decision that we discovered in the course of our review. In Section IV we address the process by which the FBI announced Comey's decision to the Department and how Department leadership reacted to his decision. In Section V we discuss how the October 28 letter was drafted, edited, and finalized. In Section VI we provide our analysis of Comey's decision.

I.   Factors Considered as Part of Comey's Decision to Notify Congress

The question of whether to notify Congress of the Midyear team's discovery of emails on the Weiner laptop was first raised during the briefing to Comey on the morning of October 27. FBI personnel involved in the decision told us that over the next 24 hours, numerous discussions occurred about whether to notify Congress of this development. Below we address the various factors relevant to this decision that Comey and others in the FBI told us they considered.

A.   Belief That Failure to Disclose Would Be an Act of Concealment

Two broad categories of longstanding Department and FBI policies, norms, and practices were potentially relevant to the decision to announce the reactivation of Midyear. First, the Department and the FBI regularly decline to comment publicly or to Congress regarding ongoing criminal investigative activity. Comey endorsed this principle in general, stating, "I believe very strongly that our rule should be, we don't comment on pending investigations."

Second, the Department has a longstanding practice of avoiding actions that could impact an imminent election, which Comey described as a "very important norm." Comey stated:

> I said to [the team] here's the way I think about it. I've lived my entire career in the Department of Justice under the norm, the principle, that we, if at all possible, avoid taking any action in the run up to an election, avoid taking any action that could have some impact, even if unknown, on an election whether that's a dogcatcher election or president of the United States....

Comey told us that the circumstances surrounding the discovery of emails on the Weiner laptop did not permit him to conform to these policies and norms, and that, in particular, remaining silent did not appear to be an option. Comey explained:

> I couldn't see a door—I said to the people inside the organization—I can't see a door labeled, no action here. I can only see two doors and both were actions. One is speak, the other is conceal. Because having testified about this multiple, multiple times, like working backwards in September, July and having spoken about it on July 5th, and told Congress, the American people, a material fact which is, this is done and there is no there there. To now restart and not just in a marginal way, in a way where we may have found the missing emails, that to not speak about that would be, in my view, an affirmative act of concealment. And so I said okay, those are the doors. One says speak, the other says conceal. Let's see what's behind the speak door. It's really bad. We're 11 days from a presidential election. Given the norm I've long operated under, that's really bad. That will bring such a storm. Okay, close that one, really bad. Open the second one. Catastrophic. And again this is something reasonable people can disagree about, but my view was to conceal at that point given all I had said would be catastrophic. Not just to the Bureau, but beyond the Bureau and that as between catastrophic and really bad, that's actually not that hard a choice. I'll take really bad over catastrophic any day. And so I said to the team, welcome to the world of really bad.

Comey testified before the Senate Judiciary Committee on May 3, 2017, and spoke at length about the Midyear investigation. When talking about the October 28 letter, Comey testified:

> [W]hen the Anthony Weiner thing landed on me on October 27 and there was a huge—this is what people forget—new step to be taken, we may be finding the golden missing emails that would change this case. If I were not to speak about that, it would be a disastrous, catastrophic concealment.

B.   Perceived Obligation to Update Congress

Comey told us that he felt he had an obligation to update Congress that the FBI was seeking a search warrant for the Weiner laptop in the Midyear investigation because the email discovery was potentially very significant and that made Comey's prior testimony no longer true. Comey stated:

> I don't think the obligation was rooted in my having promised to come back to them if I learned new evidence. I have read some of that in the open source; people saying the reason he did it is he had made a promise to Congress that he would supplement the record. No. I mean maybe I did in some form, but that's not how I thought about it.

334

I thought my obligation to Congress is—I testified under oath for 10 hours and said there's no there there; we're done.... And now that is materially untrue and that's the obligation I felt.

Comey stated that his July 5 statement was "actually irrelevant" to this obligation. Comey told us that the Department could never have closed the Midyear investigation with a "no comment." Instead, he said that, in the absence of his July 5 statement, the Department would have had to state that it conducted a "fair, honest, and independent" investigation and that the investigation was now closed. Comey stated that once that statement was made—in whatever form it came—"the decision that came in October [was] inevitable because all of a sudden that's not true."

In his testimony to the Senate Judiciary Committee, Comey stated, "I've got to tell Congress that we're restarting this, not in some frivolous way, in a hugely significant way." Comey added that "everyone on my team agreed we have to tell Congress that we are restarting this in a hugely significant way."

Comey added that the significance of the potential evidence on the Weiner laptop was a factor in assessing his obligation to notify Congress and the public. He stated:

Yeah, so I'm sitting there. It's October 27th and there's a reasonable likelihood that we are going to find material—one possibility—that will change our view of the Hillary Clinton case. Two, even if it doesn't, that we know something that is materially different than what the rest of the world knows and has relied upon since I spoke about this.... The FBI is done. There is no there there and that to conceal that, in my view, would be—subject the FBI and the Justice Department, frankly more broadly...to a corrosive doubt that you had engineered a cover up to protect a particular political candidate. And that especially given your pledges of transparency, not—I don't actually put much stock in the notion that I promised to get back to Congress, but that I had said to everybody, the credibility of the Justice enterprise is enhanced by maximal credibility, maximal transparency. I offer that transparency, and then I know something that materially changes that picture and I hide it, I think the results would be generations-long damage to the credibility of the FBI and the Justice Department. That's what I think about it.

Comey told us to put aside any hindsight bias about what was actually found on the laptop and "sit with me on October 28th and make this decision. And where you have a reasonable prospect of something that is world changing with respect to that investigation, then decide whether you speak about it or not." Comey emphasized that this was "not just any investigative step, again you have reason to believe that there are hundreds of thousands of germane emails, including which is a very important fact to me, potentially the missing BlackBerry...emails from early in her tenure." He continued, "[S]o this isn't a frolic and detour, this is, it's the reason the Department thought we had to get a search warrant, there's potentially highly significant information there."

We asked other FBI personnel about the nature of this obligation to update Congress. Rybicki told us that Comey felt he had an obligation "to basically supplement [the] record" with Congress because he had testified that the investigation was complete. Bowdich told us that he thought the obligation grew out of Comey's July 5 press conference. Bowdich stated, "The Director felt like, hey, if we don't notify them, after the July 5th notification, we could potentially be accused of concealing information. I remember him using that, that word."

Steinbach described Comey's decision and his obligation by stating:

[T]he overriding question was say nothing and get accused, worst case scenario, of covering up. Or be transparent and say we have something, we just don't know what it is, and let that course play out. And I, you know, again, I, I describe the Director as a very transparent, communicative...person. And I want to say that that transparent piece probably weighed on him more than the not saying anything piece. And also I think his, his belief that he had somehow made that pledge to Congress.

The Lead Analyst stated that at one of the meetings during this period, Comey asked everyone in the room their opinion on whether the FBI had an obligation to notify Congress. When it was his turn, the Lead Analyst told us:

I will never forget what I told him. I said, sir, every instinct in my body tells me we shouldn't do it, but I understand your argument that you have to make a, a factual representation, a factual correction to Congress to amend essentially what you told them, that otherwise, because I think that was really where he had coalesced or the discussion had, that he had made this statement to Congress, and that doing things like serving process is contrary to what he had told Congress. So he felt like he had to correct that record.

FBI Attorney 1 told us that an OGC attorney was tasked with researching whether Comey had a legal obligation to correct the record with Congress. FBI Attorney 1 stated, "I think what we decided was that he did not make a promise to come back to them. But that [the] implication was that the investigation was over." We asked FBI Attorney 1 to explain her understanding of Comey's obligation. She stated:

I think [Baker] and the Director just believed that, yes...the letter of what he said did not say I will come back to you. But they believed that he had an obligation to do so under...just general standards of candor...that we had finished the investigation. It was not finished.... I just think he felt that what he had said, the impression he had left, because he was the one testifying, was that he would come back to them. And [Baker] thought that, and [Baker] agreed with that part, definitely.

Baker told us that he believed that he was the person who first raised the issue of Comey's obligation to update Congress. Baker stated that this obligation arose because Comey had "told Congress repeatedly this thing is closed" and had now authorized "a significant step forward in the investigation." Baker stated that this obligation had nothing to do with the July 5 statement and was instead related to Comey's testimony to Congress. Baker stated that even if Comey had not done the July 5 statement, eventually "[Comey] would have had to go to Congress, talk about the FBI's investigation, talk about our conclusions. Say that we agreed or disagreed with the Department's decision. And then, having done that, he would have been in the soup in the same way at the end of October." Baker told the OIG that he believed that the perceived need to notify Congress was the overriding factor that drove the decisionmaking.

Anderson told us that she believed Comey needed to supplement his testimony to Congress because it "was such a significant issue" that "it would have been misleading by omission." Anderson stated that even though Comey did not explicitly tell Congress he would update them, it was "implied" in "his testimony overall."

C. Avoiding the Perception that the FBI Concealed the New Information to Help Clinton Win the Election

Comey told us that he was concerned that if the FBI failed to disclose the new information, it could be accused of attempting to help Clinton get elected. He stated that "to conceal that, in my view, would be—subject the FBI and the Justice Department, frankly more broadly...to a corrosive doubt that you had engineered a cover up to protect a particular political candidate."

Baker also expressed this concern. He stated:

[N]ot to notify Congress is...an action because it also potentially could have an impact on the election...so for example, [imagine] we don't say anything. We push past the election, and then we announce that, well, by the way, we've authorized a search warrant, and we found all these emails. Let's imagine, right? Because we don't know what the facts are.

We find all these emails. You guys have probably heard this story, but I'll just say it again. And it turns out that, oh, my God, there were more classified emails of a different type, or there's clear evidence that she knew what she was doing. It kind of pushes us from the probable cause thing up to the beyond a reasonable doubt. And now we're going to change our view about charging her.... If she's been elected president of the United States, then Donald Trump would say, oh my God, these people knew this beforehand and didn't say anything. This is a rigged system. This is, this, these people intentionally hid that until after the election so that they could get her elected and, and thwart me.

Steinbach also stated a similar concern. He stated:

I think weighing on everyone's mind is if, if we get through this and a week after the general election we find relevant material, the Congress and the American public will never allow the FBI to live that down. You clearly hid this from the American public. And you knew you had something, yet you waited until after, until after she became president before you disclosed that you found something relevant. That was one course of action. The other course of action is we, we state it and get accused of influencing the election beforehand.

Steinbach continued:

We felt that, again, the, the Congress, the American people, would never be able to say FBI, you withheld this. The last thing we wanted to have happen was, hey, I wouldn't have voted for her if I had known this. And so that was weighing on our minds. We wanted there to be transparency, both in November as well as in, in July. Hey, here is the set of facts. Here is the good and the bad. You, and again, I think that's, there's somebody, many feel that's not your job, but I think the discussion items were, lay out the facts and let people decide for themselves. And that, and maybe not in those exact words, that was a theme through the course of this.

Steinbach told us he did not recall if Comey "said it in exactly these words, but, in the totality, that's what he conveyed to us." Steinbach added that Comey "wanted to be transparent."

1.   Protecting the Reputation of the FBI

Several witnesses articulated a concern that failing to disclose the decision to seek the search warrant would injure the reputation of the FBI—a concern that, as discussed above, was closely related to avoiding the perception that the FBI was hiding the information to help Clinton.

Bowdich stated, "I know [Comey] really felt hung out there with Congress, and he was so worried about the institution getting hurt. He didn't, he knew it was a bad situation. But the institution getting hurt by thoughts of us concealing this information."

FBI Attorney 1 told us that the team "certainly considered" what would happen if the FBI chose not to disclose this information to Congress and the information became known after the election. She stated that would have had "a much more significant impact on the reputation of the FBI" because the FBI would have been accused of "somehow hiding" that information from Congress. We pointed out to FBI Attorney 1 that the FBI's standard practice is not to release

338

information on investigations and asked her if not sending the letter would have simply been consistent with standard practice. She responded:

> It would be, except we had already released information. And that's what I said about, maybe I would have done something differently on the July 5th [statement]. We had already released all of the information and said this is what we're doing. This is what we've decided. And then to then go back to the same stuff and...leave everybody with the impression that that's what we've decided, and then a week later, everybody finds out that we, we had reopened this investigation. I think that would have been much more detrimental. To the FBI's reputation and to the, the Justice Department's reputation.

2. Protecting the Legitimacy of a Clinton Presidency

Comey told us that he was concerned about the perceived illegitimacy of a Clinton presidency that would follow from a failure to make the October 28 disclosure. Comey stated:

> I don't remember thinking this explicitly, but I'm sure I was operating in an environment where she was going to be the next president, and I was in a position to have her be an illegitimate president the moment she was elected because I would have concealed a material development in her investigation. And the moment she took office, the FBI is dead, the Department of Justice is dead and she's dead as president....

FBI Attorney 1 expressed similar concerns to us, but said she did not express them at the time. FBI Attorney 1 stated:

> I also think it would have been detrimental.... I was careful not to discuss this. But in my mind, it was detrimental...if Secretary Clinton was elected president, then...it would have come out. It would have definitely come out that we had done the search warrant. And then, then it would have been an illegitimate, like it would have been grounds for, you know, you couldn't have elected her. She was under investigation. All of those sorts of things that would have...had more of an impact if you didn't say anything.

D. Concerns about the Electoral Impact of the Announcement

Comey told us that he decided at the time that he would not consider who would be helped or hurt by making public the reactivation of the Midyear investigation. Comey stated:

> I will not engage in the exercise of figuring out who will be helped/who will be hurt, which way this will cut, who will play it, because then I'm starting to make judgments based on a political calculation. Instead, I should think about what is the right thing to do given the circumstance

339

which we find ourselves. Where I've...made material representations and what is the best thing for the Justice institution to do given that, without regard to what may happen, so consciously I did not.

Comey described the debate within the FBI about the congressional notification as a "family conversation," where everyone was free to state their opinions and concerns. Comey specifically told us of a concern expressed by Anderson during this conversation. Comey stated:

> [O]ne important part of the family conversation about whether to send the October 28th letter was Jim Baker knew from his conversations with Trisha Anderson that one of her concerns was how should we think about the fact that this might hurt Hillary Clinton and help elect another candidate, that kind of thing, and Baker said we should raise it with the Director and that's the kind of stuff he wants you to raise and I gather he thought she might not raise it. So at our next family discussion that evening, he said let me ask you a contrarian question. You know how do you think about this? And then I think she spoke herself and said, how do you think about the fact that you might be helping elect Donald Trump? And I said, I cannot consider that at all. Down that path lies the death of the FBI because if I ever start thinking about whose political ox will be gored by this or that, who will be hurt or helped, then we are done as an independent force in American life and so I appreciate you raising it, I cannot consider it. And I was very glad she raised it because it was probably a question that was looming in lots of people's minds and I think my answer was the right answer....

Anderson stated that she did not remember exactly what she articulated in the discussions about the letter, but she told us that she had a conversation with Baker prior to the final meeting with Comey on the morning of October 28. Anderson stated:

> I do remember saying more explicitly to Jim Baker that I was worried that what we were doing was going to have an impact on the election. Was that appropriate for the Bureau? Was that, you know, did, I was concerned about that for, you know, for us as a, as an institution. And, and at least that that was how we were going to be perceived. The FBI was going to be perceived as having impacted the outcome of the election. And, you know, and sort of tied to that...had we reached the threshold, you know, that it was essential that we send this letter? And this is where, you know my, you know, my concerns about materiality and sort of fairness to the former Secretary, you know, played in. You know, in light of the fact that we're going to be perceived to be affecting the outcome of the election, is there really enough here to warrant us doing that?

Anderson stated that Baker first raised Anderson's concerns to Comey during the October 28 morning meeting and "kind of put [Anderson] on the hot seat."

340

Anderson stated that she articulated her views to Comey and told him, "I'm not so certain that this is the right thing to do." Anderson told us that a robust discussion ensued. Anderson stated that she did not recall either candidate being mentioned by name in this discussion and said any discussion of impact on the election "certainly would not have been couched in terms of" helping or hurting either candidate. Anderson added that "it would have been highly inappropriate for there to be any partisan you know, motive or interest in influencing the outcome of the election." Anderson stated, "I don't know that I walked away from the meeting feeling, you know, totally convinced that it was the right thing to do, but I also understood why the other options were worse."

After reviewing a draft of this report, Anderson clarified her testimony to the OIG. Anderson added:

> While I do not remember the specific words that I used, I recall very clearly that I did not couch my concerns in terms of the FBI's actions helping or hurting any particular presidential candidate. Rather, I asked [Comey] whether we should take into account that sending the letter might have an impact on the outcome of the election, or could be perceived as having such an impact. I stated that I had concerns about our actions having such an impact particularly given that it was unclear—and perhaps even unlikely—that the emails would be material to the investigation. I also recall raising a concern about it being unfair to the former Secretary—in a sort of due process sense—because no matter how carefully we wrote such a letter, the importance of the emails would be overinflated and misunderstood. So, in my mind, and what I believe I argued in the meeting, was that we were about to do something that could have a very significant impact on the outside world even though what we had might not be material, yet people would very likely view it as such.

We asked Baker about Anderson's concerns. Baker told us that Anderson came to him the morning of October 28 and stated:

> I've thought about this overnight. I have serious reservations about going down this road. I'm very concerned about this, Jim. Why? Well, because I'm concerned that we are going to interject ourselves into this process. We're going to interject ourselves into the election in a way that's, that potentially or almost certainly will change the outcome. And I am, I, Trisha, am quite concerned about that. And I'm concerned about us being responsible for getting Donald Trump elected.

Baker stated that Anderson was worried about "putting the thumb on the scale" in a way that is "going to hurt one candidate and benefit another one right before the election." Baker told us that he asked Anderson if she wanted to bring this up with Comey, but Baker stated that "she was reticent" to do so. Baker said that he brought the issue up with Comey during the meeting that morning in order to make sure Anderson's concern was brought to Comey's attention without attributing it to her. Baker stated that Anderson then "chimed in" and "elaborated" on her concerns once he raised the issue. Baker told us that Comey responded "[a]long the lines of like we can't think that way. We just can't think that way."

FBI Attorney 1 told us that she recalled others expressing "concern about what impact this would have on the election." Specifically, FBI Attorney 1 stated that she spoke directly with Anderson about these concerns, which they both shared. She said that Anderson spoke to Baker about this concern and Baker raised it at one of the group meetings. FBI Attorney 1 stated:

> As I was going through this, I was thinking I should not be bringing politics into this. And so I was trying to be careful about thinking about this in an apolitical way and not raising the concern as who is going to get elected, because that actually is not something that I thought we should be considering as the Bureau. I brought that up with Trisha, because she and I, you know, we're close and we talked about it. But I did not, no one, I don't think anyone brought up the outcome on the election. We talked about the policy, about, you know, that, making announcements so close in time to the election. But we didn't bring up the fact that if you do this, Trump will get elected sort of question, because I, I don't know that anyone thought it was appropriate to bring that up.

FBI Attorney 1 told us that this issue was raised with Comey in the context of having an undue influence on the election, rather the potential impact of the decision in an electoral sense. FBI Attorney 1 stated that Comey recognized the concern, but Comey framed the issue in terms of "what was our obligation...to Congress and to the people to do the right thing." FBI Attorney 1 reiterated that although the issue was discussed in terms of the proximity to the election, "we did not discuss, but if you say this, then Trump will get elected. Like, we did not in any way talk about it in those stark of terms. And so at least not in the, you know, as the group decision."

We asked other participants in the discussion about Anderson's comments. Rybicki stated that Anderson raised a concern that the notification to Congress "could help elect candidate Trump at that point." Strzok told us that someone commented that the letter "might influence the ultimate outcome of the election." Bowdich stated that Anderson made an argument against the letter, but he told us that he could not recall what that argument was.

E.   Expectation that Clinton Would Be Elected President

Comey told us that "like the rest of the world [he] assumed that Hillary Clinton was going to be elected president." When asked whether this had an impact in his decision to notify Congress, he stated:

> I think none and I tried very hard to both be that and maybe convinced myself of that.... I've often asked myself, so were you influenced in any way by the knowledge what the polls were showing? Not consciously, and in fact I tried to be very conscious about saying I

don't give a rip. I don't care. But you know if anything, I suppose like if it's unconscious, I may have been consoled that it wasn't going to make any difference anyway. I don't remember thinking that consciously, but the environment which I was operating—well I don't want to psychoanalyze myself too much more—not consciously is the honest answer.

When asked if his decision would have been the same if Clinton was expected to lose by 20 points, he stated:

[T]hat's a reasonable question.... I think I would have said still, if you conceal something, maybe the matter wouldn't have been of such intense interest if she was down 20 points all summer long or something. But a matter of intense public interest and debate that and people have relied upon your credible investigation and your word here, even if it was foreordained that she was going to lose the election, I think to hide that would have subjected this institution to justifiable withering criticism.

In a subsequent OIG interview, Comey stated: "I am sure I was influenced by the tacit assumption that Hillary Clinton was sure to be the next President."

We asked Baker if anyone raised the issue of Clinton being up in the polls and likely to win the election no matter what the FBI did. Baker said that this issue "definitely came up" and "somebody said something along those lines." Baker stated:

There was some discussion about if she, if we do this and she wins, then nobody can allege that it was a rigged system and things had been hidden to try to benefit her. Somebody may have said in that context, well, she's ahead in the polls anyway and that's probably what's going to happen, and, and so on. So I think, yes, I think that aspect of it came up in that way. But it was more like, you know, if we do this and she gets elected, then she should be thanking us.

Baker told us that he could not remember who made this comment and added, "It could have been the Director, but I don't specifically remember."

F.   Belief that Email Review Could Not Be Completed Before the Election

Each of the participants in the FBI discussions to seek the search warrant told us that no one expected the review of the Weiner laptop to be completed prior to the election. Comey told us that this fact—that the Midyear team did not expect to finish the review of the Weiner laptop prior to the election—"was a really important fact for me" in making the decision whether to make the October 28 announcement.

Comey stated that he asked the Midyear team directly during these discussions if they could "finish the review before the election." Comey said that the team told him, "There's absolutely no way we'll get that done before the

343

election. It will be long after the election." When asked why he did not just assign 30,000 people to review the laptop, Comey stated:

> Yeah, I could have, but I actually raised this and their answer was, the review has to be done by people that understand the context. If we bring in a class out of Quantico it doesn't do us any good because the quality of the work will be such that we can't rely on. It's not like searching a field for a bullet fragment...we have to put eyes on them to understand this.

We asked Comey if his decision to notify Congress would have been different if the team told him they could finish the review prior to the election. Comey stated:

> Maybe, yeah. If they could tell me with you know high confidence that this is something we can knock out in a week, maybe, yeah, maybe. But I do think it was an important consideration that we're about to undertake something of indefinite duration and so I think—maybe—I'm not certain that would make it differently, but I would have waited probably differently. If it was October 3rd and they said, we think there may be something here and we can knock it out in the next six days; I might have. Then—it's interesting—I hadn't thought about this—but then I might have been on to considering the prospect of a leak you know because I might have said, not going to do it, but what would be the effect on the Department if there's a leak about the search warrant, yeah.

Comey later added that the ultimate impact on his decision would have depended "upon how high a confidence read they could give to me that it'll be finished far enough in advance of the election to responsibly report a result." Comey reiterated:

> [I]f I had known the information or even a reasonable facsimile of the information that I was given on the 27th, three weeks earlier, I'm highly confident I would have said, let's get a search warrant and then we would have had a conversation about how soon can you finish and whether there [was] a prospect of finishing this before the election. I still would have had a very hard decision to make, but I would have been making it three weeks earlier. I don't know whether it would have led to a different place—but I certainly would have wanted to have the option to be there and to consider whether...let's make it up, three weeks' of time, does that make me think differently about the choice between speak or conceal? Is there a reasonable prospect I could run this out and have a conclusion far enough in advance of the election that if it changes the FBI's view, I could still, well you'd have to go through all that decision tree. But I don't know it would have put us in a different place, but I would have wanted to have the opportunity.

G.   Fear that the Information Would Be Leaked

We asked the FBI personnel involved in these discussions if a fear of leaks impacted the decision to notify Congress. Comey told us that he "didn't make this decision because [he] thought it would leak otherwise." Comey stated that he thought "that would be a cowardly way to make a decision." Nevertheless, Comey told us, "I kind of consoled myself, this was a hard call and you're going to get the crap beat out of you for it, but it would have come out anyway." He reiterated, however, "I [don't] want to leave you with the impression that I sent the letter to Congress because I thought it was going to leak otherwise."

Others, however, had a different recollection. Rybicki told us that, while not remembering the context, he recalled the issue of leaks being raised during these discussions. Strzok stated that the fear of leaks played a role in the ultimate decision. Strzok explained that the decision to seek a search warrant for the Weiner laptop was known to many people beyond the Midyear team and this raised a concern that the information could leak. Draft talking points that were circulated to FBI senior management on October 31 regarding the decision to send the letter to Congress, which incorporated comments by Strzok, the Lead Analyst, and Page, included the following bullet point: "It's important to note the [sic] I notified Congress <u>before</u> moving forward with additional investigative steps in this investigation, because of my commitment to transparency and because I wanted Conrgess [sic] to hear it from me first." (Emphasis in original). Page told us that her "personal belief" was that there was "a substantial and legitimate fear that when we went to seek the warrant in order to get access to the Weiner laptop, that the fact of that would leak." Page said that this concern related to the suspicion that NYO personnel had been leaking negative Clinton Foundation stories. Bowdich, Anderson, and FBI Attorney 1 told us that they did not recall a discussion of leaks during the debates about notifying Congress.

Baker told us that a concern about leaks played a role in the decision to send the letter to Congress. Baker stated:

> We were quite confident that...somebody is going to leak this fact. That we have all these emails. That, if we don't put out a letter, somebody is going to leak it. That definitely was discussed.... [If] we don't do a letter. It's either going to be leaked before or after the election, and we either find something or we don't. And either way, there's going to be claims that we tried to play games with the election, and we tried to steer it in a certain way to help Hillary Clinton and hurt Donald Trump. We're not about that. We don't, we're not making decisions on the basis of which candidate we like or don't like. We're not going to do that. And so we are just going to have to ignore all that and do what, again, what we think is right, consistent with our obligations to Congress.

Baker told us that "the discussion was somebody in New York will leak this." Baker continued, "[W]hat we discussed was the possibility that if we go forward with the search warrant and take that step, that's a step being taken in the Hillary Clinton investigation. And that's what will leak." Baker explained, "[T]he sense was that that this significant of a step is not going to go unnoticed. And if we don't put something out, somebody will leak it. That's just what we talked about."

II.   Comparison to Other Ongoing Investigations

In this section we address the Russia and Clinton Foundation investigations, both of which were ongoing in October 2016. Comey and other witnesses told us that these investigations were not discussed during deliberations regarding whether to announce to Congress the reactivation of the Midyear investigation.

A.   The Differential Treatment of the Russia Investigation

On March 20, 2017, Comey testified before Congress that the FBI began an investigation in late July 2016 into "the Russian government's efforts to interfere in the 2016 presidential election," including "investigating the nature of any links between individuals associated with the Trump campaign and the Russian government and whether there was any coordination between the campaign and Russia's efforts."

Despite the existence of this investigation into individuals associated with the Trump campaign in the fall of 2016, none of the participants in the FBI's internal discussions about the October 28 notification to Congress recalled any mention of the Russia investigation.

We asked Comey whether the existence of investigations into individuals affiliated with the Trump campaign impacted his consideration as to whether to send the October 28 notification to Congress regarding Clinton. Comey told us that "you've got to look at each case individually" and stated that comparing those investigations is "a calculation you shouldn't engage in because then you're starting to weigh political impacts of your work—who's hurt by this, who's hurt by that." Comey explained:

> Well I don't think—I shouldn't think of them in relation to each other.
> I should look at a case involving a John Smith and given our norms
> and rules around that, I don't see and I don't think the Department
> sees, a reason for treating those cases as exceptions the way we did
> the Hillary Clinton case. In part, among the considerations [in] the
> Hillary Clinton case, the whole world knew we were doing it, right?
> The candidate and her campaign themselves had talked about the
> review, the security inquiry. We know the government is working on
> this. The referral had been public, so all of that to my mind puts this
> in a different position. And counterintelligence investigations are very
> different—and for all reasons you can imagine, we are very, very
> careful about—because we don't want the adversary who's not
> necessarily the subject, but is the nation-state to know what we're
> doing or who we may have thought of to focus on, so there it would
> take even more to be the exception to the rule as I just look at—I

wouldn't look at them in relation to each other, but if I found another case where I and the Department thought that made sense to make an exception, we would.

Comey was asked during testimony before the Senate Judiciary Committee on May 3, 2017, if it was "appropriate" for Comey to comment on the Midyear investigation repeatedly and "not say anything" about the investigation involving "the Trump campaign's connections to" Russia. Comey replied, "I think I treated both investigations consistently under the same principles. People forget that we would not confirm the existence of the Hillary Clinton email investigation until three months after it began, even though it began with a public referral and the candidate herself talked about it."

Whether to make the public aware of the more general issue of Russian interference in the U.S. presidential election also arose in the fall of 2016. On October 6, the Department of Homeland Security and Office of the Director of National Intelligence issued a joint statement about election security. This statement was not drafted in connection with the FBI's Russia investigation, but Comey's reaction to it is highly relevant. The statement began, "The U.S. Intelligence Community (USIC) is confident that the Russian Government directed the recent compromises of emails from US persons and institutions, including from US political organizations." The statement then described the nature of these compromises and urged "state and local election officials to be vigilant."

As a member of the USIC, the FBI was consulted on this statement. Comey told us that he decided the FBI should not be included in the statement because he felt that it conflicted with the longstanding Department of Justice norm "that we, if at all possible, avoid taking any action in the run up to an election, avoid taking any action that could have some impact, even if unknown, on an election." Comey continued:

> It was actually that norm that drove me to say the FBI should not be putting out a statement earlier in October about the Russian hacking, that I had advocated inside the U.S. government. In fact, I drafted an op-ed from my own name in August to call out the Russians, to say here's what they are doing in our election. And our awesome interagency system, kicked that around, kicked that around, and then come October, there is then discussion about making a public statement about the Russians. And I said my view is...that the goal of a public statement is to inoculate the American people against what the Russians are doing. I think the inoculate goals have been by and large achieved because of all the press reporting on it. You had legislators talking about it. I said so there's only a marginal increase in the inoculation by an official statement from the FBI. And given that we are now a month from a presidential election—from an election, I think we can reasonably avoid that action.... And so I said, I don't think the FBI should put out such a statement; it's too late. That if we need to do it, we should have done it then and I said that's just how I've long operated.

In an October 5, 2016 email, Comey explained his position on the statement to Central Intelligence Agency Director John Brennan and Director of National Intelligence James Clapper. Comey stated, in part:

> I think the window has closed on the opportunity for an official statement, with 4 weeks until a presidential election. I think the marginal incremental disruption/inoculation impact of the statement would be hugely outweighed by the damage to the [Intelligence Community's] reputation for independence.

> I could be wrong (and frequently am) but Americans already "know" the Russians are monkeying around on behalf of one candidate. Our "confirming" it (1) adds little to the public mix, (2) begs difficult questions about both how we know that and what we are going to do about it, and (3) exposes us to serious accusations of launching our own "October surprise." That last bit is utterly untrue, but a reality in our poisonous atmosphere.

B.   The Differential Treatment of the Clinton Foundation Investigation

In 2016, the FBI had an open investigation into the Clinton Foundation. Comey refused to confirm the existence of the investigation on July 7, 2016, in testimony before the House Oversight and Government Reform Committee because the investigation was not public.

In addition, numerous witnesses told us that agents involved in the Clinton Foundation investigation were instructed to take no overt investigative steps prior to the election. We asked Yates about this instruction. Yates stated, "[Y]eah, I think there was discussion about look, if [agents on the Clinton Foundation investigation] want to go do record stuff and stuff that you can do covertly, fine. But not overtly.... And the sort of thought being we'll address that again at the end after the election was over." Yates explained that this instruction was explicit because the Department does "everything [it] can to avoid having an impact on an election." Yates continued:

> [Y]ou have to be cognizant of the fact that the actions that we take at DOJ can have an unintended impact on an election. And so that you do everything you can to avoid that.... Like if somebody wants to send you a criminal referral we generally don't initiate an investigation until after the election.... So it's, you know, sort of basic DOJ practice that I don't think anybody would dispute that you do everything you can to avoid having an impact on an election....

> And the Bureau never pushed back on that concept. This actually came up with, in the connection with Paul Manafort. And they had an investigation on Manafort and I had a lengthy discussion with [McCabe], at least one, maybe more, about how important it was at that time that our investigation not be overt. And what they were, what the Bureau was doing with respect to Manafort because that

could impact Trump even though he was no longer his campaign manager. That unless there was something they really needed to do, because they were getting records and doing that kind of, unless there was something they needed, really needed to do overt they really needed to stay under the radar screen.... Because it's not fair to impact [an election].

Axelrod echoed this point, stating that "DOJ's policy, procedure, and tradition" is to avoid overt investigative steps in "the run up to [an] election." Axelrod continued, "And [this policy] had actually been cited to the Bureau on other investigations during this election cycle," including the Clinton Foundation and Manafort investigations.

We asked Comey about the different instructions given to the Midyear investigation and the Clinton Foundation investigation. Comey told us, "The principle is take no action if it can reasonably be avoided and there was nothing about the Clinton Foundation investigation that was time sensitive." Comey continued:

The challenge of the discovery of the emails on the Weiner thing was, given the context that we had told the world, we the Justice Department and the FBI, that there was nothing there...to now be presented with all these emails that are...highly significant to that investigation, how is, where is the door labeled no action, that you either speak or you conceal. And so either one's an action, so which action should we take. So it was very different, given the context, a very different posture than the Clinton Foundation. And my worry was, I have to be careful that people in New York aren't by virtue of political enthusiasm, trying to take action that will generate noise that will have an impact on the election. No time sensitivity whatsoever to that....

III. Internal FBI Discussions Regarding the Decision to Notify Congress

A. McCabe, Strzok, and Page Text Messages on October 27

We reviewed text messages from Strzok, Page, and McCabe that indicated their disagreement with Comey's decision to notify Congress on October 28. At 4:03 p.m. on October 27, Page sent a text message to Strzok that stated, "Please, let's figure out what it is we HAVE first. What if we can't make out [probable cause]? Then we have no further investigative step." Strzok replied, "Agreed." At 9:57 p.m. on October 27, McCabe sent a text message to Page that stated, in part, "[Baker] says his meetings were mostly about the notification and statement which the boss wants to send tomorrow. I do not agree with the timing but he is insistent." Page responded, "Fwiw, I also wildly disagree that we need to notify before we even know what the plan is. If we can't get in, then no investigative step has been taken. Whatever. I hope you can get some rest tonight."

We asked Strzok about his text message exchange with Page. Strzok stated that there was a "vigorous, healthy debate" within the FBI about whether the notification to Congress was a good idea and Strzok told us that he thought the concerns expressed in Page's text message were part of that debate. Strzok told us that he ultimately agreed with Comey's decision to send the letter to Congress.

Page told us that she could not remember the context of the text messages with Strzok. Page agreed with the content of the message and stated that she did not support Comey's decision to notify Congress. Page added, "We just didn't know what we had yet. It just felt premature to me." Page also stated that there was "no guarantee" that the FBI would be able to make out probable cause for the search warrant and she felt it was "presumptuous of us to sort of say we're reopening and we're doing this before we have even a search warrant in hand." However, Page told us that she was not involved in the discussions about the letter due to McCabe's recusal.[182]

We asked McCabe about this text message exchange with Page. McCabe stated that Baker told him during a phone call that Comey planned to send a letter to Congress. McCabe told us that from his perspective—as someone who had not participated in the discussions about the letter—"it just seemed like we should have a better understanding of what we had before we made a notification."

We also showed these text messages to Comey. Comey stated he did not recall discussing the issue of congressional notification with McCabe. Comey told us that he did not remember hearing Page express these concerns during the debate over the letter, adding, "I think I would remember that."

B.   Strzok Call with Midyear SSA, Agent 1, and Agent 2 on October 28

At 5:21 a.m. on October 28, Page sent a text message to Strzok that stated, "Any plan to tell the case agents? You know, since so much of this has hinged on the credibility of 'the team.' ☹." At 5:59 a.m., Strzok sent an email to the Midyear SSA and Agents 1 and 2, stating, "Would like to talk to the three of you on a conference call at 645. Sorry for late notice."

Strzok stated that he reached out to the agents and the SSA on his own and not at Comey's suggestion. Strzok told us that he wanted to make sure the agents and the SSA knew what was happening and he wanted their input. Strzok stated:

> I think it was, hey look, we went, we briefed [Comey]. Our sense is they want us to reopen the case, and we need to get a warrant and go after it. And they're going to send a letter to Congress. What do you think about that? Are you, are you good? Are you, objections, are we horribly off-base? Are we not thinking about something?

---

[182] As discussed in Chapter Thirteen, Comey asked McCabe to drop out of the discussion about this topic on October 27, and Page left the discussion as well. McCabe formally recused himself from Clinton-related matters on November 1.

The Midyear SSA told us that Strzok called to inform him of Comey's decision to send the letter and wanted to make sure "the case agents were informed" as well. The Midyear SSA, Agent 1, and Agent 2 told us that they each ultimately agreed with the decisions to seek the search warrant and send the letter. As noted previously, Agent 2 was on the September 29 phone call with NYO about the Weiner laptop. Agent 2 told us that around this time was the first he had heard about the Weiner laptop since September 29.

C.   Agent 1's Instant Messages on October 28

After the letter was sent by the FBI to Congress on October 28, Agent 1 sent a series of instant messages to other FBI employees about the reactivation of the Midyear investigation.

Beginning at 1:46 p.m., Agent 1 exchanged the following messages with Agent 5. The sender of each message is identified after the timestamp.

> 1:46 p.m., Agent 5: "jesus christ... Trump: Glad FBI is fixing 'horrible mistake' on clinton emails... for fuck's sake."
>
> 1:47 p.m., Agent 5: "the fuck's sake part was me, the rest was Trump."
>
> 1:49 p.m., Agent 1: "Not sure if Trump or the fifth floor is worse..."
>
> 1:49 p.m., Agent 5: "I'm so sick of both..."
>
> 1:50 p.m., Agent 5: "+o(TRUMP"
>
> 1:50 p.m., Agent 5: "+o(Fifth floor"
>
> 1:50 p.m., Agent 5: "+o(FBI"
>
> 1:50 p.m., Agent 5: "+o(Average American public"

We asked both Agent 1 and Agent 5 about these messages. Agent 1 and Agent 5 both stated the reference to "fifth floor" referred to the location of the FBI WFO's Counterintelligence Division. Agent 1 continued, "Again, you know, I think a general, general theme in a lot of this is some personal comment, or, you know, complaining about common topics and leadership and, and venting." Agent 5 also described this as general complaining to Agent 1 and also as an example of her being "very tired of working" these types of cases.

Agent 1 also sent two instant messages about the Weiner laptop to FBI employees not involved in the Midyear investigation. At 2:16 p.m., Agent 1 messaged, "Yes. Its more email found through a separate matter. Not sure if they are even unique yet, but we have to make sure." At 2:25 p.m., Agent 1 messaged, "emails found through separate matter. Due diligence—my best guess—probably uniques, maybe classified uniques, with none being any different tha[n] what we've already seen." We asked Agent 1 about these instant messages. Agent 1 stated that, as of October 28, any information he had about the contents of the Weiner laptop would have come from discussions with the Midyear SSA. Agent 1 told us he did not recall precisely what he meant by these messages, but that given the seemingly small numbers of Abedin-Clinton emails the Midyear team had previously found, "I thought there was a chance that we would see more emails that we hadn't seen before." We asked Agent 1 to explain his comment about "none being any different [than] what we've already seen" and whether that indicated Agent 1 did not expect to find emails substantively different than what the Midyear team had previously reviewed. Agent 1 responded, "Maybe. That, right, right. The classified email was in a similar vein that we saw, similar activities and similar talking around. Yeah."

IV.   The FBI Informs DOJ Leadership About Comey's Decision

Department personnel were informed of Comey's decision to notify Congress around mid-day on October 27. Various discussions between FBI and Department personnel occurred over the next 24 hours. These discussions were at both the Midyear-team level and between Rybicki and Axelrod. Notably, Comey never spoke directly with either Lynch or Yates about the notification. We describe these interactions between the Department and the FBI below.

A.   FBI and DOJ Midyear Team Discussions

Strzok stated that FBI personnel assigned to Midyear "had a variety of robust discussions with" Department personnel about the letter to Congress. One such discussion occurred on October 27 after Comey had decided that the FBI should seek to review the emails on the Weiner laptop, and that Congress should be notified. According to Prosecutor 2's notes, Strzok, FBI Attorney 1 and the Midyear SSA from the FBI, and Toscas, Laufman, Prosecutor 1, and Prosecutor 2 from the Department participated in this discussion. The notes reflect that there was a discussion of whether the decision to review the Abedin emails on the Weiner laptop was inconsistent with the Midyear team's investigative approach during the investigation. For example, the notes indicate that Laufman asked, "What distinguishes this from other devices we chose not to obtain? When think of [Abedin's] email, her emails were of less probative significance." The notes reflect that Strzok responded, "Volume – 500k emails – specifically domains of interest – gap period (1st 3 months)." Strzok also stated, according to the notes, that "it is relevant that [the Weiner laptop] is in our possession." Toscas agreed that possession of the laptop was a relevant factor, stating that if the Midyear team had possessed the laptop during the investigation, it "seems like we would've looked at it." Toscas went on to state, according to the notes, "[W]ill beg the question of why we're not going to ask for all these folks' devices?" According to the notes, Prosecutors 1 and 2 pointed out that the investigative team did not previously seek to obtain devices from Clinton's senior aides. Regarding a public announcement, the notes reflect that Laufman stated, "[P]ublic announcement disproportionate to importance of what we're doing." According to the notes, when Laufman asked whether the Department would be shown a copy of the FBI's announcement in advance, Strzok responded, "I don't know."

We asked Department personnel involved in the Midyear investigation about these discussions. The Department personnel we interviewed told us they disagreed with Comey's decision to notify Congress and that they communicated that disagreement to the FBI. We summarize their concerns below.

Laufman stated that the entire CES team found the notification "highly objectionable." Laufman told us his concerns, stating:

> (A) We had a very low expectation that, that the substance of what this [the laptop] might include would be anything novel or consequential that would occasion reassessing, let alone altering the findings and analysis and recommendations we had already made.

> (B) [T]o the extent that investigative action was necessary to review the data, it's not uncommon for the Bureau to have to nail down something that arises at the end of an investigation. And we ordinarily would forgo public comment about that unless and until it's appropriate to say something about the results of that activity. In many instances, it might not be appropriate to say anything publicly about it at all....

> (C) This is October 28th. We're about a, a week away from our presidential election. And it particularly struck us as exceptionally inappropriate to make a statement that unmistakably would be construed as the Bureau's having reopened this investigation in that close a proximity to the day of the election.

We asked Laufman what he meant when he said there was a "low expectation" that this evidence would alter the outcome of the Midyear investigation. Laufman stated:

> [W]e had seen through our investigation, the types of emails that Huma Abedin had been party to. And they were just not the kinds of emails that really went to the core issues that were under legal analysis, meaning they had to do with sort of scheduling, and...I mean, as important as she is in a personal, confidential assistant manner to the former Secretary, she wasn't as substantively engaged in, in some matters that would have occasioned access to classified information or dealing with classified issues. So...we had seen quite a bit up to that point. And with respect to her, we hadn't seen her engaged via email with anybody on the types of things that were material to our legal analysis. So, assuming that what was going to be reviewed from this new dataset was consistent with that, it seemed improbable to us that it was going to, to change anything. And of course as we know now, it was a giant nothing-burger.

Prosecutor 1 stated that the notification to Congress "didn't make any sense." Prosecutor 1 told us that given Abedin's role and the evidence they had previously reviewed there was little "likelihood of finding anything of import in there." Instead of doing a public announcement, Prosecutor 1 stated, "We should just investigate it and do it as quickly as we could." We asked Prosecutor 1 about the potential presence of BlackBerry emails from early in Clinton's tenure.

Prosecutor 1 stated that the FBI mentioned that "there could be information that covered that BlackBerry period from the period at the front end of the tenure," but added:

> I felt like a lot of the analysis was based upon what, what could be in there and the opportunity cost of sort of missing out on that. Of course, to me that's a different analysis than making an announcement about it. We didn't want to be seen to be in favor of forgoing the effort entirely.

Prosecutor 1 stated that the FBI seemed "very concerned about transparency with the public" and "had already kind of decided what they were going to do" prior to consulting with the Department.

Prosecutor 2 told us that the Department was "shocked" that the FBI was even considering notifying Congress about this development. Prosecutor 2 said that she did not necessarily view the Weiner laptop as a significant development in the Midyear investigation. Prosecutor 2 stated:

> Because over the course of this investigation, we haven't sought out personal devices of anybody other than Hillary Clinton. So we haven't asked, for example, for like Huma's personal laptops, her personal BlackBerries. We have her state.gov stuff, but that's like, that of Huma's is all we've searched.

> So, there's a threshold question in my mind of whether, like, this is even something that needs to be searched. And based on the, the iffyness on that threshold question, and then the likely significance of this device, it seems totally nuts to me that they would make an announcement having no idea what is on this device, having not looked at it. And in, and in terms of like the impact that this announcement could have.

> And I remember being on the phone call like, how are you, asking like how on earth are you going to word this announcement so it's accurate and doesn't, doesn't like, you know, open a much bigger can of worms than is really the significance of this recent finding. I mean at this point...we have no idea.... We just know that like some of Huma's emails are in FBI's custody. Like, of course Huma has other emails. Like, how is this a game changer?

Prosecutor 2 also told us that she believed the FBI would not listen to any of the arguments they put forth. She stated, "[T]here's a defeated feeling at this point that like [Strzok] was given the task of like pretend to DOJ that you're hearing them out. And he was going to, you know, humor us by having this conference call, but like that nothing we said mattered on that call."

Recalling a discussion with Strzok in this time period, Toscas stated, "I was really upset and I basically said, you know this is BS. We don't talk about our stuff publicly. We don't announce things. We do things quietly." Toscas told us that the justification provided by the FBI for why it needed to notify Congress was what he called "the Comey Rule," meaning a duty to correct the record with Congress because Comey testified to "one thing" and circumstances have now changed. Toscas told us that, in his opinion, the October 28 letter demonstrates that "as soon as you deviate from normal practice" once—meaning the July 5 statement—"you're going to have to adjust to deviations all along." Toscas explained:

> One of the things that I tell people all the time, after having been in the Department for almost 24 years now, is I stress to people and people who work at all levels, the institution has principles and there's always an urge when something important or different pops up to say, we should do it differently or those principles or those protocols you know we should—we might want to deviate because this is so different. But the comfort that we get as people, as lawyers, as representatives, as employees and as an institution, the comfort we get from those institutional policies, protocols, has, is an unbelievable thing through whatever storm, you know whatever storm hits us, when you are within the norm of the way the institution behaves, you can weather any of it because you stand on the principle.

> And once you deviate, even in a minor way, and you're always going to want to deviate. It's always going to be something important and some big deal that makes you think, oh let's do this a little differently. But once you do that, you have removed yourself from the comfort of saying this institution has a way of doing things and then every decision is another ad hoc decision that may be informed by our policy and our protocol and principles, but it's never going to be squarely within them.

McCord was Acting AAG for the National Security Division at this time and she told us that she thought the notification was "a bad idea." McCord stated, "I believe there were conversations between [Toscas] and ODAG and the Bureau expressing our view that we should at least get a handle first on whether these are just duplicates because it could be a big nothing."

B.   Department and FBI Leadership Discussions

After deciding on October 27 that he needed to notify Congress, Comey told us that he instructed Rybicki to reach out to the Department about the notification. Comey stated that he told Rybicki, "I want you to tell DOJ that I think I need to inform Congress of this step. And please tell the DAG and the AG I'm happy to speak to them, but that's what I'm thinking. I welcome their feedback." Comey stated that he did not remember his specific directions to Rybicki, "but the substance would have been something like, call [Axelrod], tell him where we are and that I think we have an obligation to notify" Congress "that we're taking this step."

We asked Comey why he decided to seek the Department's advice in October, but not in July. Comey stated:

I'm not sure, I think given Loretta's position, I thought the July decision I had to do it given where Loretta had landed and that it was the decision best calculated to protect the Department.... In this circumstance, I wasn't positive I was right, making a very hard decision, I thought if they want to get involved in this, it's not necessarily a bad thing. I thought it would be a very bad thing if I was...because Loretta might well say, don't do that, don't do that in July. Here, I guess I thought about it slightly differently. I thought it was a hard call and if they wanted to weigh in on it, offer their view, say we'll take the decision, that maybe it was a little less courageous frankly than in July, I'm just thinking out loud here, maybe it was a product of having gotten the pain after July, but I'm not sure, I'll think more about that. I'm not sure. Yeah, that's my reaction to it.

Comey told us that he did not have any concerns about potential bias when consulting with Lynch on this decision. We asked Comey why that was the case given the concerns about Lynch that led to his July 5 statement. Comey replied, "Probably because I saw that reasonable people could see the framing differently than I, in the way I didn't feel that way with her refusal to step out, the semi-recusal, I think."

1. Comey's Decision Not to Engage Directly with Lynch or Yates

We asked Comey why he delegated communication with the Department to Rybicki instead of talking to Yates and Lynch directly. Comey stated:

I think because of the way, the distance they've been taking on the whole thing I wanted to offer them the opportunity to honestly to step away from it. That I wanted to offer them the opportunity—I didn't want to jam them and I wanted to offer them the opportunity to think about and decide whether they wanted to be engaged on it.

Comey emphasized that the reason he had Rybicki reach out to the Department was because he "wanted to offer them the opportunity to take this decision."

2. Phone Calls between Rybicki and Axelrod

Rybicki stated that he spoke with Axelrod on the afternoon of October 27. Rybicki told us his conversation with Axelrod was "twofold" and explained,

To let him know that the Director had decided to, the Director had decided to authorize the seeking of the search warrant. And there was no real reaction to that from [Axelrod]. I think he, I think he perhaps knew that was coming, or, he didn't seem surprised in any way. And then two was the second part that the Director felt he had the obligation to supplement the record.... [Axelrod had a] very strong reaction. You know, you know, no, we just don't do that. Right? We, you know, we don't do that.

Rybicki stated that he and Axelrod had "a series of phone calls" the rest of the day. After the initial call to Axelrod, Rybicki told us that his understanding was that Axelrod was speaking for both Yates and Lynch in their subsequent calls. We asked Rybicki why Comey and Yates did not speak directly. Rybicki stated that he "had asked whether they wanted to speak to the Director, and, and [Axelrod] said no."

Rybicki told us that he asked Axelrod to provide the FBI with any Department policy or guidance dealing with investigative activity near an election. Rybicki stated that Axelrod did not believe the congressional notification would technically violate Department policy, but was outside of "the normal course." Rybicki told us that he explained Comey's thinking to Axelrod, stating that Comey "felt strongly" and "felt he had the obligation" to notify Congress.

Axelrod stated that he received a call from Rybicki on October 27 and Rybicki informed him "that the Director was intending to send a letter to Congress notifying them" of the decision to examine the Midyear-related emails on the Weiner laptop. Axelrod described his reaction as "surprise, concern, dismay" and stated:

> I told [Rybicki] like in that initial call look, obviously I'll have to talk to folks here and, you know, call you back. But I said, but I will give you my initial reaction which is that...[this] would be [a] very bad idea. Contrary to...Department policies and procedures, both about, you know, taking overt investigative steps so close to an election and talking to the Hill about, you know, investigations.... It just struck me as incredibly problematic.

Axelrod told us that he and Rybicki "talked it through a little bit" and Rybicki asked Axelrod to send him the relevant Department policies. Axelrod told us that contacted Ray Hulser, then Section Chief of the Department's Public Integrity Section, to get information on the relevant policies.

Axelrod stated that Rybicki told him "that the Director believes he has an obligation to correct a misimpression that Congress has" that the Midyear investigation is concluded. Axelrod told us that this was "the key part" of their conversation. Axelrod stated that he asked Rybicki where Comey had promised to update Congress and Rybicki replied that it related more to the "overall tenor" of Comey's testimony to Congress. Axelrod told us that he tried to convince Rybicki that Comey and the FBI would be better served following Department policies and procedures. Axelrod continued:

> [Rybicki] never said look, I don't think that's the policy or I don't think that's the procedure or I don't understand.... [H]e was all like yeah, I get all that but this is different. This is separate. The Director has testified. The Director believes that Congress has, now has a misimpression and so it's the Director's you know, butt on the line. And he needs to do this. And you know, and if he doesn't, you know, the concern [is] it's not survivable for him.

We asked Axelrod what he understood Rybicki to mean by the comment that this would not be survivable for Comey. Axelrod stated:

> I understood that to mean that they thought that the heat the Director would get from the Hill, right, so that if this doesn't, you know, he doesn't surface it and then...afterwards when it comes out that [the] Bureau had this information but kept it quiet that there would be calls for his resignation that he wouldn't be able to survive.

Axelrod stated that Rybicki told him that the FBI was also concerned that the information would leak if no notification was made.

We asked Rybicki if he told Axelrod that failing to notify Congress would not be survivable for Comey. Rybicki told us that he did not "remember using that language." Rybicki stated, "I certainly conveyed how seriously Director Comey felt about it. But I, I don't recall, you know, the survivability of it. I just, sitting here I don't." We also asked Rybicki if he more generally conveyed that there would be "political heat and a call to resign" if Congress was not notified. Rybicki replied, "[N]ot that I can recall. I remember telling him the Director felt strongly. But I don't remember sort of political heat, calls to resign, just that he felt strongly and that he, he himself felt he had the obligation."

We asked Comey if he expressed concerns at the time about not being able to survive as the FBI Director if Congress discovered post-election that he had not notified them of this development in the Midyear investigation. As previously noted, Comey stated that it would cause "catastrophic damage" to the FBI, the Department, and to a Clinton presidency. He said that he did not remember expressing his concerns in terms of survivability, but added, "I'm sure I said something like, if I chose conceal over speak, I ought to be fired, I ought to be hung out, I would be run out of town because of the damage it will have brought to this. I'm sure I said things like that."

We asked others in FBI leadership if they heard Comey state that failing to notify Congress would not be survivable. Bowdich stated he did not recall Comey making that comment, but did remember Comey saying:

> I am going to take a huge hit on this, but it's the right thing to do. And I remember him, it struck me that not only was the organization going to take a hit, but he even, I remember him pointing and saying I am going to suffer personally from this as well. But he felt it was the right decision to make.

Anderson stated that Comey viewed sending at the letter to Congress as the option that "would do the least damage to the Bureau's long-term credibility and integrity as an institution."

Baker stated, "I think [Comey] may have said like I could be impeached" or "something along those lines." We asked Baker to explain the context for that remark. Baker stated:

It may have been during the meeting, one of the two meetings on the 28th [or] 27th.... Some of the stuff that gets talked about at those meetings...he and I talked about separately later and kind of repeated it. But at some point in time, he raised, I don't remember the context exactly. He raised the issue of, you know, potentially he could get impeached for this if he doesn't tell them this.

Baker told us that because Comey "had testified under oath, and now that something different has happened, people are going to react to this big-time" if it was leaked or the FBI told Congress "after the election or whatever."

3. Internal Department Discussions

Axelrod told us that he discussed the congressional notification with both Yates and Lynch. Yates stated that Axelrod told her that "he got a call from Rybicki about the Director writing a letter" to Congress. Yates stated:

[Rybicki told Axelrod] that the Director feels like he has a personal ethical obligation. Because he had told them that the investigation was closed. Because we had these new emails. And we agreed we should get a search warrant for the emails, by the way. I thought we should. We need to find out what's on there. But that because he had told them that it was a closed investigation he had a personal obligation to tell them that it was, an ethical obligation to tell them that they were now reviewing these new emails.

Yates also told us that she remembered "being told that FBI doesn't think it's survivable for the Director for him not to" notify Congress. Yates stated that one of the reasons that the FBI "gave for why they felt like [Comey] had to go to Congress is that they felt confident that the New York Field Office would leak it and that it would come out regardless of whether he advised Congress or not."

Lynch stated that she was told that Axelrod "had gotten a call" that the Weiner laptop "had potentially relevant emails on it" and Comey "felt that because of his prior testimony over the summer, that he had an obligation to notify Congress of it." Lynch told us that it was presented to her as the FBI was notifying the Department that Comey felt he needed to and had an obligation to make this notification. Lynch stated that this obligation was described to her as "an ethical obligation both based on testimony, but also as a matter of ethics to notify Congress of new information in this investigation." Lynch told us that she did not recall the FBI asking for the Department's feedback. Lynch continued:

And then at one point, I think [Axelrod] relayed information again from Rybicki saying that the Director's view was that he had to provide this information to Congress, that he was concerned about the information being leaked from the New York office in even more negative ways, that he was concerned about, he was very concerned about that. He expressed that to the FBI and Rybicki shared that. And that he also was concerned that if, if in fact he did not provide this information to Congress, and either it was leaked or later on we discussed it in some Department-approved way, that it was not survivable. And that was the phrase that was given to us. And both the DAG and I said, I think we both repeated the same, you know, what do you mean not survivable, one of those chorus things. And [Axelrod] said that was just the phrase that Rybicki had used. It was not survivable.... [W]e certainly took it as coming from the Director. It would not be survivable in his, in his view for either him or the FBI. I didn't think that he was thinking of the Department at large at that point, so we never got, and [Axelrod] said he did, when he heard that he said the exact same question that anybody would have, for whom? But he just got it wouldn't be survivable.

Lynch stated that Rybicki's call started a conversation within the Department about the Department's response. Lynch told us that Axelrod examined Comey's prior testimony and Department personnel discussed whether or not that created an obligation. Lynch stated:

And my view was, look, you can, you can read it any way you want, but if he's looking at it and saying it does, that's his view. You're not going to change his mind by saying here's another interpretation of this particular statement. That's not the issue. The issue is should this happen...should this be done regardless of, of what's been testified to prior or what's happened.

Lynch told us that her view was "let's find out what's on this computer before you start talking about it at all." Lynch added, "Even if you view it as I need to say something to Congress, you don't have anything to say" at this point.

Yates stated that the Department began "almost nonstop" discussion on how to respond to the FBI. Yates told us that, among the factors discussed, were the Department's policies, the lack of knowledge about what was actually on the Weiner laptop, and the fact that the Department had not yet obtained a search warrant. Yates stated that the FBI did not dispute the Department's policies. Instead, Yates stated, "It all kept coming back to, and it was always framed as this is a personal ethical obligation that Jim Comey has. Not a Department strategic decision. Not a Department even policy decision. But a personal ethical obligation that he has."

4.   Decision Not to Order Comey to Stand Down

Lynch described the Department's decision-making process to us. She stated, "[W]e had a discussion about, well, we need to make sure that at least it's conveyed that we don't want this letter to go out. We think, we think it's not only against policy but it's harmful given the calendar, meaning the timing of the election." Lynch stated that there was also "some discussion about whether either the DAG or I should call directly to the Director and whether or not that was a good idea." Lynch told us that "the staff's view" was a direct call from either of them "was not going to change anything based upon the discussions that [Axelrod] was having with Rybicki." Lynch continued:

And ultimately what we decided to do was to, was to continue to have the staff discussions and have [Axelrod] convey the strong view that neither the DAG nor I felt this letter should go out. And that we thought that it was going to cause serious problems. The response we got back was essentially the Director heard us, took that into consideration. Also took into consideration whoever he was speaking with...at the FBI, and was going to send the letter in any event.

We asked Lynch why she did not directly order Comey to stand down and not send the letter to Congress. Lynch told us:

I thought about it. I went back and forth on it. And we did in the room. We went back and forth on it. And ultimately, I did have a concern, and we had discussed this in the, in the small group also about the perception of Department leadership trying to somehow prevent information damaging to a candidate from coming out and that also being a political problem, because we also had the, we talked about it from the sense of, you know, you talk about reopening an investigation into either candidate, you know, whether we had, for example, said something about, you know, the, the Russian stuff at that point in time. We wouldn't have done that.

[B]ut the concern of appearing to put a thumb on the scale for a particular candidate was something we were wrestling with. And that's what I was wrestling with, was if in fact someone comes to you and says I have a legal, moral, and ethical obligation to do something, this is what I think is right, and then you say well you can't do it because of this policy and don't do it, then are you in fact then sort of doing the same thing only on the other side. And I will tell you, we went back and forth. Certainly I went back and forth in my mind over what to do, as to whether or not I should call him directly or have the DAG call him directly first, then have me call him. Either way, should there be a direct call to him?

We asked Lynch to respond to the criticism that she essentially abdicated her responsibility by not ordering Comey to stand down. Lynch responded:

I would say I was trying to get him to do the right thing. And I was hoping he would do the right thing. And I would say that you can have that criticism of me if you, if you would like. But I really felt that, that, frankly, when I say he didn't need me to tell him, I don't mean to say that I had no role in it at all. But this shouldn't have come up. This shouldn't have been an issue. This, this should not have been something that was being considered.

Lynch told us that she "went back and forth" on whether to order Comey to stand down, but she "thought at that point...it could lead to greater damage," meaning that Comey would disobey and send the letter anyway.

We also asked Yates why she or Lynch did not directly order Comey to stand down and not send the letter to Congress. Yates stated:

I certainly discussed it with Loretta.... [W]e looked at this and thought, all right. It was not presented to us as, again, you know, [Comey's] kind of thinking about this and he's wanting to know what you guys, and I don't mean to be sarcastic here at all. But this was really important how this was framed. It wasn't a he's seeking your view on this or he's torn and wants to know.... It was framed as he feels obligated ethically to do this. And it was like a notification. He feels obligated to do it. That's a difficult situation because, yes, either one of us had the authority to order him not to do it. But you got to play out what happens after that....

[L]et's imagine a scenario here where we order him not to do it. We're then ordering him not to do something he says he feels like he's ethically obligated to do. There are a couple options. He can say...I'm sorry that you're saying that but I feel ethically obligated and I'm going to do it anyway. So then we're in a scenario where he notifies Congress. He's been telling us it's going to come out. Because on top of this I'm ethically obligated to do it paired with that was it's going to leak out. It's going to come out and if I don't tell Congress that's going to put me in a very bad position because they're going to find out anyway and they're going to find out that I didn't tell them when I could have. So we're in a scenario where he says he's ethically obligated to do it.... [W]e weren't at all convinced that he would follow such an order not to do it. If he didn't follow the order and he did it anyway and then it comes out we were ordering him not to do it that's a very bad position for the Department of Justice. Because we're then telling the Director of the FBI not to do something he feels like he's ethically obligated to do. And it takes a bad situation and it makes it even worse because then you add what would be the perception of a concealment on top of this that we thought would be even worse for DOJ.

There's another option there which is he, we order him not to do it and he resigns. And then it comes out that that's why he's resigning. That seemed like a very real possibility to us, particularly against the backdrop of the situation with John Ashcroft in the hospital room where he had the resignation letter drafted. That wasn't even an ethical obligation. That was something where he disagreed with them about the statutory authority there. So we thought it was a very real possibility that he could resign and then it's, of course it's going to come out. And so that then is a bad situation for DOJ because it's got the concealment there as well.

So we couldn't figure out a scenario that was not going to, again, take a bad situation and make it even worse when we ordered him to do it when it had been framed as his personal ethical obligation. And we looked at it from every conceivable angle.

Axelrod stated that he participated in discussions with both Yates and Lynch about how to respond to the proposed congressional notification. Axelrod told us that he did not remember anyone advocating that Lynch order Comey not to notify Congress. Axelrod stated that there were "three possible outcomes, all of which [were] really bad" should Lynch order Comey not to send to the letter. First, Axelrod told us that Comey could obey the order and that "tees up an obstruction of Congress investigation" of Lynch because she has forbidden Comey from correcting a misimpression to Congress. Second, Axelrod stated that Comey could ignore the order and send the letter anyway, and then "you're in the same spot except the FBI Director has disobeyed a direct order from the AG so then you have to fire him." Third, Comey could resign. Axelrod told us, "[N]one of those [are] good for the institutions. None of those [are] good for the policies and the procedures or the, sort of the goals of keeping DOJ and FBI out of politics. None of those good for the AG personally."

5.   Decision Not to Engage Directly with Comey

We asked Lynch why she or Yates did not contact Comey directly. Lynch stated, "I didn't get the impression that a private conversation was going to get me any more information than we were being given before." Lynch stated that she was "surprised" that Comey did not contact her or Yates directly and noted that he had spoken directly to both of them in July. Lynch also stated that Comey "set the terms of" the conversation by starting it at the Rybicki-Axelrod level.

We asked Yates why she or Lynch did not contact Comey directly. Yates stated that the FBI decided to have Rybicki reach out to Axelrod initially and "[i]t was just a notification to" Axelrod. Yates continued:

> So we went through the thought process of is there a viable way to order him not to do it and we concluded we didn't think that there was without it blowing up in a much worse way than we were already in.... So the second step in the analysis thing is okay, if we're not going to order him should Loretta get on the phone with him? Should I get on the phone with him and talk about it? And we went through that analysis as well and we came out the same place for these reasons.

> Again, he's not saying this is a strategic or policy question he has. He feels ethically obligated. Both of us have the authority to order him not to do it. So if we call him up I can't have a conversation with him about this without telling him I think it's a huge mistake for him to do this. The feeling was is that that would be portrayed as strong-arming him when you have the authority to be able to tell him not to do it and you have this conversation with him saying, I really don't think you should do this....

Yates told us that she felt this concern about "strong-arming" was later borne out in Comey's description of the meeting with Lynch in September 2015 about whether to call the investigation a matter or investigation. Yates continued:

And then you layer on top of that this. Strategically based on my interaction with [Comey] over all of this time I felt like our best chance at being able to convince him not to do this was going to be from his own, his discussions with his own people. That I had seen in too many meetings, and understand this, that if I had raised an objection to something FBI was doing that [Comey] understandably was very defensive of his agency and he would push back hard. I didn't think there was any way in the world he was going to go back to his people and say, I just got off the phone with the AG or I just got off the phone with the DAG and they convinced me that I really don't have this personal ethical obligation I've told all of you that I have. I felt like strategically the best way to convince him not to do it was going to be to convince his people that he shouldn't do it. And he in discussions with them could come to that conclusion because he could change his mind internally. I didn't think he would change his mind through a discussion with either one of us.

Yates told us that she considered Rybicki to be his "confidant" and the person that the Department needed to convince to change Comey's mind in this situation.

We asked Axelrod why Lynch did not contact Comey directly. Axelrod stated a direct conversation on the phone could lead to "a misunderstanding" or the impression that Lynch "was leaning on" Comey. Axelrod specifically highlighted the matter/investigation meeting between Comey and Lynch in September 2015 as an example of such a misunderstanding. Axelrod also stated that everyone understood Rybicki to be "a proxy for the Director." Axelrod added:

I thought about this a lot in the aftermath, right. And I've thought...if the reaction from [Rybicki] or the FBI had ever been oh, we didn't know you guys felt that way. We didn't know what your guys' view was...then I would have both been really disappointed in myself but also wondered like oh, well if only, right, something got garbled somewhere. If only, you know, the, one of the principals had been able to speak directly to the Director we could have conveyed the message more clearly. I've never heard that...and I don't think that's the case. I was quite clear with [Rybicki] as to what our building's view.... It was clear that was not just Matt Axelrod's view but the Department's view was that the Director should not do this.... I'm sure that was his takeaway. What I put is this, doing this violates our policies and procedures and traditions.... I said repeatedly this is, you know, this is not only a really bad idea but it, it's contrary to how we do business. And actually, I used those exact words as well. It was contrary to how we do business.

6.   Comey's Reaction to the Department's Response

Comey stated that Rybicki reported that the Department "didn't wish to speak to me, but that their advice would be not to do it and that they didn't think it was necessary." Comey added that Rybicki told him that the Department "recommend[ed] against" the congressional notification and thought it was "a bad idea."

We asked Comey why he asked for the Department's feedback and then ignored the feedback that he received. Comey told us, "I thought the better view of it was that we had to. They were leaving it to me essentially and I took it, I knew that I was alone at that point in time, but my view was, as between these two options, I disagree." Comey emphasized that neither Yates nor Lynch gave him a direct order. Comey continued, "I would not have sent it if they had told me not to. Instead I got this, we recommend against it. We don't think it's consistent with our policy. But it's up to him was the message conveyed to me." Comey told us that he felt that he gave Lynch and Yates "the chance to engage," but "they didn't wish to participate, it's up to you, basically I took that as, it's up to you. We don't think it's a good idea. We advise against it. I honestly thought they were taking kind of a cowardly way out."[183]

We asked Comey if anything short of a direct order would have prevented the notification. He stated:

> I don't know what, I don't know is the answer. I don't, because I don't know what argument that I haven't thought of or that hasn't been made or that we didn't make in discussing this they would've made, so I don't know, but, so in the absence of that, if they directed me not to do it, I would not have done it.

Comey stated that he also thought the October 28 congressional notification was consistent with Department policy. He stated, "Well Department policy is we don't comment on investigations unless there's a, you know whatever the exact language is, overriding public interest. In my view there was a powerful public interest in that division between speaking and concealing, between really bad and catastrophic."

We asked Comey how Lynch or Yates could have ordered him not to send the letter if they understood it to be his personal or ethical obligation to Congress. Comey stated:

> Of course they could. They could say, I mean circumstances where a Department lawyer thinks that they need to disclose something in a particular case and their supervisor says, no we don't, we don't do that, and so you have to decide then, do you believe it's reasonable and consistent with the obligations of the lawyer for the United States or do you believe that your supervisor is doing something unethical and then you have to decide what to do about it.

---

[183] In his book, Comey stated that after he received the Department's feedback, "I briefly toyed with the idea of communicating to them that I had decided not to tell Congress, just to see what they would do if I shifted the responsibility entirely to them, but decided that would be cowardly and stupid. Once again it became my responsibility to take the hit." COMEY, *supra*, at 197.

V.   Finalizing the FBI's October 28, 2016 Letter to Congress

After Comey decided to notify Congress, the FBI began discussing internally how that notification should occur. Anderson told us that because the "animating rationale" behind the notification was to update Comey's prior testimony to Congress, the FBI decided that "a letter to Congress was the right way to go about it." The letter was transmitted on October 28.

In this section we discuss the drafting of the letter along with several key edits made during the drafting process. We also describe discussions with the Department about the letter and Comey's email to all FBI employees.

A.   October 28, 2016 Letter to Congress

At approximately 11:50 a.m. on October 28, the FBI transmitted the following letter to Congress, which we also provide as Attachment E:

> In previous congressional testimony, I referred to the fact that the Federal Bureau of Investigation (FBI) had completed its investigation of former Secretary Clinton's personal email server. Due to recent developments, I am writing to supplement my previous testimony.

> In connection with an unrelated case, the FBI has learned of the existence of emails that appear to be pertinent to the investigation. I am writing to inform you that the investigative team briefed me on this yesterday, and I agreed that the FBI should take appropriate investigative steps designed to allow investigators to review these emails to determine whether they contain classified information, as well as to assess their importance to our investigation.

> Although the FBI cannot yet assess whether or not this material may be significant, and I cannot predict how long it will take us to complete this additional work, I believe it is important to update your Committees about our efforts in light of my previous testimony.

Later that day, after the letter was made public, Clinton's lawyer, David Kendall, contacted Baker to ask about the letter. According to Baker's email to Comey and the Midyear team, during the call Kendall complained that Comey's "letter was 'tantalizingly ambiguous' and made statements that were 'inchoate and highly ominous' such that what we had done was worse than transparency because it allows people to make whatever they want out of the letter to the prejudice of Secretary Clinton." In the email, Baker stated that he told Kendall "that I could not respond to his requests at this time."

B.   Drafting the Letter and Key Edits

Comey described the drafting of the letter in the following terms:

> Our goal was to make the disclosure to Congress accurate, fair and as non-misleading as humanly possible. So we spent a lot of time that night [of October 27] on the wordsmithing of that language to give fair

366

notice that we were taking this action, but not to put us in a position where it's wildly overinterpreted one way or the other. And so the next day, the next morning, I had finally approved the language.

Comey continued:

[W]e struggled with the language of it. Everyone talks about my vague letter. Maybe it's vague, but it was structured with great care not to overstate what might be there or understate what might be there because—I think I said this in the letter, I haven't looked at it in a while—we don't know, but feel an obligation to say that we're undertaking these new investigative steps. And I think part of the public misconception about it is, and I don't know how I would have fixed this, is people have the sense that it was some sort of marginal lead, that it was a frolic and detour kind of deal. And I don't know how we could have done that, but maybe we would've been better off if there was some way to convey, yeah there could be a real deal here, but that then would be unfair because you would be overinterpreting the evidence.

In his book, Comey discussed the "carefully" chosen wording of the October 28 letter and why it contained limited content. Comey explained, "Because we didn't know what we had and what we might find, any further public statement would be inherently limited and misleading and only add confusion and damage to the FBI."[184]

FBI Attorney 1 told us that she and Strzok began drafts of the letter to Congress after leaving the initial meeting with Comey on October 27. FBI Attorney 1 stated that she and Strzok combined their drafts and presented the joint draft to Baker. FBI Attorney 1 continued, "We talked to [Baker], I remember handwritten edits that [Baker] put in, which were wordsmithing a lot of. And then it moved to email so that people could circulate it."

We identified two significant phrases in the letter that were discussed during the editing process. We discuss each below.

1.   "Appear to be Pertinent"

The letter sent to Congress stated that "the FBI has learned of the existence of emails that *appear to be pertinent* to the investigation" and noted that "the FBI cannot yet assess whether or not this material may be significant". (Emphasis added). FBI Attorney 1's first draft stated that the emails "may be relevant" and noted that "[a]t this time, it is impossible to determine if the emails are new or duplicative." Strzok's first draft stated that the emails were "related to the FBI's prior investigation" of the Clinton email server and noted that "the FBI cannot assess at this time the significance of this material." Various formulations similar to

---

[184] COMEY, *supra*, at 200-01.

these were discussed before deciding upon the language ultimately used in the letter.

FBI Attorney 1 told us that two competing considerations resulted in the language used. On the one hand, FBI Attorney 1 stated that the FBI did not want to undermine the probable cause needed to obtain the search warrant, "[s]o we couldn't say it may be relevant when we, we needed to have probable cause to actually look at" the emails. On the other hand, FBI Attorney 1 stated that the FBI did not want to overstate what was on the Weiner laptop and the FBI wanted "to make it clear that even though we were getting a search warrant, that did not mean there was a smoking gun there." Anderson echoed this stating, "I was concerned that…saying that they were relevant or were pertinent wasn't supported by where we were in the process. In other words, we hadn't put any eyes on any of the emails, so we really didn't know whether what we were going to find, you know, was or wasn't relevant."

Baker stated that he found "may be pertinent" or similar formulations to be "too vague" and "too wishy-washy." Indeed, Baker stated in an email, on October 27 at 9:51 p.m., to the FBI officials involved in drafting the letter:

> If everyone wants "may be pertinent" then fine. All I am saying is that even if they are all copies of what we already have, they are still pertinent because they are copies and indicate where else the material went and who may have had access to it. And if they only may be pertinent why are we bothering with them and putting out this public statement which we know will be a big deal.

Baker told us that because the FBI was seeking a search warrant for these emails it was "saying there is probable cause to believe this is evidence of a crime, therefore they are pertinent and we should be willing to make that statement." Baker said there was some "pushback" on this suggestion as others said "we're not 100% confident" that the emails are pertinent. Baker stated that he came up with the "appear to be pertinent" phrasing and "that seemed to thread the needle and make everybody happy."

2. "Briefed Me On This Yesterday"

The letter sent to Congress also stated that "[d]ue to recent developments, I am writing to supplement my previous testimony" and "I am writing to inform you that the investigative team briefed me on this yesterday." FBI Attorney 1's first draft stated that the FBI "has recently retrieved emails" and "today, the FBI decided to conduct additional investigative steps." Strzok's first draft stated that the FBI "recently learned of the potential existence of emails" and "earlier today, I decided the FBI will take investigative action." The joint draft submitted by FBI Attorney 1 and Strzok to the others stated that the FBI "recently learned of the existence of emails" and Comey decided "earlier today" to take investigative action on these emails.

In providing comments and edits to the draft letter, Baker stated in an email on the night of October 27, "[T]he institution has known about these for a while (albeit not long) but not 'yesterday.' What happened today was the Director's decision." Baker recommended the letter state that "I decided yesterday." We asked Baker about this recommendation. Baker stated that he could not recall the discussion about this change and also did not remember knowing at the time that Comey had been previously briefed about the Weiner laptop.

3.   Discussions About Letter With the Department

The FBI did not share a copy of the draft letter with the Department, but rather read the proposed text of the letter to Axelrod and Toscas during a telephone call. We found that, during the call, Axelrod provided feedback regarding the letter, but we did not identify any evidence showing that the FBI accepted his proposed edits.

Comey told us that he recalled telling Rybicki "to share the text of the letter with [the Department], ask for feedback." Comey further stated that it was his understanding the Department provided "a lot" of edits to the draft that were accepted. Comey said, "Yeah I think Matt Axelrod added real value, yeah, is my recollection, shaping it in a different way, shortening it at different parts."

Rybicki told us that he discussed the proposed letter with Axelrod and Toscas on the telephone "and we read it to them, and they provided some feedback."

Axelrod told us that the FBI never provided the Department with a copy of the proposed letter, but stated that he did discuss the contents of the letter with the FBI. Axelrod stated that Baker and Rybicki read portions of the letter to Axelrod and Toscas over the phone, and that he (Axelrod) suggested edits to the letter that the FBI did not accept. Axelrod stated:

So, on that phone call when they read the first sentence I said to them, to Rybicki and Baker is my memory of who was on the phone.... If that's how you start the letter the headline is going to be case reopened. We all agree that's not what we're doing. We're not reopening the case, right? Agreement voiced on the phone by FBI. Agreement voiced by [Toscas]. If that's your opening sentence that's going to be the headline, case reopened. And what you need to, what you ought to do is you're telling us that you need to send this letter because the Director believes that he's left a misimpression. But remember when I pointed you to the transcript what he said was if new information comes to light I will bring it, I will, we will take a look at it.

You, why don't you reference that? Explain why you're, what you're doing. Don't just make it seem like, you know, you're emailing them out of nowhere. Say, I previously testified. I told you that if new information came to light we would, you know, take a look at it. Some new information has come to light. We're doing exactly what I said. So that was one suggestion we made to them on the phone, which they ignored.

369

And a second suggestion we made to them on the phone was that they include some context about what the device was. In other words, that it wasn't a Hillary Clinton device but that it was...the husband of a former aide or former senior aide, right? Because, and that was important for context because...if you don't put that context in there could be a notion that something was hidden from the investigators that only recently came to light instead of something that came in sideways. But they rejected that suggestion as well.

Because I think what we, our pitch to them on the call was like, you say you need to send this letter to avoid, to correct the misimpression Congress has. You got to make damn sure that by sending the letter you don't just create a different misimpression. They ignored our two substantive suggestions. Those are the two I remember. And they sent the letter I think basically the way they had, and I didn't see the full text beforehand but basically it was, you know, what sort of, at least the parts Baker had read to us on the phone it was consistent with, it didn't, I don't think they changed a word.

Toscas said that the entire discussion about the contents of the letter was "awkward" since the Department "oppose[d] every aspect of this." Toscas stated, "But I do remember like at some point on our side feeling like...if you're going to say it, there's a way to just sort of lay it out a little bit more clearly that takes off some of the natural suspicions that are going to be created by less clear, less specific, and more ambiguous language." Toscas told us that he did not recall if the FBI accepted any of the suggested edits provided by the Department.

4.   Comey Email to All FBI Employees

At 3:08 p.m. on October 28, after news of the letter to Congress had been publicly reported, Comey sent the following message to all FBI employees:

This morning I sent a letter to Congress in connection with the Secretary Clinton email investigation. Yesterday, the investigative team briefed me on their recommendation with respect to seeking access to emails that have recently been found in an unrelated case. Because those emails appear to be pertinent to our investigation, I agreed that we should take appropriate steps to obtain and review them.

Of course, we don't ordinarily tell Congress about ongoing investigations, but here I feel an obligation to do so given that I testified repeatedly in recent months that our investigation was completed. I also think it would be misleading to the American people were we not to supplement the record. At the same time, however, given that we don't know the significance of this newly discovered collection of emails, I don't want to create a misleading impression. In trying to strike a balance, in a brief letter and in the middle of an election season, there is significant risk of being misunderstood, but I wanted you to hear directly from me about it.

VI.   Analysis of the Decision to Send the October 28 Letter

We found no evidence that Comey's decision to send the October 28 letter was influenced by political preferences. Instead, we found that his decision was the result of several interrelated factors that were connected to his concern that failing to send the letter would harm the FBI and his ability to lead it, and his view that candidate Clinton was going to win the presidency and that she would be perceived to be an illegitimate president if the public first learned of the information after the election. Although Comey told us that he "didn't make this decision because [he] thought it would leak otherwise," several FBI officials, including Baker and Strzok, told us that the concern about leaks played a role in the decision. We concluded that, in considering his choices, Comey failed to give adequate consideration to long-established Department and FBI norms, policies, and expectations that he applied in other cases. Although we acknowledge that Comey faced a difficult situation with unattractive choices, in proceeding as he did on October 28, Comey made a serious error of judgment.

Much like with his July 5 announcement, Comey engaged in ad hoc decisionmaking based on his personal views even if it meant rejecting longstanding Department policy or practice. For example, we found unpersuasive Comey's explanation as to why transparency was more important than Department policy and practice with regard to the reactivated Midyear investigation while, by contrast, Department policy and practice was more important to follow with regard to the Clinton Foundation and Russia investigations.

A.   Substantive Assessment of Comey's Decision

1.   FBI and Department Norms and Policies

Comey had ample guidance in longstanding Department and FBI policies and norms regarding making public statements about pending investigations and taking actions that might affect elections.

To start, the Department and the FBI consistently decline to comment publicly or to Congress regarding ongoing investigative activity. The "stay silent" principle exists to protect the privacy and reputational interests of the subjects of the investigation, the right to a fair trial for those subsequently accused of crimes, the integrity of an ongoing investigation or pending litigation, and the Department's ability to effectively administer justice without political or other undue outside influences. Comey endorsed this principle in general, stating, "I believe very strongly that our rule should be, we don't comment on pending investigations." This principle is embodied in several regulations and policies set forth in Chapter Two, including in policies regarding communications with Congress. USAM 1-8.030; Eric Holder, Attorney General, U.S. Department of Justice, memorandum for Heads of Department Components and all U.S. Attorneys, Communications with Congress, August 17, 2009; Robert Raben, Assistant Attorney General, U.S. Department of Justice, letter to Congressman John Linder, January 1, 2000. ("Although Congress has a clearly legitimate interest in determining how the Department enforces statutes, Congressional inquiries during the pendency of a matter pose an inherent threat to the integrity of the Department's law enforcement and litigation functions.").[185] This principle is also reflected in 28 C.F.R. § 50.2, which provides, with respect to the release of information to the news media, that "where information relating to the circumstances of...an investigation would be highly prejudicial or where the release thereof would serve no law enforcement function, such information should not be made public." 28 C.F.R. § 50.2(b)(3)(iv).[186] *See also* USAM 1-7.530, 9-11.130, 9-16.500, 9-27.760; FBI Media Policy Guide 3.1.

In addition, the Department and the FBI have long observed a norm against taking an action during the run-up to an election that could impact an election. Although there is no codified "60-day rule," Comey acknowledged that he has consistently adhered to this "take no action" norm in the past: "I've lived my entire career in the Department of Justice under the norm, the principle, that we, if at all possible, avoid taking any action in the run up to an election, avoid taking any action that could have some impact, even if unknown, on an election whether that's a dogcatcher election or President of the United States." Given the lack of a written policy, we recommend that the Department consider providing guidance to agents and prosecutors concerning the taking of overt investigative steps, indictments, public announcements, or other actions that could impact an election.

These policies and norms formed the fundamental backdrop for Comey's decision on October 28. Because of them, Comey's description of his choice as being between "two doors," one labeled "speak" and one labeled "conceal," was a false dichotomy. The two doors were actually labeled "follow policy/practice" and "depart from policy/practice." His task was not to conduct an ad hoc comparison of case-specific outcomes and risks. Rather, the burden was on him to justify an extraordinary departure from these established norms, policies, and precedent.

2.   Comey's Justification for Departing

Comey's justification for departing from established norms was that because he had previously told Congress and the public that the case was over, staying silent would be misleading. But it is hardly unique for the FBI to receive new information that might cause it to reactivate a previously closed or dormant investigation. To our knowledge, the FBI has not generally identified this circumstance as nullifying the stay silent principle.

Comey admitted that he had made no explicit promise to make a further announcement if new evidence were discovered. He stated, instead, that he had

---

[185] Current Department policy regarding communications with Congress continues to honor this principle. *See* Jefferson B. Sessions, Attorney General, U.S. Department of Justice, Memorandum for All Heads of Department Components, Communications with Congress, May 2, 2018.

[186] 28 C.F.R. § 50.2 is directed largely at preventing the prejudice to defendants or subjects from media publicity that might influence the outcome of a trial. However, it states that the guidelines it contains—including "stay silent"—are effective "from the time a person is the subject of a criminal investigation until any proceeding resulting from such an investigation has been terminated by trial or otherwise." 28 C.F.R. § 50.2(b)(1). An unfair trial is obviously not the only form of prejudice that may arise from media disclosures, especially in an investigation that does not result in a trial.

previously offered "maximal transparency" because that "enhances the credibility of the Justice enterprise," and that maintaining that transparency required him to update his July statement in October.

If so, the problem originated with Comey's elevation of "maximal transparency" as a value overriding, for this case only, the principles of "stay silent" and "take no action" that the FBI has consistently applied to other cases. The Department and the FBI do not practice "maximal transparency" in criminal investigations. It is not a value reflected in the regulations, policies, or customs guiding FBI actions in pending criminal investigations. To the contrary, the guidance to agents and prosecutors is precisely the opposite—no transparency except in rare and exceptional circumstances due to the potential harm to both the investigation and to the reputation of anyone under investigation.

Comey told us that the potentially great evidentiary significance of the newly discovered emails would have made it particularly misleading to stay silent. But we found that the FBI's basis for believing, as of October 28, that the contents of the Weiner laptop would be significant to the Clinton email investigation was overestimated. Comey and others stated that they believed the Weiner laptop might contain the "missing three months" of Clinton's emails from the beginning of her tenure when she used a BlackBerry domain, and that these "golden emails" would be particularly probative of intent, because they were close in time to when she set up her server. However, at the time of the October 28 letter, the FBI had limited information about the BlackBerry data that was on the laptop. The case agent assigned to the Weiner investigation stated only that he saw at least one BlackBerry PIN message between Clinton and Abedin. As of October 28, no one with any knowledge of the Midyear investigation had viewed a single email message, and the Midyear team was uncertain they would even be able to establish sufficient probable cause to obtain a search warrant. Even the description of the emails in the October 28 letter is at odds with Comey's emphasis on the importance of the discovery. The letter was edited to state that the emails "appear to be pertinent," because several members of the team objected to the words "are pertinent" as an unsupportable overstatement.

Moreover, the Midyear team did not treat the BlackBerry emails as if they were critical to completing a thorough investigation prior to October. Rather, the team decided during the investigation not to obtain personal devices that Clinton's senior aides used for State Department work, because, among other reasons, they did not believe obtaining those devices was necessary for a thorough investigation. Indeed, the Midyear team did not ask Abedin's attorneys to turn over Abedin's personal BlackBerry or laptop that she used during her employment at the State Department, even though Abedin told the FBI that she had given those devices to her attorneys so that they could produce her work-related emails to the State Department.

Before October 28, Comey lauded the thoroughness of the investigation and stated that declining prosecution was not a close call.[187] If the vague and general information known about the laptop contents was sufficient to "create a reasonable likelihood...that will change our view" of the case, then it is difficult to see how the investigation could have been as thorough as Comey represented given the FBI's decision not to obtain similar devices from Clinton's senior aides prior to July 5. Nor could the declination decision have been such an easy call if unseen emails to and from one of Clinton's aides could have resulted in a change in the Department's prosecution assessment.

In fact, as detailed in Chapter Nine, every pertinent fact that the FBI knew about the laptop in October was already known in late September. Yet none of the Midyear investigators thought these were "golden emails" then—a factor that contributed to the FBI's delay in acting on the information, as discussed in Chapter Nine. In short, far too little was known about these emails in October 2016 to justify departing from Department norms, policies, and precedent.

3.   Comey's Comparison of Risks and Outcomes

Instead of referring to and being guided by longstanding Department and FBI policies and precedent, Comey conducted an ad hoc comparison of the risks and outcomes associated with each option. He described the potential consequences "concealing" the existence of the emails as "catastrophic" to the FBI and the Department, because it would subject the FBI and the Department to allegations that they had acted for political reasons to protect Hillary Clinton. Instead, Comey said he chose the option that he assessed as being just "really bad."

Even within the flawed analytical construct that Comey set up, he did not assess risks evenhandedly. He assigned paramount significance to avoiding the reputational risk of staying silent: that he and the FBI would be unfairly accused of hiding the emails to protect candidate Clinton. But he appears to have placed no comparable value on the corresponding risk from making the public statement: that he and the FBI would not only be accused of violating long-standing Department and FBI policy and practice, but that he also would be unfairly accused of hyping the emails in a manner that hurt candidate Clinton. We believe that Comey's unequal assessment of these risks was the product of his belief that Clinton was going to win the election. Comey told us, "I am sure I was influenced by the tacit assumption that Hillary Clinton was sure to be the next President." This expectation likely led him to focus too heavily on what he perceived to be the consequences of not revealing the new information, namely undermining the legitimacy of Clinton's presidency and harming the reputation of the FBI. Ironically, in his effort to avoid the FBI or himself being seen as political, Comey based his decision, in part, on his assessment of the likely outcome of the political process.

---

[187] In his book, Comey stated, with respect to the July declination, that "[n]o fair-minded person with any experience in the counterespionage world (where 'spills' of classified information are investigated and prosecuted) could think this was a case the career prosecutors at the Department of Justice might pursue. There was literally zero chance of that." COMEY, *supra*, at 185.

In our view, assumptions about the outcome of an election should not affect how the FBI or the Department applies longstanding policies and norms.

We believe that Comey underestimated his own ability to address the unfair criticism that he feared would ensue if he stayed silent. Comey acknowledged to us, "I've lived my entire career in the Department of Justice under the norm, the principle, that we...avoid taking any action that could have some impact, even if unknown, on an election...." Thus, if Comey had chosen to have the FBI seek the search warrant but not send the October 28 letter, he would have had a principled response if he was asked about his decision: "This is the way we always do it, for the following good reasons." And he could have stated, accurately and in good conscience, that he applied this principle evenhandedly with respect to the Clinton email investigation and other pending FBI investigations. The FBI never commented publicly on the Russia investigation until after the election, and he refused to comment publicly about the Clinton Foundation investigation. And, earlier in October 2016, Comey declined on behalf of the FBI to participate in a U.S. Intelligence Community statement warning about Russian interference because "it exposes us to accusations of launching our own 'October surprise.'" Had he observed the same principle with respect to the Clinton email investigation, the evenhandedness of his decisions would have been apparent. Indeed, much of the criticism that Comey received for not revealing before the election information about the Russia and Clinton Foundation investigations was due to the perceived lack of evenhandness given the disclosure he made on October 28 in the Clinton email investigation.

In reaching our conclusion about the October 28 letter, we found the testimony of Deputy Assistant Attorney General George Toscas to be on point:

> One of the things that I tell people all the time, after having been in the Department for almost 24 years now, is I stress to people and people who work at all levels, the institution has principles and there's always an urge when something important or different pops up to say, we should do it differently or those principles or those protocols you know we should—we might want to deviate because this is so different. But the comfort that we get as people, as lawyers, as representatives, as employees and as an institution, the comfort we get from those institutional policies, protocols, has, is an unbelievable thing through whatever storm, you know whatever storm hits us, when you are within the norm of the way the institution behaves, you can weather any of it because you stand on the principle.

> And once you deviate, even in a minor way, and you're always going to want to deviate. It's always going to be something important and some big deal that makes you think, oh let's do this a little differently. But once you do that, you have removed yourself from the comfort of saying this institution has a way of doing things and then every decision is another ad hoc decision that may be informed by our policy and our protocol and principles, but it's never going to be squarely within them.

4.   Fear of Leaks

Comey denied that a fear of leaks influenced his decision to send the October 28 letter to Congress. However, other witnesses told us that a concern about leaks played a role in the decision. As Baker stated, "We were quite confident that.... [I]f we don't put out a letter, somebody is going to leak it. That definitely was discussed...." Numerous witnesses connected this concern about leaks specifically to NYO and told us that FBI leadership suspected that FBI personnel in NYO were responsible for leaks of information in other matters. Even accepting Comey's assertion that leaks played no role in his decision, we found that, at a minimum, a fear of leaks influenced the thinking of those who were advising him.

We also note that these discussions on October 27 and 28 were occurring at almost the same time that FBI leadership was focused on how the Midyear investigation was being publicly portrayed. As detailed in Chapter Eight, the FBI was devoting significant time and attention in October 2016 responding to both public and private criticism of the Midyear investigation. That included sending talking points to FBI SACs on October 21 for their use in responding to such criticism. Comey told us that these efforts were necessary to "protect the credibility of the [FBI] in American life." As a result, at the time Comey was deciding whether to send the October 28 letter to Congress, the FBI had just one week earlier empowered its officials to speak publicly about the FBI's handling of the Midyear investigation. In our view, this confluence of events inevitably increased the risk of leaks.

B.   Lack of Communication Between Comey and Department Leadership

As we describe above, on October 27 and 28, Comey and Lynch decided not to speak to one another, in person or by phone, about the decision to notify Congress. Instead, Comey directed Rybicki to contact Axelrod, and the Department decided to communicate its response entirely through Axelrod. Comey explained that he decided to ask Rybicki to contact Axelrod rather than speaking directly to Lynch or Yates because "...I didn't want to jam them and I wanted to offer them the opportunity to think about and decide whether they wanted to be engaged on it."

We asked Lynch and Yates why they did not call Comey or ask to meet with him after Rybicki's initial notification to Axelrod. Both Lynch and Yates told the OIG that they made an intentional strategic decision to handle discussions about the letter to Congress through Axelrod and Rybicki. Both Lynch and Yates explained that they were concerned that any direct discussion with Comey—particularly any discussion in which they told him not to send the letter—would be perceived as an attempt to prevent him from fulfilling his "personal ethical obligation" to notify Congress. Both stated that they were concerned that the fact of any such direct discussions would leak and would be portrayed as Department leadership attempting to "prevent information damaging to a candidate from coming out" (Lynch) or "strong-arming" Comey (Yates).

Lynch and Yates also told the OIG that a significant factor in their decision to handle communications through Rybicki and Axelrod was that direct discussions likely would have been ineffective. Lynch said the fact that Comey did not call her directly indicated that he did not want a real discussion and had already made up his mind to send a letter, because he would call her to discuss other issues that were not resolved. Yates stated that, based on her experience with Comey, he was likely to "push back hard" against input from Lynch or her, especially if accepting their input meant that he had to go back to his staff and explain that he was reversing his decision based on their input. She told us that she believed strategically the best way to convince him not to send the letter was to allow him to come to that conclusion through discussions with his own staff, including Rybicki. Yates told us that she considered Rybicki to be his "confidant" and the person that the Department needed to convince to change Comey's mind in this situation.

Comey's reaction to the input he received as the result of Rybicki's discussions with Axelrod suggests that these concerns were well-founded. While Comey stated that he "welcome[d]" the Department's feedback, he did not take their feedback into account when Rybicki told him that the Department "recommend[ed] against" the letter and thought it was "a bad idea." When asked why he essentially ignored the advice of Department leadership, Comey told us, "I thought the better view of it was that we had to [send the letter]. They were leaving it to me essentially and I took it, I knew that I was alone at that point in time, but my view was, as between these two options, I disagree." Comey added that he felt that he gave Lynch and Yates "the chance to engage," but "they didn't wish to participate, it's up to you, basically I took that as, it's up to you. We don't think it's a good idea. We advise against it. I honestly thought they were taking kind of a cowardly way out."

Although Comey told us that he would not have sent the October 28 letter had Lynch or Yates ordered him not to do it, we found no evidence that he or Rybicki ever conveyed this to Department leadership. Both Lynch and Yates cited Comey's description of his "personal ethical obligation" to notify Congress and his concerns about the "survivability" of failing to do so as reasons that they believed a direct order would be ineffective. As described above, Axelrod told the OIG that they considered three possible negative outcomes should Lynch order Comey not to send to the letter: Comey could obey the order and Lynch would be accused of obstructing Congress; Comey could ignore the order and send the letter anyway, and Department leadership would have to fire him; and Comey could resign. Axelrod told us, "[N]one of those [are] good for the institutions. None of those [are] good for the policies and the procedures or the, sort of the goals of keeping DOJ and FBI out of politics. None of those [are] good for the AG personally."

We acknowledge that Comey, Lynch, and Yates faced difficult choices in late October 2016. However, we found it extraordinary that Comey assessed that it was best that the FBI Director not speak directly with the Attorney General and Deputy Attorney General about how to best navigate this most important decision and mitigate the resulting harms, and that Comey's decision resulted in the Attorney General and Deputy Attorney General concluding that it would be counterproductive to speak directly with the FBI Director. We believe that open and candid communication among leaders in the Department and its components is essential for the effective functioning of the Department.

CHAPTER ELEVEN:
COMPLETION OF THE INVESTIGATION

I.   The October 30, 2016 Search Warrant

The FBI obtained a search warrant for the Midyear-related material on the Weiner laptop on October 30, 2016. The search warrant authorized the FBI to search for four categories of information on the laptop:

> 1. Data and information associated with the operation, use, maintenance, backup, auditing, and security functions of the Subject Laptop...;
>
> 2. Data and information electronically stored on the Subject Laptop related to communications with email accounts used by former Secretary of State Hillary Clinton during her tenure as Secretary of State;
>
> 3. Data and information on the Subject Laptop that might identify the person or persons who accessed classified information present on the Subject Laptop...; and
>
> 4. Data and information on the Subject Laptop that might identify activity related to a computer intrusion....

We discuss the Midyear team's decision to seek a search warrant rather than using consent to review the laptop below. We also discuss the narrow factual basis for the search warrant that the Midyear team included in the application and compare the Weiner laptop with the treatment of other devices during the main part of the Midyear investigation.

A.   Decision Not to Seek Consent from Abedin and Weiner before Seeking a Warrant

Prosecutor 1 told us that there was "some discussion" of getting consent from Weiner and Abedin to search the laptop. However, Prosecutor 1 stated that consent from both was needed and, at that point, the Midyear team's understanding was that Weiner was inaccessible because he was at a location where he did not have access to electronic devices. Prosecutor 1 continued:

> And...there was some concern about [Weiner's] attorney gladly providing consent but wanting something from SDNY for it. And our horse trading on conduct that was egregious and doing something for purposes of our case didn't seem to make much sense. I think the decision was made not to seek consent from either attorney and to get a warrant.

Prosecutor 1 told us that he believed both FBI and the Department agreed with the decision to seek a search warrant rather than consent to access the Weiner laptop.

Baker agreed that they did not want to try to deal with Weiner or his attorney, but also provided an additional explanation for not seeking consent. Baker stated:

> I think we were concerned about that being too prolonged and dragged [out]. I think that reflects some of our frustration with what had happened previously in the investigation. We're trying to get consent, and those kinds of discussions were long and drawn out. And we were just like, screw it, we're not going to deal with that. We're just going to get a damn search warrant. We're just not going to, we're not going to let DOJ take us down that road. We're just going to get a search warrant.... [A]nd in this case, we've got SDNY, and we think they'll be aggressive and they'll go get it.

After reviewing a draft of this report, Toscas and other prosecutors noted that SDNY played no substantive role in the October 30 search warrant.

B.   Factual Basis of the October 30 Search Warrant Application

The factual basis for the October 30 search warrant application, which was prepared by the Midyear team, contained limited information about what the NYO case agent had seen on the Weiner laptop and the importance of that information to the Midyear investigation. The entirety of the search warrant application that discussed what had been seen on the Weiner laptop stated:

> In executing the search of the laptop computer (the Subject Laptop) pursuant to the search warrant issued on September 26, 2016, FBI agents sorted the emails on the Subject Laptop to segregate emails within the scope of the warrant from those outside of it. As a result, the FBI reviewed non-content header information for emails on the Subject Laptop to facilitate its search. In so doing, the FBI observed non-content header information indicating that thousands of emails of Weiner's then wife, Huma Abedin (Abedin), resided on the Subject Laptop. Because Abedin's emails were outside the scope of the September 26 search warrant, the FBI did not review the content of those emails.

> ...The non-content header information that FBI agents reviewed on the Subject Laptop indicates that the emails on the Subject Laptop include emails sent and/or received by Abedin at her @clintonemail.com account and at a Yahoo! email account appearing to belong to Abedin, as well as correspondence between one or both of these accounts and State Department email accounts during and around Abedin's tenure at the State Department. The FBI's investigation of the improper transmission and storage of classified information on unclassified email systems and servers has established that emails containing classified information were transmitted through multiple email accounts used by Abedin, including her @clintonemail.com and Yahoo! email accounts.

The FBI's investigation determined that Abedin, using her various email accounts, typically communicated with Clinton's @clintonemail.com account on a daily basis. Analysis of emails in the FBI's possession revealed more than 4,000 work-related emails between Abedin and Clinton from 2009 to 2013.

The FBI's investigation established that 27 email chains containing classified information, as determined by the relevant original classification authorities, have been transmitted through Abedin's @clintonemail and/or Yahoo! accounts. Out of the 27 email chains, six email chains contained information that was classified at the Secret level at the time the emails were sent, and information in four of those email chains remains classified at that level now, while two email chains contain information that is currently classified at the Confidential level. Information in the remaining 21 email chains was classified at the Confidential level at the time the emails were sent, and of those 21 email chains, information in 16 of them remains classified as Confidential.

Given the information indicating that there are thousands of Abedin's emails located on the Subject Laptop – including emails, during and around Abedin's tenure at the State Department, from Abedin's @clintonemail.com account as well as a Yahoo! account appearing to belong to Abedin – and the regular email correspondence between Abedin and Clinton, there is probable cause to believe that the Subject Laptop contains correspondence between Abedin and Clinton during their time at the State Department. Because it has been determined by relevant original classification authorities that many emails were exchanged between Abedin, using her @clintonemail.com and/or Yahoo! accounts, and Clinton that contain classified information, there is also probable cause to believe that the correspondence between them located on the Subject Laptop contains classified information....

Noticeably absent from the search warrant application prepared by the Midyear team is both any mention that the NYO agent had seen Clinton's emails on the laptop and any mention of the potential presence of BlackBerry emails from early in Clinton's tenure. In explaining the absence of this information, Strzok stated:

I think what we were trying to do was establish as tightly as we could the fact that we believed, because I think the basis of the probable cause was that there was classified information on there.... I think it as that narrative was not designed to tell the whole story. That narrative was to, designed to demonstrate to the magistrate that we have probable cause that there was evidence of a crime on there.

We also asked Prosecutor 1 about the factual statement of probable cause outlined in the search warrant. Prosecutor 1 stated:

[T]he [probable cause] was basically that Huma Abedin had an email account. That email account communicated with email accounts where classified information was there. Classified information made it into Huma's email accounts. We believe information from those email accounts is on this computer belonging to her husband based upon whatever we could describe about what that agent saw, which we had to characterize very carefully, and so that what tethered it to the computer was basically what an agent saw doing a search warrant from another case. That's the [probable cause].

We asked Prosecutor 1 if there was any discussion of putting in information relating to the BlackBerry emails from early in Clinton's tenure. Prosecutor 1 stated:

I don't think so. If it would have helped the probable cause, I would have put it in. I don't think we had...strong enough basis to do that, or I would have put it in I'm sure. Because it, I mean we would have, anything that we could have put in there that was true and would have bolstered the probable cause, we would have put in.

We also reviewed the factual basis of the October 30 search warrant application with the NYO case agent for the Weiner investigation. The case agent told us that each of the facts related to the Weiner laptop that were included in the search warrant application were known to him "within a day or two" of September 26.

We asked Comey for his reaction to the statement that "[e]very fact in [the October 30] search warrant was known to the FBI at the highest levels—at least to the Deputy Director level—on September 28th." Comey responded, "My reaction is it likely should have moved faster and I'd want to know, to answer this I'm asking, but what would their motive be to delay?"

C. Difference in Approach to Devices during Main Investigation

As noted previously, Comey's decision on October 27 to have the FBI seek a search warrant for the Weiner laptop generated discussion among the Midyear team about how that approach differed from the approach that the Midyear team agreed upon and took during the investigation, namely to only seek Clinton's personal electronic devices and not to seek the personal electronic devices of any of her aides. In addition, in drafting the search warrant application for the Weiner laptop, a discussion occurred regarding the scope of the requested search warrant and whether it should be limited to emails between Clinton and Abedin, or whether it should include all of Abedin's emails.

Emails from the night of October 29 show that Baker expressed concerns that the draft search warrant request was too narrow. Specifically, in an email at 9:13 p.m. to FBI Attorney 1, Strzok, and Anderson, Baker stated, "The main question I [sic] have right now is why we are only seeking access to emails between Huma and Clinton. Based on the facts set forth about Huma mishandling classified information on all of her accounts, it seems to me there is [probable cause] to look at all of her emails no matter who is the other party. Am I misreading the scope of the warrant or the strength of the [probable cause]?" Strzok responded to Baker's email at 9:28 p.m., stating:

> I think the primary deficiency in trying to go after Huma's own communications is that Huma's role and expertise was far more administrative in nature than that of the other close aides to [Clinton]. That is, when it came to classified information, she was primarily a conduit to/from others to Clinton, not a generator of such information/discussion on her own. Whereas Sullivan or Mills had substantive (and sometimes classified) discussions on their own absent [Clinton's] participation, Abedin's were largely as an administrative conduit to the Sec'y. Thus, it's more challenging to articulate an expectation at the level of [probable cause] that we'd expect to find classified in her discussions not involving [Clinton]. We can't exclude it, but it's challenging.

FBI Attorney 1 responded to Strzok's email at 9:55 p.m., stating, "That's right, Pete. Plus, we can't say she mishandled on all of her accounts. Of the 27 classified emails, 26 were on her @clintonemail.com account and one was Yahoo. We also cannot say for certain that the 27 classified emails are on this particular device, which also weakens our argument generally." In response, Baker sent an email at 10:18 p.m., stating, "There is [probable cause] to believe that Huma used her email accounts to mishandle classified information. I just don't understand why that [i]s not enough to look at all her emails.... Would you please discuss with DOJ?" Baker told us that he believed the FBI should seek the authority to review all of Abedin's emails on the laptop, instead of just emails between Abedin and Clinton.

FBI Attorney 1 told us that she recalled Baker "wanting the search warrant to be broader" and in an email on October 29 FBI Attorney 1 stated that Baker's "point is there could be relevant emails that are not between Huma and HRC—particularly regarding intent." At 11:06 p.m. on October 29, FBI Attorney 1 sent Prosecutor 1 and Prosecutor 2 an email informing them of Baker's concern and adding, "I understand that the scope of our consensual searches has been limited to emails with [Clinton], but the purpose of our investigation was to look for classified information that transited the server, which would include Huma's @clintonemail. I honestly can't remember how we treated those when we got consent for the second server, and I don't [have] the letter in front of me." Prosecutor 1 responded at 11:12 p.m., "[W]e did not look through all of Huma's emails before (we searched for Clinton's addresses but did not go through all of her emails). We can discuss but that seems like a pretty big push (we only use examples of comm[uniciation]s with Clinton [to] establish [probable cause] for 793 offenses)." Five minutes later, at 11:17 p.m., FBI Attorney 1 responded, "I honestly couldn't remember how we treated Huma @clintonemail emails before given [sic]. Sounds like limiting the search to [Clinton] communications is consistent."

FBI Attorney 1 told the OIG that the Department "didn't believe that we had the [probable cause] to, to be broader than that." Baker stated that someone at either the Department or SDNY "pushed back and said no, we don't have [probable cause] for that."[188]

We asked the prosecutors about this issue. Prosecutor 1 told us that he felt "we need[ed] to treat Huma like we treated her earlier on in the investigation." Prosecutor 1 told us that it did not make sense to "expand the bounds" of what they had done before when reviewing the Weiner laptop. Prosecutor 2 also noted this, stating:

> And then there is also the issue of like we didn't look at everyone's emails over the course of this investigation. We had Huma's, some of like Huma's clintonemail.com emails on the server. And we never got consent or a search warrant to look through Huma's email on the server because, you know, the judgment was made that like that was not so significant to the investigation. So, I think from the DOJ perspective, we were kind of confused why this was such a significant development.

During this debate with FBI on October 29, Prosecutor 1 sent an email to Toscas stating, "Worried that Baker and higher ups over there (or people in the chain) are going to say DOJ was standing in their way. It just seems to me that they are pushing the bounds here all of a sudden (when they didn't do so before)." We asked Prosecutor 1 about this email. Prosecutor 1 stated that part of his concern was frustration at the FBI for requesting the search warrant be completed immediately, yet trying to suggest major changes after it was substantially completed. Prosecutor 1 stated that he also felt "it didn't make a lot of sense" for the purpose of probable cause "to talk about hypothetical conversations that could have" occurred "in order to expand the bounds of what we're trying to do with the search warrant."[189]

II.   Lynch-Comey Meeting on October 31

On Monday, October 31, Lynch requested a private conversation with Comey after the regularly scheduled Monday morning meeting between the Department and the FBI. Yates told us that she and Lynch had talked about this meeting beforehand and that Lynch told Yates that Lynch planned to make two points to Comey: (1) the October 28th letter "was a blunder," and (2) that Comey and the FBI needed to process the Weiner laptop "as fast as you can."

---

[188] As noted above, after reviewing a draft of this report, Toscas and others noted that SDNY played no substantive role in the October 30 search warrant.

[189] In comments provided to the OIG after reviewing a draft of this report, Baker stated that he "had not played a significant role, if any, in scoping the prior consent agreements or legal process used to obtain other emails in the investigation." Baker continued, "Given the intense focus on the Weiner laptop, [Baker said he] looked more closely at this warrant application and asked what [he] thought were logical questions." Ultimately, Baker stated that he "deferred to DOJ on whether there was probable cause to support the seizure of additional emails."

We asked Comey about this meeting. Comey stated:

So the two of us went into the AG's private office...and I went over to sit in a chair and she closed the door and turned around and started walking at me with her head down and her arms out and came up to me because I'm so ridiculously tall and pressed her head, her face against my solar plexus and wrapped her arms around me and hugged me and then I kind of awkwardly—I'm not a hugger because I'm a giraffe—and so I kind of patted the Attorney General's back and then the embrace—she broke the embrace and then said, "I just wanted to give you a hug."

And she went over and sat down. And then...she said, "How are you doing?" I said, "I'm doing okay." I said, "Look this is really bad, but the alternative is worse." And then she said, "Yeah would they feel better if it had leaked on November 6th?" And I just said, "Exactly Loretta." Because I hadn't made the disclosure to Congress because of the leaks—the prospect of leaks, but it actually consoled me because really you're not that important because even if you hadn't sent a letter to Congress, which was the right thing to do, it probably would have leaked anyway that you were going for a search warrant on this stuff and she obviously saw it the same way and said, "Right, would they feel better if it had leaked on November 6th?" I think she said. And I said, "Exactly."

And then she said a nice thing, "I hope you're holding up." And then she said—so we get up and start walking to the door. She's in front of me and then she turns around and says, "Try to look beat up." And so then she opens the door, we walk out, her staff is all out in the hallway and I walk out.

And then somebody puts it out within moments that the Attorney General had taken me aside to give me a woodshedding or something; it was in the media, I think, that morning. So she and I never spoke about that again, but I reasonably understood that. Her saying you did the right thing, and even if you hadn't sent the letter, it would have come out anyway and that would've been even worse and so that's—I think that's the end of the story.

We also asked Lynch about this meeting. Lynch told us that the reason she called the one-on-one meeting with Comey was primarily because she "wanted to talk to him about" leaks and she was concerned that Comey "didn't want to talk about it in front of a larger group." Lynch stated:

We went into a smaller room.... And I recall, we were both sitting down. And I recall saying we have to talk about this letter and the aftermath of it.... I don't recall my exact words, but I remember saying, you know, I know that you were aware that I did not think you should do this. But, it is done now, and we have to deal with the aftermath of it.... And I said...this has not followed what was at least

385

conveyed to me you thought you were going to do. And...I made the point that it was immediately described as the investigation was reopened, the full investigation was reopened.

And he said, you know, I was very clear...I was very careful not to say that. And I had heard over the weekend that he had been surprised or disappointed, or perhaps both, that the letter was being characterized in that way. Because that was not what he wanted to say, not what he intended to say. And I said, I understand that that wasn't your intention, but that's how it was taken.... I said, in many ways, it's the exact opposite of what you wanted to have happen. And I said, and I think it's caused a huge problem for the Department because we have this perception now that we are essentially trying to harm one of the candidates....

And I raised the possibility. I said I think you ought to think about sending another letter, a clarifying letter. You've already done this now. You have created a misimpression as to what is going on.... You need to clarify this and say that essentially you want to make it clear that this is not a reopening of the investigation. That should be conveyed in there somewhere.

And he said, how would you phrase that? And I said, you know, I have not put pen to paper. I have not wordsmithed this. And I said, and I don't think it should come from me. It needs to come from you because you gave the initial letter. I said if it comes from me, then we are essentially talking about internal DOJ fights and disagreements and everything. And that's throwing more into the public arena that shouldn't be there. He said, I agree with you on that. He said I'll think about that. I'll think about that.

...[A]t some point, I said it's clear to me that, that we're going to have to do some statement at the end of the forensic analysis. It could be part of that. Or you could do it today. I said, but I really think you need to clarify this. And he said, I hear you, I hear you. Which is a phrase that Comey uses a lot, I hear you. And he said, I will give that a great deal of thought. And he said, my concern is, and again, I don't recall the exact words, but he said I have a concern that it would do more harm than good at this point. And I said, okay, well let's think about what it would look like.

The other issue I raised with him was...I said, look, I've known you for a long time. You and I have been in the Department a long time. I said, my view is you would never have done something like this if you didn't feel tremendous pressure to do it. And I said, and I don't understand that pressure. I said, but, it was conveyed to me that you were very concerned about leaks, specifically. And I said, I can only assume that you were thinking of leaks that would have been of this information in a much, much worse way. And he said, you're right. You're exactly right about that.

Now, I knew that the laptop had been handled in a case out of New York. And so I said, you know, we have to talk about the New York office...and the concern that both you and I have expressed about leaks in the past. And I said, do you think that this was the right way to deal with the issue, the concern about leaks?... He didn't have much of a response. But we were having a conversation.... And I said, you know, I've talked, you and I have talked about that before.... [McCabe] and I have talked about them before....

And then I said, now, we've got to talk about the New York office in general. And he said yes. And I said we both work with them. We both know them. We both, you know, think highly of them. I said, but this has become a problem. And he said, and he said to me that it had become clear to him, he didn't say over the course of what investigation or whatever, he said it's clear to me that there is a cadre of senior people in New York who have a deep and visceral hatred of Secretary Clinton. And he said it is, it is deep. It's, and he said, he said it was surprising to him or stunning to him.

You know, I didn't get the impression he was agreeing with it at all, by the way. But he was saying it did exist, and it was hard to manage because these were agents that were very, very senior, or had even had timed out and were staying on, and therefore did not really feel under pressure from headquarters or anything to that effect. And I said, you know, I'm aware of that.... I said, I wasn't aware it was to this level and this depth that you're talking about, but I said I'm sad to say that that does not surprise me.

And he made a comment about, you know, you understand that. A lot of people don't understand that. You, you get that issue. I said, I get that issue. I said I'm, I'm just troubled that this issue, meaning the, the New York agent issue and leaks, I am just troubled that this issue has put us where we are today with respect to this laptop.

And he said again I hear you, I hear you. I will think about that. I will consider what to do. He said, but he said again, I'm concerned that another letter right now that isn't tied to a resolution of the forensics would just be pouring more, he didn't say more fuel on the fire, but that was the phraseology, something like that that he used. And I said, all right. I said, well, let me know what you decide about whether to do something else or not, particularly as we go through the process of finding things out.

Lynch told us that she was "sure" she "asked [Comey] if he was okay" and that she may have hugged him because she "often did." Lynch also stated that as they departed the room she joked with Comey and said "something like of course you're going to look like I beat you up." Overall, Lynch described the conversation as a "friendly" but "tough conversation" given the "serious and significant issues" involved.

Lynch's Chief of Staff stated that Lynch told her about the conversation with Comey afterwards. Lynch's Chief of Staff stated:

> [Lynch] said the Director had expressed that he needed to send the letter because he was very concerned about leaks, that it was going to leak out anyway that they had found these emails in relation to the Weiner investigation. She may have told me something else, but I don't remember. I remember that being the big thing that he had focused on.

We also reviewed McCord's notes of a meeting she attended with Lynch on October 31, after Lynch's meeting with Comey, in which the Midyear investigation was discussed. The notes reflect that Lynch stated the following:

> ...good vehicle for more clarifying stmt.
>
> need to correct misimpressions out there
>
> Told Director this morning [and] he wanted to think about it
>
> > —could recap where we were at end of last week [and] talk about process w/out details of what we're finding
> >
> > —will cont. our review [and] take approp. inv. steps
> >
> > —should come from Comey to clarify what he said Friday....

III.   FBI Review of Weiner Laptop Emails

Midyear agents obtained a copy of the Weiner laptop from NYO immediately after the search warrant was signed on October 30. The laptop was taken directly to Quantico where the FBI's Operational Technology Division (OTD) began processing the laptop. The Lead Analyst told us that given the volume of emails on the laptop and the difficulty with de-duplicating the emails that "at least for the first few days, the scale of what we're doing seem[ed] really, really big." Strzok told us that OTD was able "to do some amazing things" to "rapidly de-duplicate" the emails on the laptop, which significantly lowered the number of emails that the Midyear team would have to individually review. Strzok stated that only after that technological breakthrough did he begin to think it was "possible we might wrap up before the election."

FBI leadership, including Comey, was briefed on an almost daily basis during the review process. The Lead Analyst told us that he recalled briefing Comey on Friday, November 4, stating:

> I told [Comey], I said...I think there's a possibility we may be able to get through this before the end of the weekend. So he said if you think you can do it, you should try to. So that's what we did. We brought in, we basically put all hands on deck for [that Saturday].

The Midyear team flagged all potentially work-related emails encountered during the review process and compared those to emails that they had previously reviewed in other datasets. Any work-related emails that were unique, meaning that they did not appear in any other dataset, were individually reviewed by the Lead Analyst, Strzok, and FBI Attorney 1 for evidentiary value.

Analysts on the Midyear team subsequently drafted a document summarizing the review of the Weiner laptop entitled, "Anthony Weiner Laptop Review for Communications Pertinent to Midyear Exam." This document, dated November 15, 2016, showed that the full image of the laptop contained approximately 1,355,980 items, or files. According to the document, FBI OTD initially extracted approximately 350,000 emails from the laptop and then approximately 344,000 BlackBerry backup files.[190] The FBI determined that 4 of the 13 BlackBerry backups "were assessed to belong to Abedin." The remaining 9 BlackBerry backups were associated with Weiner. The FBI only reviewed emails to or from Clinton during the period in which she was Secretary of State, and not emails from Abedin to other parties or emails outside that period. Analyst 1 stated, "I had very strict instructions that all I was allowed to do within the case was look for Hillary Clinton emails, because that was the scope of our work." Utilizing various searches targeting Clinton's emails, the FBI reviewed in full "approximately 48,982" items on the Weiner laptop.

The FBI ultimately "identified 13 confirmed classified email chains, the content of which was duplicative of emails previously recovered during the investigation." None of these emails were marked classified, but 4 of the 13 were classified as Secret at the time sent and 9 were classified Confidential at the time sent. The FBI determined that Abedin forwarded two of the confirmed classified emails to Weiner.[191] The FBI reviewed 6,827 emails that were either to or from Clinton and assessed 3,077 of those emails to be "potentially work-related." The FBI analysis of the review noted that "[b]ecause metadata was largely absent, the emails could not be completely, automatically de-duplicated or evaluated against prior emails recovered during the investigation" and therefore the FBI could not determine how many of the potentially work-related emails were duplicative of emails previously obtained in the Midyear investigation.

---

[190] A BlackBerry backup is a file, typically found on a personal computer, containing data from a BlackBerry handheld device. The BlackBerry backup can include data from the handheld device's address book, calendar, browser, email, SMS and MMS messages, phone call logs and history, as well as pictures and other media stored on the on-board media storage. At the time the backup is created, the user can configure the specific items to be saved. As a result, not all of the above items may be found in every backup.

[191] The FBI did not determine exactly how Abedin's emails came to reside on Weiner's laptop. Analyst 2 told us that it appeared that Abedin's personal devices had been backed up on the laptop at various points in time. Documents we reviewed indicated that Abedin told the FBI that she did not know how or why this occurred.

IV.   Agent 1 Instant Messages from November 1

On November 1, Agent 1 and an FBI agent uninvolved in the Midyear investigation exchanged the following instant messages on the FBI's computer network. The sender of each message is identified after the timestamp.

> 8:31 a.m., Uninvolved Agent: "A horrible shit sandwich. Still no [grand jury] I imagine. So, you find Huma lied; BFD. No one at DoJ is going to prosecute."

> 8:33 a.m., Agent 1: "Rog – noone is going to pros[ecute] even if we find unique classified. [Grand jury] story was inaccurate – 50+ GJ subpoenas and 2703d issued,"

> 8:37 a.m., Agent 1: "...We only had several warrants and alot of consent searches on media. I would have liked to use warrants for all because the consent agreements had limited scope. Reasonable scope, but I don't like to stand on the lawn and have the occupants throw out the evidence to us."

We asked Agent 1 about these messages. Agent 1 told us that this was another example of a friend reaching out to him about the status of the Midyear investigation. Agent 1 continued:

> I think that similar to what I've said before, I think this is me venting or complaining in a vein of, you know, but I have, I have nothing to substantiate. I don't have a statement. I don't have a, I don't have an action that someone wouldn't prosecute it if, if we found it.

We asked Agent 1 about his expectation at the time of what would be found on the Weiner laptop and how that could impact the Midyear investigation. Agent 1 stated:

> I think my feeling at the time was there was a really good chance we'd find emails we hadn't seen before.... That there might not be something that could potentially be classified...but...would it be so much different than what we had already seen? I, my impression would probably be no.

V.   Comey Letter to Congress on November 6

On the afternoon of November 3, the FBI began drafting what ultimately became Comey's letter to Congress announcing that the FBI had completed its review of the emails to or from Clinton that were on the Weiner laptop. That work was completed very early on November 6. Later that same day, Comey sent his second letter to Congress, which we provide as Attachment F. This letter stated:

> I write to supplement my October 28, 2016 letter that notified you the FBI would be taking additional investigative steps with respect to former Secretary of State Clinton's use of a personal email server. Since my letter, the FBI investigative team has been working around

the clock to process and review a large volume of emails from a device obtained in connection with an unrelated criminal investigation. During that process, we reviewed all of the communications that were to or from Hillary Clinton while she was Secretary of State.

Based on our review, we have not changed our conclusions that we expressed in July with respect to Secretary Clinton.

I am very grateful to the professionals at the FBI for doing an extraordinary amount of high-quality work in a short period of time.

Comey told us that he met with the Midyear team after they had finished the review of the emails on the Weiner laptop and "went through what they had done, what they had found, and their conclusion was, it does not change our view with respect to Hillary Clinton." Comey stated that there was "more work to be done with respect to" Abedin and Weiner to understand how the emails ended up on Weiner's computer, but that the review was complete with respect to Clinton. Comey continued, "And then I said, okay, you know, basically convince me you've done it well." Once convinced, Comey stated, "I said, okay now we're done, we should notify Congress that we are done. And then we set to work on that."

Comey stated that Steinbach opposed the idea of a second letter. Comey explained:

And [Steinbach's] view was, I just think it's too late that, as I recall it...but that we've created a storm and if you try to undo the storm now, you'll simply feed the storm more or something—so words to that effect. I said, look I respect that view, but I think you're wrong. I think having spoken, that led to us having to speak, having spoken we need to, in fairness, say that we're done. You've done it well, you've been able to do it in time. So then we shared that also with DOJ, got feedback and then sent that letter. And again the goal there was to be as fair as possible while still accomplishing the goal of telling them that we've finished with respect to her.

Steinbach told us that he could not recall the specifics of the debate about the November 6 letter, but stated, "I think maybe the November 6th one I was thinking look, it's already done. Just let it, let it go, let it die. I can't remember."

The Lead Analyst told us that he raised objections to the November 6 letter during discussions with Comey. The Lead Analyst stated:

I said I, I could understand the first statement because we were reopening an investigation. We were correcting the record. But I said I don't agree that, that this time we have any obligation to do that because the investigation isn't done. We have additional investigative steps that are going to happen. We're not closed in the sense of being closed. We may have, we may have come to a, a position of understanding about what's on this laptop. But to me, that same

391

obligation, which is to me what drove us to make the first statement, does not exist now.

The Lead Analyst told us that the further investigative steps needed to complete the investigation included at least a "malware analysis" to examine the laptop for intrusion and a re-interview of Abedin. Abedin was in fact re-interviewed by the FBI on January 6, 2017. With regard to the malware analysis, the Lead Analyst explained:

> [T]he way I explain this in my thinking is, again, from my [counterintelligence] perspective, one of the key questions you're trying to answer to any of these circumstances, especially when you've been confirmed that classified information is resident on a device that it shouldn't be, is did that device get compromised by anyone. That's a part of the equation of was this of significant or negative impact to U.S. national security. If it's simply on Weiner's laptop and that's where it ended, then that's one thing. It's another thing if through this, their actions that got on Weiner's laptop and a foreign power obtained those classified, that's a separate question. So to me that's not a, that's not an insignificant aspect of this that was still completely unresolved at the time.

The Lead Analyst stated, "Then ultimately, the Director looked at me, and...he thanked me and thanked everybody for our candor, as always. And he said, but I have decided we're going to do it. And we're going to make it, you know, the statement and, that's kind of it."

At 7:52 p.m. on November 5, Page sent a text message to Strzok that stated, "I don't want to make a statement anymore." Strzok responded at 7:58 p.m., stating, in part, "Yeah I don't either. We're kind of out of the news cycle, let's leave it that way." At 8:11 a.m. on November 6, Page sent another text message to Strzok that stated, "I still don't know that we should make this statement." Strzok immediately responded, "I don't either. Imsg?"

After being shown these text messages, Strzok stated that he thought the decision to send the November 6 letter was "easier" then the decision about the October 28 letter. However, Strzok stated that he was concerned that every time the FBI acted it "invigorate[d] the news cycle." We also asked Strzok and Page about their use of iMessage, a built-in instant message service on Apple devices. As described in more detail in Chapter Twelve, Strzok and Page told us that they mostly used iMessage and personal email for personal use. However, Strzok told us could not exclude the possibility that he sent work-related information over iMessage. Similarly, Page told us that references to these other forums reflected "mostly personal use" as opposed to using them for work purposes. However, she stated that she and Strzok sometimes used these forums for work-related discussions due to the technical limitations of FBI-issued phones.

Unlike the October 28 letter, the FBI sent a draft copy of the November 6 letter to the Department and the Department participated meaningfully in the drafting process. Axelrod stated that he "insisted" upon seeing the letter and he, along with Toscas and Associate Deputy Attorney General Scott Schools, provided comments and edits.

PAGE LEFT INTENTIONALLY

BLANK

CHAPTER TWELVE:
TEXT MESSAGES, INSTANT MESSAGES, USE OF PERSONAL EMAIL, AND ALLEGED IMPROPER DISCLOSURES OF NON-PUBLIC INFORMATION

This Chapter discusses text messages from FBI-issued mobile devices and instant messages exchanged on FBI systems that raised concerns of potential bias. We describe key text messages and instant messages we identified during our review, as well as explanations for these messages that the involved employees offered during their OIG interviews. We also identified instances where FBI employees, including Comey and Strzok, used personal email accounts to conduct official government business. Lastly, we discuss allegations that Department and FBI employees improperly disclosed non-public information.

I.   Text Messages and Instant Messages

During the course of our review, we requested and received text messages from FBI-issued mobile devices and instant messages exchanged on the FBINet and SCINet Lync applications for FBI personnel involved in the Midyear investigation.[192] We also requested text messages for Department personnel involved in the Midyear investigation, but were informed that the Department does not retain text messages for more than 5 to 7 days.[193] The OIG previously expressed concerns in a 2015 report about the text message retention practices of the Department's four law enforcement components, and we recommend that ODAG consider taking steps to improve the retention and monitoring of text messages Department-wide.[194]

After receiving FBI text messages and instant messages responsive to keywords we provided to the FBI, we identified messages for certain FBI personnel

---

[192] FBINet is the FBI's computer system for information classified at the Secret level, while its SCINet system handles Top Secret and compartmented information.

[193] After reviewing a draft of this report, the Midyear prosecutors told the OIG that they did not use text messages, and that the only text messages they received were from the Midyear agents about logistical arrangements.

[194] In March 2015, the OIG issued a report pertaining to the handling of sexual harassment allegations by the Department's four law enforcement components, the FBI, the Drug Enforcement Administration (DEA), the Bureau of Alcohol, Tobacco, Firearms and Explosives (ATF), and the U.S. Marshal's Service (USMS). In that report, we noted that all four components had weaknesses detecting sexually explicit text messages and images, and that two components did not archive text messages sent and received by its employees. We therefore recommended that all four law enforcement components, in coordination with ODAG, should (1) acquire and implement technology and establish procedures to effectively preserve text messages and images for a reasonable period of time, and should make that information available to misconduct investigators and for discovery purposes; and (2) take concrete steps to acquire and implement technology to proactively monitor text message and image data for potential misconduct. *See* U.S. Department of Justice (DOJ) Office of the Inspector General (OIG), *The Handling of Sexual Harassment and Misconduct Allegations by the Department's Law Enforcement Components*, Evaluation and Inspections Division Report 15-04 (March 2016), https://go.usa.gov/xQGz4 (accessed May 9, 2018).

that raised concerns about potential bias. We then obtained all text messages and instant messages for those FBI personnel for the entire period of the Midyear investigation through July 1, 2017, to capture post-election discussions. We identified communications from five different FBI employees that we discuss in this section.[195]

First, we identified text messages exchanged between DAD Peter Strzok and Lisa Page, Special Counsel to former Deputy Director Andrew McCabe, on their FBI-issued cell phones. These text messages included political opinions about candidates and issues involved in the 2016 presidential election, including statements of hostility toward then candidate Trump and statements of support for candidate Clinton. Several of their text messages also appeared to mix political opinions with discussions about the Midyear and Russia investigations, raising a question as to whether Strzok's and Page's political opinions may have affected investigative decisions. In addition to being involved in the Midyear and Russia investigations, both Page and Strzok were also briefly assigned to the investigation conducted by Special Counsel Robert Mueller III.

Next, we identified instant messages exchanged on FBINet involving Agent 1 and Agent 5. As noted previously, Agent 1 was assigned to the Midyear investigative team and was one of the four case agents. Agent 5 was assigned to the Midyear filter team. We discussed in Chapter Five a number of Agent 1's instant messages that expressed opinions that were critical of the conduct and quality of the Midyear investigation. In addition to those messages, we identified two instant message exchanges involving Agent 1 that appeared to combine a discussion of politics with a discussion of the Midyear investigation. We also identified instant messages between Agent 1 and Agent 5 that expressed support for candidate Clinton and hostility toward first candidate and then President Trump.

Finally, we identified instant messages sent on FBINet by FBI Attorney 2. FBI Attorney 2 was assigned to the Midyear investigation, the Russia investigation, and the Special Counsel investigation. We found instant messages in which FBI Attorney 2 discussed political issues, including three instant message exchanges that raised concerns of potential bias.

In this section, we describe key text messages and instant messages we identified during our review, as well as explanations for these messages that the employees offered during their OIG interviews.

A.   Text Messages between Lisa Page and Peter Strzok

Peter Strzok is an experienced counterintelligence agent who was promoted to Deputy Assistant Director (DAD) of the Espionage Section in September 2016.

---

[195] We identified other text messages and instant messages in which FBI employees involved in the Midyear investigation discussed political issues and candidates. This Chapter does not include a discussion of every political text message or instant message that we identified. Instead, we discuss only those messages that we found raised the most significant questions of potential bias or improper motivation based on their content, timing, or the individuals involved.

As described in the previous chapters, Strzok was assigned to the Midyear investigation in August 2015 and was responsible for supervising the investigation on a daily basis. Page was named counsel to then Deputy Director Andrew McCabe in February 2016, and served as his liaison to the Midyear investigative team from February 2016 forward.

In addition to their roles in the Midyear investigation, both Page and Strzok were involved in the FBI investigation into the Russian government's efforts to interfere in the 2016 presidential election.[196] Strzok was assigned to lead the Russia investigation in late July 2016.[197] Page also worked on the Russia investigation, and told us that she served the same liaison function as she did in the Midyear investigation. Both Page and Strzok accepted invitations to work on the Special Counsel staff in 2017. Page told the OIG that she accepted a 45-day temporary duty assignment but returned to work in the Deputy Director's office at the FBI on or around July 15, 2017. Strzok was removed from the Special Counsel's investigation on approximately July 28, 2017, and returned to the FBI in another position, after the OIG informed the DAG and Special Counsel of the text messages discussed in this report on July 27, 2017.

As noted above, after finding responsive text messages between Page and Strzok that appeared to intermingle political comments with discussions of the Midyear investigation, the OIG obtained from the FBI all text messages between Strzok and Page from their FBI-issued phones for the entire period of the Clinton email server investigation as well as the period of the Russia investigation during which Strzok and Page worked on it. The OIG received more than 40,000 unique text messages between Strzok and Page in response to these requests.[198] The FBI did not provide any text messages for the period from December 15, 2016, to May 17, 2017, because of issues with the data collection and preservation software used on the FBI's Samsung S5 mobile devices. However, OIG forensic agents obtained the phones used by Strzok and Page, and recovered a large number of the text

---

[196] On March 20, 2017, then Director Comey testified before Congress that the FBI began an investigation in late July 2016 into "the Russian government's efforts to interfere in the 2016 presidential election," including "investigating the nature of any links between individuals associated with the Trump campaign and the Russian government and whether there was any coordination between the campaign and Russia's efforts."

[197] Supervision of the Russia investigation was briefly transitioned from Strzok to another Counterintelligence Division DAD in early 2017. However, AD Priestap told us that FBI leadership decided to keep Strzok involved in the Russia investigation and he was therefore reassigned back to it.

[198] The FBI produced 73,900 text messages between Strzok and Page from the period June 30, 2015, to December 1, 2016; 1,368 text messages from the period December 1 to December 14, 2016; and 2,054 text messages from the period May 18 to July 1, 2017. However, these included significant numbers of duplicates. We estimate that the number of unique text messages exchanged between Strzok and Page exceeded 40,000. The FBI pulled the majority of these text messages from Page's archives, as Strzok's text messages were not consistently preserved due to compatibility problems between the FBI's text message preservation software and the Samsung S5 cell phones used by the FBI. Issues related to the preservation of text messages affected a large number of FBI employees, and OIG forensic agents determined that the failure to preserve Strzok's text messages resulted from this compatibility issue, not from the actions of any FBI employee, including Strzok. Text message preservation resumed in May 2017, after Page received a Samsung S7 phone.

messages from this "gap" period. For the gap period, the OIG recovered 9,311 text messages from Strzok's phone and 10,760 text messages from Page's phone, some of which were duplicates or text messages exchanged with other people. Although the number and frequency of text messages is generally consistent with previous time periods, we cannot definitively say that our forensic recovery captured every text message exchanged between Page and Strzok during the gap period.[199]

The text messages between Page and Strzok covered a wide range of topics. For example, we identified a large number of routine work-related communications. Many of the text messages were of a personal nature, including discussions about their families, medical issues, and daily events, and reflected that Strzok and Page were communicating on their FBI-issued phones as part of an extramarital affair. We found that this relationship was relevant to the frequency and candid nature of the text messages and their use of FBI-issued phones to communicate. Some of these text messages expressed political opinions about candidates and issues involved in the 2016 presidential election, including statements of hostility toward candidate Trump and statements of support for candidate Clinton.

We identified three categories of text messages that raised concerns about potential bias in FBI investigations. The first were text messages of a political nature commenting on Trump and Clinton. We specifically highlight these text messages because Strzok and Page played important roles in investigations involving both Trump and Clinton, and the exchange of these text messages on an FBI-issued device potentially created an appearance of bias. The second category we identified were text messages that combined expressions of political sentiments with a discussion of the Midyear investigation, potentially indicating or creating the appearance that investigative decisions were impacted by bias or improper considerations. The third category raised similar questions with respect to the Russia investigation. We also include a fourth category of text messages that have received significant public attention. These messages are included to provide context and further explanation as to their meaning, and do not necessarily implicate potential bias in either the Midyear or Russia investigations. Examples of these four categories of text messages are discussed below.[200] We also include

---

[199] The OIG is preparing a separate report on its text message recovery efforts and findings.

[200] This Chapter includes the text messages we found most relevant to our review. However, Page and Strzok sent other text messages about candidates and issues involved in the 2016 presidential election, unrelated to the Midyear or Russia investigations, and also sent numerous text messages, both positive and negative, about other public and government officials from both political parties. These included former Maryland Governor Martin O'Malley ("And Martin O'Malley's a douche," October 14, 2015), Congressman Paul Ryan ("And I hope Paul Ryan fails and crashes in a blaze of glory," November 1, 2015), Ohio Governor John Kasich ("Poor Kasich. He's the only sensible man up there," "Exactly re Kasich. And he has ZERO appeal," March 4, 2016), former Attorney General Eric Holder ("Oh God, Holder! Turn [the television] off turn it off turn it off!!!!" "Yeah, I saw him yesterday and booed at the tv," July 27, 2016), and others. Page and Strzok told us that these additional text messages were relevant because they reflected that Trump was not singled out by them for criticism or criticized for partisan reasons.

explanations provided by Page and Strzok during their OIG interviews about these text messages.

1.   Text Messages Commenting on Trump or Clinton

In this section, we highlight examples of text messages of a political nature commenting on Trump and Clinton. We include explanations provided by Page and Strzok about their use of FBI-issued phones in general and their use of FBI-issued phones for political discussions. The sender of each text message is identified after the date.

- August 16, 2015, Strzok: "[Bernie Sanders is] an idiot like Trump. Figure they cancel each other out."[201]

- February 12, 2016, Page: "I'm no prude, but I'm really appalled by this. So you don't have to go looking (in case you hadn't heard), Trump called him the p-word. The man has no dignity or class. He simply cannot be president. With a Slur for Ted Cruz, Donald Trump Further Splits Voters http://nyti.ms/1XoICkO."

- February 12, 2016, Strzok: "Oh, [Trump's] abysmal. I keep hoping the charade will end and people will just dump him. The problem, then, is Rubio will likely lose to Cruz. The Republican party is in utter shambles. When was the last competitive ticket they offered?"

- March 3, 2016, Page: "God trump is a loathsome human."

- March 3, 2016, Strzok: "Omg [Trump's] an idiot.

- March 3, 2016, Page: "He's awful."

- March 3, 2016, Strzok: "God Hillary should win 100,000,000-0."

- March 3, 2016, Page: "Also did you hear [Trump] make a comment about the size of his d*ck earlier? This man cannot be president."

- March 12, 2016: Page forwarded an article about a "far right" candidate in Texas, stating, "[W]hat the f is wrong with people?" Strzok replied, "That Texas article is depressing as hell. But answers how we could end up with President trump."

- March 16, 2016, Page: "I cannot believe Donald Trump is likely to be an actual, serious candidate for president."

- June 11, 2016, Strzok: "They fully deserve to go, and demonstrate the absolute bigoted nonsense of Trump."

- July 18, 2016, Page: "...Donald Trump is an enormous d*uche."

---

[201] All text messages produced to the OIG reflected Greenwich Mean Time. As a result, some text messages sent late at night bore the wrong date. We have corrected times and, where necessary, dates in this report to reflect the Eastern Time Zone. In addition, some text messages used emojis and other formatting symbols, which we omitted unless they affected the meaning of the text message. We also excluded other intervening text messages that did not contribute to understanding the highlighted text messages.

- July 19, 2016, Page: "Trump barely spoke, but the first thing out of his mouth was 'we're going to win soooo big.' The whole thing is like living in a bad dream."

- July 21, 2016, Strzok: "Trump is a disaster. I have no idea how destabilizing his Presidency would be."

- August 26, 2016, Strzok: "Just went to a southern Virginia Walmart. I could SMELL the Trump support...."

- September 26, 2016, Page: Page sent an article to Strzok entitled, "Why Donald Trump Should Not Be President," stating, "Did you read this? It's scathing. And I'm scared."

- October 19, 2016, Strzok: "I am riled up. Trump is a fucking idiot, is unable to provide a coherent answer."

- November 3, 2016, Page: "The nyt probability numbers are dropping every day. I'm scared for our organization."

- November 3, 2016, Strzok: "[Jill] Stein and moron [Gary] Johnson are F'ing everything up, too."

- November 7, 2016, Strzok: Referencing an article entitled "A victory by Mr. Trump remains possible," Strzok stated, "OMG THIS IS F*CKING TERRIFYING."

- November 13, 2016, Page: "I bought all the president's men. Figure I needed to brush up on watergate."[202]

Both Strzok and Page agreed to multiple voluntary interviews with the OIG regarding, among other things, their text messages. The OIG asked Strzok and Page each to comment in general on the text messages. Strzok explained that the text messages reflected his "personal opinion talking to a friend." He stated that ingrained in FBI culture was a "bright and inviolable line between what you think personally and belief and the conduct of your official business," and that the political opinions he expressed in the text messages "never transited into the official realm. In any way. Not in discussions, not in acts." Strzok acknowledged that "it was dumb to do that all on a government device," but distinguished his private exchanges with Page from a more public forum where expressing such views might call into question the integrity of an FBI investigation. When questioned about the possibility that exchanges on his government device could be hacked, obtained by the media, or otherwise exposed to the public, he acknowledged that "I can envision a number of scenarios" where it could impact an investigation.

Strzok stated most people would have no idea of his partisan affiliation and that "[i]t was a point of pride on Midyear that we absolutely conducted that

---

[202] Among the text messages forensically recovered by the OIG in May 2018 was another exchange about "All the President's Men." On March 14, 2017, Page texted, "Finally two pages away from finishing atpm. Did you know the president resigns in the end?! ☺" Strzok replied, "What?!?! God, that we should be so lucky."

investigation and pursued the truth in a manner that was protected from bias or influence and was simply apolitical." He further stated, "I did not either in Midyear or any other case act in a vacuum.... I had subordinates, I had peers, I had supervisors," and that none of these people would say that he had acted in a biased manner in carrying out his official duties.

Page told us that these text messages reflected her personal opinions regarding candidate Trump's fitness to be president and her preference for Clinton, but that she did not allow her political views to impact investigative steps on the Midyear investigation. She stated, "Because I was on the Clinton investigation, I actually felt extremely constrained from talking to anyone about politics at all.... And so, Pete being a good friend, it was in a way a, like a safe place to sort of have a conversation about what was...the normal sort of news of the day because...we both knew that we weren't, it wasn't impacting anything that we were doing." She pointed out that many of the text messages in question were sent after the Midyear investigation was effectively concluded on July 5, 2016, at which point she said she personally felt less constrained to express an opinion. Page stated that she was "responsible for no single decision at all with respect to the case," but that her role was rather to communicate information between FBI executive leadership and the investigative team. She also said she was not the sole source of information to executive leadership.

When asked about using her FBI-issued phone for these exchanges, Page told us, "[T]he predominant reason that we communicated on our work phones was because we were trying to keep our affair a secret from our spouses." Page also said, "I guess I didn't feel like I was doing anything wrong. I'm an American. We have the First Amendment. I'm entitled to an opinion.... I saw it as, I still see it as so separate from the investigative activity we were taking in the, in Midyear that I didn't, didn't really think about it, to be honest with you."

2. Text Messages Discussing Political Sentiments and the Midyear Investigation

In this section, we highlight examples of text messages that appear to combine expressions of political sentiments with discussion of the Midyear investigation. We provide background and context where possible to assist in understanding the text messages. We also include the explanations provided by Page and Strzok about these text messages.

February 24, 2016: In connection with a discussion about how many people from the FBI and Department should be present during a potential interview of former Secretary Clinton, Page stated in a February 24, 2016 text message to Strzok, "One more thing: she might be our next president. The last thing you need us going in there loaded for bear. You think she's going to remember or care that it was more doj than fbi?" Strzok replied, "Agreed...." Page sent similar text messages to McCabe and another FBI employee around the same time, adding that having a larger number in the room "is not operationally necessary" and that "[t]his is as much about reputational protection as anything." These text messages occurred at almost the midpoint of the Midyear investigation, before Clinton's interview was formally scheduled. Ultimately, Clinton was interviewed on July 2, 2016, and there were three FBI and five Department officials in the room. Page did not attend the interview.

Both Page and Strzok told the OIG that these messages did not reflect that the FBI took into account the likelihood that former Secretary Clinton would be president when conducting her interview. Page told us that her text message was advocating that the FBI should "follow the practice we always, always follow" with respect to who would attend Clinton's interview, "and not do something that might otherwise negatively impact [Clinton's] thinking or her feeling about the FBI in general." She stated that having fewer people present in an interview is generally better for building rapport and ensuring that the right people are asking the questions, and that by "loaded for bear" she meant having a large number of interviewers in the room, which might look "like we're trying to intimidate" Clinton. Strzok told us he did not interpret Page's text message to suggest that the FBI should treat Clinton differently "because she might be the next president," and he stated that he was certain he "made no decision based on anything [Clinton] might be or become or have done."

July 26, 2016: Strzok and Page exchanged a series of text messages on July 26, 2016, while they appeared to be watching television coverage of the Democratic National Convention. In the course of this exchange, Page texted, "Yeah, it is pretty cool. [Clinton] just has to win now. I'm not going to lie, I got a flash of nervousness yesterday about trump. The sandernistas have the potential to make a very big mistake here...." Strzok responded, "I'm not worried about them. I'm worried about the anarchist Assanges who will take fed information and disclose it to disrupt. We've gotta get the memo and brief and case filing done."

Strzok told us that "the memo" he was referring to was the closing Letterhead Memorandum (LHM) summarizing the Clinton email server investigation. Strzok said he was not certain what the "brief and case filing" referred to, but speculated these could have related to a FOIA filing. When asked if his text message meant that the LHM needed to be completed because he was worried about Trump and wanted Clinton to win, Strzok said, "No, not at all." He described this exchange as a "discussion that is purely in that private, personal realm about beliefs and opinions that are personal opinions intermixed [with discussion of work tasks] because, as a work colleague, there are a lot of things going on, and they do get intermixed." Strzok stated that mixing work and personal communications in the same text message exchange, on the same device, was "dumb" and acknowledged that it could create a perception issue. He again emphasized that he never took any investigative step designed to help or hurt Clinton or Trump.

Page told us that she was not sure what the "memo and brief and case filing" referred to but that it might have been a related classified issue. She stated that she did not read Strzok's text message to connect the need to "get the memo and brief and case filing done" with his political preferences. Rather, Page stated that she thought that the use of "fed" in the text message may have been an erroneous auto-correction of an unclassified acronym of a codename and that Strzok was referring to concerns about leaks by actors like Assange (Wikileaks) "who will leak classified information."

3. Text Messages Discussing Political Sentiments and the Russia Investigation

In this section, we highlight examples of text messages that appear to combine expressions of political sentiments with discussion of the Russia investigation. We provide background and context where possible to assist in understanding the text messages. We also include the explanations provided by Page and Strzok about these text messages.

July 31, 2016: In connection with formal opening of the FBI's Russia investigation, Strzok texted Page: "And damn this feels momentous. Because this matters. The other one did, too, but that was to ensure we didn't F something up. This matters because this MATTERS. So super glad to be on this voyage with you."

Strzok told us the "other one" referred to in the text message was the Midyear investigation. He said his text message was comparing and contrasting the Midyear investigation with the Russia investigation, and reflected his view that "if there is criminal activity there [in Midyear], it is comparatively limited, versus allegations [in the Russia investigation] which are of the most extraordinarily, potentially grave conduct." He said that his assessment of the significance of the Russia investigation was not affected by his personal feelings toward Trump and that it would be the same if another campaign were involved.

August 6, 2016: In an exchange on August 6, 2016, Page forwarded Strzok a news article relating to Trump's criticism of the Khans (the Gold Star family who appeared at the Democratic National Convention) and stated, "Jesus. You should read this. And Trump should go f himself." Strzok responded favorably to the article and added, "And F Trump." Page replied, "So. This is not to take away from the unfairness of it all, but we are both deeply fortunate people." She then sent another text message, "And maybe you're meant to stay where you are because you're meant to protect the country from that menace. To that end, read this:" and forwarded a David Brooks column from the New York Times about Trump "enablers" in the Republican Party who had not opposed Trump. Strzok responded, "Thanks. It's absolutely true that we're both very fortunate. And of course I'll try and approach it that way. I just know it will be tough at times. I can protect our country at many levels, not sure if that helps...."

When asked to explain what she meant by "you're meant to protect the country from that menace," Page began by stating, "I was totally appalled that the President would insult the father of a dead service member.... And just find that unconscionable and disgusting and cruel." She also stated that the "menace" was "the potential threat to national security that Trump or his people pose if [the] predication [for the Russia investigation] is true." Strzok told us that he did not interpret Page's reference to "protect the country from that menace" to refer to Trump. He stated, "I take menace a little differently. I take, I take the menace as, again, I view any foreign interference with our electoral process to be a threat, to be a violation of law.... So when I see menace, I, you know, is that Trump, is that Russian interference, is it the combination of the two?"

August 8, 2016: In a text message on August 8, 2016, Page stated, "[Trump's] not ever going to become president, right? Right?!" Strzok responded, "No. No he's not. We'll stop it."[203]

When asked about this text message, Strzok stated that he did not specifically recall sending it, but that he believed that it was intended to reassure Page that Trump would not be elected, not to suggest that he would do something to impact the investigation. Strzok told the OIG that he did not take any steps to try to affect the outcome of the presidential election, in either the Midyear investigation or the Russia investigation. Strzok stated that had he—or the FBI in general—actually wanted to prevent Trump from being elected, they would not have maintained the confidentiality of the investigation into alleged collusion between Russia and members of the Trump campaign in the months before the election. Page similarly stated that, although she could not speak to what Strzok meant by that text message, the FBI's decision to keep the Russia investigation confidential before the election shows that they did not take steps to impact the outcome of the election.

August 15, 2016: In a text message exchange on August 15, 2016, Strzok told Page, "I want to believe the path you threw out for consideration in Andy's office—that there's no way he gets elected—but I'm afraid we can't take that risk. It's like an insurance policy in the unlikely event you die before you're 40...." The "Andy" referred to in the text message appears to be FBI Deputy Director Andrew McCabe. McCabe was not a party to this text message, and we did not find evidence that he received it.

In an interview with the OIG, McCabe was shown the text message and he told us that he did not know what Strzok was referring to in the message and recalled no such conversation. Page likewise told us she did not know what that text message meant, but that the team had discussions about whether the FBI would have the authority to continue the Russia investigation if Trump was elected. Page testified that she did not find a reference in her notes to a meeting in McCabe's office at that time.

Strzok provided a lengthy explanation for this text message. In substance, Strzok told us that he did not remember the specific conversation, but that it likely was part of a discussion about how to handle a variety of allegations of "collusion between members of the Trump campaign and the government of Russia." As part of this discussion, the team debated how aggressive to be and whether to use overt investigative methods. Given that Clinton was the "prohibitive favorite" to win,

---

[203] Although we received Page's August 8 text message to Strzok from the FBI as part of its production of text messages in 2017, Strzok's response to Page was not among those preserved by the FBI's text message preservation software, and therefore was not produced to us. The OIG's Cyber Investigations Office recovered this text message, along with others, in May 2018 through forensic analysis of a folder found on Page's and Strzok's Samsung S5 devices.

Strzok said that they discussed whether it made sense to compromise sensitive sources and methods to "bring things to some sort of precipitative conclusion and understanding." Strzok said the reference in his text message to an "insurance policy" reflected his conclusion that the FBI should investigate the allegations thoroughly right away, as if Trump were going to win. Strzok stated that Clinton's position in the polls did not ultimately impact the investigative decisions that were made in the Russia matter.

May 18, 2017: Mueller was appointed Special Counsel on May 17, 2017. The next day Strzok and Page exchanged text messages in a discussion of whether Strzok should join the Special Counsel's investigation. Strzok wrote: "For me, and this case, I personally have a sense of unfinished business. I unleashed it with MYE. Now I need to fix it and finish it." Later in the same exchange, Strzok, apparently while weighing his career options, made this comparison: "Who gives a f*ck, one more A[ssistant] D[irector]...[versus] [a]n investigation leading to impeachment?"[204] Later in this exchange, Strzok stated, "you and I both know the odds are nothing. If I thought it was likely I'd be there no question. I hesitate in part because of my gut sense and concern there's no big there there."

Strzok acknowledged that his text messages could be read to suggest that Strzok held himself responsible for Trump's victory and Clinton's defeat because of the Midyear investigation and that he viewed the Russia investigation as providing him an opportunity to "fix" this result by working on an investigation that could result in the impeachment of President Trump. However, Strzok said he strongly disagreed with this interpretation and provided a lengthy explanation for these statements. Strzok said that he wanted to "finish" the Russia investigation rather than be reassigned midway through and lose the institutional knowledge of issues being investigated by the Special Counsel. He further stated that he was referring to Russia's use of the Midyear investigation in its election interference efforts. Strzok explained, "[I]t wasn't so much the investigation about Midyear, but then how it played into, how it was being portrayed in the political environment, how it was being leveraged by the government of Russia and all the social media disseminations.... [W]e then came to see all this kind of overlap and replaying of events with regard to the involvement of Russia, and certainly the back-and-forth with some elements of the Trump campaign." When asked what he wanted "to fix," Strzok identified the misperception that "Russia wasn't involved," given that "Russia did interfere with our elections."

---

[204] Strzok expressed similar sentiments in an email to Page using his FBI UNET (unclassified) account. On May 22, 2017, at a time when Page was working for the Special Counsel but Strzok had not yet joined the Special Counsel investigation, Page forwarded Strzok a Washington Post article entitled, "Trump asked intelligence chiefs to push back against FBI collusion probe after Comey revealed its existence." Strzok responded saying, "Yup. Assuming you/team will do it via Mueller?" When Page confirmed this, Strzok responded, "God I suddenly want on this. You know why." Page replied that she would leave the Special Counsel investigation and "happily" return to her work at the FBI if Strzok really wanted to join the investigation. Strzok responded, "I'm torn. I think – know – I'm more replaceable than you are in this. I'm the best for it, but there are others who can do OK. You are different and more unique. This is yours. Plus, leaving a S[pecial] C[ounsel] (having been an SC) resulting in an impeachment as an attorney is VERY different than leaving as an investigator...."

When asked to explain his comment about working on an investigation "leading to impeachment?" Strzok denied that he had already prejudged the Russia investigation. He described himself as a person:

[W]ho has had access to the information about the, all of these cases and all of the ins and outs of what the allegations [in the Russia investigation] are. And that he has both, as it matters as a public servant, he has a professional concern about the allegations.... And he is concerned on the impact of the national security of the United States. He finds that he has an expertise and a competence in this line of work, and he feels compelled and driven to pursue that and pursue those facts where they lay.

He stated further that his professional actions, including on the staff of the Special Counsel, were not affected by political bias.

We also asked Strzok about his "no big there there" message." Strzok stated:

As I looked at the predicating information, as I looked at the facts as we understood them from...the allegations that Russia had these emails, and offered to members of the Trump campaign to release them. As we looked at the various actors, the question [was,]...was that part of a broad, coordinated effort, or was that simply a bunch of opportunists seeking to advance their own or individual agendas...which of that is it?

...My question [was] about whether or not this represented a large, coordinated conspiracy or not. And from that, as I looked at what would give me professional fulfillment, what I thought would be the best use of my skills and talents for the FBI and for the United States, whether to take, which path to take.

Page stated that she understood Strzok's reference to "unfinished business" that he had "unleashed" and needed "to fix and finish" to be "a reflection of our Director having been fired," and "the purported reason for why the Director was fired was his mishandling of the Midyear investigation, and the work force was, you know, in mutiny, and it was all about Midyear." She disagreed with the suggestion that Strzok felt responsible for Clinton's defeat in the election. She said she interpreted Strzok's reference to impeachment to mean he wanted to be involved in the Russia investigation because it was so important "it *might* lead to impeachment," not because "it *will* lead to impeachment."[205] (Emphasis added). In response to the OIG's question as to whether Strzok's text messages made it appear that he was biased against Trump from the beginning of the Special Counsel investigation, Page acknowledged that the text messages could be read that way,

---

[205] Strzok gave a similar explanation for the email he sent to Page referencing a Special Counsel investigation "resulting in an impeachment." He stated, "[W]hile it says that, I think my sense was very much, you know, where it could result in an impeachment. I am, again, was not, am not convinced or certain that it will...."

but stated, "[T]hat's just not how I read it." She stated, "He wants to finish the Russia investigation to do, right, this President fired the Director. This President's team is being investigated for potentially colluding with the Russians in the 2016 election. So, [he] want[s] to finish [his] involvement."

4.   Other Notable Text Messages

In this section, we briefly discuss other text message exchanges between Page and Strzok that have received significant public attention.

April 1, 2016: On April 1, 2016, Page sent the following text message to Strzok: "So look, you say we text on that phone when we talk about hillary because it can't be traced, you were just venting bc you feel bad that you're gone so much but it can't be helped right now." Page told us that this was an example of why she and Strzok used their work phones to conceal their affair from their spouses. Page stated, "[T]hat [text message] follows us communicating personally on our personal phones, and his wife inquiring what it is he was doing. And so my saying, tell her we're talking about Hillary is not in fact because we were talking about Hillary, but coming up with an explanation for him to provide his wife with respect to why we were on that phone."

June 30, 2016: On June 30, 2016, Strzok sent the following text message to Page: "...Just left Bill.... He changed President to 'another senior government official.'" Based on context, Strzok told us "Bill" referred to Priestap. Strzok stated:

> My recollection is that the early Comey speech drafts included references to emails that Secretary Clinton had with President Obama and I think there was some conversation about, well do we want to be that specific? Is there some, out of deference to executive communications, do we want to do that? And I remember that discussion occurring. I remember the decision was made to take it out. I know I was not the person who did it.

Strzok told us that he saw no indication that this decision was done "to curry favor or to influence anything." Page told us that she could not remember the discussion referenced in this text message. We also discuss this change to Comey's July 5 statement in Chapter Six.

July 24, 2016: On July 24, 2016, before the Russia investigation was formally opened, Page and Strzok exchanged numerous text messages in which they discuss U.S. District Court Judge Rudolph "Rudy" Contreras. Judge Contreras is also a current member of the Foreign Intelligence Surveillance Court (FISC). They discuss, among other things, Strzok hosting a social gathering and inviting Contreras. They also discuss whether Contreras would "have to recuse himself" on "espionage FISA" cases given "his friend oversees them." We asked Strzok about this exchange and his relationship with Contreras. Strzok stated that he considered Contreras a friend and explained that they met years ago when their children attended the same elementary school. Strzok stated that this text message exchange reflected that "it had been a while since he had seen" Contreras and he was telling Page that it would nice to see Contreras and find out how he was doing. Strzok continued:

> What it was not, and I will say this in response to, again, a lot of the speculation I've seen. At no time did I ever with Judge Contreras think of or in actuality reach out for the purpose of discussing any case or trying to get any decision, provide any information, or otherwise influence him with regard to any investigative matter that I or others were involved with.

Strzok told us that Judge Contreras "knew that [Strzok] worked or may have worked national security matters for the FBI," but knew nothing about the specifics of Strzok's job or any of the cases he worked. Strzok stated that he never discussed specifics of any investigation with Judge Contreras. Strzok also told us that the social gathering discussed in this text message exchange never occurred.

We also asked Strzok about the recusal discussion reflected in the text messages. Strzok stated:

> [This] came up in the context of now that he was on the FISC and that we did have a relationship, the question about, from an ethical perspective and doing the right thing from an ethical perspective, where the lines of either notifying the court and/or either his recusal or my recusal with regard to matters that might bring us in contact with each other on the professional side.

> And so the discussion which then came up...was, whether in the context of being the head of the Counterespionage Section, were there, noticing the court or at a minimum noticing [the Department's National Security Division Office of Intelligence] of that personal relationship to allow the court to make the appropriate decision, or, you know, the, the conglomeration of all of us to make the appropriate ethical decision of whether or not to do was the substance of this discussion. But all of this discussion is a consideration of doing the right, appropriate, ethical thing. It is the polar opposite of what is being suggested by some. This is, this is the flip side of that saying we want to make sure we're absolutely doing the right thing. And by the way...Judge Contreras is thoughtful and extraordinarily conscientious about ethics and doing the right thing. So this is, if anything, and what is particularly personally aggravating to me is this speaks highly to him as a person, to us as the way we were thinking about it. And it's being absolutely twisted in the, the complete opposite direction.

Strzok told us that this text message exchange was not about any particular case and represented a more general concern of what he should do.

September 2, 2016: On September 2, 2016, Page and Strzok exchanged the following text messages. The sender of each message is identified after the timestamp.

> 09:41:30, Strzok: "Checkout my 9:30 mtg on the 7th"
>
> 09:42:40, Page: "I can tell you why you're having that meeting."
>
> 09:42:46, Page: "It's not what you think."
>
> 09:49:39, Strzok: "TPs for D?"
>
> 09:50:29, Page: "Yes, bc potus wants to know everything we are doing."
>
> 09:55:21, Strzok: "I'm sure an honest answer will come out of that meeting...."

This text message exchange occurred during the period in which Midyear was effectively closed—after Comey's July 5 announcement and prior to the discovery of Midyear-related emails on the Weiner laptop in late September. Strzok told us that these text messages referenced a request by the White House to get a "comprehensive idea across the U.S. Intelligence Community" about the scope of Russian interference activities and details of what Russia was doing. Strzok stated that this was "strictly limited to Russian actors" and he did not believe any investigations of U.S. persons were part of this request. Page stated that this exchange had "nothing to do with the Clinton email investigation."

November 9, 2016: The day after the presidential election, on November 9, 2016, Page sent the following text message to Strzok: "Are you even going to give out your calendars? Seems kind of depressing. Maybe it should just be the first meeting of the secret society." We asked Page about this message. Page stated that the "calendars" referenced in this text message were "funny and snarky" calendars of Russian President Vladimir Putin in different poses, such as "holding a kitten." Page told us that Strzok had previously purchased these calendars as "dark gallows humor." Page stated that the reference to the "secret society" was also a "dark sort of" humor about Trump winning the election and concerns she and Strzok had about Trump. Page continued:

> And so, we somewhat with dark humor, but also somewhat, you know, with real concern as, of course, our Director actually gets fired, talk about, like, well, when he shuts down the, when he finds out about the investigation and shuts down the FBI, you know, we'll form a secret society so we can like continue the investigation. So that's just, that's obviously not real. I mean, that's just us being, you know, sort of snarky. But that's a, that's a joke. I mean, a reflection of that sort of joke.

Strzok stated that he "took and certainly believed [this text message] to be a joke." Strzok explained:

I had gotten a bunch of Putin 2017 calendars where he is in various, glorious displays of Russian patriotism for each month. And we were going to give it out to the, kind of the, the closer senior members of the [Russia investigation] team, just to, you know, hey, we made it to, to Election Day just as like, you know, thanks for your hard work because people, you know, had been truly working very hard....

To give that out and, you know, and Lisa, you know, saying, God, you know, and the thought was, you know, give it out like right around the election. And then my, my take of Lisa's, and I think the everyman, commonsense take of this is that it's like, God, you know, is that something you would want to, you know, want to do right now? And, you know, the secret society is entirely in jest.

B.   Instant Messages between Agent 1 and Agent 5

Agent 1 is an experienced counterintelligence agent and was assigned to the Midyear investigative team from August 2015 through the conclusion of the investigation. Agent 1 was one of four agents responsible for the day-to-day activities of the Midyear investigation. Agent 1's duties included conducting witness interviews and Agent 1 was one of the two agents who interviewed former Secretary Clinton on July 2. Agent 5 is also an experienced counterintelligence agent and was a member of the Midyear filter team. As a member of the filter team, Agent 5 was responsible for identifying privileged communications among the materials obtained by the FBI to ensure that they were not reviewed by the investigative team. Neither Agent 1 nor Agent 5 was assigned to the FBI's Russia investigation or the Special Counsel investigation.

As noted previously, we identified instant messages sent by Agent 1, often to Agent 5, that expressed opinions critical of the conduct and quality of the Midyear investigation. We discussed these message in Chapter Five. In addition to those messages, we identified two instant message exchanges that appeared to combine a discussion of politics with a discussion of the Midyear investigation. We also identified instant messages between Agent 1 and Agent 5 that expressed support for Clinton and hostility toward Trump. We discuss these messages in this section, along with explanations provided by Agent 1 and Agent 5. Because it is relevant to their explanations, we note that Agent 1 and Agent 5, who are now married, were in a personal relationship that predated their assignment to the Midyear investigation.

1.   Instant Messages Referencing the Midyear Investigation

On July 6, 2016, the day after Comey's Midyear declination announcement, Agent 1 and an FBI employee not involved with Midyear exchanged messages about the investigation. During the course of this discussion, Agent 1 described the prior weekend's activities, which included the interview of Clinton. A portion of this instant message exchange follows. The sender of each message is noted after the timestamp.[206]

> 15:07:41, Agent 1: "...I'm done interviewing the President – then type the 302. 18 hour day...."
>
> 15:13:32, FBI Employee: "you interviewed the president?"
>
> 15:17:09, Agent 1: "you know – HRC" [Hillary Rodham Clinton]
>
> 15:17:18, Agent 1: "future pres"
>
> 15:17:22, Agent 1: "Trump cant win"
>
> 15:17:31, Agent 1: "demographics dont line up"
>
> 15:17:37, Agent 1: "America has changed"

We asked Agent 1 if he thought of Clinton as the next president while conducting the Midyear investigation. Agent 1 stated, "I think my impression going into the election in that personal realm is that all of the polls were favoring Hillary Clinton." We asked Agent 1 if he treated Clinton differently because of this assumption. Agent 1 stated, "Absolutely not. I think the message they said that our leadership told us and our actions were to find whatever was there and whatever, whatever that means is what it means."

Comey sent the first letter to Congress about the Weiner laptop discovery on October 28, 2016. Agent 1 and Agent 5 exchanged instant messages about the letter and Trump's reaction to it later that day. The sender of each messages is noted after the timestamp.

> 13:46:48, Agent 5: "jesus christ... Trump: Glad FBI is fixing 'horrible mistake' on clinton emails... for fuck's sake."
>
> 13:47:27, Agent 5: "the fuck's sake part was me, the rest was Trump."
>
> 13:49:07, Agent 1: "Not sure if Trump or the fifth floor is worse..."
>
> 13:49:22, Agent 5: "I'm so sick of both..."
>
> 13:50:25, Agent 5: "+o(TRUMP"[207]
>
> 13:50:30, Agent 5: "+o(Fifth floor"
>
> 13:50:34, Agent 5: "+o(FBI"
>
> 13:50:44, Agent 5: "+o(Average American public"

---

[206] All instant messages produced to the OIG reflected Greenwich Mean Time. We have corrected times to the Eastern Time Zone as a result. In addition, some instant messages contained emojis, which we omitted unless they affected the meaning of the message. We also do not include other intervening instant messages unless they contribute to understanding the highlighted messages.

[207] The symbol used in these messages is a "sick face" emoticon. *See* IM Emoticons, *at* http://sheet.shiar.nl/emoji (last accessed April 28, 2018).

We asked both Agent 1 and Agent 5 about these messages. Agent 1 and Agent 5 both stated the reference to "fifth floor" referred to the location of the FBI WFO's Counterintelligence Division. Agent 1 continued: "Again, you know, I think a general, general theme in a lot of this is some personal comment, or, you know, complaining about common topics and leadership and, and venting." Agent 5 also described this as general complaining to Agent 1 and also as an example of her being "very tired of working" these types of cases. Agent 5 also noted that she was not involved in the review of the Weiner laptop.

2.   Instant Messages Commenting on Trump or Clinton

On August 29, 2016, Agent 1 and Agent 5 exchanged the following instant messages as part of a discussion about their jobs. The sender of each message is noted after the timestamp.

> 10:39:49, Agent 1: "I find anyone who enjoys [this job] an absolute fucking idiot. If you dont think so, ask them one more question. Who are you voting for? I guarantee you it will be Donald Drumpf."

> 10:40:13, Agent 5: "i forgot about drumpf..."

> 10:40:27, Agent 5: "that's so sad and pathetic if they want to vote for him."

> 10:40:43, Agent 5: "someone who can't answer a question"

> 10:40:51, Agent 5: "someone who can't be professional for even a second"

On September 9, 2016, Agent 1 and Agent 5 exchanged the following instant messages.

> 08:56:43, Agent 5: "i'm trying to think of a 'would i rather' instead of spending time with those people"

> 08:56:54, Agent 1: "stick your tongue in a fan??"

> 08:56:58, Agent 5: "i would rather have brunch with trump"

> 08:57:03, Agent 1: "ha"

> 08:57:15, Agent 1: "french toast with drumpf"

> 08:57:19, Agent 5: "i would rather have brunch with trump and a bunch of his supporters like the ones from ohio that are retarded"

> 08:57:23, Agent 5: ":)"

Agent 5 told the OIG these instant messages "referenced TV programming and commentary that Agent 1 and Agent 5 had recently viewed together." Agent 5 continued, "The reference was not a general statement about a particular part of the country, rather it was in jest and pertained to individuals' inability to articulate any reason why they so strongly favored one candidate over another."

On Election Day on November 8, 2016, Agent 1 and Agent 5 exchanged the following instant messages.

> 14:21:10, Agent 1: "You think HRC is gonna win right? You think we should get nails and some boards in case she doesnt"

> 14:21:56, Agent 5: "she better win... otherwise i'm gonna be walking around with both of my guns."

> 14:22:05, Agent 5: "and likely quitting on the spot"

> 14:28:43, Agent 1: "You should know;....."

> 14:28:45, Agent 1: "that"

> 14:28:50, Agent 1: "I'm....."

> 14:28:56, Agent 1: "with her."

> 14:28:58, Agent 1: "ooooooooooooooooooo"

> 14:29:02, Agent 1: "show me the money"

> 14:29:03, Agent 5: "<:o)"

> 14:29:14, Agent 5: "screw you trump"

> 14:19:18, Agent 5: "wheeeeeeeeeeeeeeeeeeeeeeeeeeee!"

> 14:29:32, Agent 5: "go baby, go! let's give her Virginia"

> 14:30:03, Agent 1: "not to my country. You just cant get up and try to appeal to all the worst things in humans and fool my country...."

> 14:30:12, Agent 1: "Just 49% of us....."

> 14:30:25, Agent 5: "let's hope it's 49% or less..."

> 14:30:31, Agent 5: "we'll find out..."

In a December 6, 2016 exchange, Agent 5 complained to Agent 1 about being required to be on call on the day of the presidential inauguration. In the middle of expressing displeasure about this, Agent 5 sent a message to Agent 1 that stated, "fuck trump." On February 9, 2017, in the context of an FBI employee receiving a presidential award for public service, Agent 5 messaged, "...I think now that trump is the president, i'd refuse it. it would be an insult to even be considered for it."

We asked Agent 1 and Agent 5 about their use of instant messaging generally and about these messages in particular. As mentioned in Chapter Five, Agent 1 told us that he believed that instant messages were not retained by the FBI and therefore used less caution with those communications than he would have with other types of communications, such as email or text messages.[208] Agent 5

---

[208] Agent 1 explained the reason for his belief that the instant messages were not retained, stating, "So my understanding of [instant messaging] in the FBI is that it was implemented about four or five years ago, roughly. Because I did internal investigations, at the time I was on the espionage

also made this point, stating that she considered these exchanges as a private "outlet" to Agent 1. Both Agent 1 and Agent 5 apologized for their use of instant messaging in this manner and told us that they were embarrassed.

We asked Agent 1 whether he believed these political discussions raised questions about the integrity or reliability of the Midyear investigation. Agent 1 stated:

> I don't based on knowing my actions. I guess I would kind of repeat what I said before. Yes, I, I have personal, a personal life, private opinions, private views. I think what happened here is that I used instant message and chat like it was my home.
>
> ...I like the job of fact-finding and having it lead you where you go. I don't start any day with an endgame in mind of let it, let it go to, go to that. That's the way I think I act, that's how I think I've acted over my whole career. That's how I, that's how I know I acted in, in this case.
>
> Yeah, I think that, I understand your question because it's an FBI system. I just unfortunately did not view it that way and did not use it that way. I used it as, as, you know, some of my worst hits here, as a, a way to relieve stress, as a way to be jocular, as a way to exaggerate, as a way to blow off steam, as a, you know, potentially get sympathy from, and then, you know, it was compounded by frustrations from other people coming to me for answers for why certain people got elected, and is it our fault, and, so I think there was a, kind of a cocktail of, of stress in this case that came out on this system like it was a conversation.
>
> So I, I don't, I don't think so based on knowing my actions and what I did knowing the actions of the people around me.

We also asked Agent 1 whether his personal beliefs impacted his investigative actions in Midyear. Agent 1 responded:

> [I]n no way do I think it, it impacted my view. I guess the best way is almost like a, it's almost like you switch on your, when, when we did our morning meetings, it was what do we have and where do we go next? It, it was just like almost, you know, like there's a, there's the professional side, the do your job side, and there's a personal side. And I think a lot of this falls into the personal side.

---

squad, my awareness was that it was not logged by the FBI because I tried to get those records for internal investigations." Agent 5 stated the she also had requested instant messages in prior internal investigations and been told that they were not preserved. Agents 1 and 5 told the OIG that they learned in April 2017 that the FBI had retained instant messages since February 2015, as the result of receiving a memorandum about preservation and criminal discovery obligations stemming from the FBI's instant messaging system. The FBI email distributing this memorandum advised employees that the FBI began preserving instant messages in February 2015 and stated, "Lync should not be used for substantive communications."

...It was only to try to do the right thing.... That's, that's the only thing, the only thought process in my head when I was, when I was doing my job.

We asked Agent 5 how she would respond to someone who read these messages and concluded the opinions expressed in them impacted the Midyear investigation. Agent 5 stated:

Well, I can see someone who doesn't know us at all saying the same, wondering, I guess, if [our political beliefs] could have impacted [the Midyear investigation]. I can tell you in no way did my political or what I understand of [Agent 1], no political anything is going to interfere with us doing our job as professionals.

I can see me going into these rants. I can see me ranting in some of these, and, you know, again, I think all of these are very personal, off-the-cuff...these are personal, private messages. I mean, you could probably even see the difference between, if you've seen anything in my [career] that I put to the file...for, you know, case-related things. I am very thorough, methodical, and I think through everything when I'm typing it. I don't even cut corners with acronyms. I, I treat that extremely seriously in my [career], and even before I became an agent.

So I, I would tell that person that part of being a professional, part of the oath that I swore here to work, I...uphold it. And I upheld it at this point. I, I do have personal beliefs and personal opinions. You know, I expressed some of those. Some of them come out in frustration. Some of them come out in jokes. I can see us quoting things kind of just to make us smile, you know, make us feel better, you know, after sometimes tough days. And...I would say in, in no way has it ever or would it ever affect the way I, I handle any investigation, any case, any professional work that I, that I put forward.

C.   FBI Attorney 2 Instant Messages

FBI Attorney 2 was assigned to the Midyear investigation early in 2016. FBI Attorney 2 was not the lead FBI attorney assigned to Midyear and he told us he provided support to the investigation as needed. FBI Attorney 2 told us that he was also assigned to the investigation into Russian election interference and was the primary FBI attorney assigned to that investigation beginning in early 2017. FBI Attorney 2 told us that he was then assigned to the Special Counsel investigation once it began. FBI Attorney 2 left the Special Counsel's investigation and returned to the FBI in late February 2018, shortly after the OIG provided the Special Counsel with some of the instant messages discussed in this section.

We identified instant messages on FBINet involving FBI Attorney 2 that discussed political issues. Most of these exchanges appeared to be jokes or attempts at humor, often involving Trump. We asked FBI Attorney 2 in general about the use of FBI instant messaging in this manner. FBI Attorney 2 told us that, in general, he regretted his use of instant messaging in this manner and noted "it's not something that I did routinely." He described these messages as "commentary" on recent political events and not connected to decisions or activities in investigations. FBI Attorney 2 stated that almost all of these messages were sent to co-workers he "considered to be" friends and he "was talking to them in that capacity," and "[n]ot in a professional capacity." FBI Attorney 2 reiterated that these messages or views had "absolutely" no impact on his work on investigations. He stated:

> I, like most people, have particular views on, on politics. I'm a bit of a news junkie when it comes to government. It's one of the main reasons I, I joined the federal workforce is because I've always found it so fascinating and interesting.

> But when it came to doing my work, I never injected this, this type of, of color commentary or this type of water cooler type talk into that. I, I maintained impartiality and just tried to work through the issues individually as they came through. So if they needed some assistance on a warrant or some assistance on, you know, potentially pursuing contacts with another government agency or something like that, like, I just, I assisted with the process more like, kind of like an XO type role I guess.

Among the general discussion of political issues by FBI Attorney 2, we identified three instant message exchanges that raised concerns of potential bias. The first of these exchanges was on October 28, 2016, shortly after Comey's October 28 letter to Congress that effectively announced the reopening of the Midyear investigation. FBI Attorney 2 sent similar messages to four different FBI employees. The timestamps of these messages are included below. The messages stated:

> 13:44:42, to FBI Employee 1: "I mean, I never really liked the Republic anyway."

> 13:44:52, to FBI Employee 2: "I mean, I never really liked the Republic anyway."

> 14:01:52, to FBI Employee 3: "As I have initiated the destruction of the republic.... Would you be so kind as to have a coffee with me this afternoon?"

> 15:28:50, to FBI Employee 4: "I'm clinging to small pockets of happiness in the dark time of the Republic's destruction"

FBI Attorney 2 described these messages as reflecting his surprise and frustration that the FBI "was essentially walking into a landmine in terms of injecting itself [into the election] at that late in the process." FBI Attorney 2 continued:

> I think that, that there is some distinguishment between my frustration at the way that the Bureau is operating itself in October in

terms of, of wading into the process at that point.... But, I think that there is a distinguishment between having reservations about the way that we were operating and just expressing the frustration about, about us coming into the process. It's like, in terms of, of, you know, what's not in here too is like, you know, we, at that point we had investigation, the Russia investigation was ongoing as well. And that information was obviously kept close hold and was not released until March. So, you know, it, it was just kind of frustration that we weren't handling both of them the same way with, with that level I guess.

FBI Attorney 2 described the "destruction" language as "hyperbolic" and "off-the-cuff commentary to friends."

The second exchange we identified occurred on November 9, 2016, the day after the presidential election. FBI Attorney 2 and another FBI employee who was not involved in the Midyear investigation exchanged the following instant messages. Note that the sender of the instant message is identified after the timestamp and intervening messages that did not contribute to the understanding of this exchange are not included.

> 09:38:14, FBI Attorney 2: "I am numb."
>
> 09:55:35, FBI Employee: "I can't stop crying."
>
> 10:00:13, FBI Attorney 2: "That makes me even more sad."
>
> 10:43:20, FBI Employee: "Like, what happened?"
>
> 10:43:37, FBI Employee: "You promised me this wouldn't happen. YOU PROMISED."
>
> 10:43:43, FBI Employee: Okay, that might have been a lie..."
>
> 10:43:46, FBI Employee: "I'm very upset."
>
> 10:43:47, FBI Employee: "haha"
>
> 10:51:48, FBI Attorney 2: "I am so stressed about what I could have done differently."
>
> 10:54:29, FBI Employee: "Don't stress. None of that mattered."
>
> 10:54:31, FBI Employee: "The FBI's influence."
>
> 10:59:36, FBI Attorney 2: "I don't know. We broke the momentum."
>
> 11:00:03, FBI Employee: "That is not so."
>
> 11:02:22, FBI Employee: "All the people who were initially voting for her would not, and were not, swayed by any decision the FBI put out. Trump's supporters are all poor to middle class, uneducated, lazy POS that think he will magically grant them jobs for doing nothing. They probably didn't watch the debates, aren't fully educated on his policies, and are stupidly wrapped up in his unmerited enthusiasm."

11:11:43, FBI Attorney 2: "I'm just devastated. I can't wait until I can leave today and just shut off the world for the next four days."

11:12:06, FBI Employee: "Why are you devastated?"

11:12:18, FBI Employee: "Yes, I'm not watching tv for four years."

11:14:16, FBI Attorney 2: "I just can't imagine the systematic disassembly of the progress we made over the last 8 years. ACA is gone. Who knows if the rhetoric about deporting people, walls, and crap is true. I honestly feel like there is going to be a lot more gun issues, too, the crazies won finally. This is the tea party on steroids. And the GOP is going to be lost, they have to deal with an incumbent in 4 years. We have to fight this again. Also Pence is stupid."

11:14:58, FBI Employee: "Yes that's all true."

11:15:01, FBI Attorney 2: "And it's just hard not to feel like the FBI caused some of this. It was razor thin in some states."

11:15:09, FBI Employee: "Yes it was very thin."

11:15:23, FBI Attorney 2: "Plus, my god damned name is all over the legal documents investigating his staff."

11:15:24, FBI Employee: "But no I absolutely do not believe the FBI had any part."

11:15:33, FBI Attorney 2: "So, who knows if that breaks to him what he is going to do."

We asked FBI Attorney 2 about this exchange. FBI Attorney 2 stated, "I'd say that we're just discussing our personal feelings on [the outcome of the election] between friends, yeah." When asked about the FBI employee meant by "[y]ou promised me this wouldn't happen," FBI Attorney 2 told us that he "did not promise [the employee] anything," and stated, "I think, again, it's just kind of the way that [the employee] and I converse. We tend to exaggerate some statements back and forth to one another." We also asked FBI Attorney 2 what he meant by "I am so stressed about what I could have done differently." FBI Attorney 2 replied:

That was a, that was a reference to, again, just in terms of the way that we opened or how long it took us to open [in October]. You know, with the, with the knowledge that the information was there [on the Weiner laptop], why we didn't work on it to, to gain access sooner, as opposed to later because it was a, a bit of a, of a gap between us learning of the information in New York and, and officially getting the case reopened again....

Just in terms of like what I could have done to, to either have accelerated the process or to, like how I expressed to [FBI Attorney 1] that I didn't know if this was the correct way for the Bureau to be doing this notification, et cetera. Whether, you know, I could have said something differently to her that would have resonated in, or, or

418

would have been part of the discussion. But I wasn't anywhere near the, the room deciding on these factors....

It was just kind of like a discussion on how I could have either moved the process along more quickly or more efficiently at a, at a more, at an earlier time, or whatnot.

When asked if he thought earlier action on the Weiner laptop would have alleviated the need to send the letter to Congress, FBI Attorney 2 stated:

Well, not, not, I don't think that that would have alleviated the need for the letter in the Director's eyes. But if we would have opened a few weeks earlier, as opposed to at that time, two weeks before the election, I think it, you know, it would have given more time for the FBI's actions and, and required and, and necessary investigation to, to occur to allow the, the public a chance to make their own decision-making.

FBI Attorney 2 again reiterated that his "personal political feelings or beliefs...in no way impacted" his work on the Midyear or Russia investigations.

The third exchange we identified was on November 22, 2016. FBI Attorney 2 sent an instant message to FBI Attorney 1 commenting on the amount of money the subject of an FBI investigation had been paid while working on the Trump campaign. FBI Attorney 1 responded, "Is it making you rethink your commitment to the Trump administration?" FBI Attorney 2 replied, "Hell no." and then added, "Viva le resistance." FBI Attorney 1 responded that Trump was "going to eliminate all of our pensions in order to pay for people like" the person discussed in the instant message exchange, and FBI Attorney 1 and FBI Attorney 2 then began a discussion of federal pension and retirement issues.

We asked both FBI Attorney 2 and FBI Attorney 1 about this exchange. FBI Attorney 2 stated:

So, this is in reference to an ongoing subject. And then following that, like I interpreted [FBI Attorney 1's] comment to me as being, you know, just her and I socially and as friends discussing our particular political views, to which I see that as more of a joking inquiry from her. It's not something along the lines of where I'm not committed to the U.S. Government. I obviously am and, you know, work to do my job very well and to continue to, to work in that capacity. It's just the, the lines bled through here just in terms of, of my personal, political view in terms of, of what particular preference I have. But, but that doesn't have any, any leaning on the way that I, I maintain myself as a professional in the FBI.

We asked FBI Attorney 2 if "Viva le resistance" signaled he was going to fight back against President Trump. FBI Attorney 2 responded:

419

That's not what I was doing.... I just, again, like that, that's just like the entire, it's just my political view in terms of, of my preference. It wasn't something along the lines of, you know, we're taking certain actions in order to, you know, combat that or, or do anything like that. Like that, that was not the intent of that. That was more or less just like, you know, commentary between me and [FBI Attorney 1] in a personal friendship capacity where she is just making a joke, and I'm responding. Like, it's not something that, that I personally believe in that instance.

FBI Attorney 2 acknowledged that both he and FBI Attorney 1 were assigned to the Russia investigation at this point in time and he "can understand the, the perception issues that come from" this exchange.

FBI Attorney 1 stated that she and FBI Attorney 2 were friends and often had discussions unrelated to work. She acknowledged that that this was "not the right place to make those kind of comments." We asked FBI Attorney 1 what she meant by the message, "Is it making you rethink your commitment to the Trump administration?" She stated, "I think what I meant was are you going to leave the government and start working to get more money." We also asked FBI Attorney 1 what she understood FBI Attorney 2 to mean when he messaged, "Viva le resistance." FBI Attorney 1 told us, "I think it was a joke obviously. But I think it was intended to say that, you know, he was committed to continuing to work for the Bureau, for these cases." FBI Attorney 1 stated that nothing about this exchange affected her work on the Russia investigation.

D.   Analysis

The conduct of the five FBI employees described in sections A, B, and C of this Chapter has brought discredit to themselves, sowed doubt about the FBI's handling of the Midyear investigation, and impacted the reputation of the FBI. As described in Chapter Five, our review did not find documentary or testimonial evidence directly connecting the political views these employees expressed in their text messages and instant messages to the specific investigative decisions we reviewed in Chapter Five. Nonetheless, the conduct by these employees cast a cloud over the FBI Midyear investigation and sowed doubt the FBI's work on, and its handling of, the Midyear investigation. Moreover, the damage caused by their actions extends far beyond the scope of the Midyear investigation and goes to the heart of the FBI's reputation for neutral factfinding and political independence.

We were deeply troubled by text messages sent by Strzok and Page that potentially indicated or created the appearance that investigative decisions were impacted by bias or improper considerations. Most of the text messages raising such questions pertained to the Russia investigation, which was not a part of this review. Nonetheless, when one senior FBI official, Strzok, who was helping to lead the Russia investigation at the time, conveys in a text message to another senior FBI official, Page, that "we'll stop" candidate Trump from being elected—after other extensive text messages between the two disparaging candidate Trump—it is not only indicative of a biased state of mind but, even more seriously, implies a willingness to take official action to impact the presidential candidate's electoral prospects. This is antithetical to the core values of the FBI and the Department of Justice. Moreover, as we describe in Chapter Nine, in assessing Strzok's decision to prioritize the Russia investigation over following up on the Midyear-related investigative lead discovered on the Weiner laptop in October 2016, these text messages led us to conclude that we did not have confidence that Strzok's decision was free from bias.

Each of the five employees expressed remorse about using FBI devices and systems for these discussions, and each also stated that they intended these messages to be private conversations. Several of the employees also expressed the belief that their messages would not be preserved or would be exempt from public disclosure under FOIA. We found this reliance on the "private" nature of these messages to be misplaced. Because these messages were exchanged on government systems and devices, they were never "private." Every Department employee sees a notice each time he or she logs onto the Department's network informing him or her that there is no reasonable expectation of privacy in communications exchanged on government systems.[209] We recommend that the FBI add a similar warning banner to all of the FBI's mobile phones and devices.

Indeed, rather than being "private" communications, these messages were at all times potentially subject to being reviewed by others (including the OIG) and to being disclosed to the public. This point seems even more obvious in light of the significant congressional and public interest generated by the Midyear and Russia investigations. The employees exchanging text messages and instant messages are trained law enforcement agents or attorneys, and should have known that these messages were potentially subject to release in response to FOIA requests, subject to disclosure in civil litigation, or discoverable as impeachment evidence even in the absence of the OIG investigation.[210] We note that these messages also

---

[209] After reviewing a draft of the report, Page told the OIG that the Samsung phones used by the FBI do not include any such warning banner. The OIG confirmed with the FBI that this is accurate. However, the notice on the FBI's computer system applies to "all devices [or] storage media attached to this network or to a computer on this network," and alerts users that they "have no reasonable expectation of privacy regarding any communication transmitted through or data stored on this information system. At any time the government may monitor, intercept, search and/or seize data transmitted through or data stored on this information system." In addition, a recent Department training stated, "DOJ systems are not your personal systems. That means you have no reasonable expectation of privacy about maintaining any personal information, data, or applications on Department systems, networks, or devices." Department of Justice, Office of the Chief Information Officer, 2018 Annual DOJ Cybersecurity Awareness Training, at 14.

[210] For example, FBI Records Management Training warns FBI employees to be careful about what they say in emails and text messages:

Remember, that emails and texts messages should be treated the same way as paper correspondence. So be aware of what you write. It may be released through FOIA, and be made widely available one day.

Of course, many of our records also end up in court. In civil cases, the FBI must turn over all relevant evidence, including emails and text messages. While all documents are viewed for privilege and redacted prior to release, there is no claim of privilege covering inappropriate or embarrassing statements. Such as, the governor is a block

421

potentially implicate the FBI's or prosecutors' disclosure obligations in any prosecutions resulting from the investigations at issue.[211]

We do not question that the FBI employees who sent these messages are entitled to their own political views. Indeed, federal statutes and regulations explicitly protect the right of federal employees to "express...opinion[s] on political subjects and candidates" and to "exercise fully, freely, and without fear of penalty or reprisal, and to the extent not expressly prohibited by law, their right to participate or to refrain from participating in the political processes of the Nation"—provided such expression "does not compromise his or her efficiency or integrity as an employee or the neutrality, efficiency, or integrity of the agency or instrumentality of the United States Government in which he or she is employed."[212] While these employees did not give up their First Amendment rights when they became employed by the FBI, Supreme Court decisions make clear that the FBI retains the authority—particularly as a law enforcement agency—to impose

---

head. Although what we turn over in criminal cases can be more targeted, such as witness statements and exculpatory and impeachment evidence. Just as in civil cases, emails and text messages that fit into one of these categories must be turned over regardless whether they are embarrassing or worded inappropriately....

Even though it's a casual medium, we can't take a casual attitude towards email. All email, even a text or a PIN message, can be instantly copied, archived, filed, and disseminated. Just like a memo or a 302, emails reflect on the professionalism of the employee, and potentially the FBI as a whole. Inappropriate, offensive language, ill-advised humor, off-color references, and poorly thought out remarks have no place in any FBI communication. And it doesn't matter if that communication was intended as a record or a non-record.

[211] *See* USAM § 9-5.001, Policy Regarding Disclosure of Exculpatory and Impeachment Information; *see also United States* v. *Johnson,* 14-CR-00412-TEH, 2015 WL 2125132, at 3-4 (N.D. Cal. May 6, 2015) (ordering the disclosure of racist text message(s) sent or received by a police officer involved in maintaining a crime scene); *Linetsky* v. *City of Solon*, Case No. 1:16-CV-52, 2016 WL 5402615 (N.D. Ohio Sept. 28, 2016) (ordering an assistant prosecutor to produce in discovery all text messages between the prosecutor and law enforcement personnel pertaining to the plaintiff's prior criminal case); *United States* v. *Marcus Mumford*, Case No. 3:17-CR-0008-JCC, 2017 WL 652448, at 2-3 (D. Ore. Feb. 16, 2017) (finding, during prosecution of Ammon Bundy's attorney in connection with a scuffle with U.S. Deputy Marshals, that "the Marshals' government issued cell phones are subject to discovery and should any texts reveal hostility towards Defendant or in any way casts doubt on their credibility, they must be produced.").

[212] 5 U.S.C. §§ 7321, 7323(c); 5 C.F.R. § 734.402. FBI policy similarly provides that FBI employees retain the right to participate in various specified political activities, as long as such activity is not performed in concert with a political party, partisan political group, or a candidate for partisan political office. The list of political activities includes the right of an FBI employee to "[e]xpress his or her opinion as an individual privately and publicly on political subjects and candidates," and to "otherwise participate fully in public affairs, except as prohibited by other Federal law, in a manner which does not compromise his or her efficiency or integrity as an employee or the neutrality, efficiency, or integrity of the agency or instrumentality of the United States Government in which he or she is employed." FBI Office of Integrity and Compliance, FBI Ethics and Integrity Program Policy Directive and Policy Guide, § 7.4.2 (Feb. 2, 2015).

certain restrictions on its employees' speech in the interest of providing effective and efficient government.[213]

We believe the messages discussed in this chapter—particularly the messages that intermix work-related discussions with political commentary—potentially implicate provisions in the FBI's Offense Code and Penalty Guidelines, which provides general categories of misconduct for which FBI employees may be disciplined. This includes the provisions relating to Offense Codes 1.7 (Investigative Deficiency – Misconduct Related to Judicial Proceedings), 3.6 (Misuse of Government Computer(s)), 3.11 (Misuse of Government Property, Other), 5.21 (Unprofessional Conduct – Off Duty), and 5.22 (Unprofessional Conduct – On Duty).[214] However, we did not identify any prior FBI misconduct investigations under these provisions that involved a similar fact pattern or similar issues.[215]

At a minimum, we found that the employees' use of FBI systems and devices to send the identified messages demonstrated extremely poor judgment and a gross lack of professionalism. This is not just because of the nature of the messages, but also because many of the messages commented on individuals (Clinton and Trump) who were inextricably connected to the Midyear and Russia investigations. The FBI is charged with the investigation of many important and sensitive matters, including some that generate intense public interest and debate. It is essential that the public have confidence that the work of the FBI is done without bias or appearance of partiality, and that those engaged in it follow the

---

[213] The Supreme Court has held that public employees do not forfeit their right to freedom of speech by virtue of their public employment. *See Pickering* v. *Bd. of Educ.*, 391 U.S. 563, 568 (1968). However, when a citizen enters government service, he accepts certain limitations on his First Amendment rights. *See Garcetti* v. *Ceballos*, 547 U.S. 410, 418 (2006). In *Pickering*, the Supreme Court recognized that a public employer has an interest in regulating the speech of its employees. The Court strove to "arrive at a balance between the interests of the [public employee], as a citizen, in commenting upon matters of public concern and the interest of the State, as an employer in promoting the efficiency of the public services it performs through its employees." To strike this balance, the Supreme Court has set forth a two-step inquiry to determine whether a public employee's speech is entitled to protection. *See Lane* v. *Franks*, 134 S.Ct. 2369, 2378 (2014). First, the court must determine the threshold question of whether the employee spoke as a private citizen on a matter of public concern. *See Garcetti*, 547 U.S. at 418. If not, the employee has no First Amendment claim. If so, the second step is to establish "whether the relevant government entity had an adequate justification for treating the employee differently from any other member of the general public." *Id.*

[214] These messages may also implicate other Department-wide Rules, such as Department of Justice Information Technology Security Rules of Behavior for General Users Version 10 (January 1, 2017).

[215] In 2012, "racy texts" exchanged between two FBI agents and an FBI informant were used to impeach the agents in the prosecutions of several defendants for violations of the Foreign Corrupt Practices Act. According to a Washington Post article about the case, which ended without convictions, the foreman of the jury stated that the "texts were one of many things that point[ed] to an absolutely amateurish operation" by the government. *See* Del Quentin Wilbur, *Racy Texts Hurt Justice's Largest Sting Operation Targeting Foreign Bribery*, Wash. Post, Feb. 13, 2013. This case and the Washington Post article about the impact of the text messages are used in the Department's training on electronic discovery as an example of what not to say in text messages. However, the OIG learned that the agents involved in that case were not investigated or disciplined for misconduct, and that their text messages were handled as a performance issue. Both agents remain employed by the FBI.

facts and law wherever they may lead and without any agenda or desired result other than to see that justice is done.

Although we found no documentary or testimonial evidence directly connecting the political views these employees expressed in their text messages and instant messages to the specific Midyear investigative decisions we reviewed in Chapter Five, the messages cast a cloud over the FBI investigations to which these employees were assigned. Ultimately, the consequences of these actions impact not only the senders of these messages but also others who worked on these investigations and, indeed, the entire FBI.

We therefore refer this information to the FBI for its handling and consideration of whether the messages sent by the five employees listed above violates the FBI's Offense Code of Conduct.

Additionally, we recommend that the FBI (1) assess whether it has provided adequate training to employees about the proper use of text messages and instant messages, including any related discovery obligations, and (2) consider whether to provide additional guidance about the allowable uses of FBI devices for any non-governmental purpose, including guidance about the use of FBI devices for political conversations.

II.   Use of Personal Email

As mentioned above, we identified several instances in which Comey and Strzok used personal email accounts for official government business. When questioned, Page also told us she used personal email for work-related matters at times. We briefly discuss these issues below.

On September 21, 2016, the Department issued a Policy Statement detailing the records retention policy for email communications. The Policy Statement contained the following guidance for the use of personal email accounts:

> In general, DOJ email users should not create or send record emails or attachments using non-official email accounts. However, should exigent circumstances require the use of a personal account to conduct DOJ business, the DOJ email user must ensure that the communicated information is fully captured in a DOJ recordkeeping system within 20 days. If sending the email from a non-official account, the email user must copy his or her DOJ email address as a recipient. If receiving a DOJ business-related email on a non-official account, the DOJ email user must forward the business-related email to his or her DOJ email account. Once the user has ensured the capture of the email information in the DOJ account, the DOJ email should be removed from the non-official account.

See DOJ Policy Statement, Electronic Mail and Electronic Messaging Records Retention (approved on September 21, 2016).

A.   Comey

We identified numerous instances in which Comey used a personal email account (a Gmail account) to conduct FBI business. We cite five examples of such use in this section and include information provided by Comey and Rybicki about Comey's use of a personal email account.

On November 8, 2016, Comey forwarded to his personal email account from his unclassified FBI account a proposed post-election message for all FBI employees that was entitled "Midyear thoughts." This document summarized Comey's reasoning for notifying Congress about the reactivation of the Midyear investigation. In late December 2016, Comey forwarded to his personal email account from his unclassified FBI account multiple drafts of a proposed year-end message to FBI employees. On December 30, 2016, Comey forwarded to his personal email account from his unclassified FBI account proposed responses to two requests for information from the Office of Special Counsel.[216] The forwarded email included two attachments: (1) a certification for Comey to sign; and (2) a list of FBI employees with information responsive to this request, including their titles, office, appointment status, contact information, and duty hours. On January 6, 2017, Comey forwarded to his personal email account from his unclassified FBI account an email from Rybicki to Kortan highlighting language that needed to be corrected in a Wall Street Journal article. In mid-March 2017, Comey sent from his personal email account to his own and Rybicki's unclassified FBI accounts multiple drafts of Comey's proposed opening statement for his March 20, 2017 testimony to the House Intelligence Committee.

We asked Comey about his use of personal email for FBI business and showed him the November 8, 2016 email with Rybicki as an example. Comey stated:

> I did not have an unclass[ified] FBI connection at home that worked. And I didn't bother to fix it, whole 'nother story, but I would either use my BlackBerry, must have been or Samsung...my phone, I had two phones—a personal phone and a government phone. Or if I needed to write something longer, I would type it on my personal laptop and then send it to Rybicki, usually I copied my own address.... Yeah. And so I would use, for unclassified work, I would use my personal laptop for word processing and then send it into the FBI.

We asked Comey if he had any concerns about conducting FBI business on his personal laptop or personal email. Comey stated that he did not and explained:

> Because it was incidental and I was always making sure that the work got forwarded to the government account to either my own account or Rybicki, so I wasn't worried from a record-keeping perspective and it

---

[216] This refers to the federal agency responsible for investigating violations of the Hatch Act, not to Special Counsel Robert Mueller III.

was, because there will always be a copy of it in the FBI system and I wasn't doing classified work there, so I wasn't concerned about that.

Comey stated that he did not use his personal email or laptop for classified or sensitive information, such as grand jury information. Comey told us that he only used his personal email and laptop "when I needed to word process an unclassified [document] that was going to be disseminated broadly, [such as a] public speech or public email to the whole organization." We asked Comey if the use of personal email in this manner was in accordance with FBI regulations. Comey replied, "I don't know. I think so, but I don't know. I remember talking to Jim [Rybicki] about it at one time, and I had the sense that it was okay."

We also asked Rybicki about Comey's use of a personal email account. In response to the OIG's questions and in consultation with Comey, Rybicki sent the OIG an email on April 20, 2017, that stated:

> In rare circumstances during his tenure, Director Comey sends unclassified emails from his official FBI.gov email account address to [his Gmail account]. This permits him to open attachments and use his personal laptop to then work on a speech or other content intended for wide dissemination. He then sends drafts or the completed text to his official FBI.gov email account or to another FBI.gov email account from [his Gmail account]. He opened this personal account at about the time he became Director....

> To ensure a high level of cybersecurity, Director Comey routinely deletes all emails from his [Gmail] account each day, and then clears the deleted messages folder. He began this practice about two years ago.

> The Director does not recall receiving and/or seeking advice concerning the use of these accounts.

We found that, given the absence of exigent circumstances and the frequency with which the use of personal email occurred, Comey's use of a personal email account on multiple occasions for unclassified FBI business to be inconsistent with the DOJ Policy Statement.

B.   Strzok and Page

During our review, we identified several instances where Strzok used his personal email account for government business. Examples included an email chain forwarded to Strzok's personal email account on December 10, 2016, discussing a draft congressional response, and draft versions of emails on his personal email account that Strzok eventually sent to other FBI employees using his government account. Most troubling, on October 29, 2016, Strzok forwarded from his FBI account to his personal email account an email about the proposed search warrant the Midyear team was seeking on the Weiner laptop. This email included a draft of the search warrant affidavit, which contained information from the Weiner investigation that appears to have been under seal at the time in the Southern

District of New York and information obtained pursuant to a grand jury subpoena issued in the Eastern District of Virginia in the Midyear investigation.[217]

We asked Strzok about these emails and his use of personal email account for FBI business. Strzok stated:

> My general practice was not to use personal email for FBI business. The times that I did it was when it wasn't possible or there, there were problems with the FBI systems. In the case of I think the one issue that came out was...the one about the draft affidavit for the Weiner laptop.
>
> Our phones at the time had significant limitations specifically to that. You couldn't view redlines. And so, and, but yet you could on an iPhone. So I remember in the case of that search warrant forwarding it over so I could see what DOJ changed and their comment bubbles in regard to that. There were some other times where I was either out of the office. I think a lot of those were either I was on travel or certainly over the weekends. It is very cumbersome on the old iPhones, or on the old Samsungs of the Bureau because of the way they autocorrect spelling and the nature of the...keyboard, it is difficult to write anything of length whatsoever. So there were times that, I mean, I think there's one where I was very aggravated with a set of circumstances that had unfolded. I was going to tell my boss about it, and I remember talking with Lisa [Page] saying, hey look, did I hit the right tone in this because I wanted to, you know, just be respectful, but at the same time convey my frustration.
>
> I wrote that on my home computer, because it's easier to type it out. I think there was one that might be a holiday greeting that I sent to Bill [Priestap]. But, again, the sort of thing that, you know, for, for convenience, but because on the one hand it was bulky to, our technology was crappy, and it was impossible on the rare occasion I would write these things. And then send them to, you know, my account and forward it on. So it got incorporated and picked up into the FBI system.

Strzok told us that his understanding was that FBI policy discouraged the use of personal email and devices, but "there are allowances made" where "it is not practical or possible to use your [FBI] device." Strzok stated that he would double delete any work-related emails in his personal account.[218]

---

[217] The OIG previously notified the respective U.S. Attorney's Offices about Strzok's actions.

[218] We requested access to Strzok's personal email account. Strzok agreed to produce copies of work-related emails in his personal account but declined to produce copies of his personal emails. Strzok subsequently told the OIG that he had reviewed the emails residing in his personal mailboxes and found no work-related communications. We determined that we lacked legal authority to obtain the contents of Strzok's personal email account from his email provider, which requires an Electronic Communications Privacy Act (ECPA) search warrant to produce email contents. Strzok's email

We also identified numerous references in text messages between Page and Strzok about using "Imessage" (or "Imsg") or a personal email account. A number of these messages reference work-related discussions on those forums. We asked Strzok and Page about this. Strzok stated, "Typically, we would iMessage personal things." We asked Strzok if he and Page ever exchanged work-related information on iMessage. Strzok told us, "I do not recall that. I can't exclude it ever, ever happening, but I don't recall ever sending work-related stuff on, on iMessage."

Page told us that references to these other forums reflected "mostly personal use" as opposed to using them for work purposes. However, she stated that she and Strzok sometimes used these forums for work-related discussions due to the technical limitations of FBI-issued phones. Page explained:

> [I]n particular, the autocorrect function is the bane of literally every agent of the FBI's existence because those of us who care about spelling and punctuation, which I realize is a nerdy thing to do, makes us crazy because it takes legitimate words that are spelled correctly and autocorrects them into gobbledygook. And so, it is not uncommon for either one of us to just either switch to our personal phones or, or in this case, where it was going to be a, a fairly substantive thing that he was writing, to just save ourselves the trouble of not doing it on our Samsungs. Because they are horrible and super-frustrating.

Page also noted that she and Strzok would often use personal email accounts to send news articles to one another.

We refer to the FBI the issue of whether Strzok's use of personal email accounts violated FBI and Department policies. As noted above, Page left the Department on May 4, 2018.

III. Allegations that Department and FBI Employees Improperly Disclosed Non-Public Information

Among the issues we reviewed were allegations that Department and FBI employees improperly disclosed non-public information. We found that Department and FBI officials raised considerable concerns about alleged leaks of information, particularly in October 2016, regarding the Midyear investigation and the Clinton Foundation investigation.

---

provider's policy applies to opened emails and emails stored for more than 180 days, which ECPA otherwise permits the government to obtain using a subpoena and prior notice to the subscriber. *See* 18 U.S.C. § 2703(a), (b)(1)(B)(i); COMPUTER CRIME AND INTELLECTUAL PROPERTY SECTION, U.S. DEPARTMENT OF JUSTICE, SEARCHING AND SEIZING COMPUTERS AND OBTAINING ELECTRONIC EVIDENCE IN CRIMINAL INVESTIGATIONS at 129-30 (2009). In addition, although we learned that a non-FBI family member had access to Strzok's personal email account in 2017, Strzok told the OIG that no one else had access to his personal email account during the period in question (*i.e.*, late October 2016).

As we describe in Chapter Eleven of this report, Lynch and Comey discussed their concerns about leaks on October 31, 2016. Additionally, on October 26, 2016, Lynch raised her concerns about leaks with McCabe and the head of the FBI New York Field Office (NYO), with specific focus on leaks regarding the FBI's high-profile investigation into the death of Eric Garner, as we detailed in our February 2018 misconduct report concerning McCabe.[219] McCabe told us that he "never heard [Lynch] use more forceful language." The head of FBI NYO confirmed that the participants got "ripped by the AG on leaks." These widespread concerns about leaks led Comey, following the 2016 election, to instruct the FBI's Inspection Division (INSD) to investigate whether confidential information was being improperly disclosed by any FBI employees.[220]

Concerns about the impact of possible leaks on the Midyear investigation, particularly in the October 2016 time period, are described in Chapters Ten and Eleven. Several FBI officials told us that their concerns about potential leaks were a factor that influenced them in the discussions about the possibility of sending a notification letter to Congress on October 28, 2016, regarding the FBI's discovery of Clinton-related emails on the Weiner laptop. As then FBI General Counsel Baker starkly characterized that decision to us, "[I]f we don't put out a letter, somebody is going to leak it."

Against this backdrop, and as noted at the time the OIG announced this review, we examined allegations that Department and FBI employees improperly disclosed non-public information. We focused, in particular, on the April/May and October 2016 time periods. We have profound concerns about the volume and extent of unauthorized media contacts by FBI personnel that we have uncovered during our review.

Our ability to identify individuals who have improperly disclosed non-public information is often hampered by two significant factors. First, we frequently find that the universe of Department and FBI employees who had access to sensitive information that has been leaked is substantial, often involving dozens, and in some instances, more than 100 people. We recognize that this is a challenging issue, because keeping information too closely held can harm an investigation and the supervision of it. Nevertheless, we think the Department and the FBI need to consider whether there is a better way to appropriately control the dissemination of sensitive information.

---

[219] U.S. Department of Justice (DOJ) Office of the Inspector General (OIG), *Report of Investigation of Certain Allegations Relating to Former FBI Deputy Director Andrew McCabe,* Oversight & Review Report (February 2018), https://oig.justice.gov/reports/2018/o20180413.pdf (accessed May 14, 2018).

[220] One of those investigations led to INSD raising questions about McCabe's conduct and resulted in the OIG taking over the matter from INSD. Ultimately, the OIG found that McCabe himself had authorized others in the FBI to disclose information regarding the FBI's Clinton Foundation investigation just days prior to the election.

Second, although FBI policy strictly limits the employees who are authorized to speak to the media, we found that this policy appeared to be widely ignored during the period we reviewed.[221] We identified numerous FBI employees, at all levels of the organization and with no official reason to be in contact with the media, who were nevertheless in frequent contact with reporters. The large number of FBI employees who were in contact with journalists during this time period impacted our ability to identify the sources of leaks. For example, during the periods we reviewed, we identified dozens of FBI employees that had contact with members of the media. Attached to this report as Attachments G and H are link charts that reflects the volume of communications that we identified between FBI employees and media representatives in April/May and October 2016.[222]

In addition to the significant number of communications between FBI employees and journalists, we identified social interactions between FBI employees and journalists that were, at a minimum, inconsistent with FBI policy and Department ethics rules. For example, we identified instances where FBI employees received tickets to sporting events from journalists, went on golfing outings with media representatives, were treated to drinks and meals after work by reporters, and were the guests of journalists at nonpublic social events. We will separately report on those investigations as they are concluded, consistent with the Inspector General (IG) Act, other applicable federal statutes, and OIG policy.

The harm caused by leaks, fear of potential leaks, and a culture of unauthorized media contacts is illustrated in Chapters Ten and Eleven, where we detail the fact that these issues influenced FBI officials who were advising then Director Comey on consequential investigative decisions in October 2016. The FBI updated its media policy in November 2017, restating its strict guidelines concerning media contacts, and identifying who is required to obtain authority before engaging members of the media, and when and where to report media contact. We do not believe the problem is with the FBI's policy, which we found to be clear and unambiguous. Rather, we concluded that these leaks highlight the need to change what appears to be a cultural attitude. Accordingly, we recommend that the FBI evaluate whether (a) it is sufficiently educating its employees about both its media contact policy and the Department's ethics rules, and (b) its disciplinary penalties are sufficient to deter such improper conduct.

---

[221] The Media Policy in effect both at the time of these events and currently authorizes only four employees at FBI Headquarters to speak directly to the media without prior authorization. This list includes the Director, Deputy Director, Associate Deputy Director, and the Assistant Director of the Office of Public Affairs (OPA). All other headquarters employees are required to coordinate with OPA prior to any contact with the media. In FBI Field Offices (FO), only the head of the FO and a designated Public Affairs Officer are authorized to speak to the media. The policies require these authorized FO officials to coordinate with OPA on stories with national interest.

[222] These charts do not reflect communications that occurred between media representatives and FBI employees who were working in a public affairs capacity or were otherwise authorized to speak directly to the media.

CHAPTER THIRTEEN:
WHETHER FORMER DEPUTY DIRECTOR ANDREW MCCABE SHOULD HAVE RECUSED FROM CERTAIN MATTERS

I.   Introduction

In this chapter we address whether former FBI Deputy Director Andrew McCabe should have recuse himself from the Clinton email server and Clinton Foundation investigations prior to November 1, 2016.[223] We also address whether McCabe violated his recusal obligations after he recused himself from those investigations on November 1, 2016.[224]

II.   Timeline of Key Events

Aug 10, 2014	Andrew McCabe becomes Assistant Director in Charge of the FBI Washington Field Office (WFO).
Feb 25, 2015	McCabe's wife, Dr. Jill McCabe, receives a call from the Virginia Lieutenant Governor's office asking her to consider a state senate run.
Mar 7, 2015	McCabe accompanies Dr. McCabe to Richmond and the two meet with Governor McAuliffe to discuss her potential run for state senate.
Mar 9-13, 2015	McCabe contacts Director Comey's Chief of Staff and Deputy Director Giuliano to discuss Dr. McCabe's potential run.
Mar 11, 2015	McCabe obtains advice from FBI ethics official Patrick Kelley and FBI General Counsel Baker.
Mar 12, 2015	Dr. McCabe announces candidacy for state senate.
April 29, 2015	McCabe documents his recusal from all Virginia public corruption cases.

---

[223] This chapter has been written to avoid reference to Law Enforcement Sensitive (LES) information. Attached to this report at Appendix Two is a non-public LES appendix containing the complete, unmodified version of Chapter Thirteen.

[224] The OIG's review focused on McCabe's conflict of interest obligations. Other allegations against McCabe arising from his wife's 2015 campaign for state senate were not within the OIG's jurisdiction and therefore not within the scope of this review. Specifically, in a December 1, 2017, letter to Deputy Attorney General Rosenstein, Senator Charles Grassley expressed concern that McCabe may have violated the Hatch Act. *See* The Honorable Charles Grassley, letter to Rod Rosenstein, Deputy Attorney General, U.S. Department of Justice, December 1, 2017. The Hatch Act generally governs the political activity of federal employees to protect the federal workforce from partisan political influence. The law's restrictions on political activity are codified at 5 U.S.C. §§ 7321-7326. The U.S. Office of Special Counsel (OSC) has jurisdiction over potential Hatch Act violations.

July 10, 2015	FBI opens the Clinton email investigation.
Fall 2015	Dr. McCabe's campaign committee (McCabe for Senate) receives a combined total of ~ $675,000 from a Political Action Committee controlled by McAuliffe ($467,500 in monetary contributions) and from Virginia Democratic Party ($207,788 in in-kind contributions). McCabe states he was not aware of these contributions until October 2016.
Sep 6, 2015	McCabe leaves WFO and becomes Associate Deputy Director for the FBI.
Nov 3, 2015	Dr. McCabe defeated in state senate election.
January 2016	FBI opens Clinton Foundation investigations.
Feb 1, 2016	McCabe becomes Deputy Director for the FBI.
Oct 23, 2016	The *Wall Street Journal* publishes article disclosing McAuliffe contributions to Dr. McCabe's campaign, triggering discussions with Director Comey about whether McCabe should be recused from Clinton-related investigations.
Nov 1, 2016	McCabe formally recuses himself from participating in Clinton-related investigations, but the decision is not announced externally and only to a limited group internally.

III. Relevant Standards and Procedures

In this section we summarize the statutes, regulations, and FBI policies relevant to the conflict of interest and recusal issues.

A. Financial Conflict of Interest Statute

18 U.S.C. § 208 is the criminal conflict of interest statute addressing financial interest conflicts. It prohibits an executive branch employee from "participating personally and substantially" in a particular matter in which the employee knows he (or other persons whose interests are imputed to him, including the employee's spouse) have a disqualifying financial interest. The particular matter must also have "a direct and predictable effect" on the financial interest. 5 C.F.R. § 2635.402. Direct and predicable effect is defined by regulations to include "a close causal link between any decision or action to be taken in the matter and any expected effect of the matter on the financial interest." 5 C.F.R. § 2635.402(b)(1). However, a particular matter does not have a direct effect on a financial interest, "if the chain of causation is attenuated or is contingent upon the occurrence of events that are speculative or that are independent of, and unrelated to, the matter." *Id*.

B.   Executive Branch Regulations Addressing Appearance Concerns and Impartiality in Performing Official Duties

The Office of Government Ethics (OGE) promulgates the *Standards of Ethical Conduct for Employees of the Executive Branch* (Standards of Ethical Conduct or OGE regulations). *See* 5 C.F.R. Chapter XVI, Subchapter B., Part 2635. 5 C.F.R. § 2635.101 identifies general principles applying to all executive branch employees. One principle addresses appearance concerns and states that: "[e]mployees shall endeavor to avoid any actions creating the appearance that they are violating the law or the ethical standards set forth in this part."[225] 5 C.F.R. § 2635.101(b)(14). *See also* Executive Order 12674 (as modified by Executive Order 12731) on Principles of Ethical Conduct for Government Officers and Employees, section 101(n).

Conflicts of interest for federal employees are addressed in the OGE regulations at 5 C.F.R. §§ 2635.401 – 2635.403 and 2635.501 – 2635.503. Section 502(a), relating to "Personal and business relationships," provides:

> Where an employee knows that a particular matter involving specific parties is likely to have a direct and predictable effect on the financial interest of a member of his household, or knows that a person with whom he has a covered relationship is or represents a party to such matter, and where the employee determines that the circumstances would cause a reasonable person with knowledge of the relevant facts to question his impartiality in the matter, the employee should not participate in the matter unless he has informed the agency designee of the appearance problem and received authorization from the agency designee in accordance with paragraph (d) of this section.

5 C.F.R. § 2635.502(a).

Section 502(a) thus identifies two categories of circumstances creating conflicts of interest that require recusal. The first is where an employee knows that a "particular matter involving specific parties is likely to have a direct and predicable effect on the financial interest of a member of his household." Section 402(b)(1) defines "direct and predicable effect," as described above in connection with 18 U.S.C. § 208.

The second category of conflict requiring recusal occurs if the employee knows that a person with whom the employee has a "covered relationship" is or represents a party to the "particular matter." Section 502(b) defines "covered relationships" to include, among other things, persons who are members of the employee's household, persons who are relatives with whom the employee has a

---

[225] 5 C.F.R. § 2635.101(b)(8) is the general principle which states that "[e]mployees shall act impartially and not give preferential treatment to any private organization or individual." In this chapter we address McCabe's recusal obligations and do not discuss whether McCabe's conduct demonstrated that he acted with bias or partiality.

"close personal relationship," and persons with whom the employee has certain financial relationships. 5 C.F.R. § 2635.502(b).

Where either of these two circumstances is present and the employee determines that these circumstances "would cause a reasonable person with knowledge of the relevant facts to question [the employee's] impartiality in the matter, the employee should not participate in the matter" unless he or she has obtained authorization to do so from a designated agency ethics official. 5 C.F.R. § 2635.502(a). Thus, the "reasonable person" test is the standard for determining whether the circumstances could raise a fair question about an employee's impartiality thereby creating an appearance concern.[226] Section 502 encourages the employee to seek the assistance of his supervisor, an agency ethics official, or the agency designee in making a recusal determination. 5 C.F.R. § 2635.502(a)(1). Section 502 also empowers the employee's supervisor to request the agency designee to make a determination about whether recusal is required. 5 C.F.R. § 2635.502(c). The agency designee may also make such a determination on his or her own initiative. *Id*.

In addition to the specific circumstances described above, section 502(a)(2) contains a catchall provision that addresses impartiality concerns in any "other circumstances." It states:

> An employee who is concerned that circumstances other than those specifically described in this section would raise a question regarding his impartiality should use the process described in this section to determine whether he should or should not participate in a particular matter.

Section 502(a)(2) gives the employee the option to invoke the section 502 process (i.e., seeking a recusal determination or waiver from the agency designee) for these "other circumstances." *See also* 5 C.F.R. § 2635.501(a). For example, where the unique circumstances of "a personal friendship, or a professional, social, political or other association not specifically treated as a covered relationship" raise an appearance question, the employee may elect to use the section 502 process. Office of Government Ethics (OGE) 99 x 8, Memorandum to Designated Agency Ethics Officials Regarding Recusal Obligation and Screening Arrangements, April 26, 1999 at 2.

The OGE has made clear that while employees are "encouraged" to use the process provided by section 502 (a)(2), "[t]he election not to use that process should not be characterized, however, as an 'ethical lapse.'" OGE 94 x 10(1), Letter to a Departmental Acting Secretary, March 30, 1994; *see also*, OGE 01 x 8 Letter to a Designated Agency Ethics Official, August 23, 2001. Further, a note in section 502 states that "[n]othing in this section

---

[226] The "reasonable person" standard is also the test for the general appearance principle in section 101 referenced above. 5 C.F.R. § 2635.101(b)(14) ("Whether particular circumstances create an appearance that the law or these standards have been violated shall be determined from the perspective of a reasonable person with knowledge of the relevant facts.").

shall be construed to suggest that an employee should not participate in a matter because of his political, religious or moral views."

A recused employee is prohibited from participating in the matter unless authorized by the agency designee based on a determination that the Government's interest "in the employee's participation outweighs the concern that a reasonable person may question the integrity of the agency's programs and operations." 5 C.F.R. § 2635.502(d). The authorization could allow for partial participation by adjusting the employee's duties to "reduce or eliminate the likelihood that a reasonable person would question the employee's impartiality." 5 C.F.R. § 2635.502(d)(6).

C.   Department of Justice Regulation Requiring Disqualification Arising from Personal or Political Relationships

28 C.F.R. § 45.2 is a Department of Justice regulation which addresses recusal arising from a Department employee's personal or political relationships.[227] Section 45.2(a) states that no Department employee "shall participate in a criminal investigation or prosecution if he has a personal or political relationship with" any person or organization that is the subject of the investigation or prosecution or with any person or organization that the employee "knows has a specific and substantial interest that would be directly affected by the outcome of the investigation or prosecution."

Section 45.2(c)(1) defines "political relationship" to mean:

[A] close identification with an elected official, a candidate (whether or not successful) for elective, public office, a political party, or a campaign organization, arising from service as a principal adviser thereto or a principal official thereof.

In an April 2017 memorandum, the FBI's then-chief ethics official, while acknowledging that the syntax of this definition is not "crystal clear," wrote that section 45.2(c)(1) appears to require that in order to have a "close identification" with an elected official or candidate, the "employee must be or have been a 'principal adviser' to the official or candidate."[228]

Section 45(c)(2) defines "personal relationship" in part to mean "a close and substantial connection of the type normally viewed as likely to induce partiality." It presumes an employee has a personal relationship with a parent, sibling, child, or spouse, and states that whether an employee's relationships are "'personal' must

---

[227] 28 C.F.R. § 45.2 implements 28 U.S.C § 528, which states that the Attorney General shall promulgate rules and regulations which require the disqualification of Department Employees "from participation in a particular investigation or prosecution if such participation may result in a personal, financial, or political conflict of interests, or the appearance thereof."

[228] Patrick W. Kelley, Deputy Designated Agency Ethics Official & Assistant Director, Office of Integrity and Compliance, FBI, memorandum for the FBI Deputy Director, Recusal, April 11, 2017. Kelley retired from the FBI on February 28, 2018.

be judged on an individual basis with due regard given to the subjective opinion of the employee."

Unlike other ethics provisions that contain language imputing to the employee a relative or spouse's conflicts of interest, section 45.2 does not have language imputing to the Department employee a relative or spouse's political or personal relationships.

Section 45.2(b) requires an employee "who believes that his participation may be prohibited by paragraph (a) of this section" to report the matter to his supervisor. If the supervisor determines that the employee has a personal or political relationship as described in paragraph (a), "he shall relieve the employee from participation" unless he determines that the relationship will not render the employee's "service less than fully impartial and professional," and the "participation would not create an appearance of a conflict of interest likely to affect the public perception of the integrity of the investigation or prosecution."

D. What Constitutes "Participation" Under the Regulations

18 U.S.C. § 208 prohibits an employee from participating "personally and substantially" in a matter in which he has a disqualifying financial interest. *See also* 18 U.S.C § 207(a)(1). The OGE regulations define "personal and substantial" and states in part: "[t]o participate substantially means that the employee's involvement is of significance to the matter...it requires more than official responsibility, knowledge, perfunctory involvement, or involvement on an administrative or peripheral issue." 5 C.F.R. § 2635.402(b)(4).

In contrast, 5 C.F.R. § 2635.502 and 28 C.F.R. § 45.2 both use the term "participate" without qualification and neither the OGE nor DOJ regulations contain definitions describing the type of "participation" to be avoided by recused employees. Section 502(e) states that "[d]isqualification is accomplished by not participating in the matter." The OGE has provided general guidance on the scope of an employee's recusal obligations and stated that a proper recusal requires "that an employee avoid any official involvement in a covered matter." OGE 99 x 8 at 2. The OGE has offered the following advice to ethics officials to share with employees who "may not fully appreciate the meaning of the term 'recuse'":

> An employee should refrain, abstain, refuse, relinquish, forebear, forgo, hold off, keep away, give up, decline, desist, discontinue, end, cancel, close, quit, terminate, stop, halt, cease, drop, stay away, shun, avoid participation in the matter before him or her. In other words, just don't do it.

Id. at n.2.

E. FBI Procedures and Ethics Officials

The Department's ethics program is administered by the Designated Agency Ethics Official (DAEO), the Assistant Attorney General for Administration, and the Departmental Ethics Office. *See* DOJ Order 1200.1, part 11, chapter 11-1, B.1, 4.

The Deputy Designated Agency Ethics Official (Deputy DAEO) is the person to whom the DAEO delegates the responsibility and authority for the management of the ethics program within each Department component. *Id*. at B.3. Patrick W. Kelley was the FBI's Deputy DAEO and Assistant Director for the FBI's Office of Integrity and Compliance during the time period of our review.

The FBI Director's authority as the FBI's Agency Designee has been delegated to the FBI's Deputy DAEO. *See* James B. Comey, Director, Federal Bureau of Investigation, memorandum for Lee J. Lofthus, Assistant Attorney General for Administration, Department of Justice, November 12, 2013 at 2. Consequently, for FBI employees—including the Deputy Director of the FBI—the FBI's Deputy DAEO may make ethics determinations on his own, without approval or consultation with the Department's DAEO, the Departmental Ethics Office, or the FBI Director.[229]

Within the FBI, all Chief Division Counsel (CDC) and other employees designated by the Deputy DAEO may act as "ethics counselors." FBI Ethics and Integrity Program Policy Guide, 2.2.3(a). Ethics counselors' duties include providing advice regarding the standards of ethical conduct to employees in their offices, channeling questions requiring formal ethics determinations to the Deputy DAEO and forwarding any written advice to the Deputy DAEO. *Id* at 2.2.3(b). Employees with ethics questions are directed to contact the ethics counselors designated in their respective offices. *Id*. at 2.3(b). FBI policy states that disciplinary action is generally not taken against an employee who engaged in conduct relying in good faith on the advice of an ethics counselor. *Id*. at 2.3(c)

IV. Factual Findings

A. Background Facts

1. Andrew McCabe

McCabe began his career with the FBI in 1996 as a Special Agent in the New York Field Office. McCabe served in a variety of leadership positions in the FBI during his career, including as Assistant Director for the Counterterrorism Division and Executive Assistant Director for the National Security Branch. He served as Assistant Director in Charge (ADIC) of the FBI's Washington Field Office (WFO) from August 2014 until September 2015. On September 6, 2015, McCabe became Associate Deputy Director of the FBI, responsible for the FBI's non-operational divisions. On February 1, 2016, McCabe became Deputy Director of the FBI, overseeing all FBI domestic and international investigative and intelligence activities. McCabe became Acting Director of the FBI on May 9, 2017, when FBI Director James Comey was fired. McCabe served as Acting Director until August 2, 2017, when Christopher Wray became the new FBI Director. At that time, McCabe

---

[229] Ethics determinations for the Director are made by the Deputy Attorney General. *See* DOJ Order 1200.1 at part 11, chapter 11-1, C2.1.

resumed his duties as Deputy Director, a position he held until January 29, 2018, at which point he went on annual leave but remained an FBI employee. In February 2018, the OIG issued a misconduct report regarding McCabe to the FBI.[230] On March 16, 2018, Attorney General Sessions terminated McCabe's employment with the FBI.

2.   FBI Clinton Investigations

The FBI opened the Clinton server email investigation when McCabe was the ADIC of WFO and opened the Clinton Foundation investigations after McCabe became FBI Associate Director.

3.   Dr. McCabe Meets Governor McAuliffe in February 2014

In February 2014, then-Governor Terry McAuliffe visited the hospital where Dr. Jill McCabe practiced to advocate for expansion of Medicaid coverage in Virginia. McCabe told us that, by coincidence, his wife, Dr. McCabe, was working at the hospital that day and was present at the time of Governor McAuliffe's visit. McCabe told the OIG that Dr. McCabe had not previously met Governor McAuliffe until his visit to her hospital that day.

4.   Recruitment to Run for Virginia State Senate in February 2015

A year later, on February 25, 2015, Dr. McCabe received a phone call from an aide to then-Virginia Lieutenant Governor Ralph Northam. That day, Dr. McCabe emailed her husband and said the aide had asked if she would consider running for Virginia State Senate against the incumbent in District 13. McCabe told us that Dr. McCabe had not previously met Lieutenant Governor Northam.

McCabe said that Dr. McCabe was subsequently invited to, and agreed to attend, a Democratic caucus meeting in Richmond on March 7, 2015, which would provide an opportunity for her to discuss a potential run with other elected officials. According to McCabe, a Virginia State Senator told Dr. McCabe that Governor McAuliffe was scheduled to speak at the meeting and they might have an opportunity to speak to him as well, although it was "not a guarantee" that they would talk with the Governor.

5.   The McCabes' Meeting with Governor McAuliffe in March 2015

McCabe accompanied Dr. McCabe on her trip to Richmond on March 7.

---

[230] *See* U.S. Department of Justice (DOJ) Office of the Inspector General (OIG), *A Report of Investigation of Certain Allegations Relating to Former FBI Deputy Director Andrew McCabe*, Oversight and Review Division (February 2018).

a. Conversation with Richmond Special Agent in Charge (SAC) on March 6

McCabe said the day before the March 7 trip he spoke to the Special Agent in Charge of the FBI's Richmond Field Division (Richmond-SAC), to let him know he would be in Richmond with Dr. McCabe because she was considering a state senate run and they were going to a meeting "to talk with more people about this prospect." McCabe also said he talked to Richmond-SAC to get his impressions on Richmond and the state legislature and that Richmond-SAC "was very positive about it." McCabe told the OIG that Richmond-SAC was the first FBI employee with whom he discussed the March 7 trip.

Richmond-SAC told us that McCabe called to tell him he would be coming to Richmond with his wife to meet with the Governor as she was considering a run for office. Richmond-SAC said McCabe asked if he would "get in the way of anything" by going to meet with state legislators. Richmond-SAC said he did not have any investigative concerns with him meeting the Governor or state legislators, although he warned McCabe that if McCabe met with Governor McAuliffe, he would "be tethered to the Clintons" forever, and this could impact McCabe's future in government.

b. The McCabes' Meeting with McAuliffe on March 7

McCabe told us that on March 7 he and Dr. McCabe drove to Richmond for the Democratic caucus meeting where they met with a Virginia State Senator. According to McCabe, the State Senator told them "there's been a change of plans" and that Governor McAuliffe wanted to speak to Dr. McCabe at the Governor's mansion. The three then drove to the mansion in the McCabes' car.

McCabe said they met with Governor McAuliffe at the mansion for 30 to 45 minutes. He said the Governor made it very clear that his number one priority was expanding Medicaid, and that "they" (from the context, apparently referring to the Virginia Democratic Party and himself) planned to target a few state senate seats. McCabe said the Governor explained why they thought Dr. McCabe would be a good candidate and that he said she could expect to spend a lot of time fundraising. According to McCabe, Governor McAuliffe said that he and the Democratic Party would support Dr. McCabe's candidacy. However, McCabe told us to the best of his recollection they did not discuss financial support nor did they say they would support Dr. McCabe "in the form of financial backing." McCabe also said there was no mention of the Governor's Political Action Committee (PAC), the Clintons, or Clintons' associates providing financial assistance. McCabe said that Dr. McCabe asked McAuliffe questions about the nature, demands, and logistics of the legislative session and the amount of time she would have to spend in Richmond because she "had no intention ever of leaving her medical profession." McCabe said the Governor asked him about his occupation and McCabe told him he worked for the FBI but that they did not discuss McCabe's work or any FBI business.

According to McCabe, after the meeting at the Governor's mansion, he and Dr. McCabe rode with the Governor to a hotel, where the Governor delivered his speech. McCabe said they were at the hotel for 20 to 25 minutes, standing in the audience listening to the speech and returned with the Governor to the mansion where the McCabes had left their car. McCabe said they stayed for another 20 to 30 minutes at the mansion for an unrelated event before returning home in their car.[231] McCabe told us the March 7 meeting was the first and only time he had ever met McAuliffe.

c. Follow-up Conversation with Richmond SAC on March 8

Richmond-SAC told us that McCabe called him probably the following day (March 8) and described the meeting with Governor McAuliffe. According to Richmond-SAC, McCabe said it was a "surreal meeting" with the Governor at the mansion. Richmond-SAC said McCabe told him that from the mansion they were whisked away to a function at a hotel and that the Governor, without Dr. McCabe having committed to a run, introduced her as someone that they believed could unseat the incumbent senator in District 13. Richmond-SAC said McCabe told him that he would address any ethics issues.

6. Dr. McCabe's Campaign

Dr. McCabe announced her run for the Virginia State Senate on March 12, 2015. In FBI responses to Congressional inquiries in December 2016, the FBI stated that, to the best of McCabe's recollection, his role in Dr. McCabe's campaign "included providing transportation to his spouse in their personal vehicle on two occasions to public events; attending one public debate as a spectator; and appearing in a family photo which was used in a campaign mailer."[232]

Dr. McCabe's campaign committee, McCabe for Senate, received substantial monetary contributions in 2015 from Common Good VA, a PAC controlled by then-Governor McAuliffe, as well as in-kind contributions from the Virginia Democratic Party. According to state campaign finance records, Common Good VA donated a total of $467,500 to McCabe for Senate, the vast majority of which was contributed in October 2015. The Virginia Democratic Party provided a total of $207,788 in the form of campaign mail production in September and October 2015. The combined total of $675,288 from the Governor's PAC and the party represents approximately 40 percent of the total contributions raised by Dr. McCabe for her state senate campaign during the 2015 election cycle, according to the records.

On June 26, 2015, Hillary Clinton was the featured speaker at a fundraiser in Fairfax, Virginia hosted by the Virginia Democratic Party and attended by Governor McAuliffe. News accounts at the time indicated that the party raised more than

---

[231] McCabe said he did not remember what the unrelated event was about.

[232] The FBI also stated in the letter that McCabe's campaign activities were permissible under the Hatch Act. We discuss the FBI's Congressional responses in further detail below.

$1,000,000 at the fundraiser.[233] McCabe told us he was not aware of the June 2015 fundraiser until the October 2016 news accounts and that neither he nor his wife attended the event.[234]

McCabe told us that during his wife's campaign he was generally unaware of the nature and source of donations to her campaign, including the contributions from Governor McAuliffe's PAC and the Virginia Democratic Party. According to McCabe, he learned of these details for the first time from the October 23, 2016, *Wall Street Journal* article, discussed below. He told us he was not aware of the Clintons or anyone on their behalf ever contributing to Dr. McCabe's campaign.

B. McCabe Discusses Wife's Candidacy with FBI Officials, Seeks Ethics Advice, and Recuses from Various FBI Investigations

1. Meeting with Comey's Chief of Staff; Extent of Director Comey's Knowledge or Approval

McCabe said that the week following the March 7 meeting with Governor McAuliffe, he spoke to Chuck Rosenberg, Director Comey's then-Chief of Staff. He said he told Rosenberg that his wife was considering a state senate run and that they had traveled to Richmond and met with Governor McAuliffe. McCabe said they had a "fulsome discussion about everything that was involved," and that he described the information they had gathered, although he could not recall whether he flagged for Rosenberg the fact that his wife's campaign could receive financial support from the Democratic Party or other sources influenced by McAuliffe. McCabe said he told Rosenberg that his wife would not run if the Director had "any concerns about it reflecting negatively" on the FBI or McCabe. McCabe said that Rosenberg called him back a few hours later and said he had spoken to the Director "and he's totally comfortable with it." McCabe told us the ethics issues were foremost on his mind and that he believed he talked to Rosenberg about the efforts he (McCabe) would take with the FBI's chief ethics official, Patrick Kelley, to address conflict of interest and recusal issues. McCabe said he believed that the Director's approval would have been with the understanding that McCabe would address all conflict and recusal issues as required.

Rosenberg told us that he recollected one brief in-person conversation in his office with McCabe at the time his wife was considering a run for the state senate. Rosenberg said that McCabe told him that his wife was considering a run and asked whether Rosenberg thought that would be problematic. Rosenberg said he told

---

[233] *See* Jim Nolan, *Clinton Rouses Virginia Democrats at Party Fundraiser at GMU*, Richmond Times-Dispatch, Jun. 27, 2015, 2015 WLNR 19664828; Patrick Wilson, *Clinton Makes Her First Campaign Appearance in Virginia*, The Virginian-Pilot, Jun. 27, 2015, 2015 WLNR 18860380; Rachel Weiner, *At George Mason Arena, Clinton Goes on the Attack*, Wash. Post, Jun. 28, 2015, 2015 WLNR 18937709.

[234] Clinton also appeared with Governor McAuliffe at a campaign rally in Alexandria, Virginia on October 23, 2015. Laura Vozzella, *Clinton Stirs Up Crowd in Alexandria, Va., at Afternoon Rally*, Wash. Post, Oct. 23, 2015, https://www.washingtonpost.com/news/post-politics/wp/2015/10/23/clinton-stirs-up-crowd-in-alexandria-va-at-afternoon-rally (accessed March 27, 2018). McCabe also told us that neither he nor his wife attended this event.

McCabe he did not believe there would be any issues with it, but that McCabe should talk to Kelley. He told us he probably also said to McCabe that he would think about it further and let McCabe know if something ended up concerning him about the situation. Rosenberg said he told McCabe that his wife was a private citizen and so long as her campaign does not interfere with his FBI work, he did not see why there would be an issue. Rosenberg said he did not recall a subsequent conversation with Director Comey about this issue, but he believed McCabe's recollection that Rosenberg called McCabe back and said the Director had no issue with it was correct because that sounded like what he would have done.

Rosenberg said the conversation with McCabe was at "a fairly abstract level" and he assumed that that the ethics questions would be addressed with Kelley. Rosenberg said he told McCabe as long as "he was careful about recusals" and talked to Kelley it seemed okay to him.

Comey told us he did not recall Rosenberg having asked him whether he had any concerns with a potential run for office by ADIC McCabe's wife at the time she was considering a run. Comey said he believes he learned for the first time that Dr. McCabe had run for office in a causal conversation with her at an event in July 2016 (about 8 months after she lost the election), and that he recalled being surprised about that fact. Comey told us that assuming McCabe's recollection was accurate, then it is likely that Rosenberg described the issue in passing to him and said he had "checked it out and it's all good" and Comey said "ok, no sweat."

2.   Conversation with Deputy Director Giuliano

McCabe told us he also spoke about his wife's potential run with his direct supervisor, then-Deputy Director Mark Giuliano, on March 9, the Monday after their visit to Richmond. McCabe said he described the "whole situation" to Giuliano in a "robust conversation" in which he described why his wife was interested in a possible run and the "sensitivities" of her run relative to his position, and that he identified WFO's public corruption program. He said Giuliano responded by directing him to talk to Kelley to identify a "clear path forward" that avoided any Hatch Act or recusal problems. McCabe said Giuliano did not express any reservations and that Giuliano said "…good for her…she's getting involved and trying to do the right thing."

By contrast, Giuliano told us that he advised McCabe, when McCabe told him that his wife was planning to run, that it was a "bad idea." According to Giuliano, McCabe responded by saying, "she's supported me for all these years; I need to support her; what do I need to do?" Giuliano said he told McCabe to consult Kelley and FBI attorneys, and that he believes McCabe ultimately "dotted every 'I' and crossed every 'T' that he needed to" on the issue. Giuliano also told us that he ensured that McCabe was recused from appropriate WFO investigations.

3.   Meeting with Acting Chief Division Counsel on March 10

McCabe and WFO's Acting Chief Division Counsel (A-CDC), met on March 10, 2015, the day before a meeting McCabe scheduled with Kelley. McCabe said he had an in-depth conversation with A-CDC when they met and that he asked her to attend the meeting with Kelley.

A-CDC confirmed that she and McCabe had a conversation on March 10 in which McCabe described to her many details, including that he and his wife had met that weekend with McAuliffe at the governor's mansion. A-CDC told us, and her contemporaneous notes corroborate, that McCabe identified public corruption investigations and other areas of potential conflicts. She said that he wanted her to identify the conflict parameters he would work under if his wife decided to run. She responded by suggesting a "taint team" review process to identify potential conflict cases. A-CDC said that McCabe was also very concerned with telling WFO employees about his wife's run for fear that they would feel pressured to vote for her. A-CDC said that McCabe told her that he had already notified the Director and the Deputy Director.

4.   Meeting with Kelley and Baker on March 11

McCabe met with Kelley at his office at FBI Headquarters on March 11, 2015. The meeting was also attended by A-CDC and FBI General Counsel James Baker, who joined halfway through the meeting. According to McCabe, Kelley addressed two areas in their discussions: the Hatch Act restrictions on McCabe's activities during the campaign, and conflict of interest and other issues to consider in the event Dr. McCabe won her race. They did not discuss how to address donations to Dr. McCabe's campaign or the possibility that they could create an appearance of a conflict of interest if made by individuals who may be under investigation by the FBI, or closely affiliated with individuals under investigation by the FBI. McCabe said that they also discussed a process in which ongoing and future cases would be identified for potential recusal, with A-CDC serving as a "filter" of cases and the WFO's Special Agents in Charge (SACs) tasked with bringing potential conflict cases to A-CDC for a recusal decision. McCabe said that in the meeting they "hammered out the details of how they would do this collaboratively" and that Kelley was satisfied that such a process was "an abundantly cautious way to approach the issue." McCabe said that they had minimal discussion regarding considerations in the event Dr. McCabe won, but that Kelley said a win by her might trigger other recusal issues and that they would "cross that bridge" when they got to it.

According to McCabe, the filtering arrangement they discussed was to take effect immediately. McCabe told us that in the March 11 meeting it was his "strong belief" that his wife would run because the "all-clear report" from Rosenberg was the "last hurdle" prior to her decision to run. Dr. McCabe announced her run for the state senate the next day, March 12, 2015.

According to A-CDC, during the March 11 meeting Kelley and Baker were concerned with potential Hatch Act violations and said they did not think there would be case conflict of interest issues unless Dr. McCabe won her election. A-CDC told us that McCabe said they should nonetheless proceed as if there are conflicts of interest.

Kelley told us that Hatch Act considerations were the focus of most of the March 11 meeting. Kelley said that once the Hatch Act questions were resolved they discussed what to do with WFO investigations and that McCabe, A-CDC, or both said they had put measures in place to screen investigations for conflicts. Kelley's notes of the March 11 meeting are contained in an Ethics Advice Tracker, an OIC electronic form used to memorialize advice provided. The Tracker stated that in the meeting they "reviewed disqualification/recusal requirements" and that McCabe had "already put in place filtering arrangements within his office." A-CDC said that they did not memorialize a filter process or issue written instructions immediately, but that they put in place a "stopgap measure" of funneling all public corruption matters through the Criminal Division SAC, Acting SAC, or someone from the CDC's office to assess potential conflicts until they had implemented a formal process.

McCabe told us that after the March 11 meeting, he expected A-CDC to document the recusal, speak to the Acting SAC about the filtering process, and work with the Acting SAC to list any cases from which he would be recused. McCabe said that he did not necessarily expect to hear about the specific cases that he had been recused from. McCabe told us that at a regularly scheduled meeting of the WFO SACs, the same week as the March 11 meeting, he informed the SACs of his wife's decision to run for state senate and of the filtering arrangement that they had put in place for identifying potential conflict cases.

5. McCabe Recusal EC Issued on April 29

The A-CDC documented McCabe's recusals in an Electronic Communication (EC) dated April 29, 2015, which was approved by McCabe.[235] The EC was sent to all of the WFO's SACs and began by referencing Dr. McCabe's run for state senate and stating that prior to her announcement, McCabe had consulted FBI officials "to identify limitations on his participation in her campaign and to identify areas where Dr. McCabe's campaign may present potential conflicts of interest." It then referenced the March 11 meeting and stated that they had "also addressed with AD Kelley and GC Baker the potential for conflicts of interest." The EC stated that A-CDC and the Acting SAC of the Criminal Division (A-SAC), in which the public corruption squads were located, had "identified several areas" where McCabe's "dissociation would be appropriate," including:

> [A]ll public corruption investigations arising out of or otherwise connected to the Commonwealth of Virginia present potential conflicts, as Dr. McCabe is running for state office and is supported by the

---

[235] A-CDC told us she drafted the EC on her own and did not coordinate the writing of the EC with Kelley or any others in OIC or OGC. A-CDC said McCabe was the approving official on the EC because he was her direct supervisor. When we asked Kelley whether McCabe's supervisor or some other official should have approved the EC given that its subject matter was about his recusal, he said he believed it was "fine" for McCabe to approve it and make a record of the recusal in the system. Kelley provided two reasons. First, he said the EC work flow process requires a supervisor to approve its creation and McCabe is A-CDC's supervisor. Second, he said that substantively the EC does not so much reflect on the decision to recuse as it describes the administrative measures that would be taken to implement the recusal protocols.

Governor of Virginia. Therefore, out of an abundance of caution, the ADIC will be excluded from any involvement in all such cases.

The April 29 EC then stated that supervising case agents in the WFO's Criminal Division had conducted "an initial review" of pending investigations to identify cases that present a potential conflict of interest, that these cases were identified to A-CDC and would be included in the matters in which McCabe "may take no part, either by being briefed or in the decision-making process."

The EC next identified a screening protocol for future or other ongoing cases requiring the CDC to review any investigations that may present "an actual or perceived conflict of interest" and make the recusal determination. The EC concluded by stating: "This protocol will be reassessed and adjusted as necessary and at the conclusion of Dr. McCabe's campaign in November, 2015."

A-CDC told us she did not recall why she did not document the recusal until April 29 and that it was "always the plan" to memorialize the recusal in an EC.

C.   No Reassessment of Conflict/Recusal when McCabe becomes ADD or after Dr. McCabe Loses Election

McCabe left the WFO and became the FBI's Associate Deputy Director (ADD) in September 2015, while his wife's campaign was ongoing. The ADD primarily has administrative responsibilities rather than operational ones.

When we asked McCabe if he had any conversations with anyone about whether the April 29 EC and its provisions traveled with him to his new position as ADD, he said he did not recall having any such conversations.

Dr. McCabe lost her race for the state senate on November 3, 2015. As noted above, the April 29 EC stated that the recusal protocol would "be reassessed and adjusted … at the conclusion of Dr. McCabe's campaign in November 2015." When we asked McCabe about the language related to reassessment, he told us no one approached him at the end of his wife's campaign to discuss the issue with him.

D.   Participation in Clinton Email and Clinton Foundation Investigations

1.   McCabe Not Recused as ADIC, ADD, or DD

As described in this report, until he recused himself from the Clinton email and Clinton Foundation investigations on November 1, 2016, McCabe had an active role in the supervision of the Clinton email investigation after he became the Deputy Director in February 2016. He also had oversight of the Clinton Foundation investigations when he became Deputy Director. When McCabe served as ADD, he did not have supervision over the Clinton email investigation, but he was occasionally present at meetings where the matter was discussed, according to

McCabe and an FBI response to Congressional inquiries.[236] In July 2015, when the Clinton email investigation was opened, McCabe was serving as the ADIC in the WFO. He told us he had no recollection of participating in any discussions about the opening of the case and only learned after the fact that the WFO had provided personnel to the Clinton email investigation team.

2.   Recusal Concerns Related to Clintons Raised in May 2015 when McCabe is ADIC

McCabe said that he never heard of any concerns that his wife's run for office presented a conflict for him in Clinton matters until October 2016, as detailed below. He also told us that until that time, he did not consider addressing a potential Clinton conflict because neither he nor his wife had any connection to Hillary Clinton, his wife's campaign received no support from her, and whatever relationship Hillary Clinton had to Governor McAuliffe did not appear to McCabe to be grounds for a conflict. We found one instance prior to October 2016 in which concerns were raised about a potential conflict for McCabe in Clinton-related matters, although we found no evidence that these concerns were brought to McCabe's attention. As described below, these concerns were raised by WFO personnel in May 2015, shortly after the April 29 EC was issued.

a.   Complaint Regarding Clinton

On May 4, 2015, a private attorney emailed Director Comey to request that the FBI open a public corruption investigation into Hillary Clinton, citing public allegations related to the Clinton Foundation and her use of a private email server while she was Secretary of State. Comey forwarded the complaint to Deputy Director Giuliano, who in turn forwarded it the next day to McCabe, stating: "[p]rovided to WFO for whatever action you deem appropriate."

On May 5, 2015, McCabe, who was out of the country on vacation, forwarded the email to A-SAC and directed her to have the complaint reviewed and to contact the private attorney and "conduct a standard assessment of these allegations." McCabe copied Giuliano on this email. A few hours later, McCabe sent a follow up email to A-SAC stating, "To be clear, we are info gathering at this point. Please do not open a case or assessment until we have the chance to discuss further." A-SAC responded by stating she understood and added that they had "already discussed the issue in coordination with [the Department's Public Integrity Section] and [FBI Headquarters] as this is not the first complaint on this matter. We are following established protocol and guidelines for these types of complaints." McCabe responded to A-SAC, "Great. Thanks." He also forwarded to Chuck Rosenberg the

---

[236] McCabe told us that when he was ADD and Deputy Director Giuliano was absent, McCabe filled in for him at meetings, although McCabe said he did not recollect doing so at any meetings related to the Clinton email investigation. Giuliano also told us that for a period of about two weeks before he departed the FBI and McCabe became the Deputy Director, McCabe shadowed Giuliano and he coached McCabe as he took over his new position.

first email he sent to A-SAC and described to Rosenberg his subsequent instructions to A-SAC to hold off on opening a case or assessment.

Rosenberg told us he vaguely recalled the email thread but he did not recall McCabe's email to him or his response to McCabe, which was "[u]nderstood... [e]njoy your vacation". He said he does not recall the email thread prompting any concerns at headquarters about McCabe working on Clinton matters and that he would not have made a connection with a Clinton matter and Dr. McCabe and Governor McAuliffe.

b. Supervising Case Agent and A-SAC Raise Concerns About McCabe Participating in Decisions Related to Clinton

A-SAC forwarded the email thread to a supervising case agent in the Criminal Division the same day who replied "ADIC should recuse himself from this matter in my opinion." The supervising case agent told us he was concerned because, among other things, he knew "the Clintons and McAuliffe are hard to separate," and that McAuliffe ran her 2008 campaign for President. He also described his concerns as being protective of McCabe's interests by anticipating how any participation by him on a Clinton matter would play out in the press since "the ADIC's wife has benefited from her relationship to McAuliffe."

A-SAC told us that her concern on the nature of a potential Clinton conflict "was overall [public corruption], and Clinton specifically because of just the broader relationship between McAuliffe and Clinton." A-SAC said she spoke to A-CDC who reached out to Kelley. A-SAC said she also addressed her concerns with another SAC in WFO and the then-Chief of the Public Corruption Section of CID (PCS-Chief). PCS-Chief told us he recalls speaking to A-SAC about concerns she had although he did not recall the specifics of those concerns or the identity of the matter. PCS-Chief told us he passed along A-SAC's concerns to one of his superiors. A-SAC said she did not know whether PCS-Chief or anyone else prompted McCabe in the May 5 time period about a potential Clinton conflict.

c. A-CDC and Kelley's Communications and Nonrecusal Decision

On May 5, A-CDC emailed Kelley and stated:

I have an issue I would like to run by you regarding ADIC McCabe's potential conflicts of interest and his wife's campaign. Should be fairly quick, but I would appreciate your opinion on how we are handling a particular matter.

A-CDC's email to Kelley did not identify the subject of the potential conflict of interest. Kelley and A-CDC spoke by phone the following morning, May 6, which Kelley documented in an Ethics Advice Tracker dated May 7, 2015. In the Tracker, Kelley summarized the advice he provided to A-CDC as follows:

Q re necessity of recusal of her ADIC. Relates to ADIC's spouse running for partisan office which we have discussed and worked out recusal arrangements, etc. This matter concerns a separate investigation where there may be a relationship between certain persons. Advised that relationship in the investigations was not enough to warrant recusal. Details too sensitive to be included here.

A-CDC told us she did not remember why she reached out to Kelley and did not recall discussing with anyone a potential McCabe conflict with Clinton-related matters. Likewise, Kelley told us that he did not recall his conversation with A-CDC or whether the advice memorialized in the Tracker related to a potential conflict regarding Clinton. (The Tracker did not reference Clinton or otherwise identify the subject of the potential conflict of interest.)

Kelley said that the first time he remembers hearing about a recusal question regarding Clinton-matters was in October 2016, as discussed below. Kelley also told us that in the May 2015 time frame he would have said there is no need for McCabe to recuse from Clinton-matters on the basis of the relationship between Governor McAuliffe and Clinton because their relationship is tangential: "[T]he question is, are McAuliffe's relationships to Clinton imputed to Ms. McCabe. And frankly, I think that's a bridge too far. I can't see that we should impute all of McAuliffe's relationships to McCabe."

We found no evidence that McCabe was ever made aware of the concerns raised by A-CDC, A-SAC, or the supervising case agent. We also found no evidence that Kelley consulted with or questioned McCabe, who was out of the country on vacation, regarding A-CDC's concerns before reaching his conclusions and providing the advice to A-CDC on May 7.

E.   Clinton Email and Clinton Foundation Investigations Recusals

1.   October 23, 2016 *Wall Street Journal* Article

On October 23, 2016, the Wall Street Journal (WSJ) published online an article stating that a political-action committee (PAC) run by Virginia Governor McAuliffe and the Virginia Democratic Party (over which the article reported McAuliffe "exerts considerable control") collectively donated nearly $675,000 to the 2015 unsuccessful state senate campaign of the wife of Andrew McCabe.[237] The article described McAuliffe as "an influential Democrat with long-standing ties to Bill and Hillary Clinton" and noted that McCabe was an FBI official "who later helped oversee the investigation into Mrs. Clinton's email use." The article contained an official FBI statement that McCabe "played no role" in his wife's 2015 state senate campaign and was promoted to FBI Deputy Director months after his wife's defeat

---

[237] *See* Devlin Barrett, *Clinton Ally Aided Campaign of FBI Official's Wife*, WALL ST. J, Oct. 23, 2016, https://www.wsj.com/articles/clinton-ally-aids-campaign-of-fbi-officials-wife-1477266114 (accessed June 11, 2018). A print version of the article was published in the WSJ on Monday, October 24, 2016.

"where,...he assumed for the first time, an oversight role in the investigation into Secretary Clinton's emails."[238] According to the article, FBI officials stated that McCabe's supervision of the Clinton email investigation in 2016 did not present a conflict or ethics issues because his wife's campaign was over by then. The article went on to note that when the Clinton email investigation was launched in July 2015, Mr. McCabe was "running the FBI's Washington, D.C., field office, which provided personnel and resources to the Clinton email probe."

Among other things, the article stated that McAuliffe could recall having met only once with McCabe, on March 7, 2015, when he and other state Democrats met with the couple to urge Dr. McCabe to run. It stated that after the March 7 meeting, McCabe sought ethics advice from the FBI "and followed it, avoiding involvement with public corruption cases in Virginia, and avoiding any campaign activities or events."

2. Internal Deliberations and Recusals from Clinton Email and Clinton Foundation Investigations

Immediately following online publication of the October 23 WSJ article, there was substantial public discussion as to whether McCabe's oversight of the Clinton email investigation had been appropriate in light of the information in the article. In the week that followed the article, discussions ensued within the FBI over whether McCabe should recuse from Clinton-related matters. These discussions took on additional significance on October 27, when Comey was briefed by the FBI Clinton email investigation team regarding the Weiner laptop issue.

a. Comey and Baker Responses to Article

Comey told us he was "frustrated" that he had not known about the facts raised in the October 23 WSJ article earlier and that he had a conversation with McCabe about this. Had he known them earlier, Comey said he believed it "highly likely as a prudential matter" that he would have had someone else take on McCabe's role in the Clinton email investigation, even if presented with an opinion from Kelley finding no requirement for recusal under the ethics rules. Comey said although he did not believe there was an actual conflict, "because of the nature of the [Clinton email] matter" he would not have permitted McCabe to participate as it would have been "used to undercut the credibility of the institution." He said, "I don't buy this. I think it's crap, but it brings a vector of attack to this institution

---

[238] The "played no role" reference in the FBI statement was derived from information provided by McCabe and was approved in advance by McCabe. Soon after publication of the October 23 WSJ article, the "played no role" statement came under public criticism. Subsequently, in its December 14 letter to Senator Grassley (described below) relating to alleged conflict of interest issues involving McCabe, the FBI removed the "played no role" language from a draft of the letter and instead stated in its final letter: "To the best of his recollection, Mr. McCabe's only activities related in any way to the campaign included providing transportation to his spouse in their personal vehicle on two occasions to public events; attending one public debate as a spectator; and appearing in a family photo which was used in a campaign mailer, all of which are permissible under the Hatch Act."

and why would I open a vector of attack to this institution, its credibility is its bedrock, when I don't need to."

Comey said that while as a lawyer he could see the alleged conflict was a "triple bank shot," a few days after the October 23 WSJ article the necessity of seeking a search warrant on the Weiner laptop was a "mushroom cloud" making "much more significant" the question of whether to notify Congress. He said that given these elevated stakes he did not need the "baggage" of an alleged conflict for McCabe brought into the decisions that would be "heavily scrutinized" and he did not have time to "get a legal opinion" or even for "thoughtful analysis" on whether McCabe should participate in the decisions. He said there was enough in the news articles to counsel against McCabe's involvement. He said that while initially he viewed the conflict allegations as "a PR thing" that needed to be managed, "it became hugely significant to me once [the Clinton email investigation] awoke from the dead." Comey said he told McCabe, "I don't need you on this because I don't see it as that close a call."[239]

Baker told us that in the wake of the October 23 WSJ article, he and Comey had one-on-one conversations in which they discussed the issues it raised. Baker said that he believes he and Comey first learned from the October 23 WSJ article that Dr. McCabe's campaign received large contributions attributed to McAuliffe. He said he and Comey concluded that McCabe should recuse himself from the Clinton email investigation "out of an abundance of caution." Baker said that they agreed that it would be best if McCabe recused himself rather than being recused by Comey and that Comey instructed Baker to attempt to persuade McCabe to do so.

b.   McCabe Excluded from Weiner Laptop Meeting on October 27

As described above in Chapter Nine, on October 27 at 10:00 a.m., Comey held a meeting with the Clinton email investigation team to discuss obtaining a search warrant for a set of Clinton-related emails the FBI had discovered on a laptop belonging to Anthony Weiner, and taking additional steps in the Clinton email investigation. Lisa Page, McCabe's special counsel, attended the meeting. McCabe was out of town, but joined the meeting via conference call. After the meeting began, Baker suggested, and Comey agreed, that McCabe should leave the call. Comey told us that he asked McCabe to drop off the call, and McCabe was "very unhappy about it."

Accounts differ about the reason stated on the October 27 call for excluding McCabe. McCabe told the OIG that the reason stated on the call for dropping him related to the potential for discussion about classified information. However, Comey, Baker, and Page all told us that Comey asked McCabe to leave the call out of an abundance of caution because of appearance issues following revelations in

---

[239] Comey told us he did not recall his weighing in on whether McCabe should recuse from the Clinton Foundation investigation and said he did not remember knowing that McCabe ultimately recused from the Clinton Foundation investigation at the same time he recused from the Clinton email investigation.

the October 23 WSJ article about the campaign donations to Dr. McCabe from McAuliffe-associated PACs.

McCabe discussed the issue of his participation in the Clinton email matter further with Comey and Baker by telephone later that day. After these conversations, McCabe sent a text message to Page stating, "I spoke to both. Both understand that no decision on recusal will be made until I return and weigh in."

c.   Baker and Kelley Meet on October 27

Baker and Kelley met on October 27 to discuss the allegation of a conflict of interest raised by the October 23 WSJ article. Kelley said that he concluded, along with Baker, that although the facts did not require McCabe to recuse, it was "desirable" to recuse because of appearance concerns, so he recommended it. Baker told us that Kelley concluded that while McCabe was not legally required to recuse from Clinton matters he recommended recusal because of appearance concerns and out of an abundance of caution.

An Ethics Advice Tracker from the October 27 meeting memorializing the discussion and advice Kelley rendered states:

> Cited to and discussed DOJ rule at 28 C.F.R. 45.2, conflict of interest statute at 18 USC 208, SOC rules on impartiality at 5 CFR 2635.502, and appearance standard at 5 CFR 2635.101(b)(14). Based on facts, advised that I saw no legal requirement for disqualification but, on balance, there was an appearance issue and would recommend recusal.

d.   Kelley's Rationale for Recusal

Although Kelley did not issue a formal opinion in October 2016, he told us that if he had put his advice in writing he was "confident" he would have said recusal of McCabe in the Clinton-related matters was not required. He said his recommendation that it was nonetheless desirable for McCabe to recuse was based on the allegations in the press and potential adverse publicity for the FBI were McCabe not to recuse, the fact that the FBI could "avoid a fight" while "preserving its equities" in having another senior leader take on McCabe's role, and, on a personal level, making "life easier for the people who are under attack or under scrutiny." While Kelley said McCabe's recusals were desirable, he also told us that the question of whether a recusal is required under the standards of conduct is based on the reasonable person standard, see 5 C.F.R. § 2635.101(b)(14), and not on the "Washington Post test," i.e., the likelihood that certain facts may become the subject of a news article. He said that while the likelihood of adverse publicity could factor into the reasonable person standard and that "we all have in the back of our mind how is this going to read in the Post…we have to make the decision based not on what's in the Washington Post but on what a reasonable person would take away if that person knew the relevant facts, and sometimes that's very nuanced." In a memorandum Kelley wrote in April 2017, Kelley described McCabe's Clinton-related investigation recusals as "not required by law or regulation" and done by McCabe "out of an abundance of caution, and to avoid further speculation in some quarters about the propriety of [his] continued participation."

Kelley told us he did not believe that a reasonable person would question McCabe's impartiality because Dr. McCabe had no relationship to Clinton, and while the relationship between the Governor and Clinton is close, he did not believe that meant "we can impute that relationship or should impute that relationship to Ms. McCabe and then turn around and impute that imputed relationship to Mr. McCabe…it's too tangential to say recusal is required."

e.   Baker and McCabe Conversation on October 31

McCabe and Baker spoke about recusal by phone while McCabe was out of town on October 27, but no decision was made. McCabe told us he had conversations with Baker after returning to the office on October 31 and that Baker said to him that Kelley's view was that he should recuse.[240] Baker told us that he had a series of conversations with McCabe culminating in a "very intense" conversation in which Baker told McCabe that he believed he needed to recuse himself and that it was better that he do it "than have the boss order him to do it." He said McCabe "was not happy about it" and "had lots of questions" and they had a "good argument back and forth."

McCabe said that he had numerous discussions with Baker and Page during this time in which he expressed his view that he should not recuse out of abundance of caution as it "would unfairly create a negative inference over the work that the [Clinton email investigation] team had done with [his] participation over the previous" months. McCabe said Baker presented him with his argument that there existed connections among Hillary Clinton and McAuliffe and his wife, but it seemed to McCabe to be too "attenuated" to call for recusal.

McCabe said that the size of the contributions that came to light in the October 23 WSJ article was a relevant new fact for Baker in creating an appearance concern. McCabe said he countered by arguing that the size of the contributions should not determine whether a conflict is present, that you have a conflict at $1 as you do at $200,000, and while Baker agreed with his analysis that there was no legal conflict, Baker was focused on the "external impression of my involvement in the case."

McCabe said Baker's response to his concerns was to acknowledge that while he may be right on the law and facts that he was not required to recuse, Baker believed he should recuse in light of the news article, in an abundance of caution, for the sake of perception, and given Kelley's view. McCabe said he believed there was "a very clear inevitable negative impact to being overly cautious." McCabe said that in his discussions with Baker he asked whether he would be ordered to recuse

---

[240] McCabe and Page both told us that neither of them spoke directly to Kelley about Clinton matter recusals in October 2016, but wished they had because they would learn in 2017 that Kelley's view was the same as theirs — that there was no basis in fact or law that required McCabe to recuse from the Clinton matters.

and Baker told him "if the Director thinks you should, then it's better to recuse yourself than to be…directed; [b]etter to recuse voluntarily, than involuntarily."

f.   McCabe and Comey Meeting on November 1

On November 1, McCabe and Comey spoke in the Director's office. McCabe told us he said to Comey that he did not believe he should recuse from the Clinton email investigation and presented the arguments he made to Baker in their earlier conversations. McCabe said that Comey responded by saying he made a good argument but told him that in light of the external perception from the negative media attention he should recuse. McCabe told us that when he argued that his recusal at this late stage may call into question his earlier participation, Comey acknowledged that recusal could have such a negative impact, but said that given the media attention he should nonetheless recuse. McCabe said that although Comey did not explicitly order him to recuse, given what Baker said about a request from the Director to recuse, he told Comey that he would recuse.

Comey told us that in his conversation with McCabe, McCabe said that the allegations of conflict as to the Clinton email investigation were akin to a "triple cushion bank shot" and that therefore it was unreasonable for him to seek an opinion from Kelley on the alleged Clinton conflict. Comey said McCabe also told him that, although he did not believe there was a legal basis for recusal, he thought it was "prudent" for him to step aside.

Comey also said that in a conversation with McCabe he "made clear to him [his] disappointment" that these facts were not brought to his attention earlier.

g.   November 1 Recusal Emails

On November 1, soon after his meeting with Comey, McCabe sent emails to FBI executives and officials overseeing the Clinton Foundation investigation and the Clinton email investigation informing them that he was recusing himself from those investigations. The emails stated:

> As of today I am voluntarily recusing myself for the ongoing [Clinton email investigation / Clinton Foundation investigation]. I will continue to respond to congressional requests for historical information as necessary.

McCabe told us that the timing of the recusals from the Clinton Foundation and Clinton email investigations were not on different tracks and he believed that a recusal rationale based on a perceived Clinton-related conflict as to the Clinton email investigation logically extended to the Clinton Foundation investigation.

The FBI did not publicize McCabe's recusals from these Clinton investigations despite the rationale that the recusals were at least in part intended to address the public perception of a potential conflict. In fact, even within the FBI, McCabe's recusal decision was only shared with a limited audience, primarily those copied on the email and those aware of the recusal discussions. McCabe told us that he thought the decision to recuse was a mistake, so to be "very public" and publicize it "would just compound the mistake."

3. Participation in Clinton Foundation Investigation after November 1

In this section we summarize three instances in which McCabe took actions related to the Clinton Foundation investigation after his November 1 recusal.

a. Call to NY ADIC Following November 3 *Wall Street Journal* Article

On November 3, 2016, the WSJ published another story on the Clinton Foundation investigation.[241] That evening, McCabe emailed the ADIC of the FBI New York Office, William Sweeney, and stated, "This is the latest WSJ article. Call me tomorrow." According to Sweeney's calendar notes on November 4 and testimony to the OIG, McCabe and Sweeney spoke for approximately 10 minutes around 7 a.m., regarding "leaks and WSJ article" and that McCabe was "angry." Sweeney's calendar notes also reflect that McCabe expressed to him: "will be consequence[s] and get to bottom of it post elect[ion]. Need leaks to stop. Damaging to org."[242]

McCabe told the OIG that he did not recall the details of the conversation on November 4, but it was "probably about leaks" to the media. McCabe said he would not have viewed his conversation with Sweeney as participating in the Clinton Foundation investigation but rather as a "logical follow-up to an ongoing conversation" he had been having with Sweeney for several weeks over the general issue of leaks coming out of the New York office. He said he was not transacting on the case, making decisions, or asking about the case, but rather telling Sweeney that he needed to address unauthorized media disclosures by getting his "people under control." Additionally, McCabe told us he did not believe his recusal from the Clinton Foundation investigation encompassed his general responsibilities to address the issue of FBI leaks.

b. Email to Kortan on November 3 *Wall Street Journal* Article

Also on the evening of November 3, McCabe emailed the latest WSJ article to Kortan and stated: "I am curious as to why I keep stumbling across these things with no notice whatsoever from my OPA machine?... I would like to discuss solutions tomorrow." Kortan told us he did not recall the email from McCabe or any subsequent conversation with McCabe. McCabe said his email to Kortan was

---

[241] *See* Devlin Barrett and Christopher Matthews, *Secret Recordings Fueled FBI Feud in Clinton Probe*, WALL ST. J., Nov. 3, 2016, https://www.wsj.com/articles/secret-recordings-fueled-fbi-feud-in-clinton-probe-1478135518 (accessed June 11, 2018).

[242] As detailed in a separate OIG misconduct report, McCabe had himself authorized the disclosure of sensitive information about the Clinton Foundation investigation to the Wall Street Journal, which was included in an article published on October 30 as well as in the November 3 article he discussed with Sweeney.

intended to address a "persistent frustration" he had over not receiving timely notice by OPA of news articles of interest. McCabe told us he did not know if he had a subsequent conversation with Kortan in which Kortan provided an explanation for why OPA did not send him the article. However, McCabe said that Kortan may not have brought the November 3 WSJ article to his attention in the first place because McCabe had recused himself from the Clinton Foundation investigation. When we asked McCabe whether in retrospect he should have asked Kortan to be briefed or kept up to speed on matters he was recused from, he said, "no, no" and reiterated that may have been why Kortan did not bring the article to his attention.

F.   Decision Not to Disclose McCabe's Recusals to Congress

Soon after the publication of the October 23 WSJ article, the FBI received three Congressional requests for information regarding the facts and allegations in the article. One was a letter from Senator Charles E. Grassley to Director Comey dated October 28, 2016, requesting answers to 12 questions, including one which stated: "What steps are you taking to mitigate the appearance of a conflict of interest in the Clinton email investigation and to reassure Congress and the American people that the investigation was not subject to political bias?"

On December 14, 2016, the FBI sent its response to Senator Grassley's letter, signed by the then-Acting Assistant Director (AAD) for the FBI's Office of Congressional Affairs (OCA). The December 14 letter did not explicitly address Senator Grassley's question concerning mitigation steps taken or otherwise disclose McCabe's November 1 recusal from the Clinton email investigation. Instead, the last two sentences of the corresponding paragraph in the final December 14 letter stated:

> Dr. McCabe lost the election for state senate on November 3, 2015, months before Mr. McCabe, as DD, assumed responsibility for the Clinton email investigation. Based on these facts, it did not appear that there was a conflict of interest – actual or apparent – that required recusal or waiver.

We attempted to determine who made the decision not to disclose the November 1 recusal of McCabe from the Clinton email investigation in the December 14 response to Senator Grassley, and for what reason.

Beginning in early December 2016, the OCA AAD and another OCA staff member circulated several drafts of the response to Senator Grassley. One draft included the sentence: "On October [?], 2016, out of an abundance of caution, Mr. McCabe recused himself from further participation in the [Clinton email] investigation." Lisa Page responded in an email that stated, "No way on [that] sentence. During our conversation with Jim [Baker] last week, both of us express[ed] our overwhelming interest in protecting that fact as long as possible." Page told us she believed the "both of us" reference was to herself and McCabe, but was not sure. Page told us she believed that McCabe's recusal, if revealed, would have been misused for political purposes and further inflamed the claims that Comey and McCabe were biased in favor of Clinton. Page also said she was not sure who made the ultimate decision on whether to disclose McCabe's recusal. She said that she did not know whether McCabe weighed in on this decision.

McCabe told us he did not have a recollection of any discussion, including with Comey, regarding whether to reveal his recusal from the Clinton email investigation in the December 14 letter. He said Page's "protect the fact" comment in her email reflected their thinking at the time that to reveal that information would create a "potentially damaging misimpression of the case" and that although he did not recall specifically discussing this issue with Comey, he believed Comey was also of that view.

Comey said he had "some recollection" that his Chief of Staff, James Rybicki, presented him with two options being considered, one sentence urged by McCabe and his staff would respond narrowly, the other would volunteer the fact of McCabe's recusal. Comey told us he did not recall the details of his participation in the decision on how to answer, but he said he recalled seeing the proposed language and hearing about an internal conflict that McCabe did not want the FBI to volunteer that he had recused from the Clinton email investigation. Comey told us that although he does not recall how he responded to the issue as it was presented to him, he assumes he would have agreed to the final language so long as it was "technically accurate I'm okay with answering it narrowly." Rybicki told us he had a vague recollection of the Grassley letter, but could not recall any discussions regarding whether to disclose McCabe's November 1 recusal to Congress or whether the issue was presented to Comey.

The OCA AAD told us he did not specifically recall who made the decision not to disclose McCabe's recusal, but that he believes McCabe likely made the decision. However, the OCA AAD said he did not remember having a conversation with McCabe about disclosing his recusal in the December 14 letter or providing him a draft with the proffered recusal language in it.

V.   OIG Analysis

A.   Recusal Issues

In this section we analyze whether McCabe should have been recused from the Clinton investigations prior to November 1, 2016 and whether he adhered to the terms of his recusal once he was recused.

1.   Summary of Findings

We found that McCabe was not required to recuse from the Clinton-related investigations under section 502(a) or any of the other relevant authorities. We also determined that, at the time McCabe became Deputy Director and thus had authority over Clinton-related investigations, no one in the FBI considered the question of whether Dr. McCabe's campaign raised recusal concerns as to Clinton-related investigation. This issue was not considered until after publication of the October 23 WSJ article and led to McCabe recusing himself from Clinton-related investigations on November 1, 2016. We found that McCabe did not fully comply with his November 1 recusal in a few instances related to the Clinton Foundation investigation as detailed below.

We found that FBI ethics officials and attorneys did not fully appreciate the potential significant implications to McCabe and the FBI from campaign donations to Dr. McCabe's campaign. The FBI did not implement any review of campaign donations to assess potential conflicts or appearance issues that could arise from the donations. On this issue, we believe McCabe did what he was supposed to do by notifying those responsible in the FBI for ethics issues and seeking their guidance. Had the FBI put in place a system for reviewing campaign donations to Dr. McCabe, which were public under Virginia law, the sizable donations from McAuliffe's PAC and the Virginia Democratic Party may have triggered prior consideration of the very appearance concerns raised in the October 23 WSJ article.

2.   Recusal from Clinton-Related Investigations

We agree with FBI chief ethics officer Kelley and found that the relevant authorities did not require McCabe to recuse himself from Clinton-related investigations. With regard to the financial conflicts provisions in Sections 208 and 502(a), there is no evidence of any financial or business ties between the McCabes and the Clintons or their Foundation. Further, there is no evidence that Hillary Clinton provided political or financial support to Dr. McCabe's 2015 senate campaign. The fact that McAuliffe supported Dr. McCabe's campaign, and was a known associate of Hillary Clinton, did not create any connection between the Clinton email investigation and Dr. McCabe's financial interests. Indeed, by the time McCabe became Deputy Director and assumed supervisory responsibilities for any Clinton-related matters, Dr. McCabe had already lost her election, and no developments in the Clinton-related matters could have any plausible impact on Dr. McCabe's financial interests, let alone a direct and predictable one as required under Sections 208 or 502(a).

In addition, because neither McCabe nor Dr. McCabe had a political or personal relationship with Clinton, McCabe was not obligated to recuse under 28 C.F.R. § 45.2. As discussed above, "political relationship" under section 45.2 is defined to mean "a close identification with an elected official, a candidate (whether or not successful) for elective, public office, a political party, or a campaign organization, arising from service as a principal adviser thereto or a principal official thereof." "Personal relationship" is defined as a "close and substantial connection of the type normally viewed as likely to induce partiality." Neither McCabe nor Dr. McCabe, who had never even met Clinton, served as a "principal adviser" to Clinton or had a "close and substantial connection" to Clinton sufficient to meet the definitions of political and personal relationships in section 45.2.

Although McCabe was not required by law or regulation to recuse from the Clinton-related investigations, he recused from these investigations on November 1, 2016, at the urging of Director Comey, who told us that he did not learn about McAuliffe's financial support of Dr. McCabe's candidacy until it was revealed in the October 23 WSJ article. Voluntary recusal is always permissible with the approval of a supervisor or ethics official, even where the elements in section 502(a) are not present.

We did not find fault with McCabe for not considering, prior to the October 23 WSJ article, whether to recuse himself under the "other circumstances" provision of section 502(a)(2) or the "appearance" provision of section 101(b)(14) of the Standards of Ethical Conduct.[243] However, we were troubled by the fact that the FBI ethics officials and attorneys did not fully appreciate the potential significant implications to McCabe and the FBI from campaign contributions to Dr. McCabe's campaign and did not implement any review of those campaign donations. Thus, while the same factual circumstances that led to McCabe's recusal on November 1, 2016 were present at the time McCabe became Deputy Director on February 1, 2016, the FBI ethics officials, McCabe, and Comey only learned of them as a result of the October 23 WSJ article. Had the FBI put in place a mechanism to review the campaign's donation information, it would have been in a position to consider these issues earlier.

We believe McCabe did what he was supposed to do by notifying those responsible in the FBI for ethics issues and seeking their guidance. Thereafter, he was entitled to rely on those ethics officials to identify any ethics issues that were implicated by Dr. McCabe's candidacy.

Campaign donations to a spouse's campaign present complicated questions under section 502(a), as well as under the financial conflict of interest statute. They also may present significant appearance issues under section 502(a)(2). The fact that the FBI did not apparently recognize the issues, and the potential importance of them, became evident when the October 23 WSJ article was published. Under Virginia law, the identity of contributors and their donation amounts was available to the public. Had the FBI reviewed the campaign donations to Dr. McCabe, they would have observed the $675,288 from McAuliffe's PAC and the Virginia Democratic Party, which may have resulted in earlier consideration of the very appearance concerns raised in the October 23 WSJ article. The predictable result of the WSJ article triggered the October 2016 controversy, which led to Comey's decision to ask McCabe to recuse himself from Clinton-related investigations.

We further determined that the FBI's decision to keep McCabe's recusal from Clinton matters a secret made no sense. The apparent purpose of that recusal was to address allegations concerning the propriety of McCabe's continued participation in the Clinton-related investigations, which would be used to undercut the FBI's credibility. This purpose is generally accomplished by informing the public that McCabe was recused. However, the FBI did not publicize McCabe's recusal. As a related matter, we do not believe that the FBI acted wisely in deciding not to reveal McCabe's recusal to Senator Grassley in response to a question to which this fact

---

[243] As noted above, McCabe told us that neither he nor his wife attended the June 2015 fundraiser in Virginia and that he was unaware that the Clintons or anyone on their behalf ever contributed to Dr. McCabe's campaign. He said neither he nor his wife have ever met the Clintons.

was reasonably responsive. Again, the recusal decision served no function in protecting the FBI's reputation if it was kept secret.

We considered whether McCabe violated his voluntary recusal from Clinton-related matters after November 1. Recusal "is accomplished by not participating in the matter." 5 C.F.R. § 2635.502(e). Exposure to case related information by a recused employee when attending a meeting or briefing, including receiving information about news articles related to the recused matter, is a form of participation that must be avoided. We found no evidence that McCabe continued to supervise investigative decisions in the Clinton-related matters after that day. We did find that McCabe, prompted by a follow-up WSJ article of November 3, 2016, made inquiries about the steps the FBI was taking to address media leaks relating to the Clinton Foundation and exhorting managers to stop the leaking. McCabe's conduct in inquiring about media leaks appears to have been consistent with instructions that Comey told us he gave McCabe about taking action on media leaks in the Clinton Foundation investigation. However, McCabe's conduct was not fully consistent with his recusal, as the discussion of the Clinton Foundation investigation in the November 3 WSJ article was the very basis for his call and admonitions to Sweeney, the NY ADIC. McCabe told us he did not believe his recusal from the Clinton Foundation investigation encompassed his general responsibilities to address FBI leaks. But McCabe's November 1 recusal email contained one exception, which allowed him to continue to respond to Congressional requests for information, and it did not carve out an exception allowing him to continue addressing the leaks about the Clinton Foundation investigation.

Similarly, McCabe encroached on his recusal obligations when he forwarded the November 3 WSJ article to OPA chief Kortan and asked why he (McCabe) kept seeing such articles without prior notice from OPA. While McCabe told us that his email to Kortan was intended to express a generalized frustration with lack of prior notice by OPA, McCabe acknowledged that he should not have asked Kortan to keep him up to speed on matters he was recused from. McCabe also said that may have been the very reason Kortan did not bring the November 3 WSJ article to his attention.[244]

---

[244] In March 2017, news accounts reported allegations that McCabe failed to disclose in his Public Financial Disclosure Report (OGE Form 278e) for 2016, the amount of salary his wife received from her employer and the campaign donations she received in 2015. However, such disclosures are not required by OGE Form 278e. First, the OGE regulation addressing the financial disclosure report expressly states that the report does not need to disclose the amount of the spouse's income. See 5 C.F.R. § 2634.309(1). Second, according to the OGE regulations, while campaign funds need not be included in the financial disclosure report "if the individual has authority to exercise control over the fund's assets for personal use rather than campaign or political purposes, that portion of the fund over which such authority exists must be reported." 5 C.F.R. § 2634.311(a). However, the OGE regulations do not require reporting gifts that are received by a spouse "totally independent" of the spouse's relationship to the filer. 5 C.F.R. § 2634.309(a)(2). While we did not investigate individual donations to Dr. McCabe's campaign committee, during our review we did not find evidence suggesting that Dr. McCabe received campaign donations because of McCabe.

B.   Conclusion

We agreed with Kelley, the FBI's chief ethics official, that McCabe was not at any time required to recuse from the Clinton-related investigations under the relevant authorities. However, following the October 23 WSJ article and discussions with Comey, McCabe recused from the Clinton-related investigations on November 1, 2016. Once McCabe recused himself, he was required to cease participation in those matters. Voluntary recusal is always permissible with the approval of a supervisor or ethics official, even where the elements in section 502(a) are not present. We found that McCabe did not fully comply with his recusal in a few instances related to the Clinton Foundation investigation.

We also found that the FBI ethics officials and attorneys did not fully appreciate the potential significant implications to McCabe and the FBI from campaign contributions to Dr. McCabe's campaign and did not implement any review of those campaign donations. We therefore recommend that ethics officials consider implementing a review of campaign donations when Department employees or their spouses run for public office.

CHAPTER FOURTEEN:
WHETHER FORMER ASSISTANT ATTORNEY GENERAL PETER J. KADZIK SHOULD HAVE RECUSED FROM CERTAIN MATTERS

I. Introduction

This chapter addresses allegations that former Department of Justice (Department or DOJ) Assistant Attorney General (AAG) for the Office of Legislative Affairs (OLA) Peter J. Kadzik improperly disclosed non-public information to the Clinton campaign and/or should have been recused from participating in certain matters.

The allegations regarding Kadzik stem from the public release of certain emails of John D. Podesta, Jr., the 2016 chairman of the Hillary Clinton presidential campaign and longtime friend of Kadzik. Beginning in October 2016, Wikileaks released Podesta emails, including emails between Kadzik and Podesta. Among the emails released by WikiLeaks was a May 19, 2015 email from Kadzik to Podesta with the subject line "Heads up" and which included information concerning a Department Freedom of Information Act (FOIA) litigation and a congressional oversight hearing. Shortly before that email, Kadzik had made efforts to assist his son in obtaining a position with the 2016 Clinton campaign.

On or about November 2, 2016, Department leadership determined that Kadzik's May 19, 2015 "Heads up" email to the chairman of the Clinton campaign created an appearance of a conflict of interest and required Kadzik to recuse himself from Clinton-related matters. The Department's Office of Professional Responsibility (OPR) subsequently conducted an inquiry and determined that Kadzik did not disclose privileged or confidential Department information in the email to Podesta.

The OIG's investigation included reviewing investigative materials, documents, and emails from several DOJ components including OLA, OPR, and the Civil Division. The OIG also interviewed numerous witnesses, including Kadzik, then Principal Assistant Deputy Attorney General (PADAG) Matt Axelrod, Associate Deputy Attorney General Scott Schools, and the current and former Departmental Ethics Directors. Two relevant witnesses who worked in OLA under Kadzik, but are no longer with the Department, declined our request for an interview or were unable to schedule an interview.[245]

As detailed below, we found that Kadzik demonstrated poor judgment by failing to recuse himself under Section 502(a)(2) of the Standards of Ethical Conduct prior to November 2, 2016. First, Kadzik did not recognize the appearance of a conflict that he himself had created when he initiated an effort to obtain

---

[245] The Inspector General Act of 1978, as amended, does not provide the OIG with the authority to compel non-Department employees to participate in interviews.

employment for his son with the Clinton campaign while he was participating in senior staff meetings where Clinton-related matters were discussed and signing letters to Congress regarding Clinton-related matters on behalf of the Department. Second, Kadzik created an appearance of a conflict when he sent Podesta the "Heads up" email that included government information about the FOIA litigation in an effort to be helpful to the Clinton campaign without knowing whether the information had yet been made public. His willingness to do so raised a reasonable question about his ability to act impartially on Clinton-related matters in connection with his official duties.

Additionally, although Department leadership ultimately decided to recuse Kadzik from Clinton-related matters upon learning of Kadzik's "Heads up" email to Podesta, Kadzik subsequently forwarded several emails communicating information related to Clinton-related matters within the Department and indicated his intent to speak with staff about those matters. We therefore concluded that Kadzik exercised poor judgment by failing to strictly adhere to his recusal.

Lastly, because the government information in the "Heads up" email had in fact been released publically, we did not find that Kadzik released non-public information or misused his official position.

II.   Timeline of Key Events

Jun 17, 2014   Kadzik is confirmed as AAG for OLA.

Jan 25, 2015   FOIA litigation is initiated seeking the release of former Secretary of State Clinton's emails.

Mar 2, 2015   The New York Times reports that Clinton exclusively used personal email to conduct government business while Secretary of State.

Apr 12, 2015   Clinton announces candidacy for President of the United States. John Podesta serves as her campaign chairman; Brian Fallon, former DOJ Office of Public Affairs Director, serves as her campaign spokesman; and Jennifer Palmieri serves as her Director of Communications.

Apr 23, 2015   Kadzik emails Fallon asking for a job for his son with the Clinton campaign.

Apr 30, 2015   Fallon emails Kadzik asking for his son's resume and stating that Palmieri would be reviewing resumes over the weekend. Kadzik replies, sending his son's resume and noting that Kadzik's wife and Palmieri went to college together.

May 5, 2015   Kadzik's son emails Podesta his resume and asks for a job with the Clinton campaign. Podesta forwards the email to Palmieri, who replies that Kadzik's wife had contacted her and that she told Kadzik's wife that there were currently no openings with the campaign but positions might become available in July. (Email released by WikiLeaks).

May 18, 2015	Department files a proposed schedule for the release of the Clinton emails with the court in the FOIA litigation.
	Politico reports on the Department FOIA filing and proposed schedule for the release of the Clinton emails.
May 19, 2015	Kadzik sends Podesta the "Heads up" email about the FOIA filing and proposed schedule for the release of the Clinton emails, and about a congressional oversight hearing, which could include questions about the Clinton emails. (Email released by WikiLeaks).
	Civil Division Chief testifies at the congressional oversight hearing.
Jul 10, 2015	FBI opens the Clinton email investigation.
Jan 2016	FBI opens Clinton Foundation investigation.
Nov 1, 2016	WikiLeaks releases the May 5 email chain that begins with Kadzik's son asking Podesta for a job with the Clinton campaign.
Nov 2, 2016	WikiLeaks releases Kadzik's May 19 "Heads up" email to Podesta.
~ Nov 2, 2016	PADAG Axelrod tells Kadzik to recuse himself from Clinton-related matters.
Nov 8, 2016	Presidential Election
Dec 2016	OPR conducts an inquiry and finds that Kadzik did not send privileged or confidential information in his May 19, 2015 "Heads up" email to Podesta.
Jan 19, 2017	Kadzik's last day with the Department.

III. Relevant Standards

In this section we identify the regulations from the Standards of Ethical Conduct for Employees of the Executive Branch Standards of Ethical Conduct), 5 C.F.R. Part 2635, relevant to our analysis.

A.   Personal and Business Relationships Creating an Appearance of a Conflict 5 C.F.R. § 2635.502

Personal and Business Relationships Creating an Appearance of a Conflict 5 C.F.R. § 2635.502 (Section 502) establishes the analytical framework for determining when a federal employee has an appearance of a conflict of interest. As discussed in greater detail in Chapter Thirteen of this report, Section 502 requires an employee to consider the appearance of his participation in a particular matter involving specific parties (1) that is likely to have a direct and predictable effect on the financial interest of a household member or (2) if the employee has a covered relationship with someone who is a party or represents a party to the matter. Section 502 also includes catchall provision which may apply to "other circumstances" that would lead a reasonable person to question an employee's impartiality in a matter.

A recused employee is prohibited from participating in the matter unless authorized by the agency designee based on a determination that the Government's interest "in the employee's participation outweighs the concern that a reasonable person may question the integrity of the agency's programs and operations." 5 C.F.R. § 2635.502(d). According to OGE, a proper recusal requires "that an employee avoid any official involvement in a covered matter." OGE 99 x 8 at 2.

B.   Use of Non-public Information 5 C.F.R. § 2635.703

Section 703 of the Standards of Ethical Conduct, 5 C.F.R. § 2635.703, states: "An employee shall not...allow the improper use of nonpublic information to further his own private interest or that of another, whether through advice or recommendation, or by knowing unauthorized disclosure."

C.   Use of Public Office for Private Gain 5 C.F.R. § 2635.702

Section 702 of the Standards of Ethical Conduct, 5 C.F.R. § 2635.702, states: "An employee shall not use his public office...for the private gain of friends, relatives, or persons with whom the employee is affiliated in a nongovernmental capacity...."

According to commentary to Section 702, "[i]ssues relating to an individual employee's use of public office for private gain tend to arise when the employee's actions benefit those with whom the employee has a relationship outside the office...". 57 Fed. Reg. 35030 (Aug. 7, 1992).

IV.   Factual Findings

A.   Background

1.   Peter J. Kadzik

Peter J. Kadzik was confirmed as the Assistant Attorney General (AAG) for the Office of Legislative Affairs (OLA) on June 17, 2014, and served in the position until January 19, 2017. As OLA AAG, Kadzik reported to the Deputy Attorney General. Kadzik had re-joined the Department as a Deputy Assistant Attorney General in OLA in 2013 after several decades in private practice. Early in his legal career, Kadzik served as an Assistant United States Attorney in the United States Attorney's Office for the District of Columbia.

Kadzik is married to "LM." LM previously served as a political appointee in former-President Bill Clinton's administration. "RS" is Kadzik's child from a prior marriage, who was 24 years old at the time of these events.[246]

2.   John D. Podesta, Jr.

John D. Podesta, Jr. is an attorney who served as chairman of the 2016 Clinton presidential campaign. During his career, Podesta also served in various high-level positions in both the Bill Clinton and Barack Obama administrations, including as White House Chief of Staff to Bill Clinton and as Counselor to Obama.

Kadzik and Podesta have a long standing personal and professional relationship which, during the Bill Clinton administration, included Kadzik serving as Podesta's lawyer in 1998 during the Independent Counsel investigation. Kadzik's relationship with Podesta was known at the time of and raised during his confirmation for the OLA AAG position.

Kadzik told the OIG that neither he nor his wife had any business, contractual, or financial relationship with Podesta or the Clinton campaign while he served as OLA AAG. He said that he did not serve as an officer, director, trustee, general partner, agent, attorney, consultant, contractor, or employee of Podesta, Clinton, or the Clinton campaign. Kadzik said that neither he nor Podesta had performed any legal work for the other in the past five years.

3.   Office of Legislative Affairs

The Office of Legislative Affairs (OLA) is responsible for managing the Department's relationship with Congress and advancing its interests on Capitol Hill. Among its responsibilities, OLA prepares nominees for confirmation hearings and Department witnesses for congressional hearings; responds to congressional inquiries and oversight requests; advises and assists Department leadership on a variety of congressional matters; and advocates for the Department's legislative priorities. When answering congressional inquiries and preparing nominees and employees for hearings, OLA routinely coordinates with the relevant DOJ investigative, litigation, and administrative components.

As OLA AAG, Kadzik reviewed and signed letters on behalf of the Department responding to Congressional inquiries, prepared the highest level nominees and witnesses for congressional testimony, and represented OLA at the daily senior staff

---

[246] We have anonymized Kadzik's wife and son by giving them initials as pseudonyms. We refer to Kadzik's wife as "LM" and his son as "RS."

465

meetings. Senior staff meetings were generally attended by the Attorney General (AG) and members of her staff, the Deputy Attorney General (DAG) and her Principal Assistant Deputy Attorney General (PADAG), as well as the Directors of OLA and the Office of Public Affairs (OPA).[247] At the senior staff meeting, among other things, attendees discussed sensitive information regarding Department cases and investigations and coordinated matters and information that were expected to become public or to be the source of public commentary and questions.

Kadzik told the OIG that his role was that of the Department's liaison with Congress and that as such, he was "not involved" in Department investigations. He stated that, "[t]o the extent that I corresponded with Congress, it was based on information provided to my office by the relevant component within the Department. So I didn't participate in any investigations."

Department cases and investigations are often the subject of Congressional inquiries. As discussed below, OLA received numerous congressional inquiries related to the Clinton matters.

4. Ethics Training and Obligations

All Department employees are responsible for complying with Department policies as well as the Standards of Ethical Conduct for Employees of the Executive Branch, codified in 5 C.F.R. Part 2635, which include rules and regulations governing conflicts of interest, use of nonpublic information, and misuse of position. The Department provides training and resources to ensure all employees are aware of their ethical responsibilities and are able to obtain ethics advice as specific questions and situations arise. The ethics program includes annual mandatory ethics training, and a Deputy Designated Agency Ethics Official (DDAEO) in each Department component, among other things. A designated DDAEO works within OLA.

Kadzik acknowledged participating in the Department's annual ethics training. He also acknowledged that OLA employees are subject to the same ethics rules and regulations as all other Departmental employees even though OLA employees are not assigned to investigative or litigation teams.

5. Kadzik's Recusals

As a presidential appointee, Kadzik was required to enter an ethics agreement indicating that he understood and would comply with the conflict of interest laws and regulations and submit the financial disclosure form required by the provisions of the Ethics in Government Act of 1978.[248] After he was confirmed,

---

[247] The Office of Public Affairs is the Department's principal point of contact for the news media.

[248] The Ethics Agreement was signed by Kadzik and Lee Lofthus, the AAG for Administration and the Department's Designated Ethics Official, and sent to the Director of Office of Government Ethics (OGE).

Kadzik also sent a 2014 recusal memorandum to various Department components (including OLA) listing the matters from which he was recused and identifying the OLA DDAEO as the individual who would evaluate his need to recuse himself (serve as his "gatekeeper") and the individuals who would serve in his capacity as Acting OLA AAG on those matters.[249]

Kadzik's 2014 recusal memorandum stated that for matters from which he had recused, all communications should be with the Acting OLA AAG and "in no event should there be any discussions with [Kadzik]." Email shows that after the initial 2014 memorandum, Kadzik emailed the OLA DDAEO when he recused himself from additional matters involving clients of his former law firm, clients of his wife's business, and personal matters. Kadzik told the OIG that he likely orally informed the OLA DDAEO, his deputies, and chief of staff when he was recused from Clinton-related matters on or about November 2, 2016, as discussed below.

B. Events Preceding the "Heads Up" Email from Kadzik to Podesta (March through May 2015)

This section focuses on the events in the spring of 2015 leading up to the "Heads up" email from Kadzik to Podesta, which included information about the FOIA litigation and a congressional oversight hearing.

1. OLA Clinton-Related Work

On March 2, 2015, the New York Times reported that Clinton exclusively used a personal email account to conduct government business while serving as Secretary of State. The same day, the Department filed its initial response (Answer) in a FOIA litigation seeking Clinton's email and other documents during her tenure as Secretary of State.[250]

At the time, both Lynch and Yates were awaiting confirmation for the positions of Attorney General and Deputy Attorney General, respectively.[251] In order to prepare Lynch and Yates to answer questions related to the former Secretary of State's exclusive use of a personal email account (and the applicable federal laws and regulations), Kadzik's principal deputy drafted the briefing paper on the topic on March 18, 2015, and Kadzik added edits on March 21, 2015, after the document was reviewed by personnel in the Office of the Attorney General (OAG), Office of the Deputy Attorney General (ODAG), and the OPA.[252] The briefing

---

[249] Emails show that Kadzik coordinated his recusal memorandum with OLA's DDAEO. The individual who served as OLA's DDAEO under Kadzik has since retired from the Department and declined our requests for an interview.

[250] The FOIA litigation discussed in this report is *Leopold v. U.S. Dep't of State*, 15-cv-123 (D.D.C.).

[251] Congress confirmed Attorney General Lynch on April 23, 2015, and Deputy Attorney General Yates on May 13, 2015.

[252] Despite the OIG's repeated attempts, Kadzik's principal deputy in OLA, who is no longer with the Department, was unable to accommodate the OIG's request for an interview.

paper contained potential questions and the Department's vetted answers on the topic as approved by personnel in OLA, the Civil Division, and the Office of the Attorney General. Briefing papers are used to help prepare nominees and employees to speak publicly on a Department issue or concern.[253] Emails show that OLA (in conjunction with other components) scheduled "moots" or preparatory sessions with Lynch and Yates to prepare them to answer questions related to the State Department emails, among other issues, in March, April, and May 2015.

OLA also responded to congressional inquiries related to Clinton's use of email during her tenure as Secretary of State. Emails show that Kadzik coordinated with the Office of the Attorney General and the White House with respect to nominee-Lynch's response to an April 2, 2015 congressional inquiry asking whether Lynch would commit to an investigation into Clinton's use of an email server and appoint a special counsel. Kadzik also replied on May 21, 2015, on behalf of the Attorney General, to an April 22, 2015 Congressional inquiry into whether Clinton was lobbied while Secretary of State by an unregistered agent of a foreign power associated with the Clinton Foundation.

In addition to preparing nominees Lynch and Yates, OLA participated in the preparation of the Director of the Office of Information Policy (OIP) and the Chief of the Civil Division to answer questions related to the State Department emails at their respective hearings. The OIP Director testified on a panel addressing open government at a Senate Judiciary Committee hearing on May 6, 2015.[254] After the hearing, the OLA employee who accompanied the OIP Director emailed Kadzik that the majority of questions were directed to the panelist from the State Department regarding Clinton's emails.

The Civil Division Chief testified on a panel on general oversight at a House Judiciary Committee hearing on May 19, 2015.[255] Although prepared to answer, the Civil Division Chief was not asked questions related to the State Department emails at the hearing. After the hearing, Kadzik sent an email complementing the several DOJ division leaders who testified.

On May 18, the evening prior to the Civil Division Chief's testimony before the House Judiciary Committee, the Department filed a proposed schedule for the production of former Secretary of State Clinton's emails as required by the court in the FOIA litigation. According to the proposed schedule, the State Department emails would be released in January 2016.

---

[253] At the time, both Lynch and Yates were U.S. Attorneys and therefore they could be provided with Department information as part of their briefing materials.

[254] The hearing was titled "Ensuring an Informed Citizenry: Examining the Administration's Efforts to Improve Open Government."

[255] The hearing was before the Judiciary Subcommittee on Regulatory Reform, Commercial and Antitrust Law and titled "Ongoing Oversight: Monitoring the Activities of the Justice Department's Civil, Tax and Environment and Natural Resources Divisions and the U.S. Trustee Program."

2. 2016 Clinton Campaign Staffed and Announced

In early 2015, Clinton was preparing to announce her candidacy for President. Prior to her announcement, in February 2015, Podesta left his position in the White House as Counselor to the President to become Chief of Staff for the Clinton campaign. In mid-March 2015, Brian Fallon announced that he would be leaving his position as the Director of OPA at the end of the month to become the Clinton campaign's national spokesperson. Clinton formally announced her candidacy for President on April 12, 2015.

Kadzik told the OIG that neither he nor his wife sought employment with the campaign or discussed the prospect of employment with the campaign with Podesta or other campaign members.

3. Kadzik Assists Son's Job Search

Also in early 2015, Kadzik's son "RS" was looking for employment opportunities and sought a job with the Clinton campaign. Emails show that Kadzik's wife forwarded Kadzik her edited version of RS's resume on March 22, 2015, and that RS sent his resume to Kadzik and his wife for their "final review" on April 1, 2015.

According to RS's resume, he lived in New York City and had worked for Kadzik's wife's public affairs firm since December 2014 (approximately 3 months). Emails indicate that RS was paid for hourly work performed from January to March 2015.

Kadzik told the OIG that he did not support his son financially other than paying for his cell phone. He said that he did not declare his son a dependent on his 2015 tax returns and provided a redacted copy of his 2015 return to the OIG.

On April 23, 2015, shortly after he left the Department and on the day Lynch was confirmed as Attorney General, Fallon sent an email from his Clinton campaign address to Kadzik's Department address that included a single word on the subject line "Congrats!" Kadzik replied:

Thanks! Hope all is well with you, [Fallon's wife], the kids, and the candidate. Let me know if you or someone else needs a great assistant; my 25 year old son is ready for [Hillary Rodham Clinton].

One week later, on April 30, 2015, Fallon replied to Kadzik:

Can you send me his resume? Unfortunately I do not get an assistant but Palmieri is hiring one and will be looking over resumes this weekend.

Within the hour, Kadzik emailed RS asking for his current resume and then forwarded RS's resume to Fallon stating "Here you go. Again, thanks. FYI, [Palmieri] and my wife [LM], went to college together."

469

Kadzik told the OIG that he did not recall sending Fallon the emails requesting a job for his son. Kadzik also said that his son was neither hired nor offered a job by the Clinton campaign and that he found employment with a digital education company in New York City in August 2015.

4. Kadzik's Son Separately Seeks Employment with the Clinton Campaign

According to an email released by Wikileaks, on May 5, 2015, one week after Kadzik emailed Fallon his son's resume, RS emailed his resume directly to Podesta.[256] In his email to Podesta, RS said he was sending Podesta his resume at the suggestion of Kadzik and his wife, LM. Podesta then forwarded RS's email to at least two other campaign workers, one of whom was Palmieri, the campaign's Director of Communications. Podesta's email stated "Do you need any help in [headquarters] or states? [Kadzik] and [LM's] son." Palmieri replied:

> Heard from [LM], too. Told her we did not have openings for rest of quarter but can open back up in July.

Kadzik told the OIG that he did not recall when RS applied for a position with the Clinton campaign, whether he and his wife suggested that RS send his resume to Podesta, or whether he spoke to his wife about any discussions with Palmieri on RS's behalf. Kadzik also said that he did not know whether his wife or son ever followed up with Podesta, Fallon, Palmieri, or anyone else associated with the campaign for a job for RS, but that he (Kadzik) did not.

5. Kadzik Gives Podesta a "Heads Up"

On May 19, 2015, Kadzik sent from his personal email account the "Heads up" email to Podesta. There is no timestamp on the email. Kadzik wrote:

---

[256] This email was published by WikiLeaks on November 1, 2016. WikiLeaks obtained emails from Podesta's personal email account and released those emails online in the weeks leading up to the November 2016 election. Some of these emails, including this email from RS to Podesta, were not sent to or from a DOJ email address, and as such we were not able to authenticate them. Where the only source for an email was the WikiLeaks publication, we have identified the email as such.

"In January of [2017], our Intelligence Community determined that Russian military intelligence—the GRU—had used WikiLeaks to release data of US victims that the GRU had obtained through cyber operations[.]" Director Pompeo Delivers Remarks at CSIS, April 13, 2017, available at https://www.cia.gov/news-information/speeches-testimony/2017-speeches-testimony/pompeo-delivers-remarks-at-csis.html (accessed April 25, 2018). The OIG is cognizant of the fact that the release of emails discussed in this chapter may be part of this cyber operation and our review of this material is in no way intended to validate or justify WikiLeaks' data releases.

We note that the fact that the email became public after Podesta's email was allegedly hacked and then released by WikiLeaks did not excuse or minimize Kadzik's conduct. While Department leadership did not publically acknowledge the authenticity of the illegally hacked emails, Axelrod confronted Kadzik (who then authenticated the email), recognized the appearance of the conflict and its impact on the integrity of the Department, and ensured Kadzik's recusal.

There is a [House Judiciary Committee] oversight hearing today where the head of our Civil Division will testify. Likely to get questions on State Department emails. Another filing in the FOIA case went in last night or will file in this am that indicates it will be awhile (2016) before the State Department posts the [Clinton] emails.[257]

Kadzik told the OIG that he did not recall, but does not deny sending the "Heads up" email to Podesta and that he "apparently" sent the email to Podesta to identify two important events of the day.

Kadzik told the OIG that no one in the Clinton campaign asked him for information regarding the FOIA litigation and that he did not send the email to try to help his son get a job with the campaign. Kadzik also said he did not send any other "heads up" type emails or otherwise communicate about Department matters to Podesta.[258]

Kadzik also said he did not speak with Podesta about Clinton after the Department opened an investigation into the Clinton email server in July 2015. Kadzik told the OIG that he distinguished speaking to Podesta about the FOIA litigation and the Clinton email investigation. "Whether [the email server investigation] was criminal or a security review, [], it was now the Department doing something as a Department, rather than the Department defending FOIA litigation, which was all public."

C. Kadzik's Subsequent OLA Work Related to or Referencing Clinton

In the time between spring 2015 and the day in November 2016 when Kadzik was recused from Clinton-related matters, the FOIA litigation continued and the FBI opened an investigation into Clinton's use of a private email server and an investigation related to the Clinton Foundation. These cases generated Clinton-related inquiries from Congress to which Kadzik responded both in testimony and in letters.

OLA continually responded to congressional inquiries and prepared Department employees to respond to congressional inquiries related to Clinton's email server and the Department's investigation. The inquiries corresponded to various aspects of the Department's actions and investigative choices including:

---

[257] Wikileaks published this email on November 2, 2016. We have no independent source for this email. Kadzik told us he did not recall it, but did not allege that it was inauthentic or inaccurate. Moreover, Kadzik acknowledged its authenticity to Axelrod when the "Heads up" email was released.

[258] Kadzik's "Heads Up" email was not the only email of this type sent to the Clinton campaign. According to emails later released by WikiLeaks, on May 18, 2015, the same evening the Department filed its proposed schedule for releasing the emails, an unidentified Department employee emailed the FOIA filing to Fallon at Fallon's personal email address and wrote "This was filed tonight." Fallon forwarded the email to campaign members including Podesta. As noted above, Fallon left the Department at the end of March 2015 to join the campaign. Kadzik told the OIG that he had no participation in, or knowledge of, the May 18 email to Fallon with the FOIA filing.

requests to appoint a special counsel; decisions to grant immunity; potential perjury charges; the Lynch/Bill Clinton tarmac conversation; Comey's July 5, 2016 and Lynch's July 6, 2016 announcements regarding the email server investigation and declination; congressional access to FBI investigative documents; additional FOIA inquiries; and Comey's October 28 and November 6, 2016 letters to Congress regarding the FBI review of additional Clinton related emails.[259] OLA also coordinated its hearing preparation and congressional responses with the appropriate components which, with respect to the Clinton-related matters, included, depending on the specific question, the OAG, ODAG, OPA, the Civil Division, the National Security Division (NSD), and the FBI. Thus while Kadzik had no role in the conduct of the underlying Clinton litigation and investigation, he reported on and defended the Department's actions with respect to its handling of a wide variety of Clinton-related matters.

In addition, Kadzik, along with his FBI counterpart (the then Acting Assistant Director of the FBI's Office of Congressional Affairs), and representatives from the Department of State and Office of the Director of National Intelligence were called to testify before Congress on September 12, 2016, to address congressional access to and redactions of FBI investigative material from the email server investigation.

The last letters that Kadzik signed before the 2016 election were sent on October 31, 2016, to several senators who had written to the Attorney General and FBI Director after receiving the FBI Director's October 28, 2016 letter announcing the review of additional Clinton related emails. Kadzik wrote, in part, "We assure you that the Department will continue to work closely with the FBI and together dedicate all necessary resources and take appropriate steps as expeditiously as possible."

Kadzik told the OIG that he had no role in the email server investigation and that to his memory, in response to a congressional inquiry, met with Department attorneys on the investigative team on only one occasion to discuss the terms of the immunity agreements.

With respect to letters from Congress, Kadzik approved standardized language which OLA used to respond with consistency. For example, when asked about the Clinton email investigation, OLA consistently responded: "Any investigation related to this referral will be conducted by law enforcement professionals and career attorneys in accordance with established Department policies and procedures which are designed to ensure the integrity of all ongoing investigations" and when asked about a special counsel OLA consistently responded by acknowledging the authority and stating that the "authority is rarely exercised."

Axelrod also told the OIG that Kadzik had "no role" in the email server investigation. Axelrod said that the investigative information pertaining to that investigation was closely held, not discussed in senior staff meetings, and not

---

[259] We note that upon receiving a September 2016 congressional inquiry requesting the appointment of special counsel, Kadzik specifically requested the latest Department filing in the FOIA litigation.

discussed with Kadzik. However, Axelrod stated that Kadzik worked "on things related to [the Clinton email investigation]." Axelrod also said that Kadzik likely had more access to information regarding the FOIA litigation for the Clinton emails since that was a civil matter in litigation and discussed in senior staff meetings.

D.   Response to WikiLeaks Release

The WikiLeaks release of Podesta/Kadzik emails on November 1 and 2, 2016, generated inquiries about Kadzik's conduct from several sources.

Axelrod told us that when WikiLeaks released the "Heads up" email, he contacted Kadzik, who authenticated the email and, after searching his emails, assured Axelrod that there were no other similar emails (referencing Departmental matters) that could be released by WikiLeaks.

The Acting Director of OPA emailed Kadzik on November 2 stating that he wanted to speak with Kadzik. The same day the OPA Acting Director informed the press that Kadzik's "Heads up" email contained "public information" that Kadzik sent "in his personal capacity" and was not sent "during work hours." The OPA Acting Director told us that he made the statements attributed to him in the press and said that while he did not specifically recall the conversation with Kadzik, he did not dispute that the information came from Kadzik.[260]

The then Director of the DOJ Ethics Department told us that she contacted the OLA DDAEO about the "Heads up" email and asked whether it contained non-public Departmental information. She said the OLA DDAEO assured her that the information in the email was public when Kadzik sent the email. The then Ethics Director nevertheless expressed concern to us that a Department leader had sent an email to a third party without knowing whether the Department-related information in the email had been made public.

Also following the disclosure, the Department's Office of Professional Responsibility (OPR) initiated an inquiry into whether Kadzik had disclosed privileged or confidential Department information to the Clinton campaign. OPR submitted questions for Kadzik's written response and, in December 2016, closed the inquiry after determining that the Kadzik's "Heads up" email contained only public information and personal opinion. Among other things, OPR found that on May 18, 2015, the Department filed with the court the document containing the proposed schedule for the release of the Clinton emails; the media reported the schedule the same evening; and Kadzik sent his "Heads up" email to Podesta on May 19, 2015, the following day. OPR concluded that Kadzik's email did not include privileged or confidential information. OPR did not consider Kadzik's conduct in terms of other ethical standards including recusal.

---

[260] The Acting OPA Director said that he spoke to the reporter off the record and should not have been quoted because the Department did not want to acknowledge illegally obtained emails.

E.   Kadzik Is Recused

Axelrod told us that after Wikileaks posted the "Heads up" email, he concluded that Kadzik should be recused from all Clinton-related matters. He stated the email created an appearance problem because high level DOJ employees should not be giving a "heads up" to a campaign and that Kadzik had admitted he did not know whether the schedule in the FOIA litigation had been publicly filed at the time he sent Podesta the email. Axelrod stated that the recusal was not because of Kadzik's personal relationship with Podesta but because Kadzik sent the "Heads up" email. Axelrod said that "it was a feeling that, right, DOJ folks, especially like senate confirmed senior leaders, but really anyone in DOJ shouldn't be, you know, it wasn't good practice to be emailing sort of people involved in sort of political campaigns to, right. It's not our job to give campaigns a head's up. It's our job to do our work free from politics."

Axelrod said that because Kadzik was a presidential appointee, Axelrod probably discussed the matter with the Deputy Attorney General and possibly the Attorney General and Associate Deputy Attorney General. Axelrod said that in those discussions, "the decision was made was made [that Kadzik] should...be screened off from...things Clinton related."

Axelrod said that he told Kadzik that he needed to be recused on all Clinton-related matters and that Kadzik should recuse himself. Axelrod said that Kadzik "understood" but was not "wild about" the need to recuse himself. He said that Kadzik was not on the email server investigative team or the FOIA litigation team but it was an appearance issue and someone else needed to sign the Department's letters to Congress.

Associate Deputy Attorney General (ADAG) Scott Schools told the OIG that after the "Heads up" email was posted, Axelrod called him and they agreed that Kadzik should be recused from Clinton-related matters because of the appearance problem. In a subsequent telephone call, Axelrod informed Schools that Kadzik did not agree with, but was willing to abide by, the decision to recuse himself from the Clinton-related matters. Axelrod also asked if Kadzik's recusal needed to be documented. Schools said that there was no requirement to document the recusal and told the OIG that while the decision to recuse was not difficult, the rationale was nuanced and might be over scrutinized if the document was subject to a FOIA request.

According to Schools, Kadzik's principal deputy in OLA later called him to ask whether OLA should be informed of Kadzik's recusal. Schools told her that she could inform OLA personnel about Kadzik's recusal but told the OIG that he did not know if she had.[261]

Kadzik told us Axelrod called him "on or about November 2, 2016" and said that "in light of the controversy, I should recuse myself from anything further

---

[261] As noted above, despite the OIG's repeated attempts, Kadzik's principal deputy, who is no longer with the Department, was unable to accommodate the OIG's request for an interview.

concerning the Clinton emails." Kadzik said that since he "had nothing to do with the Hillary Clinton email investigation or [FOIA] litigation," the recusal only meant he would not review and sign anymore letters to Congress about the matters.

Kadzik said that he would have informed his OLA deputies, OLA DDAEO, and chief of staff of his recused status but did not recall the conversation or who stood in his place as Acting OLA AAG for those matters. He said it was likely that it was his principal deputy, as she was "the oversight person."

Axelrod said that Kadzik's principal deputy took over his responsibilities on Clinton-related matters – that she took Kadzik's place in the discussions related to the Clinton email investigation during the week before the election and then generally handled the Clinton related matters through the rest of Kadzik's term as OLA AAG, which ended on January 19, 2017.

Kadzik told the OIG that he could not recall how Axelrod defined the scope of his recusal but that, as a practical matter, Kadzik understood that he would no longer sign letters to Congress on behalf of the Department that were related to the Clinton emails and that he was not aware that any letters came in after November 2, 2016. Kadzik said that he "wasn't participating in anything with respect to Hillary Clinton and the emails other than signing letters to Congress." Kadzik also said that despite his recusal, he never had to leave a meeting because the Clinton email server investigation was never discussed. However, Axelrod and the OPA Acting Director told us that Kadzik was replaced by his principal deputy for a time at senior staff meetings after WikiLeaks released the "Heads up" email. Axelrod said that the principal deputy replaced Kadzik because the discussions involved Clinton-related matters.

Though Kadzik said he told his deputies and the OLA DDAEO that he was recused, emails show that Kadzik subsequently sent and received emails about Clinton-related matters.

Kadzik forwarded various congressional inquiries about Clinton-related matters to ODAG, OAG, OAAG, OLA, and FBI personnel that had also been sent to his principal deputy. When we asked why he did not leave the matter for his principal deputy to handle, Kadzik said he forwarded the emails to the persons who he thought could respond to the inquiries and that action was no different than reminding his principal deputy that he was recused.

We also asked Kadzik about two Clinton-related emails forwarded to him by his principal deputy. Kadzik's principal deputy sent one email on November 3, 2016, with the notation "FYSA" (for your situational awareness) and another on November 6, 2016, with the notation "I've got it. (Calls throughout today. All the right people looped.)" Kadzik said he did not know why his principal deputy sent him emails after he was recused, that he had not asked her to keep him informed of the matter despite his recused status, and that he did not believe the "looped in" email "[broke] the recusal." As noted previously, we were unable to ask the principal deputy about these emails because she did not make herself available for an interview.

There is evidence that on two other occasions, Kadzik may have spoken with his principal deputy and DDAEO directly about Clinton-related matters. On November 4, 2016, Kadzik's principal deputy forwarded him an email from a Senate Judiciary staffer asking whether there would soon be an official update on the Weiner laptop email review. Kadzik replied, "Call me later this am." Kadzik told the OIG that he did not recall receiving the email, responding to his principal deputy, or whether he ultimately spoke with her. On November 28, 2018, when the OLA DDAEO asked Kadzik and his principal deputy about the Mills immunity agreements with respect to a FOIA request, Kadzik replied "Will circle back with both of you tomorrow." Kadzik said he asked that they circle back to "find out what she was asking about."

In contrast, emails also show that with respect to other (non-Clinton related matters) on which Kadzik was recused, he reminded or informed the persons on the email of his recused status.

V.   Analysis

We analyze Kadzik's actions with respect to three regulations from the Standards of Ethical Conduct for Employees of the Executive Branch (Standards of Ethical Conduct), 5 C.F.R. Part 2635: Personal and business relationships, 5 C.F.R. § 2635.502 (Section 502); Use of non-public information, 5 C.F.R. § 2635.703 (Section 703); and Use of public office for private gain, 5 C.F.R. § 2635.702 (Section 702).

A.   Whether Kadzik Should Have Been Recused Prior to November 2 from Clinton-Related Matters under Section 502 of the Standards of Ethical Conduct

Section 502 of the Standards of Ethical Conduct, 5 C.F.R. § 2635.502 establishes the analytical framework for determining when a federal employee has an appearance of a conflict of interest that merits recusal. As discussed above, Section 502 requires an employee to consider the appearance of his participation in a particular matter involving specific parties (1) that is likely to have a direct and predictable effect on the financial interest of a household member, or (2) if the employee has a covered relationship with someone who is a party or represents a party to the matter. Section 502 also includes catchall provision which may apply to "other circumstances" that would lead a reasonable person to question an employee's impartiality in a matter.

1.   Whether There Was a Particular Matter Involving Specific Parties

The threshold issue for a Section 502(a) analysis is whether there is a "particular matter involving specific parties" before the Department. A "particular matter involving specific parties" denotes a specific proceeding which affects the legal rights of the parties such as an investigation or litigation. 5 C.F.R. § 2640.102(l).

During Kadzik's tenure as OLA AAG, the Department defended the Department of State in a FOIA litigation filed in January 2015 seeking emails from Clinton's personal server during her tenure as Secretary of State, among other things. The Department also initiated the Clinton email investigation in July 2015. Both the FOIA litigation and the email server investigation are "particular matters involving specific parties," as each is a discrete litigation or investigation. Clinton and others were specific subjects of the Clinton email investigation, and the FOIA litigation involved particular plaintiffs and defendants.[262] Therefore, we include both the FOIA litigation and the email server investigation in our analysis (and for the ease of the reader refer to both as "Clinton-related matters.")

2. Whether Kadzik Should Have Recused Because of his Son's Efforts to Obtain Employment with the Clinton Campaign

We next considered whether Kadzik was required to recuse from the Clinton-related matters because of Kadzik and his son RS's efforts to obtain employment for his son with the Clinton campaign.

Under the "financial interests" provisions of Section 502(a), recusal would be required if the Clinton-related matters were likely to have a direct and predictable effect on the financial interest of a member of Kadzik's household. A direct and predictable effect requires a causal link between a decision on the matter and the effect on the specified financial interest and cannot be attenuated or dependent on the occurrence of speculative events. 5 C.F.R. §§ 2635.502(b)(2), 2635.402(b)(1).

Kadzik told the OIG that his son lived in New York City and supported himself financially. Kadzik also provided a redacted copy of his 2015 federal tax returns on which he did not declare his son as a dependent.

Even if the Clinton-related matters could affect his son's financial interests, RS was not a member of Kadzik's household. Therefore, we found that RS's efforts to obtain employment with the Clinton campaign did not require Kadzik to recuse himself from Clinton-related matters under the financial interest provision of Section 502(a).

Under the "covered relationship" provision of Section 502(a), recusal would be required if Kadzik had a covered relationship with a party or with someone who represents a party to a matter. Section 502 defines "covered relationship" to include a "person for whom the employee's...dependent child is, to the employee's knowledge,...seeking to serve as an...contractor or employee." This is the only category of "covered relationship" potentially applicable with respect to Kadzik's

---

[262] Although Clinton was not a named party to the FOIA litigation, it is possible that she would be considered a "party" within the meaning of Section 502 because the litigation centered around her use of a private server and sought emails stored on it. OGE does not take a narrow or strictly legal view of what it means to be a party under Section 502. OGE letter 01 x 8. As detailed below, we were not required to reach this issue. The FOIA litigation indisputably had specific parties, even if Clinton was not one of them.

son.[263] If RS was a dependent child, Kadzik would have had a covered relationship with a party to the particular matter since RS was seeking employment with the Clinton campaign and Clinton was clearly a party to the Clinton email investigation and may have been a party to the FOIA litigation. 5 C.F.R. § 2635.502(b)(1)(iii).

We did not find that RS was a "dependent child." In April 2015, Kadzik's son was 24 years old.[264] Kadzik said that his son was supporting himself financially while living in New York City and that Kadzik only covered the cost of his son's cell phone. Kadzik also told the OIG that he did not declare his son as a dependent on his 2015 tax returns and provided a redacted copy of his 2015 return to the OIG confirming this fact. Thus we found no evidence of a covered relationship based on Kadzik and his non-dependent son's efforts to obtain employment for his son with the Clinton campaign.[265]

The "other circumstances" provision in Section 502 applies when a federal employee is concerned that "other circumstances" would cause a reasonable person to question his impartiality. As with all Section 502 provisions, the conflict may be self-identified by the employee or directed by management. OGE Memorandum 04 x 5.

Kadzik did not self-identify a potential appearance of a conflict under the "other circumstances" provision based on his, his wife's, and his son's efforts to get his son a job with the Clinton campaign. In April and May 2015, Kadzik, his wife, and son reached out to personal acquaintances in the Clinton campaign in an attempt to obtain a job for his son RS with the campaign. At the same time, Kadzik was participating in senior staff meetings where Clinton-related matters were discussed and signing letters to Congress regarding Clinton-related matters on behalf of the Department.

We believe that these circumstances would cause a reasonable person to question Kadzik's impartiality in Clinton-related matters during the time RS was seeking employment with the Clinton campaign. We therefore concluded that under the "other circumstances" provision of Section 502(a)(2), Kadzik should have either recused himself from Clinton-related matters beginning in April 2015, when he initiated employment solicitations to the Clinton campaign, until RS was no longer seeking employment with the campaign, or disclosed these circumstances to the appropriate Department ethics officer so that the Department could have considered whether Kadzik should be recused.

According to OGE, self-identification under the "other circumstances" provision is permissive, but not required, and therefore the failure to recuse under

---

[263] Although RS was a relative of Kadzik's with whom he who presumably had a "close personal relationship," this fact did not create a "covered relationship" because RS was not a party to the Clinton-related investigations, nor did he represent a party.

[264] Kadzik wrote in the email to Fallon that his son was 25 years old; however, his son would not turn 25 until later in the year.

[265] Because RS was not a dependent child, and no other "covered relationship" appears to be in issue, we were not required to determine whether Clinton was a "party" to the FOIA litigation.

the provision is not an ethics violation. "Employees are encouraged to use the process provided by [the "other circumstances" provision], [but] the 'election not to use that process cannot appropriately be considered to be an ethical lapse.'" OGE letter 01 x 08 citing OGE letter 94 x 10(2); *see also* OGE 97 x 8, OGE 95 x 5; OGE 94 x 10. Instead, according to the former Departmental Ethics Director, the failure to self-identify under the "other circumstances" is evidence of an employee's judgment and may reflect on whether the employee has the judgment necessary for a particular Department position.

Although Kadzik did not commit an ethics violation by failing to recuse himself under Section 502(a)(2), we found that his failure to recognize the appearance of a conflict by participating in Clinton-related matters when he, his wife, and his son were trying to get his son a job with the Clinton campaign demonstrated poor judgment.

3. Whether Kadzik Should Have Recused from Clinton-Related Matters in May 2015 by Reason of Sending the "Heads Up" Email to Podesta

According to Kadzik, Axelrod told him he should recuse himself from Clinton-related matters "on or about" November 2, 2016, after learning that Kadzik had sent the "Heads up" email to Podesta on May 19, 2015. Axelrod told us that the "Heads up" email to Podesta raised appearance concerns because Kadzik communicated with a partisan campaign about Department matters and provided information without knowing whether it had yet been made public.[266]

As noted, Kadzik sent the "Heads up" email in May 2015. He continued to participate in senior staff meetings, prepare Department employees for hearings, and respond to inquiries about Clinton-related matters between May 19 and November 2, when Axelrod instructed him to recuse himself. We therefore analyzed whether Kadzik should have recused himself under Section 502 in May 2015 rather than waiting for Axelrod to do it a year and a half later.

We determined that the "Heads up" email did not require Kadzik to recuse under the personal or financial interests provision of Section 502(a). Neither sending the email nor any other aspect of Kadzik's relationship with Podesta or the

---

[266] We also note that long standing Department policies addressing employee participation in political activity place greater restrictions on the political activities of presidential appointees than does the Hatch Act. The Department's stated purpose for further restricting the political activities of political appointees is to ensure that "there is not an appearance that politics plays any part in the Department's day to day operations." Among other things, Department policy prohibited Kadzik from participating in political activity "in concert" with a political party, partisan group, or candidate for partisan political office, even when off duty. We believe that it is a close question whether Kadzik violated Department policy by acting "in concert" with the campaign when he sent Podesta the "Heads up" email. Even if Kadzik did not violate the letter of the Department's policy, he certainly intended to provide assistance, however small, directly to Podesta, the campaign Chairman, which was inconsistent with the stated intent of the policy. *See* James M. Cole, Deputy Attorney General, U.S. Department of Justice, memorandum for All Department of Justice Non-Career Employees, July 14, 2014, https://www.justice.gov/sites/default/files/jmd/legacy/2014/03/24/pol-activ-dag-noncareer-employees.pdf (accessed June 6, 2018).

Clinton campaign gave Kadzik or a member of his household a financial interest that would be affected by the outcome of the Clinton-related investigations. We are not aware of any evidence that Kadzik or any member of his household had any business, contractual, or financial relationship of any kind with Podesta, Clinton, or the Clinton campaign, or any other financial interest that would be affected by any Clinton-related matters pending in the Department of Justice.

Nor did the facts create a "covered relationship" within the definition in Section 502(b)(1). For example, Kadzik did not serve as, or seek to serve as, an officer, director, trustee, general partner, agent, attorney, consultant, contractor, or employee of Podesta, Clinton, or the Clinton campaign. See 5 C.F.R. § 2635.502(b)(1).

We therefore turned to the question of whether Kadzik's "Heads up" email to the Clinton campaign was an "other circumstance" that would raise a question about Kadzik's impartiality with respect to Clinton-related matters within the meaning of Section 502(a)(2). As noted above, according to OGE, self-identification under the "other circumstances" provision is permissive, but not required. Therefore, the failure to recuse oneself under the provision may be bad judgment, but not an ethics violation.

The "Heads up" email reflected an effort by Kadzik to be helpful to the Clinton campaign. Kadzik sent government information (the proposed schedule for the release of the Clinton emails in the FOIA litigation) to a partisan campaign without knowing whether it had been made public. Kadzik's May 2015 "Heads up" email explicitly stated that he did not know whether the Department had yet filed the proposed schedule in court. Similarly, according to Axelrod, Kadzik admitted in November 2016 that he did not know whether the information had been released publically when he sent the email to Podesta. Because Kadzik admittedly did not know that the information had been released publically when he sent the "Heads up" email to Podesta, Department leadership decided that Kadzik should be recused from Clinton-related matters. As discussed below, Kadzik actually used information he acquired in his official position with the intention to assist the campaign in a manner that would have been a misuse of office but for a fact that Kadzik did not definitely know — that the proposed schedule had already been made public.[267]

---

[267] After reviewing a draft of this chapter, Kadzik's attorney submitted a letter to the OIG which, among other things, stated that "Mr. Kadzik learned the information he shared with Mr. Podesta from the Politico article." However, Kadzik's attorney provided no evidentiary basis for the statement, and it conflicts with the content of the May 19, 2015 "Heads up" email and is inconsistent with Kadzik's previous statements to the Department. The Politico article (that Kadzik provided to OPR in response to the inquiry that arose because of his "Heads up" email) clearly states that the proposed schedule was "filed in U.S. District Court in Washington" on "Monday night." Yet Kadzik wrote in his Tuesday morning email that he did not know if the document had yet been filed and admitted the same to Axelrod in November 2016. In addition, in his December 2016 written response to OPR's inquiry, Kadzik wrote that he "did not recall" the source from which he learned the information in his email and cited the Politico article only to establish that the information had been made public when he sent it to Podesta.

Kadzik's willingness to do that raised a reasonable question about whether he would be willing or inclined to act partially toward the Clinton campaign in connection with his official duties, which sometimes touched on Clinton-related matters. At minimum, this created an appearance problem with respect to Kadzik's ability to act impartially that justified Axelrod in recusing him from further participation in Clinton-related matters.

We believe that Kadzik used poor judgment not only in sending the email to a partisan campaign without knowing whether its content was public, but also in failing to recognize how his action would impact the Department and in failing thereafter to recuse himself from Clinton-related matters pursuant to Section 502(a)(2).

B.   Whether Kadzik Violated the Terms of his Recusal after November 2, 2016

In this section, we discuss whether Kadzik violated the terms of his recusal after Axelrod instructed him to recuse from Clinton-related matters on or about November 2, 2016.

Shortly after his confirmation, Kadzik signed an ethics agreement with JMD (for OGE's approval) which identified the scope of his recusals and sent a 2014 memorandum to various leadership components and OLA identifying the specific matters from which he would be recused. Kadzik's memorandum stated that no one should communicate with him about the matters from which he was recused. Furthermore, Kadzik demonstrated his knowledge that a recusal included communications when he received emails related to other recused matters and replied notifying the sender that he was recused.

Communicating about a matter is considered participation and employees should not communicate with others about matters from which they have been recused.[268] Occasionally, a recused employee may receive communications about the matter in an email, telephone call, or meeting. On those occasions, recused employees are trained to clearly identify their recusal to the sender of the email, the caller, or meeting attendees (as the employee leaves the meeting room or the discussion is tabled). While an inadvertent communication would not be considered "participation" in violation of the recusal, repeated and unaddressed communications may evidence a violation of the recusal or a lack of respect for both the process and the Department that would represent poor judgment.

We found that Kadzik forwarded several emails communicating information related to Clinton-related matters within the Department after his recusal and indicated his intent to speak with staff about those matters. In each of those

---

[268] We recognize that Kadzik did not have complete visibility into all Department matters (particularly the closely-held Clinton email investigation). However, recusals not only serve to prevent an employee from affecting a particular investigation or litigation, but also serve to prevent an employee from receiving and misusing Department information. Once an employee is recused from a matter, the employee must fully respect the recusal and cease all participation or seek a determination by the agency designee under section 502(d).

instances his principal deputy also was copied on the incoming email and aware of Kadzik's recusal. In none of those instances did Kadzik either respond to the incoming email informing the sender that he was recused from Clinton-related matters or advise the recipients of his forwarded emails that he was recused from Clinton-related matters. By contrast, when Kadzik received emails related to other matters from which he was recused, he appropriately responded to the senders alerting them to or reminding them of his recusal.

We therefore found that Kadzik understood his responsibilities when contacted about matters from which he was recused, and that he exercised poor judgment when he failed to fully respect his post-November 2 recusal. Kadzik argued that his post-recusal participation was not substantial. However, even if this was a mitigating factor, we could not substantiate his assertion because Kadzik told us he was unable to recall details of his activities during this time. In addition, as noted previously, his principal deputy and his ethics advisor (OLA DDAEO), neither of whom still work for the Department, did not make themselves available to speak with us.

Ultimately, once Department leadership made the decision that Kadzik should be recused from Clinton-related matters, Kadzik was required to cease all participation.

C. Whether Kadzik Improperly Used Non-Public information in Violation of the Standards of Ethical Conduct

We next consider whether Kadzik violated Section 703 of the Standards of Ethical Conduct, 5 C.F.R. § 2635.703, which states: "An employee shall not...allow the improper use of nonpublic information to further his own private interest or that of another, whether through advice or recommendation, or by knowing unauthorized disclosure."

In December 2016, OPR conducted an inquiry to consider whether Kadzik disclosed privileged or confidential Department information to the Clinton campaign and determined that Kadzik's "Heads up" email contained public information and personal opinion. Among other things, OPR found that on May 18, 2015, the Department filed with the court the document containing the proposed schedule for the release of the Clinton emails; the media reported the schedule the same evening; and Kadzik sent his "Heads up" email to Podesta on May 19, 2015, the following day. OPR concluded that Kadzik's email did not include privileged or confidential information.

Although OPR did not specifically address Kadzik's compliance with Section 703, the fact that the information in Kadzik's "Heads up" email did not include nonpublic information also requires the finding that Kadzik did not violate Section 703.

D. Whether Kadzik Misused His Public Office for Private Gain in Violation of the Standards of Ethical Conduct

We next consider whether Kadzik violated Section 702 of the Standards of Ethical Conduct, 5 C.F.R. § 2635.702, which states: "An employee shall not use his public office...for the private gain of friends, relatives, or persons with whom the employee is affiliated in a nongovernmental capacity...". According to commentary to Section 702, "[i]ssues relating to an individual employee's use of public office for private gain tend to arise when the employee's actions benefit those with whom the employee has a relationship outside the office...". 57 Fed. Reg. 35030 (Aug. 7, 1992).

We found that Kadzik learned of the proposed schedule for the release of the Clinton server emails in his capacity as a Department employee. We also found that Kadzik sent the information to a longtime personal friend and professional colleague, Podesta, with whom Kadzik had a relationship outside the office. Further, we found that Kadzik believed that the information would be of benefit to the Clinton campaign.[269] However, as discussed above, the information included in the "Heads up" email was public at the time that Kadzik sent it. Therefore we did not find that these facts amounted to a violation of Section 702.

---

[269] In his email, Kadzik also said that the Civil Division Chief may be asked questions about the Clinton emails in the congressional hearing scheduled that day. However, Kadzik's opinion was not based on nonpublic information, as notice of the hearing had been posted on the committee's website and congressional interest in the Clinton emails was public information. We note that the Civil Division Chief was not asked questions about the Clinton email server during the hearing.

PAGE LEFT INTENTIONALLY

BLANK

CHAPTER FIFTEEN:
FBI RECORDS VAULT TWITTER ANNOUNCEMENTS

I.   Introduction

On November 1, 2016, in response to multiple Freedom of Information Act (FOIA) requests, the FBI Records Management Division's Records/Information Dissemination Section (RIDS) posted records to the FBI Records Vault, a page on the FBI's public website, concerning the "William J. Clinton Foundation" (Clinton Foundation). The bulk of those records concerned the 2001 investigation into the pardon of Marc Rich. The @FBIRecordsVault Twitter account announced this posting later that same day.[270] This Twitter announcement or "tweet" followed a series of 20 tweets released from the @FBIRecordsVault account on October 30, 2016, after a year-long dormant period during which no tweets announcing FOIA releases on the FBI Records Vault had been issued. One of the 20 tweets on October 30, 2016, concerned a release of records for Fred C. Trump, the father of then candidate Donald Trump.

Several newspaper reports suggested that the timing of the Clinton Foundation tweet—coming four days after FBI Director James Comey had announced the re-opening of the Hillary Clinton email investigation—was "further evidence of FBI meddling" in the 2016 election.

The FBI Inspection Division (INSD) conducted a review of the circumstances leading to the Clinton Foundation tweet that focused particularly on the causes of the one-year dormant period and the circumstances surrounding the release of 20 tweets on October 30, 2016, which as noted above included the Fred C. Trump information. INSD's investigation found that: (1) the materials responsive to the FOIA requests were "properly posted" to the FBI Records Vault and (2) a technical malfunction that began in October 2015 and went unnoticed caused the @FBIRecordsVault Twitter account to cease posting automatic Twitter announcements about records posting to the Vault. The malfunction was corrected with a software update on October 30, 2016. After this correction, INSD found that the tweet function operated properly—automatically posting overdue tweets on the @FBIRecordsVault Twitter feed for FOIA releases posted during the dormant period on the FOIA Vault page—and then functioning as intended from that point forward, to include the November 1, 2016 tweet concerning the Clinton Foundation. Therefore, INSD concluded that the tweet concerning the Clinton Foundation was not affected by the software malfunction that prevented the issuance of other tweets for the one-year period.

The OIG conducted this follow-up review focused in particular on the circumstances surrounding the November 1, 2016 FOIA posting on the FBI Records

---

[270] The posting date for the records on the Vault is October 31, 2016, but the RIDS Section Chief and a RIDS analyst told us that October 31 reflects the date when the records were uploaded into the system to be reviewed by RIDS and OPA personnel, but not the date the records were published for the public.

Vault and the subsequent tweet announcing the posting. The purpose of this review was to determine whether there was any evidence that improper political considerations were a factor in the timing of these events. As part of this investigation, the OIG reviewed FOIA requests received by the FBI on the Clinton Foundation prior to November 1, 2016, documents associated with the FBI's processing of these requests, and email records for individuals involved in processing and releasing the requests. The OIG interviewed eight individuals from RIDS and the FBI's Office of Public Affairs (OPA).

Based on our investigation, we found no evidence to indicate that improper political considerations influenced the FBI's processing and release of the Clinton Foundation documents or the use of an FBI Twitter account to publicize the release. The evidence indicates that the FOIA requests related to the Clinton Foundation were processed according to RIDS' internal procedures like other similarly-sized requests. Likewise, we found no evidence to indicate that the FOIA response was either expedited or delayed in order to impact the 2016 Presidential election. Below are the factual findings and conclusions reached by the OIG's investigation.

II.   Background

This section discusses the laws, regulations, guidance, and procedures governing the FBI's activities in receiving, researching, processing, and responding to FOIA requests and, in appropriate cases, publicly releasing documents produced in response to FOIA requests by posting such documents on the FBI Records Vault.

A.   Freedom of Information Act, 5 U.S.C. § 552

The *Freedom of Information Act*, 5 U.S.C. § 552 (FOIA), requires federal agencies to make agency records available to the public and sets forth the specific requirements to do so along with guidance on records and information exempt from public release. On June 30, 2016, the *FOIA Improvement Act of 2016* (the FOIA Improvement Act), Public Law No. 114-185, 130 Stat. 538, updated 5 U.S.C. § 552 with a notable change pertinent to this case regarding when an agency must release previously-requested records to the public. Before the FOIA Improvement Act, FOIA permitted agencies to proactively release records, "which, because of the nature of their subject matter, the agency determines have become or are likely to become the subject of subsequent requests for substantially the same records."[271] This wording, often referred to as the "frequently requested record" provision of FOIA, allowed agencies latitude to decide when to make these records available and for how long.[272] However, the FOIA Improvement Act now also requires agencies to publicly release records once they have received three or more requests for the same or substantially similar records. This is commonly referred to as the "rule of

---

[271] 5 U.S.C. § 552(a)(2)(D) (2009).

[272] 5 U.S.C. § 552(a)(2)(D) (2009).

three."[273] An agency may also pre-emptively release the records if it believes they will receive additional requests for the records.[274]

Under FOIA, agencies are authorized to withhold information from public release that is specifically exempt from release under 5 U.S.C. § 552(b), traditionally referred to as FOIA exemptions. Exemptions cover material such as classified information, trade secrets, personnel and medical files, and law enforcement information.[275] Under this provision however, the agency is tasked with redacting the information that cannot be disclosed, but releasing as much of the requested information as possible.[276]

In sensitive law enforcement matters, FOIA allows a law enforcement agency to "treat the records as not subject to the requirements of [FOIA]."[277] This is known as a FOIA exclusion, which "provide[s] protection in three limited sets of circumstances where publicly acknowledging even the existence of the records could cause harm to law enforcement or national security interests."[278] The first exclusion protects records in an ongoing criminal investigation, the release of which could "reasonably be expected to interfere with enforcement proceedings."[279] The second exclusion protects from the acknowledgment of confidential informant records.[280] The last exclusion protects the FBI's classified foreign intelligence, counterintelligence, and international terrorism records.[281] The Department's Office of Information Policy (OIP) requires Department components—including the FBI—to obtain OIP's approval to use a FOIA exclusion.[282]

FOIA allows agencies to expedite the processing of records in cases where the requester can "demonstrate[] a compelling need" or in other situations as defined by each agency.[283] A "compelling need" is defined in FOIA as a situation where not receiving the requested records quickly "could reasonably be expected to pose an imminent threat to the life or physical safety of an individual" or in situations where individuals who disseminate information demonstrate an "urgency

---

[273] 5 U.S.C. § 552(a)(2)(D)(ii) (2016).

[274] 5 U.S.C. § 552(a)(2)(D)(ii).

[275] 5 U.S.C. § 552(b).

[276] 5 U.S.C. § 552(b).

[277] 5 U.S.C. § 552(c)(1).

[278] Department of Justice, Office of Information Policy, Implementing FOIA's Statutory Exclusion Provisions, Aug. 15, 2014, https://www.justice.gov/oip/blog/foia-guidance-6.

[279] 5 U.S.C. § 552(c)(1)(B)(ii).

[280] 5 U.S.C. § 552(c)(2).

[281] 5 U.S.C. § 552(c)(3).

[282] 36 C.F.R. § 16.6(g)(1) (2017).

[283] 5 U.S.C. § 552(a)(6)(E)(i).

to inform the public concerning actual or alleged Federal Government activity."[284] If the agency grants the request, it must process the FOIA request "as soon as practicable."[285]

B.   The FBI FOIA Process

RIDS oversees the FBI's FOIA program. This section describes the RIDS FOIA process, their coordination with other FBI entities on "high visibility" and "rule of three" requests, and the posting of FOIA requests on the FOIA Vault.

1.   Records/Information Dissemination Section's FOIA Process

FBI Policy Directive 0481D, Freedom of Information Act and Privacy Act Requests, February 8, 2012, establishes the FBI's FOIA and Privacy Act programs and provides top-level guidance. It sets forth that the FBI's policy is to respond to FOIA and Privacy Act requests within 20 business days (the requirement set forth in the FOIA) and establishes an over-arching list of responsibilities for various offices within the FBI to assist RIDS to meet that goal. Policy Directive 0481D provides no additional procedural guidance beyond this top-level listing of roles and responsibilities. With the exception of Policy Directive 0481D, RIDS does not have any formal rules or manuals that outline the FBI's FOIA process.[286]

FOIA requests received by the FBI are initially reviewed during a weekly meeting by senior RIDS personnel, including the section chief, assistant section chief, and unit chiefs. During that meeting, "high visibility" and complex requests are identified, as well as those that may qualify for expedited treatment (if requested). RIDS personnel told us that high visibility requests are generally those dealing with current political issues; anything dealing with a significant issue or person of interest to the public and the FBI; or items that have potential to impact the FBI. According to RIDS personnel, the RIDS Section Chief and Assistant Section Chief normally determine which requests will be designated high visibility requests. As detailed below, responses to high visibility requests receive a higher level of supervisory review at the end of the process, and are also made available to the public on the FBI Records Vault.

Following intake, a FOIA request is then submitted to the Work Process Unit (WPU) in RIDS for initial processing. FOIA analysts send the requestor an acknowledgement of the request and provide them a FOIA number. They then search the FBI's central records system, including Sentinel and the Automated Case Support (ACS) system, and contact relevant FBI personnel to locate responsive

---

[284] 5 U.S.C. § 552(a)(6)(E)(v). The Department's FOIA Regulations add two more categories in which the Department may grant expedited processing: the loss of substantial due process rights or matters of widespread and exceptional media interest in which there exist possible questions about the government's integrity that affects public confidence. 28 C.F.R. § 16.5(e)(1)(i)-(iv).

[285] 5 U.S.C. § 552(a)(6)(E)(iii).

[286] As a result, the following description of the FBI's process is based on interviews with RIDS managers and analysts.

records. If no records are found, the FBI communicates this fact to the requestor. If responsive records are identified, they are compiled, quality checked, and then uploaded into the FOIA Document Processing System.

Once the collection of documents has been completed, the response is placed in a workflow "queue" to await processing by a RIDS disclosure analyst in one of the RIDS processing units. The FBI has established four separate workflow "queues" based on the volume of responsive documents. Responses that qualify for expedited treatment under FOIA are moved to the front of the appropriate workload queue. All other responses enter the queue from the back, in a "First In, First Out" order.

According to the RIDS Section Chief, requests with 50 or fewer pages of responsive documents enter the "small" queue and are typically processed within approximately 4 months from the date of the request to the date of the response.[287]

Requests generating between 50 and 950 pages of responsive documents are directed to the "medium" queue and are typically completed in approximately 9 to 10 months. Completion time for requests placed in the "large" queue, those that generate 950 to 8,000 pages of relevant documents, is approximately 2 and a half years. The fourth queue, for extra-large requests that generate over 8,000 pages of responsive documents, can take upwards of 4 years to fulfill. For larger requests, requestors do not have to wait the full time period for documents; RIDS provides interim releases in batches of 500 pages at a time.

RIDS personnel explained that once a request has worked its way to the front of the appropriate workflow queue, a supervisor assigns the responsive documents to a disclosure analyst for processing. Processing the documents involves a line-by-line review of the documents to identify and redact information exempt from release under the FOIA. After the disclosure analyst's review is complete, RIDS experts and supervisors conduct a quality review. If the request is not a high visibility request, the analyst finalizes the release, sends the appropriate correspondence to the requestor, and closes the matter.

Responses to high visibility requests are subject to additional management review before being released to the requestor or posted to the FBI Vault, including by the RIDS Section Chief and the FOIA attorney supporting RIDS, to ensure accurate and proper application of exemptions, classification decisions, and redactions and to spot any other potential issues. The processing analyst drafts a "high visibility" memorandum to accompany the package through these additional reviews. According to the RIDS Section Chief, the designation of a request as "high visibility" does not mean it will be processed quicker than any other request, unless it otherwise qualifies for expedited treatment. Rather, these requests are processed according to the same prioritization procedures as other FOIA requests.

---

[287] The average processing times are based on regular analysis of queue processing times by RIDS personnel in order to provide estimated completion dates to FOIA requestors.

2. Release of FOIA Documents on the FBI Vault

The FBI Records Vault is a page on the FBI.gov public website. Requests posted to the FBI Records Vault fall into one or both of the following categories: high visibility requests or requests that meet the "rule of three" standard as defined in the 2016 updates to FOIA.

Although OPA manages the overall FBI.gov public website, RIDS is responsible for the content and postings for the FBI Records Vault page. According to RIDS personnel, in the fall of 2016, once RIDS management determined that a post would be made to the FBI Records Vault, RIDS would notify the RMD chain of command, OPA's National Press Office, and often the General Counsel's FOIA Litigation Unit Chief of the upcoming post. To assist historians and researchers who use the FBI Records Vault, RIDS would often ask the FBI Historian to draft a summary of the documents to accompany the posting on the FBI Records Vault. The purpose of RIDS's notification to the National Press Office was to allow the National Press Office an opportunity to prepare for any media inquiries and to notify OPA management and FBI executive management as necessary.

Ultimately, once all these offices had been notified of the upcoming post, and a summary had been drafted to be posted with the responsive documents, the RIDS Section Chief made the final determination of when to post the documents.[288] Postings could be delayed by the Section Chief and Assistant Section Chief of RIDS, as well as the Office of Public Affairs and FBI executive management. The RMD Section Chief told us that postings could only be delayed for short periods of time to give FBI executive management notice that information with high public interest was about to be posted. Once the release was posted to the FBI Records Vault, the @FBIRecordsVault Twitter account was configured to automatically announce (auto-tweet) the addition of new content to the FBI Records Vault.

III. Findings

This section presents our findings with regard to the timeline of events and our analysis of whether there were any improper political considerations involved with the timing of the FOIA release and its associated tweet.

A. Facts

1. Timeline

Nov 10, 2015   FBI Records Management Division (RMD) receives the first FOIA request for documents relating to the Clinton Foundation. Several subsequent requests for the same or similar materials are later combined with the initial request for processing.

---

[288] The Assistant Section Chief of RIDS could make the determination in the absence of the Section Chief.

Dec 17, 2015	Records/Information Dissemination Section (RIDS) analysts begin searching for responsive documents.
May 12, 2016	RIDS analysts complete the search for responsive documents. The resulting collection (the "Clinton Foundation documents") is placed in the "medium workflow queue" to await processing for release on a "First In, First Out" basis.
Aug 15, 2016	RIDS begins reviewing the Clinton Foundation documents for exempt and classified material.
Oct 25, 2016	RIDS completes its review and redaction of the documents. Because RIDS had designated this release as a "high visibility" response, it receives review by the RIDS Assistant Section Chief and the FBI Office of Public Affairs (OPA) prior to release to the requesters and to the FBI Records Vault. The FBI Historian is asked to draft a summary of the documents' contents to accompany the release to the Vault.
Oct 28, 2016	OPA informs RIDS that it concurs with the proposed release of the Clinton Foundation documents.
Oct 31, 2016	OPA requests RIDS to postpone posting the Clinton Foundation documents for one day because of workload resulting from Director Comey's October 28 letter to Congress announcing reactivation of the Clinton email investigation.
Nov 1, 2016	RIDS publishes the Clinton Foundation documents on the FBI Records Vault. The posting is announced on a system-generated tweet from @FBIRecordsVault.

2.   Detailed Chronology

The first Clinton Foundation request received by RMD on November 10, 2015, sought any and all records about the Clinton Foundation. Between November 11 and December 15, 2015, the request was pending assignment for initial processing. The Work Processing Unit opened a request for the Clinton Foundation on December 15. Materials from six subsequent, similar requests were later combined with this request.[289] These multiple requests met the "rule of three" standard for posting on the FBI's FOIA Vault page. The Clinton Foundation request was designated as a high visibility request during processing due to its subject and the expectation it could attract media attention. The request was not designated for "expedited" treatment.

---

[289] The subsequent requests were dated April 1, 2016; July 13, 2016; July 14, 2016; August 16, 2016; August 17, 2016; and August 30, 2016.

Between December 17, 2015, and May 12, 2016, RIDS analysts searched for and gathered material responsive to the request. During this initial phase, RIDS identified additional documents that were responsive to the FOIA request but potentially qualified for a FOIA exclusion. The RIDS Section Chief stated to the OIG that when they located these documents, he coordinated with the relevant investigative section chief and determined the FBI should seek Department approval to use a FOIA exclusion. The RIDS Section Chief explained to the OIG that the Department's policies required the FBI to "write up an exclusion" for approval by OIP. The Director of OIP ultimately approved the FBI's use of an exclusion for these documents on July 25, 2016.

Responsive materials also included documents involving a closed 2001 FBI investigation probing whether donations to the Clinton Foundation had been made to influence former President Clinton to pardon Marc Rich. After discovering the Marc Rich records on May 9, 2016, the RIDS Section Chief released the records to the medium processing queue.

In the three months between May 12 and August 15, 2016, the documents collected in response to the request (the "Clinton Foundation documents") were in the medium workflow queue awaiting processing. During this timeframe, additional relevant records were located and added to the documents already in the queue, but the request remained in the medium queue.

On August 16, 2016, the Clinton Foundation request entered the processing and review phase in which the analyst reviewed the pages for exempted material and performed a declassification review, and the supervisor performed a quality review. Because the Clinton Foundation request had been designated as a high visibility request, it received additional review by the FOIA Unit Chief, the RIDS Assistant Section Chief and the RIDS Section Chief.

On October 25, 2016, the RIDS Assistant Section Chief notified two individuals in OPA's National Press Office—the Unit Chief and a Public Affairs Specialist—and the FBI Historian via email that documents responsive to the Clinton Foundation request, a high visibility FOIA release, were ready for their review prior to release. The Assistant Section Chief noted in his email that RIDS planned to post the FOIA response to the FBI Records Vault on October 28 or 31, 2016. The Assistant Section Chief noted in his email that "the timing, of course, may draw attention" to this release and provided a copy of the high visibility memo drafted by the FOIA review unit, which provided a brief overview of the substance of the release. The Assistant Section Chief told us and the recipients stated that they understood this statement to refer to the short time before the 2016 election and thus the expected media interest in any release involving the Clintons. In the email the Assistant Section Chief also requested that the FBI Historian write a synopsis for the FBI Records Vault posting.

On October 26, the National Press Office Unit Chief sent an email to the Public Affairs Specialist in her office and the FBI Historian stating, "Can you give this [reviewing the Clinton Foundation documents] priority in the event we need to consider timing?" According to the Unit Chief, her timing concern involved the election being close and with the potential media coverage, needing to allot time to review documents to be prepared for any issues that might arise after the documents were released. The Unit Chief told us that the press office wanted to review the documents in order to determine whether to alert FBI executive management, potentially including the FBI Director, to the potential media coverage. She stated that her reference to the timing was not to make it a high priority to ensure that it was released prior to the election, but that it meant "that they need[ed] to stop what they're doing and review this so that we can make a decision if we need to, or raise it to another level."

On October 27, the Public Affairs Specialist provided the high visibility memorandum and about 15 pages of the FOIA release documents to the Assistant Director (AD) of OPA, Michael Kortan, for his review. The FBI Historian told us that in response to the request from RIDS and the National Press Office Unit Chief, he drafted a synopsis to accompany the release of records and sent it to the National Press Office Unit Chief on October 27, 2016. That same day, the FBI Historian also emailed the Assistant Section Chief with a short summary of the release to accompany the FBI Records Vault posting, and cautioned the Assistant Section Chief not to make the post "live" before checking back with the Public Affairs Specialist on whether OPA was ready for the release.

On Friday, October 28, the Public Affairs Specialist emailed RIDS to say that OPA reviewed the FOIA response, and had no issues with the proposed release.

On Monday, October 31, the Public Affairs Specialist sent an inquiry to RIDS at 9:17 a.m. asking whether the responsive materials had been released to the requester yet. When the RIDS Assistant Section Chief responded that they were in the process of posting it to the FBI Records Vault, the Public Affairs Specialist requested an hour delay to give AD Kortan an additional heads-up. As a result, RIDS planned for an 11:30 a.m. release and informed OPA. The Public Affairs Specialist then called the RIDS Section Chief and requested to delay the posting for a full day. The RIDS Section Chief stated that the Public Affairs Specialist told him they needed the delay because they were overwhelmed by the reaction to Director Comey's announcement regarding the Clinton email investigation and "that there's not any way [the National Press Office] can deal with this today." However, the Public Affairs Specialist told us she could not recall the reason for the delay. The National Press Office Unit Chief stated that this was a typical delay needed to ensure that AD Kortan had the time to review the documents and make notifications to executive management. The RIDS Section Chief agreed to delay the posting until the next day.

On the morning of November 1, the RIDS Section Chief sent an email to members of his team as well as individuals in OPA stating that RIDS was ready to make the Clinton Foundation documents public on the FBI Vault site. In the absence of further delay requests or other inputs from OPA, the RIDS Section Chief approved the public posting of the materials and instructed one of his subordinates, a Supervisory Government Information Specialist (SGIS), to publish it on the FBI Records Vault. The SGIS then posted the FOIA records.[290]

Witnesses told us that the fact that the presidential election was just a week ahead was not a factor in deciding when to release the Clinton Foundation documents to the public, though they knew the timing would call attention to their release. They stated that the FBI does not take into account elections in deciding how to process FOIA requests or when to release responsive documents to the public. Witnesses told us that there was no FOIA equivalent to the Election Year Sensitivities guidance that addresses overt investigative steps and the timing of charges. Further, they told us that there were no discussions about delaying the release of the Clinton Foundation documents until after the election and that the fact that the release occurred the week before the election was a coincidence.

In response to OIG inquiries regarding the processing and the timing of the release, the RIDS Assistant Section Chief emphasized that FOIA is a release statute and presumes release: "[T]he legal duty under the FOIA is to release something...when it's ready to be released...[i]rrespective of any timing, irrespective of any election. [The] FOIA statute says when something is ready to be released, we release it." He also stated, "We deal with the most sensitive issues...every day.... [Y]ou have to stick to the process." The RIDS Section Chief told us that the only guidance they received regarding the timing of FOIA releases came "from the Director himself when he released [a summary of Hillary Rodham Clinton's July 2, 2016 interview with the FBI]."[291] The FBI had received criticism for releasing the documents on a Friday to minimize press attention. The Section Chief told us that, in a message to the FBI, he understood Comey to say that the FBI does not "hold onto anything for political purposes" and "when it's ready it goes out." The attorney supporting RIDS stated that in her interactions with RIDS management, "they have always been very clear that the FOIA process operates rather independently of any politics with a small p or the big P for that matter, that may be going on." She added:

> [T]he way that RIDS works, it's such a massive beast that it's essentially a machine.... And it could be the dogcatcher case next to the Hillary Clinton case, and you're going to handle them the same. The next one in your queue pops up, you're going to work it until it's done, and then you're going to move onto your next one. So, the FOIA process...does not sort of cherry pick the things that we want to handle at any particular time in any particular way, either fast or slow.

---

[290] The public FBI Records Vault webpage indicates that the Clinton Foundation documents were posted on October 31, 2016. However, the RIDS Section Chief and the SGIS told us that this date refers to when the documents were uploaded to the system for review by RIDS and OPA. The documents were not made available to the public until November 1, 2016.

[291] On September 2, 2016, the FBI posted Hillary Clinton's July 2, 2016 interview with the FBI concerning allegations that classified information was improperly stored or transmitted on a personal email server she used during her tenure.

Later on November 1, a system-generated tweet from @FBIRecordsVault announced the posting on FBI's Records Vault. Shortly thereafter, NPO began receiving inquiries from the media questioning the timing of the posting of the records and the associated tweet. The SGIS stated that he received multiple inquiries about the tweet because individuals within OPA and RMD were concerned that he had manually tweeted the release. The SGIS told us he informed the individuals who called that he had not manually tweeted concerning the release. He then checked the Twitter feed on his phone and realized the attention it was getting, so he looked into what happened. The SGIS stated he then learned about the issues with the automatic Twitter feed, that those issues had been corrected on October 30, and that upon correction the system released multiple tweets concerning posts over the prior year.

B. Analysis

In order to determine whether the Clinton Foundation release was impacted by any improper political motivation, we examined two issues. First, we explored whether the Clinton Foundation request was handled differently than other similarly-sized, high visibility FOIA requests. Next, we also examined whether any FBI officials improperly attempted to affect the timing of the processing or release of the responsive documents to either advance or harm the prospects of either presidential candidate.

We found no evidence that the Clinton Foundation request was handled any differently than other FOIA requests. Within RIDS, all of the individuals we interviewed told us that the Clinton Foundation request was processed just like any other FOIA request. The RIDS Section Chief told us the FOIA process is a regimented process based on workload queues, and that the Clinton Foundation request "just fell right into line with this [process]" and this request "was a number on somebody's spreadsheet." The RIDS Assistant Section Chief said that they followed "the business process at the time."

We found no evidence that anyone in RMD or OPA expedited or delayed the processing or posting of the request for any improper purpose. The RIDS Section Chief stated that the Clinton Foundation request was processed according to its size queue and consistent with that queue's processing timeline. Our review of the timeline for the processing of this request confirmed the Section Chief's assessment. RIDS located over 500 pages responsive to the request, putting the request in the medium queue with a stated average processing time of 9-10 months.[292] The request was received on November 10, 2015, and was posted on November 1, 2016—just under 12 months. The RIDS Section Chief told the OIG that the response did not meet the average processing time because it was "an unusual request" due to the potential FOIA exclusion, "which totally skew[ed] what happen[ed]." However, the RIDS SGIS who monitors the FOIA processing time

---

[292] We did not perform an independent audit of RIDS' medium queue, but utilized the averages as reported to us by the RIDS Section Chief and Assistant Section Chief.

statistics, told the OIG that the time it took RIDS to produce this response "wasn't off of the, off-timing," and he did not think anyone had rushed it or slowed it down.

Additionally, the individuals we interviewed told us that there were no efforts to delay the release of the Clinton Foundation documents until after the election or efforts to expedite the release before the election. In fact, all of the witnesses we spoke to said that at no time were there any discussions about holding the Clinton Foundation release until after the election or ensuring that it was released before the election. The RIDS Section Chief told us that "there was no actual timing involvement to get it out before the election." The RIDS Assistant Section Chief said there were no internal discussions about whether to hold the release until after the election. He told us that "FOIA is a disclosure action.... There was no consideration of [timing]." The National Press Office Unit Chief told us that documents are released when they are ready for release, regardless of the date or time period they fall under. She stated that OPA might ask for a delay of a few hours or a day or two if they needed time to review the documents, but would not hold back releasing information for a substantial period of time. The witnesses interviewed denied taking any action, or delaying any action, with regard to the FOIA request in order to assist or harm either candidate's prospects in the election. None of the witnesses had knowledge of any attempt to do so.

CHAPTER SIXTEEN:
CONCLUSIONS AND RECOMMENDATIONS

I.   Conclusions

The Clinton email investigation was one of the highest profile investigations in the FBI's history; however, it is just one of thousands of investigations handled each year by the approximately 35,000 FBI agents, analysts, and other professionals who dedicate their careers to protecting the American people and upholding the Constitution and the rule of law. Through the collective efforts of generations of FBI employees, the FBI has developed and earned a reputation as one of the world's premier law enforcement agencies.

The FBI has gained this reputation, in significant part, because of its professionalism, impartiality, non-political enforcement of the law, and adherence to detailed policies, practices, and norms. However, as we outline in this report, certain actions during the Midyear investigation were inconsistent with these long-standing policies, practices, and norms.

First, we found that several FBI employees who played critical roles in the investigation sent political messages—some of which related directly to the Midyear investigation—that created the appearance of bias and thereby raised questions about the objectivity and thoroughness of the Midyear investigation. Even more seriously, text messages between Strzok and Page pertaining to the Russia investigation, particularly a text message from Strzok on August 8 stating "No. No he's not. We'll stop it." in response to a Page text "[Trump's] not ever going to become president, right? Right?!," are not only indicative of a biased state of mind but imply a willingness to take official action to impact a presidential candidate's electoral prospects. This is antithetical to the core values of the FBI and the Department of Justice. While we did not find documentary or testimonial evidence that improper considerations, including political bias, directly affected the specific investigative actions we reviewed in Chapter Five, the conduct by these employees cast a cloud over the entire FBI investigation and sowed doubt about the FBI's work on, and its handling of, the Midyear investigation. It also called into question Strzok's failure in October 2016 to follow up on the Midyear-related investigative lead discovered on the Weiner laptop. The damage caused by these employees' actions extends far beyond the scope of the Midyear investigation and goes to the heart of the FBI's reputation for neutral factfinding and political independence.

Second, in key moments, then Director Comey chose to deviate from the FBI's and the Department's established procedures and norms and instead engaged in his own subjective, ad hoc decisionmaking. In so doing, we found that Comey largely based his decisions on what he believed was in the FBI's institutional interests and would enable him to continue to effectively lead the FBI as its Director. While we did not find that these decisions were the result of political bias on Comey's part, we nevertheless concluded that by departing so clearly and dramatically from FBI and Department norms, the decisions negatively impacted the perception of the FBI and the Department as fair administrators of justice.

Moreover, these decisions usurped the authority of the Attorney General and upset the well-established separation between investigative and prosecutorial functions and the accountability principles that guide law enforcement decisions in the United States.

As we further outline in this report, there was a troubling lack of any direct, substantive communication between Comey and then Attorney General Lynch in advance of both Comey's July 5 press conference and his October 28 letter to Congress. With regard to the July 5 events, Comey affirmatively concealed his intentions from Lynch. When he did finally call her on the morning of July 5—after the FBI first notified the press—he told her that he was going to be speaking about the Midyear investigation but that he would not answer any of her questions, and would not tell her what he planned to say. During that call, Lynch did not instruct Comey to tell her what he intended to say at the press conference. With respect to the October 28 letter, Comey chose not to contact Lynch or then Deputy Attorney General Yates directly; rather, he had FBI Chief of Staff Rybicki advise Yates's senior advisor (then PADAG Axelrod) that Comey intended to send a letter to Congress and that Comey believed he had an obligation to do so. Given these circumstances, Lynch and Yates concluded it would be counterproductive to speak directly with Comey and that the most effective way to communicate their strong opposition to Comey about his decision was to relay their views to him through Axelrod and Rybicki. We found it extraordinary that, in advance of two such consequential decisions, the FBI Director decided that the best course of conduct was to not speak directly and substantively with the Attorney General about how best to navigate these decisions and mitigate the resulting harms, and that Comey's decision resulted in the Attorney General and Deputy Attorney General concluding that it would be counterproductive to speak directly with the FBI Director.

This is not the first time the Department and the FBI have conducted a politically-charged investigation, and it will not be the last. To protect the institutions from allegations of abuse, political interference, and biased enforcement of the law, the Department and the FBI have developed policies and practices to guide their decisions. In the vast majority of cases, they are followed as a matter of routine. But they are most important to follow when the stakes are the highest, and when the pressures to divert from them—often based on well-founded concerns and highly fraught scenarios—are the greatest. No rule, policy, or practice is perfect, but at the same time, neither is any individual's ability to make judgments under pressure or in what may seem like unique circumstances. It is in these moments—when the rationale for keeping to the ordinary course fades from view and the temptation to make an exception is greatest—that the bedrock principles and time-tested practices of the Department and the FBI can serve their highest purpose. This notion was most effectively summarized for us by DAAG George Toscas, who was the most senior career Department official involved in the daily supervision of the Midyear investigation:

> One of the things that I tell people all the time, after having been in
> the Department for almost 24 years now, is I stress to people and
> people who work at all levels, the institution has principles and there's

always an urge when something important or different pops up to say, we should do it differently or those principles or those protocols you know we should—we might want to deviate because this is so different. But the comfort that we get as people, as lawyers, as representatives, as employees and as an institution, the comfort we get from those institutional policies, protocols, has, is an unbelievable thing through whatever storm, you know whatever storm hits us, when you are within the norm of the way the institution behaves, you can weather any of it because you stand on the principle.

And once you deviate, even in a minor way, and you're always going to want to deviate. It's always going to be something important and some big deal that makes you think, oh let's do this a little differently. But once you do that, you have removed yourself from the comfort of saying this institution has a way of doing things and then every decision is another ad hoc decision that may be informed by our policy and our protocol and principles, but it's never going to be squarely within them.

There are many lessons to be learned from the Department's and FBI's handling of the Midyear investigation, but among the most important is the need for Department and FBI leadership to follow its established procedures and policies even in its highest-profile and most challenging investigations. By adhering to these principles and norms, the public will have greater confidence in the outcome of the Department's and the FBI's decisions, and Department and FBI leaders will better protect the interests of federal law enforcement and the dedicated professionals who serve these institutions.

II.   Recommendations

For these reasons, and as more fully described in previous chapters, we recommend the following:

1.   The Department and the FBI consider developing practice guidance that would assist investigators and prosecutors in identifying the general risks with and alternatives to permitting a witness to attend a voluntary interview of another witness, in particular when the witness is serving as counsel for the other witness.

2.   The Department consider making explicit that, except in situations where the law requires or permits disclosure, an investigating agency cannot publicly announce its recommended charging decision prior to consulting with the Attorney General, Deputy Attorney General, U.S. Attorney, or his or her designee, and cannot proceed without the approval of one of these officials.

3.   The Department and the FBI consider adopting a policy addressing the appropriateness of Department employees discussing the conduct of uncharged individuals in public statements.

4.	The Department consider providing guidance to agents and prosecutors concerning the taking of overt investigative steps, indictments, public announcements, or other actions that could impact an election.

5.	The Office of the Deputy Attorney General consider taking steps to improve the retention and monitoring of text messages Department-wide.

6.	The FBI add a warning banner to all of the FBI's mobile phones and mobile devices in order to further notify users that they have no reasonable expectation of privacy.

7.	The FBI consider (a) assessing whether it has provided adequate training to employees about the proper use of text messages and instant messages, including any related discovery obligations, and (b) providing additional guidance about the allowable uses of FBI devices for any non-governmental purpose, including guidance about the use of FBI devices for political conversations

8.	The FBI consider whether (a) it is appropriately educating employees about both its media contact policy and the Department's ethics rules pertaining to the acceptance of gifts, and (b) its disciplinary provisions and penalties are sufficient to deter such improper conduct.

9.	Department ethics officials consider implementing a review of campaign donations when Department employees or their spouses run for public office.

ATTACHMENT A

U.S. Department of Justice

Office of the Deputy Attorney General

Associate Deputy Attorney General   Washington, D.C. 20530

June 11, 2018

MEMORANDUM

TO: Michael E. Horowitz
             Inspector General
             U.S. Department of Justice

FROM: Scott N. Schools
             Associate Deputy Attorney General
             Office of the Deputy Attorney General

SUBJECT: Response to "A Review of Various Actions by the Federal Bureau of
             Investigation and Department of Justice in Advance of the 2016 Election"

The Department of Justice (Department) appreciates the review your office conducted regarding various actions by the Federal Bureau of Investigation (FBI) and the Department in advance of the 2016 election and the resulting report of investigation. This response addresses only the report and recommendations as they pertain to the Department as the FBI is responding separately.

Based on the findings in the report, your office made six recommendations for the Department to consider. The Department concurs in Recommendations 1-5 and 9 and will expeditiously consider taking steps in response to them.

cc: Hon. John Demers
        Assistant Attorney General
        National Security Division

        Hon. Christopher Wray
        Director
        Federal Bureau of Investigation

ATTACHMENT B

June 12, 2018

The Honorable Michael E. Horowitz
Inspector General
U.S. Department of Justice
Washington, D.C.

Dear Mr. Horowitz:

The Federal Bureau of Investigation (FBI) greatly values the opportunity to review and respond to the forthcoming Report entitled "A Review of Various Actions by the Federal Bureau of Investigation and Department of Justice in Advance of the 2016 Election." The FBI's formal response is enclosed, including a Law Enforcement Sensitive portion appended at the end.

The FBI recognizes and appreciates the importance of the Inspector General's oversight role and thanks you for the thoroughness of your Report and recommendations regarding FBI actions and policies.

Sincerely yours,

Christopher A. Wray
Director

Enclosure

FBI RESPONSE TO THE REPORT OF
THE DEPARTMENT OF JUSTICE'S OFFICE OF THE INSPECTOR GENERAL

The mission of the Federal Bureau of Investigation (FBI or Bureau) is to protect the American people and uphold the Constitution of the United States. Within this mission, the FBI has certain priorities, including protecting the United States against terrorist attack, foreign intelligence operations and espionage, cyber-based attacks and high-technology crimes, combatting public corruption at all levels, protecting civil rights, and combating major criminal offenses. Sometimes, the investigations and operations conducted by the FBI in furtherance of its mission may cut against the personally held views of certain Special Agents and other employees supporting those cases. There is nothing inherently wrong with this; indeed, the Constitution contains robust protections for personally held and espoused beliefs and the freedom of association. The FBI endeavors to, and as reflected in the Department of Justice (DOJ) Office of the Inspector General's (OIG) "A Review of Various Actions by the Federal Bureau of Investigation and Department of Justice in Advance of the 2016 Election" Report, succeeds in its efforts, to maintain separation between personally held views and the actual work of the FBI. Nevertheless, proper oversight is required in order to ensure this separation remains effective, that the mission comes first regardless of personal view, that all investigations proceed objectively, and that the American people maintain their trust and confidence that the critically important work of the FBI remains unbiased and apolitical. The FBI appreciates the key role of the DOJ Office of the Inspector General (OIG) in the oversight process.

Below, the FBI sets forth a response to the findings and recommendations contained in the OIG Report. The FBI recognizes that mistakes were made. These mistakes were errors of judgment, violations of or disregard for policy, or, when viewed with the benefit of hindsight, simply not the best courses of action. They were not, in any respect, the result of bias or improper considerations. Further, the OIG Report focuses on the conduct of several individuals acting in extraordinary and unprecedented circumstances. None of the actions or conduct faulted by the OIG impugn the integrity of the FBI as an institution, or of the Bureau's dedicated 37,000-person workforce as a whole.

I.   **Summary of FBI Response**

The FBI identified eight (8) focal points, specific to the FBI, in the OIG Report: (1) conduct creating a perception that political bias could have influenced certain actions or decisions; (2) violation of or disregard for DOJ or FBI policies by former Director James Comey's July 5, 2016, announcement and October 28, 2016, letter; (3) issues involving media contacts, leaks, and ethics rules on acceptance of gifts; (4) former Deputy Director Andrew McCabe's recusal obligations; (5) the use of personal email accounts; (6) missteps in certain investigatory processes; (7) insubordination by former Director Comey; and (8) the potentially improper use of FBI systems and devices to exchange messages, the related referrals for investigation, and the creation of additional warning banners and guidance.

The FBI's accepts the OIG's findings that certain text messages, instant messages, and statements, along with a failure to consistently apply DOJ and FBI interview policies, were inappropriate and created an appearance that political bias might have improperly influenced investigative actions or decisions. The Bureau also agrees with the OIG that, despite these errors

1

and the damage they may have caused to the FBI's reputation, there was no evidence of bias or other improper considerations affecting the handling of the Midyear Exam (MYE) investigation. The FBI is taking immediate remedial actions to reinforce the importance of maintaining a work environment free from the appearance of political bias. This includes a review of whether the intermixing of work-related discussions with political commentary implicates any of the FBI's Offense Codes and Penalty Guidelines. It will further include political bias training, Hatch Act training, and, as applicable, will also include a review of how the FBI staffs, structures, and supervises sensitive investigations.

The FBI also accepts the OIG's findings that former Director Comey's July 5, 2016, announcement violated DOJ's media policy and may have violated regulations regarding the public release of information, and that his October 28, 2016, letter was a serious error in judgment. In the judgment of the OIG, there was no evidence that these actions were the result of bias, political preference, or an effort to influence the election. The Bureau takes seriously its obligations to control public statements, especially those related to charging recommendations in criminal investigations and uncharged conduct. Accordingly, the FBI has issued a revised media policy, will act to further ensure that all personnel are aware of the new policy and the serious consequences for non-compliance, and will provide further training on media contact and the limited authority to release information.

The OIG also identified a need to change the "cultural attitude" regarding media contacts and leaks at the FBI. The Director has ordered the Office of Integrity and Compliance (OIC), the Office of the General Counsel (OGC), and the Office of Professional Responsibility (OPR) to review how personnel are trained regarding the media policy and related ethics rules, including those related to the acceptance of gifts, and whether current disciplinary penalties are adequate to deter unauthorized media contact or leaks.

The OIG made several determinations regarding former Deputy Director McCabe's recusal from the Clinton-related investigations. Because he may not have fully complied with his voluntary recusal obligations, the FBI OIC has been instructed to review recusal policy and training, and make updates as necessary to help more quickly identify and mitigate actual or perceived conflicts of interest.[1] The FBI OGC and OIC have also been directed to work together to develop a framework for earlier notification of potential conflicts caused by campaign contributions to covered persons and to provide additional training on recusal obligations and conflicts of interest. The Director has called for the framework to be completed within 60 days.

Upon finding that former Director Comey, Lisa Page, and Peter Strzok used personal email accounts for unclassified FBI business, the OIG referred Mr. Strzok for an investigation into whether his actions violated FBI and DOJ policies. This referral will be investigated and adjudicated pursuant to FBI and DOJ policies. While, there is no finding or indication that any classified material ever transited former Director Comey's, Ms. Page's, or Mr. Strzok's personal devices or accounts, the FBI OGC and OIC have been tasked to evaluate whether additional training and messaging would reinforce the existing policies and protocols on the use of non-FBI

---

[1] The OIG's findings and recommendations related to other recusal issues and contained in the Law Enforcement Sensitive (LES) Appendix Two, are addressed separately in the appended LES response.

devices and accounts and further minimize any non-compliance, and to report back to the Director on their findings within 60 days.

The OIG concluded that certain MYE investigatory missteps were made. The FBI accepts the OIG's conclusions that, in hindsight, it could have taken additional or different investigatory actions, including moving more quickly to secure a search warrant for Anthony Weiner's laptop, and staffing the investigation differently so as to avoid affecting the MYE investigation when senior members of the MYE team were assigned to the Russia investigation. The FBI appreciates, however, that the OIG recognized that many of the identified missteps were judgment calls by seasoned investigators and prosecutors, and that there was no evidence that any decision was made as the result of bias or other improper considerations. This includes the decision not to seek personal devices from former Secretary Clinton's senior aides, the prioritization of the Russia investigation at the time, and the delay in seeking a search warrant for the Weiner laptop. The FBI is convening a working group to provide recommendations, within 120 days, for the staffing, structuring, and supervision of sensitive investigations to help avoid or mitigate similar missteps in the future.

The OIG also stated that former Director Comey was insubordinate by intentionally concealing from DOJ his intentions regarding the July 5, 2016, announcement and instructing his subordinates to do the same. The FBI does not condone insubordination at any level. Compliance with policy – and the chain of command as appropriate – will be reinforced through training.

In its review of collected materials, the OIG found that several FBI employees had exchanged text messages, instant messages, or both, that included political statements hostile to or favoring particular candidates, and appeared to mix political opinion with discussions about the MYE investigation. The OIG found no evidence to connect the political views expressed by these employees with the specific investigative decisions, but referred five employees for investigation into whether the messages violated the FBI's Offense Codes and Penalty Guidelines. The FBI will handle these referrals pursuant to the FBI's disciplinary investigation and adjudication processes, and will impose disciplinary measures as warranted. The OIG separately recommended that the FBI add privacy warning banners to FBI-issued mobile devices and consider assessing whether employees are properly trained on the use of text messages and instant messages, as well as whether it should provide additional guidance about the use of FBI devices for non-governmental purposes. Although the FBI has clear and unambiguous warnings related to the use of FBI Information Technology and Systems, including FBI-issued devices, the Executive Assistant Director of the Information and Technology Branch has been directed to implement the suggested warnings in the most technologically expeditious and feasible manner. The Bureau will also provide renewed training on the governing policies related to device use.

Each of these areas is discussed in more detail below.

II.   Detailed Response to the Eight Focal Points of the OIG Report

While the OIG Report contains several findings of poor judgment, violations of or disregard for policy, and investigatory actions that might have benefitted from a better decision-making process, it contains no finding that any error in judgment, violation of policy, or investigatory action was motivated by political bias or other improper considerations. This is critical to the operation of the FBI and the ability of the American people to count on the FBI to act impartially and objectively. For the same reasons, it is equally important to note again that the OIG Report is narrowly focused on the handful of individuals who were the most deeply involved in running the MYE investigation, and does not generally find fault with the FBI's policies, practices, or procedures as they pertain to investigations, ethical conduct, or media contacts.

1. **Conduct creating a perception that political bias could have influenced certain actions or decisions**

The OIG identified several separate acts that created an appearance that political bias could have influenced certain actions or decisions. The FBI accepts that text messages exchanged over FBI-issued devices by certain FBI employees, primarily Peter Strzok and Lisa Page, demonstrated extremely poor judgment and a lack of professionalism. The FBI also accepts that the content of these messages, critical of political candidates, brought discredit upon those exchanging them and harmed the FBI's reputation. Similarly, the FBI accepts that the decision to allow Cheryl Mills and Heather Samuelson to be present during the interview of former Secretary Clinton was inconsistent with typical investigative strategy and created an appearance that political bias could have influenced this decision, especially when viewed in the light of messages exchanged between Mr. Strzok and Ms. Page.[2]

Despite the appearance of bias created by these actions, the OIG found no evidence that bias affected any investigatory decision or action. As determined by the OIG, there was no evidence of bias or other improper considerations in former Director Comey's instruction to complete the MYE investigation "promptly." Likewise, the OIG considered multiple decisions and actions taken by the MYE team related to obtaining evidence, interview timing and procedures, and the use of consent or immunity agreements. No evidence of bias or other improper considerations was found by the OIG in the MYE team's: use of consent, rather than subpoenas, search warrants, or other legal process to obtain evidence; decisions regarding how to limit consent agreements; decision not to seek personal devices from former Secretary Clinton's senior aides; decisions to enter into immunity agreements; decisions regarding the timing and scoping of former Secretary Clinton's interview, or to proceed with the interview with Cheryl Mills and Heather Samuelson present; and, the decision to obtain testimony and other evidence from Ms. Mills and Ms. Samuelson by consent agreement and with act-of-production immunity.

Although no bias or other improper consideration was found in the FBI's decisions or actions, the appearance of bias is disconcerting and potentially damaging to the FBI's ability to perform its mission. Accordingly, the FBI is instituting new political bias training, drawing from, among other sources, the training, guidance, and practices of the federal judiciary. To commence within 120 days, training will begin with senior leadership and the Senior Executive Service (SES) ranks, with the objectives of discussing the OIG Report, lessons learned, and the need for scrupulous, unwavering adherence to the policies and procedures intended to combat potential political bias. After this initial training, the Director will require all employees to

---

[2] Identifying a different type of potential bias, the OIG Report also found it improper for Ms. Page to comment on or consider how the approach to interviewing former Secretary Clinton might affect the FBI's interests if she won the presidency. The FBI agrees with this finding.

undergo similar training to reinforce the importance of maintaining a work environment free from political bias. The training will cover multiple areas, including at a minimum ethics and integrity, objectivity, and the avoidance of political bias, and will occur across multiple settings, such as Special Agent in Charge onboarding, Senior Executive Service onboarding, Senior Leader courses, Leading People courses, and the Basic Field Training Course. If necessary, supplementary Hatch Act and ethics training may also be required.

Additionally, the Director has tasked the Associate Deputy Director with establishing a working group to provide recommendations, within 120 days, on the staffing, structuring, and supervising of sensitive investigations in order to ensure that the full suite of the FBI's investigative strengths, a balance of operational experience, and proper resources are provided such that every future sensitive investigation is conducted to the highest standards of the Bureau. This will include, among other things, consideration of when and whether to increase field office participation in such matters, and when and whether it would be beneficial to team agents from different components and backgrounds to leverage respective skill sets and experiences, *e.g.*, drawing on the experience of public corruption agents when conducting counterintelligence investigations.

Disciplinary referrals from the OIG Report will be handled pursuant to the FBI's disciplinary investigation and adjudication processes. Any allegation of misconduct by an FBI employee is reviewed, and if merited, investigated by either the FBI Inspection Division or the DOJ OIG, as occurred here. At the conclusion of the investigation, the matter is referred to the FBI's OPR for adjudication. FBI employees must maintain the highest standards of personal and institutional responsibility. The FBI OPR ensures that the FBI maintains its rigorous standards of integrity and professionalism by impartially adjudicating allegations of employee misconduct. OPR's prompt, thorough, and fair adjudication of employee misconduct cases materially enhances confidence in and support for the FBI and its mission. With that said, the FBI OPR has already opened and is conducting investigations, or has concluded misconduct investigations arising out of or related to the conduct identified in the Report. It would not be appropriate to comment here on any particular individual who was or may be the subject of such an investigation.

2. Violation of or disregard for DOJ or FBI policies by former Director James Comey's July 5, 2016, announcement and October 28, 2016, letter

The OIG found that former Director Comey violated DOJ's media policy, and potentially regulations related to the public release of information, when he made his July 5, 2016, announcement. He was also found to have committed a serious error in judgment by sending his October 28, 2016, letter, in disregard of FBI and DOJ policy, without DOJ approval, and in usurpation of the Attorney General's authority. The FBI does not contest these findings.

The FBI will implement the OIG's recommendation that the FBI adopt a policy on the appropriateness of employees addressing uncharged conduct in public statements. The Director is also tasking the FBI's OGC to develop, within 30 days, guidance requiring prior consultation with DOJ preceding any public reference to FBI charging recommendations in criminal investigations.

Pursuant to the new FBI media policy, FBI personnel authorized to communicate with the media must abide by DOJ guidelines contained in 28 CFR 50.2 "Release of information by personnel of the [DOJ] relating to criminal and civil proceedings," and in the U.S. Attorney's Manual Title 1-7.000 "Confidentiality and Media Contacts Policy." This would include receiving advanced approval by the appropriate United States Attorney or Assistant Attorney General before communicating with the media about a pending investigation or case, except in emergency circumstances. Training on these policies will be included in the training described above.

3. Issues involving media contacts, dissemination of information, and leaks

The OIG's conclusion that there is a need to change the "cultural attitude" regarding media contacts and leaks at the FBI is troubling. The FBI is acutely aware of the damage unauthorized communications or leaks can cause to investigations, prosecutions, the personal lives of those involved in the case or who may be subjects or targets, and the reputation of the Bureau. Leaks or unauthorized communications are not taken lightly, are never condoned, and may result in discipline, up to and including termination, and potentially prosecution. Given the conclusions reached in the OIG report, the Director instructed the Assistant Director of OPR to review whether current disciplinary penalties are adequate to deter unauthorized media contact or leaks and to report back on their adequacy, or the need for additional penalties, within 30 days.

The FBI protects information on a need-to-know basis and, to reinforce the limitations on sharing that information, revised its media policy effective November 15, 2017. As an additional step, the FBI will ensure that, within 30 days, all personnel are fully aware of the media policy and the serious potential consequences for noncompliance. The new media policy restricts who is authorized to communicate with the media (*i.e.*, within FBI Headquarters, the Director, Deputy Director, Associate Deputy Director, Assistant Director of the Office of Public Affairs, and designated OPA staff; in a field office, the Assistant Director in Charge or Special Agent in Charge, designated public affairs officer, or other personnel specifically authorized by the field office head). The new policy requires that "all contact with members of the media about FBI matters must be reported" to the relevant Headquarters or field office officials. It also requires that personnel "must immediately notify their supervisors if contact with a member of the media concerns suspected classified or grand jury subject matter." The policy also requires conformance with DOJ guidelines contained in 28 CFR 50.2 "Release of information by personnel of the [DOJ] relating to criminal and civil proceedings," and in the U.S. Attorney's Manual Title 1-7.000 "Confidentiality and Media Contacts Policy." The FBI's policies, training, and disciplinary measures related to media contact and ethics rules, combined with any additional policies and training developed after this review, will sufficiently mitigate the risk and continue to deter this type of misconduct.

4. Former Deputy Director Andrew McCabe's recusal obligations

The OIG found that the former Deputy Director and the Bureau acted appropriately with regard to his involvement in and recusal from the Clinton-related investigations. The OIG concurred with the FBI's determination that former Deputy Director McCabe was not required to recuse from those investigations and found that he notified the appropriate persons in the FBI to seek guidance on ethics issues. The OIG Report also makes clear that former Deputy Director McCabe generally abided by his voluntary recusal from Clinton-related matters after November 1, 2016, in that there is no evidence that he continued to supervise investigative decisions in those matters after his recusal. The FBI agrees with the OIG that in a few instances, the former Deputy Director did not fully comply with his voluntary recusal.

Based on the OIG's findings related to the analysis of recusal decisions and recusal obligations, in particular the finding that FBI ethics officials and attorneys did not fully appreciate the potential significant implications of campaign contributions to Dr. McCabe's campaign, and the ninth recommendation in the OIG Report, the FBI's OGC and OIC have been directed to work together to develop a framework for earlier notification of potential conflicts caused by campaign contributions to covered persons and to provide additional training on recusal obligations and conflicts of interest. The Director has mandated that the framework be completed within 60 days.

5. The use of personal email accounts by former Director Comey and Peter Strzok

The OIG found that former Director Comey used personal email accounts for unclassified FBI business, absent exigent circumstances, in contravention of FBI and DOJ policy. The OIG also found that Peter Strzok and Lisa Page used personal email accounts for unclassified FBI business. Although former Director Comey and Ms. Page are no longer employed by the FBI, the OIG referred Mr. Strzok for an investigation into whether his use of personal email accounts violated FBI or DOJ policy. The FBI will handle this referral pursuant to the FBI's disciplinary investigation and adjudication processes. The FBI notes that there is no finding or indication in the OIG Report that any classified material ever transited former Director Comey's, Ms. Page's, or Mr. Strzok's personal devices or accounts.

The Bureau will evaluate whether additional training and messaging would clarify and reinforce the existing policies and protocols on the use of non-FBI devices and accounts and further minimize any non-compliance by FBI personnel. Further, the Director has tasked the Executive Assistant Director of the Information and Technology Branch with evaluating the benefits of consolidating existing relevant policies and guidance concerning the use of personal devices and accounts for FBI business, in order to underscore the requirement for exigency in such use.

6. Missteps in certain investigatory processes

Two complex, exceptionally important investigations were being conducted concurrently by the FBI in 2016, MYE and the Russia influence investigation. The FBI sought to staff both investigations with the people it thought at the time were the best qualified (as it always does). Both were close-hold, sensitive, and multifaceted. At the highest levels of leadership then in the FBI, judgment calls and decisions were made regarding how each investigation should proceed and how investigatory actions should be prioritized. The OIG questioned some of the judgment calls and decisions, including reassigning senior members from the MYE team to the Russia influence investigation, the delay in seeking a search warrant for Anthony Weiner's laptop, and the decision by agents and prosecutors not to subpoena or seek search warrants for the personal devices of three senior aides to former Secretary Clinton. The FBI agrees that it could have moved more quickly to secure a search warrant for Weiner's laptop and could have staffed the two investigations differently to minimize any detrimental effect to the MYE investigation. The addition of staff or resources may have impacted how agents and prosecutors decided what devices to seek and review, even if their judgment that certain devices were likely of limited evidentiary value remained the same.

While the OIG was critical of these judgment calls and decisions, it did not find that these were the result of bias or other improper considerations. Rather, the OIG specifically concluded that there was no evidence of bias or improper considerations in the decision not to seek the personal devices from former Secretary Clinton's senior aides, the lack of urgency in seeking a search warrant for the Weiner laptop, and the prioritization of the Russia influence investigation.

As previously described, in an effort to learn from its past decisions, good and bad, the FBI is establishing a working group to provide recommendations for the staffing, structuring, and supervision of sensitive investigations to help avoid or mitigate similar missteps in the future.

7. Insubordination by former Director Comey

The OIG found that former Director Comey was insubordinate when he intentionally concealed from DOJ his intentions regarding the July 5, 2016, announcement and instructed his subordinates to do the same. The FBI does not condone insubordination at any level and will institute training to ensure compliance with policy and the chain of command, as appropriate.

8. The potentially improper use of FBI systems and devices to exchange messages, the related referrals for investigation, and the recommendations to create additional warning banners and guidance.

The OIG found that several FBI employees had exchanged text messages, instant messages, or both that included political statements. The OIG also found that some messages appeared to mix political opinion with discussions about the MYE investigation. The OIG concluded there is no evidence to connect the political views expressed by these employees with the specific MYE investigative decisions. Regarding the messages, the FBI will handle the OIG's referrals pursuant to its disciplinary investigation and adjudication processes and will impose disciplinary measures as warranted.

Based on its review of these messages, the OIG separately recommended that the FBI add privacy warning banners to FBI-issued mobile devices and consider assessing whether employees are properly trained on the use of text messages and instant messages and whether it should provide additional guidance about the use of FBI devices for non-governmental purposes. FBI employees sign a Rules of Behavior Agreement expressly consenting to the monitoring of data communications over FBI information systems (emails, facsimile, computer database use and data storage, digital transmission of data, but not voice communications). This agreement form must be signed before access to any FBI Information Technology or Information Systems is granted. Existing policy also advises employees that "FBI personnel using FBI information systems have no reasonable expectation of privacy." Further, the warning banners that appear at login on the FBI's computer systems expressly apply to "all devices [or] storage media attached to this network or to a computer on this network." Although the FBI has clear and unambiguous warnings related to the use of FBI Information Technology and Systems, including FBI-issued devices, the Executive Assistant Director of the Information and Technology Branch has been directed to implement the suggested warnings in the most technologically expeditious and feasible manner. The Bureau will also provide enhanced training on the governing policies related to device use, including but not limited to the use of FBI Information Technology and Systems for political conversations.

* * * *

In addition to the focal points addressed above, which the FBI believes are responsive to findings and recommendations in the OIG report, one other specific and narrow recommendation deserves a brief response.

The OIG recommends that the Office of the Deputy Attorney General (ODAG) consider taking steps to improve the retention and monitoring of text messages Department-wide. The Bureau already goes to great lengths, within the restrictions imposed by existing technology and practicality, to capture and retain text messages sent or received on FBI-issued devices. Still, the FBI stands ready to work with ODAG to improve its processes and capabilities.

III.   Conclusion

The FBI appreciates the role of the OIG, its dedication to its task, and the thoroughness of its investigation in bringing to light ways in which the FBI can improve the performance of its mission. The Bureau also appreciates the finding that there was no evidence that bias or improper considerations affected its investigative actions or decisions. Further, while the OIG Report focused on only a handful of individuals, as described above, the FBI is reviewing the recommendations of the OIG and will be taking action that applies far more broadly to FBI leadership, career Special Agents and Intelligence Analysts, and all the various personnel that make the FBI the premiere law enforcement and national security agency in the world. The FBI is extraordinarily cognizant of the need to maintain impartiality and objectivity, and to make certain that the American people trust it to always do so.

ATTACHMENT C

From:	STRZOK, PETER P. (CD) (FBI)
Sent:	Friday, May 06, 2016 6:08 PM
To:	MCCABE, ANDREW G. (DO) (FBI); PRIESTAP, E W. (CD) (FBI); ███████████████ (FBI); PAGE, LISA C. (OGC) (FBI)
Subject:	RE: Midyear Exam --- UNCLASSIFIED

Classification: UNCLASSIFIED
==

Understood and will do.

From: MCCABE, ANDREW G. (DO) (FBI)
Sent: Friday, May 06, 2016 5:32 PM
To: PRIESTAP, E W. (CD) (FBI); STRZOK, PETER P. (CD) (FBI); ██████████████ PAGE, LISA C. (OGC) (FBI)
Subject: FW: Midyear Exam --- UNCLASSIFIED
Importance: High

Classification: UNCLASSIFIED
==

Folks:

The Director composed the below straw man in an effort to compose what a "final" statement might look like in the context of a press conference. This was really more of an exercise for him to get his thoughts on the matter in order, and not any kind of decision about venue, strategy, product, etc.

The Director asked me to share this with you four, but not any further. The only additional people who have seen this draft are Jim Rybicki and Jim Baker. Please do not disseminate or discuss any further.

I do not know if the boss will want to discuss this at the Monday update but please review it before the meeting just in case.

Thanks

Andrew G. McCabe
Deputy Director
Federal Bureau of Investigation

███████████████

From: COMEY, JAMES B. (DO) (FBI)
Sent: Monday, May 02, 2016 7:15 PM
To: MCCABE, ANDREW G. (DO) (FBI); BAKER, JAMES A. (OGC) (FBI); RYBICKI, JAMES E. (DO) (FBI)
Cc: COMEY, JAMES B. (DO) (FBI)
Subject: Midyear Exam --- UNCLASSIFIED

Classification: UNCLASSIFIED
==

I've been trying to imagine what it would look like if I decided to do an FBI only press event to close out our work and hand the matter to DOJ. To help shape our discussions of whether that, or something different, makes sense, I have spent some time crafting what I would say, which follows. In my imagination, I don't see me taking any questions. Here is what it might look like:

Good afternoon folks. I am here to give you an update on our investigation of Secretary Clinton's use of a private email system, which began in late August.

After a tremendous amount of work, the FBI has completed its investigation and has referred the case to the Department of Justice for a prosecutive decision. What I would like to do today is tell you three things: (1) what we did; (2) what we found; (3) what we have recommended to DOJ.

But I want to start by thanking the many agents, analysts, technologists, and other FBI employees who did work of extraordinary quality in this case. Once you have a better sense of how much we have done, you will understand why I am so grateful and proud of their efforts.

So, first: what we have done over the last eight months.

The investigation began as a referral from the Intelligence Community Inspector General in connection with Secretary Clinton's use of a private email server during his time as Secretary of State, focused on whether classified information was transmitted on that private system.

Our investigation focused on whether there is evidence that classified information was improperly stored or transmitted on that private system, in violation of a federal statute that makes it a felony to mishandle classified information either intentionally or in a grossly negligent way, or a second statute that makes it a misdemeanor to remove classified information from appropriate systems or storage facilities.

Consistent with our counterintelligence responsibilities, we have also investigated to determine whether there is evidence of computer intrusion in connection with the private email server by any foreign power, or hackers on behalf of a foreign power.

I have so far used the singular term, "email server," in describing the referral that began our investigation. It turns out to have been more complicated than that. Secretary Clinton used several different servers and providers of those servers during her four years at the State Department, and used numerous mobile devices to view and send email on that private domain. As new servers and providers were employed, older servers were taken out of service, stored, and decommissioned in various ways. Piecing all of that back together to gain as full an understanding as possible of the ways in which private email was used for government work has been a painstaking undertaking, requiring thousands of hours of effort.

For example, when one of Secretary Clinton's original private servers was decommissioned in 20xx, the email software was removed. Doing that didn't remove the email content, but it was like removing the frame from a huge finished jigsaw puzzle and dumping the pieces on the floor. The effect was that

2

millions of email fragments end up unsorted in the server's un-used – or "slack" – space. We went through all of it to see what was there, and what parts of the puzzle could be put back together.

FBI investigators have also read all 34,000 emails provided by Secretary Clinton to the State Department in spring 2015. Where an email was assessed as possibly containing classified information, the FBI referred the email to the U.S. government agency that was the likely "owner" of the information in the email so that agency could make a determination as to whether the email contained classified information at the time it was sent or received, or whether there was reason to classify the email now, even if its content was not classified at the time it was sent (this is the process sometimes referred to as "up classifying").

From that group of 34,000 emails that had been returned to the State Department in 2015, the FBI sent xxxx emails to agencies for classification determinations. Of those, xxxx have been determined to contain classified information at the time they were sent or received. Xxxx of those contained information that was Top Secret at the time they were sent; xxxx contained Secret information at the time; and xxxx contained Confidential information. Separate from those, a total of xxxx additional emails were "up classified" to make them Secret or Confidential; the information in those had not been classified at the time the emails were sent.

The FBI also discovered xxxx work-related emails that were not in the group of 34,000 that were returned by Secretary Clinton to State in 2015. We found those additional emails in a variety of ways. Some had been deleted over the years and we found traces of them on devices that supported or were connected to the private email domain. Others we found by reviewing the archived government email accounts of people who had been government employees at the same time as Secretary Clinton, including high-ranking officials at other agencies, with whom a Secretary of State might naturally correspond. This helped us recover work-related emails that were not among the 34,000 produced to State. Still others we recovered from the laborious review of the millions of email fragments dumped into the slack space of the server decommissioned in 20xx.

All told, we found xxxx emails that were not among those produced to the State Department last year. Of those, we assessed that xxxx possibly contained classified information at the time they were sent or received and so we sent them to other government agencies for classification determinations. To date, agencies have concluded that xxxx of those were classified at the time they were sent or received, xxx at the Secret level and xxxx at the Confidential level. There were no additional Top Secret emails found. Finally, none of those we found have since been "up classified."

I should add here that we found no evidence that any of the additional work-related emails we found were intentionally deleted in an effort to conceal them. Our assessment is that, like many users of private email accounts, Secretary Clinton periodically deleted emails or emails were purged from the system when devices were changed. Because she was not using a government account, there was no archiving of her emails, so it is not surprising that we discovered emails that were not on Secretary Clinton's system in 2015, when she produced the 34,000 emails to the State Department.

It could also be that some of the additional work-related emails we recovered were among those deleted as "personal" by Secretary Clinton's lawyers when they reviewed and sorted her emails for production in 2015. We have conducted interviews and done technical examination to attempt to understand how that sorting was done. Although we do not have complete visibility because we are

3

not fully able to reconstruct the electronic record of that sorting, we believe our investigation has been sufficient to give us reasonable confidence there was no intentional misconduct in connection with that sorting effort.

The lawyers doing the sorting for Secretary Clinton in 2015 did not individually read tens of thousands of emails, as we did; instead, they used search terms to try to find all work-related emails among the more than 60,000 total emails remaining on Secretary Clinton's private system in 2015. It is highly likely their search terms missed some work-related emails, and that we found them, for example, in the mailboxes of other officials or in the slack space of a server. It is also likely that there are other work-related emails that they did not produce to State and that we did not find elsewhere, and that are now gone because they deleted all emails they did not return to State, and the lawyers cleaned their devices in a such a way as to preclude forensic recovery.

And, of course, in additional to our technical work, we interviewed many people, from those involved in setting up and maintaining the various iterations of Secretary Clinton's private server to staff members with whom she corresponded on email, to those involved in the email production to State, and finally, Secretary Clinton herself.

Lastly, we have done extensive work with the assistance of our colleagues elsewhere in the Intelligence Community to understand what indications there might be of compromise by hostile actors in connection with the private email operation.

That's what we have done. Now let me tell you what we found.

There is evidence to support a conclusion that Secretary Clinton, and others, used the private email server in a manner that was grossly negligent with respect to the handling of classified information. For example, seven email chains concern matters that were classified at the TS/SAP level when they were sent and received. These chains involved Secretary Clinton both sending emails about those matters and receiving emails from others about the same matters. There is evidence to support a conclusion that any reasonable person in Secretary Clinton's position, or in the positon of those government employees with whom she was corresponding about these matters, should have known that an unclassified system was no place for such an email conversation. Although we did not find clear evidence that Secretary Clinton or her colleagues intended to violate laws governing the handling of classified information, there is evidence that they were extremely careless in their handling of very sensitive, highly classified information.

Similarly, the sheer volume of information that was properly classified as Secret at the time it was discussed on email (that is, excluding the "up classified" emails) supports an inference that the participants were grossly negligent in their handling of that information.

We also developed evidence that the security culture of the State Department in general, and with respect to use of unclassified email systems in particular, was generally lacking in the kind of care for classified information found elsewhere in the government.

With respect to potential computer intrusion by hostile actors, we did not find direct evidence that Secretary Clinton's personal email system, in its various configurations since 2009, was successfully hacked. But, given the nature of the system and of the actors potentially involved, we assess that we

4

would be unlikely to see such direct evidence. We do assess that hostile actors gained access to the private email accounts of individuals with whom Secretary Clinton was in regular contact from her private account. We also assess that Secretary Clinton's use of a private email domain was both known by a large number of people and readily apparent. Given that combination of factors, we asses it is reasonably likely that hostile actors gained access to Secretary Clinton's private email account.

So that's what we found.

Finally, with respect to our recommendation to the Department of Justice. In our system, the prosecutors make the decisions about whether charges are appropriate based on evidence the FBI has helped collect. Although we don't normally make public our recommendations to the prosecutors, we frequently make recommendations and engage in productive conversations with prosecutors about what resolution may be appropriate, given the evidence. In this case, given the importance of the matter, I think unusual transparency is in order.

Although there is evidence of potential violations of the statute proscribing gross negligence in the handling of classified information and of the statute proscribing misdemeanor mishandling, my judgment is that no reasonable prosecutor would bring such a case. At the outset, we are not aware of a case where anyone has been charged solely based on the "gross negligence" prohibition in the statute. All charged cases of which we are aware have involved the accusation that a government employee intentionally mishandled classified information. In looking back at our investigations in similar circumstances, we cannot find a case that would support bringing criminal charges on these facts. All the cases prosecuted involved some combination of: (1) clearly intentional misconduct; (2) vast quantities of materials exposed in such a way as to support an inference of intentional misconduct; (3) indications of disloyalty to the United States; or (4) efforts to obstruct justice. We see none of that here.

Accordingly, although the Department of Justice makes final decisions on matters such as this, I am completing the investigation by expressing to Justice my view that no charges are appropriate in this case.

I know there will be intense public disagreement in the wake of this result, as there was throughout this investigation. What I can assure the American people is that this investigation was done competently, honestly, and independently. No outside influence of any kind was brought to bear. I know there were many opinions expressed by people who were not part of the investigation -- including people in government – but none of that mattered to us. Opinions are irrelevant, and they were all uninformed by insight into our investigation, because we did the investigation in a professional way. Only facts matter, and the FBI found them here in an entirely apolitical and professional way. I couldn't be prouder to be part of this organization.

# # #

5

ATTACHMENT D

**Statement by FBI Director James B. Comey on the Investigation
of Secretary Hillary Clinton's Use of a Personal Email System**

July 5, 2016

[As Prepared for Delivery]

Good morning. I'm here to give you an update on the FBI's investigation of Secretary Clinton's use of a personal email system during her time as Secretary of State.

After a tremendous amount of work over the last year, the FBI is completing its investigation and referring the case to the Department of Justice for a prosecutive decision. What I would like to do today is tell you three things: what we did; what we found; and what we are recommending to the Department of Justice.

This will be an unusual statement in at least a couple ways. First, I am going to include more detail about our process than I ordinarily would, because I think the American people deserve those details in a case of intense public interest. Second, I have not coordinated or reviewed this statement in any way with the Department of Justice or any other part of the government. They do not know what I am about to say.

I want to start by thanking the FBI employees who did remarkable work in this case. Once you have a better sense of how much we have done, you will understand why I am so grateful and proud of their efforts.

So, first, what we have done:

The investigation began as a referral from the Intelligence Community Inspector General in connection with Secretary Clinton's use of a personal email server during her time as Secretary of State. The referral focused on whether classified information was transmitted on that personal system.

Our investigation looked at whether there is evidence classified information was improperly stored or transmitted on that personal system, in violation of a federal statute making it a felony to mishandle classified information either intentionally or in a grossly negligent way, or a second statute making it a misdemeanor to knowingly remove classified information from appropriate systems or storage facilities.

Consistent with our counter-intelligence responsibilities, we have also investigated to determine whether there is evidence of computer intrusion in connection with the personal email server by any foreign power, or other hostile actors.

I have so far used the singular term, "email server," in describing the referral that began our investigation. It turns out to have been more complicated than that. Secretary Clinton used

1

several different servers and administrators of those servers during her four years at the State Department, and used numerous mobile devices to view and send email on that personal domain. As new servers and equipment were employed, older servers were taken out of service, stored, and decommissioned in various ways. Piecing all of that back together -- to gain as full an understanding as possible of the ways in which personal email was used for government work -- has been a painstaking undertaking, requiring thousands of hours of effort.

For example, when one of Secretary Clinton's original personal servers was decommissioned in 2013, the email software was removed. Doing that didn't remove the email content, but it was like removing the frame from a huge finished jigsaw puzzle and dumping the pieces on the floor. The effect was that millions of email fragments end up unsorted in the server's un-used – or "slack" – space. We searched through all of it to see what was there, and what parts of the puzzle could be put back together.

FBI investigators have also read all of the approximately 30,000 emails provided by Secretary Clinton to the State Department in December 2014. Where an email was assessed as possibly containing classified information, the FBI referred the email to any U.S. government agency that was a likely "owner" of information in the email, so that agency could make a determination as to whether the email contained classified information at the time it was sent or received, or whether there was reason to classify the email now, even if its content was not classified at the time it was sent (that is the process sometimes referred to as "up-classifying").

From the group of 30,000 emails returned to the State Department, 110 emails in 52 email chains have been determined by the owning agency to contain classified information at the time they were sent or received. Eight of those chains contained information that was Top Secret at the time they were sent; 36 chains contained Secret information at the time; and 8 contained Confidential information, which is the lowest level of classification. Separate from those, about 2,000 additional emails were "up-classified" to make them Confidential; the information in those had not been classified at the time the emails were sent.

The FBI also discovered several thousand work-related emails that were not in the group of 30,000 that were returned by Secretary Clinton to State in 2014. We found those additional emails in a variety of ways. Some had been deleted over the years and we found traces of them on devices that supported or were connected to the private email domain. Others we found by reviewing the archived government email accounts of people who had been government employees at the same time as Secretary Clinton, including high-ranking officials at other agencies, people with whom a Secretary of State might naturally correspond.

This helped us recover work-related emails that were not among the 30,000 produced to State. Still others we recovered from the laborious review of the millions of email fragments dumped into the slack space of the server decommissioned in 2013.

With respect to the thousands of emails we found that were not among those produced to State, agencies have concluded that 3 of those were classified at the time they were sent or received, 1 at the Secret level and 2 at the Confidential level. There were no additional Top Secret emails found. Finally, none of those we found have since been "up-classified."

2

I should add here that we found no evidence that any of the additional work-related emails were intentionally deleted in an effort to conceal them. Our assessment is that, like many email users, Secretary Clinton periodically deleted emails or emails were purged from the system when devices were changed. Because she was not using a government account – or even a commercial account like Gmail – there was no archiving at all of her emails, so it is not surprising that we discovered emails that were not on Secretary Clinton's system in 2014, when she produced the 30,000 emails to the State Department.

It could also be that some of the additional work-related emails we recovered were among those deleted as "personal" by Secretary Clinton's lawyers when they reviewed and sorted her emails for production in 2014.

The lawyers doing the sorting for Secretary Clinton in 2014 did not individually read the content of all of her emails, as we did for those available to us; instead, they relied on header information and used search terms to try to find all work-related emails among the reportedly more than 60,000 total emails remaining on Secretary Clinton's personal system in 2014. It is highly likely their search terms missed some work-related emails, and that we later found them, for example, in the mailboxes of other officials or in the slack space of a server.
It is also likely that there are other work-related emails that they did not produce to State and that we did not find elsewhere, and that are now gone because they deleted all emails they did not return to State, and the lawyers cleaned their devices in such a way as to preclude complete forensic recovery.

We have conducted interviews and done technical examination to attempt to understand how that sorting was done by her attorneys. Although we do not have complete visibility because we are not able to fully reconstruct the electronic record of that sorting, we believe our investigation has been sufficient to give us reasonable confidence there was no intentional misconduct in connection with that sorting effort.

And, of course, in addition to our technical work, we interviewed many people, from those involved in setting up and maintaining the various iterations of Secretary Clinton's personal server, to staff members with whom she corresponded on email, to those involved in the email production to State, and finally, Secretary Clinton herself.

Last, we have done extensive work to understand what indications there might be of compromise by hostile actors in connection with the personal email operation.

That's what we have done. Now let me tell you what we found:

Although we did not find clear evidence that Secretary Clinton or her colleagues intended to violate laws governing the handling of classified information, there is evidence that they were extremely careless in their handling of very sensitive, highly classified information.

For example, seven email chains concern matters that were classified at the Top Secret/Special Access Program level when they were sent and received. These chains involved

3

Secretary Clinton both sending emails about those matters and receiving emails from others about the same matters. There is evidence to support a conclusion that any reasonable person in Secretary Clinton's position, or in the position of those government employees with whom she was corresponding about these matters, should have known that an unclassified system was no place for that conversation. In addition to this highly sensitive information, we also found information that was properly classified as Secret by the U.S. Intelligence Community at the time it was discussed on email (that is, excluding the later "up-classified" emails).

None of these emails should have been on any kind of unclassified system, but their presence is especially concerning because all of these emails were housed on unclassified personal servers not even supported by full-time security staff, like those found at Departments and Agencies of the U.S. Government – or even with a commercial service like Gmail.

Separately, it is important to say something about the marking of classified information. Only a very small number of the emails containing classified information bore markings indicating the presence of classified information. But even if information is not marked "classified" in an email, participants who know or should know that the subject matter is classified are still obligated to protect it.

While not the focus of our investigation, we also developed evidence that the security culture of the State Department in general, and with respect to use of unclassified email systems in particular, was generally lacking in the kind of care for classified information found elsewhere in the government.

With respect to potential computer intrusion by hostile actors, we did not find direct evidence that Secretary Clinton's personal email domain, in its various configurations since 2009, was successfully hacked. But, given the nature of the system and of the actors potentially involved, we assess that we would be unlikely to see such direct evidence. We do assess that hostile actors gained access to the private commercial email accounts of people with whom Secretary Clinton was in regular contact from her personal account. We also assess that Secretary Clinton's use of a personal email domain was both known by a large number of people and readily apparent. She also used her personal email extensively while outside the United States, including sending and receiving work-related emails in the territory of sophisticated adversaries. Given that combination of factors, we assess it is possible that hostile actors gained access to Secretary Clinton's personal email account.

So that's what we found. Finally, with respect to our recommendation to the Department of Justice:

In our system, the prosecutors make the decisions about whether charges are appropriate based on evidence the FBI has helped collect. Although we don't normally make public our recommendations to the prosecutors, we frequently make recommendations and engage in productive conversations with prosecutors about what resolution may be appropriate, given the evidence. In this case, given the importance of the matter, I think unusual transparency is in order.

4

Although there is evidence of potential violations of the statutes regarding the handling of classified information, our judgment is that no reasonable prosecutor would bring such a case. Prosecutors necessarily weigh a number of factors before bringing charges. There are obvious considerations, like the strength of the evidence, especially regarding intent. Responsible decisions also consider the context of a person's actions, and how similar situations have been handled in the past.

In looking back at our investigations into mishandling or removal of classified information, we cannot find a case that would support bringing criminal charges on these facts. All the cases prosecuted involved some combination of: clearly intentional and willful mishandling of classified information; or vast quantities of materials exposed in such a way as to support an inference of intentional misconduct; or indications of disloyalty to the United States; or efforts to obstruct justice. We do not see those things here.

To be clear, this is not to suggest that in similar circumstances, a person who engaged in this activity would face no consequences. To the contrary, those individuals are often subject to security or administrative sanctions. But that is not what we are deciding now.

As a result, although the Department of Justice makes final decisions on matters like this, we are expressing to Justice our view that no charges are appropriate in this case.

I know there will be intense public debate in the wake of this recommendation, as there was throughout this investigation. What I can assure the American people is that this investigation was done competently, honestly, and independently. No outside influence of any kind was brought to bear.

I know there were many opinions expressed by people who were not part of the investigation – including people in government – but none of that mattered to us. Opinions are irrelevant, and they were all uninformed by insight into our investigation, because we did the investigation the right way. Only facts matter, and the FBI found them here in an entirely apolitical and professional way. I couldn't be prouder to be part of this organization.

# # #

5

ATTACHMENT E

U.S. Department of Justice

Federal Bureau of Investigation

Washington, D.C. 20535

October 28, 2016

Honorable Richard M. Burr
Chairman
Select Committee on Intelligence

Honorable Devin Nunes
Chairman
Permanent Select Committee on Intelligence

Honorable Charles E. Grassley
Chairman
Committee on the Judiciary

Honorable Robert Goodlatte
Chairman
Committee on the Judiciary

Honorable Richard Shelby
Chairman
Committee on Appropriations
Subcommittee on Commerce, Justice, Science
  and Related Agencies

Honorable John Culberson
Chairman
Committee on Appropriations
Subcommittee on Commerce, Justice,
  Science and Related Agencies

Honorable Ron Johnson
Chairman
Committee on Homeland Security and
  Governmental Affairs

Honorable Jason Chaffetz
Chairman
Committee on Oversight and
  Government Reform

Dear Messrs Chairmen:

In previous congressional testimony, I referred to the fact that the Federal Bureau of Investigation (FBI) had completed its investigation of former Secretary Clinton's personal email server. Due to recent developments, I am writing to supplement my previous testimony.

In connection with an unrelated case, the FBI has learned of the existence of emails that appear to be pertinent to the investigation. I am writing to inform you that the investigative team briefed me on this yesterday, and I agreed that the FBI should take appropriate investigative steps designed to allow investigators to review these emails to determine whether they contain classified information, as well as to assess their importance to our investigation.

Although the FBI cannot yet assess whether or not this material may be significant, and I cannot predict how long it will take us to complete this additional work, I believe it is important to update your Committees about our efforts in light of my previous testimony.

Sincerely yours,

James B Comey

James B. Comey
Director

1 – Honorable Dianne Feinstein
   Vice Chairman
   Select Committee on Intelligence
   United States Senate
   Washington, DC 20510

1 – Honorable Patrick J. Leahy
   Ranking Member
   Committee on the Judiciary
   United States Senate
   Washington, DC 20510

1 – Honorable Barbara Mikulski
   Ranking Member
   Committee on Appropriations
   Subcommittee on Commerce, Justice, Science
     and Related Agencies
   United States Senate
   Washington, DC 20510

1 – Honorable Thomas R. Carper
   Ranking Member
   Committee on Homeland Security and
     Governmental Affairs
   United States Senate
   Washington, DC 20510

1 – Honorable Adam B. Schiff
   Ranking Member
   Permanent Select Committee on Intelligence
   U.S. House of Representatives
   Washington, DC 20515

1 – Honorable John Conyers, Jr.
   Ranking Member
   Committee on the Judiciary
   U.S. House of Representatives
   Washington, DC 20515

1 – Honorable Michael Honda
   Ranking Member
   Committee on Appropriations
   Subcommittee on Commerce, Justice, Science
     and Related Agencies
   U.S. House of Representatives
   Washington, DC 20515

1 – Honorable Elijah E. Cummings
   Ranking Member
   Committee on Oversight and
     Government Reform
   U.S. House of Representatives
   Washington, DC 20515

ATTACHMENT
F

U.S. Department of Justice

Federal Bureau of Investigation

November 6, 2016

Honorable Richard M. Burr
Chairman
Select Committee on Intelligence

Honorable Devin Nunes
Chairman
Permanent Select Committee on Intelligence

Honorable Charles E. Grassley
Chairman
Committee on the Judiciary

Honorable Robert Goodlatte
Chairman
Committee on the Judiciary

Honorable Richard Shelby
Chairman
Committee on Appropriations
Subcommittee on Commerce, Justice,
 Science and Related Agencies

Honorable John Culberson
Chairman
Committee on Appropriations
Subcommittee on Commerce, Justice,
 Science and Related Agencies

Honorable Ron Johnson
Chairman
Committee on Homeland Security and
 Governmental Affairs

Honorable Jason Chaffetz
Chairman
Committee on Oversight and
 Government Reform

Dear Messrs. Chairmen:

I write to supplement my October 28, 2016 letter that notified you the FBI would be taking additional investigative steps with respect to former Secretary of State Clinton's use of a personal email server. Since my letter, the FBI investigative team has been working around the clock to process and review a large volume of emails from a device obtained in connection with an unrelated criminal investigation. During that process, we reviewed all of the communications that were to or from Hillary Clinton while she was Secretary of State.

Based on our review, we have not changed our conclusions that we expressed in July with respect to Secretary Clinton.

I am very grateful to the professionals at the FBI for doing an extraordinary amount of high-quality work in a short period of time.

Sincerely yours,

James B. Comey
Director

cc: See next page

1 – Honorable Dianne Feinstein
Vice Chairman
Select Committee on Intelligence

1 – Honorable Adam B. Schiff
Ranking Member
Permanent Select Committee on Intelligence

1 – Honorable Patrick J. Leahy
Ranking Member
Committee on the Judiciary

1 – Honorable John Conyers, Jr.
Ranking Member
Committee on the Judiciary

1 – Honorable Barbara Mikulski
Ranking Member
Committee on Appropriations
Subcommittee on Commerce, Justice,
  Science and Related Agencies

1 – Honorable Michael Honda
Ranking Member
Committee on Appropriations
Subcommittee on Commerce, Justice,
  Science, and Related Agencies

1 – Honorable Thomas R. Carper
Ranking Member
Committee on Homeland Security and
  Governmental Affairs

1 – Honorable Elijah E. Cummings
Ranking Member
Committee on Oversight and
  Government Reform

ATTACHMENT G

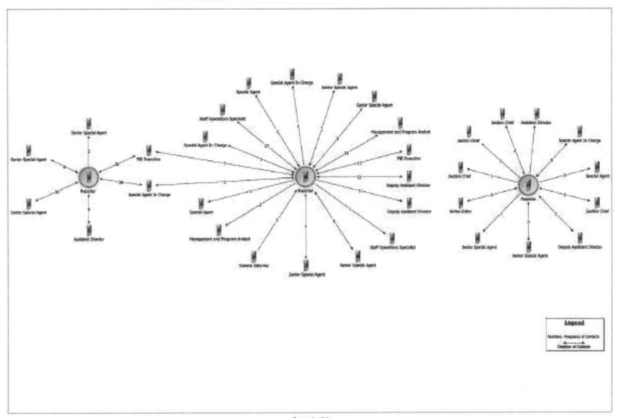

ATTACHMENT
H

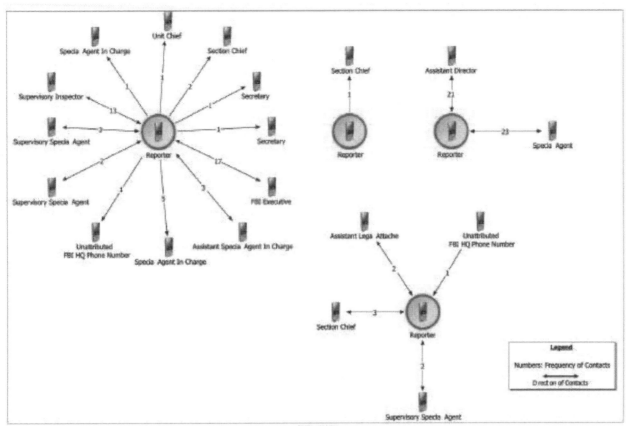

APPENDIX ONE

CLASSIFIED

APPENDIX TWO

LAW ENFORCEMENT SENSITIVE

The Department of Justice Office of the Inspector General (DOJ OIG) is a statutorily created independent entity whose mission is to detect and deter waste, fraud, abuse, and misconduct in the Department of Justice, and to promote economy and efficiency in the Department's operations.

To report allegations of waste, fraud, abuse, or misconduct regarding DOJ programs, employees, contractors, grants, or contracts please visit or call the DOJ OIG Hotline at oig.justice.gov/hotline or (800) 869-4499.

Made in the USA
Coppell, TX
11 December 2019